Foundations
of American Education

L. Dean Webb
Arizona State University

Arlene Metha
Arizona State University

K. Forbis Jordan
Arizona State University

Merrill, an imprint of
Macmillan Publishing Company
New York

Maxwell Macmillan Canada
Toronto

Maxwell Macmillan International
New York   Oxford   Singapore   Sydney

Cover photo: © 1991: Carla A. Sansone
Editor: Linda A. Sullivan
Developmental Editor: Linda Kauffman Peterson
Production Editor: Jonathan Lawrence
Art Coordinator: Ruth A. Kimpel
Photo Editor: Gail L. Meese
Cover Designer: Cathleen Norz
Production Buyer: Patricia A. Tonneman
Illustrations: Diphrent Strokes

This book was set in New Baskerville by Carlisle Communications, Ltd. and was printed and bound by Arcata Graphics/Halliday. The cover was printed by Phoenix Color Corp.

Macmillan Publishing Company
866 Third Avenue
New York, NY 10022

Macmillan Publishing Company is part of the
Maxwell Communication Group of Companies.

Maxwell Macmillan Canada, Inc.
1200 Eglington Avenue East, Suite 200
Don Mills, Ontario M3C 3N1

Library of Congress Cataloging-in-Publication Data
Webb, L. Dean.
    Foundations of American education/ L. Dean Webb, Arlene Metha, K. Forbis Jordan.
      p.   cm.
    Includes bibliographical references and index.
    ISBN 0-675-21204-9
    1. Education—United States. I. Metha, Arlene. II. Jordan, K.
Forbis (Kenneth Forbis), (date). III. Title.
LA217.2.W43 1992
370'.973 —dc20 91–17403

CIP

Printing: 1 2 3 4 5 6 7 8 9   Year: 2 3 4 5

Preface

Teaching is one of the most rewarding and challenging professions. In writing this book, our primary challenge has been to help persons interested in elementary and secondary education develop an understanding of the historical and philosophical roots of education, current developments, and projected futures so that they can make informed decisions about entering education and the profession of teaching. There is general agreement about the need for able persons in education; however, the decision to become a teacher should be deliberated carefully because of the critical and demanding role of the teacher, the diverse duties and responsibilities related to teaching, and the commitment of time and energy required to be a successful teacher.

A critical part of being informed about teaching is developing an understanding of the history and philosophy of elementary and secondary education, the current status of the field, the pressures for change on the schools, the role of the teacher, and the teaching/learning process. Educational foundation books often address one or more of these elements, but neglect other vital considerations. To overcome this deficiency, we have drawn upon both the historical knowledge base about education and emerging developments to prepare a comprehensive discussion of educational foundations. This book will be a valuable resource to the instructor in educational foundations and also to the student who is seeking an expanded information base about elementary and secondary education and teaching.

Rather than developing the book around a series of loosely related topics, we have used a sequenced presentation: the historical and philosophical background of elementary and secondary education, the relationship between schools and society, the law and its effect on schools, the organization and financing of elementary and secondary schools, the current and evolving process of teaching and learning, and the recent and contemplated changes in the role of the teacher, including the challenge of working with diverse populations and at-risk students. We have used an interdisciplinary approach in selecting and presenting the content; attention has been given to both the theoretical and the applied aspects of education. Our goal has been to prepare a text that includes a balance of past, present, and future applications of education in a context that students and professors will find both readable and challenging.

Orientation of the Text

Sequenced Presentation

We used the sequential approach in presenting material to help students develop an understanding of the historical and philosophical background and current and future context of elementary and secondary education. This organization will help students place the subsequent discussions of the organization of schools, school curriculum, and teaching/learning processes in a broader perspective. One effect of this sequential organizational approach is to help the student develop an understanding of the different influences on the organization and operation of American elementary and secondary education. Those influences include not only the historical and philosophical background of education, but current and projected political and social values, financial and legal developments, and emerging knowledge about teaching and learning, as well as technological developments. The sequenced presentation emphasizes that education takes place in a socio-political context and is subject to a variety of influences. We believe that this sequenced approach enhances both teaching and learning so that students will have a better understanding of the educational process and of teaching as a career.

Interdisciplinary Emphasis

In preparing the text, we have utilitzed material from various social sciences. We have incorporated historical material to provide an extensive discussion of the evolution of schooling for the past several centuries. The philosophical roots of American education have been identified and discussed. Sociology, economics, the politics of education, administration, finance, and law have been used to provide an understanding of the current and developing context of education. We have used material from psychology in the discussion of learning and teaching and the future of education.

Theoretical and Applied Aspects of Education

Based on current research, we place special emphasis on making connections between the theoretical content and the applied world of teaching. Unlike many foundations texts that concentrate primarily on pedagogical knowledge and academic skill domains, this text provides a comprehensive application of research and theory to actual classroom/educational situations and practice. Through margin notes, vignettes, and discussion questions the educational implication of research and theory are reinforced in ways that will be understandable to both practicing and prospective teachers.

Balance of the Past, Present, and Future

We have included a series of chapters that trace the historical development of education. They contain information regarding the current status and context of elementary and secondary education in America. We have illustrated different ways in which education is in a state of change. Since the mid-1980s, the school reform movement has focused major public attention on education. In this text we have addressed various ways in which school reform has had an impact on schools and classrooms. Throughout the discussion, we have emphasized the need for schools to be sensitive to the multicultural composition of the student body, expand the uses of technology in classrooms, recognize the changing role of the teacher, and change the focus of educational programs so that they will be more responsive to societal changes. The final chapter of the text explores the changing societal trends, technological advances, and their impact on education.

Readability

Many of us often think that we understand education because we have attended school for several years, but then we find that education has its share of jargon and special language. In this text we have tried to minimize the use of specialized terms and to present the material in an interesting way to stimulate reader interest. We hope that our enthusiasm for education will be obvious to you and that you will be challenged by our style of presentation. Our goal is to do more than help you understand the basic concepts about elementary and secondary education; we want you to think about education and its foundations and hope that you will seek answers to some of today's unanswered questions about education. To foster this transfer of current knowledge and the continuing search for new knowledge, we have written this book for the student. Our goal is that you find this text interesting and readable, and that it will encourage and help your learning.

Pedagogical Aids

Several special features have been designed to help the student in using the text for study and review. They also provide some direction for the overall use of the text by teachers and students.

Vignettes

The basic concepts of each chapter are reflected in the opening vignettes. They may be used to stimulate interaction about the overall content of the chapter or as springboards in expanding the discussion.

Chapter Objectives

At the start of each chapter, objectives come before the more detailed material. These may be used as guides for class discussion and also will be a good tool for you to use in studying and reviewing the material.

Margin Notes and Key Terms

To help you understand the meaning of concepts as you read and review, we have included notes in the margins of each chapter. Key terms have been identified in italic type in the text, referenced at the end of each chapter, and defined in a glossary at the end of the book.

Discussion Topics

At the end of each chapter, a series of discussion questions or topics provide an overview of the basic concepts in the chapter. They may be used as oral or written assignments, topics for class discussion, or review topics.

Special Features

Each chapter contains pedagogical features designed to enrich the learning opportunities by including historical notes and discussion stimulators drawn from current and past educational developments, current issues, or applications of educational principles in real-life situations. These special features appear under the following designations:

- *Historical Notes* provide background information about specific educational developments that have resulted in changes in education or about individuals who have exerted leadership in some aspect of education. They supplement the other content of the text and illustrate the educational contributions made by various role models.

- *Ask Yourself* features contain a series of questions that expand upon the text and stimulate exploration of specific concepts and issues in greater depth. These enrichment activities may be used by groups of students or by individuals.

- *Controversial Issues* present a dichotomy of arguments, pro and con, concerning a variety of educational issues. The controversy surrounding the educational issues is suggested to identify a wide range of values concerning important educational concepts and beliefs.

- *For Future Reference* illustrates practical and helpful educational guides for the prospective teacher. It is hoped that such guides and actual classroom aids will be relevant to the professional development of tomorrow's teachers.

Figures and Tables

The text makes extensive use of figures and tables to enhance and extend content. These visual organizers add an important dimension to the chapters.

Summary

We have presented a brief summary at the end of each chapter. These key points can be used in reviewing the chapter and identifying its important concepts. The summary also provides transition to the next chapter.

Glossary

The glossary at the end of the text defines the key terms identified throughout the book. This will help you refresh your memory about the terms and provide consistent definitions in the use of terms throughout the book.

References

A complete list of references at the end of each chapter provides bibliographic information for all references we have cited. They can be used as beginning points of identifying sources and topics for research papers and further study.

Special Emphases

We have emphasized several special areas that make this text different from some of the other materials in the field:

- The discussion of the historical and philosophical roots of education not only provides an in-depth overview of the development of education over time, but applies those time dimensions to current practice.

- The emphasis placed on a variety of social, economic, and political developments that affect the schools will be useful in understanding to what extent our educational institutions have or have not changed.

- The sections on law and the teacher provide valuable information to the prospective teacher.

- The sections on the financing and organization of the schools will be timely and valuable as shared governances and site-based decision making expand the role of the teacher in educational decision making.

- Current research on the changing role of the teacher in the learning process will raise important questions about the profession of teaching and one's attitudes about students.

- The recognition of the importance of curriculum, instruction, and the impact of tomorrow's technology will expand the text's usefulness and contribution to the field of education.

Acknowledgments

This textbook reflects the work of many persons in addition to the authors. First, we recognize the teachers and other educators who each day work to provide learning opportunities for the youth of America. Second, we wish to acknowledge the contributions of the scholars who have provided the past and present record of the development of elementary and secondary education and the researchers and policy analysts who are charting the future. Third, we recognize the various persons who supported this effort.

We extend our special thanks and appreciation for the assistance and guidance of our developmental editor, Linda Peterson. She guided us, digested the reviews, made helpful suggestions, listened to our problems, and provided a good mixture of patience and encouragement during development of the manuscript. Special recognition is also extended to the copyeditor, Sheryl Rose; the production editor, Jonathan Lawrence, who worked closely with us during the final stages of the manuscript; and Linda Sullivan, our editor on the project.

To the various reviewers we extend our sincere thanks for their constructive comments as they helped us refine the manuscript. Their efforts helped us shape the book in many positive ways. For their participation, we offer our thanks to Mary Lee Batesko, Georgian Court College; Myra J. Baughman, Pacific Lutheran University; Malcolm B. Campbell, Bowling Green State University; Duane Christian, Texas Tech University; Warren B. Fruechtel, Edinboro University of Pennsylvania; Dwight Hare, Mississippi State University; Robert Kinderman, Kutztown University; James C. Lawlor, Towson State University; Miles Lovelace, Northeast Missouri State University; William R. Martin, George Mason University; John W. McLure, The University of Iowa; Franklin Parker, Western Carolina University; Trevor J. Phillips, Bowling Green State University; Marjorie P. Quimby, Ball State University; Jack Rasmussen, Weber State College; Hans Schieser, DePaul University; and Beverly Shaklee, Kent State University.

We especially appreciate the many ways in which Terri Trimble provided assistance. Without her coordination, patience, and supervision this project might never have been brought to completion. Finally, we wish to acknowledge the invaluable contributions made by our research assistants, Cathy Freericks, Teresa Lyons, John McDonough, and Rick Trammel. Their various roles were too diverse to describe, and their comments and large and small contributions were a critical element in the successful completion of the project.

L. Dean Webb
Arlene Metha
K. Forbis Jordan

Contents in Brief

Part One
The Teaching Profession   1

    Chapter 1
    Status of the Profession   2

    Chapter 2
    Development of the Profession   36

Part Two
Historical Foundations of Education   61

    Chapter 3
    American Education: European Heritage and Colonial Experience   62

    Chapter 4
    American Education: From Revolution to the Twentieth Century   100

    Chapter 5
    Modern American Education: From the Progressive
    Movement to the Present   140

Part Three
Philosophy and Its Impact on the Schools   171

    Chapter 6
    The Major Philosophies   172

    Chapter 7
    The Impact of Educational Theories on Educational Practice   198

Part Four
The Schools and Society   235

    Chapter 8
    School and Society   236

    Chapter 9
    Achieving Equity in Education   272

    Chapter 10
    Students at Risk   310

Part Five
Legal and Political Control and Financial Support   345

Chapter 11
Legal Framework for the Public Schools   346

Chapter 12
Teachers, Students, and the Law   378

Chapter 13
Organizing and Administering Elementary
and Secondary Schools   416

Chapter 14
Financing Public Education   444

Part Six
Curriculum and Instruction   475

Chapter 15
The School Curriculum: Development and Design   476

Chapter 16
Instructional Practices in Today's Schools   504

Chapter 17
Effective Schools and Teachers   534

Part Seven
Projections for the Future   559

Chapter 18
Education for the Twenty-First Century   560

Appendix A
Selected Federal Legislation Supporting Education   585

Appendix B
Selected National Education Reports: 1982–1989   589

Glossary   591

Contents

Part One
The Teaching Profession   1

Chapter 1
Status of the Profession   2

The Teacher and Teaching: Definitions   4
Profile of the Teaching Profession   5
Why Become a Teacher?   6
Avenues to the Profession   7
Ask Yourself: Do I Want To Be a Teacher?   8
Teacher Preparation   8
Teacher Certification   16
Historical Note: Rules Regulating a Schoolmaster
in New Amsterdam in 1661   17
Teacher Supply and Demand   21
Salary and Other Compensation   22
How the Public Views the Schools and Teaching   29

Chapter 2
Development of the Profession   36

Teaching as a Profession   38
Requirements of a Profession   38
Ask Yourself: How Do I Feel About Teaching as a Profession?   43
The Professionalization of Teaching   43
Career Development   50
Teachers' Organizations   54
Historical Note: The Birth of Teachers' Unions   56

Part Two
Historical Foundations of Education   61

Chapter 3
American Education: European Heritage
and Colonial Experience   62

European Background of American Education   64

Ask Yourself: Does Corporal Punishment
Have a Place in the Classroom?   70

Historical Note: Life of the Medieval University Student   74

Education in Colonial America   83

Chapter 4
**American Education: From Revolution
to the Twentieth Century**   100

Education in the Revolutionary and Early National Period   102

For Future Reference: Peer Tutoring   107

Education in the Nineteenth and Early Twentieth Centuries   110

Historical Note: Zeal for Learning Among Freedmen, 1868   132

Chapter 5
**Modern American Education: From the
Progressive Movement to the Present**   140

The Twentieth Century Unfolds   142

The Progressive Era in American Education   145

Sputnik and After   155

Controversial Issues: Merit Pay   167

For Future Reference: Promoting Attitudes
Conducive to AIDS Prevention Behavior   168

Part Three
Philosophy and Its Impact on the Schools   171

Chapter 6
The Major Philosophies   172

What Is Philosophy?   174

Approaches to the Study of Philosophy   174

Branches of Philosophy   175

Idealism   178

Controversial Issues: Should Moral Education or
Values Education Be a Responsibility of the School?   179

Ask Yourself: What is My Philosophy of Life?   180

Realism   184

Neo-Thomism   187

Experimentalism   188

Existentialism   192

Chapter 7
The Impact of Educational Theories on Educational Practice   198

Theories of Education   200

Perennialism   201

Historical Note: St. Thomas Aquinas   202

Progressivism   205

Behaviorism   210

Essentialism   214

Reconstructionism   218

Existentialism   224

Analytic Philosophy of Education   228

Identifying Your Philosophy of Education   230

Ask Yourself: What Is My Philosophy of Education?   231

Part Four
The Schools and Society   235

Chapter 8
School and Society   236

Some Basic Concepts   238

Agents of Socialization   238

The Purposes and Expectations of Schooling   244

The Inequality of Educational Opportunity   247

Historical Note: The Concept of Social Class   249

For Future Reference: Strategies for Eliminating
Sex-Related Differences in Outcomes   266

Chapter 9
Achieving Equity in Education   272

Desegregation   274

Controversial Issues: Parental Public School Choice   279

Education of Children with Disabilities   281

For Future Reference: Mainstreaming Strategies
for Students with Behavioral Problems   282

Compensatory Education   287

Multicultural and Bilingual Education   289

Indian Education   294

Promotion of Sex Equity   297

Adult and Continuing Education   300

Vocational Education   303

Chapter 10
Students at Risk   310

At-Risk Children and Youth   312

Identifying the At-Risk Student   312

Drug and Alcohol Use and Abuse   313

Cult Participation   318

Suicide   321

Controversial Issues: The School's Role in
Suicide Prevention   324

Dropping Out of School   326

Teenage Pregnancy   328

AIDS   331

Child Abuse and Sexual Abuse   333

For Future Reference: Indicators of Sexual Abuse   335

Running Away and Homelessness   335

Delinquency and Teen Violence   337

Part Five
Legal and Political Control and Financial Support   345

Chapter 11
Legal Framework for the Public Schools   346

Federal Constitutional Provisions Affecting Education   348

State Constitutional Provisions Affecting Education   353

Statutory Law   354

Case Law   355

Administrative Law   357

Attorney General Opinions   357

Powers and Organization of the Courts   358

Historical Note: U. S. Supreme Court Justices   363

Church-State Relations   363

Ask Yourself: What Is My Opinion on Censorship?   370

Chapter 12
Teachers, Students, and the Law   378

Teacher Rights and Responsibilities   380

For Future Reference: Guidelines for Classroom Copying   386

Student Rights and Responsibilities   401

Controversial Issues: No Pass, No Play   405

Chapter 13
**Organizing and Administering Elementary
and Secondary Schools**   **416**

The Context of the Public Schools   418

The Federal Government and Public Education   418

State Educational Agencies   422

Intermediate Educational Service Agencies   426

Local School Districts   428

Historical Note: Ella Flagg Young,
Pioneer School Administrator   436

Attendance Centers—The Local School   437

Controversial Issues: Site-or School-Based Management?   439

Private Education   440

Chapter 14
Financing Public Education   **444**

Financing the Schools   446

Education—An Expense or an Investment?   447

Public Policy Goals in School Finance   448

Ask Yourself: Issues of Equity   449

The Courts and School Finance   449

State School Finance Equalization Programs   451

Sources of Tax Revenue for Schools   454

Local School District Planning and Budgeting   458

Historical Note: The Lotteries and Education   460

Nontax Sources of School Revenues   460

Federal Aid for Elementary and Secondary Schools   462

Differences Among the States   465

School Finance Issues of the 1990s   466

Part Six
Curriculum and Instruction   **475**

Chapter 15
The School Curriculum: Development and Design   **476**

Forces Influencing the Curriculum   478

Curriculum Development   487

Patterns of Curriculum Organization   488

For Future Reference: Practical Hints for
Preparing and Stating Learning Objectives   490

The Hidden Curriculum   496

Controversial Issues: The Subject-Centered
and Student-Centered Curricula   498

The Curriculum Cycle   499

Chapter 16
Instructional Practices in Today's Schools   **504**

Schools for All   506

Instructional Goals and Objectives   506

Organizing for Instruction   509

Historical Note: Maria Montessori and the
Montessori Method   510

Mastery Learning   512

Teaching Strategies   514

Ask Yourself: A Checklist for Critical Thinkers   522

Technology and Instruction   522

Issues and Trends in Curriculum and Instruction   524

Chapter 17
Effective Schools and Teachers   **534**

Impact of Schools on Student Learning   536

Effective Schools   537

Ask Yourself: How Will Adoption of the Effective
Schools Concept Affect You as a Teacher?   543

Characteristics of Effective Teachers   543

Effective Principals   548

Historical Note: The Effective Principal   551

Business–Education Partnerships   553

Part Seven
Projections for the Future   **559**

Chapter 18
Education for the Twenty-First Century   **560**

Societal Trends for the Twenty-First Century   562

Historical Note: Nostradamus—
Astrologer, Physician, and Futurist   564

Ask Yourself: Are You a Futurist?   578

Futures Education   578

Appendix A
Selected Federal Legislation Supporting Education   **585**

Appendix B
Selected National Education Reports: 1982–1989   **589**

Glossary   **591**

Author Index   **I-1**

Subject Index   **I-9**

Special Features

Historical Note

Rules Regulating a Schoolmaster in
New Amsterdam in 1661   17

The Birth of Teachers' Unions   56

Life of the Medieval University Student   74

Zeal for Learning Among Freedmen, 1868   132

St. Thomas Aquinas   202

The Concept of Social Class   249

U. S. Supreme Court Justices   363

Ella Flagg Young, Pioneer School Administrator   436

The Lotteries and Education   460

Maria Montessori and the Montessori Method   510

The Effective Principal   551

Nostradamus—Astrologer, Physician, and Futurist   564

Ask Yourself

Do I Want To Be a Teacher?   8

How Do I Feel About Teaching as a Profession?   43

Does Corporal Punishment Have a Place in the Schools?   70

What Is My Philosophy of Life?   180

What Is My Philosophy of Education?   231

What Is My Position on Censorship?   370

Issues of Equity   449

A Checklist for Critical Thinkers   522

How Will Adoption of the Effective Schools
Concept Affect You as a Teacher?   543

Are You a Futurist?   578

Controversial Issues

Merit Pay   167

Should Moral Education or Values Education
Be a Responsibility of the School?   179

Parental Public School Choice   279

The School's Role in Suicide Prevention   324

No Pass, No Play   405

Site- or School-Based Management?   439

The Subject-Centered and Student-Centered Curricula   498

For Future Reference

Peer Tutoring   107

Promoting Attitudes Conducive to
AIDS Prevention Behavior   168

Strategies for Eliminating Sex-Related
Differences in Outcomes   266

Mainstreaming Strategies for Students
with Behavioral Problems   282

Indicators of Sexual Abuse   335

Guidelines for Classroom Copying   386

Practical Hints for Preparing and
Stating Learning Objectives   490

Part One

The Teaching Profession

Status of the Profession   **Chapter 1**
Development of the Profession   **Chapter 2**

Chapter 1
Status of the Profession

Education is the one investment that means more for our future, because it means the most for our children. . . . The nation will not accept anything less than excellence in education.

President George Bush
State of the Union Address
January 31, 1990

Dr. Flynn enters the room of a patient who was recently admitted to University Hospital complaining of severe abdominal pain. Several interns follow Dr. Flynn to the patient's bedside. Dr. Flynn begins to ask the patient a series of questions. After the patient responds, Dr. Flynn turns to one of the interns and asks for a diagnosis. The intern gives a diagnosis. Dr. Flynn follows with a series of questions related to the basis for the diagnosis and possible treatment.

The ABC Corporation has just initiated a new data management plan. All middle managers have been told to report to the conference room at 8:30 A.M. on Monday. Upon arrival, the director of human resources introduces Ms. Dominguez from Data Resources, the retailer of the software supporting the new data management plan. Ms. Dominguez distributes a packet of materials and spends the remainder of the day with the managers, reviewing the materials in the packet, pre-senting additional information from overheads, and showing a video related to the data management plan.

Mr. Pell stops at Amy Black's desk and answers a question. He moves to the desk of another student, observes the student writing in a workbook, points to something the student has written, and then, in a low voice, tells the student that the response is not correct and explains why. He continues around the room, stopping at almost every desk to make some remark. After about 10 minutes he goes to the front of the room and says, "Class, it appears that several people are having problems with this assignment. Let's review how to divide one fraction by another fraction." Mr. Pell walks to the blackboard and begins talking.

Which of the above individuals, Dr. Flynn, Ms. Dominguez, or Mr. Pell, is a teacher? Why? What defines the act of teaching?

There is no one right answer to the questions "What is a teacher?" and "What defines the act of teaching?" Teaching has been considered by some to be the most noble of the professions. H. G. Wells went so far as to say that "The teacher, whether mother, priest, or schoolmaster, is the real maker of history." Perhaps you are asking yourself, "what is a teacher? What is this profession of teaching all about?" And, perhaps most importantly, "Should I become a teacher?" This chapter presents an overview of the teaching profession. After studying the chapter you should be able to:

- Provide a demographic overview of America's teaching force.

- Discuss the public's views of the schools and the teaching profession.

- Evaluate your motives for becoming a teacher, as well as those commonly cited by others.

- Describe the preparation of teachers and the concerns related to program and student quality and minority participation.

- Discuss current issues related to certification, including testing, alternative certification, emergency certification, and interstate certification.

- Compare projected data related to teacher supply with that projected for demand and explore the factors contributing to supply and demand.

- Identify the determinants of teacher compensation and approaches to salary determination, including incentive pay and extracurricular pay.

The Teacher and Teaching: Definitions

Put most simply, a teacher is one who instructs others. A more formal definition from Good's *Dictionary of Education* (1973) defines a teacher as "a person employed in an official capacity for the purpose of guiding and directing the learning experiences of pupils or students in an educational institution, whether public or private" (p. 586). Teaching is defined in the same work as "the act of instructing in an educational institution" (p. 588). A well-known educator and writer in the field of education, B. O. Smith (1987), provides five definitions of teaching:

1. The descriptive definition of teaching: Defines teaching as imparting knowledge or skill.

2. Teaching as success: Defines teaching as an activity such that X learns what Y teaches. If X does not learn, Y has not taught.

3. Teaching as intentional activity: Defines teaching as intended behavior (i.e., paying attention to what is going on, making diagnoses, changing one's behavior) for which the aim is to induce learning.

4. Teaching as normative behavior: Defines teaching as a family of activities, including training, instructing, indoctrinating, and conditioning.

5. The scientific or technical definition of teaching: Defines teaching by the coordinating propositions; teaching is not explicitly defined, but its meaning is implicated in the sentences where it occurs (e.g., "The teacher gives feedback.").

Perhaps the most provocative definition defines the teacher as an artist and teaching as an art. This definition sees the person of the teacher as the essential ingredient in teaching and subscribes to the saying that "teachers are born, not made" (Dawe, 1984). N. L. Gage (1984), a leading theorist in education, describes teaching as an instrumental or practical art, not a fine art:

> As an instrumental art teaching departs from recipes, formulas, and algorithms. It requires improvisation, spontaneity, the handling of a vast array of considerations of form, style, pace, and rhythm, and appropriateness in ways so complex even computers must lose the way. (p. 88)

Although Gage rejects the possibility of a science of teaching, he does believe in the necessity of establishing a scientific basis for the art of teaching—a research basis consisting of scientifically developed knowledge about relationships between variables. The stronger the scientific basis, the greater the potential to improve teaching.

Do you believe that teachers are "born, not made"? In your experience as a student, have you been exposed to teachers who were "artists" in the classroom?

Profile of the Teaching Profession

Whatever definition is used, there is little argument that the teacher is the central element in the educational system. It is of interest to review what we know about the teacher in American society today. Table 1.1 presents some characteristics of public and private teachers.

As indicated in the table, the teaching force is predominantly female and white. Public school teachers are almost equally divided in terms of degree status: about half have a bachelor's degree and about half have higher than a bachelor's degree. The degree attainment of public school teachers was higher overall than that of private school teachers. However, private school teachers experience smaller pupil-teacher ratios at the secondary level and in combined schools than

Table 1.1: Selected Characteristics of Public and Private School Teachers, 1986

Teacher Characteristics	Public School Teachers	Private School Teachers
Sex (Percent)		
Male	31	24
Female	69	76
Race/ethnicity (Percent)		
White, non-Hispanic	90	92
Black, non-Hispanic	7	4
Other	3	4
Highest degree (Percent)		
Bachelor's	51	66
More than bachelor's	48	30
Average number of pupils per class		
Elementary	24	20
Secondary	25	17
Average number of hours per week spent on school-related activities	49	50[1]
Years of full-time teaching experience (Percent)		
Less than 5	12[1]	25
5–9	21[1]	27
10 or more	68[1]	48

Source: U.S. Department of Education, National Center for Education Statistics. (1989). *Digest of education statistics, 1989.* Washington, DC: U.S. Government Printing Office.

[1]U.S. Department of Education, National Center for Education Statistics. (1989). *The condition of education.* Washington, DC: U.S. Government Printing Office.

Table 1.2: Historical Summary of Public Elementary and Secondary School Statistics: United States, 1869–70 to 1986–87

	1869–70	1879–80	1889–90	1899–1900	1909–10	1919–20
Total enrollment (in thousands)	6,872	9,867	12,723	15,503	17,814	21,578
Total instructional staff (in thousands)	—	—	—	—	—	678
Total teachers, librarians and other nonsupervisory staff (in thousands)	201	287	364	423	523	657
Men	78	123	126	127	110	93
Women	123	164	238	296	413	585

do public school teachers. Both groups of teachers report spending about 50 hours per week in school-related activities. Public school teachers as a group have more experience than private school teachers. In fact, 68% of the public school teachers have 10 or more years of experience.

The number of teachers and other instructional personnel employed in the public school systems of the United States has grown over the years as enrollments have increased. Table 1.2 gives a historical summary of public elementary and secondary school enrollments, number of instructional staff, and number of teachers, librarians, and other nonsupervisory staff. As can be seen, in the years since 1950 the total number of teachers, librarians, and other nonsupervisory staff more than doubled. The growth in staff reflects not only enrollment increases, but the steady reduction in pupil-teacher ratios, legislation requiring increased services and specialized personnel, and the increased utilization of teacher aides, librarians, guidance counselors, and other instructional support personnel.

Why Become a Teacher?

There are many reasons why an individual might choose a career in teaching. Very few teachers would be able to identify a single reason for entering the profession. For some an important reason might be a practical consideration such as job security, or something as forthright as the fact that their first career choices were blocked (i.e., they didn't make it into medical school or into professional sports). Others may even be attracted by the long summer vacations. Some less positive reasons might be that teaching is convenient; it is a job that is respectable and not too demanding while going to law school, supporting a spouse through professional or graduate school, looking for a

1929–30	1939–40	1949–50	1959–60	1969–70	1979–80	1986–87
25,678	25,434	25,112	36,087	45,619	41,645	39,837
880	912	962	1,464	2,253	2,441	2,540[1]
843	875	914	1,387	2,131	2,300	2,400[1]
140	195	195	402	691	782	—
703	681	719	985	1,440	1,518	—

Source: U.S. Department of Education, National Center for Educational Statistics. (1989). *Digest of educational statistics, 1989* (Table 35). Washington, DC: U.S. Government Printing Office.

[1]National Education Association. (1987). *Estimates of school statistics, 1986–87*. Washington, DC: National Education Association.

good business connection, or marking time while trying to determine what one really wants to do (Kohl, 1976).

All of the above are indeed motives for becoming a teacher, but they are not the primary motives. Over the years, numerous researchers have asked teachers what attracted them to the profession. The three reasons given most consistently are: (1) a desire to work with young people; (2) a desire to make a contribution to society/a belief in the importance of teaching to society; and (3) an interest in a certain field and an excitement in sharing it with others.

The reasons one has for becoming a teacher have a significant effect on the ultimate satisfaction one finds in the job. For this reason, Herbert Kohl (1976), elementary school teacher and well-known, outspoken educator, suggests that prospective teachers question themselves about what they expect to gain from or give to teaching. Several sets of questions suggested by Kohl to guide you in this inquiry are found on page 8.

Avenues to the Profession

There are a number of ways to become a teacher. The most traditional is to complete a baccalaureate teacher education program. For the increasing number of individuals who already have college degrees and are entering the profession the two options are: (1) enrolling as a postbaccalaureate student and taking only enough courses to become a teacher without obtaining a graduate degree, or (2) enrolling in a master's degree program leading to teacher certification. At some institutions, undergraduates majoring in fields

1. What reasons do you have for wanting to teach? Are they all negative (e.g., because the schools are oppressive, or because I need a job and working as a teacher is more respectable than working as a cab driver or salesperson)? What are the positive reasons for wanting to teach? Is there any pleasure to be gained from teaching? Knowledge? Power?

2. Why do you want to spend so much time with young people? Do you feel more comfortable with children? Have you spent much time with children recently, or are you mostly fantasizing how they would behave? Are you afraid of adults? Intimidated by adult company? Fed up with the competition and coldness of business and the university?

3. What do you want from the children? Do you want them to do well on tests? Learn particular subject matter? Like each other? Like you? How much do you need to have students like you? Are you afraid to criticize them or set limits on their behavior because they might be angry with you? Do you consider yourself one of the kids? Is there any difference in your mind between your role and that of your prospective students?

4. What do you know that you can teach to or share with your students?

5. With what age youngster do you feel the greatest affinity or are you most comfortable with?

6. Do you have any sex-based motives for wanting to work with young people? Do you want to enable them to become the boy or girl you could never be? For example, to free the girls of the image of prettiness and quietness and encourage them to run and fight, mess about with science and get lost in the abstraction of math? Or to encourage boys to write poetry, play with dolls, let their fantasies come out, and not feel abnormal if they enjoy reading, acting, or listening to music?

7. What kind of young people do you want to work with?

8. What kind of school should you teach in?

9. How comfortable would you be teaching in a multiracial or multicultural setting? Do you feel capable of working with a culturally diverse student population?

---

other than education are able to accumulate enough teacher education credits to qualify for certification. And in a few states it is still possible for candidates with no teacher education course work to apply directly to the state department of education for certification after having completed one or more years of successful teaching experience under a *provisional certificate*. In the next section we will review teacher education programs, the most common avenue into the profession.

Teacher Preparation

Assumptions about the general quality of teacher preparation programs, as well as the faculty and students in those programs, are central to much of the debate about reform in teacher education. Opinions vary on the present quality of the programs and on what reforms are needed. But before we review the various reform proposals, let us look at teacher education programs as they exist today, and see in what ways they are changing to meet the demands of the profession and its clientele.

Program Characteristics

The formal education of teachers takes place in about 1,200 different departments, schools, or colleges of education in the United States. Teacher education programs usually consist of four areas: (1) a general studies requirement, (2) the major and minor areas of specialization, (3) a professional studies component, and (4) a student teaching experience. The general studies or liberal arts portion of the program, as well as the academic major portion, are generally similar to those required of other students at the college or university. The professional studies component usually consists of courses in teaching methods, curriculum, foundations, and educational psychology.

Preparation programs for elementary school teachers are somewhat different from those for secondary school teachers. Depending on the organization of the institution, students completing preparation programs for secondary school teachers may have a major in education or a major in the subject field to be taught. Generally, the number of hours taken by the secondary education student in the subject field is the same as for noneducation majors, though there may be some differences in specific courses.

Although a growing number of institutions are requiring that students preparing to be elementary school teachers have a minor in a content area, elementary education is considered their major. They are not expected to be a subject matter specialist, but must be prepared to teach the full range of subject matter studied in the self-contained elementary classroom. Consequently, they take courses in the content and methods of elementary reading, science, math, social studies, or other subjects. "Although these courses frequently carry the label 'Methods of . . . ,' they actually describe the curriculum content as well as appropriate methods for teaching that content, and they show how these are related both to each other and to the child's development" (Egbert, 1985, p. 17).

How did you determine your preference for elementary or secondary teaching?

Figure 1.1 graphically depicts the typical preparation programs for elementary and secondary teachers and gives the percentage of each program devoted to each area. As the graphs show, the general studies and student teaching requirements are approximately the same for both programs; they differ in the percentage of time spent in professional studies and in other academic studies. Overall, secondary education students average 10 semester hours more to complete their program than elementary majors.

In addition to the internship or student teaching experience, teacher preparation programs increasingly include *field or clinical experiences* such as classroom observation or tutoring prior to student teaching. A survey of American Association of Colleges of Teacher Education (AACTE) institutions found that 86% required early field experiences (AACTE, 1987). Typically,

Figure 1.1: Elementary and Secondary Education Program Requirements

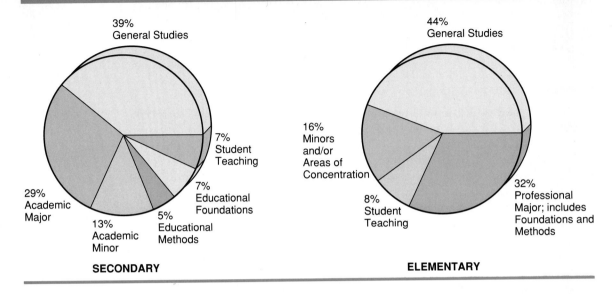

39%
General Studies

7%
Student
Teaching

7%
Educational
Foundations

29%
Academic
Major

5%
Educational
Methods

13%
Academic
Minor

SECONDARY

44%
General Studies

16%
Minors
and/or
Areas of
Concentration

8%
Student
Teaching

32%
Professional
Major; includes
Foundations and
Methods

ELEMENTARY

special education students spend 166 clock hours in field experience, early childhood and elementary students 140 hours, and secondary education students 90 hours (Galluzzo & Arends, 1989). When added to the average of 360 hours reportedly spent in student teaching, today's teacher education student is receiving significantly more clinical experiences than those trained even a decade ago.

Quality of Teacher Education Programs

Have you experienced any bias or negative responses to your desire to become a teacher? Have you felt any of the "less than" stigma?

It is not uncommon for teacher education programs to be viewed as less rigorous than, for example, science, engineering, or business programs on college and university campuses. Although many of today's largest and most prestigious universities began as "normal schools," or teacher training institutions, the schools or colleges of education on these same campuses often find themselves viewed with a more critical eye than colleges of engineering, business, or law. But is this negative perception justified? Is there reason to believe that the majority of the teacher preparation programs in the country today are not quality programs? Let us examine the facts.

Admission Standards

One of the charges that have been leveled against teacher education is that admission standards are too low. However, the facts do not support this allegation. For example, a study of the 103 institutions that are members of the Association of Colleges and Schools of Education in State Universities and Land Grant Colleges and Affiliated Private Universities (ACSE) found that the admission and graduation requirements of colleges of education were generally higher than the requirements of other undergraduate programs in the

Increasingly, students are given the opportunity to gain clinical experience in the classroom, often beginning with their first professional teacher education course.

same institutions (Ishler, 1984). Since this survey, admission requirements have been raised in most institutions in response to criticisms and state mandates (Galluzzo & Arends, 1989).

In addition to raising grade point averages and course requirements for admission, an increasing number of states require students to pass a test before being admitted to a teacher education program: 32 states currently have such requirements. The most commonly used instruments are the Pre-Professional Skills Test and a similar instrument, the California Basic Education Skills Test (CBEST), both published by the Educational Testing Service (ETS).

Program Rigor

Another challenge to the quality of teacher preparation programs is their alleged lack of "rigor." Again, the data do not support this allegation. When asked to rate the "rigor" of their teacher education courses in comparison to noneducation courses, one-third (33%) of the education students responding to a survey at AACTE institutions said the education courses were more rigorous than the noneducation courses, 30% said they were as rigorous, and 27% said they were less rigorous (AACTE, 1987).

Do you believe you are enrolled in a quality teacher education program? Is there room for improvement?

Students were then asked to compare the rigor of their specific secondary education methods course with a comparable course in five different content areas: English, history, foreign languages, science, and math. Only one-fourth of the students viewed the secondary methods courses as less rigorous than the English courses. Similar results were true for comparisons with history (27%) and foreign language (30%) courses. Perhaps most surprisingly, only one-half of the students perceived science and math courses to be more rigorous than secondary education methods courses.

Quality of Teacher Education Students

Although student quality is difficult to assess, one of the most commonly accepted measures is academic ability. Unfortunately, over the past decade or more the average standardized test scores of high school students indicating an interest in becoming a teacher have declined. A major factor contributing to the decline has been the fact that "the best and the brightest" women and minorities, those who historically had few fields open to them but teaching, began to enter law, medicine, engineering, and other professional fields in increasing numbers. In fact, the entering classes of many law and medical schools are now over 50% female. An additional factor is that because of the teacher surplus in the 1970s, many people who might have entered teaching chose other careers (Borkow & Jordan, 1983).

The national studies critical of teachers and teacher preparation have looked at the test scores of high school students who express an intent to enter teacher education or college entrants who declare teacher education as their intended major. However, many of these individuals either never actually go on to college, or once there often change majors several times. When we look at those students who are actually admitted or enroll in a teacher education program, the data present a much more positive view of the quality of teacher education students.

For example, a study at Michigan State University showed ACT and SAT scores of a representative sample of entering teacher candidates to be at or above the average for all MSU students. Additionally, no significant differences were found in the high school grade point average of teacher candidates (mean g.p.a. = 3.14) and nonteaching majors (mean g.p.a. = 3.07) (Book, Freeman, & Brousseau, 1985). More recent data collected by the AACTE Research About Teacher Education (RATE) Project support the conclusion that the SAT and ACT scores of teacher education students compare favorably with other undergraduate students. Additionally, the typical teacher education student was rated in the top 30% of his or her high school graduating class (Galluzzo & Arends, 1989).

Minority Participation

Minority teachers are needed in the schools for a variety of reasons, perhaps the most important being their presence as role models. These models

"help young children develop an appreciation for diversity, and cultural difference. Without visible examples of diversity, broadened thinking and experience are not only out of sight, but unfortunately out of mind" (Bass de
Martinez, 1988, p. 13). Yet one of the major concerns of teacher preparation
programs today is the declining number of minority students and subsequently minority teachers. The decline in minority enrollments is especially
distressing because it has been occurring at the same time that minority enrollments in the public schools have been increasing. It has been predicted that
by the year 2000, 50% of the students in urban schools will be minorities, but
less than 5% of the teachers will be (Grant & Gillette, 1987). "This means an
average student who might be exposed to forty teachers during his or her
public school career can at best expect to be exposed to only two minority
teachers" (Nicklos & Brown, 1989, p. 146).

Obstacles to Participation

The problem of attracting minorities into careers in education is com-
pounded by the fact that proportionately fewer minorities, especially blacks,
are going to college today compared to a decade ago (Graham, 1987). Of those
who do attend college, many are choosing other careers. Once teaching was
one of the few, if not the only, means of upward social mobility, but minorities
are now making advances in other professions (Nicklos & Brown, 1989).

The entrance of minority students into teaching is being further threatened by the various gatekeeping measures proposed by the reform initiatives.
The imposition of higher SAT or ACT requirements for college admissions, as
well as testing requirements for entry into teacher education programs and for
certification, have had an adverse effect on minority students and prospective
teachers. The pass rates for minorities on these tests are significantly lower
than for Anglos. This has been especially true in the southern states where
about half the nation's black teachers are prepared (Graham, 1987; Nicklos &
Brown, 1989).

The possibility that teacher education might become a five-year (or
longer) program is seen as a further discouragement to minorities (Waters,
1989). With the number of minorities entering and completing college down,
it follows that fewer would enter postbaccalaureate or advanced degree programs. The factors of funding and long-term financing must also be considered. The Carnegie Forum has estimated that given the decreasing number of
minorities currently completing college, colleges of education would have to
produce 50,000 minority masters of teaching each year when hiring rates
reach 200,000 teachers per year in the 1990s, to replace those already in the
teaching force, let alone meet the demand associated with changing population demographics (Bass de Martinez, 1988).

Strategies for Improvement

Some recommendations have been made for increasing the number of
minorities in teacher education. These include increased recruitment efforts,
especially at the precollege level; increased support services and other retention
efforts at all levels; scholarship programs, loan forgiveness, and low-interest

The projected demographics of student populations support the pressing need for preparing greater numbers of minority teachers.

loan programs; ensuring that testing and evaluation programs minimize the influence of handicapping conditions, poverty, race, and ethnicity on entry to the profession; creating new forms of postbaccalaureate teacher education programs aimed specifically at minorities (Haberman, 1988), and various proposals designed to make the profession more attractive (Holmes Group, 1986). If these recommendations are not implemented and these efforts are not successful, "we may soon have a teacher force composed overwhelmingly of people from majority backgrounds teaching students who are primarily from low income and minority backgrounds" (Holmes Group, 1986, p. 66).

Recommendations for Teacher Education in the School Reform Reports

Beginning with the *Nation at Risk* report in 1983 from Secretary of Education Terrel H. Bell's National Commission on Excellence in Education, 13 major national reform reports have presented a variety of recommendations related to improving teacher education. The reports took different approaches in their recommendations and observations about ways to improve teacher education, which can be classified into several broad areas: length of program; program content, admission, performance and exit standards; and clinical experiences. In our discussion, while noting other reports, we will focus on the two that have received the most attention in the literature related to teacher preparation: *A Nation Prepared: Teachers for the 21st Century* (1986), the report of the Carnegie Forum on Education's Task Force on Teaching as a Profession; and the report of the Holmes Group (a group of deans of colleges of education at research universities), *Tomorrow's Teachers: A Report of the Holmes Group* (1986).

Length of Program

The consensus among the reports is that teacher education programs should be at least five years in length. The rationale for this recommendation, as the Carnegie report explains, is that four years of college is not enough time for the prospective teacher to master the subjects to be taught and gain the skills to teach them. Consequently, both the Carnegie Forum and the Holmes Group recommend abolishing the undergraduate teacher education major and requiring a bachelor's degree as a prerequisite for the professional study of teaching. The National Commission on Excellence in Teacher Education report (*A Call for Change in Teacher Education*, 1983), the Boyer report (*High School: A Report on Secondary Education in America*, 1983) and other reform reports, while not necessarily calling for the abolition of undergraduate teacher education, presume that adequate preparation of teachers would require a more lengthy program than currently exists in most colleges of education.

Do you recognize that there may be content areas in which you need further training? Have you considered enrolling in more courses to supplement your knowledge in these areas?

Program Content

A major focus of all the reports is on the actual content of the programs. A major theme is that teachers must be knowledgeable in the content of the subjects they are to teach, that greater emphasis must be placed on academic knowledge in teacher training, and that teachers must demonstrate competence in their academic disciplines. Accordingly, a consistent recommendation is to require students to have a major in an academic discipline. As already noted, both the Carnegie and Holmes reports called for the completion of a bachelor's degree in the major prior to entrance into teacher education.

Some of the reports are concerned with the liberal arts curriculum received by prospective teachers. According to the Holmes Group, "most undergraduate programs lack coherence and a focus on enduring questions and ideas" (Murray, 1986, p. 30). Thus, "the reform of teacher education must be coupled with changes in the education that undergraduates receive in the arts and sciences" (Murray, 1986, p. 30).

The Professional Curriculum

Another major concern of the reform reports relates to program content in the professional curriculum. The Carnegie Forum, for example, speaks of a need to develop a new professional curriculum based on systematic knowledge of teaching and including internships and residences in the schools. Several other reports have recommended the development of a "core of essential courses" that would focus on teaching and learning theory and would include research on teaching. As a consequence, one of the major identifiable trends in teacher preparation today is the effort to document the knowledge bases for teacher preparation (Cruickshank & Cruz, 1989).

John Goodlad's (1983) report, *A Place Called School,* gave perhaps the greatest attention to professional education. He recommended that: (1) teachers have an interest in both the learner and the subject to be taught; (2) teachers understand and practice pedagogical techniques designed to keep students overtly and covertly engaged in learning; (3) faculties from the academic disciplines be involved in the teacher education program by using a team-teaching approach in the methods courses; (4) teachers understand human development and be sensitive to individual differences; and (5) the content of teacher education programs include components that prepare teachers to use alternate teaching methods, diagnostic tests, evaluation feedback, and praise for students (Jordan, 1988).

Admission, Performance, and Exit Standards

Many of the reports included recommendations related to admission, performance, and exit standards for the teacher preparation program. A variety of recommendations were made, including making more careful selection of candidates, raising g.p.a. entrance requirements, and requiring candidates to pass skills tests. The Holmes Group recommended that prospective teachers be required to pass a written test in each subject to be taught.

Have you completed a precertification examination? Do you believe the examination made a fair estimate of your knowledge and skills?

It is in this area of recommendations that the most demonstrable action has been taken. State legislatures and boards of education have mandated various entry, exit, or certification requirements, the most common being the passage of an examination (see section on Competency Testing).

Clinical Experiences

Several of the reports, especially the more recent ones, recommend increasing the clinical experiences provided in teacher education programs. For example, the master in teaching degree proposed in the Carnegie report includes internship and programs, each lasting nine months. Like others, this report considers the field component to be essential to the teacher preparation program. Both the Carnegie report and the report of the Holmes Group go so far as to suggest the establishment of "clinical schools" or "professional development schools" that would serve the same function in education as do teaching hospitals in medicine.

Teacher Certification

To qualify for teaching, administrative, and many other positions in the public schools, an individual must acquire a valid certificate or license. The *certification* or licensure requirement is intended to ensure that the holder has met established state standards and is therefore qualified for employment in

Historical Note:
Rules Regulating a Schoolmaster in New Amsterdam in 1661

1. He shall take good care, that the children, coming to his school, do so at the usual hour, namely at eight in the morning and one in the afternoon.

2. He must keep good discipline among his pupils.

3. He shall teach the children and pupils the Christian Prayers, commandments, baptism, Lord's supper, and the questions with answers of the catechism, which are taught here every Sunday afternoon in the church.

4. Before school closes he shall let the pupils sing some verses and a psalm.

5. Besides his yearly salary he shall be allowed to demand and receive from every pupil quarterly as follows: For each child, whom he teaches the a b c spelling and reading, 30 st.; for teaching to read and write, 50 st.; for teaching to read, write, and cipher, 60st.; from those who come in the evening and between times pro rata a fair sum. The poor and needy, who ask to be taught for God's sake he shall teach for nothing.

6. He shall be allowed to demand and receive from everybody, who makes arrangements to come to his school and comes before the first half of the quarter preceding the first of December next, the school dues for the quarter, but nothing from those who come after the first half of the quarter.

7. He shall not take from anybody, more than is herein stated. Thus done and decided by the Burgomasters of the City of Amsterdam in N. N., November 4, 1661.

Notice that the New Amsterdam schoolmaster was paid more for those students receiving instruction beyond the ABCs. The practice of paying secondary teachers more than elementary teachers was practiced well into this century. Also notice the schoolmaster was *required* to give religious instruction, a prohibition today.

Source: Finegan, T. (Ed.) (1921). *Free schools: A documentary history of the free school movement in New York State.* Quoted in S. Cohn (Ed.). (1974). *Education in the United States, a documentary history, Vol. 1.* New York: Random House.

the area specified on the certificate. The certification process is administered by the state education agency. The certificate can be obtained in one of two ways: assessment by the state agency of the candidate's transcripts and experiences against a particular set of course and experience requirements, or, more typical, the "approved program approach." In this case, candidates who have graduated from a teacher preparation program approved by the state to prepare teachers are automatically certified upon graduation (Zimpher, 1987).

Specific state certification requirements may include a college degree (all states require a bachelor's degree as a minimum), recommendation of a college or employer, minimum credit hours in designated curricular areas, a student teaching experience, evidence of specific job experience, "good moral character," attainment of a minimum age, United States citizenship, the signing of a loyalty oath affirming support of the government, and, in recent years, the passing of a state prescribed competency exam.

What are the personal requirements for certification in your state or the state in which you plan to teach?

Competency Testing

The number of states requiring some form of competency testing as a requisite for initial certification has increased dramatically in the past decade, from 13 in 1980 to 48 in 1990 (U.S. Department of Education, 1989a). The increase in the testing of teachers can be attributed directly to the public's growing concern about the quality of education and the quality of teachers, and reflects the public's demand for accountability "to insure that teachers do, indeed, possess the basic skills, academic knowledge, and professional skills necessary for successful teaching" (Sandefur, 1985, p. 21). The most commonly used instruments are the National Teacher Examination (NTE); the Pre-Professional Skills Test (PPST), a test taken prior to admission to the teacher education program; and state-developed tests. Testing is in one or more of four areas: basic skills, professional knowledge, general knowledge, and a specialty area.

The major concerns that have been voiced in regard to the precertification testing of teachers are much the same as those raised in regard to preadmission testing: fairness and impact on the available pool of teachers. That is, although testing does produce quantitative results and reduces some of the subjectivity that might exist in qualification and employment decisions, there is concern that these tests may measure the wrong things and may not measure those aspects of competence that are needed for success in the classroom (i.e., they lack content validity). There is also concern that the tests may be poorly designed, may be inappropriately used (e.g., as the basis for arbitrary layoffs), and may have an adverse impact on minority populations. Moreover, testing tends to reduce the available pool of prospective teachers without any real assurance "that this small group will be superior to those excluded on any criterion other than the ability to take tests" (Lines, 1985, pp. 618–19).

Impact on Minorities

The results of teacher testing indicate that disproportionate percentages of blacks and Hispanics fail. For example, in California, 76% of the Anglo test takers passed the CBEST, as opposed to 26% of blacks and 19% of Hispanics. In Texas, the pass rate for Anglos was 62%, for blacks, 10%, and for Hispanics, 19% (Smith, 1984). The Educational Testing Service reports that unless there is significant change, by the year 2000 the percentage of minorities in the teaching force will be cut almost in half. This decline will be taking place at the same time that the number of minority students in the public schools will be increasing dramatically (Anrig, 1986).

Prospects for a National Proficiency Examination

Although there has been considerable opposition to most of the competency exams in use among the states, both the *National Education Association (NEA)* and the *American Federation of Teachers (AFT)* have supported proposals for a national proficiency examination for licensing new teachers. Under the proposals a national board would be created to develop and administer the exam, which would be similar to those required by the legal and medical professions. While supporting a national teachers' exam, these professional organizations and many other organizations and individuals continue to be critical of the use of a single test as an absolute screening device. Most agree with NEA past-president Mary Hatwood Futrell that successful classroom performance should be determined by a number of criteria, with the score on one test being but one aspect of a comprehensive teacher assessment program.

Recertification

Acquiring certification once does not mean that a teacher is certified for life. An increasing number of states have adopted testing or other requirements for the recertification of experienced teachers. This is one of the reform efforts intended to bring greater efficiency and effectiveness to American education. Historically, to obtain recertification a teacher needed to earn a specified number of graduate hours during an allotted period. Within the last decade, however, the practice of meeting recertification requirements through district-sponsored, in-service training has become an increasingly common alternative (Hanes & Rowls, 1984).

Alternative Certification Programs

In response to the shortage of qualified teachers in some teaching areas, almost half the states have adopted *alternative certification* plans. Despite the objections of the teachers' unions, if the predicted teacher shortages do in fact occur, alternative certification plans will undoubtedly become even more popular. These programs differ from traditional certification programs in target audience, training, and length of training, but not, it is intended, in program content, rigor, or expected outcomes (Smith, Nystrand, Ruch, Gideonse, & Carlson, 1985). They are aimed at noneducation college graduates who have an academic major in a subject matter field taught in the schools. These programs hope to attract qualified recent college graduates or mid-career persons to the teaching profession. Although many such programs were originally intended to address the shortages in math and science, most are open to those with majors in any teaching field.

Alternative certification programs may be offered through the hiring school district (as in California), a college or university (e.g., Arkansas), or a partnership of the two. The typical alternative certification program includes: (1) a formal instructional component including the philosophical, historical, and sociological foundations of education as well as methods courses; (2) an intensive field practicum; and (3) the close supervision of the participant by school district and/or college or university personnel. In the more common programs, students first complete the equivalent of one semester of formal coursework and then complete a semester that combines student teaching and coursework (Aldeman, 1987). The AACTE recommends that alternative certification programs utilize selective admission standards that assess subject matter competency as well as personal characteristics and incorporate a comprehensive assessment of professional competency (AACTE, 1989).

If noneducation graduates can prepare for teaching in one year of study, why can't education graduates also be prepared in one year?

State alternative certification programs have met with varying degrees of success. In New Jersey, 10% of beginning teachers enter the profession through the program. In California, district interns represent less than 1% of the state's new teachers. Among the states with alternative certification programs, the average is 3%. In those states where participants' performances have been evaluated, they have performed at least as well as traditionally trained candidates (McKibbin, 1988).

Alternative certification programs provide professionals outside of education the opportunity to recareer into teaching.

Emergency Certification

Almost all states have some provision for granting *emergency or temporary certificates* to persons who do not meet the specified degree, course, or other requirements when districts cannot employ fully qualified teachers. Emergency certificates are issued with the presumption that the recipient teacher will obtain the credentials or will be replaced by a regularly certified teacher. In most instances the request for the emergency certificate must be made by the employer. However, in only nine states is the district required to verify the need, and in only six states is the recipient required to hold a bachelor's degree. Unlike alternative certification, emergency certification ignores professional education training. Although many professional educators believe that hiring untrained teachers makes a mockery of efforts to improve the teaching profession, the practice of awarding emergency certificates has spread. Only Vermont and Virginia have no form of emergency certificates (Roth, 1986).

Interstate Certification

A matter of concern related to state certification for any profession is whether the certification granted by one state will be recognized by other states. The increasing mobility of teachers has encouraged state certification authorities to establish interstate reciprocity. It is to the advantage of each state to facilitate the employment of qualified educators and to increase the availability of educational personnel, not to establish barriers to employment. To this end, 32 states, the District of Columbia, and the overseas dependents schools have entered into Interstate Certification Agreement Contracts with one or more other states to recognize each other's teaching certificates and credentials. The initiation of a national teachers' examination such as those proposed by the NEA or the AFT could result in greater teacher certification reciprocity among the states.

Teacher Supply and Demand

The Supply Side

The supply of teachers is a function of: (1) the number of college graduates entering teaching, (2) the number of former teachers, and (3) the number of "trained but never served" teachers in the workforce. Despite the fact that enrollments in schools, colleges, and departments of education increased significantly in the last half of the 1980s, as of the end of the decade this had not resulted in any significant increase in the number of bachelor's degrees awarded in education. However, there has been some increase in the number of noneducation graduates entering teaching. Among the most important reasons why more persons are not preparing for careers as teachers are: (1) the reduced earning power of teachers relative to other professions;

(2) the opening of career opportunities in other fields for women and minorities; (3) the increase in certification requirements; (4) the low status image of teaching held by college students; and (5) the decline in the quality of the teacher's working environment (Hawley, 1986). The number of returning teachers and the number of individuals who were trained as teachers but never entered the profession is far greater than the number of students preparing to teach. One of the major unknown factors in projecting teacher supply and demand is what percentage of these individuals would enter teaching if salaries and working conditions were improved and the status of the profession were enhanced.

Reasons for Increased Demand

Although the supply of new teachers is projected to decline, the demand for additional teachers is expected to increase, principally because of enrollment increases, teacher attrition, reduced pupil-teacher ratios, and increased requirements for high school graduation. Enrollments are expected to increase at the elementary level until 1997, declining slightly in the remainder of the decade. At the secondary level, enrollments will increase throughout the 1990s.

Teacher attrition is a serious problem. Significant numbers of the current teaching force are becoming eligible for retirement. Many others are considering leaving the teaching field. The continued lowering of pupil-teacher ratios has also contributed to an increased demand for teachers. Pupil-teacher ratios have declined from 21.7 at the elementary level and 18.8 at the secondary level in 1975, to 19.2 and 15.2 respectively in 1988, and are projected to be 17.6 and 14.7 in 2000 (U.S. Department of Education, 1989b). Last, each of the major reform reports recommended increased coursework for high school graduation, thereby requiring additional teachers.

Table 1.3 gives the projected demand for classroom teachers through the year 2001. As can be seen, the demand for both elementary and secondary teachers is expected to show an overall increase through the 1990s, rising steadily from the mid-1990s.

While a shortage of teachers is expected nationwide, supply and demand will vary among states, school districts, and disciplines. Inner-city and rural districts especially will experience shortages. Shortages are also expected in such fields as special education, foreign languages, bilingual education, art, music, physics, mathematics, gifted and talented, and physical sciences.

Salary and Other Compensation

The issues associated with teachers' salaries have become more visible as a result of the publicity given both to employee activism and to the findings of the various reform reports. These reports combined with the possibility of a teacher shortage emphasize the need to make beginning teachers' salaries

Table 1.3: Trends in the Demand for New-Hiring of Classroom Teachers in Public Elementary and Secondary Schools, 1991–2001			
Fall of Year	Projected Demand for More Teachers (in thousands)		
	Total	Elementary	Secondary
1991	201	105	96
1992	190	95	95
1993	210	103	107
1994	208	100	108
1995	209	112	107
1996	217	108	109
1997	220	108	112
1998	218	110	108
1999	223	111	112
2000	227	114	113
2001	225	112	113

Source: U.S. Department of Education, National Center for Education Statistics. (1990). *Projection of education statistics to the year 2001, an update* (Tables 35 and 36). Washington, DC: U.S. Government Printing Office.

more competitive with those of other professions and to establish incentive plans (e.g., merit pay, career ladders, master teacher) for experienced teachers (Bell, 1984).

Historically, teachers' salaries have not only lagged behind those of other professionals with comparable training and responsibility, but behind those of many of the technical and semiskilled occupations. However, with renewed public interest in the quality of education, teacher compensation has generally improved. Figure 1.2 depicts the trend in average annual salaries of teachers since 1960 in both current and constant dollars (adjusted for inflation). Since school year 1980–81, teachers' salaries have increased 19% in 1989–90 constant dollars. In 1988 the average salary was $30,788.

Have the financial benefits of the teaching profession entered your decision to become a teacher?

Determinants of Compensation

A number of factors determine the salary and other compensation of education personnel. These factors include:

1. *Supply and demand.* The economic concept of supply and demand suggests that as teachers' salaries rise, more people will enter the profession, and as the supply of teachers increase, salaries will decrease.

2. *Ability to pay.* The financial ability of a state or school district to pay teachers' salaries is determined by their tax bases (e.g., income per capita or assessed value of property per pupil).

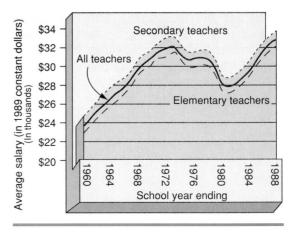

Figure 1.2: Trends in Average Annual Salary of Public School Teachers

Source: U.S. Department of Education, National Center for Education Statistics. (1990). *The Condition of Education 1990* (p. 91). Washington, DC: U.S. Government Printing Office.

3. *Cost of living.* The standard most often used for determining salary increases is the *cost-of-living index,* which is a measure of the change in the price of goods purchased by consumers.

4. *Prevailing wage rate.* The second most important determinant of current wage increases is the comparability of current rates of pay with those of neighboring school districts (Beebe, 1983).

5. *Unionization.* If school district employees are unionized, wages and other conditions of employment may be determined through the process of collective bargaining.

6. *Government regulations.* Both state and federal governments have enacted numerous pieces of legislation regarding compensation to educational personnel. The major pieces of federal legislation dealing directly with compensation are the Fair Labor Standards Act, which is concerned with minimum pay, overtime pay, child labor, and equal pay; the Equal Pay Act of 1963, which prohibits sex discrimination in pay and requires "equal pay for equal work"; the Age Discrimination in Employment Act Amendments of 1978, which protect employees from age discrimination in employment; Title VII of the Civil Rights Act of 1964 and the Equal Employment Opportunity Act of 1972, which protect against discrimination in compensation; and the Pregnancy Discrimination Act of 1978.

Salary Schedules

More than 90% of teacher salary schedules across the nation are based on the *single salary schedule* format. The single salary schedule pays equivalent salaries for equivalent preparation and experience. The trend toward the adoption of a single salary schedule for teachers began in the first quarter of the twentieth century, and before the end of the third quarter had come to dominate direct compensation. The position system it replaced based salaries on positions within the school system (elementary teacher, secondary teacher, librarian, counselor, etc.). The single salary schedule has not always been favored by teachers' groups, but it is popular with boards of education because it is easy to understand and to administer (Educational Research Service, 1984).

There are two basic dimensions to the single salary schedule: a *horizontal dimension* made up of columns that correspond to levels of academic preparation (e.g., bachelor's degree, master's degree, master's degree plus 30 hours, doctor's degree), and a *vertical dimension* of rows of "steps" that correspond to the years of teaching experience. There is no standard number of columns or rows in a teacher's salary schedule, although there are usually more rows than columns so that the schedule tends to form a vertical matrix (see Table 1.4).

Initial Placement

The initial vertical placement of a new teacher on a specific vertical step on a scale is determined by a consideration of several factors, the most common of which is previous teaching experience. To receive credit for any previous years of teaching the teacher usually must have taught for 75% of the school year. Most school districts place a limit on the number of years of teaching experience credited toward initial placement on the salary schedule. Factors that bear on this decision are whether the experience is in or out of the district or in or out of the state (Educational Research Service, 1984).

Other factors that are considered in making the initial placement on the schedule are credit for related experience, credit for military service, and credit for other experience. Some districts recognize related experience such as public library experience for librarians or recreational experience for physical educators. Others grant full or partial credit for military service or for experience in the Peace Corps, VISTA, or the National Teachers Corps.

Advancement

Vertical advancement from one step to the next within the scale is normally automatic after a stipulated period of time, usually one year, although longer periods may be required for advancement to the higher steps. Although teachers' groups have continued to advocate automatic advancement, in an increasing number of districts certain restrictions are being placed on vertical advancement. Advancement at specified points is contingent on additional units of academic credit or completion of in-service training programs; annual advancement is contingent on satisfactory performance; and advancement is based on merit (Educational Research Service, 1984).

To provide for teachers who have reached the maximum number of steps in a particular scale, some salary schedules also provide for supermaximum or long-term service increments beyond the highest step in the scale. Whereas in most instances the awarding of this increment is based solely on the attainment of a specific number of years' experience above the highest number recognized on the schedule, in some cases a performance or merit evaluation is required before the award is made.

Previous Years of Experience	Line	A B.A.	B B.A. + 15	C B.A.+30	D B.A.+45 or M.A.
	2	21,507			
0	3	22,983	23,722	24,461	25,200
1	4	23,648	24,387	25,126	25,865
2	5	24,534	25,273	26,012	26,751
3–4	6	25,428	26,167	26,906	27,645
5	7		27,083	27,822	28,561
	8		28,416	29,155	29,894
	9			30,488	31,227
	10			32,280	33,019
	11				34,811
	12				36,603
	13				
	14				
	Longevity A				
	Longevity B				
	Longevity C				

Table 1.4: Typical Single Salary Schedule for Teachers

Incentive Pay Plans

School districts across the country are under increased pressure to improve the performance of their teachers. Teacher incentive plans are perceived as one strategy that will attract and retain good teachers and motivate them to greater performance. The term *merit pay* is often used synonymously with *incentive pay*. However, the concepts are different. By definition, merit pay is differential pay awarded to individuals with the same job description on the basis of the quality of their performance. This differential compensation may be a one-time bonus or a permanent increase. The concept of incentive pay, on the other hand, includes not only merit pay but various other proposals that in effect pay teachers more for different kinds or amounts of work (e.g., master teacher plans or career ladder plans). In this section we will discuss only merit pay; master teacher plans and career ladder plans are covered in the following chapter.

Merit Pay

Merit pay for teachers is not a new concept. Prior to the widespread adoption of the single salary schedule many district salary plans had a merit component. However, school districts' experiences with merit pay in the past have been more negative than positive. Astuto and Clark (1985) noted that merit pay plans have been: "(1) difficult to initiate, (2) hard to sustain, (3) based on process rather than product measures of performance, and

E	F	G M.A.+45 or Ed.S.	H	I M.A.+75 Ed.D.,Ph.D.
M.A.+15	M.A.+30		M.A.+60	
25,939	26,678	27,417	28,156	28,895
26,604	27,343	28,082	28,821	29,560
27,490	28,229	28,968	29,707	30,446
28,384	29,123	29,862	30,601	31,340
29,300	30,039	30,788	31,517	32,256
30,633	31,372	32,111	32,850	33,589
31,966	32,705	33,444	34,183	34,922
33,758	34,497	35,236	35,975	36,714
35,550	36,289	37,028	37,767	38,506
37,342	38,081	38,820	39,559	40,238
39,422	40,161	40,900	41,639	42,378
		43,178	43,917	44,656
		44,042	44,795	45,549
		44,905	45,674	46,442
		45,769	46,552	47,335

Source: Mesa, Arizona Public Schools, 1990–91.

(4) supported with modest budgeting allocations" (p. 3). They also report that more school districts that have tried merit pay systems have dropped them than have retained them. A major reason for abandoning merit pay plans is the effect they have on morale (Coffman & Manarino-Leggett, 1984). The paradox of merit pay is that those plans that truly reward superior service threaten the self-esteem of the majority of teachers (ERIC, 1981).

In spite of past experiences or current controversy, support for merit pay has grown. Several of the reform reports recommend that teachers be paid for recognized performance rather than solely on the basis of experience or academic credentials, the underlying assumption being that financial incentives based on job performance will improve the quality of teachers and instruction. And both the National Education Association and the American Federation of Teachers have acknowledged the political necessity of accommodating demands for recognition of merit (Johnson, 1984).

A growing number of states and local school districts are experimenting with merit pay plans. The typical plan involves an evaluation conducted by the principal with teacher input into the process. The St. Louis suburb of Ladue, Missouri has one of the oldest plans still in operation. Under its plan, merit pay is based on evaluation points assigned by the principal, although a teacher committee recommends the criteria for evaluation. Each teacher may receive up to 15 points annually with each point being worth $300. The average evaluation is 10 points, worth $3,000 in merit pay.

Compensation for Extracurricular Activities

At one time extracurricular activities were considered normal duties that teachers had to assume as part of their work. In the 1950s, as teacher salaries began to lose ground in a rising economy and as many teachers sought to sup-

Table 1.5: Supplements for Athletic and Nonathletic Extracurricular Activities as Percentage of Teachers' Salaries, 1983

Activity	Percentage of Teachers' Salaries
Football head coach	11.1
Director of athletics	10.9
Basketball	9.9
Senior high band	8.7
Wrestling	8.2
Director of music	8.0
Swimming	7.5
Track	7.4
Hockey	7.3
Football assistant coach	7.3
Baseball	7.3
Gymnastics	6.6
Volleyball	6.5
Softball	6.5
Soccer	6.4
Senior high vocal	5.5
Tennis	5.4
Cross country	5.3
Speech	5.3
Orchestra	5.1
Golf	5.0
Debate	4.9
Drama (per play)	4.9
Junior high band	4.9
Drama (coach)	4.8
Cheerleading	4.5
Yearbook	4.4
Auxiliary (drill team)	3.8
Newspaper	3.7
Student Council	3.5
Junior high vocal	3.1
Miscellaneous clubs	2.8
Class sponsor	2.7
Magazine	2.3

Source for supplemental pay: Welch, E. W. (1983). *Extra pay for extra duties of teachers 1982–83.* Arlington, VA: Educational Research Service.

Source for 1982–83 annual teachers' salaries: National Center for Education Statistics. (1987). *The condition of education* (Table 1:20). Washington, DC: U.S. Department of Education.

plement their incomes by working second jobs, teachers' organizations became more aggressive in seeking additional compensation for time spent in extracurricular activities (Greene, 1971). Now it is common practice for districts to provide supplemental pay for extracurricular assignments. As indicated by the listing in Table 1.5, supplements are paid for a variety of extracurricular activities.

Indirect Compensation: Employee Benefits and Services

Indirect compensation, commonly referred to as fringe benefits, is the "in-kind payments employees receive in addition to payments in the form of money" (Henderson, 1985, p. 432). The cost of indirect compensation is significant, averaging over 30% of wages.

Indirect compensation can be classified as either employee benefits or employee services. Many benefits, including health and life insurance, long-term disability protection, payment of professional employment-related expenses, and leaves with pay (sick leave, personal leave, sabbatical leave), are voluntarily provided by the school district. Certain other benefits, namely Social Security, worker's compensation, and retirement plans, are required by law. In most states retirement benefits are financed jointly by teacher and public contributions. In several states, in an attempt to increase compensation but not increase state aid to education, school districts are required to pay not only the employer's share toward retirement, but also the employee's share. This benefit has great appeal to employees because it has a significant impact on net income while not increasing gross taxable income. Consequently, in an increasing number of school districts this provision has become a popular item for negotiation. Employee services are not required by law but "enable the employee to enjoy a better lifestyle or to meet social or personal obligations while minimizing employment-related cost" (Henderson, 1985, p. 434). Employee services include such items as credit unions, counseling, subsidized food services, or social and recreational programs.

Do you have any interest in becoming involved in any extracurricular activities? Which?

How the Public Views the Schools and Teaching

Rating the Schools

Each year the public's perceptions of the schools and issues related to the schools is assessed by the *Gallup Poll of the Public's Attitudes Toward the Public Schools.* The poll "has become a barometer, closely watched and debated each year by educators and policymakers" (U.S. Department of Education, 1989a, p. 64). In 1990, the Gallup Poll results indicated that 41% of the public surveyed gave their local schools grades of A or B, down 2% from the previous year and up 9% from five years earlier. Table 1.6 shows the ratings given to the local schools and to schools in the nation as a whole. As was true in every past poll, raters were more likely to give the schools in their community higher ratings than the schools nationally. Parents with children in the public schools also rated them higher than those with no children or those with children in private schools.

Table 1.6: Ratings Given the Public Schools, 1990

Ratings	Local Public Schools %	National Totals %	Public School Parents %	Nonpublic School Parents %
A&B	41	21	23	18
A	8	2	2	1
B	33	19	21	17
C	34	49	51	50
D	12	16	14	24
Fail	5	4	4	5
Don't know	8	10	8	3

Source: Elam, S. M. (1990). The 22nd annual Gallup poll of the public's attitudes toward the public schools. *Phi Delta Kappan, 72,* 50.

Rating the Teachers

In some years the Gallup poll asks the national sample to rate not only the schools, but also school personnel. Table 1.7 presents the findings from the latest survey. About one-half (49%) of the respondents gave the public school teachers a grade of A or B, as they have in previous polls. Public school parents graded the teachers higher than did nonpublic school parents, just as they had graded the schools higher. Elementary school teachers received higher grades than high school teachers from both public and nonpublic school parents.

Table 1.7: Public Grading of Local Public School Teachers

	A&B %	A %	B %	C %	D %	Fail %	Don't Know %
All Teachers							
National totals	49	15	34	25	6	3	17
Public school parents	64	24	40	25	7	2	2
Nonpublic school parents	44	12	32	31	9	5	11
High School Teachers							
National totals	43	12	31	24	8	3	22
Public school parents	51	17	34	24	8	2	15
Nonpublic school parents	39	11	28	26	14	4	17
Elementary School Teachers							
National totals	53	18	35	21	4	2	20
Public school parents	71	30	41	17	5	1	6
Nonpublic school parents	51	14	37	29	8	3	9

Source: Gallup, A. M., & Clark, D. L. (1987). The 19th annual Gallup poll of the public's attitudes toward the public schools, *Phi Delta Kappan, 69,* 26–27.

One of the strongest indicators of the perception held of any profession is whether people want their children to enter it. The 1990 Gallup Poll asked parents if they would like to have their child take up teaching as a career. The results showed an increase in the percentage of positive responses from eight years past, from 45% to 51%. Interestingly, and positively, college-educated and high-income parents were as likely as poorly educated and low income to perceive teaching as a desirable career for their children (Elam, 1990).

Summary

There are as many definitions of "teacher" as there are reasons for becoming a teacher. It is important that those considering the profession evaluate their perceptions and expectations of teaching and their motives for considering teaching as their chosen profession.

After a period of serious criticism of the teaching profession and teacher preparation, the status of the profession appears to be improving. There is still a shortage of minority teachers, but more and more bright and talented individuals are entering the teaching profession, either through traditional baccalaureate programs or through the growing number of alternative certification programs. These programs have responded to the recommendations of various reform reports and have raised admission standards and taken steps to improve quality. And a greater percentage of the practicing teaching force reports being satisfied with teaching as a career.

As the current demand for teachers intensifies, various proposals for differential compensation have been made in an effort to attract qualified individuals into teaching. The next chapter discusses other efforts to make teaching more attractive by increasing professionalization and reviews other professional opportunities available to teachers.

Key Terms

Alternative certification
American Federation of Teachers (AFT)
Certification
Cost-of-living index
Emergency (temporary) certificate
Field (clinical) experience

Incentive pay
Indirect compensation
Merit pay
National Education Association (NEA)
Provisional certificate
Single salary schedule

Discussion Questions

1. What is your perception of what a teacher is and does? How is your perception reflected in your responses to the questions following the opening scenario?

2. What are the advantages and disadvantages of teaching as a career? Have you considered teaching as a career? If yes, what motivated you to prepare to become a teacher?

3. What strategies should be used to attract more top-quality students into teaching?

4. Should people be required to complete a teacher training program to become a teacher? Should there be any minimum requirements?

5. The public has increasingly expressed support for the competency testing of teachers. In your opinion, should prospective teachers be required to pass a competency test?

6. The public has also shown increasing support for merit pay for teachers. What are the pros and cons of merit pay? To what extent are financial incentives likely to improve job performance?

References

Aldeman, N. E. (1987). An examination of teacher alternative certification programs. In L. M. Rudner (Project Director), *What's happening in teacher testing.* Washington, DC: U.S. Department of Education.

American Association of Colleges of Teacher Education (AACTE). (1985). 1985 report to the profession: Data show . . . *AACTE Briefs, 6*(6), 1, 3–13.

American Association of Colleges of Teacher Education. (1987). *Teaching teachers: Facts & figures.* Washington, DC: AACTE.

American Association of Colleges of Teacher Education. (1989). Alternative preparation for licensures: A policy statement. *AACTE Briefs, 10*(5), 5–6.

Anrig, G. R. (1986). Teacher education and teacher testing: The rush to mandate. *Phi Delta Kappan, 68,* 447–451.

Astuto, T. A., & Clark, D. L. (1985). *Merit pay for teachers: An analysis of state policy options,* Educational Policy Studies Series, No. 1. Bloomington, IN: Indiana University School of Education.

Bass de Martinez, B. (1988). Political and reform agendas' impact on the supply of black teachers. *Journal of Teacher Education, 38,* 10–13.

Beebe, R. J. (1983). Determining the competitiveness of school district salaries. *NASSP Bulletin, 67* (461), 84–92.

Bell, T. H. (1984). State education statistics. *National Forum, 64* (2), 34–37.

Book, C., Freeman, D., & Brousseau, B. (1985). Comparing academic backgrounds and career aspirations of education and non-education majors. *Journal of Teacher Education, 36* (3), 27–30.

Borkow, N. B., & Jordan, K. F. (1983). *The teacher workforce: Analysis of issues and options for federal action.* Washington, DC: Congressional Research Service, Library of Congress.

Boyer, E. L. (1983). *High school: A report on secondary education in America.* New York: Harper & Row.

Carnegie Forum on Education and the Economy. (1986). *A nation prepared: Teachers for the 21st century.* Washington, DC: Carnegie Forum.

Coffman, C. Q., & Manarino-Leggett, P. (1984). What do teachers think of merit pay? Study lists important variables. *NASSP Bulletin, 65* (475), 94–96.

Cruickshank, D. R., & Cruz, Jr., J. (1989). Trends in teacher preparation. *Journal of Teacher Education, 40* (3), 49–56.

Dawe, H. A. (1984). Teaching a performing art. *Phi Delta Kappan, 65,* 548–552.

Educational Research Service. (1984). *Methods of scheduling salaries for teachers.* Arlington, VA: Educational Research Service.

Egbert, R. L. (1985). The practice of preservice teacher education. *Journal of Teacher Education, 36,* 16–22.

Elam, S. M. (1990). The 22nd annual Gallup poll of the public's attitudes toward the public schools. *Phi Delta Kappan, 72,* 47.

ERIC Clearinghouse of Educational Management. (1981). What do you know about merit pay for teachers? *NASSP Bulletin, 65,* 94–96.

Gage, N. L. (1984). What do we know about teaching effectiveness? *Phi Delta Kappan, 66,* 87–93.

Galluzzo, G. R., & Arends, R. I. (1989). The RATE Project: A Profile of Teacher Education Institutions. *Journal of Teacher Education, 40*(4), 56–58.

Good, C. V. (Ed.). (1973). *The dictionary of education.* New York: McGraw-Hill.

Goodlad, J. J. (1983). *A place called school: Prospects for the future.* New York: McGraw-Hill.

Graham, P. A. (1987). Black teachers: A drastically scarce resource. *Phi Delta Kappan, 68,* 598–605.

Grant, C. A., & Gillette, M. (1987). The Holmes report and minorities in education. *Social Education, 51,* 517–521.

Greene, J. E. (1971). *School personnel administration.* New York: Chilton Book Company.

Haberman, M. (1988). Proposals for recruiting minority teachers: Promising practices and attractive detours. *Journal of Teacher Education, 39* (4), 38–44.

Hanes, M. L., & Rowls, M. D. (1984). Teacher recertification: A survey of the states. *Phi Delta Kappan, 66,* 123–126.

Hawley, W. D. (1986). Toward a comprehensive strategy for addressing the teacher shortage. *Phi Delta Kappan, 67,* 712–718.

Henderson, R. I. (1985). *Compensation management: Rewarding performance* (4th ed.). Reston, VA: Reston Publishing.

Holmes Group. (1986). *Tomorrow's teachers: A report of the Holmes Group.* East Lansing: Holmes Group.

Ishler, R. E. (1984). Requirements for admission to and graduation from teacher education. *Phi Delta Kappan, 66,* 121–22.

Johnson, S. M. (1984). *Pros and cons of merit pay.* Bloomington, IN: Phi Delta Kappa Educational Foundation.

Jordan, K. F. (1988). Teacher education recommendations in the school reform reports. In K. Alexander & D. H. Monk (Eds.), *Attracting and compensating America's teachers* (pp. 21–47). Cambridge, MA: Ballinger.

Kohl, H. R. (1976). *On teaching.* New York: Schocken Books.

Lines, P. M. (1985). Testing the teachers: Are there legal pitfalls? *Phi Delta Kappan, 66,* 618–622.

McKibbin, M. D. (1988). Alternative teacher certification programs. *Educational Leadership, 46* (3), 32–35.

Murray, F. B. (1986). Goals for the reform of teacher education: An executive summary of the Holmes Group report. *Phi Delta Kappan, 68* (1), 28–32.

National Commission on Excellence in Education. (1983). *A nation at risk: The imperative for educational reform.* Washington, DC: U.S. Government Printing Office.

National Commission on Excellence in Teacher Education. (1985). *A call for change in teacher education.* Washington, DC: American Association of Colleges for Teacher Education.

Nicklos, L. B. & Brown, W. S. (1989). Recruiting minorities into the teaching profession: An educational imperative. *Educational Horizons, 67,* 146.

Roth, R. A. (1986). Emergency certificates, misassignment of teachers, and other "dirty little secrets." *Phi Delta Kappan, 67,* 725–727.

Sandefur, J. T. (1985). State assessment trends. *AACTE Briefs, 6,* 21–23.

Smith, B. O. (1987). Definitions of teaching. In M. J. Durkin, (Ed.), *The international encyclopedia of teaching and teacher education.* New York: Pergamon Books.

Smith, D. C., Nystrand, R., Ruch, C., Gideonse, H., & Carlson, K. (1985). Alternative certification: A position statement of AACTE. *Journal of Teacher Education, 36* (3), 24.

Smith, G. P. (1984). Minority teaching force dwindles with states' use of standard tests. *AACTE Briefs, 5* (3), 12–13, 16.

U.S. Department of Education, National Center for Education Statistics. (1989a). *The condition of education.* Washington, DC: U.S. Government Printing Office.

U.S. Department of Education, National Center for Education Statistics. (1989b). *Projection of education statistics* (Table 33). Washington, DC: U.S. Government Printing Office.

Waters, M. M. (1989). An agenda for educating black teachers. *The Educational Forum, 53,* 267–279.

Zimpher, N. L. (1987). Certification and licensing of teachers. In J. M. Durkin (Ed.), *International encyclopedia of teaching and teacher education.* New York: Pergamon Books.

Chapter 2
Development of the Profession

A teacher who is attempting to teach without inspiring the child to learn is hammering on a cold iron.

Horace Mann (1796–1859)

As a new teacher, you must make decisions about the meaning of your commitment to teaching as a profession. Both of the active teacher organizations in the school district have contacted you about becoming a member. You also have considered joining the local and national organization related to your teaching area. You face a variety of choices in selecting the professional organizations that you will join and the professional activities to which you will devote your time. You have been concerned about the implications of being merely a "joiner" or becoming a contributing member in the organization.

Will you join the local affiliate of the National Education Association or the American Federation of Teachers? Will you restrict your membership to the local organization and not join the state or national organizations? Will you also join the professional organization related to the subject or grade level at which you are teaching? What responsibilities do you have when you join a professional organization?

Teaching is a complex and challenging occupation. The extent to which it is a profession is a point of continuing controversy. A profession is composed of its individual members, and the extent to which teaching is a profession will be determined by the cumulative commitment and activities of individual teachers. As you read and discuss this chapter and the related activities, consider the following outcome objectives and their impact on you as a potential teacher.

- Evaluate the duties of elementary and secondary school teachers in terms of the recognized criteria for a profession.

- Identify the factors that should be considered in teacher evaluations.

- Compare the license renewal requirements in your state with the career development requirements in a typical local school district.

- Differentiate between teacher licenses and teacher certificates.

- Identify the programs and services provided by the major teacher organizations in your state and local school districts.

- Describe the programs and services provided by the professional organization for your teaching field.

Teaching as a Profession

Is teaching a profession? Many references are made to the "profession of teaching," but the actual status of teachers continues to be a matter of discussion. Few would contend that teaching has attained the status of medicine or law, but some might argue that teaching as an occupation compares favorably with the ministry, accounting, engineering, and similar professions.

Elementary and secondary school teaching is one of the most challenging and stimulating occupations, but teachers often are confronted with frustrations in their day-to-day work. Expectations for teachers include:

- planning activities
- guiding the learning of the students in the classroom
- keeping records
- providing necessary reports
- maintaining adequate information about students
- communicating with parents

Within the past several years, various factors have contributed to an increase in the status of teachers. Some of them are:

1. Standards for teacher education programs have been raised.
2. State licensing requirements have been increased.
3. Additional use has been made of entry-level examinations for teachers.
4. Professional certification programs are being developed.
5. Teaching has come to be viewed as a career rather than an interim occupation.

What satisfactions do you think you will derive from being a teacher?

Changes like these have increased satisfaction with teaching as a career and have contributed to a growing recognition of teaching as a profession. Figure 2.1 shows responses on a recent national survey to several questions about teacher satisfaction. There has been some improvement in the mid-to-late 1980s in the extent to which teachers feel respected by society and even more of a shift in how teachers feel about their salaries. The improvements in respect and salary appear to have influenced the willingness of a greater percentage of teachers to advise a young person to pursue a career in teaching. And the percentage of teachers expressing satisfaction with teaching increased by 7% over the period 1985 to 1989.

Requirements of a Profession

Teachers may have improved their status and made progress in a variety of ways, but many observers still question whether teaching meets the recog-

Figure 2.1: Indicators of Teacher Satisfaction

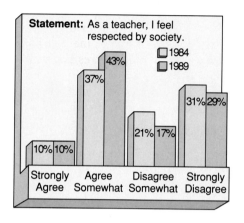

Statement: As a teacher, I feel respected by society.
☐ 1984
☐ 1989

43%, 37%, 31%, 29%, 21%, 17%, 10%, 10%

Strongly Agree / Agree Somewhat / Disagree Somewhat / Strongly Disagree

Statement: My job allows me the opportunity to earn a decent salary.
☐ 1984
☐ 1989

39%, 29%, 26%, 25%, 37%, 28%, 8%, 9%

Strongly Agree / Agree Somewhat / Disagree Somewhat / Strongly Disagree

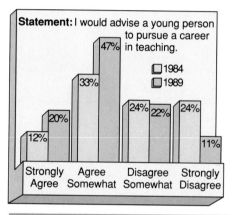

Statement: I would advise a young person to pursue a career in teaching.
47%, 33%, 24%, 22%, 24%, 20%, 12%, 11%
☐ 1984
☐ 1989

Strongly Agree / Agree Somewhat / Disagree Somewhat / Strongly Disagree

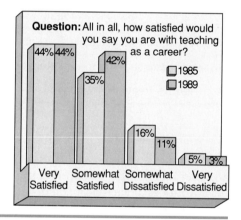

Question: All in all, how satisfied would you say you are with teaching as a career?
44%, 44%, 42%, 35%, 16%, 11%, 5%, 3%
☐ 1985
☐ 1989

Very Satisfied / Somewhat Satisfied / Somewhat Dissatisfied / Very Dissatisfied

Source: Harris, L., Kagay, M., & Leichenko, S. (1989). *The American teacher.* New York: Metropolitan Life Insurance Co. Reprinted with permission.

nized criteria for a *profession.* Definitions of a profession vary from short, simple statements to lengthy, complex descriptions; the following simplified definition is from a basic source book for education: "An occupation involving relatively long and specialized preparation on the level of higher education and governed by its own code of ethics" (Good, 1973).

More complex criteria for classifying an occupation as a profession are presented in Figure 2.2. The summary criteria discussed in this chapter include advanced knowledge and specialized preparation, provision of essential services to society, exercise of discretion, autonomy and freedom from direct supervision, standardized output and performance standards, code of professional standards, and professional organizations.

Figure 2.2: Criteria for Classifying an Occupation as a Profession

According to the National Labor Relations Act, the occupation must:

- Be an intellectual endeavor
- Involve discretion and judgment
- Have an output that cannot be standardized
- Require advanced knowledge
- Require a prolonged period of specialized study

In addition, the American Association of Colleges of Teacher Education calls for:

- Provision of essential services to society
- Decision making in providing services
- Organization into one or more professional societies for the purpose of socialization and promotion of the profession
- Autonomy in the actual day-to-day work
- Agreed upon performance standards
- Relative freedom from direct supervision

Advanced Knowledge and Specialized Preparation

Although teaching requires a period of specialized study, policy makers and members of the academic community do not agree on the course of study that produces a teacher or the order in which the courses should be taken. For instance, several recent education reform reports advocate that professional education courses be delayed until completion of general education and academic major requirements, or even until after completion of the baccalaureate degree. Other reports suggest that college graduates with no professional education courses should be permitted to serve as intern teachers, but with a higher level of supervision than that traditionally provided for beginning teachers (Jordan, 1987).

Many teacher educators also now believe that a specific body of knowledge can be identified that is necessary and appropriate for the education of teachers. Admission standards for teacher education programs have been raised, as have course requirements. However, until that specific body of knowledge or specialized field of study has been clearly articulated and implemented, teaching does not appear to meet this basic criterion of a profession.

Provision of Essential Services to Society

Academic observers may not agree that teaching has attained the status of a profession, but the public perception suggests that teachers provide an essential service to society. Although the public and the teachers may not always agree about the exact nature of this service, the importance of education in a democratic society has always been recognized: "If a nation expects to be ignorant and free in a state of civilization, it expects what never was and never will be." This often quoted statement by Thomas Jefferson reinforces the importance of education to the preservation of the nation. Teachers play a critical role in the educational process.

The Exercise of Discretion

Given the physical setting of the schools and the variety of decisions that a teacher must make during the typical school day, teachers routinely exercise discretion and judgment in providing services to their students. However, teachers are not free agents. They function in an educational environment that is larger than an individual classroom, constrained by school policies and regulations, adopted curriculum guides, and state requirements. Such district-wide concerns as scope and sequence of instruction must be considered. The typical teacher has a group of students for a period of one year, but the educational experiences in that classroom during the year will influence the learning patterns of those students over a period of years. Thus, it would appear that teachers' decisions should be in harmony with the school district's overall plan and policies.

Autonomy and Freedom from Direct Supervision

Teachers have a relatively high degree of autonomy in their actual day-to-day work, and the degree of direct supervision is rather limited. However, some recent school improvement recommendations may limit the discretion of the teacher by requiring greater uniformity in teacher-student relationships and interaction.

From a different perspective, when compared with independent, fee-charging professionals, teachers have less autonomy and freedom. Teachers function in the social setting of a school with other teachers. The culture of the school requires a degree of structure and interaction among both teachers and students. In addition, parents and taxpayers have an interest in ensuring that teachers act like responsible professionals. Some degree of supervision is necessary to provide the desired assurances.

Standardized Output and Performance Standards

There appears to be near-universal acceptance of the concept of individual differences among students; however, some of the recent school reform proposals appear to assume that the work of teachers can be standardized and uniformly measured. The latter issue has emerged in discussions about proposals related to merit pay, master teachers, career ladders, and related teacher evaluation issues. Critical questions in implementing these proposals include what to consider in reviewing a teacher's performance, and whether the performance review team is to include practicing members of the profession or only school administrators.

Should teacher pay be based on student performance?

Code of Professional Standards

An additional unresolved issue in determining whether teaching meets the criteria of a profession is whether practicing teachers are to assume responsibility for policing their peers and enforcing a code of professional standards. The alternative is for teachers to be monitored or policed by a public agency, typically at the state level. Such bodies usually are referred to as professional practices boards or commissions. Their purpose is to take appropriate disciplinary action against teachers following a review of reports of questionable professional conduct. A relatively small number of teachers whose professional performance appears to have been inadequate has been used to justify the need for review by the profession or by these bodies.

Professional Organizations

Teaching appears to meet this criterion of a profession because of the two national organizations for teachers—the National Education Association and the American Federation of Teachers. These bodies serve the functions of socialization and promotion of the profession. Questions might be raised, however, about the extent to which these organizations have developed programs to enhance the profession and to transmit and enhance skills and knowledge throughout the teacher's career.

Unresolved Questions

Previous observations suggest that some questions about the professional status of teachers remain unresolved. A consistent theme in recommendations about teachers in the education reform reports of the 1980s called for:

- increased preservice requirements
- higher standards for entrance and continued service
- greater emphasis on career advancements for teachers

These admonitions suggest that the various reform groups were applying at least one of the traditional criteria for a profession in their statements about the expectations of teachers. This level of recognition lends credibility to the concept of teaching as a profession.

When compared with the recognized professions, there are some ways in which public school teaching is different. Typically, a recipient of a professional service may choose which person will provide the service. In contrast, parents or students often have little choice in the assignment of a teacher. Also, many of the professions certify the competencies of their members. Currently, states have licensing requirements that serve as minimum standards for teachers, but emergency licenses are issued when teacher shortages develop.

You may want to ask yourself some questions to assess how you feel about teaching as a profession. Some of the questions you might ask yourself are presented on page 43.

| ? |

Ask Yourself:
How Do I Feel About Teaching as a Profession?

1. In addition to classroom duties, what responsibilities do I have as a professional teacher? With what organizations should I affiliate and what should be my motives for joining these various organizations?

2. How do I feel about teachers "policing" their own ranks? Should teachers be involved in the evaluation of colleagues? What should I do if I become aware of a colleague's unprofessional or unethical behavior?

3. What is the difference between a professional association and a union? Are the NEA and AFT unions or professional associations?

4. How do I feel about collective bargaining for teachers? Because teachers engage in collective bargaining, does that diminish their professional standing? How would I feel about withholding professional services in order to move negotiations along between a teachers' association and a school district?

The Professionalization of Teaching

Great strides in the professionalization of teachers have been made in the past several decades. In the first half of this century, many preparation programs for teachers provided initial licensing after successful completion of a few weeks of summer school following high school graduation. As discussed in Chapter 1, current programs typically involve intensive, structured four- and five-year preparation; these programs conclude with the awarding of a bachelor's or a master's degree. Other evidence of the increased professionalization of teaching may be found in the development of professional standards, teacher competency testing, increased opportunities for professional development, and the adoption of codes of professional standards.

Development of Professional Standards

The school reform movement appears to have given new impetus to the interest in developing professional standards for teachers. Various school reform groups including the Carnegie Forum on Education and the Economy and the Holmes Group have called for higher standards for teachers and the development of a national teacher certification process. One model for this concept is found in the medical specialty groups through which medical doctors are granted special professional recognition by their peers when they meet prescribed standards. In discussions about the development of a national certification program, some confusion has arisen because of a misunderstanding of the technical differences between teacher certification and teacher licensing.

Historically, a person fulfilled the legal requirements to teach when a college or university certified to the appropriate state agency that the person had completed the required teacher education coursework and field experiences. The state licensing body then granted a license to teach to the person.

These licenses, often referred to as teaching certificates, are issued for a spec-ified period and may be renewed upon satisfactory teaching experience and completion of coursework or continuing education units.

The concept of a professional teacher certificate discussed in the educa-tion reform literature is different. Certificates would be issued to those teach-ers who sought certification, whose performance merited special recognition, and who had demonstrated a commitment to teaching as a career. Certifica-tion would be voluntary rather than compulsory. As opposed to the teaching license that is issued by a state agency, certificates would be awarded by vol-untary, nongovernmental certification boards that have no formal legal au-thority. The current references to state-issued teaching certificates would be replaced by a state licensing process for teachers.

National Board for Professional Teaching Standards

With participation from the major teachers' organizations, initial steps have been taken to create the National Board for Professional Teaching Stan-dards. This voluntary group is planning to develop a system for adopting standards and awarding certificates to practicing teachers. Preliminary discus-sions suggest that teachers seeking certification will be required to submit documentation after a few years of successful experience to a state or national board consisting of professional educators.

For the next several years, considerable attention likely will be devoted to the relationships between teacher certification and licensing. Some misunder-standing may be inevitable because historically the terms have been used interchangeably in many states.

Competency Testing of Practicing Teachers

Competency testing of practicing teachers is designed to screen out of the teaching force those persons who are deficient in basic skills and knowledge. Proposals for such testing normally anticipate that the testing program will be a requirement for recertification. Required in only three states (Arkansas, Georgia, and Texas) in 1990, this practice is the subject of considerable con-troversy. Issues are related to contentions that:

- Retesting to determine competency is not required of other occupations such as the legal or medical professions.

- Competency in the classroom cannot be determined by pencil and paper tests.

- The current tests may have a discriminatory impact on minority teachers.

The NEA has been strongly opposed to testing current teachers, but the AFT has been supportive of testing current teachers under certain conditions.

Quality vs. Quantity

As discussed in Chapter 1, in the 1980s various observers of American education raised questions about the quality and quantity of elementary and

Should teachers be reexamined periodically to ensure that they understand and can teach new developments in their field?

secondary school teachers. Issues of quality have been related to the abilities, competencies, and preparation of current and future teachers. Issues of quantity have been related to the relationship between the projected supply of teachers and the estimated vacancies in the schools.

Quality and quantity concerns interact because higher quality requirements, or increased standards for teachers, may affect the quantity of persons eligible to enter teaching or the willingness of current teachers to remain in teaching. One position is that higher standards will shrink the pool of aspirants; an opposite position is that higher standards will contribute to a higher level of prestige for teaching and result in more able college students pursuing teaching as a career.

Another concern about quality is the relative ability of practicing teachers. No one knows what effect the recent state and national interest in higher standards for schools will have on the continued quality of the teaching staff. The increased standards may contribute to a higher status for teaching and education, or higher standards may be viewed as an encroachment on the freedom of the teacher. If the former is the case, experienced quality teachers may be more likely to remain in teaching, and a higher quality of student may be attracted to teaching. If the higher standards are viewed as an encroachment, some experienced teachers may desert the classroom in favor of other occupations.

Changes in societal and individual perception of teaching as a career may also influence the career decisions of a major reservoir of teaching talent not currently in the teaching force. Many concerns about the staffing of schools would be alleviated if the pool of persons who are graduates of teacher education programs but are not currently teaching should decide to enter teaching. Changes in the nation's economic conditions and employment market and improved working conditions and financial rewards for teachers could result in significant numbers of this group deciding to enter teaching (Fox, 1987).

Teacher Evaluation

Teachers are evaluated in a variety of ways. Students, parents, fellow teachers, and administrators have been evaluating teachers since the opening of the first school. Unfortunately, evaluation procedures often have been informal, unsystematic, and based on randomly gathered anecdotal information. For these reasons, considerable progress has been made in identifying the goals of the activity and developing formal teacher evaluation procedures.

The theoretical purpose of any local school district's formal teacher evaluation program is to improve the teaching and learning conditions by improving the overall performance of the teachers in the school district. The two most common evaluation procedures used to accomplish this are:

- systematic gathering and reporting of information about the performance of an individual teacher for the purpose of helping the teacher improve performance

- providing information that can be used in making decisions about retention or dismissal of the teacher

As a beginning teacher, what will you expect from a teacher evaluation program?

The optimal result of the teacher evaluation program will be to help the practicing teacher to improve classroom performance.

The school reform movement in the 1980s drew additional attention to teacher evaluation. A common theme in the various reform reports was the need to improve the performance of practicing teachers through the designation of master teachers, creation of career ladder programs, and development of merit pay systems. Each proposal assumed that an objective evaluation system would be used to determine which teachers would receive the additional compensation and recognition, and also that teacher performance could be enhanced by developing and implementing improved teacher evaluation procedures.

Any discussion of the evaluation of teachers eventually centers around a series of what, how, and who questions. As illustrated below, these questions vary in their complexity.

What to Evaluate?

Common courtesy dictates that the person being evaluated have prior knowledge as to what is being evaluated. Yet this may be the most difficult task in the evaluation process. The challenge is to identify the components of the evaluation and the behaviors and information that are to be observed, secured, and recorded during the evaluation process. A major difficulty is that the "what" cannot be answered until the observable elements have been identified. The concept of teaching as a profession assumes more than the identification of behaviors or practices indicative of "good teaching" by school administrators or outside experts. There must also be development of some degree of consensus between the person being evaluated and that person's professional peers.

How to Conduct the Evaluation?

Good practice also dictates that the person be told "how" the evaluation information is to be gathered, including the procedures and criteria to be used. This involves a determination of the types of information to be provided by the teacher, the number of classroom observations, the process for making the assessment, and the methods to be used in informing the teacher as to the relative level of performance.

A second "how" question is related to the process that will be used in making decisions about the content, design, and implementation of the evaluation program. A study of the participants in this decision process provides an opportunity to evaluate both the strength of the local teachers' organization and the administrative philosophy of the school district. Involvement and participation suggest positive attributes that should contribute to an overall supportive and positive instructional climate in the school district. Confrontation and lack of involvement likely will be further evidenced in a lack of professional respect and isolation between teachers and administrators.

Who Does the Evaluation?

One facet of the "who" question is related to the role of the profession in evaluating its own members—teachers evaluating teachers. A second facet of the "who" question is the role of the immediate supervisor or building principal in visiting, observing, and communicating with teachers concerning the relative quality of their performance and the steps that should be taken to improve. A third facet of the "who" question is the extent to which the evaluation team should include the school district's central office administrators and teachers from both inside and outside the school district.

Currently, the major interests are that evaluations be:

- conducted in a more systematic manner
- based on criteria related to acceptable levels of classroom performance as a teacher
- based on an adequate number of observations

Depending on the procedures, quality of communication, and human relations skills found in a school district, the evaluation system can contribute to either an increase or a decline in teacher morale and performance.

Observation and evaluation by peers and administrators have become an integral part of the organized efforts to improve teacher performance and enhance the learning opportunities for students.

Professional Development

Completion of the teacher preparation program does not mean that a person has mastered all that one needs to know in order to be an effective teacher. In fact, most observers recognize that teachers need to develop professionally by continuing to learn about the process of teaching and their subject areas as long as they are in the profession.

An increasing number of avenues for personal and *professional development* are open to teachers. Many choose to join the professional organization most closely related to their teaching field. This membership provides access to various professional materials, but the most critical benefit probably will be the contacts with other teachers, offering the possibilities for a professional peer support network. Other methods of growth might include the development of a personal professional library and an independent study program.

An alternative professional development program, a more structured approach, is to enroll in an advanced degree program in a college or university. The challenge of this approach is to develop an individualized program and select components that will improve competencies, as well as meet degree requirements.

Professional Ethics

Various professions have codes of ethics that serve as standards for behavior of members of the profession. Codes of ethics do not have the status of law, but indicate the aspirations of members of the profession and provide standards by which to judge conduct. In some instances, the professional organization monitors and enforces the code of ethics for its membership. In others, a public agency may assume the monitoring and enforcement role. Reporting of noncompliance can come from a variety of sources including professional peers, clients, supervisors, and the public at large.

The NEA has adopted a code of ethics for the education profession. The NEA Code of Ethics, presented in detail in Figure 2.3, contains two sections: commitment to students and commitment to the profession. The student section notes the expectations of fair, equitable, and nondiscriminatory treatment of students. The section on commitment to the profession contains standards of personal conduct in the performance of professional duties and relationships to others.

In an earlier era, codes of conduct for teachers were adopted by local school boards. These codes often were related to personal as well as professional conduct, regulating such things as marital status, style of clothing, and places in the community that were "off limits" to teachers. In those days, failure to abide by the requirements was used as justification for dismissal or other punitive action against the teacher. The requirements of yesteryear are quite different from the current concept of codes of ethics that focus on professional conduct. Responsibility for enforcement now resides with the profession rather than with a local school district's governing body.

Figure 2.3: Code of Ethics of the Education Profession

Preamble

The educator, believing in the worth and dignity of each human being, recognizes the supreme importance of the pursuit of truth, devotion to excellence, and the nurture of democratic principles. Essential to these goals is the protection of freedom to learn and to teach and the guarantee of equal educational opportunity for all. The educator accepts the responsibility to adhere to the highest ethical standards.

The educator recognizes the magnitude of the responsibility inherent in the teaching process. The desire for the respect and confidence of one's colleagues, of students, of parents, and of the members of the community provides the incentive to attain and maintain the highest possible degree of ethical conduct. The *Code of Ethics of the Education Profession* indicates the aspiration of all educators and provides standards by which to judge conduct.

The remedies specified by the NEA and/or its affiliates for the violation of any provision of this *Code* shall be exclusive and no such provision shall be enforceable in any form other than one specifically designated by the NEA or its affiliates.

Principle I: Commitment to the Student

The educator strives to help each student realize his or her potential as a worthy and effective member of society. The educator therefore works to stimulate the spirit of inquiry, the acquisition of knowledge and understanding, and the thoughtful formulation of worthy goals.

In fulfillment of the obligation to the student, the educator—

1. Shall not unreasonably restrain the student from independent action in the pursuit of learning.

2. Shall not unreasonably deny the student access to various points of view.

3. Shall not deliberately suppress or distort subject matter relevant to the student's progress.

4. Shall make reasonable effort to protect the student from conditions harmful to learning or to health and safety.

5. Shall not intentionally expose the student to embarrassment or disparagement.

6. Shall not on the basis of race, color, creed, sex, national origin, marital status, political or religious beliefs, family, social or cultural background, or sexual orientation unfairly—

    a. Exclude any student from participation in any program

    b. Deny benefits to any student

    c. Grant any advantage to any student

7. Shall not use professional relationships with students for private advantage.

8. Shall not disclose information about students obtained in the course of professional service, unless disclosure serves a compelling purpose or is required by law.

Figure 2.3: *continued*

Principle II: Commitment to the Profession
The education profession is vested by the public with a trust and responsibility requiring the highest ideals of professional service.

In the belief that the quality of the services of the education profession directly influences the nation and its citizens, the educator shall exert every effort to raise professional standards, to promote a climate that encourages the exercise of professional judgement, to achieve conditions which attract persons worthy of the trust to careers in education, and to assist in preventing the practice of the profession by unqualified persons.

In fulfillment of the obligation to the profession, the educator—

1. Shall not in an application for a professional position deliberately make a false statement or fail to disclose a material fact related to competency and qualifications.

2. Shall not misrepresent his/her professional qualifications.

3. Shall not assist any entry into the profession of a person known to be unqualified in respect to character, education, or other relevant attribute.

4. Shall not knowingly make a false statement concerning the qualifications of a candidate for a professional position.

5. Shall not assist a non-educator in the unauthorized practice of teaching.

6. Shall not disclose information about colleagues obtained in the course of professional service unless disclosure serves a compelling professional purpose or is required by law.

7. Shall not knowingly make false or malicious statements about a colleague.

8. Shall not accept any gratuity, gift, or favor that might impair or appear to influence professional decisions or actions.

Source: NEA Handbook, Washington, DC: National Education Association, 1986–87.

Career Development

Traditional career opportunities in teaching probably were more accurately career opportunities in education. Elementary and secondary school teaching was often viewed as a necessary entry-level experience before one became a school administrator or college professor in the humanities, sciences, or professional education. Recent changes in teacher salary schedules and teachers' roles have improved professional opportunities and rewards. As a result, persons are encouraged to consider elementary and secondary school teaching as a life career.

Career Ladders

Various states included the *career ladder* concept in their school reform programs in the 1980s. (See Figure 2.4 for Tennessee's Career Ladder Program.) This concept provides different status titles, pay levels, and lengths of contract for teachers at different levels of the career ladder. At the first level the beginning or apprentice teacher might receive an entry-level salary with

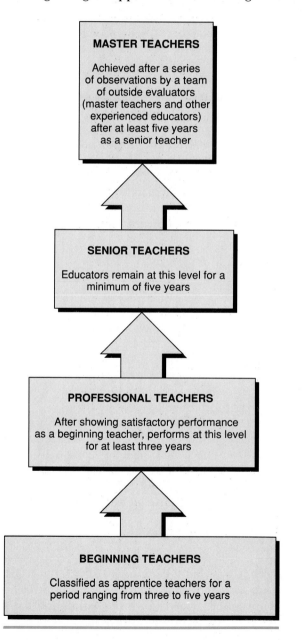

Figure 2.4: Sample Career Ladder (Tennessee)

MASTER TEACHERS

Achieved after a series of observations by a team of outside evaluators (master teachers and other experienced educators) after at least five years as a senior teacher

SENIOR TEACHERS

Educators remain at this level for a minimum of five years

PROFESSIONAL TEACHERS

After showing satisfactory performance as a beginning teacher, performs at this level for at least three years

BEGINNING TEACHERS

Classified as apprentice teachers for a period ranging from three to five years minimal increases. At the end of the three- to five-year apprenticeship, if the person were retained, promotion would be made to the second level.

The second-level professional teacher would receive a higher base salary with additional annual step increases. A person would stay at this level for a minimum of three years if performance were satisfactory, but might stay at this level for a career.

The third-level senior teacher would receive a higher base salary with additional annual step increases. A person would stay at this level for a minimum of five years if performance were satisfactory, and could stay at this level for a career if there were no aspirations to become a master teacher. Most of a district's experienced teachers might be in this group.

If a person desired to attain the fourth level of master teacher, an application and dossier would have to be submitted to a committee of administrators and master teachers. The process would include visitations and classroom observations by this committee and administrators from other school districts. Members of the team would recommend whether the person should be designated a master teacher. Master teachers on a career ladder usually would have a full-year contract and would be involved in various types of curriculum development work during the months when school is not in session. The decision to seek the status of master teacher is voluntary; a teacher can continue to teach indefinitely without attaining the classification of master teacher.

Master Teacher Concept

In addition to the use of the term in the context of career ladders, the concept of the *master teacher* has been used in other ways. In some instances, the master teacher might be given special status, pay, and recognition, but would remain in the classroom as a role model for other teachers. In others, the master teacher might be released from a portion of the regular classroom assignment to work with other teachers in a supportive, nonsupervisory role. Such activities may involve classroom observations and suggestions for improvement or leadership roles in curriculum development activities.

The key consideration is that the master teacher would have the opportunity to continue as a classroom teacher for most of the time, but would be provided with other professional tasks. These tasks can be personally and professionally rewarding as well as beneficial to the school and other teachers. Opportunities to participate in professional activities outside the classroom contribute to a sense of professional renewal and provide recognition of competency.

Mentoring

The formal and informal relationships that a beginning teacher develops with experienced teachers often are referred to as peer socialization or *mentoring*. These interactions can be invaluable sources of information and support for the beginning teacher. In contrast to other professions in which an entry-level employee often is made a junior member of a team consisting of persons with a range of experience, the beginning teacher typically is assigned a classroom of students in an elementary school or a series of classes in a secondary school and expected to assume the same responsibilities as an experienced teacher.

The concept of mentoring usually involves the development of a support relationship between a beginner and an experienced teacher. The mentor provides basic information about the operation of the school as well as advice, counsel, and support that the beginner may seek when confronted with problems. The goal of such programs is to establish a relationship and an initial professional contact that will develop into a collegial relationship.

In a recent national survey of teachers, the concept of mentor teacher was viewed favorably by 82% of the teachers familiar with the concept. Possible reasons for support include teachers' perception that the mentor teacher would provide some help in the day-to-day task of teaching, a reduction of the isolation experienced by the novice teacher, and expanded possibilities of career advancement as a teacher (Harris, Kagay, & Leichenko, 1989).

Self-Renewal

The routine of teaching is tempered by the excitement of new students arriving each semester or school year. However, the continuing pressures of the classroom and the possibilities of teaching the same grade level or the same subject for several decades can have a depressing effect on even the most

Experienced and beginning teachers can work together in a mentoring relationship or a "buddy" system and share experiences to improve student and teacher performance.

enthusiastic person. Traditionally, self-renewal has been viewed as the responsibility of the individual teacher; however, experience suggests that school districts can benefit from the development of joint self-renewal or professional renewal efforts with teachers (McLaughlin, Pfeifer, Swanson-Owens, & Yee, 1986).

Local school districts use a variety of approaches to address the teacher "burnout" problem. Among the renewal programs available in various school districts across the country are:

- sabbaticals for advanced study

- periodic change of school or teaching assignment

- attendance at workshops or professional conferences

- visitation programs

Another option involves providing teachers with alternative assignments in curriculum or staff development programs. The purpose of such programs is to recognize outstanding teachers who receive a break from the classroom while continuing to engage in professionally challenging experiences of benefit to the local school district.

Teachers' Organizations

Teachers often find themselves confronted with the choice of which and how many organizations to join. They may affiliate with one of the national teachers' organizations and also with organizations whose focus is on a particular subject or educational specialty. An important consideration may be a person's level of commitment to the organization and its program or the extent to which the person intends to become involved in the organization's activities.

National Teachers' Organizations

The National Education Association is the larger of the two national teachers' organizations. Its members are found in all types of school districts. In contrast, the American Federation of Teachers has fewer total members with activities that are concentrated in the nation's urban areas. The membership of both organizations includes professional educators other than classroom teachers, and some persons hold membership in both organizations. The NEA's membership is estimated to be about 2 million; the AFT's membership has been estimated at more than 500,000.

For almost 100 years, the NEA was the umbrella organization for higher as well as elementary and secondary educators. (See the Historical Note on p. 56 for a short history of the NEA.) Various teacher specialty and administrator organizations were under the NEA umbrella, and individuals held membership in the specialty group and the overarching organization. Until the 1960s, leadership roles in the NEA and its state affiliates often were held by school superintendents and higher education personnel. Starting in the 1960s, elementary and secondary school classroom teachers assumed the leadership roles. The administrator organizations became independent of the NEA, and teachers occupied a greater portion of the organization's membership. The organization's program now focuses more on services to teachers and state and local teacher organizations.

In contrast, teachers always have provided the leadership for the AFT. Although the organization has included building principals among its members, central office administrators have been viewed as district management and considered to be in an adversarial relationship with teachers.

Each organization provides a variety of professional development activities and services for their members. Publications include national research reports, a journal for members (*Today's Education* [NEA] and *Changing Education* [AFT]), and a variety of handbooks and related documents. Most of these publications are oriented toward improving teacher performance and working conditions or providing source information about the status of American education. Both organizations conduct annual conferences at the state and national level and provide a variety of workshop training activities related to either professional or organizational development.

What national teachers' organization was more active in the schools you attended? Were you aware of your teachers being active in their professional organizations?

Action at the State Level

In addition to their national headquarters and national programs, each national teacher organization has units at the state level and in local school districts. The NEA has been more active at the state level; the organization has served as an advocate for teacher tenure and certification statutes, revisions in state school finance programs, initiation of federal aid for education, and related educational improvements. The AFT also supports many similar activities, but the general perception has been that the AFT's strength has been concentrated in the organizational units at the local school district level.

Action at the Local Level

Both organizations have encouraged teachers to negotiate about salaries and working conditions with local school district administrators and school boards. The AFT has been bargaining for decades; the NEA started major initiatives in this area in the 1960s. During the intervening years, in most of the states, teachers have become actively involved in formal and informal negotiations with school boards. In some states the actions are voluntary; in others, school boards are required by state law to enter into a contract with the local teachers' organizations about salaries and working conditions. The result has been an increase in the control and input that teachers have over conditions related to their pay and conditions of employment.

Historical Note:
The Birth of Teachers' Unions

In 1857, teachers' organizations from 10 states joined to form the National Teachers Association (NTA). In 1870, the NTA merged with the American Normal School Association and the National Association of School Superintendents to form the National Education Association (NEA). Although the NEA was concerned with broad educational issues, at the beginning it was dominated primarily by college presidents and school superintendents and had no division for classroom teachers. The organization did not concern itself with teacher welfare. Further, the NEA leaders would not have thought that such action was professional. At this point, the NEA was in no sense a labor union.

The first teachers' labor union was the Chicago Teachers Federation (CTF), formed in 1897. In 1902, the CTF affiliated with the Chicago Federation of Labor. This action was condemned by the Chicago school board. The CTF eventually severed the tie when it lost a battle against the school board's arbitrary decision against union membership. Even with this setback, the CTF continued to grow. In New York City, another union, the Interborough Association of Women Teachers, claimed 12,000 members in the early 1900s. This was the largest local teachers' union in the country. Unions also were formed in many other cities as teachers sought to follow the lead of the growing labor union movement and improve their working conditions through organizational representation and membership.

Action on National Education Reform Commissions

During the 1980s, representatives of both the NEA and the AFT have served on several of the school reform commissions. In their participation in the reform reports, the primary goals of both organizations have been the same:

- to enhance the professional status of teaching
- to improve the working conditions of teachers
- to increase the overall pay for teachers
- to create a more positive attitude toward teachers and education

Specialized Organizations for Teachers

In addition to the general organizations for all teachers, professional organizations have been formed for each discipline. Professional development activities provided by the subject matter organizations typically include a publication program and conferences and workshops for members.

Some specialized organizations such as the Council for Exceptional Children (CEC) include as their members parents and interested citizens as well as professional educators; others such as the National Conference of Teachers of English (NCTE), the National Council for Teachers of Mathematics (NCTM), the National Council for the Social Studies (NCSS), and the National Science Teachers Association (NSTA) draw their members from teachers at all levels of education. These groups typically do not become involved in direct discussions with school officials about working conditions of teachers; however, they may adopt statements of principles about total teaching load, textbook selection procedures, and selection and use of instructional materials. In this way, the specialized organizations do assume an advocacy role for changes in state or federal legislation related to their teaching area.

Examples of other organizations oriented to specific support roles in the schools include the American Library Association (ALA) and the American Association for Counseling and Development (AACD). A broader-based organization is the Association for Supervision and Curriculum Development (ASCD), which includes teachers, administrators, and college professors. Specialized organizations for school district central office personnel and building principals include the American Association of School Administrators (AASA), the National Association of Secondary School Principals (NASSP), and the National Association of Elementary School Principals (NAESP). With some exceptions, these groups tend to be stronger at the state and national levels. For example, both the National Association of Secondary School Principals and the American Association of School Administrators recently have initiated assessment programs to improve the personal and professional knowledge and skills of administrators.

Teachers gather at national meetings to share ideas and address national educational issues.

Teachers' Organizations and Public Policy Issues

Both the NEA and the AFT assume an active role in promoting various federal education programs to improve elementary and secondary education. In addition, most of the subject matter organizations also have representatives who provide advice and counsel to Congress and the Department of Education on legislation, regulations, and administrative procedures. Recently, the Council for Exceptional Children worked for passage and implementation of both state and federal legislation related to education of the handicapped. The National Science Teachers Association and the National Council for Teachers of Mathematics supported federal legislation to improve elementary and secondary school instruction in science and mathematics. Many educational interest groups also were involved in the recent reauthorization of federal elementary and secondary education programs for educationally disadvantaged and at-risk youth.

Summary

The status of teaching as a profession remains unclear. Although the standards have been raised, the changes may not be sufficient to qualify teaching as a profession. In the past decade, progress has been made toward the professionalization of teachers. New certification standards under discussion would replace the current process with a licensing procedure. To ensure that new teachers possess basic skills, competency testing has been adopted by many states. Advances have been made in procedures for evaluating teachers, and local school districts are providing increased opportunities for professional development.

The effect of efforts to reform education on teacher quality and quantity is not known. Higher standards may drive out teachers or may attract more as the reputation of the profession increases. The tradition of teaching being viewed as a stepping-stone to careers in administration and higher education is being replaced by teaching being seen as a career in itself. As job rewards have increased, other changes in working conditions have made teaching more attractive. The expansion of practices such as the career ladder concept, master teaching programs, and opportunities for self-renewal contribute to maintaining and fostering the positive aspects of the profession.

In Chapter 3, you will have the opportunity to step back and reflect on the historical origins of Western educational thought and practice. You will also see their influence on the educational process and profession of today.

Key Terms

Career ladder	Mentoring
Competency testing	Profession
Master teacher	Professional development

Discussion Questions

1. In what ways does teaching differ from professions such as law, medicine, and accounting?

2. What is the current status of the efforts to start a national certification program for teachers?

3. What are the provisions for collective bargaining for teachers in your state?

4. What responsibility does the beginning teacher have for continued professional development? What are the professional development requirements for teachers in school districts with which you are familiar?

5. What types of tests must a person pass before becoming a teacher in the state in which you intend to seek employment?

6. What steps are taken to monitor the extent to which teachers comply with codes of ethics in school districts with which you are familiar?

7. What reasons might there be for not joining a professional organization?

References

Eaton, W. E. (1975). *The American Federation of Teachers, 1916–61.* Carbondale, IL: Southern Illinois University Press.

Fox, J. N. (1987). The supply of U.S. teachers. In K. Alexander & D. H. Monk (Eds.), *Attracting and compensating America's teachers* (pp. 49–68). Cambridge, MA: Ballinger.

Good, C. V. (Ed.). (1973). *Dictionary of education.* New York: McGraw-Hill.

Harris, L., Kagay, M., & Leichenko, S. (1989). *The American teacher.* New York: Metropolitan Life Insurance Co.

Howsam, R. B., et al. (1985). *Educating a profession.* Washington, DC: American Association of Colleges of Teacher Education.

Jordan, K. F. (1987). Teacher education recommendations in the school reform reports. In K. Alexander & D. H. Monk (Eds.), *Attracting and compensating America's teachers* (pp. 21–47). Cambridge, MA: Ballinger.

McLaughlin, M. W., Pfeifer, R. S., Swanson-Owens, D., & Yee, S. (1986). Why teachers won't teach. *Phi Delta Kappan, 67,* 420–426.

National Labor Relations Act. (1991). 29 USC 160, Section 2.

U.S. Department of Education, National Center for Education Statistics. (1986). *The condition of education 1986.* Washington, DC: U.S. Government Printing Office.

U.S. Department of Education, National Center for Education Statistics. (1987). *The condition of education 1987.* Washington, DC: U.S. Government Printing Office.

Part Two

Historical Foundations of Education

American Education: European Heritage and Colonial Experience **Chapter 3**

American Education: From Revolution to the Twentieth Century **Chapter 4**

Modern American Education: From the Progressive Movement to the Present **Chapter 5**

Chapter 3

American Education: European Heritage and Colonial Experience

Only the educated are free.

Plato

In his tenth Annual Report, the great American educator Horace Mann said, "I believe in the existence of a great, immutable principle of natural law . . . which proves the absolute right of every human being that comes into the world to an education; and which, of course, proves the correlative duty of every government to see that the means of that education are provided for all." The United States Supreme Court, in Brown v. Topeka *(1954), commented: "Today education is perhaps the most important function of state and local governments. Compulsory school attendance laws and the great expenditures for education both demonstrate our recognition of the importance of education to our democratic society. It is required in the performance of our most basic*

public responsibilities, even service in the armed forces. It is the very foundation of good citizenship. . . . Such an opportunity (of an education), where the state has undertaken to provide it, is a right which must be made available to all on equal terms." Yet, since the Constitution makes no mention of education, the question of whether it should be considered one of the fundamental rights implicitly guaranteed has been one of continued debate.

In your opinion, is the right to an education one of those inalienable rights that should be guaranteed by the government? Why? What are the implications of your decision?

When the courts consider cases like *Brown* which involve interpretation of the Constitution or specific laws, they often review historical records and consider the context of the time to try to determine the intent of the lawmakers. Similarly, studying the history of education helps educators to understand the development of educational thought and practice and to evaluate present educational institutions, theories, and practices in the light of past successes and failures. To help you develop insights into the European and colonial background of American education presented in this chapter, keep the following learning objectives in mind:

- Contrast Spartan and Athenian education.

- Compare Aristotle's and Plato's educational philosophies.

- Explain the contribution of Quintilian to the development of European educational thought and practice.

- Describe the impact of the Reformation on the provision of education.

- Identify the contributions of Bacon, Comenius, Locke, Rousseau, Pestalozzi, Herbart, and Froebel to current educational practice.

- Describe the curriculum in the elementary and secondary schools and the forces that shaped it.

- Compare education in the New England, Middle Atlantic, and Southern colonies.

European Background of American Education

Education in Ancient Societies

The oldest known schools were those of Sumer, an area lying between the Tigris and Euphrates rivers in Mesopotamia. They date from the third millennium B.C. Most of these schools were connected with a temple and taught writing and some calculations. The Sumerian language was not alphabetic, but consisted of 600 or more characters. Writing was done on clay tablets called cuneiform tablets, so a school was called the Tablet House or *edubba*.

Although the first known schools were in Sumer, the Greeks are considered the first real educators in the Western world, "for they were the first western peoples to think seriously and profoundly about educating the young, the first to ask what education is, what it is for, and how children and men should be educated" (Castle, 1967, p. 11). However, while the Greeks were interested in education, they were not all in agreement as to what form it should take. For example, the content and approach to education in the two principal city-states, Sparta and Athens, were quite different.

Education in Sparta

Sparta was predominantly a military state, and education reflected Spartan life. The maintenance of military strength was the most important goal of the government. The welfare of the individual came second to the welfare of the state, life was regimented by the state, and severe limits were placed on individual freedoms. Creative or strictly intellectual pursuits were discouraged. The aim of the educational system was to inculcate patriotism and the ideal of the sacrifice of the individual to the state, as well as to develop and train physically fit and courageous warriors.

At the age of seven boys were enrolled in state military companies where they lived in public barracks and ate at common tables. Training was concerned with cultivating the four great virtues: prudence, temperance, fortitude, and obedience. A system of exercise and games, becoming more military as the boys got older, was designed to make them obey commands, endure hardships, and be successful in battle. Dance and music were taught, but they too involved military and moral themes. Only minimal attention was given to reading and writing.

Girls in Sparta received no formal education. They were trained at home by their mothers in the ideals of the state and housewifery. They were also organized by troops and engaged in competitive sports. Their physical training was so that they might produce strong sons for the state.

Education in Athens

Where Sparta was renowned for its military preeminence, Athens was a democracy that held the individual in the highest regard. There was no compulsory education in Athens, except for two years beginning at age 18 when military training was required of all males. Schools in Athens were private and were restricted to those who could afford the fees.

Military education remains a viable educational option in the United States.

Education in Athens prior to 479 B.C. (the defeat of Sparta), referred to as "the old education," consisted of sending boys aged 7 to 14 to several schools: the *didascaleum* or music school; the home or building of the *grammatistes* for the study of reading, writing, and arithmetic; and the *palestra* for physical education. After age 14 formal education stopped, although some youth continued their education at the *gymnasia* where more severe physical training, somewhat military in nature, was received. From age 18 to 20 a program involving military, public, and religious service was required of all young men; upon completion full citizenship was granted. The aim of educating males in the Athenian state was to prepare a cultivated, well mannered, physically fit and agile individual ready for participation in Athenian citizenship.

The traditional view of the education of girls in Athens is that they only received instruction at home. Yet archaeological evidence seems to point to a different conclusion. Various pottery and statues depict girls going to school (e.g., a girl holding a tablet in one hand and a purse containing her astragals in the other), as well as reading, writing, and engaging in sports. However, it is uncertain how widespread these practices were (Beck, 1964).

What parallels do you see between modern educational systems and those of Sparta and Athens?

Sophists. The "new Greek education" (post–479 B.C.) continued much the same at the elementary level. At the secondary level, however, a new element was introduced—the Sophists, traveling teachers who charged admission to their popular lectures. Many of them were foreigners lured to Athens by its reputation and its success in defeating the Persians. Among the Sophists were the *skeptics,* who did not value knowledge for its own sake and therefore taught practical skills, especially the art of persuasion, which had easy application to public life. Other Sophists were the *rhetoricians,* who were concerned with the use of words in terms of plausibility, expedience, and political or legal success (Bowen, 1972). Their critics, including Plato, charged that they "brought to Athens a divesting spirit of critical rejection of the traditional beliefs and attitudes" and that behind their claim to teach the art of rhetoric "lay the presumption that success in public life, to be defined in terms of power, was more or less the supreme achievement possible to man" (Barrow, 1976, p. 14).

In the absence of a legal profession, some Sophists developed the practice of logography, the writing of speeches, which their clients could deliver in courts of law. Sets of speeches and handbooks on rhetoric were sold. Schools of rhetoric grew in size and number. Two of the more famous Sophists were Gorgras, a renowned orator who in his seventies was still enthralling the audience at the Olympic Games of 407 B.C., and Protagoras. The latter was considered to be so brilliant that he could charge a student as much as $10,000. Even Plato esteemed Protagoras as a man of sterling quality. Protagoras is considered the father of European grammar and philosophy (Meyer, 1972).

Socrates (469–399 B.C.).   Socrates accepted as his starting point the Sophists' position that man is the measure of all things. However, in contrast to the Sophists, he did not commercialize his teaching and accepted no fees. He also disagreed with the use of knowledge merely to achieve success or gain power, but believed that knowledge was ethically and morally important to all men. According to Socrates, knowledge was virtue. He also believed knowledge was eternal and universal.

To Socrates the purpose of education was not to perfect the art of rhetoric, but to develop in the individual his inherent knowledge and to perfect the ability to reason. Socrates believed that education and society were inextricably related: society was only as good as its schools. If education was successful in producing good citizens, then society would be strong and good.

Can you recall an example of the application of the Socratic Method in your own educational experience?

Socratic Method.   Socrates employed a dialectical teaching method that has come to be known as the *Socratic Method* and is similar to the inquiry method practiced today. Using this method Socrates would first demolish false or shaky opinions or assumptions held by the student while disclaiming any knowledge himself. Then, through a questioning process based on the student's experiences and analyzing the consequences of responses, he led the student to a better understanding of the problem. Finally, he brought the student to a discovery of general ideas or concepts that could be applied to new problems.

> "What is courage?" he would casually ask a soldier.
> "Courage is holding your ground when things get rough."
> "But supposing strategy required that you give way?"

"Well, in that case you wouldn't hold—that would be silly."

"Then you agree that courage is neither holding or giving way."

"I guess so. I don't know."

"Well, I don't know either. Maybe it might be just using your head. What do you say to that?"

"Yes—that's it; using your head, that's what it is."

"Then shall we say, at least tentatively, that courage is presence of mind—sound judgment in time of stress?"

"Yes." (Meyer, 1972, p. 26)

Plato (427–347 B.C.). Socrates' most famous pupil was Plato. Plato founded the Academy, a school of higher learning that admitted both males and females. Fees were not charged, but donations were accepted. As a teacher Plato practiced a variety of methods. Sometimes he employed the Socratic Method. At other times he assigned individual exercises and problems. Sometimes he lectured, though according to Meyer (1972), he was too technical and lecturing was reported not to have been his best performance. Plato's theory of education is most clearly put forward in *The Republic* and the *Laws*. In *The Republic* Plato begins by accepting Socrates' premise that "knowledge is virtue." He then expounds on the nature of knowledge and lays out the framework for both a political and social system, including an educational system. Plato believed that the state should operate the educational system. The aim of the schools was to discover and develop the abilities of the individual, to aid the individual in discovering the knowledge of truth that is within each of us, and to prepare the individual for his or her role in society. The curriculum was to include reading, especially the classics, writing, mathematics, and logic. Plato also emphasized the physical aspects of education. However, games and sports, as well as music, were important not for the purpose of entertainment but to improve the soul and achieve moral excellence.

Although Plato advocated universal education, he presumed that few possessed the capacity to reach its final stages. Those who passed the successive selection tests and reached the highest levels of wisdom and devotion to the state were to rule the state—the philosopher was to be king (Good & Teller, 1969). Education, then, is the means by which one arrives at the ultimate good. In the process it promotes the happiness and fulfillment of the individual (because he is sorted into the social office to which he is most fitted), as well as the good of the state. Plato's belief in leadership by the most intelligent has been espoused by countless since, including some of the founders of our nation. His belief in unchanging ideas and absolute truths has earned him the title of "the Father of Idealism."

Aristotle (384–322 B.C.). Aristotle was Plato's most famous student. For 20 years he studied and taught at the Academy. However, as the picture at the beginning of this chapter aptly reminds us, although the two agreed on many issues, they differed in some important respects. In the picture Plato is shown pointing heavenward as Aristotle points earthward. And that, metaphorically, was the main difference between them: Plato was the idealist, the lover of the metaphysical; Aristotle was a realist, the more scientific of the two (Winn &

Jacks, 1967). If Plato's concern for the idea served as the basis for Idealism, Aristotle provided the basis for Realism.

It is probably fair to say that Aristotle has had more of an impact on education than either Socrates or Plato, perhaps because he gave the most systematic attention to it. Like Plato he believed in the importance of reason. However, unlike Plato he dismissed "mere intellectual ponderings as insufficient to the advancement of knowledge. What was needed in addition was a diligent and unsparing scrutiny of all observable phenomena" (Meyer, 1972, p. 32). Aristotle is credited with the introduction of the scientific method of inquiry. He systematically classified all branches of existing knowledge and was the first to teach logic as a formal discipline. He believed that reality was to be found in an objective order.

Whereas Plato believed that knowledge is a virtue in itself and that wisdom is good, Aristotle maintained that goodness or virtue rests on deeds, not knowledge. He further maintained that man is a rational being and that the most important activity a man can do is to use his intellect fully. By doing so he attains happiness and accumulates knowledge.

Like Plato, Aristotle believed in the importance of education to the functioning of society and that education should be provided by the state; unlike Plato, he did not believe in educating girls. The aim of education, he felt, is the achievement of the highest possible happiness of the individual by the development of the intellect through the cultivating of habits and the specific use of inductive and deductive reasoning (Bowen, 1972). An additional aim is to produce the good person and good citizen. "The good person should have goodness of intellect which may be achieved by instruction, and goodness of character attained through conditioning of the control of habits" (Gillett, 1966, p. 36).

Last, Aristotle believed that there was a common core of knowledge that was basic to education, which included reading, writing, music, and physical education. This belief in a "core" of knowledge has prevailed through the centuries and is the basis for the core course requirement in American schools and colleges today.

Education in Rome

The Roman conquest of Greece in the second century B.C. brought thousands of Greek slaves to Rome and brought Romans into contact with Greece and its culture. The educational theories of the Greeks had a great impact on the Romans and by the end of the first century they dominated Roman education. The formal Roman school system that evolved (and which influenced education throughout Europe for centuries) was composed of the elementary school, known as the *ludus*, and the secondary school or grammar school. At the ludus children aged 7 to 12 were taught reading, writing, and accounting. Girls could attend the ludus, but usually that was as far as their education extended. *Grammar schools* were attended by upper class boys aged 12 to 16 who learned grammar (either Greek or Latin) and literature. From age 16 to 20 boys attended the school of rhetoric where they were instructed in grammar, rhetoric, dialectic, music, arithmetic, geometry, and astronomy. Universities were founded during the early years of the Roman Empire. Philosophy, law, mathematics, medicine, architecture, and rhetoric were the principal subjects taught.

Quintilian (35–95 A.D.). The most noteworthy Roman educator was Quintilian. His influence on Roman schooling has had a subsequent impact on education through the centuries. Quintilian was so respected that he was made a senator and was the first known endowed (state-supported) professor (Wilkins, 1914). His *Institutio Oratoria (Education of the Orator)*, published in 95 A.D., is considered to be "the most thorough, systematic and scientific treatment of education to be found in classical literature, whether Greek or Roman" (Monroe, 1939, p. 450).

Quintilian believed education should be concerned with a person's whole intellectual and moral nature, and should have as its goal the production of the effective moral man in practical life (Monroe, 1939). Accordingly, in addition to instruction in grammar and rhetoric, Quintilian recommended a broad literary education that included music, astronomy, geometry, and philosophy. Such an education was to take place in the schools, preferably the public schools, not at home with private tutors as had been the earlier practice in Rome. Public (i.e., group) education, he maintained, provided the opportunity for emulation, friendships, and learning from the successes and failures of others. Progressive for his time, Quintilian (cited in Monroe, 1939) disapproved of corporal punishment:

> first because it is a disgrace . . . and in reality . . . an affront; secondly, because if a boy's disposition be so abject as not to be amended by reproof, he will be hardened . . . (by) stripes. Besides, after you have coerced a boy with stripes, how will you treat him when he becomes a young man, to whom such terror cannot be held out? (pp. 466–467)

The "Ask Yourself" on page 70 will help you examine your position on corporal punishment in the schools.

In many other respects Quintilian's views seem remarkably modern. Recognizing that "study depends on the good will of the student, a quality that cannot be secured by compulsion," Quintilian supported holidays because "relaxation brings greater energy to study, and also games because it is the nature of young things to play" (Castle, 1967, p. 138). He believed in the importance of early training to child development. Of the proper methods of early instruction Quintilian said: "Let his instruction be an amusement to him; let him be questioned and praised; and let him never feel pleased that he does not know a thing . . . let his powers be called forth by rewards, such as that age prizes" (cited in Monroe, 1939, p. 455). He also maintained that children should not be introduced to specific subject matter until they are mature enough to master it. Last, Quintilian emphasized the importance of recognizing individual differences when prescribing the curriculum. He charged the teacher to "ascertain first of all, when a boy is entrusted to him, his ability and disposition . . . when a tutor has observed these indications, let him consider how the mind of his pupil is to be managed" (cited in Monroe, 1939, p. 465).

In what ways are the educational ideas of Quintilian relevant today?

70

The Roman system of education spread throughout western Europe. The schools of medieval Europe retained the standard curriculum of the Roman schools: grammar, rhetoric, logic, mathematics, geometry, music, and astronomy. And Latin has remained the language of the scholar until recent times. Figure 3.1 provides an overview of education in Sparta, Athens, and Rome.

Education in the Middle Ages

The period between the end of the Roman Empire (476 A.D.) and the fourteenth century is known as the Middle Ages. The Germanic tribes that conquered the Romans appropriated not only their land but much of their culture and their Catholic religion. The Roman Catholic Church became the dominant force in society and in education. By the end of the sixth century public education had all but disappeared, and what remained took place under the auspices of the church. At the secondary level, monastic schools, originally established to train the clergy, educated boys in the established disciplines of the Roman schools. Theology was studied by those preparing for the priesthood. One important function of the monastic schools was preserving and copying manuscripts. Had it not been for the monastic schools, many of the ancient manuscripts we have today would have been lost.

Alcuin and the Palace School

Another type of school, the palace school, was established by the Emperor Charlemagne (742–814). Charlemagne brought one of the most revered

Figure 3.1: Education in Ancient Societies

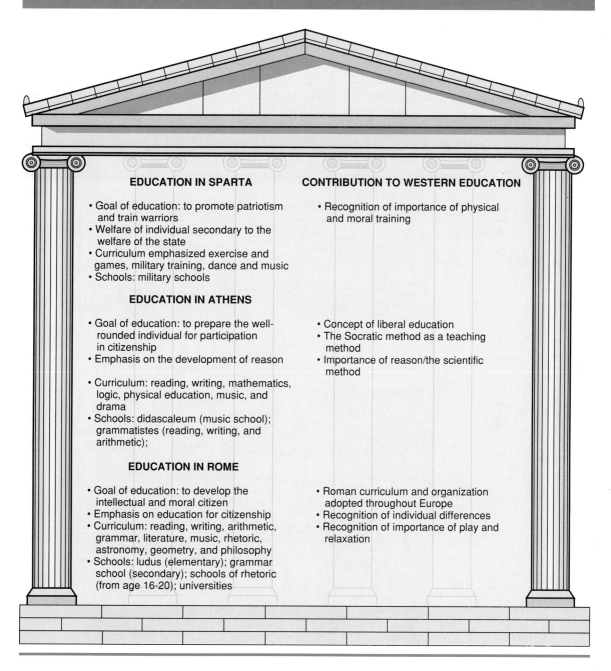

EDUCATION IN SPARTA

- Goal of education: to promote patriotism and train warriors
- Welfare of individual secondary to the welfare of the state
- Curriculum emphasized exercise and games, military training, dance and music
- Schools: military schools

EDUCATION IN ATHENS

- Goal of education: to prepare the well-rounded individual for participation in citizenship
- Emphasis on the development of reason

- Curriculum: reading, writing, mathematics, logic, physical education, music, and drama
- Schools: didascaleum (music school); grammatistes (reading, writing, and arithmetic);

EDUCATION IN ROME

- Goal of education: to develop the intellectual and moral citizen
- Emphasis on education for citizenship
- Curriculum: reading, writing, arithmetic, grammar, literature, music, rhetoric, astronomy, geometry, and philosophy
- Schools: ludus (elementary); grammar school (secondary); schools of rhetoric (from age 16-20); universities

CONTRIBUTION TO WESTERN EDUCATION

- Recognition of importance of physical and moral training

- Concept of liberal education
- The Socratic method as a teaching method
- Importance of reason/the scientific method

- Roman curriculum and organization adopted throughout Europe
- Recognition of individual differences
- Recognition of importance of play and relaxation

scholars and teachers of his age, Alcuin of York (England), to his court to establish a school. Through Alcuin's efforts, the school became an important force in education in Europe. Charlemagne and all the members of his family studied at the school, and many future teachers, writers, and scholars were trained there.

During this time the curriculum consisted of what was called the *seven liberal arts,* which included the *trivium* (grammar, rhetoric, and logic) and the *quadrivium* (arithmetic, geometry, music, and astronomy; see Figure 3.2). The term "liberal arts," if not the exact subjects, is still used today to describe that

Figure 3.2: Tower of Knowledge, Showing Stages of Medieval Education

Source: Reisch, G. (1504). *Margarita Philosophica* (2nd ed.). Argentinae (Strassbourg): Johannes Schottus.

portion of the college curriculum that is not concerned with technical or professional studies.

Thomas Aquinas (1225–1274)

The most important scholar and philosopher of the Middle Ages was the Dominican monk St. Thomas Aquinas. His philosophy, called *scholasticism* or Thomism, is the foundation of Roman Catholic education. Aquinas was able to reconcile religion with the rediscovered ancient philosophies, particularly the rationalism of Aristotle. He believed that human beings possess both a spiritual nature, the soul, and a physical nature, the body. He also maintained that man is a rational being and that through the deductive process of rational analysis man can arrive at truth. When reason fails, man must rely on faith. Thus reason supports what man knows by faith: reason and faith are complementary sources of truth. In accordance with this philosophy, the schools were to teach both the principles of the faith and rational philosophy. The curriculum was to contain both theology and the liberal arts.

The Medieval Universities

During the later part of the Middle Ages, as the Crusades opened Europe to other parts of the world and as many of the Greek masterpieces were rediscovered, there was an intellectual revival that manifested itself not only in scholasticism but in the establishment of several of the world's great universities. The University of Salerno, established in 1050 A.D., specialized in medicine; the University of Bologna (1113 A.D.) in law; the University of Paris (1160 A.D.) in theology; and Oxford University (1349 A.D.) in liberal arts and theology. By the end of the Middle Ages some 80 universities were in existence (Meyer, 1972). Some, such as the University of Paris, grew out of a cathedral school, in this case Nôtre-Dame. Others evolved from associations called *universitas*, which were chartered corporations of teachers and students, organized for their protection against interference from secular or religious authorities.

At first most universities did not have buildings of their own but occupied rented space. The curriculum at the undergraduate level followed the seven liberal arts. Classes started soon after sunrise. The mode of instruction was lecture in Latin, with the teacher usually reading from a text he had written. Student guilds or unions, commonplace at the time, ventured to tell the professors how fast to speak. At Bologna the students wanted to get full value for their fees and required the professors to speak very fast. By contrast, the Parisian students insisted on a leisurely pace and when the authorities ordered some acceleration, the students not only "howled and clamored" but threatened to go on strike (Meyer, 1972). More exciting than the lectures were the *disputations* at which students presented and debated opposing intellectual positions. The disputations also served to prepare students for the much dreaded day when they would defend their theses. The Historical Note on page 74 provides a brief glimpse of the life of the university student in medieval times. Note the differences and similarities with today.

Of all the institutions that have survived from medieval times to the present, with the exception of the Catholic Church, the university bears the

If the student guild or union were in effect today, what changes might it recommend for undergraduate education?

Historical Note:
Life of the Medieval University Student

Although academic life was rigorous, students had many privileges. They were exempt from military service and from paying taxes. A student who shaved his head and assumed a few other burdens became one of the clerical class and was allowed some of the benefits associated with it. For example, if he broke what would be considered civil law he was tried under church law, not civil law. However, in keeping with his clerical status the student was required to be celibate. If he did stray, he could continue with his studies, but lost his privileges and could receive no degree.

Medieval students were not without vices. Taverns often surrounded the universities and at the taverns were women and gambling. More seriously, students at Oxford were said to roam the streets at night, assaulting all who passed. In Rome the stu-dents went from tavern to tavern committing assault and robbery. At Leipzig they were fined for throwing stones at professors, and at Paris they were excommunicated for shooting dice on the altars of Nôtre-Dame.

Although these acts were the exceptions rather than the rule, such actions, as well as the attitude of the students, who held townspeople in low regard, were sufficient to lead to open hostilities between "town" and "gown." Some separation exists between town and gown in many university communities today, perhaps a legacy from our medieval ancestors.

Source: Based on accounts in Meyer, A. E. (1972). *An educational history of the western world.* New York: McGraw-Hill Book Company.

closest resemblance to its ancient ancestors. As it was then, it is still an organization of students and professors dedicated to the pursuit of knowledge. It still grants the medieval degrees: the bachelor's, the master's, and the doctor's. In most universities students are still required to study a given curriculum and if they seek the doctorate are required to write a thesis or dissertation and to defend it publicly. The gowns worn at academic ceremonies today are patterned after those worn by our medieval ancestors. And deans, rectors, and chancellors still exist, though their duties have changed (Meyer, 1972).

Education During the Renaissance

The Renaissance began in the fourteenth century and reached its high point in the fifteenth century. It is so called because it represented a *renaissance* or rebirth of interest in the humanist aspects of Greek and Latin thought. When Constantinople fell to the Muslims in 1453 many Byzantine scholars came to Italy, bringing with them the works of classical antiquity that had been forgotten in the West, most notably Quintilian's *Education of the Orator.* The influence of this treatise, great as it had been in imperial Rome, was even greater in the Renaissance (Woodward, 1906). Quintilian was viewed as the prime authority on Roman educational ideals. It is symbolic of the respect given Quintilian that Erasmus, the most noted educator of the Renaissance, should apologize for touching on the aims or methods of teaching "seeing that Quintilian has said in effect the last word on the matter" (Woodward, 1906, p. 10).

During the Middle Ages the Catholic Church was dominant and emphasis was on the hereafter. In the fourteenth and fifteenth centuries the increase in trade and commerce, the increase in science and technology, the growth of the Italian city-states, and the rise of a new aristocracy whose wealth came from trade and banking brought an end to the old social, economic, and political order and in so doing brought a greater concern for the here than the hereafter.

Humanism

The dominant philosophy of the Renaissance was *humanism*. Rejecting scholasticism and the model of the cleric as the educated man, the humanists considered the educated man to be the man of learning described in the classics. The first products of the Renaissance in education can be seen in the famous *court schools* operated by Vittorino da Feltre at Mantua from 1423 to 1446 and by Guarino da Verona at Ferrara from 1429 to 1469. Like the school of Alcuin in the ninth century, they were connected to the courts of reigning families. Like many modern preparatory boarding schools, they housed boys aged 8 or 10 to age 20. They emphasized what Woodward called the "doctrine of courtesy"—the manners, grace, and dignity of the antique culture (Woodward, 1906). At the court schools a humanist curriculum was taught that included not only the seven liberal arts, but reading, writing, and speaking in Latin, study of the Greek classics, and, for the first time, the study of history. Following the teachings of Quintilian, games and play were also emphasized, individual differences were recognized, and punishment was discouraged. The goal was to produce the well-rounded, liberally educated *courtier*—the ideal personality of the Renaissance.

Erasmus (1466–1536)

The foremost humanist of the Renaissance was Desiderius Erasmus of the Netherlands. Although Erasmus was not a prolific writer, what he wrote was full of charm and wit, and as a result was widely read. His *Colloquies,* textbooks on Latin style, also contained instruction in religion and morals and were among the most important textbooks of his time. In *Upon the Method of Right Instruction* he proposed the systematic training of teachers. His views on pedagogy are found in his treatise *Of the First Liberal Education of Children.* It contained much that had been advanced by Quintilian: the abolition of corporal punishment, the value of play and games, and the necessity of understanding the student's individual needs and abilities. Erasmus was also one of the first educators to understand the importance of politeness. "Erasmus knew perfectly well that politeness has a moral side, that it is not a matter of pure convention, but that it proceeds from the inner disposition of a well-ordered soul. So he assigns it an important place in education" (Laurie, 1968, p. 56).

The educational program of Erasmus was characteristic of the humanist school, which can be described as:

> return to the ancients; classical tongues to be studied in the sources, and no longer in barbarous manuals; rhetorical exercises to be substituted for useless and obscure dialectic; the study of nature to animate and vivify literary studies;

the largest possible diffusion of human knowledge without distinction of age or sex. (Laurie, 1968, p. 55)

Education During the Reformation

Speculate on the impact of the invention of the printing press on education.

That period of history known as the Reformation formally began in 1517 when an Augustinian monk and professor of religion named Martin Luther nailed his *Ninety-five Theses,* questioning the authority of the Catholic Church, to the door of the court church in Wittenburg, Germany. In the years that followed a religious revolution swept the European continent, resulting in a century of war and reformation of the Church. Those who protested the authority (and abuses) of the Church came to be known as Protestants. The invention of the printing press enabled their doctrine to be spread rapidly.

Vernacular Schools

In disavowing the authority of the Church the Protestant reformers stressed the authority of the Bible over that of the Church. They also stressed the responsibility of each man for his own salvation. Therefore it was necessary that each person be able to read the Scriptures and, as a corollary, to be educated. The initial product of this belief was the establishment of *vernacular schools*—primary or elementary schools that offered instruction in the mother tongue or "vernacular" and a basic curriculum of reading, writing, mathematics, and religion.

Vernacular schools were established throughout Germany by Philip Melanchthon and Johann Bugenhagen following Luther's teachings. Melanchthon in particular is noted for his advocacy of universal elementary education and has been called the "Schoolmaster of Germany." Elementary schools also began to appear in other Protestant strongholds, especially those that followed the teachings of John Calvin, such as in the Netherlands, in Scotland, and in the canton of Geneva (Switzerland) where Calvin established a theocratic dictatorship.

Luther (1483—1546)

Martin Luther believed that every child should have a free and compulsory elementary education. Education should be supported by the state and the state should have the authority and responsibility to control the curriculum, the textbooks, and the instruction in the schools. His *Letters to the Mayors and Aldermen of All Cities of Germany in Behalf of Christian Schools* stressed the spiritual, economic, and political benefits of education. The curriculum was to include classical languages, which were to be learned by practice. Grammar, mathematics, science, history, physical education, music, and didactics were all considered important. Theology was taught and study of Protestant doctrines was accomplished through the catechism (a question and answer drill).

Although formal schooling was important to the establishment of a "priesthood of believers," Luther thought such public instruction should occupy only part of the day. At least one or two hours a day should be spent at home in vocational training, preparing for an occupation through an apprenticeship. Secondary schools, designed primarily as preparatory schools for the clergy, taught Hebrew as well as the classical languages, rhetoric, dialectic, history, mathematics, science, music, and gymnastics. A university education, whose purpose was seen as providing training for higher service in the government or the Church, was available only to those young men who demonstrated exceptional intellectual abilities.

Calvin (1509–1564)

John Calvin's views on education were very similar to those of Luther. He too stressed the necessity of a universal, compulsory, state-supported education that would not only enable all individuals to read the Bible themselves and thereby attain salvation, but would profit the state through the contributions of an educated citizenry. The school was also seen as a place for religious indoctrination. Calvin also supported a two-track educational system consisting of common schools for the masses and secondary schools teaching the classical, humanist curriculum for the preparation of the leaders of church and state. Calvin's influence was widespread, especially in the colonies of the New World.

The Reformation in England

In contrast to what was taking place on the continent, the Protestant Reformation in England did not lead to an increase in the number of schools, but to a decrease. When Henry VIII broke with the Catholic Church and closed the Catholic monasteries, the monastic schools were also closed. Under Elizabeth I such schools as existed were placed under the regulation of the Anglican Church. The few secondary (Latin grammar) schools that continued to exist were established by a town council or by an individual benefactor and were narrow and sectarian in nature. Uniform textbooks were required throughout the country, the curriculum was rigid, and discipline was severe.

Calvinism spread to England. The English Calvinists, called Puritans, aspired to reform or purify the Anglican Church, which had maintained much of the structure of the Catholic Church. Persecuted for their efforts and seeking religious freedom, the Puritans were important in the settlement of the American colonies.

The Jesuits

While the Reformation was taking place outside the Catholic Church, a Counter-Reformation in the Church resulted in the formation of the Society of Jesus, or Jesuits, by Ignatius of Loyola (1491–1556). The Jesuits became a teaching order and were instrumental in the establishment of a number of secondary schools and universities throughout Europe. Their major contribution to education was in the training of teachers. They established, perhaps for the first time in history, a specific plan for the selection, training, and supervision of teachers.

Which of the major colleges and universities in the United States were founded and are operated by the Jesuits?

Later European Educational Thought

The Reformation not only opened the door to the questioning of religious dogma and superstition, but to investigation of the laws of nature. The Reformation gave way to the Age of Enlightenment or Reason, so called because of the great reliance placed on reason and scientific inquiry. Philosophers and scholars of the period believed that observation and scientific inquiry were the avenues to the discovery of the "natural laws" that dictated the orderly operation of the universe.

Bacon (1561–1626)

Francis Bacon, an English philosopher, was central to this movement. He was also important to education because of the emphasis he placed on scientific inquiry rather than on accepting previously derived hypotheses of deductive logic or the writings of the past. He emphasized the need for education to develop what today is termed "critical thinking skills." The Utopia described in his *The New Atlantis* envisioned a research university not inconsistent with modern ideas.

Comenius (1592–1670)

Bacon had a major influence on Jan Amos Comenius, a Moravian bishop. Like Bacon he was a proponent of what is termed *sense realism,* which is the belief that learning must come through the senses. Accordingly, education must allow children to observe for themselves and experience by doing. Children can best learn to write by writing, to talk by talking, to sing by singing, and to reason by reasoning. The notion of sensory learning was later expanded by Locke, Rousseau, and Pestalozzi.

Like Bacon, Comenius believed in the scientific method and an ordered universe that could be discovered through reason. He proposed a set of teaching methods based on these beliefs that incorporated both the deductive method and whatever instructional method was most appropriate for the specific developmental stage of the child. Comenius is said to be the first educator to propose a theory of child growth and development.

Comenius proposed that teaching be straightforward and simple and proceed from the concrete to the abstract, that it deal with things before symbols, and that it have practical application. He affirmed Quintilian's beliefs in regard to individual differences, motivation, and corporal punishment. Finally, he believed in a general learning, *paideia,* which should be possessed by all educated persons.

Comenius is also known for his Latin textbooks which were used throughout Europe. The texts were very popular, not only because they attempted to teach Latin through the use of the vernacular, but because they were among the first textbooks to contain illustrations.

Comenius has had a profound effect on Western education through his influence on the thinking of such educational leaders as Horace Mann, John Dewey, Robert Hutchins, and Mortimer Adler. Mortimer Adler's dedication to *The Paideia Program: An Educational Syllabus* (1984) reads:

To
John Amos Comenius
Who, more than 300 years ago
envisaged the educational ideal that
The Paideia Program aims to realize
before the end of this century.

Locke (1632–1704)

Although the English philosopher John Locke is best known for his political theories, which served as the basis for the American and French constitutions, he also had a profound influence on education. He held views very
similar to others in the school of sensory reasoning. Locke taught the *tabula
rasa* concept of the human mind, which says that we come into the world with
our minds a blank slate. We then learn through sensation. "A sound mind in
a sound body is a short but full description of a happy state in the world" are
his first words in *Some Thoughts Concerning Education* (Axtell, 1968, p. 114).
The sound body needs fresh air, recreation, exercise, and good hygiene. The
sound mind, like the sound body, needs exercise and discipline. The curriculum he recommended included, beyond the three R's, history, geography,
ethics, philosophy, science, and conversational foreign languages, especially
French. Mathematics was also emphasized, not to make the scholar a mathe-
matician, but to make him a reasonable man. Locke believed the goal of
education was to create the moral, practical individual who could participate
effectively in the governing process.

Rousseau (1712–1778)

In the later part of the eighteenth century an educational movement
called *naturalism* developed. Its emphasis on freedom and the individual
formed the basis for modern educational theory and practice. The forerunner
of the movement was Jean-Jacques Rousseau. Like Locke, Rousseau is perhaps best remembered for his political theories. His book *Social Contract* had a
strong influence on the thinking of those involved in both the French and
American revolutions. Although he was never an educator, Rousseau expounded a theory and philosophy of education that influenced many educators, including John Dewey and the progressive educators of a century or
more later. Rousseau has also been called the "father of modern child psychology" (Mayer, 1973).

Like Comenius, Rousseau believed in stages of children's growth and
development and in the educational necessity of adapting instruction to the
various stages. His major thoughts on education are contained in his novel
Emile, which puts forward the ideal education for a youth named Emile. He
contends that the child is inherently good and that it is society that corrupts
the natural goodness of man. Like Locke he was concerned with the physical
growth and health of the child. The education of Emile is to be child-centered,
concerned with developing his natural abilities. He is to learn by his senses
through direct experience and is not to be punished. Emile's education is to

*How does
Rousseau's
belief in the
inherent
goodness of the
child compare to
the doctrine of
original sin?*

progress as he is ready and as his interests motivate him. Finally, he is taught a trade in order to prepare him for an occupation in life.

Pestalozzi (1746–1827)

Johann Heinrich Pestalozzi was a Swiss educator who put Rousseau's ideas into practice. Pestalozzi has had a profound impact on education throughout much of the Western world. The Prussian government sent teachers to be instructed by him, and educators came from all over the world, including the United States, to observe and study his methods. He was made a citizen of the French Republic and knighted by the czar of Russia. Horace Mann and Henry Barnard came under his influence. Edward A. Sheldon, superintendent of schools in Oswego, New York, established a teacher training school at Oswego in 1861 that followed Pestalozzi's methods.

Pestalozzi's philosophy of education incorporated the child-centered, sensory experience principles of Rousseau. He believed with Rousseau in the natural goodness of human nature and the corrupting influence of society. He also supported Rousseau's idea of individual differences in "readiness" to learn. His belief in the development of the total child to his or her maximum potential has been given its greatest recognition in the movement for the education of the disadvantaged during the second half of the twentieth century.

Perhaps more than Rousseau, Pestalozzi recognized the importance of human emotions in the learning process. It was important, he believed, that the child be given feelings of self-respect and emotional security. It also was important that the teacher treat students with love. In fact, it can be said that the ideal of love governs Pestalozzi's educational philosophy. Pestalozzi was especially fond of poor children and did everything in his power to improve their condition (Mayer, 1973).

Like Comenius, Pestalozzi believed that instruction must begin with the concrete and proceed to the abstract. Materials should be presented slowly, in developmental order from simple to complex, from known to unknown. The *object lesson* centers on concrete materials within the child's experience, involves discussion and oral presentation, and replaces rote learning. For example, "in an arithmetic lesson dealing with the number 'three,' the child should handle three objects, then progress from sight and touch to abstract concepts of number and the idea contained in the word 'three' " (Gillett, 1966, p. 218).

Herbart (1776–1841)

One of the Prussian educators who studied under Pestalozzi was Johann Friedrich Herbart. Herbart believed that the aim of education should be the development of moral character. His pedagogical theory included three key concepts: *interest, apperception,* and *correlation.* Instruction can only be successful if it arouses interest. Interests are derived from both nature and society, and thus the curriculum should include both the natural and social sciences. All new material presented to the child is interpreted in terms of past experiences by the process of apperception. Additionally, ideas are reinforced and organized in the mind by the process of correlation (Gillett, 1966).

The child-centered philosophy of Pestalozzi influenced education practice throughout the western world.

Herbart maintained that any suitable material could be learned if presented systematically. The five steps in the Herbartian methodology included:

1. *Preparation*—preparing the student to receive the new material by arousing interest or recalling past material or experiences

2. *Presentation*—presenting the new material

3. *Association*—combining old and new ideas

4. *Generalization*—formulating general ideas or principles

5. *Application*—applying the ideas or principles to new situations

Herbart's ideas had a significant influence on American education. The National Herbartian Society, founded in 1892, ten years later became the

National Society of the Scientific Study of Education. Herbart made the study of educational psychology of paramount importance. He demonstrated the significance of methodology in instruction. But, perhaps most importantly, his greatness "lies in his faith that education ultimately could become a science" (Mayer, 1973, p. 282).

Froebel (1782–1852)

Friedrich Froebel was the third member of what Gillett (1966) called the nineteenth century's "famous pedagogical triumvirate" that broke with subject-centered instruction and created a new concern for the child. Froebel is known for the establishment in 1837 of the first kindergarten and for providing the theoretical basis for early childhood education. Although Froebel accepted many of Pestalozzi's ideas associated with child-centeredness,

The learning of social cooperation and playing creatively with objects are important in early childhood education according to Froebel.

Froebel was more concerned with activity than Pestalozzi, but less concerned with observation. According to Froebel, the primary aim of the school should be self-development through self-expression. Self-expression took place through games, singing, or any number of creative and spontaneous activities, which were to be part of an *activity curriculum*. Froebel was also concerned with the development of creativity in children. He viewed the classroom as a miniature society in which children learned social cooperation.

Froebel developed highly stylized materials which were mass produced and used throughout the world. They were designed to aid self-expression and bring out the "divine effluence" (the fundamental unity of all nature with God) within each child. *Mother and Nursery Songs* was a collection of songs, poems, pictures, instructions, games, and suggested activities designed for instruction of the young at home (Gillett, 1966). In the kindergarten, *gifts* and *occupations* were used. The gifts were play objects that did not change their form (e.g., wooden spheres or cubes), symbols of the fundamentals of nature. The occupations were materials used in creative construction or design activities whose shape changed in use (e.g., clay or paper). Used together they were said to ensure the progressive self-development of the child.

Recall your own experience in the primary grades. To what extent was your educational experience similar to Froebel's activity curriculum?

One of Froebel's pupils, Margaretha Schurz, opened the first kindergarten in the United States in Watertown, Wisconsin. John Dewey adopted many of Froebel's principles and used them in his famous laboratory school at the University of Chicago. Today, the kindergarten is recognized for its importance in the educational process and as a socializing force. It is the cornerstone of our educational system.

Table 3.1 gives an overview of the educational theories we have discussed and their influence on Western education.

Education in Colonial America

The English, the predominant settlers of the American colonies, had the greatest influence on the educational system that emerged in the colonies, but the French and Spanish also played a role. The French empire once spread from Canada to Louisiana. French priests, particularly the Jesuits, followed explorers and fur traders into the wilderness to convert and educate the Native Americans. The Catholic influence on education, which can still be seen today in cities as far apart as Quebec and New Orleans, can be traced to the French Jesuits and to orders of teaching nuns.

The Spanish empire was no less vast, containing at various times the entire Southwest, Florida, and California. Spanish Catholic priests, especially the Franciscans, also followed the explorers and sought to convert and educate the Native Americans. Their vast array of missions stretched throughout the Southwest and into California. The missions often included schools where Native Americans were taught not only the Spanish language but agricultural and vocational skills.

Table 3.1: Western European Educational Thought, 1200 A.D.–1850 A.D.

Theorist	Educational Theories	Influence on Western Education
Aquinas (1225–1274)	Human beings possess both a spiritual and a physical nature. Man is a rational being. Faith and reasons are complementary sources of truth.	Provided basis for Roman Catholic education.
Erasmus (1466–1536)	The liberally educated man is one educated in the seven liberal arts, steeped in the classics and in rhetoric. Systematic training of teachers is needed. Follower of Quintilian.	Advanced the need for the systematic training of teachers and a humanistic pedagogy. Promoted the importance of politeness in education.
Luther (1483–1546)	Education is necessary for religious instruction, the preparation of religious leaders, and the economic well-being of the state. Education should include vocational training.	Provided support for concept of free and compulsory elementary education. Promoted concept of universal literacy.
Calvin (1509–1564)	Education serves both the religious and political establishment: elementary schools for the masses where they could learn to read the Bible and thereby attain salvation; secondary school to prepare the leaders of church and state.	Concept of two-track system and emphasis on literacy influenced education in New England and ultimately the entire nation.
Bacon (1561–1626)	Education should advance scientific inquiry. Understanding of an ordered universe comes through reason.	Provided major rationale for the development of critical thinking skills. Proposed the concept of a research university.
Comenius (1592–1670)	Learning must come through the senses. Education must allow the child to reason by doing. There is a general body of knowledge (*paideia*) that should be possessed by all.	Provided theory of child growth and development. Concept of *paideia* profoundly influenced numerous Western educational leaders.
Locke (1632–1704)	Children enter the world with their minds like a blank slate (*tabula rasa*). The goal of education is to promote the development of reason and morality.	Provided philosophical basis for American and French revolutions. Provided support for the concept of the reasonable man and the ability and necessity for the reasonable man to participate in the governing process.

Table 3.1: *continued*		
Theorist	Educational Theories	Influence on Western Education
Rousseau (1712–1778)	Major proponent of naturalism, which emphasized individual freedom. The child is inherently good. Children's growth and development goes through stages, which necessitates adaptation of instruction. Education should be concerned with the development of the child's natural abilities.	Naturalism provided basis for modern educational theory and practice. Father of modern child psychology.
Pestalozzi (1746–1827)	Education should be child-centered and based on sensory experience. The individual differences of each child must be considered in assessing readiness to learn. Each child should be developed to his or her maximum potential. Ideal of love emphasized the importance of emotion in the learning process. Instruction should begin with the concrete and proceed to the abstract.	Concept of maximum development of each child provided support for education of the disadvantaged. Pestalozzian methods exported throughout Europe and to the United States, one of the earliest theories of instruction formally taught to teachers.
Herbart (1776–1841)	The aim of education should be the development of moral character. Any material can be learned if presented systematically: preparation, presentation, association, generalization, and application. Instruction must arouse interest to be successful. Education is a science.	Elevated the study of educational psychology. Demonstrated the significance of methodology in instruction. Advanced the concept that education is a science and can be studied scientifically.
Froebel (1782–1852)	The aim of education should be to ensure self-development through self-expression. Self-expression takes place through an activity curriculum. The school should promote creativity and bring out "divine effluence" within each child.	Established first kindergarten. Provided theoretical basis for early childhood education.

English Settlement

The first English settlement in North America was at Jamestown (Virginia) in 1607. In 1620, the Pilgrims, a group of Separatist Puritans (Protestants who wanted not only to purify but to separate from the Church of England), settled at Plymouth (Massachusetts). Ten years later a group of nonseparatist Puritans founded the Massachusetts Bay Colony. This colony became a focal point of migration and other New England colonies (Rhode Island, New Haven [Connecticut], New Hampshire, Maine) developed from this base (Cohen, 1974). Many of the colonists who came to the New World were filled with a sense of religious commitment, largely Protestant, which shaped their views on life and education. However, settlers in different regions developed varying conceptions of society and education (Gutek, 1986). These variations are explored in the following sections.

Education in the New England Colonies

According to Cubberley (1934), the Puritans who settled New England "contributed most that was of value for our future educational development" (p. 14). The New England colonists sustained a vigorous emphasis on education even in the hostile new environment. In fact, by 1700 the New England colonies could boast of literary rates that were often superior to those in England (Cohen, 1974).

Initially the Puritans attempted to follow English practice regarding the establishment and support of schools by relying on private benefactors and limiting the role of the state. However, the general absence of wealthy Puritan migrants soon led to the abandonment of this practice and, because of fears that parents were neglecting the education of their children, to a more direct role for the state (Cohen, 1974).

First Education Laws

The Massachusetts Law of 1642 ordered the selectmen of each town to ascertain whether parents and masters (of apprentices) were, in fact, providing for the education of their children. The selectmen were also to determine what the child was being taught. The child of any parent or master failing to meet his obligation could be apprenticed to a new master who would be required to fulfill the law. Although the law neither specified schools nor required attendance, it is said to have established the principle of compulsory education. Five years later, the Education Law of 1647 ordered every township of 50 households to provide a teacher to teach reading and writing, and all townships of 100 or more households to establish a grammar school. Although there was no uniform compliance nor administration of these laws, they show how important education was to the Puritans and demonstrate their belief in the necessity of a literate citizenry for the functioning of political society. The laws also served as models for other colonies and are considered the first education laws in America.

Religious Influence

In New England, as in the other colonies, the institutions of secular government, including education, were closely aligned with the dominant religious group. The Puritans brought with them many of the educational views of the Reformation, namely that education was necessary for religious instruction and salvation, as well as for good citizenship. As the Massachusetts Law of

1642 explained, there was a need to ensure the ability of children "to read and understand the principles of religion and the capital laws of this country." This purpose is also evidenced by the first words of the Massachusetts Education Law of 1647, also called the "old Deluder Satan Law": "It being one chief project of that old deluder, Satan, to keep men from knowledge of the Scriptures." The founding of Harvard College in 1636 was also based on religious motives—to ensure that there would be an educated ministry for the colony. Fearful that there would be no replacements for the ministers who first came with them, the colonists dreaded "to leave an illiterate Ministry to the churches, when our present Ministers should lie in the Dust" (Cubberley, 1934, p. 13).

How do the basic purposes of education in Colonial America compare with those of today?

Elementary School

The New England colonists not only shared Calvin's view of the aim of education, they also adopted the two-track system advocated by Calvin and other scholars of the Reformation. Town schools and *dame schools* were established to educate the children of the common folk in elementary reading, writing, and mathematics. The dame schools were held in the kitchen or living room of a neighborhood woman, often a widow, usually a person with minimal education herself, who received a modest fee for her efforts. So-called "writing" or "reading schools" were concerned with the teaching of these disciplines and also were operated on a fee basis. *Charity* or *pauper schools* were operated for the children of the poor who could not afford to attend other schools.

Education was also made available as a result of the apprenticeship system whereby a child was apprenticed to a master to learn a trade. In addition, the master was required by the terms of the indenture to ensure that the apprentice received a basic education. For some children this was the avenue by which they learned what little reading and writing they knew.

Instruction in the schools was primarily religious and authoritarian. Students learned their basic lessons from the *hornbook*, so called because the material was written on a sheet of parchment, placed on a wooden board, and covered with a thin sheath of cow's horn for protection (see Figure 3.3). The board had a handle with a hole in it so it could be strung around the child's neck.

The New England Primer

The *New England Primer* was used with slightly older children. The primer is an excellent example of the interrelationship between education and religion. Although different editions of the primer varied somewhat in the 150 years of its publication, which began in 1690, it usually featured an alphabet and spelling guide, followed by one of the things that made the primer famous—24 little pictures with alphabetical rhymes as illustrated in Figure 3.4.

The primer also included the Lord's Prayer, the Creed, the Ten Commandments, a listing of the books of the Bible, and a list of numbers from 1 to 100, using both Arabic and Roman numerals. Another prominent feature of the primer was a poem, the exhortation of John Rogers to his children, from John Foxe's *Book of Martyrs,* with a picture of the martyr burning at the

Source: Littlefield, G. E. (1965). *Early Schools and School-Books of New England* (p. 111). New York: Russell & Russell, Inc. Reprinted with permission.

stake as his wife and children look on. The primer ended with a shortened version of the Puritan catechism (Ford, 1962).

Secondary Grammar Schools

Secondary grammar schools existed for the further education of the male children of the well-to-do. They also served as preparatory schools for the university where the leaders of the church and political affairs were to be trained and which required proficiency in Latin and Greek for admission. The Boston Latin School, established in 1635, became the model for similar schools throughout New England.

Education at the grammar school was quite different from that at the dame or town school. The emphasis was on Latin, with some Greek and occasionally Hebrew. Other disciplines included those necessary for the education of the Renaissance concept of the educated man. The course of study in the grammar school lasted fairly intensively for six to seven years, although students "tended to withdraw and return, depending on familial need and circumstances; and since school was conducted on a year-round basis and

Figure 3.4: An Alphabet Including Both Religious and Secular Jingles

A
In *Adam's* Fall
We Sinned all.

B
Thy Life to Mend
This *Book* Attend.

C
The *Cat* doth play
And after flay.

D
A *Dog* will bite
A Thief at night.

E
An *Eagles* flight
Is out of fight.

F
The Idle *Fool*
Is whipt at School.

G
As runs the *Glass*
Mans life doth pass.

H
My *Book* and *Heart*
Shall never part.

J
Job feels the Rod
Yet blesses GOD.

K
Our *K I N G* the
good
No man of blood.

L
The *Lion* bold
The *Lamb* doth hold.

M
The *Moon* gives light
In time of night.

N
Nightingales sing
In Time of Spring.

O
The *Royal Oak*
it was the Tree
That sav'd His
Royal Majestie.

P
Peter denies
His Lord and cries.

Q
Queen *Esther* comes
in Royal State
To Save the JEWS
from dismal Fate

R
Rachel doth mour,
For her first born.

S
Samuel anoints
Whom God appoint:

T
Time cuts down all
Both great and small.

U
Uriah's beauteous Wife
Made *David* seek his
Life.

W
Whales in the Sea
God's Voice obey.

X
Xerxes the great did
die,
And so must you & I,

Y
Youth forward slips
Death soonest nips.

Z
Zacheus he
Did climb the Tree
His Lord to see,

Source: Ford, P. L. (Ed.). (1962). *The New England Primer.* New York: Teachers College Press.

instruction organized around particular texts, it was fairly simple for a student to resume study after a period of absence" (Cremin, 1970, p. 186).

University Curriculum

The curriculum of the university in the early colonial period was also based on the classically oriented pattern of English universities. As Cohen (1974) described it:

> The undergraduate courses revolved around the traditional Trivium and Quadrivium but without musical studies, the Three Philosophies (Metaphysics, Ethics, Natural Science), and Greek, Hebrew, and a chronological study of ancient history. As in English universities logic and rhetoric were the basic subjects in the curriculum. . . . Compositions, orations, and disputations were given the same careful scrutiny as at English universities. (p. 66)

Education in New England During the Later Colonial Period

Social and Economic Changes.   The Age of the Enlightenment or Age of Reason that swept the Western world in the seventeenth century had found its way to the shores of the American colonies by the eighteenth century. As in Europe it brought greater concern for independent rationality, a repudiation of supernatural explanations of phenomena, and a greater questioning of traditional dogma. At the same time that the Enlightenment was sweeping the colonies, the population of the colonies increased rapidly and its economy outgrew its localized base of farming and fishing. Trade and commerce increased and a new mercantile gentry emerged (Cohen, 1974). The mercantile activities of the new middle class called for a freer environment and increased religious toleration.

Changes in Education: Birth of the Academy.   It was inevitable that the educational system would change to meet the needs of the intellectual, economic, and social order. The writing and dame schools began to give way to town schools. The curriculum at the elementary level, while still dominated by reading and writing, placed greater importance on arithmetic than before. Greater concern was also shown for practical and vocational training at both the elementary and secondary levels.

Many grammar schools, however, refused to change their classical curricula. As a result, numerous *academies* and private venture schools sprang up in the larger towns, teaching subjects useful in trade and commerce. If the prestigious Boston Latin School would not teach mathematics, there were others who would. The newspapers of the time were filled with advertisements for these schools. One such 1723 advertisement appearing in New York City read:

Which would you prefer to attend, the Boston Latin School or Mr. Walton's school? Why?

> There is a school in New York, in the Broad Street, near the Exchange, where Mr. John Walton, late of Yale College, Teacheth Reading, Writing, Arethmatick, whole Numbers and Fractions, Vulgar and Decimal, The Mariners Art, Plain and Mercators Way; Also Geometry, Surveying, the Latin Tongue, the Greek and Hebrew Grammers, Ethicks, Rhetorick, Logick, Natural Philosophy and Metaphysicks, all or any of them for a Reasonable Price. The School from the

first of October till the first of March will be tended in the Evening. If any Gentlemen in the Country are disposed to send their Sons to the said School, if they apply themselves to the Master he will immediately procure suitable Entertainment for them, very Cheap. Also if any Young Gentlemen of the City will please to come in the Evening and make some Tryal of the Liberal Arts, they may have the opportunity of Learning the same things which are commonly Taught in Colledges. (Seybolt, cited in Rippa, 1984, p. 77)

Growth of Colleges.   During this period several colleges were founded in the New England colonies: Collegiate School, now Yale University, in 1701; the College of Rhode Island, now Brown University, in 1764; and Dartmouth College in 1769. The colleges of this era also reflected the growing secularism of the society. This was manifested in a broadened curricula. In 1722 Harvard established its first professorship in secular subjects—mathematics and natural philosophy. By 1760 the scientific subjects accounted for 20% of the student's time. Another manifestation of the growing secularism was the change in graduates' careers. Theology remained the most popular career, but an increasing number of graduates were turning to law, medicine, trade or commerce as the New England colleges became centers of independence, stimulation, and social usefulness (Cohen, 1974).

Education in the Middle Colonies

The New England colonies had been settled primarily by English colonists who shared the same language, traditions, and religion. The settlers of the middle colonies (New York, New Jersey, Pennsylvania, Delaware) came from a variety of national and religious backgrounds. Most had fled Europe because of religious persecution and were generally more distrusting of secular authority than the New England colonists. Thus, while the schools in the middle colonies were as religious in character as those in New England, because of the diverse religious backgrounds it was not possible for the government in any colony to agree on the establishment of any one system of state-supported schools and it fell to each denomination to establish its own schools. The consequence of this pattern of pluralistic, parochial schooling was the absence of any basis for the establishment of a system of public schools or any basis for state support or regulation of the schools.

New York

The colony of New Netherlands was established in 1621 by the Dutch. Initially, New Netherlands was similar to the New England colonies. Schools were supported by the Dutch West India Company and were operated by the Dutch Reformed Church. After the colony was seized by the British and became the royal colony of New York (1674), state responsibility and support was withdrawn, and except for a few towns that maintained their own schools, formal schooling became a private concern. Education at the elementary level was by private tutors for the upper class, private venture schools for the middle class, and denominational schools for the lower class.

Most notable of the denominational schools were those operated by a missionary society of the Church of England, the Society for the Propagation of the Gospel in Foreign Parts (SPG). The apprenticeship system also was very strong in New York and provided the means by which some children gained an elementary education. However, since few towns established their own schools and the provision of education was principally left to the will or ability of parents to send their children to private or denominational schools, the illiteracy rate was high (Cohen, 1974).

Education at the secondary level was even more exclusively private or parochial. The private venture secondary schools were few in number and questionable in quality.

Higher education was absent for any but the few who could afford to leave the colony. It was not until 1754 that the first institution of higher education, Kings College, now Columbia University, opened in the colony.

New Jersey

As in New York, education in New Jersey was primarily private and denominational. The religious diversification was great and each of the sects— Dutch Reformed, Puritan, Quaker, German Lutheran, Baptist, Scotch-Irish Presbyterian—established its own schools. The SPG also operated schools for the poor. A few towns, mainly those in the eastern region settled by the Puritans, established town schools. Secondary education was limited. Because of the primarily rural, agrarian economy, the private venture secondary schools found in the other middle colonies were lacking. However, the proximity to New York and Philadelphia did provide access to their secondary institutions for those who could afford it (Cohen, 1974).

It is in the realm of higher education that the colony of New Jersey most distinguished itself. Prior to the Revolution it had founded more colleges than any other colony: the College of New Jersey, now Princeton University, in 1746; Queens College, now Rutgers University, in 1766.

Pennsylvania

The Pennsylvania colony was founded in 1681 by a Quaker, William Penn. The Quakers, or Society of Friends, were very tolerant of other religions; consequently, a number of different religious groups or sects settled in Pennsylvania. William Penn advocated free public education, and the Pennsylvania Assembly enacted a law in 1683 providing that all children be instructed in reading and writing and be taught "some useful trade or skill." Yet the colony did not develop a system of free public education, primarily because of the great diversity among the settlers. A few community-supported schools were established, but as in the other middle colonies, formal education was primarily a private or denominational affair.

However, the major difference between this Middle Atlantic colony and the others was that the various denominations did, in fact, establish a fairly widespread system of schools in Pennsylvania. The SPG founded a number of charity schools, including a school for black children in Philadelphia. The Moravians also established a number of elementary schools, including the first nursery school in the colonies, and were active in efforts to Christianize and educate the Native Americans. They devised a written script for several Native American languages and translated the Bible and other religious materials into these languages. In their pedagogical practices they were influenced by the Moravian bishop Jan Amos Comenius (Gutek, 1986).

The Quakers were the most significant denomination in terms of educational endeavors. They believed that all were created equal under God, a principle that led not only to the education of both sexes and to the free admission of the poor, but to the education of blacks and Native Americans. A school for black children was established in Philadelphia as early as 1700.

Schools were also established at the secondary level by the various denominations. The Moravians established a boarding school for girls at Bethlehem, one of the first in the colonies. Since the Quakers do not have a ministry, they were not as interested in the establishment of secondary schools leading to that vocation. In their secondary schools they emphasized practical knowledge rather than the classical curriculum studied at most secondary schools at that time.

A number of private secondary schools were opened during the later colonial period, many offering such practical subjects as navigation, gauging, accounting, geometry, trigonometry, surveying, French, and Spanish. Among them was Benjamin Franklin's Philadelphia Academy, opened in 1751.

Benjamin Franklin (1706–1790)

Franklin was strongly influenced by the writings of John Locke and was a proponent of practical education. In his *Proposals Relating to the Education of Youth in Pennsylvania* he laid out the plan for a school in which English was to be the medium of instruction rather than Latin. This break with tradition was important, for in effect it proposed that vernacular English could be the language of the educated person. Franklin also proposed that students be taught "those Things that are likely to be most useful and most ornamental. Regard being had to the several Professions which they are intended" (Gillett, 1969, p. 138).

From this statement of principle Franklin went on to detail the specific subject matter:

> All should be taught "to write a fair hand" and "something of drawing"; arithmetic, accounts, geometry, and astronomy; English grammar out of Tillotson, Addison, Pope, Sidney, Trenchard, and Gordon; the writing of essays and letters; rhetoric, history, geography, and ethics; natural history and gardening; and the history of commerce and principles of mechanics. Instruction should include visits to neighboring farms, opportunities for natural observations, experiments with scientific apparatus, and physical exercise. And the whole should be suffused with a quest for benignity of mind, which Franklin saw as the foundation of good breeding and a spirit of service, which he regarded as "the great aim and end of all learning." (Cremin, 1970, p. 376)

As time passed Franklin's academy gave less emphasis to the practical studies and came to more closely resemble the Latin grammar school. Before he died Franklin declared the academy a failure as measured against his initial intent (Cremin, 1970).

Founding of the University of Pennsylvania.   Franklin was also instrumental in the founding in 1753 of the College of Philadelphia, now the University of Pennsylvania. Unlike its sister institutions, the College of Philadelphia was nonsectarian in origin (although it later came under Anglican control). The curriculum of the college was perhaps more progressive than at other institutions. Students were allowed a voice in the election of courses and the curriculum emphasized not only the classics but mathematics, philosophy, and the natural and social sciences. A medical school was established in connection with the college. The college appointed as the first professor of chemistry in the colonies Dr. Benjamin Rush (Cohen, 1974), one of the signers of the Declaration of Independence, a noted physician, and the father of American psychiatry.

Delaware

Which states today have the highest concentration of denominational schools? How has this changed since colonial times?

Delaware, founded in 1638 as a Swedish colony, New Sweden, fell under Dutch control in 1655, then under the rule of the English with their conquest of New Netherlands. Education in Delaware was greatly influenced by Pennsylvania. Pennsylvania's general abandonment of the responsibility for the provision of education to private or denominational groups after 1683 was followed in Delaware. Although a number of elementary schools were established in the colony, the level of literacy remained low. During the colonial period formal secondary level instruction was available on a very limited basis and no institution of higher education was established (Cohen, 1974).

Education in the Southern Colonies

Social and Economic Systems

The Southern colonies (Maryland, Virginia, the Carolinas, and Georgia) differed in significant ways from the New England and Middle Atlantic colonies. The Southern colonies were royal colonies administered by governors responsible directly to the king. The prevailing view was that it was the responsibility of parents to educate their children, not the government. Consequently, no legislation was enacted requiring local governments to establish or support schools. And, where religious dissatisfaction was the principal motivation for the settling of New England, the reason for settlement of the Southern colonies, where the Church of England was the established church, was primarily economic.

Rather than small farms and commerce, the economy of the Southern colonies was based on the plantation and slave system. The plantation system created distinct classes dominated by the aristocratic plantation owners. The relatively small population of the Southern colonies was widely dispersed. This factor limited the growth of any public or universal system of education.

Elementary and Secondary Education

As a result of the social and economic structure of the Southern colonies, educational opportunities were largely determined by social position. The children of the plantation owners and the wealthy commercial classes in the Tidewater cities received their education from private tutors or at private Latin grammar schools before being sent to a university. In the early colonial period it was common for the children of the plantation aristocracy to be sent to England to receive their secondary or, more often, their university education. However, this practice was on the decline by the later colonial period (Cohen, 1974; Gutek, 1986).

For the majority of the other classes the only education available was at the elementary level, informally through the apprenticeship system or formally at endowed (free) schools, charity schools, denominational schools, "old field schools," or private venture schools. Virginia was the most active of the Southern colonies in attempting to ensure the education of apprenticed children, especially orphaned children. Often this education took place in so-called "workhouse" schools.

The endowed or free schools were few in number and actually were not free except to a small number of poor boys. The charity schools were primarily those operated by the SPG. The influence of the SPG in the Southern colonies was significant and represented "the nearest approach to a public school organization found in the South before the Revolution" (Cohen, 1974, p. 129). Schools operated by other denominations were also established in the Southern colonies. In some rural areas where other schooling was not available, several small planters or farmers might build a schoolhouse on an abandoned tobacco field. These "old field schools" generally charged a fee and offered only the most basic education. Private venture elementary schools were found in some of the largest cities.

At the secondary level, except for the private venture schools only a very small number of schools existed. And even the number of private venture schools was limited. As a result of the public neglect of education, overall the educational level of the Southern colonies was below that of most of the Northern colonies, especially those in New England.

Higher Education: The College of William and Mary

The only institution of higher education established in the South prior to the Revolutionary War was the College of William and Mary, established in 1693 to train ministers for the Church of England. Like Harvard, its sister institution in New England and the only older institution of higher education in the colonies, it also originally offered the traditional curriculum. But by the first quarter of the eighteenth century it began to broaden its curriculum. In fact, one educational historian states that by 1779 its curriculum was probably the most advanced in the United States (Cohen, 1974).

Figure 3.5 presents an overview of education in colonial America.

Figure 3.5: Education in Colonial America

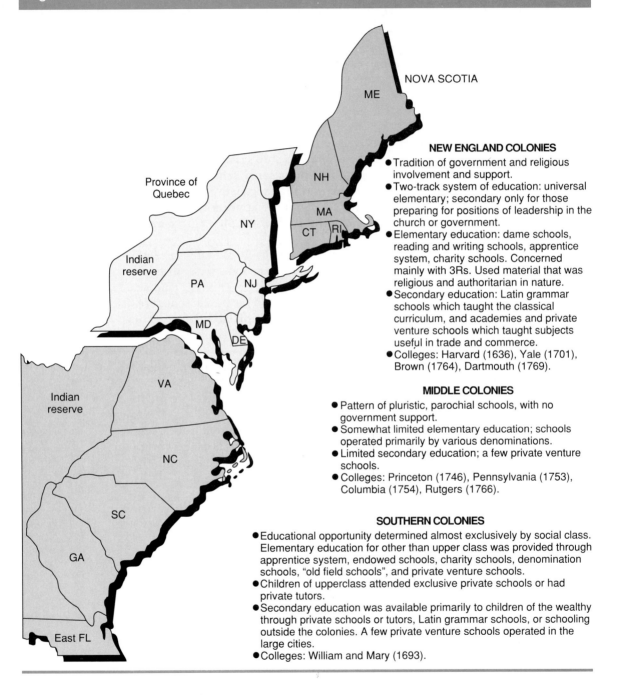

NEW ENGLAND COLONIES

- Tradition of government and religious involvement and support.
- Two-track system of education: universal elementary; secondary only for those preparing for positions of leadership in the church or government.
- Elementary education: dame schools, reading and writing schools, apprentice system, charity schools. Concerned mainly with 3Rs. Used material that was religious and authoritarian in nature.
- Secondary education: Latin grammar schools which taught the classical curriculum, and academies and private venture schools which taught subjects useful in trade and commerce.
- Colleges: Harvard (1636), Yale (1701), Brown (1764), Dartmouth (1769).

MIDDLE COLONIES

- Pattern of pluristic, parochial schools, with no government support.
- Somewhat limited elementary education; schools operated primarily by various denominations.
- Limited secondary education; a few private venture schools.
- Colleges: Princeton (1746), Pennsylvania (1753), Columbia (1754), Rutgers (1766).

SOUTHERN COLONIES

- Educational opportunity determined almost exclusively by social class. Elementary education for other than upper class was provided through apprentice system, endowed schools, charity schools, denomination schools, "old field schools", and private venture schools.
- Children of upperclass attended exclusive private schools or had private tutors.
- Secondary education was available primarily to children of the wealthy through private schools or tutors, Latin grammar schools, or schooling outside the colonies. A few private venture schools operated in the large cities.
- Colleges: William and Mary (1693).

Summary

The schools of the United States can trace their ancestry to those of ancient Greece and Rome. Educational idealism is based on the philosophy of Plato. The scientific method popularized in the twentieth century is rooted in the philosophy of realism espoused by Aristotle. And a number of the more progressive educational positions of this century were advanced by the Roman educator Quintilian: opposition to corporal punishment, advancement of the concept of readiness learning, and support for the recognition of individual differences in learners.

The concept of universal public education that we enjoy today was a product of the Reformation. It was brought to New England by the Puritans who held the view that education was necessary for religious instruction and salvation, as well as for good citizenship. However, the earliest American educational systems were not free, were limited at the secondary levels, and, in ways that would be prohibited today, were dominated by the religious establishment. In the next chapter we will continue to trace the evolution of the American educational system from the Revolution to the twentieth century.

Key Terms

Academy	Object lesson
Activity curriculum	*Paideia*
Charity (pauper) school	Scholasticism
Dame schools	Sense realism
Grammar school	Seven liberal arts
Hornbook	Socratic method
Humanism	*Tabula rasa*
Naturalism	Vernacular schools

Discussion Questions

1. How would Aristotle and Plato answer the question posed at the beginning of this chapter: Should the right to an education be guaranteed by the government?

2. What impact did the Reformation have on the education of common people?

3. What ideas of Pestalozzi and Froebel are in practice in the schools of your community?

4. Describe the status of higher education in colonial America.

5. Contrast education in the New England, Middle Atlantic, and Southern colonies. Do any legacies of these differences remain today?

6. What was the contribution of the apprenticeship system to education in the colonies?

References

Adler, M. J. (1984). *The Paideia program: An educational syllabus.* New York: Macmillan Publishing Co.

Axtell, J. L. (Ed.). (1968). *The educational writings of John Locke.* Cambridge, England: Cambridge University Press.

Barrow, R. (1976). *Plato and education.* London: Routledge & Kegan Paul.

Beck, A. G. (1964). *Greek education 450–350 B.C.* London: Methuen & Co.

Bowen, J. (1972). *A history of Western education, 1.* London: Methuen & Co.

Carriedo, R. A., & Goren, P. D. (1979). Year round education through multitrack schools. *Policy Briefs,* No. 10. San Francisco, CA: Far West Laboratory.

Castle, E. B. (1967). *Ancient education and today.* Baltimore, MD: Penguin Books.

Cohen, S. S. (1974). *A history of colonial education, 1607–1776.* New York: John Wiley & Sons.

Cremin, L. A. (1970). *American education: The colonial experience, 1607–1783.* New York: Harper & Row.

Cubberley, E. P. (1934). *Readings in public education.* Cambridge, MA: Riverside Press.

Ford, P. L. (Ed.). (1962). *The New England primer.* New York: Columbia University Teachers College.

Gillett, M. (1966). *A history of education: Thought and practice.* Toronto: McGraw-Hill.

Gillett, M. (Ed.). (1969). *Readings in the history of education.* Toronto: McGraw-Hill.

Good, H. G., & Teller, J. D. (1969). *A history of Western education.* Toronto: Collier-Macmillan.

Gutek, G. L. (1986). *Education in the United States.* Englewood Cliffs, NJ: Prentice-Hall.

Laurie, S. S. (1968). *Studies in the history of educational opinion from the Renaissance.* London: Frank Cass & Co.

Mayer, F. (1973). *A history of educational thought.* Columbus, OH: Merrill.

Meyer, A. E. (1972). *An educational history of the Western world.* New York: McGraw-Hill.

Monroe, P. (1939). *Source book of the history of education for the Greek and Roman period.* New York: Macmillan.

Rippa, S. A. (1984). *Education in a free society.* New York: Longman.

Wilkins, A. S. (1914). *Roman education.* Cambridge, England: Cambridge University Press.

Winn, C., and Jacks, M. (1967). *Aristotle.* London: Metheun & Co.

Woodward, W. H. (1906). *Studies in education during the age of the Renaissance, 1400–1600.* Cambridge, England: Cambridge University Press.

Chapter 4

American Education: From Revolution to the Twentieth Century

Those who cannot remember the past are condemned to repeat it.

Santayana

The Boston Examiner   *Thursday, July 13, 1867*

New U.S. Commissioner of Education Deplores Training of Teachers

In an address last evening to the National Education Association meeting in New York, Mr. Henry Barnard, the newly appointed United States Commissioner of Education, commented on the inadequate training possessed by the vast majority of teachers who teach our young. According to Commissioner Barnard,

"Too many of those we have chosen to be the guides and guardians of the nation's youth have little knowledge beyond that which they are attempting to impart. Indeed, we might well question whether their knowledge is superior to that of many of their fellow townsmen. Not only is the depth and breadth of their knowledge of the curriculum matter a subject of concern, but where knowledge is possessed, there exists most often an absence of any training in pedagogy." The commissioner went on to say that "teachers will not be elevated to that place in society and receive that compensation they so richly deserve until they are required to undertake a special course of study and training to qualify them for their office."

Do these comments sound familiar? Which of the concerns expressed by Barnard remain concerns today? Which are no longer concerns?

At the time Henry Barnard made these remarks, the nation was less than 100 years old, but had already more than tripled in size and increased tenfold in population. Before the century was over, the population would double again. The educational system grew with the nation, sometimes responding to, sometimes leading social and economic changes.

As you study the history of American education from the birth of the nation to the beginning of the present century, think about the following objectives:

Describe the impact of Thomas Jefferson and Noah Webster on American education in the early nineteenth century.

Identify the contributions that monitorial schools, Sunday schools, infant schools, and free school societies made to the expansion of educational opportunities in the early national period.

- Compare the curriculum and purposes of the academy with that of the grammar school and the high school.

- Discuss the development of common schools in the United States and the role that Horace Mann, Henry Barnard, Emma Willard, and Catherine Beecher played in that development.

- Outline the development of secondary education in the United States.

- Discuss the factors leading to the growth of higher education in nineteenth-century America.

- Compare the educational opportunities provided to Native Americans, Hispanic Americans, and black Americans in the nineteenth century.

- Trace the development of teacher education in the United States.

Education in the Revolutionary and Early National Period

On July 4, 1776, the 13 colonies declared their independence from England. Education was one of the casualties of the war that followed. Pulliam (1987) described the state of education during the war years:

> Illiteracy increased because rural schools had to close their doors and even the larger town Latin grammar schools were crippled. British occupation of New York caused schools to be abandoned there. New England schools continued to operate but they suffered from a lack of funds and teachers.
>
> Higher education was restricted in part because many talented teachers were Loyalists. Books were scarce since they came from England and colonial printers could not maintain their presses without outside supplies. Yale College was broken up into groups centered in different towns, while Harvard's buildings and those of the College of Rhode Island housed provincial troops. Dartmouth had neither money nor books, and classes had to be discontinued at the College of Philadelphia. The College of New Jersey and William and Mary also suffered but were not closed.
>
> British support, as in the case of the Anglican Society for the Propagation of the Gospel was cut off and never revived. Lack of money and the interruption of the normal economic process made the operation of educational institutions almost impossible. Teachers and scholars joined the fighting forces while school buildings were converted into barracks. Tory or Loyalist teachers were turned out of their schools. Sometimes the schools were burned and libraries scattered or destroyed. (p. 51)

What would be the impact of a major war on colleges and universities today?

Articles of Confederation and the Constitution

After the war the leaders of the new nation set about the business of devising a government that would encompass the ideas for which they had fought. The first attempt at self-governance under the Articles of Confederation provided little authority to the central government and established no executive or judicial branches. When this government proved inadequate, delegates from each state met in the summer of 1787 and drafted the Constitution, which after ratification in 1789 launched the new republic. Perhaps because of the former colonists' suspicion of a strong central government, or perhaps because of the association of education with theology, neither the Articles of Confederation or the Constitution mentioned education.

Northwest Land Ordinances

Despite the fact that neither the Articles of Confederation or the United States Constitution mentioned education, there can be no doubt that the nation's founders recognized the importance of education to a country in which the quality of representation depended on citizens' ability to make informed choices at the ballot box. Their concern is made clear by both the legislation they enacted and congressional testimonies.

Even before the adoption of the Constitution, Congress enacted two ordinances that contained articles supportive of education. The Land Ordinance of 1785, which provided for a rectangular survey of the Northwest Territory, set aside the 16th section of land in each township for the support of education. Article Three of the Northwest Ordinance of 1787, which incorporated the Northwest Territory, proclaimed: "Religion, morality, and knowledge being necessary to good government and the happiness of mankind, schools and the means of education shall be forever encouraged."

The Founding Fathers and Education

George Washington devoted a major portion of his first address to Congress to the importance of education: "There is nothing which can better deserve your patronage than the promotion of science and literature. Knowledge is in every country the surest basis of public happiness" (Madsen, 1974, p. 66).

The replies from the Senate and House expressed their agreement. From the Senate: "Literature and Science are essential to the preservation of a free constitution; the measures of government should therefore be calculated to strengthen the confidence that is due to that important truth." And from the House: "The promotion of science and literature will contribute to the security of free government" (Madsen, 1974, p. 66).

The Founding Fathers were aware that changing their form of government was only the beginning of the revolution. As Benjamin Rush, a proponent of a national university and universal education, remarked: "We have changed our form of government, but it remains to effect a revolution of our principles, opinions, and manners, so as to accommodate them to the forms of government we have adopted" (Cremin, 1982, p. 1). Rush and his compatriots worked untiringly at devising endless versions of political and educational arrangements. Although they differed on many details, there were at least four beliefs common to their discussions: (1) that the laws of education must be relative to the form of government; hence a republic needs an educational system that motivates citizens to choose public over private interest, (2) that what was needed was a truly American education purged of all vestiges of older, monarchical forms and dedicated to the creation of a cohesive and independent citizenry, (3) that education should be genuinely practical, aimed at the improvement of the human condition, with the new sciences at its heart, and (4) that American education should be exemplary and a means through which America could teach the world the glories of liberty and learning (Cremin, 1982).

Is there a place in today's educational system for a system of federally operated national universities as proposed by Dr. Rush?

Thomas Jefferson

While many of the Founding Fathers expressed their views on the importance of education, perhaps none is so well known for his educational views as Thomas Jefferson (1743–1826). Jefferson, who was strongly influenced by the philosophy of Locke, believed that government must be by the consent of the governed and that men were entitled to certain rights that could not be abridged by the government. Jefferson was one of the chief proponents of the addition of a Bill of Rights to the Constitution. As Rippa (1984) noted, "Few statesmen in American history have so vigorously strived for an ideal (liberty); perhaps none has so consistently viewed education as the indispensable cornerstone of freedom" (p. 68).

Plan for a State Education System. Jefferson's *Bill for the More General Diffusion of Knowledge,* introduced in the Virginia legislature in 1779, provided for the establishment of a system of public schools that would provide the masses with the basic education necessary to ensure good government, public safety, and happiness. Under the bill each county would be subdivided into parts called *hundreds;* each hundred was to provide an elementary school, supported by taxes. Attendance would be free for all white children, male and female, for three years. The curriculum would be reading, writing, arithmetic, and history. Jefferson believed that through the study of history students would learn to recognize tyranny and support democracy. The bill went on to propose that the state be divided into 20 districts and that a boarding grammar school be built at public expense in each district. Those attending would be not only those boys whose families could afford the tuition, but the brightest of the poorer students from the elementary schools whose tuition would be paid by the state. The curriculum of the grammar school was to include Latin, Greek, geography, English, grammar, and higher mathematics. Finally, upon completion of grammar school, ten of the scholarship students would receive three years' study at the College of William and Mary at state expense. The remaining scholarship students, according to Jefferson, would most likely become masters in the grammar schools.

Although this plan, viewed in today's light, appears strikingly elitist, in Jefferson's day it was considered excessively liberal and philanthropic. In fact, it was defeated by the Virginia legislature, no doubt in large part because of the unwillingness of the wealthy to pay for the education of the poor. Nonetheless, the plan is considered important because it removed the stigma of pauperism from elementary schooling (Rippa, 1984) and because it proposed a system of universal, free, public education, if only for three years.

Founding the University of Virginia. Jefferson's interest in education also extended to establishing the University of Virginia. After leaving the presidency in 1809 he devoted much of his energies to that effort. Sometimes called "Mr. Jefferson's University," no college or university ever bore so completely the mark of one person. He created the project in every detail: he designed the buildings and landscape (even bought the bricks and picked out the trees to be used as lumber), chose the library books, designed the curriculum, and selected the students and faculty. The university opened in 1825, a year before Jefferson's death on July 4, 1826, exactly 50 years after the adoption of the immortal document he wrote—the Declaration of Independence (Rippa, 1984).

Noah Webster

It was a teacher, Noah Webster (1758–1843), who had the most influence on education in the new republic. Where the nation's founders had sought political independence from England, Webster sought cultural independence (Gutek, 1986). Like many of his contemporaries, Webster believed in the relationship between nationalistic aims and the educational process, that the primary purpose of education should be the inculcation of patriotism, and that what was needed was a truly American education rid of European influence (Madsen, 1974). These goals could best be accomplished, he believed, by creating a distinctive national language and curriculum. To this end Webster prepared a number of spelling, grammar, and reading books to replace the English texts then in use, an American version of the Bible, and what became the world-famous *American Dictionary of the English Language.*

Of his textbooks the most important was the *Elementary Spelling Book,* published in 1783, often referred to as the "blue-back speller" because of the color of the binding. By 1875, 75 million copies of the speller had been sold (Spring, 1990), many of which were used again and again. The book included both a federal catechism with political and patriotic content and a moral catechism whose content was related to respect for honest work and property rights, the value of money, the virtues of industry and thrift, the danger of drink, and contentment with one's economic status (Rippa, 1984; Spring, 1990). According to the noted historian Henry Steele Commager, "No other secular book had ever spread so wide, penetrated so deep, lasted so long" (cited in Rippa, 1984, p. 74).

Webster supported the concept of free schools in which all American children could learn the necessary patriotic and moral precepts. As a member of the Massachusetts legislature he worked for the establishment of a state system of education and is credited by some as initiating the common school movement, which culminated in Horace Mann's work in the 1830s (Spring, 1990). He also supported the education of women as they would be the mothers of future citizens and the teachers of youth. However, he envisioned a rather limited and "female" education for them and counseled parents against sending their daughters to "demoralizing" boarding schools. A staunch patriot whose proposals sometimes bordered on the fanatic (e.g., the proposal that the first word a child learned should be "Washington"), Webster has been called the "Schoolmaster of the Republic."

What textbook in your elementary or secondary education had the greatest influence on you? Why?

Educational Innovations

Although Webster and others promoted the establishment of a uniquely American education, some of the major innovations in American education in the first quarter of the nineteenth century were of European origin. Among these were the monitorial school, the Sunday school, and the infant school. The period also witnessed the efforts of the free school societies and, more importantly, the rise of the academies. Each of these made a contribution, but the primary pattern of schooling that developed in the first half of the nineteenth century emerged from the common school movement, which is discussed in the next section. However, a review of these alternatives illustrates how the country, in the absence of established state systems, was searching for a suitable educational pattern for the new and developing nation (Gutek, 1986).

Monitorial Schools

Monitorial schools originated in England and were brought to America by a Quaker, Joseph Lancaster. In the Lancasterian monitorial system one paid teacher instructed hundreds of pupils through the use of student teachers or monitors who were chosen for their academic abilities. Monitorial education was concerned with teaching only the basics of reading, writing, and arithmetic. The first monitorial school in the United States was opened in New York City in 1806 and the system spread rapidly throughout the states. One such school in Pennsylvania was designed to accommodate 450 students:

> The teacher sits at the head of the room on a raised platform. Beneath and in front of the teacher are three rows of monitors' desks placed directly in front of the pupils' desks. The pupils' desks are divided into three sections . . . and each section is in line with one of the rows of monitors' desks . . . . a group of pupils would march to the front of the room and stand around the monitors' desks, where they would receive instruction from the monitors. When they finished, they would march to the rear part of their particular section and recite or receive further instruction from another monitor. While this group was marching to the rear, another group would be marching up to the front to take their places around the monitors. When finished, the pupils would march to the rear, and the group in the rear would move forward to the second part of their section to receive instruction from yet another monitor. Because each of the three sections had a group in front, one in the rear, and one in the middle working on different things, a total of nine different recitations could be carried on at one time. (Spring, 1990, pp. 56–57)

The monitorial system was attractive not only because it provided an inexpensive system for educating poor children, but because submission to the system was supposed to instill the virtues of orderliness, obedience, and industriousness. As already noted, the system gained wide appeal. Governor De Witt Clinton of New York declared the system "a blessing sent down from heaven to redeem the poor" (Spring, 1990, p. 56). However, in time the system declined. It appeared to be suited only for large cities with large numbers of students rather than small towns and rural areas. It was also criticized because it only afforded the most basic education. Yet, instead of being an educational dead end, as depicted by many educational historians, Lancasterian monitorialism may have been the model for the factorylike urban schools that emerged in the United States in the late nineteenth century (Gutek, 1986). And, as noted in "For Future Reference" on page 107, the monitorial system epitomized an instructional strategy that has experienced a revival in recent years, peer tutoring.

For Future Reference:
Peer Tutoring

The monitorial system practiced in early eighteenth century America employed an instructional strategy that has been around for many centuries—peer tutoring. For example, the teaching of the Talmud has traditionally been done by pairing students and making them responsible for each other's learning. The Decurion system introduced into Jesuit education in the 1500s involved 10 students grouped for instruction by a student monitor (Levine, 1986). And, although monitorial schools disappeared, the practice of more able students helping less able students learn was a prominent feature of the one- and two-room schools which dominated so much of early and rural America into the 1900s.

More recently, beginning in the late 1960s, the concept of peer or cross-age tutoring has seen a revival in schools across the U.S. Research over the last two decades has shown peer tutoring to be a cost-efficient means of increasing academic outcomes, that the gains to tutors are usually as much as if not more than those to tutees, that it results in improved self-concept and social skills for both tutor and tutee, and that it is usually associated with high rates of time on task. In fact, studies have found that students often rate the peer tutoring period as their favorite time of the day (Topping, 1989).

Peer tutoring can take a variety of formats that may involve the pairing of all students in a classroom or the pairing of older students from one grade with younger students from a lower grade. It can take place in the classroom all at once or on a rotational basis with some students engaged in peer tutoring while others are engaged in other learning activities. It can also take place in a tutoring center or some other space set aside for this activity, during the lunch period, or before or after school.

Should you decide that this is a strategy you would like to try in your classroom, the following steps to implementation have been found to be important to the program's success:

1. Secure the support of school administrators and parents. Obtain parental permission for participating students.

2. Establish clear and measurable program goals and objectives.

3. Select and match students. If cross-age tutoring is to be used, the age and ability difference should not be so great as to create disinterest or boredom. A common practice is to rank order students by skills, mastery, or scores in a particular area, divide the class in half, and then pair the highest ranked tutor with the highest ranked tutee, and so on in descending order. In any case, pairing relationships should consider student interests, personalities, and tutoring potential.

4. Conduct an orientation for students explaining the purposes of the program, what behaviors are expected of them, and appropriate instructional strategies.

5. Although contact time will vary with program content and objectives, a minimum of three sessions per week is desirable, with a session length of 15–30 minutes.

6. Provide for frequent monitoring of tutorial sessions of both tutor and tutee learning.

7. Conduct an ongoing evaluation of the program to determine its success and plan improvements.

Free School Societies: Charity Schools

*What are the
commonalities of
the charity
schools of the
1800s and public
education today
in relation to
educating the
poor?*

The Lancasterian system was considered ideal for the schools operated by the various free school societies. These societies operated charity schools for the children of the poor in urban areas. In some instances, as in New York City, they received public support. Overall they were not a major factor in the history of education; nonetheless, for a period they did provide the only education some children received. For example, by 1820 the Free School Society of New York City (renamed the Public School Society in 1826 and placed under the city department of education in 1853) was teaching more than 2,000 children (Cremin, 1982).

Sunday Schools

Another educational plan introduced to America was the *Sunday school,* begun by Robert Raikes in 1780 in England. The first Sunday school in America opened in 1786 in Virginia. Its purpose was to offer the rudiments of reading and writing to children who worked during the week, primarily in the factories of the larger cities, and to provide them with an alternative to roaming the streets on Sunday. Although the Bible was commonly its textbook, originally the Sunday school was not seen as an adjunct of the church and was not intended to promote conversion. In 1815 these schools were still few in number and catered to a small number of children from lower-class homes. By 1830, however, their initial practical purpose had been superseded by religious interests and they had become primarily religious institutions operated by Sunday school societies with an evangelical mission. They grew in number, reaching out to the frontier and becoming available to children from homes of all sorts. In new communities they often paved the way for the common school (Cremin, 1982).

Infant Schools

The *infant school* was originated in England by Robert Owen, who also established one of the first infant schools in the United States at his would-be Utopia, a collective at New Harmony, Indiana. Established primarily in the eastern cities, these schools were taught by women and were designed for children aged four to seven who, because they would go to work in a factory at a very early age, probably would not receive any other schooling. The primary schools designed along this model did not survive long. However, in a few cities the primary schools had been designed as preparatory to entry into the elementary school and often became part of the town school system. In the 1850s the idea behind this form of infant school was revived in the form of the kindergarten by the followers of Froebel.

The Growth of the Academy

More significant in foreshadowing the coming changes in patterns of formal schooling was the growth of the academy. Although today the term *academy* brings to mind an exclusive private institution with a college-preparatory curriculum, or perhaps military training, in the late eighteenth and nineteenth centuries the term was more broadly applied. As we have seen, Franklin's academy and similar institutions were interested in providing an alternative to the traditional curriculum of the Latin grammar schools by providing a "practical" education.

The real growth of the academy occurred after the Revolutionary War and probably reached its height in the 1820s. The variations among academies were great. Some were indeed prestigious and exclusive. Others were nothing more than log cabins. Stimulated by the founding of the United States Military Academy at West Point in 1802 and the Naval Academy at Annapolis in 1848, many were established as military schools. Admission to some was open to all comers, others catered to special clients. Some were boarding schools, some were day schools. Some were teacher-owned, others were organized by groups of parents or individuals, and yet others by denominations or various societies. Their curriculum usually depended, at least in part, on the students who were enrolled, but most offered an education beyond the three R's. In the larger academies Latin and Greek were offered along with English grammar, geography, arithmetic, and other studies deemed "practical" or in demand. The academies are also noted for the importance placed on science in the curriculum. By the end of the early national period some of the larger academies were also offering courses designed to provide preparation for teaching in the common schools (Cremin, 1982; Madsen, 1974).

Academies for Women

A number of the academies were established for women and are important for the role they played in extending educational opportunities to women. Some bore the name seminaries and were important in the training of female teachers, teaching being about the only profession open to women at the time. In 1821 the Troy Female Seminary in New York was opened by Emma Willard, a lifelong activist for women's rights. Opposed to the finishing school curriculum of the female boarding schools, Willard proposed a curriculum that was "solid and useful." Mount Holyoke Female Seminary, founded in 1837 by Mary Lyon, provided a demanding curriculum that included philosophy, mathematics, and science.

Catherine Beecher, the sister of Harriet Beecher Stowe, founded both the Hartford Female Seminary (1828) and the Western Institute for Women (1832). Beecher was a strong supporter of the common school and saw her task as focusing the attention of the nation on the need for a corps of female teachers to staff the common schools. She set forth a plan for a nationwide group of teacher training seminaries. Although the plan was not adopted, her efforts on behalf of the common school were a force in its acceptance, and her work on behalf of women pointed to a new American consensus concerning female roles (Cremin, 1982). Following the path forged by the female seminaries in New England, seminaries sprang up in other regions of the country, being especially popular in the South.

By the mid-nineteenth century there were more than 6,000 academies in the United States enrolling 263,000 students. The academy is considered

Do schools separated by gender have a place in today's world? What are the advantages and disadvantages of separate schools for women and men?

Mount Holyoke College, pictured here in an 1880s photograph, has remained a female-only institution.

by most educational historians as the forerunner of the American high school. Its broad range of curricular offerings responded to the demands of the growing middle class and demonstrated that there was an important place in the educational system for a secondary educational institution for non–college-bound as well as college-bound youth. The broadened curriculum combined with the more liberal entrance requirements allowed the entrance of people of various religious and social backgrounds and was a major step in the democratization of American secondary education (Rippa, 1984).

Figure 4.1 gives an overview of the nineteenth-century educational institutions we have discussed.

Education in the Nineteenth and Early Twentieth Centuries

The Common School Movement

The period 1830–1865 has been designated the age of the common school movement in American educational history. It is during this period that the American educational system as we know it today began to take form. Instead of sporadic state legislation and abdication of responsibility, state systems of education were established. State control as well as direct taxation for the support of the *common schools*—publicly supported schools attended *in common* by all children—became accepted practices.

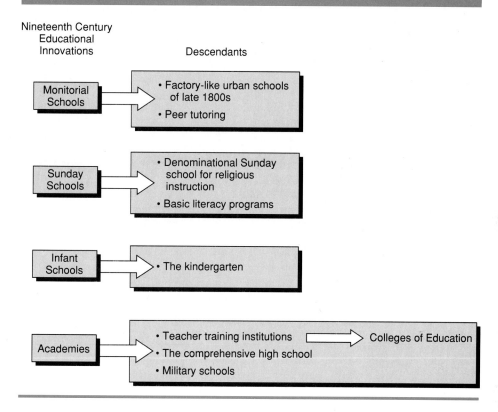

Figure 4.1: Nineteenth-Century Educational Innovations and Their Twentieth-Century Descendants

Nineteenth Century Educational Innovations

Descendants

Monitorial Schools

- Factory-like urban schools of late 1800s
- Peer tutoring

Sunday Schools

- Denominational Sunday school for religious instruction
- Basic literacy programs

Infant Schools

- The kindergarten

Academies

- Teacher training institutions → Colleges of Education
- The comprehensive high school
- Military schools

Moving Forces

Demands of a Larger and More Urban Population. The common school movement was the product of a variety of economic, social, and political factors. Between 1830 and 1860, 1,234,566 square miles of territory were added to the United States. During the same period the population exploded from 13 million to 32 million (see Table 4.1). Of this growth, 4 million came from immigration.

Not only was there an increase in immigration, but the national origins of the immigrants were different. Whereas before this era the majority of immigrants had come from Northern Europe and shared much the same cultural and religious backgrounds as the inhabitants of their new homeland, beginning in the 1830s and 1840s larger numbers came from Ireland, Germany, and Southern Europe and were often Roman Catholic. At the same time, the United States was rapidly changing from a predominantly rural nation to one that was scattered with cities. In 1820 there were only 12 cities in the then 23 states with a population of over 10,000; by 1860 the number had increased to 101 and 8 had a population of over 100,000 (Binder, 1974).

Table 4.1: Area and Population of the United States, 1790–1890		
Year	Land Area (square miles)	Population
1790	864,746	3,929,214
1800	864,746	5,308,483
1810	1,681,824	7,239,881
1820	1,749,462	9,638,453
1830	1,749,462	12,865,020
1840	1,749,462	17,069,453
1850	2,940,042	23,191,876
1860	2,969,640	31,443,321
1870	2,969,640	39,818,449
1880	2,969,640	50,155,783
1890	2,969,640	62,947,714

Source: U.S. Bureau of the Census. (1975). *Historical statistics of the United States, colonial times to 1970* (p. 8). Washington, DC: U.S. Government Printing Office.

The growth in the cities was a result of the growth in industrialization. For example, in 1807 only 15 cotton mills were in operation in the United States; by 1831 there were 801 mills employing 70,000 workers (Rippa, 1984). These changing economic and social patterns gave rise to an increasing urban population, which included concentrations of children who needed schooling, a more industrialized economy that required a trained work force, and in certain areas a Roman Catholic population that challenged Protestant domination.

Demands of the Working Class.   In this context the common schools were seen by the working class, who could not afford to educate their children at private expense, as avenues for upward social and economic mobility. Critical of pauper or charity schools, the newly emerging workingmen's organizations were open in their support of tax-supported common schools. The common schools were seen as providing the education necessary for protection against the tyranny of the upper class and necessary for equal participation in a democratic form of government. The leaders of business and industry also supported common schools. They saw them as a means of ensuring a supply of literate and trained workers.

Social Control.   The dominant English-speaking, upper-class Protestants saw a different merit in the common schools. This group viewed the common schools as agencies of social control over the lower socioeconomic classes. According to Gutek (1986), social control in this context meant

> imposing by institutionalized education the language, beliefs, and values of the dominant group on outsiders, especially on the non-English speaking immigrants. Common schools were expected to create such conformity in

American life by imposing the language and ideological outlook of the dominant group. For example, by using English as the medium of instruction, the common schools were expected to create an English-speaking citizenry; by cultivating a general value orientation based on Protestant Christianity, the schools were expected to create a general American ethic. (pp. 87–88)

Most social groups also saw the common schools as a means of controlling crime and social unrest. Knowledge was seen as "the great remedy for intemperance: for in proportion as we elevate men in the scale of existence . . . so do we reclaim them from all temptation of degrading vice and ruinous crimes" (Binder, 1974, p. 32).

Needs of the Frontier.   Interest in the establishment of common schools was not limited to the industrialized regions of the east. As the frontier moved steadily westward, the one-room schoolhouse, often the only public building in a community, became the symbol of civilization and the center of efforts to keep literacy, citizenship, and civilization alive in the wilderness (Gutek, 1986).

Extended Suffrage.   On the political front, the age of the common school coincided with the age of the common man. In the early years of the republic the right to vote in many states was limited to those who owned property. Gradually this began to change and many states, especially those on the frontier, extended suffrage to all white males. In 1828 the first "common man" was elected president–Andrew Jackson. The result of the extension of suffrage was not only increased office-holding by the common man, but an increased pressure for direct taxation to support common schools.

Education Journals and Organizations.   The movement for common schools began in the northeast. To some extent the public had been introduced to the basic ideas of the common school movement through the writings of individuals like Webster and Rush and through the arguments for social and moral reform made by the leaders of the charity school movement and the Lancasterian monitorial system. However, perhaps the two most important mechanisms for spreading the ideology of the common school were educational periodicals and educational organizations.

Between 1825 and 1850 more than 60 educational journals came into existence (Spring, 1990). Among the most important were the Massachusetts *Common School Journal,* founded and edited by Horace Mann; the *Connecticut Common School,* edited for several years by Henry Barnard; and the prestigious *American Journal of Education,* also edited from 1855 to 1881 by Henry Barnard. Among their other material, these journals printed part or all of several reports (e.g., the Cousin Report and the Stowe Report) describing and praising the Pestalozzian reforms of Prussian education (Rippa, 1984).

Do you subscribe to any educational journals? Which do you read regularly?

Of the educational organizations, the most noteworthy were the American Institute of Instruction, the Western Literary Institute and College of Professional Teachers, and on a more national scale, the American Lyceum. By 1839 there were 4,000–5,000 local lyceums in the United States actively presenting programs, mutual instruction, and informative lectures in favor of school reforms. Cremin (1982) credits the educational organizations with spearheading the common school movement, "articulating its ideals, publicizing its goals, and instructing one another in its political techniques; indeed, in the absence of a national ministry of education, it was their articulating, publicizing, and mutual instruction in politics that accounted for the spread of public education across the country" (p. 176).

Horace Mann

If any one person were to be given the title "Father of American Education," that person would be Horace Mann (1796–1859). Elected to the Massachusetts legislature in 1827, Mann, a brilliant orator, soon became the spokesperson for the common school movement. He led a campaign to organize the schools in Massachusetts into a state system and to establish a state board of education.

Upon the creation of the state board of education in 1837 Mann gave up his political career and a chance at the governorship to become the board's first secretary and the chief state school officer. He served in this position for 12 years and used it as a platform for proclaiming the ideology of the common school movement, as well as other educational ideals. In addition to his numerous lectures, editorships, and other writings, each year Mann wrote a report to the legislature reciting current educational practice and conditions and making recommendations for improvement. These reports were distributed in other states and abroad, and were significant in influencing educational legislation and practice throughout the country.

In his own state, Mann campaigned vigorously to increase public support for education and public awareness of the problems facing education in the form of dilapidated, unsanitary facilities and substandard materials, as well as the shortcomings of the local school committees. Mann was also critical of the status of the teaching profession and the training of teachers. As a result of his efforts, state appropriations to education were doubled, 50 new secondary schools were built, textbooks and equipment were improved, and teachers' salaries in Massachusetts were raised more than 50%. Mann also fought for the professional training of teachers and established three normal schools (teacher training institutions), the first such schools in America. The first of these normal schools was established in 1839 at Lexington, Massachusetts.

In his Tenth Annual Report (1846) Mann asserted that education was the right of every child and that it was the state's responsibility to ensure that every child was provided an education. Although Mann himself did not promote compulsory attendance but *regular* attendance, this report was instrumental in the adoption by the Massachusetts legislature of the nation's first compulsory attendance law in 1852.

Like several prominent educators of his time, Mann had visited the Prussian schools and observed the Pestalozzian methods. His Seventh Report (1843) gave a positive report of his observations. A humanitarian in all things (treatment of the mentally ill, abolition of slavery, etc.), he was particularly impressed with the love and rapport shared by the teachers and students involved in these schools. He also shared Pestalozzi's and Catherine Beecher's belief that women were the better teachers for the common schools.

The view Mann expounded on the role of the common school in promoting social harmony and ensuring the republic would be guided by an intelligent, moral citizenry was not original or unique. But at a time when the common school movement was spreading across the nation, when it came to defining its basic principles and articles of faith, he was unquestionably the chief spokesperson (Binder, 1974). The measure of his respect by contemporaries is reflected in a review of one of his annual reports by a Scottish newspaper not given to praising things American, the *Edinburgh Review:* "The volume is, indeed, a noble monument of civilized people; and, if America were sunk beneath the waves, would remain the fairest picture on record of that ideal commonwealth" (cited in Cremin, 1982, p. 142).

Henry Barnard

The other major leader of the common school movement was Henry Barnard (1811–1900). Like Mann he served in the state (Connecticut) legislature, worked to establish a state board of education, and then became the board's first secretary (1838–1842). He then served in a similar capacity in Rhode Island (1845–1849), as chancellor of the University of Wisconsin, president of St. John's College, and the first U.S. commissioner of education.

The American Journal of Education and Teachers' Institutes.   Much of Barnard's influence on educational theory and practice came through his numerous lectures and writings, and more importantly, through his editorship of the *American Journal of Education,* the only educational journal of national significance at the time. The journal served not only to popularize education but to keep teachers informed of educational innovations and ideas from both home and abroad. Barnard is also credited with initiating the *teachers' institute* movement. These were meetings, lasting for a few days to several weeks, at which teachers met to be inspired by noted educators, instructed in new techniques, and informed of the most modern material (Binder, 1974).

Barnard's greatest success lay in his democratic philosophy, "schools good enough for the best and cheap enough for the poorest," and as a disseminator of information about better schools. He is sometimes called the "Father of American School Administration" (Pulliam, 1987).

State Support

The idea of having universal common schools was one thing, but paying for them through direct taxation of the general public was another. Until the 1820s or 1830s, the only really free education was that provided by the charity schools, or in certain other schools if the parents were willing to declare themselves paupers. Often local or county taxes levied on specific activities, for example liquor licenses or marriage fees, provided partial support for the schools, but the remainder of the expenses were charged to the parents in the form of a *rate bill*. The rate bill was, in effect, a tuition fee based on the number

How does the practice of some districts of charging fees for participation in extracurricular activities affect the participation of the children of the poor?

of children. Even though the fee might be small, poor parents often could not afford it, so their children either did not attend school or took turns attending.

In some states, legislation provided for the establishment of school districts and allowed the districts to levy a school tax if the majority of the voters agreed. However, if the tax proceeds were insufficient to support the schools, the rate bill was used.

State support for the schools was very limited. One of the emphases of the common school movement was greater state support. Beginning in the first quarter of the nineteenth century several states began to provide aid for public schools from either permanent school funds (derived largely from the sale of public lands), direct taxation, or appropriations from the general fund. Conditions were usually placed on the receipt of such funds; for example, that local support must equal or exceed state support or that the schools must be kept open a minimum length of time.

By 1865 systems of common schools had been established throughout the northern, midwestern, and western states, and more than 50% of the nation's children were enrolled in public schools. The lowest enrollments were in the South where the common school movement had made little progress.

As the common school movement progressed, the pressure to make these schools completely tax supported increased. Massachusetts was the first state to do away with the rate bill, in 1827. Pennsylvania's Free School Act of 1834 was a model for eliminating the pauper school concept. Although other states soon followed these examples and by constitutional or legislative enactment adopted the concept of public support for public schools open to all children, it was not until 1871 that the last state (New Jersey) abolished the rate bill, making the schools truly free.

State Control

Creation of State Superintendents of Education.   As is usually the case, increased support is accompanied by increased efforts to control. The effort to establish some control or supervision was marked by the creation of an office of state superintendent or commissioner of education and a state board of education. In 1812 New York became the first state to appoint a state superintendent, Gideon Hawley. His tenure in office was filled with such controversy that in 1821 he was removed from office and the position was abolished and not recreated until 1854. Nonetheless, by the outbreak of the Civil War, 28 of the 34 states had established state boards of education and chief state school officers. By and large these officers and boards were vested with more supervisory power than real control. Initially their major responsibilities were involved with the distribution of the permanent school funds and the organization of a state system of common schools.

Creation of Local School Districts and Superintendents.   The creation of a state system of common schools paralleled the establishment of school districts and the establishment of local and county superintendents. The New England states instituted the district system in the early years of the nineteenth century and it spread westward during the next three decades. Local supervision was

The one-room schoolhouse was the symbol of free, public education in rural and frontier America.

provided by the district or county superintendent whose primary duty was to supervise instruction. The development of the position of county superintendent of schools helped bring about some degree of standardization and uniformity in areas that had numerous small, rural school districts (Gutek, 1986). The evolution of the office of city school superintendent quickly followed that of the district and county office. The first city superintendent was appointed in Buffalo in 1837, and was quickly followed in Louisville, St. Louis, Providence, Springfield, Cleveland, Rochester, and New Orleans. One of the major responsibilities of the early city superintendents was to develop a uniform course of study. This development was concurrent with the establishment of graded schools (Spring, 1990).

Organization and Curriculum

The common schools varied in terms of size, organization, and curriculum, depending on their location. In rural areas the one- or two-room school was dominant; progress was not marked by movement from one grade to another, but by completing one text and beginning another. In larger cities

*What would be
the advantages
of attending a
one- or two-room
rural school over
a large, urban
school? The
disadvantages?*

and towns, grading had been introduced. On the frontier, where there remained some distrust for too much education, the curriculum was often limited to the three R's; in larger cities it tended to be more broad. A great variety of textbooks appeared and their authors began to practice the more modern educational teachings. For example, the extremely popular *McGuffey Readers* continued to teach "the lessons of morality and patriotism, but the stern, direct preachments of earlier schoolbooks were replaced or supplemented by stories and essays designed to appeal to youthful interest" (Cremin, 1982, p. 96). Rote learning, drill, and practice did not disappear from the classroom, but a more progressive approach that placed a value on the sensitivities and individuality of the child was making some inroads.

Secondary School Movement

Public *secondary schools* offering education beyond the elementary school did not become a firmly established part of the American educational scene until the last quarter of the nineteenth century. However, the beginnings of the movement occurred well before the Civil War. Perhaps not unexpectedly, the lead was taken by those states that had been first to establish systems of common schools. Boston inaugurated the high school movement in 1821 with the opening of the English Classical School, renamed the Boston English High School in 1824. Then as now the school was open to boys only. In calling for community support the Boston school committee made it clear that they wished to provide an alternative to the Latin grammar school and to provide locally "an education that shall fit him (the child) for active life, and shall serve as a foundation for eminence in his profession, whether Mercantile or Mechanical" (Binder, 1974, p. 107). Such an education, as we have seen, could otherwise be obtained only by sending the child to a private academy.

Ten years later, in 1831, the first American *comprehensive* (and coeducational) *high school*, offering both English and classical courses of study, was opened in Lowell, Massachusetts. In 1838 Philadelphia opened a coeducational high school with three tracks: a four-year classical curriculum, a four-year modern language curriculum, and a two-year English curriculum.

Slow Beginnings

In the years before the Civil War the high school movement expanded slowly. By 1860 there were only 300 high schools in the nation compared to more than 6,000 academies. Of the 300, more than 100 were located in Massachusetts. Massachusetts was unique in requiring communities of 50 families or more to provide secondary level education (Binder, 1974).

The slow growth of the high school can be partially explained by the fact that, unlike the common school, the high school was not being overwhelmingly demanded by the masses. It appeared to be more a reformer's response to urbanization and industrialization. Middle or upper class reformers, adopting the philosophy and rhetoric of the common school advocates, viewed their efforts as democratizing secondary education and providing a means of maintaining social values and promoting economic progress. As a result, prior to the Civil War most high schools were located in urban areas; it was there that a sufficient number of students and sufficient tax support were most often found.

The Movement Grows as Industry and the Economy Grow

The years after the Civil War were marked by rapid industrial growth and technological change. These trends intensified the demand for skilled workers. A great tide of immigration brought people who needed not only skills but knowledge of American values and ideals. The mood of the masses changed and a high school education was increasingly seen as necessary to the full realization of one's social and economic goals. Economic growth also created a larger tax base that could be used to support an expanded educational system. As a consequence, the number of public high schools increased. During the 1880s the number of high schools surpassed the number of academies, and by 1890 there were 2,526 public high schools enrolling 202,063 students, compared to the 1,632 private academies with their 94,391 students (Gutek, 1986).

Herbert Spencer and the "Practical Curriculum"

The design of the curriculum of the high school was influenced by the English philosopher Herbert Spencer (1820–1903) who applied many of Darwin's concepts of evolution and the idea of the "survival of the fittest" to education. In his book *Education,* Spencer poses and answers the question, "What knowledge is of most worth?" He concluded that it was not the "ornamental" education predominant in English schools of the time, which emphasized a classical education. Rather, he maintained, it is one that is practical and emphasizes the study of science. The aim of education should be "to prepare us for complete living." This can best be done by a curriculum that prepares the individual first for direct self-preservation (health), next for indirect self-preservation (earning a living), then parenthood, followed by citizenship, and last, use of leisure time. By placing the useful or practical first and the arts last, such a curriculum was a reversal of the traditional curriculum of the grammar school.

If you were designing a curriculum for "complete living" for today, what would be its essential features?

Tax Support, Compulsory Attendance and the Decline of Illiteracy

The public secondary school movement was given further impetus by the finding of the Michigan Supreme Court in the famous *Kalamazoo* case (1874). By its ruling that the legislature could tax for the support of both elementary and secondary schools the court provided the precedent for public support of secondary education. By the end of the century the publicly supported high school had replaced the academy in most communities and had become an established part of the common school system in every state.

The *Kalamazoo* decision having quashed the argument that public funds could not be used for secondary education, compulsory attendance laws soon followed. The passage of child labor laws and the increasing demand for an educated workforce were also instrumental in driving the adoption of compulsory attendance laws. By 1918 all states had enacted laws requiring full-time attendance until the child reached a certain age or completed a certain grade. One result of this increase in school attendance was the declining illiteracy rate: from 20% of all persons over 10 years of age in 1870, to 7.7% in 1910 (Graham, 1974).

Illiteracy rates varied by segment of the population. As a result of the pre–Civil War prohibition on teaching blacks in most Southern states and inadequate education after the war, blacks had the highest illiteracy rate, 30.4% in 1910. The illiteracy rate was also high among the older population, which had not been the beneficiary of universal, compulsory education. Whites who were the children of a foreign-born parent had the lowest illiteracy rate, 1.1%. Literacy rates also varied by region. The South, which not only had the most blacks but also had been the slowest in developing systems of common schools, had the highest illiteracy rate (Graham, 1974).

The Committee of Ten

As previously noted, in its origins the high school had been viewed as a provider of a more practical education. The need to assimilate the children of the new immigrants and the more technical demands of industry placed additional pressures on the schools to include a curriculum that could be immediately useful and that included vocational training (Graham, 1974). However, there were educators who did not share this esteem for the "practical curriculum." In 1892, in an effort to standardize the curriculum, the National Education Association established the Committee of Ten. The committee was chaired by Charles Eliot, the president of Harvard University, and was largely composed of representatives of higher education. The two major recommendations of the committee were: (1) early introduction to the basic subjects, and (2) uniform subject matter and instruction for both college-bound and terminal students. While four curricula were recommended (classical, Latin-scientific, modern language, and English), the entire curriculum was dominated by college-preparatory courses. Using the psychology of mental discipline as a theoretical rationale, the Committee claimed that the recommended subjects would be used profitably by both college-bound and terminal students because they trained the powers of observation, memory, expression, and reasoning (Gutek, 1986).

The Seven Cardinal Principles of Secondary Education

The view of the Committee of Ten was immediately challenged by many educators; within 25 years there was little support for its position. In 1918 the National Education Association appointed another committee, the Commission on the Reorganization of Secondary Education, to review the curriculum and organization of secondary education in light of the many changes that had swept American society. The commission issued its seven *Cardinal Principles of Secondary Education,* which identified what should be the objectives of the high school curriculum:

- health

- command of fundamental processes

- worthy home membership

- vocational preparation

- citizenship

- worthwhile use of leisure time

- ethical character

As compared to the recommendations of the Committee of Ten, only one of these, command of fundamental processes, was concerned with college preparation. Instead, the commission viewed the high school as a much more comprehensive institution in terms of both integration of the various ethnic, religious, and socioeconomic groups, and accommodation of the various educational goals of students. Figure 4.2 shows the development of secondary schools in the United States.

Patterns of Curricular Organization

By the mid-1920s the essential shape of the American comprehensive high school was apparent. It was an institution that offered a range of curricula to students of differing abilities and interests. Four basic patterns of curricular organization were in evidence: (1) the college preparatory program, which included courses in English language and literature, foreign languages, mathematics, the natural and physical sciences, and history and social sciences; (2) the commercial or business program, which offered courses in bookkeeping, shorthand, and typing; (3) the industrial, vocational, home economics, and agricultural programs; and (4) a modified academic program for students who planned to terminate their formal education upon high school completion. The typical high school program was four years and was attended

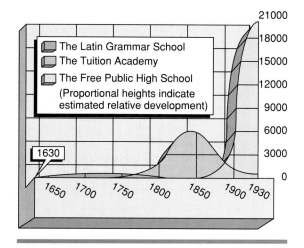

Figure 4.2: The Development of Secondary Schools in the United States, 1630–1930

Source: Cubberley, E. P. (1948). *The history of education* (p. 699). Cambridge, MA: Riverside Press.

by students aged 14 to 18. Exceptions were the six-year combined junior-senior high schools (Gutek, 1986).

The Junior High School

Did you attend a junior high school? If so, what educational experiences do you recall that reinforce the positive value of the junior high school over other organizational plans?

The two-year and three-year *junior high schools* offering grades 6 and 7, or 6, 7, and 8, which also began to appear in some urban districts, were an outgrowth of the Committee of Ten's recommendation that academic work begin earlier and that elementary schooling be reduced from eight to six years. Their growth was also encouraged by the work of G. Stanley Hall, who wrote the first book on adolescent development and emphasized the developmental differences between childhood and preadolescence, which called for a reorganization of the eight–four system. Others felt greater opportunity for industrial and commercial training should be given before high school. As a result of these and other proposals, in 1909 junior high schools were established in Columbus, Ohio and Berkeley, California. Other cities soon followed, and the junior high school became commonplace in the United States after 1930 (Pulliam, 1987).

Higher Education

As was discussed in the preceding chapter, nine colleges were founded during the colonial period. In the period after the Revolution and before the Civil War, the number increased dramatically. Although a large number did not survive, the net result was a twentyfold increase in the number of colleges that did survive, compared to a tenfold increase in the population during this period (Madsen, 1974). This increase was a result of both the fact that as people moved westward they wanted colleges close at hand and the fact that many denominations chose to establish their own colleges rather than have their members educated at colleges operated by other denominations. Thus, of the colleges founded before 1860, less than 10% were state institutions.

By and large the colleges were very small. For example, it was not until after the Civil War that Harvard had a graduating class of 100. During the late colonial and early national periods the curriculum of the colleges became more "liberal," but it retained its heavy classical overlay and its emphasis on religion.

In 1816 the New Hampshire legislature, dominated by the more liberal Jeffersonian Republicans and concerned by what appeared to be the antiliberal sentiments of the board of trustees, enacted legislation to convert Dartmouth College from a private to a state institution. In the *Dartmouth College* case (Trustees of Dartmouth College, 1819), the U.S. Supreme Court upheld the original contract from the king of England which had given private status to the college. The effect of the case was not only to establish the principle that the state could not impair contracts, but to provide a secure foundation for the system of private colleges we have today.

Patterned after the English universities of Oxford and Cambridge, American colleges offered professional studies in theology, medicine, and eventually in law. Lecture and recitation remained the most common modes of instruction. Discipline was strict and the entire atmosphere authoritarian. As a result, student riots sometimes occurred: in 1807 over half the student body of Princeton was suspended; in 1830 Yale experienced the "bread and butter rebellion"; and on one occasion over half the senior class at Harvard was expelled. Intercollegiate athletics being unheard of, literary and debating societies provided some outlet for student enthusiasm (Madsen, 1974).

Growth of Public Institutions

The first state institutions of higher education were established in the South: the University of Georgia in 1785, the University of North Carolina in 1789, the University of Tennessee in 1794, and the University of South Carolina in 1801. In the second quarter of the nineteenth century the same nationalistic, democratic spirit that gave rise to the common school movement also produced an increase in public institutions of higher education. These appeared largely in the Midwest: Indiana University in 1820, the University of Michigan in 1837, and the University of Wisconsin in 1848.

State institutions, unlike denominational institutions, were publicly supported and controlled. In contrast to an emphasis on classical languages and philosophy, their curriculum tended to emphasize the sciences and modern languages. The growth of public institutions was also enhanced by the federal land-grant policy, which granted two townships of land to each state when it entered the union for the support of institutions of higher education.

The Morrill Acts and the Establishment of Land-Grant Institutions

By the mid-nineteenth century there was growing recognition among farmers and laborers that equality of opportunity required an education that would contribute to an improved economic condition. Finding the majority of the existing colleges unresponsive and irrelevant to their needs, they urged the establishment of a new institution, the industrial college. In response, the first Morrill Act was passed by Congress and signed by President Lincoln in 1862. The act granted 30,000 acres of land to each state for each senator and representative it had in Congress based on the 1860 census. The income from the land was to be used to support at least one college that would "teach such branches of learning as are related to agriculture and mechanical arts, . . . in order to promote the liberal and practical education of the industrial classes in the several pursuits and professions of life."

The Second Morrill Act of 1890 provided for direct annual grants of $15,000 (increasing annually to $25,000) to each state to support land-grant colleges. The bill also provided that no grant would be given to any state that denied admission to its land-grant colleges because of race without providing "separate but equal" institutions.

As a result of the Morrill Acts, 65 new land-grant colleges were established. Among the first of the new institutions of higher education were the universities of Maine (1865), Illinois and West Virginia (1867), California (1868), Purdue and Nebraska (1869), Ohio State (1870), and Arkansas and Texas A & M (1871). Seventeen states, mostly in the South, also established separate land-grant colleges for blacks under the provisions of the Second

Morrill Act. The Morrill Acts provided both the foundation for a new type of curriculum at government expense and powerful incentives for greatly expanded state systems of higher education (Rippa, 1984).

Higher Education for Women

Significant developments were also being made in the higher education of women during this period. As discussed earlier, a number of women's seminaries or colleges had been opened prior to the Civil War. A few coeducational colleges also existed before the Civil War (e.g., Oberlin, 1833; Antioch, 1853; and the State University of Iowa, 1858). However, it was not until after the Civil War that women's higher education really began to flourish. Several women's colleges (e.g., Vassar, 1865; Wellesley, 1875; Smith, 1875; Radcliffe, 1879; and Bryn Mawr, 1880) were established which offered programs comparable to those found in the colleges for men. In addition, an increasing number of formerly all-male institutions began admitting women, albeit selectively. By 1880 about half the colleges and universities admitted women (Pulliam, 1987). However, while a wide curriculum was open to them, teaching remained the most accessible and socially acceptable.

The Emergence of the Modern University

In the last decades of the nineteenth century and the first decades of the twentieth century, two other institutions made their appearance on the higher educational scene in America: the university and the *junior college*. In contrast to the small, single-purpose, largely undergraduate colleges, the emerging universities were large and multipurpose. Influenced by the German universities where many of them had studied, American professors and college presidents worked to establish graduate programs and emphasize research. By the end of the nineteenth century, the American university had come to look much as we know it today with an undergraduate college of liberal arts and sciences, a graduate college, and various professional colleges.

Founding of Junior Colleges

Have you ever attended a junior or community college? Would you support the movement toward having all lower division education take place at these institutions?

The initiative for the establishment of junior colleges came in the late nineteenth century from a number of university presidents who viewed the first two years of higher education as more appropriate to secondary education. They wanted to free their faculty from what they considered secondary education responsibilities so that they could devote themselves more to research and graduate education. In 1901 the first public junior college was established, the Joliet (Illinois) Junior College. Although initially established to offer courses that would transfer to four-year institutions, it soon began to offer terminal and vocational programs too (Gutek, 1986). In 1907 California passed a law permitting school boards to offer high school graduates courses similar to those required during the first two years of college (Rippa, 1984). By the early 1920s the concept of the junior college was well established. During the late 1920s, encouraged by the Smith-Hughes Act which provided federal aid to vocational education, junior colleges developed more extensive vocational and technical education programs. In subsequent decades they not only expanded rapidly, but as their goal was expanded to include serving the broad-based needs of the community, they became transformed into today's community colleges (Gutek, 1986).

Table 4.2 lists some of the individuals we have been discussing who had an important effect on American education and the development of the elementary, secondary, and university school systems.

Table 4.2: They Made It Happen: Important Figures in Eighteenth- and Nineteenth-Century American Education History

Benjamin Franklin (1706–1790)	Established Franklin Academy in 1751 with a practical curriculum as an alternative to the Latin grammar school. Proposed first state school system.
Thomas Jefferson (1743–1826)	Proposed state system of free and universal elementary education and selected publicly supported secondary and higher education. Founded the University of Virginia (1825).
Noah Webster (1758–1843)	"Schoolmaster of the Republic." Sought to create a distinctive national language. Published a number of widely used spelling, grammar, and reading books, as well as a dictionary.
Joseph Lancaster (1778–1838)	Originated monitorial system of mass instruction in England in 1798; first monitorial school in U.S. in 1806. Concept widely promoted by Lancaster in U.S.
Robert Raikes (1735–1811)	Popularized Sunday schools in England to offer basic reading and writing to children who worked during the week. Practice brought to U.S. in late eighteenth century.
Robert Owen (1771–1858)	Originated infant schools in England for children of poor factory workers. Transplanted to the United States, infant schools evolved into primary schools. Founded community of New Harmony, Indiana.
Emma Willard (1787–1870)	Women's rights activist. Founded Troy Female Seminary in 1821, first U.S. institution of higher education for women, to train female teachers in the subject areas and pedagogy.
Mary Lyon (1797–1849)	Founded Mount Holyoke Female Seminary in 1837, the first permanent women's college in the U.S.
Catherine Beecher (1800–1878)	Founded Hartford Female Seminary. Supporter of common school movement. Advocated nationwide system of teacher training seminaries.
Horace Mann (1796–1859)	"Father of American Education." State superintendent of education in Massachusetts. Spokesperson for common school movement. Established first normal schools in U.S.
Henry Barnard (1811–1900)	Leader of common school movement. First U.S. commissioner of education. Editor of *American Journal of Education.* Initiated teachers' institutes.
Charles Eliot (1834–1926)	President of Harvard University (1869–1909). Chaired the Committee of Ten (1892), which recommended a classical curriculum for the secondary schools.

Education of Minorities

The progress of education in the United States has not been uniform across all regions, socioeconomic classes, or races. To many the schoolhouse door was closed and the promise of equal educational opportunity an unrealized dream. Native Americans, Hispanic Americans, and black Americans in particular have had to struggle to realize the promise of an equal education.

Education of Native Americans

The formal education of Native Americans was initiated by missionaries who equated education with Christianity and the virtues of civilized life. The Society for the Propagation of the Gospel and the Moravians were among the more active of the missionary groups. Just as education for the white colonists was primarily for the purpose of training for the ministry, so too it was hoped that education would equip Native Americans to become missionaries to their people. However, the efforts of missionary or philanthropic groups was limited, and the town and grammar schools enrolled few Native Americans. Efforts to provide any higher education were even more limited. In 1653 a college was founded at Harvard to instruct Native American students in the same classical education received by whites. Dartmouth College was originally established for the education of Native Americans, but was soon dominated by the children of the white colonists.

The initial response to the formal, traditional education offered by the colonists was distrust and rejection. Benjamin Franklin quoted one Native American leader as saying:

> Several of our young people were formerly brought up at the colleges of the Northern Provinces; they were instructed in all your Sciences; but, when they came back to us, they were bad Runners, ignorant of every means of living in the Woods, unable to bear either Cold or Hunger, knew neither how to build a Cabin, take a Deer, or kill an Enemy, spoke our Language imperfectly, were therefore neither fit for Hunters, Warriors, nor Counsellors; they were totally good for nothing. (cited in Kidwell & Swift, 1976, p. 335)

Treaties and Mission Schools.   During the first century of the new republic much of the education of the Native Americans came about as a result of federal legislation or negotiated treaties. According to the terms of the treaties, 389 of which were signed with various tribes between 1778 and 1871, in return for relinquishing their land, the Native Americans were given money payments, guarantees of the integrity of the land they retained, and promises of educational services (Kidwell & Swift, 1976). The predominant means by which the federal government met its obligation to provide educational services was through support of mission schools operated on the reservation. These schools concentrated on the three R's, some vocational and agricultural training, and, of course, religion. Instruction was given in the native tongue, as this was viewed as the best way to lead the Native Americans to conversion. In 1917 this arrangement, which in effect constituted government support of sectarian education, ended (Butts, 1978).

Boarding Schools.   The decline of the mission schools was accompanied by the establishment of three other forms of Native American education: the off-reservation boarding school, the reservation day school, and public schools. The off-reservation boarding school was a product of the *assimilation* approach that became popular in the post–Civil War decades. This approach advocated the incorporation of Native Americans into the predominant white culture and was established on the belief that the most lasting and efficient way this assimilation could take place was to remove children from their tribal setting and subject them, in a strict disciplinary setting, to an infusion of American language and customs.

The first major boarding school was established in 1879 at Carlisle, Pennsylvania by General Richard Pratt. Vocational and industrial training was emphasized at this and other off-reservation boarding schools. By the turn of the century, 25 off-reservation boarding schools had been established (Szasz, 1977). However, they were subject to much criticism. The physical and living conditions were often inadequate. The dropout rate was high. Students more often returned to the reservation rather than enter white society, and upon return to the reservation found they were either unable to apply the training they had received, or that it was irrelevant.

Class at Carlisle Indian boarding school, circa 1900.

Reservation Day Schools and Public Schools. The reservation day schools offered several advantages over the off-reservation boarding school; not only were they less expensive, they were more acceptable to parents. As a consequence, day schools increased in number after the turn of the twentieth century.

Although Native Americans in the eastern United States who were not under the jurisdiction of the federal government had already been attending off-reservation public schools, a newer phenomenon was the public school located on the reservation. These schools initially had been built to accommodate the white people who rented land on some reservations. The on-reservation public schools tended to encourage not only assimilation, but learning. As one Indian agent wrote, "Indian children progress much faster when thrown in contact with white children than they do when they are all kept together with whites excluded" (Szasz, 1977, p. 11).

The Meriam Report. In the 1920s the appalling living conditions and reprehensible treatment of Native Americans were brought to public view by a number of reformers determined to improve their plight. In response the Bureau of Indian Affairs (BIA) commissioned the Brookings Institution for an independent study of Native American life in the United States. The report, called the Meriam Report, documented the intolerable conditions of Native American life and pointed out that much of their poverty was caused by their loss of land. It also criticized the BIA educational program, exposing the inadequate industrial training, overcrowded dormitories, inadequate diet, and physical punishment in the boarding schools and encouraged the construction of day schools that could also serve as community centers. The report accused the reservation system of creating isolation and concluded that the best way to improve the living standards of Native Americans was to educate them so they could be assimilated into white society (Kidwell & Swift, 1976).

The Meriam Report marked the beginning of a change in BIA policy. After 1928 BIA appropriations for education increased dramatically, efforts were made to deal with conditions in government schools, and curriculum reform was initiated. Soon a major share of the BIA's budget was allocated to education, with the goal of assimilating Native Americans into the mainstream society.

How successful have been efforts to assimilate Native Americans into mainstream society? Should these efforts continue?

Education of Hispanics

The story of the involvement of the United States in the education of Hispanics is largely to be told in relation to the Spanish-speaking peoples of the southwestern United States and begins with the acquisition of this territory from Mexico in 1848 at the end of the Mexican-American War. For the Mexicans who chose to remain in the territory after the U.S. takeover, or for those who fled across the border in the years that followed, life became marked by discrimination, prejudice, and segregation. Although segregation was not imposed by law (*de jure*) as it was for blacks in the South, it nonetheless existed by practice (*de facto*): separate schools and/or classes, poorer facilities, fewer well-trained teachers, and smaller budgets. English was used for instruction, whether understood or not, and the use of Spanish in the classroom or playground was often forbidden (Butts, 1978).

Any improvement in the educational condition of Mexican-American children was hampered by the attitudes of many of their parents who failed to see the value of an education that was aimed at undermining their traditional beliefs and culture. It was also hampered by the articulated views of the larger society, including many educators, that Mexican-Americans were mentally inferior. Many Mexican-American children also suffered the additional handicap of migrancy. Often those who traveled from place to place working in the fields did not attend school at all. Few attended beyond the primary years, and their failure was viewed as natural by educators and the Anglo society in general. Such schooling as they did receive emphasized learning English, vocational and manual arts training, health and hygiene, and the adoption of such American core values as cleanliness, thrift, and punctuality (Carter & Sequra, 1979).

During the Depression years many rural Mexican-Americans moved to the cities, bringing their problems to a wider consciousness. Also during the 1930s and 1940s greater attention was given to the concerns of Mexican-Americans in some states, especially California and New Mexico (Carter & Sequra, 1979). However, it would not be until a quarter century later that any marked progress was made as the "consciousness and conscience of the nation began to stir under the proddings of a new generation of Anglo liberals and especially new Chicano leadership" (Butts, 1978, p. 251).

Education of Blacks

Although blacks came to America before the Puritans, 20 having been sold to the colonists at the Jamestown colony in 1619, their educational history was anything but similar. The vast majority of blacks living in the United States during the first 300 years of its history lived in the South and, until after the Civil War, as slaves. On the eve of the Civil War there were about 4 million black slaves and one-half million free blacks out of a total population of 31 million.

Education of Slaves.   For the slaves, education was virtually nonexistent. In the colonial period some missionary or philanthropic groups had provided limited and sporadic schooling, but by the third decade of the nineteenth century the rise of militant abolitionism and the fear of slave revolts had led to the enactment of the so-called "Black Codes" which, among other things, prohibited the education of slaves. As Pifer (1973) described the pre–Civil War status of education for the slave:

> Education was thought to give the slave too high an opinion of himself and access to such pernicious ideas as those expressed in our Declaration of Independence, namely, that all men are created equal and have certain inalienable rights. In short, education was dangerous. Nevertheless, some slaves and some whites, at great personal risk, defied these harsh laws and engaged in

clandestine learning and teachings, but the sum total of education for slaves, all the same was meager. (p. 8)

Education of Free Blacks Prior to the Civil War.   The education of free blacks in the South (some 10% of the free blacks did reside in the South) was also very limited. Before the institution of the Black Codes, black apprentices benefited from the requirement that apprentices be taught to read and write. But under the codes this requirement was repealed in some states as it applied to blacks. Outside the South, in some communities the children of free slaves did attend public schools or the private schools established by various religious, philanthropic, or abolitionist societies. The SPG was one of the most active groups in these efforts.

In the decades preceding the Civil War, as common school systems were developed in the North, blacks more often than not found themselves in segregated schools. An important legal support for this segregation (and also the legal basis for segregation for the remainder of the century) was provided by the Massachusetts Supreme Court decision in *Roberts v. City of Boston* (1850), which said that separate but equal schools did not violate the rights of the black child.

Despite the difficulties, some free blacks did obtain an education. The outbreak of the Civil War in 1861 found about 4,000 blacks in schools in the slave states and 23,000 in the free states (West, 1972). A few blacks even obtained a higher education. A small number went abroad to England or Scotland, a few attended the limited number of American colleges that admitted blacks, notably Oberlin in Ohio and Berea in Kentucky, and others attended the three black colleges established before 1860: Cheyney State College (1839) and Lincoln University (1854) in Pennsylvania and Wilberforce University (1856) in Ohio.

Many of the free blacks who gained a higher education prior to 1860 did so under the auspices of the American Colonization Society, which was established in 1817 to send free blacks to the colony of Liberia in Africa, founded by the society in 1822. The education of the free blacks was undertaken to provide the doctors, lawyers, teachers, clergy, and civil servants needed by the colony. Although not all those educated by the Society went to the colony, or if they went did not remain, enough did so to provide the colony and the Republic of Liberia, which it became in 1847, with its leadership elite (Pifer, 1973).

Reconstruction.   The period of Reconstruction (1865–1877) following the Civil War brought new factors to bear on education in the South in general and education of blacks in particular. One such force was the hundreds of teachers who, supported by various northern churches and missionary societies, moved to the South to educate those who had been liberated. Another factor was the emergence of charitable *educational foundations*, philanthropy in a new form. The first of these, established in 1867, was the Peabody Fund for the Advancement of Negro Education in the South. It later merged with the Slater Fund to support industrial education and teacher preparation. Among the others, the largest was the General Education Board set up by John D. Rockefeller in 1902 (Pifer, 1973; West, 1972).

Another major force affecting black education in the South during this period was the Freedmen's Bureau. The bureau was responsible for the establishment of some 3,000 schools, and by 1869 some 114,000 students were in attendance in bureau schools (the Historical Note on page 132 gives the account of one teacher in a freedmen's school). These schools followed the New England common school model in terms of their curriculum (reading, writing, grammar, geography, arithmetic, and music) and moral outlook (the importance of certain values and the responsibility of citizenship), but added a new dimension—industrial training. In the view of northern educators, industrial training would prepare blacks for the occupations they were most suited to perform in the South (Gutek, 1986).

Hampton and Tuskegee Institutes.   Industrial education was the basic mission of the Hampton Institute, founded in 1868 by a representative of the Freedmen's Bureau, General Samuel Chapman Armstrong. Booker T. Washington attended the institute and developed the educational ideas that led to the establishment of his Tuskegee Institute in 1880. Some, such as W. E. B. DuBois, who in 1907 co-founded the National Association for the Advancement of Colored People, argued against what they viewed as a position of accommodation or compromise and protested that it was wrong for blacks to be given only one educational direction (industrial) and whites several. However, to Washington and others who supported industrial education, this approach appeared the most immediate and practical way for blacks to improve their economic and social position.

Washington's efforts were successful: 10 years after its founding Tuskegee had a faculty of 88 and a student body of 1,200, making it one of the largest institutions of higher education in the South. It is also significant to note that Tuskegee, and even more so the Hampton Institute, were important as centers for the training of black teachers. In fact, as one historian reminds us, the traditional attention given to Hampton as an agricultural and industrial school has obscured the fact that Hampton was founded and maintained primarily to train black teachers for the South. Indeed, between 1872 and 1890, 604 of Hampton's 723 graduates became teachers (Anderson, 1978).

Black Colleges and Universities.   In addition to Hampton and Tuskegee, several other distinguished black colleges and universities were established in the immediate post–Civil War years. These include Atlanta University, founded in 1865 by the American Baptist Mission Society; Howard University, chartered in 1868 by the Congregationalists; Fisk University, established in 1866 by the American Missionary Association; and Mehary Medical College, originally Walton College, founded in 1865 by the Methodist Episcopal Church. Somewhat later, as a result of the Second Morrill Act of 1890, black land-grant colleges were established in each of the southern and border states—17 in all (Pifer, 1973).

The topic of segregated universities is currently being revisited in discussions of the place of all-women colleges, Hispanic universities, etc. What is your position on voluntary segregated institutions of higher education?

Historical Note:
Zeal for Learning Among Freedmen, 1868

Dear Brethren and Sisters;

Since I last wrote I have commenced my school and have now been teaching just four weeks. Everything was finally arranged so that on Monday Nov. 30th I opened school with twenty-five scholars. Since then the number has been steadily increasing and now it numbers forty-two with a prospect of large additions after their great holiday Christmas week is past.

From all the accounts of Freedmen's schools which I had heard and read previous to coming here I expected to find them anxious to learn but after all, I confess I was unprepared for the amount of zeal manifested by most of them for an education. I can say as one did of old, "The half had not been told me." I am surprised each day by some new proof of their anxiety to learn.

Nearly all ages, colors, conditions and capacities are represented in my school. Ages ranging from five to sixty-five; Colors from jet-black with tight curling hair to pale brunette with waving brown hair.

Some, a few of them could read quite readily in a second reader and many more knew the alphabet and were trying patiently to spell out short easy words, while by far the greater number could not distinguish a letter. I have had as many as nineteen in my alphabet class at one time but it is now reduced to four.

One old woman over sixty, after spending three weeks on the alphabet and finally conquering it, said she wanted to learn to spell Jesus first before spelling easy words for said she, "Pears like I can learn the rest easier if I get that blessed name learned first." So now she looks through the Bible for that name and has learned to distinguish it at sight from other words. The older members of the school are as quiet and orderly as I could desire but the children are not so very different from other children. They love mischief and play and the prevailing vice among them is deceit. But education has all the charm of novelty to them and they learn with astonishing rapidity. They come to school as well provided with books as children usually do.

Your Sister in Christ,

Pamelia A. Hand

Source: Reprinted by permission of Macmillan Publishing Company from *The Black American and Education* (pp. 73–74) by Earle H. West. Copyright © 1972 by Merrill Publishing Company.

Segregated Public Schools.   Yet another factor changing the face of education in the South during the Reconstruction period was legislation leading to the establishment of tax-supported public or common school systems. Many freedmen recently elected to state legislatures were a force in this movement. Many of these black legislators as well as some white legislators advocated integration in the newly established schools. In fact, many of the state statutes or constitutional provisions established the schools without making reference to either integration or segregation. However, none of the southern states actually instituted an integrated system, and what began as custom became law in all the southern states. Yet the efforts of the various groups and agencies did result in a dramatic reversal of the educational status of black Americans: from a literacy rate estimated at 5% or 10% at the outbreak of the Civil War to one of 70% by 1910.

From the end of Reconstruction through the turn of the century a system of racial segregation was established in the South that remained in effect until the desegregation movement of the 1950s and 1960s. The practice of segregation was sanctioned by the 1896 U.S. Supreme Court decision in *Plessy v. Ferguson,* which said that separate railroad cars did not violate the Constitution. But the "separate but equal" doctrine, while always producing separate, rarely produced equal. After the 1870s the federal government effectively withdrew from the promotion of the civil and educational rights of blacks.

During this same period, ever-increasing numbers of white children from immigrant and lower socioeconomic families were entering the enlarged public school system; between 1880 and 1895 white enrollment in the public schools increased 106% compared to 59% for black enrollment (Frazer, cited in Hare & Swift, 1976). The "rise of the poor whites" placed increased financial demands on public revenues and often resulted in funds being diverted from black schools to improve other schools (Gutek, 1986). To this was added the disenfranchisement of blacks by many southern states and the delegation of authority to local school boards to divide state education funds as they saw fit. From the court approval of segregation, the loss of political power, and the decreased financial support emerged the "separate but inferior" system that marked so much of the South until after the middle of the twentieth century.

Teacher Education

The formal training of teachers in the United States did not begin until the nineteenth century. In colonial America teachers at the elementary level were often young men who taught for only a short time before studying for the ministry or law. Given the strong relationship between church and education, more often than not they were chosen more for their religious orthodoxy than their educational qualifications. In fact, they were often viewed as assistant pastors and in addition to their teaching they were expected to perform various duties related to the functioning of the church. In many small communities the minister himself was the schoolmaster.

Unfortunately, too often the "career teachers" were individuals who had been unsuccessful at other occupations or those whose personal character and civil conduct left something to be desired. It was also not uncommon in colonial America to find teachers who were indentured servants—persons who had sold their services for a period of years in exchange for passage to the New World. Perhaps the closest to any teacher preparation was that received by those individuals who entered teaching after serving as apprentices to schoolmasters. In fact, the educational historian Pulliam (1987) refers to the apprenticeship training received by Quaker teachers as the first teacher education in America.

A distinction was made between teachers at the elementary level and those at the secondary level, not in the teacher training they received, but in the higher status the secondary teachers held in society and the higher education they possessed. Teachers in the Latin grammar schools and academies were normally graduates of secondary schools and not uncommonly had received some college education, while those at the elementary level very often had little more than an elementary education themselves.

Although most histories of education identify the Colombian School at Concord, Vermont, established by the Reverend Samuel Hall in 1823, as the first formal teacher training institution, a good argument can be made that the first such institution was actually the previously mentioned Troy Female Seminary opened by Emma Willard in 1821 (Spring, 1990). Willard established the seminary to train female teachers in both the subject areas and in pedagogy. Each graduate received a signed certificate confirming her qualifications to teach. Long before the first state-supported normal schools in Massachusetts were opened by Horace Mann, the Troy Seminary had prepared 200 teachers for the common schools (Rippa, 1984). In fact, this and other academies were responsible for not only expanding educational opportunities for women, but for preparing a large number of individuals for the teaching profession.

Establishment of Normal Schools

The greatest force, however, in increasing the professional training of teachers was the establishment of *normal schools*. As we have seen, Horace Mann, Henry Barnard, Catherine Beecher and others who worked for the establishment of common school systems recognized that the success of such systems was dependent upon the preparation of a sufficient quantity of adequately trained teachers. This in turn demanded the establishment of institutions for the specific training of teachers, that is, normal schools. These educational leaders also believed that the teaching force for the common schools should be female, not only because women supposedly made better teachers at the elementary level, but because they were less expensive to hire. The fact that at least the latter was true is shown in Table 4.3, which compares the salaries of men and women teachers from the years 1841 to 1864, as well as the salaries of teachers in rural areas with those in cities.

The growing enrollments in the common schools also created a growing demand for teachers. The response in one state after another was the estab-

Table 4.3: Average Weekly Salaries of Teachers, 1841–1864

| Year | Rural | | City | |
	Men	Women	Men	Women
1841	$4.15	$2.51	$11.93	$4.44
1845	3.87	2.48	12.21	4.09
1850	4.25	2.89	13.37	4.71
1855	5.77	3.65	16.80	5.79
1860	6.28	4.12	18.56	6.99
1864	7.86	4.92	20.78	7.67

Source: From *The American School, 1642–1985: Varieties of Historical Interpretation of the Foundations and Development of American Education* by Joel Spring. Copyright © 1986 by Longman Publishing Group. Reprinted with permission from Longman Publishing Group.

lishment of normal schools. The New York State Normal School at Albany, the next established (1844) after those in Massachusetts, was headed by David P. Page. His book, *Theory and Practice of Teaching or the Motives and Methods of Good School Keeping,* published in 1847, became the standard text in teacher education. By 1875 at least 70 normal schools were receiving some state support, and by 1900 there were a reported 345 normal schools in the United States (Pulliam, 1987).

Admission to the normal school required only an elementary education. The course of study lasted one or two years and included a review of material to be taught in the elementary school, instruction in methods of teaching, "mental philosophy" (i.e., educational psychology), and classroom management. Overriding the curriculum was a concern for the development of moral character. A prominent feature of these normal schools was the model school, the forerunner of the laboratory school, where the students could practice teaching.

Teacher Institutes

Despite the spread of normal schools, in some places, even reform-minded Massachusetts, as late as 1900 only a bare majority of teachers had attended normal schools. Before this time, and even into the twentieth century, the most important institution in the training of teachers was the teacher institute. A common practice of school districts was to hire individuals with no formal training, with the condition that their continued employment depended on attendance at a teacher institute. The typical institute met once or twice a year for from several days to four weeks, usually in the summer months. In less populous areas the institutes were often conducted by the county superintendent of schools. Some were offered in connection with institutions of higher education. The primary purpose of the institute was to provide a brief course in the theory and practice of teaching. Great emphasis was placed on elevating the moral character of the teacher (Spring, 1990).

Normal School Curriculum and Standards Strengthened

Toward the end of the nineteenth century the character of the normal school began to change. Not only was the burgeoning population creating an increased demand for elementary or common school teachers, but the secondary school movement created a concomitant demand for secondary school teachers. To meet this demand, normal schools began to broaden their curriculum to include the training of secondary school teachers. At the same time, they began to require high school completion for admission. The passage of teacher certification statutes that specified the amount and type of training required of teachers contributed to the expansion of the normal school program from two to three years and eventually, during the 1920s, to four years. By this time the normal schools were beginning to call themselves state teachers' colleges. In time, with the broadening of the curriculum to embrace many of the liberal arts, the "teacher" designation was dropped and most became simply "state colleges." Some of these former normal schools have become the largest and most respected universities in the United States.

Are you attending or have you ever attended a college or university that began as a normal school? What influence has this history had on the institutional climate?

Universities Enter Teacher Training

During the late nineteenth century the universities also became increasingly involved in teacher education. Teacher training at the college or university level had been offered at a limited number of institutions as early as the 1830s, but it was not until toward the end of the nineteenth century that universities entered the field of teacher preparation to any measurable extent (Pulliam, 1987). Their involvement stemmed in part from the increased demand for secondary school teachers. The universities had always been institutions for the education of those who taught in the grammar schools, academies, and high schools. However, they did not prepare these students as teachers *per se,* but as individuals who had advanced knowledge of certain subject matter. The increased demand for secondary school teachers, the late entrance of the normal schools into the training of secondary school teachers, and the growing recognition that the professionalization of teaching demanded study of its theory and practice led to the increased involvement of universities in teacher education. The University of Iowa established the first chair of education in 1873, other midwestern universities followed, and in 1892 the New York College for the Training of Teachers (Teachers College) became a part of Columbia University. After the turn of the century teacher training departments became commonplace in the universities.

Summary

The Founding Fathers recognized the importance of education to the development of the new nation. As the nation marched through the nineteenth century and became an industrial giant, the demand for skilled workers and the demand of the working class who saw education as a path to success combined to expand the offering of publicly supported education through the secondary school. The growth of higher education can also be attributed to these forces. Indeed, today it is the recognition of education's importance to our national prominence and its vital role in assuring our continued economic prosperity that has served as the motivation for much of the current activity to reform our nation's schools.

Unfortunately, while the educational opportunities afforded much of the population were greatly expanded in the nineteenth century, the history of the education of minorities was basically one of neglect and segregation. It would not be until the third quarter of the twentieth century that any marked progress would be made in improving the education of Native Americans, Mexican-Americans, and blacks. In the next chapter many of these efforts will be detailed, as well as those designed to improve the professional training of teachers.

Key Terms

Assimilation

Common school

Comprehensive high school

De facto segregation

De jure segregation
Educational foundations
Infant school
Junior college
Junior high school

Normal school
Rate bill
Secondary school
Sunday school
Teachers' institute

Discussion Questions

1. In what ways do Henry Barnard's concerns in the opening of the chapter echo the concerns regarding teacher education expressed in the reform reports of the 1980s?

2. In what ways were Thomas Jefferson's plans for an educational system elitist? Egalitarian?

3. What was the significance of each of the following to expanding educational opportunities in the U.S.?
   a. monitorial schools
   b. Sunday schools
   c. infant schools
   d. free school societies

4. Describe the contribution of Horace Mann and Henry Barnard to the common school movement.

5. What influence did Prussian education have on American education in the early nineteenth century?

6. Describe the impact of the Second Morrill Act on the provision of education to minorities in the U.S.

7. What impact has the historical neglect of the education of minorities had on their education and on the educational system today?

8. What was the contribution of Emma Willard to women's education? To teacher education?

9. Compare the role of the university with that of the normal school in the education of teachers.

References

Anderson, J. D. (1978). The Hampton model of normal school industrial education, 1868–1900. In V. P. Franklin & J. D. Anderson (Eds.), New perspectives on black educational history. Boston: G. K. Hall.

Binder, F. M. (1974). The age of the common school, 1830–1865. New York: John Wiley & Sons.

Butts, R. F. (1978). Public education in the United States. New York: Holt, Rinehart and Winston.

Carter, T. P., & Sequra, R. D. (1979). Mexican Americans in school: A decade of change. New York: College Entrance Examination Board.

Cremin, L. A. (1982). *American education: The national experience, 1783–1876.* New York: Harper and Row.

Frazer, D., Hare, N., & Swift, D. W. (1976). Black education. In D. W. Swift (Ed.), *American education: A sociological view.* Boston: Houghton Mifflin.

Graham, P. A. (1974). *Community & class in American education.* New York: John Wiley & Sons.

Gutek, G. L. (1986). *Education in the United States.* Englewood Cliffs, NJ: Prentice-Hall.

Kidwell, C. S., & Swift, D. W. (1976). Indian education. In D. W. Swift (Ed.), *American education: A sociological view.* Boston: Houghton Mifflin.

Levine, M. (1986). Docemur docendo (He who teachers, learns). *American Educator, 10*(3), 22–25.

Madsen, D. L. (1974). *Early national education, 1776–1830.* New York: John Wiley & Sons.

Pifer, A. (1973). *The higher education of blacks in the United States.* New York: Carnegie Corporation.

Plessy v. Ferguson, 163 U.S. 537, 16 S. Ct. 1138 (1896).

Pulliam, J. D. (1987). *History of education in America.* Columbus, OH: Merrill.

Rippa, S. A. (1984). *Education in a free society.* New York: Longman.

Roberts v. City of Boston, 59 Mass. (5 Cush.) 198 (1850).

Spring, J. (1990). *The American school 1642–1985,* 2d ed. New York: Longman.

Stuart et al. v. School District No. 1 of the Village of Kalamazoo, 30 Michigan 69 (1874).

Szasz, M. C. (1977). *Education and the American Indian.* Albuquerque, NM: University of New Mexico Press.

Topping, K. (1989). Peer tutoring and paired reading: Combining two powerful techniques. *The Reading Teacher, 42,* 488–494.

Trustees of Dartmouth College v. Woodward, 17 U.S. (4 Wheat) 518 (1819).

West, E. (1972). *The Black American and education.* Columbus, OH: Merrill.

Chapter 5

Modern American Education: From the Progressive Movement to the Present

Human history becomes more and more a race between education and catastrophe.

H. G. Wells
The Outline of History *(1920)*

In the 1930s, faculty and students at Oglethorpe University created a "time room" where artifacts from the history of civilization were preserved in their original form, on film and on paper. Film footage was also included that presented a verbal and visual condensed version of significant events in the history of the world up to that time.

Suppose you and your classmates were requested to create a time room on the history of American education. What artifacts would you include in your room? If you made a video chronicle of education, what would it include?

As you may have discovered in answering the above questions, capturing the most noteworthy happenings from a period of time, whether in a capsule, a room, or a chapter is a challenge. The challenge becomes greater the more rapidly changing the times and the more diverse the areas to be included.

In this chapter the history of American education begun in Chapters 3 and 4 is brought to the present. Although covering a relatively short period of time from a historical perspective, this period has witnessed the most rapid expansion of education in our nation's history and some of the most marked changes. So much has taken place that we could not focus in detail on every contributing personality or intervening variable. Consider the following objectives as you study this chapter:

- Identify the major economic, political, and social forces affecting education in the twentieth century.

- Describe the progressive education movement in the United States.

- Compare the impact of the Great Depression, World War II, and the Cold War on education.

- Evaluate the progress of the civil rights movement and the War on Poverty.

- Outline the developments in education during the 1970s and 1980s.

- Trace the fluctuation of federal support for education in the twentieth century.

The Twentieth Century Unfolds

The People and Nation Grow

The twentieth century brought marked changes in American social, economic, political and educational life. Population growth continued at a staggering rate: from 50 million in 1880 to 76 million in 1900 and 106 million in 1920. Although birth rates declined, improvements in medicine and sanitation led to lower infant mortality and cut the overall death rate. A significant portion of the population growth was the result of immigration. In the two decades before the turn of the century, an average of almost 500,000 immigrants per year arrived in this country. The numbers grew to more than 1 million per year in 1905–07, 1910, and 1913–14 (U.S. Bureau of the Census, 1975).

At the same time that the population was experiencing rapid growth it was becoming increasingly urban. According to the 1920 census, for the first time in our nation's history, the number of those living in towns of 2,500 (54.2 million) exceeded those living in rural areas (51.6 million). Although the westward movement continued throughout the late nineteenth and early twentieth centuries, by 1890 the frontier was closed; that is, the Bureau of Census could not draw a line of demarcation beyond which the population was less than two persons per square mile.

America experienced growth not only at home, but on the international scene. In the last years of the nineteenth century and the beginning of the twentieth century the United States acquired Guam, the Philippines, Puerto Rico, the Hawaiian Islands, the Virgin Islands, and the Panama Canal Zone. The nation also engaged in a war with Spain, landed troops in Mexico, Nicaragua, and Haiti, helped put down a revolt in China, and in 1917 entered the fight to make the world safe for democracy.

Economic Growth

The economic growth of the United States during this period was even more profound than the population growth. Whereas the population increased less than fourfold in the post–Civil War to pre–World War I period, production increased tenfold (Gray & Peterson, 1974). This was a period of rapid growth for the railroads and other transportation and communication industries. The expansion of the railroads brought an end to the frontier and linked all parts of the nation, as did an ever-expanding network of telephone lines. At the same time, the transatlantic cable and transworld shipping linked this nation with others. The expansion in the transportation industry opened up new markets for the growing agricultural and manufacturing industries. By 1920 the United States had become the largest manufacturing nation in the world.

Paradoxically, this period of stellar economic growth is also regarded as a dark chapter in American history because of the abuses in industry (Gray & Peterson, 1974). The business leaders who helped bring about the growth and contributed to the abuses have been referred to as "robber barons," and the business and political corruption of the era touched every aspect of American life. The plight of workers (including children) in factories, the unsafe and unsanitary working conditions, the horrors of industrial accidents, and descriptions of life in the poverty-ridden slums filled the tabloids and stirred political and social reforms.

Politics and Reform

Antitrust legislation was enacted in an attempt to control monopolies and their unfair business practices. The progressive movement which emerged at the turn of the century was responsible for a flood of labor legislation addressed at regulating the labor of women and children, wages and hours, and health and safety conditions. Workers also sought to improve their plight through labor unions. Increased union activity met with harsh resistance and persecution; violence and loss of life were not uncommon. Yet by 1920 one-fifth of all nonagricultural workers in the nation were organized; in view of employer hostility, this was a considerable achievement (Kirkland, 1969).

In the political arena the progressive movement gained momentum in the years after 1900. Decrying the excesses of big business, the progressives challenged the cherished ideal of limited government and urged the government to protect consumers against unfair monopolistic practices, workers (particularly women and children) against exploitation, and the less fortunate against any form of social injustice. Reform became the "order of the day" on the local, state, and national levels as progressives sought to wrest control of government from the business community and use it to bring about social change. At the same time, progressives maintained a firm belief in representative democracy and individual freedom.

Forces in Education

Significant changes in the educational arena accompanied those in the social, economic, and political arenas. The urbanization of the population and the popularity of the automobile made possible the building of larger schools and contributed to the consolidation of rural school districts. The number of school districts in the United States continued to decrease gradually from over 130,000 at the turn of the century to approximately 15,500 in 1990. State control of education increased in a number of areas: certification of teachers, specification of requirements for teacher education programs, specification of curricular requirements for public elementary and secondary schools, establishment of minimal standards for school facilities, and provisions for financial support.

At the same time, the size of the school population increased more rapidly than the overall population. In the three decades between 1890 and 1920 the school-age population increased 49% and school enrollments 70%. The growth in the student population was accompanied by an 80% growth in the number of teachers and other nonsupervisory personnel. During the same period the average length of the school term increased by 27 days. More teachers and longer terms translated into significant increases in expenditures (see Table 5.1).

For a number of years the average length of the school term has been 180 days. Do you support current efforts to extend the school year? Why or why not?

Table 5.1: Historical Summary of U.S. Public Elementary and Secondary School Statistics, 1870–1930 (all dollars unadjusted)

	1870	1880	1890	1900	1910	1920	1930
Enrollments							
Total school age (5–17 yrs.) population (thous.)	12,055	15,066	18,543	21,573	24,009	27,556	31,417
Total enrollment in elementary and secondary schools (thous.)	6,872	9,867	12,723	15,503	17,814	21,578	25,678
% of population aged 5–17 enrolled in public schools	57.0	65.5	68.6	71.9	74.2	78.3	81.7
(in private schools)	(NA)	(NA)	(9.5)	(6.4)	(5.2)	(4.9)	(7.8)
Attendance							
Average daily attendance (thous.)	4,077	6,144	8,154	10,633	12,827	16,150	21,265
Average length of school terms (in days)	132.2	130.3	134.7	144.3	157.5	161.9	172.7
Average number of days attended per pupil enrolled	78.4	81.1	86.3	99.0	113.0	121.2	143.0
Instructional staff							
Total classroom teachers/nonsupervisory staff (thous.)	201	287	364	423	523	657	843
Men	78	123	126	127	110	93	140
Women	123	164	238	296	413	565	703
Average annual salary of instructional staff	$189	$195	$252	$325	$485	$871	$1,420
Finance							
Total revenue receipts (thous.)	(NA)	(NA)	$143,195	$219,766	$433,064	$970,120	$2,088,557
Percent of revenue receipts from:							
Federal government	(NA)	(NA)	(NA)	(NA)	(NA)	.3	.4
State government			18.2	17.3	15.0	16.5	16.9
Local government			67.8	67.7	72.1	83.5	82.7
Total expenditures per pupil in ADA	$16	$13	$17	$20	$33	$64	$108

Source: U.S. Department of Education, National Center for Education Statistics. (1982). *Digest of Education Statistics. 1982* (Table 27). Washington, DC: U.S. Government Printing Office.

The Progressive Era in American Education

The Beginnings of Progressive Education

The progressive reform movement, which had such a widespread impact on political, social, and economic life, also found expression in education. Progressive education traces its intellectual roots to Rousseau and its beginnings in this country to Francis W. Parker, superintendent of schools in Quincy, Massachusetts, and later head of the Cook County Normal School in Chicago. Parker studied in Europe and became familiar with the work of Pestalozzi and Froebel. He shared their belief that learning should emanate from the interests and needs of the child and that the most appropriate curriculum was an activity-based one that encouraged children to express themselves freely and creatively.

The practice school of Cook County Normal School was organized as a model democratic community. Art was an integral part of the curriculum, as were nature studies, field trips, and social activities. Rather than deal with multiple, discrete subject matter, the curriculum attempted to integrate subjects in a way that made it more meaningful to the learner. In all things Parker's aim was to make the child the center of the educational process.

Dewey

Among the parents of children at Parker's school in Chicago was John Dewey, professor of philosophy and pedagogy at the University of Chicago. Dewey was impressed with the philosophy and methods of the school and in 1896 established his own laboratory school at the University of Chicago. Through his many writings and articulation of his philosophy, Dewey provided the intellectual foundation for progressive education. In fact, Dewey was said to be "the real spokesman for intellectual America in the Progressive Era" (Bonner, 1963, p. 44).

First and foremost Dewey was a philosopher. He was one of the founders of the philosophy known as pragmatism, which holds that there are no absolutes: truth is that which results from the application of scientific thinking to experience. Scientific thinking, in turn, involves data gathering, hypothesis formulation, and testing.

Dewey's educational theories reflected his philosophy. He rejected the old, rigid, *subject-centered curriculum* in favor of the *child-centered curriculum* in which learning came through experience, not rote memorization, the classroom was a miniature of society, the problem-solving method was the preferred approach, and motivation was at the center of the learning process. The goal of education was to promote individual growth and to prepare the child for full participation in our democratic society.

Dewey maintained that the child should be viewed as a total organism and that education is most effective when it considers not only the intellectual but the social, emotional, and physical needs of the child. He thought that education was a lifelong process and that the school should be an integral part of community life, a concept that gave support to the development of the community school. Dewey wrote some 500 articles and 40 books. His influence was felt not only in philosophy and education, but law, political theory, and social reform. He left an imprint on American education that has been unparalleled in this century. His classic *Democracy and Education* (1916) provided perhaps the strongest statement of his educational theories and provided the rationale for a generation of educators who were part of what was to be known as the progressive education movement.

Progressive Education Association

The formation of the Progressive Education Association (PEA) in 1919 gave what previously had been a "rather loosely joined revolt against pedagogical formalism" a vigorous organizational voice (Cremin, 1962). The association adopted seven guiding principles:

1. The child should be given the freedom to develop naturally.

2. Interest provides the motivation for all work.

3. The teacher should be a guide in the learning process, not the taskmaster.

4. The scientific study of pupil development should be promoted by the refocusing of information to be included on school records.

5. Greater attention should be given to everything that affects the child's physical development.

6. The school and home should cooperate to meet the natural interests and activities of the child.

7. The Progressive School should be a leader in educational movements. (*Progressive Education*, 1924, pp. 1–2)

What activity in your educational experience was the best example of creative self-expression? Was it intended as such by the teacher, or did it take place by accident?

The Progressive Education Association published a journal, *Progressive Education,* from 1924 to 1955. The journal became the forum for the educational opinions of its membership. In its early years *Progressive Education* devoted considerable space to the concept of "creative self-expression." According to Harold Rugg, professor at Teachers College, Columbia University and a leading spokesperson for the PEA, creative self-expression was the essence of the progressive education movement. In 1928, Rugg and Ann Schumaker published *The Child-Centered School*, an interpretive survey of progressive pedagogical innovations across the country (Cremin, 1962).

Another well-known spokesperson for progressive education, William H. Kilpatrick, was also on the faculty at Teachers College. Kilpatrick translated Dewey's philosophy into a practical methodology, the *project method*. The project method was an attempt to make education as "lifelike" as possible. At the heart of the educative process was to be "wholehearted purposeful activity," activity consistent with the child's own goals. Kilpatrick, while sharing Dewey's belief in the importance of problem-solving, went beyond Dewey in his child-centered emphasis and in his rejection of any organized subject matter (Cremin, 1962).

Higher Education

The influence of the progressive education movement was also felt in higher education. The great model of progressive higher education was the University of Wisconsin. The Wisconsin model was based on the idea that "the obligation of the university was to undertake leadership in the application of science to the improvement of the life of the citizenry in every domain" (Cremin, 1988, p. 246). This was to be accomplished through faculty research and service, the training of experts, and extended education.

College and university enrollments rose steadily during the pre–World War I years and then surged after the war, partly as a result of those who had come to higher education as part of the Student's Army Training Corps and then stayed after the war ended. Enrollments rose from almost 600,000 in 1919–20 to 1.1 million in 1929–30.

Most of these students were seeking a professional or technical education, primarily in education, business, and engineering, and enrolled not in the universities but in the growing number of junior colleges and the teacher education institutions. The number of junior colleges increased from 52 in 1920 to 277 in 1930, to 456 in 1940 (U.S. Bureau of the Census, 1975); the number of colleges for teachers grew from 45 in 1920 to four times that number by 1940 (Pulliam, 1987). The normal schools across the country were as typical of the progressive service orientation in higher education as the state universities: "they presumed to prepare scientifically trained experts; they extended their learning to all comers; and they prided themselves on their sensitivity to popular need" (Cremin, 1988, p. 248).

The Child Study Movement

During the first two decades of the twentieth century, as the progressive movement was gaining momentum, two other related movements were also taking place that would have far-reaching consequences—the child study and measurement movements. The child study movement began with the pioneering work of G. Stanley Hall. Hall established a center for applied psychology at Johns Hopkins University in 1884, the year Dewey graduated from the same institution. Later, as president of Clark University, he brought together the first group of scholars interested in the scientific study of the child through the careful observation of children at school or at play and at various stages of development (Pulliam, 1987).

Hall and his colleagues recognized that emotional growth and personality development were just as important as cognitive development in understanding the child. They saw the child as an evolving organism and believed that once educators understood how the child developed they would be better able to foster that development (Perkinson, 1977). These early efforts were important in laying the foundation for educational psychology and for the recognition and inclusion of this discipline in teacher education. Child study, the stage theory of learning propounded by theorists such as Jean Piaget, the specialties of child and adolescent psychology, as well as developmental psychology and the study of exceptional children, all owe their beginnings to Hall's work (Pulliam, 1987).

The Measurement Movement

Another cornerstone of educational psychology was laid by Lewis M. Terman, Edward L. Thorndike, and other psychologists involved in the development of the measurement movement. Although intelligence and aptitude tests had been in use for some time, the real breakthrough came when the French psychologists Alfred Binet and Theodore Simon developed an instrument based on an intelligence scale that allowed comparison of individual intelligence to a norm. Of the many adaptations of the Binet-Simon scale the most important for education was the so-called Stanford revision by Lewis Terman of Stanford University. It was also Terman who developed the *intelligence quotient* (IQ), a number indicating the level of an individual's mental development. Meanwhile, Thorndike and his students at Columbia developed scales for measuring achievement in arithmetic, spelling, reading, language, and other areas (Cremin, 1962).

World War I was a major factor in the growth of the measuring movement. The military needed a massive mobilization of manpower. It also needed a way to determine which men were suited for service and for what type of service. Out of this need a number of group intelligence tests were developed and ultimately were administered to hundreds of thousands of recruits.

One unexpected result of this massive testing was the discovery of a large number of young men with educational (as well as physical) deficiencies: approximately one-quarter of all recruits were judged illiterate. Deficiencies were particularly high among rural youth.

Have you ever taken a test that you felt was biased in terms of race, ethnicity, or gender? What positive benefits have you gained from taking national standardized tests?

Within a decade of the end of the war, the measurement movement had become a permanent part of American education. According to Heffernan (1968), the "apparent objectivity of the test results had a fascination for school administrators and teachers. Certainty seemed somehow to attach to these mathematically expressed comparisons of pupil achievement" (p. 229). Throughout the country students were classified, assigned, and compared on the basis of tests. Often the tests were used wisely to diagnose learning difficulties and assess individual differences. Unfortunately, they were also used to make comparisons without consideration of differences in school populations, to make judgments about the quality of teaching, and most distressing, to make subjective judgments about students' potential (Heffernan, 1968). Regrettably, these misuses of tests continue today.

Education During the Great Depression

The crash of the stock market in October 1929 ushered in the greatest depression our nation has ever experienced. The period was marked by the failure of banks and businesses, the closing of factories, mass unemployment, bread lines, soup kitchens, and tent cities. Unemployment was particularly high among minorities and young people. As many as 6,000,000 young people were out of school and unemployed in 1933–35. Many had no occupational training or experience. In a labor market overrun with experienced workers, they had few opportunities for employment (National Policies Commission, 1941).

The Depression also had a serious impact on the operation of schools. In many states, especially in the hard-pressed South and Southwest, schools were closed or the school year shortened. In school districts throughout the land local school boards were unable to pay their teachers and issued them promissory notes agreeing to pay them when revenues were collected. And in almost every school district the number of teachers was reduced, class size increased, and the number of courses in the high school curriculum cut (Gutek, 1986).

Until the Great Depression the relationship of the federal government to education was clear: Education was viewed as a function of the states and local school districts. These entities were responsible for operating educational programs. Beginning in 1933 with the creation of the Civilian Conservation Corps (CCC) and later the National Youth Administration (NYA), this established relationship changed markedly. The CCC and the NYA were two of the federal emergency agencies created under President Roosevelt's New Deal to provide "work relief" for the unemployed. The CCC provided temporary work for over 2 million people 18–25 years of age on various conservation projects, including reforestation, wildlife preservation, flood control, and forest fire prevention. The NYA administered two programs, a work relief and employment program for needy out of school youth aged 16–25, and a program that provided part-time employment to needy high school and college students to help them continue their education. At its peak in 1939–40 approximately 750,000 students in 1,750 colleges and 28,000 secondary schools participated in NYA programs.

When it became clear to officials of both the CCC and the NYA that many of the participants lacked not only vocational skills but basic skills in reading, writing, and arithmetic, they moved to meet those needs by means of educational activities operated and controlled by the agencies themselves. In time Congress changed the authorizing language of each agency to include an educational function. Although both these measures were terminated as the war economy stimulated employment, the fact that the federal government actually operated and controlled educational activities that could have been offered by state or local educational systems marked a departure from the past that was of concern to many educators, including the National Education Association (National Policies Commission, 1941).

Other New Deal programs provided relief to the financially depressed schools. The Public Works Administration (PWA) provided assistance for the building of numerous public buildings, including almost 13,000 schools. The Works Projects Administration (WPA) provided employment for teachers in adult education, art education, and nursery schools. Under a program that became the forerunner of the National School Lunch Program, the Department of Agriculture distributed surplus foods to the schools.

What effects do pronounced economic upswings and downswings have on the public schools and colleges and universities?

The Civilian Conservation Corps offered youth both employment and educational opportunities.

Indian New Deal

Several New Deal measures were directed at improving the plight of Native Americans and became known as the Indian New Deal. The Indian New Deal was an attempt to remedy the conditions described by the Meriam Report. Among the actions taken was the cessation of the sale of allotted Indian land, the organization of tribal councils as legal bodies, the investment of the Bureau of Indian Affairs with the right to contract with states for educational services, and the ending of the boarding school system (although because of distance constraints several off-reservation boarding schools still exist). The Johnson-O'Malley Act of 1934 provided supplemental funds to public schools to provide for the special needs of transportation, school lunches, or other expenses, such as those associated with graduation (Kidwell & Swift, 1976).

Native American education was also the beneficiary of other programs of Roosevelt's New Deal—the Works Projects Administration, the Public Works Administration, and the Civilian Conservation Corps—as they provided job training, income, and improvements on the reservations, including construction of schools and roads and conservation of land, water, and timber. The total result of the New Deal was "the most dynamic program of Indian education in the history of the Indian Service" with a "curriculum more suited to the needs of the child; . . . community day schools and a decreased emphasis on boarding schools; and a better qualified faculty and staff" (Szasz, 1977, p. 48).

George C. Counts and the John Dewey Society

The experience of the Depression had a significant impact on many progressive educators who came to believe that the schools had a responsibility to redress social injustices. At the 1932 convention of the Progressive Education Association, in an address entitled "Dare Progressive Education Be Progressive," George C. Counts challenged the child-centered doctrine and called on educators to focus less on the child and more on society, to "face squarely and courageously every social issue, come to grips with life in all its stark reality . . . develop a realistic and comprehensive theory of welfare, fashion a compelling and challenging vision of human destiny . . ." (Perkinson, 1977). In effect, Counts asked the schools to take the lead in planning for an intelligent reconstruction of society. Although the *social reconstructionism* movement never gained much of a foothold in American education, it served to associate progressive education in the minds of many people with "an economic radicalism that smacked of socialism and communism" and ultimately contributed to its growing unpopularity in the postwar years (Spring, 1976).

Counts was joined in his deep concern about socioeconomic conditions in America and his belief that educators should do something to address them by liberal progressive educators such as William H. Kilpatrick and Harold Rugg. In 1935 these individuals joined with other social reformers to form the John Dewey Society for the Study of Education and Culture and began publishing a journal, *The Social Frontier,* which became the focus of educational extremism during the 1930s. The position of Counts and his contemporaries was sharply criticized by many conservative progressives and was responsible for a deepening schism within the Progressive Education Association.

The Eight Year Study

During this same period a significant study was being conducted by the Progressive Education Association. The Eight Year Study (1932–1940) involved 30 high schools willing to experiment with their curriculum to discover the effectiveness of progressive educational approaches in preparing students for college. The results, published in 1942, showed that students from progressive high schools not only achieved higher than students from traditional high schools, but also were better adjusted socially.

Turning Tides

Although progressive education and innovations such as the community school and the project method were popular, protests against the child-centered ideal and its lack of emphasis on fundamentals gained momentum under another professor of education at Teachers College, William Bagley, and other educators associated with *essentialism* (Pulliam, 1987). The essentialists believed that the basic function of education should be to preserve and transmit those skills, arts, and sciences that have endured through time and are necessary for the continuation of civilization. Like Arthur Bestor in the 1950s and the reform reports in the 1980s, Bagley looked at American education and judged it to be weak, lacking in rigor, full of "frills," and inadequate in preparing youth for productive participation in society. The essentialists were also critical of the social reconstructionists and argued that instead of attempting to reconstruct society, educators would serve society better by preparing citizens who possessed the knowledge of the fundamental skills and subjects that provide a basis for understanding and for the collective thought and judgment essential to the operation of our democratic institutions (Bagley, 1938).

The Influence of War

As the war with Nazi Germany spread in Europe and American factories increasingly were called on to supply the Allied war effort, the American economy began to recover from the Depression. Once this country entered the war, every institution, including the schools, was dominated by the war effort (see Figure 5.1). According to a statement made by the National Education Association shortly after the attack on Pearl Harbor:

> When the schools closed on Friday, December 5, they had many purposes and they followed many roads to achieve those purposes. When the schools opened on Monday, December 8, they had but one dominant purpose—complete, intelligent, and enthusiastic cooperation in the war effort. (Education Policies Commission, 1942, p. 3)

Figure 5.1: A War Policy for American Schools, A Statement of the Educational Policies Commission of the National Educational Association

The responsibilities of organized education for the successful outcome of the war involve at least the following activities:

- Training workers for war industries and services.

- Producing goods and services needed for the war.

- Conserving materials by prudent consumption and salvage.

- Helping to raise funds to finance the war.

- Increasing effective manpower by correcting educational deficiencies.

- Promoting health and physical efficiency.

- Protecting school children and property against attack.

- Protecting the ideals of democracy against war hazards.

- Teaching the issues, aims, and progress of war and the peace.

- Sustaining the morale of children and adults.

- Maintaining intelligent loyalty to American democracy.

Source: Educational Policies Commission. (1942). *A war policy for American schools.* Washington, DC: National Education Association.

Impact on Schools

The war had a heavy impact on the schools. Not only did large numbers of teachers leave the classroom for the battlefield, but enrollment dropped significantly as youth chose not to return to school or to go to work. High school enrollments declined from 6.7 million in 1941 to 5.5 million in 1944 (Knight, 1952). In addition, financial support, already low because of the Depression, was further reduced as funds were diverted from education to other purposes. Some assistance was provided by the Lanham Act of 1941 to school districts overburdened by an influx of children from families employed in defense industries or on military bases. The so-called "impact aid" continues today under the provisions of Public Laws 815 and 874.

Colleges and universities were also affected by the war. Enrollments declined sharply; the enrollment of civilian students was cut almost in half between 1940 and 1944. There was also a severe reduction in instructional staff and revenues. Institutional income in 1944 and 1945 was only 67% of what it had been in 1940 (Knight, 1952). Income would have been reduced even more dramatically had it not been for the large research projects commissioned by the federal government. These vast research enterprises transformed many universities into what Clark Kerr has termed "federal grant universities" (Kerr, 1963).

Colleges and universities also played a vital role in preparing men for military service, for war industries, and for essential civilian activities. By the end of 1943, 380,000 men were involved in specialized training in 489 colleges and universities, many as part of the Army Specialized Training Program and the Navy College Training Program (Knight, 1952).

What is your position in the current debate about the appropriateness of ROTC on college and university campuses?

The Postwar Years

Toward the end of the war, in an effort to assist veterans whose schooling had been interrupted by military service, the Servicemen's Readjustment Act of 1944 was passed. The G.I. Bill of Rights, as it became known, provided benefits to 7.8 million veterans of World War II to help them further their education. The benefits subsequently were extended to veterans of the Korean, "Cold," and Vietnam wars; eventually almost 15 million veterans were involved. The G.I. Bill also initiated a great postwar popularization of higher education. More men and women representing a greater age range and social, economic, cultural and racial groups attended colleges and universities than ever before (Cremin, 1988) (see Table 5.2).

In addition, while returning servicemen filled college and university classrooms after the war, within a decade the postwar "baby boom" hit the public schools. Between 1946 and 1956 kindergarten and elementary school enrollments increased 37%, from 17.7 million to 24.3 million (U.S. Bureau of the Census, 1975).

Life Adjustment Education

In the postwar years progressive education came under major criticism by those who held it responsible for the decline in educational standards in this

Table 5.2: Institutions of Higher Education, Faculty, and Enrollments, 1919–20 to 1986–87			
	1919–20	**1929–30**	**1939–40**	**1949–50**
Total institutions	1,041	1,409	1,708	1,851
Total faculty	48,615	82,386	146,929	245,722
Total enrollment	597,880	1,100,737	1,494,203	2,659,021

country. By the 1950s it had become identified with an educational program known as *life adjustment education.* Life adjustment education was introduced in 1945 at a vocational education conference sponsored by the U.S. Office of Education. Fully supported by this office and spurred on by a series of conferences, state and national commissions, and numerous publications, it was seen by many as a natural outgrowth of progressive education. Focusing on that majority of youth who do not attend college, life adjustment education stressed functional objectives such as vocation and health and rejected traditional academic studies. In many ways life adjustment education was indistinguishable from many other versions of progressive education already well established in schools across the country (Ravitch, 1983).

Critics of progressive education found in life adjustment education a perfect target: "it continued an abundance of slogans, jargon, and various anti-intellectualism; it carried the utilitarianism and group conformism of latter-day progressivism to its ultimate trivialization" (Ravitch, 1983, p. 70). The outpouring of criticism, coming at the same time as the teacher shortage and the onset of the baby boom, made it clear that the schools were in the middle of a crisis that could not be ignored. Throughout most of the 1950s the "crisis in education" and the debate over contemporary practices filled the pages of national journals (Ravitch, 1983).

The Critics and the Decline of Progressive Education

One of the foremost critics of progressive education at this time was Arthur Bestor. In his most famous critical study, *Educational Wastelands,* Bestor deplored the anti-intellectual quality of American schools, which he argued had been caused by progressive education. Bestor advocated a rigorous curriculum of well-defined subject matter disciplines and the development of the intellect as the primary goal of education. Bestor later became one of the founders of the Council on Basic Education, an organization dedicated to the promotion of a basic academic curriculum. Two other leading critics of the contemporary educational scene were former Harvard president James Conant and Admiral Hyman Rickover. Their criticisms foreshadowed the back to basics movement of the 1970s.

But in the end it was not its critics that killed progressive education. It died because it was no longer relevant to the time. The great debate about Amer-

1959–60	1969–70	1979–80	1986–87
2,008	2,525	3,152	3,406
380,554	450,000	675,000	722,000
8,639,847	8,004,660	11,569,899	12,504,501

Source: U.S. Department of Education, National Center for Education Statistics. (1989). *Digest of Education Statistics 1989* (Table 147). Washington, DC: U.S. Government Printing Office.

ican education continued until 1957 when the Soviet Union launched Sputnik, the first space satellite. Then, in a nation suddenly concerned with intelligence and the need for increased science and mathematics skills, progressive education seemed out of step. By the time it disappeared in the mid-1950s it had strayed far from the "humane, pragmatic, open-minded" approach proposed by Dewey,

> though surely the influence of its pioneers was present whenever projects, activities, and pupil experiences had been intelligently integrated into subject-matter teaching, wherever concern for health and vocation had gained a permanent place in the school program, and whenever awareness of individual differences among children had replaced lockstep institution and rote memorization. (Ravitch, 1983, p. 80)

Table 5.3 lists the contributions of major figures from the progressive era to American educational history.

Sputnik and After

Few times in history has a single event had such an impact on education as the launching of Sputnik in October 1957. The event seemed to confirm the growing fear that the United States was losing in the Cold War technological and military races with the Soviet Union because of a shortage of trained teachers, engineers, and students.

Curriculum Reforms

Reacting to public pressures, in 1958 the federal government passed the National Defense Education Act (NDEA). By directing significant federal funding to specific curricular areas, particularly mathematics, science, and modern foreign languages, the federal government for the first time attempted to influence the curriculum in general elementary and secondary education. The NDEA sponsored the efforts of academic specialists engaged in large-scale projects to revise the curriculum according to the latest theories

Table 5.3: They Made It Happen: Important Figures from the Progressive Era in American Educational History

Francis W. Parker (1837–1902)	Principal of Cook County Normal School in Chicago (1883–1896) and director of the University of Chicago School of Education (1901–1902). Began progressive education movement.
John Dewey (1859–1952)	Noted philosopher and educator. Advanced philosophy that became known as pragmatism or progressivism. Provided intellectual foundation and rationale for the progressive education movement.
Harold Rugg (1886–1960)	One of the founders and leading spokespersons of the Progressive Education Association. Leader in social reconstructionist movement.
William H. Kilpatrick (1871–1965)	Professor at Teachers College, Columbia University (1909–1938). Leader of progressive education movement and the Progressive Education Association. Originator of the project method.
G. Stanley Hall (1844–1924)	Psychologist, professor (taught Dewey) and president of Clark University (1889–1919). Founder of the child study movement. Important in providing foundation for the fields of child and adolescent psychology and the study of exceptional children.
Lewis M. Terman (1877–1956)	Pioneer in the measurement movement. Developed Stanford-Binet test using the intelligence quotient (IQ), a measure of mental development.
Edward L. Thorndike (1874–1949)	Experimental psychologist. Major early contributor to the measurement movement and educational psychology. Developed instruments to measure achievement in a number of academic areas.
George C. Counts (1889–1974)	President of the American Federation of Teachers (1934–1942). Professor at Teachers College, Columbia University (1927–1956). Critic of the child-centeredness of progressive education.
William Bagley (1874–1946)	Educator and theorist. Critic of progressive education. Founder and spokesperson for the essentialist movement.
Arthur Bestor (1879–1944)	Pioneer in adult education in U.S. President of the Chautauqua Institution. Critic of progressive education. Cofounder of Council on Basic Education.

If a major federal initiative such as the NDEA were being considered to fund programs to meet today's educational demands, what specific programs would you recommend be funded?

and methods. Soon the "new math," "new chemistry," "new grammar," and other "new" revisions were being developed and introduced in the schools. Summer institutes were held for teachers to train them in the use of the new materials and methods. The NDEA also provided funding for science, mathematics, and foreign language laboratories; media and other instructional material; and improvement of guidance, counseling, and testing programs, especially those efforts directed at identification and encouragement of more capable students. Student loans and graduate fellowships were also funded under the NDEA.

The curriculum reforms initiated by the NDEA of 1958 and an expanded version of that act in 1964 were further stimulated by James Conant's widely publicized study of secondary education, *The American High School Today* (1959), which recommended increased rigor and an academic core of English, mathematics, science, and the social sciences. Underlying these curricular reforms was the learning theory of Jerome Bruner, which stressed the teaching of the structure of the disciplines (i.e., the major concepts and methods of inquiry of the discipline) and the stage concept of child development formulated by Jean Piaget. According to Bruner some form of the structure of a discipline could be taught to students at each stage of their cognitive development. These theories gave credence to the *spiral curriculum* sequencing pattern whereby subject matter is presented over a number of grades with increasing complexity and abstraction.

The NDEA set the stage for the federal government's increased involvement in education. In the decade that followed, the federal government waged another war in which it became, for perhaps the first time in our nation's history, a major force in the educational arena. This war was the War on Poverty.

Education and the War on Poverty

In the early 1960s large numbers of Americans became aware that at least one-quarter of the population had been bypassed by the postwar prosperity and lived in dire poverty. The results were rising crime rates, a decline in qualified manpower for military service, and a number of other social and economic problems. Books, reports, and high-impact media coverage such as Edward R. Murrow's documentary on migrant farm workers, "Harvest of Shame," brought a flood of interest in the elimination of poverty. As a result, the Democratic administrations of John F. Kennedy in 1963 and Lyndon B. Johnson in 1964 declared a War on Poverty. In an effort to win the war, federal legislation was passed to subsidize low-income housing, improve health care, expand welfare services, provide job retraining, undertake regional planning in depressed areas such as Appalachia, and improve inner city schools (Church & Sedlak, 1976).

Education was viewed as a major factor in the elimination of poverty. Poor children as well as those of certain minority groups, it was noted, consistently failed to achieve. In the optimistic view of many politicians, social scientists, and educators, the "cultural deprivation" (i.e., lack of middle-class attitudes and incomes) of the poor was attributable to a lack of education, and if the poor were provided the skills and education for employment they could achieve middle-class economic and social status and break the "cycle of poverty" (Zigler & Valentine, 1979).

Federal Education Legislation

The War on Poverty on the education front was waged by a number of initiatives. The Vocational Education Act of 1963 more than quadrupled federal funds for vocational education. The purpose of the act was to enhance occupational training opportunities for persons of all ages through the provision of financial assistance to vocational and technical programs in high schools and nonbaccalaureate postsecondary institutions. The Manpower Development and Training Act, enacted the same year, was directed at providing retraining for unemployed adults.

Presidents Johnson and Kennedy declared a war on poverty, using education as a major weapon in the fight.

The Economic Opportunity Act (EOA) of 1964 established the Job Corps to train youth between 16 and 21 in basic literacy skills and for employment, and also established a type of domestic Peace Corps, Volunteers in Service to America (VISTA). Perhaps the most popular and controversial component of the EOA was Project Head Start, a program aimed at disadvantaged children three to five years old who would not normally attend preschool or kindergarten. President Johnson called Head Start a "landmark," not only in education but in "the maturity of our democracy." Head Start, he foretold, would "strike at the basic cause of poverty" by addressing it at its beginnings—the disadvantaged preschool child. As the name suggests, the intent of the program was to give disadvantaged children a head start in the educational race so that once in school they might be on equal terms with children from nondisadvantaged homes. The Head Start Program, while perhaps not living up to all President Johnson's expectations, has proven since its initiation in 1965 to be the most successful of the compensatory education programs.

The major piece of educational legislation enacted as part of the War on Poverty was the Elementary and Secondary Education Act of 1965 (ESEA). The most far-reaching piece of federal education legislation to date, the ESEA provided over $1 billion in federal funds to education. Although it was directed at specific programs, populations, and purposes, it represented more general aid than previous federal aid programs.

The ESEA included five major sections or titles. The largest, receiving about 80% of the funds, was Title I (now Chapter 1), which provided assistance to local school districts for the education of children from low-income families. The compensatory education programs funded through Title I were intended to maintain the educational progress begun in Head Start. Title I was to become the major education component of the War on Poverty (Spring, 1976). Other sections of the ESEA provided funds for library resources, textbooks, and instructional materials; supplemental education centers; educational research and training; and strengthening state departments of education. The act was expanded in 1966 and 1967 to include programs for Native American children, children of migrant workers, the handicapped (Title VI) and children with limited English-speaking ability (Title VII).

In the same year that the ESEA was passed, Congress passed the Higher Education Act, which provided direct assistance to institutes of higher education for facilities construction and library and instructional improvement, as well as loans and scholarships to students. The year 1965 also saw the establishment of the National Foundation of the Arts and the Humanities to promote and encourage production, dissemination, and scholarship in the arts and humanities.

In 1967 the Educational Professions Development Act was signed into law by President Johnson. In 1968, the last year of Johnson's Great Society, the Vocational Education Act was expanded and its funding authorization doubled. In addition, the Higher Education Act was amended to consolidate previous legislation involving higher education and a number of new program initiatives.

Between the years 1963 and 1969 Congress passed more than two dozen major pieces of legislation affecting education. These laws dramatically increased federal involvement in education and provided vast sums of money for elementary and secondary schools, vocational schools, colleges and universities. In 1963–1964 federal funds for elementary and secondary schools totaled almost $900 million. By 1968–1969 this had rocketed to $3 billion, and the federal government's share of the financing of education had risen from 4.4% to 8.8%. Perhaps equally as important as the increased funding was the shift in emphasis from identifying the gifted, which had marked the 1950s, to a concern for the disadvantaged.

Have you been a beneficiary of any federally sponsored educational program? What educational benefits did you receive from this participation?

The Civil Rights Movement

The Brown Decision

The schools not only were given a major role in the War on Poverty, they became a stage for much of the drama of the civil rights movement. The *Brown v. Board of Education of Topeka* decision of 1954, which ordered an end to legalized segregation in education, stated that segregated educational facilities are inherently unequal and generate a feeling of inferiority that affects the child's motivation to learn. However, instead of being the climax of the struggle for racial equality in education, *Brown* marked the beginning of the civil rights revolution. Although the civil rights movement began with blacks, perhaps because the basic vision of what was wrong was most visible in the history of blacks in America, the general principles of the movement were later applied to advancing the rights of women, racial and ethnic groups, the aged, and the handicapped (Sowell, 1984).

The *Brown* decision met with massive nationwide resistance in the form of legal maneuvers and violence, resulting in countless confrontations between federal authorities who sought to enforce the law and local police or citizens who sought to obstruct it. The most dramatic physical confrontations occurred

> in 1957 when President Eisenhower sent federal troops to Little Rock to insure that black students were safely enrolled, over the objections of the state's governor, in Central High School; in 1962 when large numbers of federal marshals were required to force James Meredith's enrollment at the University of Mississippi over the objections of the state authorities, an incident in which two lives were lost; and in 1963 when President Kennedy nationalized the Alabama National Guard to enforce the integration at the state university. (Church & Sedlak, 1976, p. 446)

At the same time that school desegregation was making limited progress (see Chapter 9 for a discussion of desegregation), the civil rights movement was gaining momentum on other fronts. Freedom rides, sit-ins, boycotts, and other forms of nonviolent protest both appealed to the national conscience and focused national attention on a movement that would not be denied. President John F. Kennedy pressed for the passage of a federal civil rights statute that would end segregation in public facilities, attack discrimination in employment, and require nondiscriminatory practices in programs and institutions receiving federal funds. Five days after his assassination, his successor, Lyndon B. Johnson, appeared before Congress and sought its passage, declaring it the most fitting honor of his memory. The Civil Rights Act of 1964, when passed, became one of the most significant pieces of social legislation in the United States in this century (Spring, 1976).

The Civil Rights Act and Desegregation

To what do you attribute the increase in the number of incidences of racial violence in the schools and on college and university campuses?

The Civil Rights Act of 1964 further involved the federal government in the activities of the schools. Title VI of the Act prohibits discrimination against students on the basis of race, color, or national origin in all institutions receiving federal funds. Title VII forbids discrimination in employment based on race, religion, national origin, or—as of 1972—sex. The act authorized the withholding of federal funds from any institution or agency violating the law. It also authorized the U.S. attorney general to take legal action to achieve school desegregation and provided federal financial assistance to school districts attempting to desegregate.

The passage of the Civil Rights Act of 1964 and the education acts of 1965 combined with the growing intolerance of the Supreme Court to the resistance to the *Brown* decision to create a "carrot-and-stick" mechanism that dramatically increased the pace of school desegregation. Federal expenditures for education, including higher education, increased from $4.5 billion in 1966, to $8.8 billion in 1970, to $13.4 billion in 1974, to $19.5 billion in 1983 —"thus the carrot; and the Supreme Court continued to strike down devices for evading school desegregation—thus the stick" (Cremin, 1988, p. 264). As detailed in Chapter 9, in a series of decisions between 1968 and 1972 the Supreme Court struck down *de jure* segregation in the South and *de facto* segregation in the North.

Further Advances

The civil rights movement in education also made advances on other fronts. Previously, instruction in most schools was given only in English. In the 1960s attention was turned to the growing Hispanic population of the large cities and states outside the Southwest. In 1968 the Bilingual Education Act was passed, which gave federal funds to school districts to provide bilingual education to low-income students with limited English proficiency. Additional support for bilingual education was provided by the 1974 *Lau v. Nichols* decision by the Supreme Court, which said that schools must provide special language programs for non-English-speaking children. In response, Congress passed the Bilingual Education Act of 1974, which provided for bilingual education for *all* children with limited English ability as a means of promoting educational equity (Cremin, 1988). At the same time, the Indian Education Act of 1972 and the Indian Self-Determination and Education Assistance Act of 1975 expanded the rights of Native Americans in regard to the education of their youth, and sought to ensure increased educational opportunity for those youth.

Title IX of the 1972 Education Amendments, which prohibited discrimination against employees and students in educational programs receiving federal funds, was a major victory in the extension of the civil rights movement to women. And in 1975, the landmark Education for All Handicapped Children Act established the right of all handicapped children to a free and appropriate education. Each of these topics is covered in greater detail in later chapters.

Social Unrest

The late 1960s and 1970s also saw a series of urban riots and the sometimes passive, sometimes violent student rights and anti-Vietnam War movements, which began with protests on college campuses but often spilled into the streets. Both movements tended to have a negative impact on the civil rights movement through a subliminal process of guilt by association. Many members of academia as well as the larger society became disenchanted with the civil rights movement, "not because they disagreed with or were unsympathetic to its legitimate claim, but because the Student Rights Movement, which they strongly opposed, got its impetus, simulation, and example from the Civil Rights Movement" (Tollett, 1983, p. 57). A campaign against demonstrations and riots and for the restoration of law and order helped put Richard Nixon in the White House in 1969 and reelect him in 1972.

During the 1980s the civil rights movement was slowed considerably by the actions of both the courts (see Chapters 9 and 12) and the Reagan administration. The budget of the Office of Civil Rights was cut, investigations were "cursory," and enforcement and compliance were loosened. The Department of Justice not only seemed uninterested in enforcing civil rights plans, it attempted to block efforts to broaden the scope of civil rights and to strengthen affirmation action. The current status of the various civil rights interests (e.g., desegregation, discrimination, education of minority and special populations) is discussed elsewhere in this text.

The 1970s: Retreat and Retrenchment

During the Nixon administration (1969–1974) support for many of the initiatives begun during the Kennedy and Johnson administrations was reduced. The hallmark of the Republican administrations of the 1970s and 1980s was transfer of responsibility for domestic programs from the federal government to state and local governments (see Table 5.4). However, the 1970s did witness increased attention to the needs of handicapped persons. The Vocational Rehabilitation Act of 1973 sought to increase the physical access of handicapped persons to educational institutions and vocational training and employment. And during the Ford administration (1974–1977) the Education for All Handicapped Children Act of 1975 (now the Individuals with Disabilities Education Act) was enacted (see Chapter 9).

Under the Carter administration (1977–1981) the federal education budget was increased, from 8.8% of the total elementary and secondary revenues in 1977 when Carter took office, to 9.8% in 1980, his last year in office (see Table 5.4). Under his administration a Department of Education was established. Keeping his campaign promise to the National Education Association, Carter was able to overcome congressional opposition and in 1979 legislation was passed to elevate the Office of Education to department status, making its secretary a member of the president's cabinet. Carter appointed Shirley Hufstadler, a federal appeals court judge, as the first secretary of education. The appointment of a federal judge was indicative of the Carter administration's commitment to enforcing legislation directed at protecting civil rights and promoting equality of educational opportunity (Ravitch, 1983).

The 1970s was a decade marked by economic uncertainty. Presidents Nixon, Ford, and Carter fought unsuccessfully to curb inflation, reduce unemployment, reduce the federal deficit, and reduce the imbalance of foreign trade. The impacts of rapid inflation and the energy crisis (resulting from the oil embargo of the United States by the Organization of Petroleum Exporting Countries in 1973) were sorely felt by the schools. At the same time that operating costs were spiraling and the salary demands of teachers hurt by inflation were becoming more strident, revenues were declining.

The decline in revenues was a result of two forces: (1) the "revolt" of taxpayers against rising taxes, especially property taxes, which are the major source of tax revenues for the schools, and (2) a decline in enrollments, which

Table 5.4: Public Elementary and Secondary School Revenues, by Source, 1940–1987 (in thousands of dollars)

School Year Ending	Federal Amount	Federal Percent of Total	State Amount	State Percent of Total	Local Amount	Local Percent of Total	Total
1940	39,810	1.8	684,354	30.3	1,536,363	68.0	2,260,527
1950	155,848	2.9	2,165,689	39.8	3,115,507	57.3	5,437,044
1952	227,711	3.5	2,478,596	38.6	3,717,507	57.9	6,423,816
1954	355,237	4.5	2,944,103	37.4	4,567,512	58.1	7,866,852
1956	441,442	4.6	3,828,886	39.5	5,416,350	55.9	9,686,677
1958	486,484	4.0	4,800,368	39.4	6,894,661	56.6	12,181,513
1960	651,639	4.4	5,768,047	39.1	8,326,932	56.5	14,746,618
1962	760,975	4.3	6,789,190	38.7	9,977,542	56.9	17,527,707
1964	896,956	4.4	8,078,014	39.3	11,569,213	56.3	20,544,182
1966	1,996,954	7.9	9,920,219	39.1	13,439,686	53.0	25,356,858
1968	2,806,469	8.8	12,275,536	38.5	16,821,063	52.7	31,903,064
1970	3,219,557	8.0	16,062,776	39.9	20,984,589	52.1	40,266,923
1971	3,753,461	8.4	17,552,566	39.4	23,205,265	52.1	44,511,292
1972	4,467,969	8.9	19,133,256	38.3	26,402,420	52.8	50,003,645
1973	4,525,000	8.7	20,843,520	40.0	26,749,412	51.3	52,117,930
1974	4,930,351	8.5	24,113,409	41.4	29,187,132	50.1	58,230,892
1975	5,811,595	9.0	27,211,116	42.2	31,422,528	48.8	64,445,239
1976	6,318,345	8.9	31,776,101	44.6	33,111,627	46.5	71,206,073
1977	6,629,498	8.8	32,688,903	43.4	36,004,134	47.8	75,322,532
1978	7,694,194	9.4	35,013,266	43.0	38,735,700	47.6	81,443,160
1979	8,600,116	9.8	40,132,136	45.6	39,261,891	44.6	87,994,143
1980	9,503,537	9.8	45,348,814	46.8	42,028,813	43.4	96,881,165
1981	9,768,262	9.2	50,182,659	47.4	45,998,166	43.4	105,949,087
1982	8,419,359	7.4	54,573,117	47.9	51,006,513	44.7	113,998,987
1983	8,623,079	7.1	57,557,593	47.7	54,578,820	45.2	120,759,492
1984	8,801,655	6.8	61,603,642	47.8	58,523,611	45.4	128,928,908
1985	9,282,798	6.7	69,138,507	49.0	62,588,260	44.4	141,009,565
1986	9,786,607	6.5	75,331,882	49.8	66,214,293	43.8	151,332,782
1987	9,958,558	6.2	80,433,129	50.0	70,516,575	43.8	160,908,262

Sources: U.S. Department of Education, Office of Educational Research and Improvement. (1986). *Department of educational statistics, 1985–1986* (p. 80). Washington, DC: Government Printing Office; National Education Association. (1987). *Estimates of school statistics, 1986–1987* (p. 21). West Haven, CT: National Education Association.

brought about a reduction in state revenues, since most states, to a large extent, base their aid to local school districts on enrollment. In 1971, for the first time since World War II, the total number of elementary and secondary students enrolled in the public schools declined (see Figure 5.2). This decline and its accompanying reduction in revenues led to various efforts to "trim the budget," including program cuts, teacher layoffs, and in extreme cases school closures.

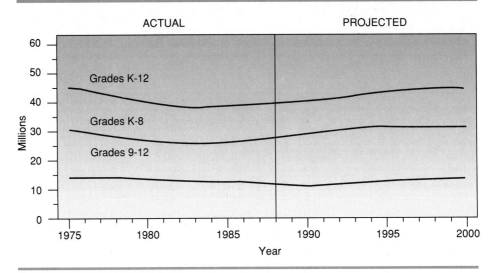

Figure 5.2: Enrollment in Public Elementary and Secondary Schools, by Grade Level, with Projections, Fall 1975–Fall 2000

Source: U.S. Dept. of Education, National Center for Education Statistics. (1989). *Projections of education statistics to 2000.* Washington, DC: U.S. Government Printing Office.

The Reagan Administration

The election of Ronald Reagan in 1980 brought a resurgence of conservatism in both politics and education. "Reaganomics," as his economic policy was called, involved lowering taxes to stimulate investment and reducing federal spending for social programs, including education. The Education Consolidation and Improvement Act of 1981 sought to consolidate the massive array of federal aid programs into several large block programs. However, Reagan's proposal for the entire block was less than what formerly had been spent for the ESEA alone. In fact, in every budget request made while he was in office, President Reagan proposed reductions in federal spending for education. Fortunately, Congress appropriated more than the president requested. Nonetheless, from fiscal years 1980 to 1989 federal funds for elementary and secondary education declined by 17%, and for higher education declined by 27% (U.S. Department of Education, 1989).

The 1980s also saw a renewal of public debate about the condition of American education. Where Sputnik and technological competition with the Russians had focused attention on the educational system in the 1950s, in the 1980s it was economic competition with the Japanese that brought the educational system into the forefront of public debate.

The decade of the 1980s saw the issuance of a number of national reports on the status of education, which echoed the criticisms of the 1950s (see Appendix B). Once again the schools were said to lack academic standards and rigor and to neglect intellectual training. Again there was a call for reform and a return to the basics. A major difference in the two periods is that the response of the federal government to the cry for reform was not massive legislation and an infusion of funds, but to define the reform agenda, promote school–business partnerships, and encourage state and local governments to initiate reform efforts.

Accepting the recommendations of the national reports and the rhetoric of the Reagan administration, the states have adopted a number of measures intended to improve the quality of both the teachers and the graduates of the nation's schools. In perhaps the most dramatic action thus far, Kentucky has proposed to replace the state department of education with an agency that provides assistance to schools but has no regulatory power; give school councils composed of parents, teachers, and principals the responsibility for hiring staff, deciding on curriculum, and setting disciplinary standards; and provide significant rewards or sanctions to schools based on student performance on state-imposed assessment measures. Minimum curricula standards, increased graduation requirements, testing of students, minimum academic standards for participation in athletics, increased emphasis on homework and study skills, testing of teachers, and merit pay for teachers (see the discussion of merit pay on page 167) are among the more popular initiatives adopted by other states. Each of these issues is discussed in other chapters of this text.

A Look Ahead

As the 1990s begin, a number of initiatives and issues dominate both the popular and the professional literature. The appropriate role of the schools in AIDS prevention continues to be an area of concern and controversy (see "For Future Reference" on page 168). Open enrollment plans, parental choice, voucher plans, school-based management, and teacher empowerment are being advanced as strategies to make the schools more accountable and efficient. *Restructuring*, the buzzword of the 1990s, refers to a number of prescriptions: year-round schools, longer school days and years, recast modes of governance, alternative funding patterns, all-out commitments to technology, and various combinations of these and other proposals (Kaplan, 1990).

For the first time in our nation's history, state and national leaders have joined in setting goals for the schools. The National Governors' Association and the Bush administration in early 1990 approved six education goals to be accomplished by the year 2000:

- *Readiness*—All children in America will start school ready to learn.

- *School completion*—The high school graduation rate will increase to at least 90%.

- *Student achievement and citizenship*—American students will leave grades 4, 8, and 12 having demonstrated competency over challenging subject matter including English, mathematics, science, history and geography.

- *Mathematics and science*—U.S. students will be first in the world in mathematics and science achievement.

- *Adult literacy*—Every adult American will be literate and will possess the knowledge and skills necessary to compete in a global economy and exercise the rights and responsibilities of citizenship.

- *Drug-free, safe, and disciplined schools*—Every school in America will be free of drugs and violence and will offer a disciplined environment conducive to learning.

At the same time, the recurring cycles of changing liberal and conservative values that have been observed in the broader society (Schlesinger, 1986) have led to the prediction that the 1990s will be marked by a more liberal national mood and that this mood will be reflected in education. It is predicted that during the Bush administration we will see a number of proposals that reflect a greater concern for social issues, a more progressive philosophy of education, and a desire for not only a "kinder and gentler America" but a "kinder and gentler school." Among these proposals are:

President Bush and the nation's governors approve the first ever national goals for education.

Controversial Issues:
Merit Pay

Several of the reform reports of the 1980s advocated merit pay for the teachers—that part or all of the teacher's pay be based on performance. The 1988 Gallup poll of the public's attitudes toward the public schools also showed support for merit pay. The 1989 poll of teachers, on the other hand, found them to be 2 to 1 against merit pay. The reasons often given in favor of or against merit pay are:

Reasons For

1. Merit pay would reward good teachers and provide the incentive for them to stay in education.

2. The public would be more willing to support the schools if they knew that teachers were paid according to merit.

3. Rewarding performance is consistent with the standard applied to other workers and professions.

4. Teachers would be encouraged to improve their performance and students would be the beneficiaries.

Reasons Against

1. There is little agreement about what is good teaching or how it should be evaluated.

2. Evaluation systems are often subjective and potentially inequitable.

3. Competition creates morale problems for people doing the same job.

4. There is no evidence that merit pay systems will improve the quality of education by improving teacher performance.

Why do you oppose or favor merit pay? Are you familiar with a school system where merit pay is in operation? What effect has merit pay had on education in that system?

- Efforts to recruit and promote female principals and superintendents.

- Proposals related to the empowerment of teachers and students.

- Curricular reforms that stress character development and the individuality of students.

- Instructional strategies designed to maximize cooperation, creativity, and the development of critical thinking skills and social responsibility.

- A stronger research focus on "whole-brain learning," dropout prevention, and learning styles.

- Efforts to improve school climate so that teaching and learning are more enjoyable.

- Greater emphasis on drug education, sex education, and global education.

- Increased use of differentiated staff, incentive pay plans, and alternative certification.

- More staff development activities in the areas of motivational techniques and multicultural awareness. (McDaniel, 1989, pp. 17–18)

For Future Reference:
Promoting Attitudes Conducive to AIDS Prevention Behavior

Every classroom teacher has some responsibility for AIDS education—not just the science teacher, the health teacher, the physical education teacher. An effective AIDS education program includes learning activities designed to foster attitudes that reinforce preventative behaviors—activities that can be a part of the curriculum of every classroom teacher.

Following are some learning experiences you might consider for future use in your classes (Yarber, 1987):

- Answering hypothetical letters from teenagers with questions about AIDS for a newspaper advice column.

- Role playing a discussion about AIDS prevention with a possible sex partner.

- Simulating a community task force that is developing a policy for dealing with students with AIDS in the school.

- Writing an editorial for the school or local newspaper on the need for AIDS education in the schools.

- Practicing using the AIDS National Hotline.

- Practicing problem solving by using a typical AIDS prevention problem faced by adolescents.

You can probably think of other activities. What is important is that the activities provide opportunities for students to engage in problem solving and decision making and practice health-promoting skills.

The final chapter of this text presents a more detailed look at the future of education.

Summary

Much of the history of education in this century can be seen in terms of a swing from one view of education to another. The progressive education movement, which began at the turn of the century and continued to gain popularity through the 1930s, gave way in the post–World War II years to a more conservative view of the purpose of education, which was a response to a perceived decline in the nation's technological supremacy. In the 1960s the tide turned again in favor of a more liberal and child-centered approach and schools became a vital weapon in the War on Poverty.

The late 1970s and 1980s once again saw a renewed interest in basics and a national cry for reform of the entire educational system. Signs that the cycle is beginning to change are already evident, leading a number of educators and social scientists to predict that the 1990s will be marked by a return to a more progressive orientation in an attempt to create "kinder, gentler schools." Other predictions about the future of education are found in Chapter 18. Before that, however, we will turn our attention to a number of topics, including an exploration of the major philosophies of education in Chapter 6.

Key Terms

Child-centered curriculum
Essentialism
Intelligence quotient
Life adjustment education
Project method

Restructuring
Social reconstructionism
Spiral curriculum
Subject-centered curriculum

Discussion Questions

1. What criteria did you use in deciding what artifacts to include in your "time room" or video on the history of education?

2. Compare the high school curricula of 1930, 1960, and 1990.

3. Describe the impact of the two world wars on American higher education.

4. To what extent have the schools either changed society or adapted to changes in society in this century?

5. Trace the changing involvement of the federal government in education in the twentieth century. What has been the impact of declining federal financial support?

6. What have been the most significant positive and negative changes in education during your lifetime? What changes/reforms do you think need to be made?

References

Bagley, W. C. (1938). An essentialist platform for the advancement of American education. *Educational Administration and Supervision, 24*, 241–56.

Bonner, T. N. (1963). *Our recent past: American civilization in the twentieth century.* Englewood Cliffs, NJ: Prentice-Hall.

Brown vs. Board of Education, 347 U.S. 463 (1954).

Church, R. L., & Sedlak, M. W. (1976). *Education in the United States.* New York: The Face Press.

Conant, J. B. (1959). *The American high school today.* New York: McGraw-Hill.

Cremin, L. A. (1962). *The transformation of the school.* New York: Alfred A. Knopf.

Cremin, L. A. (1988). *American education: The metropolitan experience, 1876–1980.* New York: Harper & Row.

Education Policies Commission. (1942). *A war policy for American schools.* Washington, DC: National Education Association.

Gray, R., & Peterson, J. M. (1974). *Economic development of the United States.* Homewood, IL: Richard D. Irwin.

Gutek, G. L. (1986). *Education in the United States: An historical perspective.* Englewood Cliffs, NJ: Prentice-Hall.

Heffernan, H. (1968). The school curriculum in American education. In *Education in the states: Nationwide development.* Washington, DC: Council of Chief State School Officials.

Kaplan, G. (1990). Pushing and shoving in videoland U.S.A.: TV's version of education (and what to do about it). *Phi Delta Kappan, 71,* K11–K12.

Kidwell, C. S., & Swift, D. W. (1976). Indian education. In D. W. Swift (Ed.), *American education: A sociological view.* Boston: Houghton Miffin.

Kirkland, E. C. (1969). *A history of American economic life* (4th ed.). New York: Appleton-Century-Crofts.

Knight, E. W. (1952). *Fifty years of American education.* New York: The Ronald Press.

McDaniel, T. R. (1989). Demilitarizing public education: School reform in the era of George Bush. *Phi Delta Kappan, 71,* 15–18.

National Policies Commission. (1941). *The Civilian Conservation Corps, the National Youth Administration, and the public schools.* Washington, DC: National Education Association.

Perkinson, H. J. (1977). *The imperfect panacea: American faith in education, 1965–1976* (2d ed.). New York: Random House.

Progressive Education. (1924). 1, 2.

Pulliam, J. D. (1987). *History of education in America* (4th ed.). Columbus, OH: Merrill.

Ravitch, D. (1983). *The troubled crusade—American education, 1945–1980.* New York: Basic Books.

Schlesinger, A. M. (1986). *The cycles of American history.* Boston, MA: Houghton Mifflin.

Sowell, T. (1984). *Civil rights: Rhetoric or reality.* New York: William Morrow.

Spring, J. (1976). *The sorting machine: National educational policy 1945.* New York: David McKay.

Szasz, M. C. (1977). *Education and the American Indian.* Albuquerque, NM: University of New Mexico Press.

Tollett, K. S. (1983). *The right to education: Reaganism, Reganomics, or human capital?* Washington, DC: Institute for the Study of Educational Policy, Howard University, 47.

U.S. Bureau of the Census. (1975). *Historical statistics of the United States, colonial times to 1970.* Washington, DC: U.S. Government Printing Office, Series H 316-326.

U.S. Department of Education, National Center for Education Statistics. (1989). *Digest of education statistics, 1989.* Washington, DC: U.S. Government Printing Office.

Yarber, W. L. (1987). *AIDS education: Curriculum and health policy.* Bloomington, IN: Phi Delta Kappa Educational Foundation.

Zigler, E., & Valentine, J. (Eds.). (1979). *Project Head Start: A legacy of the War on Poverty.* New York: The Face Press.

Part Three

Philosophy and Its Impact on the Schools

The Major Philosophies **Chapter 6**
The Impact of Educational Theories on Educational Practice **Chapter 7**

Chapter 6
The Major Philosophies

As Plato understood, there is really only one serious political topic. It is more serious than war, or even the New Federalism. It is the upbringing of children.

George F. Will, 1941

It is late Friday afternoon and classes have been dismissed at John F. Kennedy High School. A few students are left in the chemistry laboratory cleaning equipment and in the visual arts and industrial arts classrooms putting the finishing touches on their semester projects, which are due on Monday. The sound of a lonely basketball, dribbling in the nearby gymnasium, echoes down the corridor. The school seems rather eerie in its stark quietude—a far cry from the loud sounds and activities of an hour before.

The faculty lounge also is empty except for a group of four teachers in a heated discussion. Ms. Jenkins, who has taught an introductory biology course for the past seven years, appears agitated over the school district's new policy concerning electives. She makes a passionate argument to the rest of her colleagues at the table, alleging that it is a mistake to allow students a choice in determining their own curriculum. Her major thesis is that adolescents are not capable of making such

choices and if left to their own whims will opt for the easiest, least demanding courses, and will avoid the mathematics, life sciences, and physical sciences courses that most colleges and universities require.

Mr. Rhodes, a soft-spoken and gentle individual who has taught courses in anthropology, sociology, and psychology for the past three years, attempts to argue an opposing viewpoint. He directs his comments to the entire group, but his attention is focused primarily on Ms. Jenkins. His counterargument is that adolescents, and even very young children, are capable of decision making. In fact, according to Mr. Rhodes, most individuals, if left on their own, will choose what is good for them and are capable of making quality educational decisions at a very early age.

Do you agree with Ms. Jenkins or Mr. Rhodes? What additional arguments might you give to support your position?

The opposing viewpoints of Ms. Jenkins and Mr. Rhodes are examples of basic philosophic issues. Their different points of view concerning choice reflect their different personal philosophies as well as their philosophies of education.

For many, philosophy connotes a certain type of abstract or theoretical thinking that seems far removed from the day-to-day life of the elementary or secondary classroom teacher. However, every teacher and every classroom reflects a set of assumptions about the world. Those principles or assumptions comprise one's personal philosophy as well as one's educational philosophy. In this chapter, we will outline some of the basic philosophic questions as well as review some of the major traditional (idealism, realism, and neo-Thomism) and contemporary (experimentalism and existentialism) philosophies.

As you study the philosophies outlined in this chapter, you will probably begin to question your own personal philosophy. To help you better understand the philosophies and where your personal philosophy fits within that framework, consider the following objectives:

- Explain the relationship between general philosophy and a philosophy of education.

- Discuss the three approaches to the study of philosophy.

- Describe the three branches of philosophy.

- Compare the metaphysics of idealism, realism, neo-Thomism, experimentalism, and existentialism.

- Compare the epistemology of idealism, realism, neo-Thomism, experimentalism, and existentialism.

- Compare the axiology of idealism, realism, neo-Thomism, experimentalism, and existentialism.

- Identify the philosophies that take an optimistic view of human nature and those that take a pessimistic view.

- Discuss your philosophy of life and how it has changed over time.

What Is Philosophy?

One formal definition of philosophy as a discipline of inquiry states that philosophy is "the rational investigation of the truths and principles of being, knowledge, or conduct" (*Random House Dictionary*, 1986). Perhaps the most simple, yet comprehensive definition is that philosophy is "love of wisdom and the search for it."

The formal study of philosophical thought enables us to better understand our own philosophy of life: who we are, why we are here, and where we are going. Whereas our philosophy of life enables us to recognize the meaning of our personal existence, our *philosophy of education* enables us to recognize certain educational principles that define our views about the learner, the teacher, and the school. To teach without a firm understanding of one's philosophy of life and philosophy of education would be analogous to painting a portrait without the rudimentary knowledge and skills of basic design, perspective, or human anatomy. Although you may not have thought about your personal philosophy in a formal sense, you certainly have personal beliefs that have shaped your life. After you have studied and discussed Chapter 6, you should be able to better articulate your own philosophy of life.

Approaches to the Study of Philosophy

According to Wingo (1974) there are three main approaches to the study of philosophy: (1) descriptive, (2) normative, and (3) analytic. The descriptive approach is concerned with learning about various schools of philosophic thought and how the philosophers associated with these schools created the thought or position. The normative approach is concerned with values. It is not interested in "what is" (which is the goal of descriptive philosophy) but rather, "what *ought* to be." Using this approach, the philosophic thought is explored and critiqued and determinations are made as to rightness and wrongness. The analytic approach is concerned with an analysis of language, concepts, and theories. The goal of analytic philosophy is to improve our understanding of education by clarifying our educational concepts, beliefs,

Figure 6.1: Approaches to the Study of Philosophy		
Approach	Definition	Example
Descriptive	Learning about various schools of philosophic thought.	Idealism stresses the world of the mind and ideas. Realism stresses the world of physical things.
Normative	Learning about values or "what ought to be."	Should birth control information be dispensed in health classes on high school campuses?
Analytic	Learning how to analyze language, concepts and theories.	Explain the concept of discipline and its application to your philosophy of education.

arguments, and assumptions. For example, an analytic philosophy of education would attempt to understand such questions as: What is experience? What is understanding? What is readiness? (See Figure 6.1 for further descriptions of these approaches to the study of philosophy.)

Jonas Soltis (1978), a noted philosopher of education, has suggested that the descriptive and normative approaches to the study of philosophy can be combined. To Soltis, these approaches represent the traditional view of philosophy as a discipline that seeks an understanding of human life, including the way the world is, the way it ought to be, and what is good, right, and suitable. In a manner similar to Wingo, Soltis described the analytic approach to the study of philosophy as a more contemporary view that seeks a more precise language by examining and questioning certain concepts. Also, according to Soltis, the various approaches to philosophy are not mutually exclusive and can be incorporated.

In fact, in Chapters 6 and 7 we incorporate all three approaches to the study of philosophy. The descriptive approach is utilized in the presentation of the major philosophies in Chapter 6 and the theories of education are discussed in Chapter 7. The analytic approach with its analysis of selected educational concepts and the normative approach with the construction of educational values embedded in the philosophy of education are also introduced in Chapter 7.

Branches of Philosophy

Although there is much discussion about which school of philosophic thought is most accurate, relevant, or even complete, there is general agreement concerning the basic components or branches of philosophy: metaphysics, epistemology, and axiology. These branches are concerned with the answers to the three basic questions that are important in describing any philosophy:

- What is the nature of reality?
- What is the nature of knowledge?
- What is the nature of values?

The framework these questions provide enables us to study the major schools of philosophy from a descriptive approach. These branches and questions are elaborated upon in the following section and summarized in Figure 6.2.

Metaphysics: What Is the Nature of Reality?

Of the three basic questions, "What is the nature of reality?" is perhaps the most difficult to answer because its elements are vague, abstract, and not easily

Figure 6.2: Summary of Branches of Philosophy

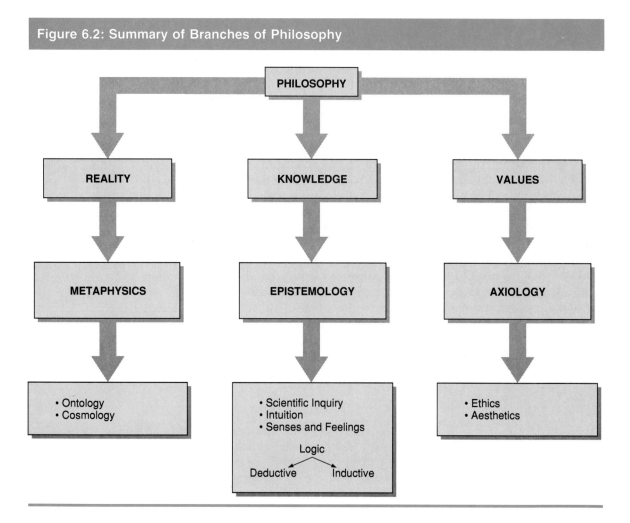

identifiable. According to two recognized educational philosophers, Van Cleve Morris and Young Pai (1976):

> Some individuals . . . consider reality a kind of "given" quality or "ground" of the human situation. We are unable to discuss the nature and character of this ground because we can never truly know it; there is nothing against which we can see it. It is . . . basically irrational or a-rational, possibly even transitional, or beyond the reach of human mentality, and hence not subject to intelligent study. (p. 28)

The branch of philosophy that is concerned with the nature of reality and existence is known as *metaphysics*. Metaphysics is concerned with the question of the nature of the person or self. It addresses such questions as whether human nature is basically good, evil, spiritual, mental, or physical. Metaphysics can be subdivided into the areas of ontology and cosmology.

Ontology raises some fundamental questions about what we mean by the nature of existence and what it means for anything "to be." *Cosmology* raises questions about the origin and organization of the universe, or cosmos.

Should schools concern themselves with questions regarding the origin of the universe? Why or why not?

Epistemology: What Is the Nature of Knowledge?

The branch of philosophy that is concerned with the investigation of the nature of knowledge is known as *epistemology*. To explore the nature of knowledge is to raise questions about the limits of knowledge, the sources of knowledge, the validity of knowledge, the cognitive processes, and how we know. There are several ways to know, including scientific inquiry, intuition, the senses, feelings, and logic. Logic is a key dimension in the traditional philosophies. Logic is primarily concerned with making inferences, reasoning, or arguing in a rational manner, and includes the traditional subdivisions of deduction and induction. *Deductive logic* involves deducing a concrete application from a general principle. *Inductive logic,* on the other hand, typically begins with a combination of facts or true examples and from these facts a general principle or rule is formulated. Figure 6.3 further describes these two types of logic.

Axiology: What Is the Nature of Values?

Where epistemology explores the question of knowledge, *axiology,* the study of the nature of values, seeks to determine what is of value. To evaluate, to make a judgment, to value, literally means applying a set of norms or standards to human conduct or beauty. Axiology is divided into two spheres: ethics and aesthetics. *Ethics* is concerned with the study of human conduct and examines moral values—right, wrong, good, bad. *Aesthetics* is concerned with values in beauty, especially in the fine arts.

One of the current debates in education centers around the question of whether moral education or values education should be a responsibility of the school. "Controversial Issues" on page 179 poses arguments for and against the place of ethics in the classrooms; "Ask Yourself" on page 180 lists

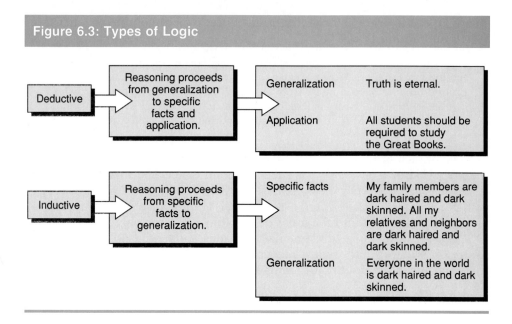

Figure 6.3: Types of Logic

a number of questions that are asked by the three branches of philosophy. The questions provide a framework for you to examine and perhaps articulate your own philosophy of life. Your answers to these questions also reflect some of the basic assumptions you hold, which will determine how you view your students and their capacity to learn, how you view the curriculum and its subject matter, how you view the evaluation process, and how you view the general classroom environment. Your philosophy of life and philosophy of education are interdependent and provide a basis for your view of life, as well as your view of teaching.

Idealism

Idealism is considered the oldest philosophy of Western culture, dating back to ancient Greece and the time of Plato. For the idealist, the world of the mind and ideas is primary.

Metaphysics

Idealism stresses the reality of the mind, soul, and spirit. For the idealist, nothing exists or is real except for an idea in the mind of the person or the mind of God, the Universal Mind. The universe can be explained as a creative and spiritual reality that includes the notions of permanence, order, and certainty. Morris and Pai (1976) suggest that there are two major divisions of reality in the world: apparent reality and real reality.

Controversial Issues:
Should Moral Education or Values Education Be a Responsibility of the School?

Although axiology or the study of values is a major component or branch of all philosophies, the question of whether virtue or ethics should be taught in the school remains a controversial issue. The history of American education confirms that the didactic teaching of moral values, including religious values, was once a central feature of the school. Today, some parents and educators are suggesting that ethical questions and moral dilemmas do indeed have a place in the educational enterprise. Others have expressed strong opinions against the school's role in moral or values education. The arguments, pro and con, concerning moral education or values education are:

Arguments For

1. The teaching of values is not a new phenomenon and follows the earlier works of Plato, Aristotle, Dewey, and Piaget who linked values to cognitive development, which has a place in the classroom.

2. Teachers can serve as an important value model for their students.

3. The discussion of moral dilemmas integrates critical thinking and ethics, which develops moral reasoning skills.

4. The school is the best place for assisting learners to understand their own attitudes, preferences, and values. The role of the school is to help students sort through value confusion so they can live by their values.

5. Students should become as adept in critical thinking principles of morality as we expect them to be in science and social studies.

Arguments Against

1. The teaching of values is not the purview of the school, but the family and church.

2. Too many teachers lecture their students about the importance of certain "appropriate" values without demonstrating those values by their own actions or behaviors.

3. No individual is "valueless," thus all teachers, by the nature of their position, have the potential of imposing their values on their students.

4. The function of the school is to educate, not proselytize or indoctrinate, therefore moral education and values education do not belong in the classroom.

What is your view of moral education or values education?

Apparent reality is made up of day-to-day experiences. "This is the region of change, of coming and going, of being born, growing, aging, and dying; it is the realm of imperfection, irregularity, and disorder; finally, it is the world of troubles and suffering, evil and sin" (Morris & Pai, 1976, p. 47). *Real reality*, on the other hand, is the realm of ideas and is therefore the realm of eternal truths, perfect order, and absolute values. For the idealist, real reality reigns above apparent reality, since real reality embodies perfection and eternal ideas that do not change.

If you were an idealist, what eternal ideas would you recommend be taught in the schools?

Ask Yourself:
What Is My Philosophy of Life?

Philosophic Questions	Branches of Philosophy
1. Are human beings basically good or is the essential nature of the human being evil?	What is the nature of reality? (Metaphysics—ontology)
2. What causes certain events in the universe to happen?	What is the nature of reality? (Metaphysics—cosmology)
3. What is your relationship to the universe?	What is the nature of reality? (Metaphysics—cosmology)
4. What is your relationship to a higher being (God)?	What is the nature of reality? (Metaphysics—ontology)
5. To what extent is your life basically free?	What is the nature of reality? (Metaphysics—ontology)
6. How is reality determined?	What is the nature of reality? (Metaphysics—ontology)
7. What is your basic purpose in life?	What is the nature of reality? (Metaphysics—ontology)
8. How is knowledge determined?	What is the nature of knowledge? (Epistemology)
9. What is truth?	What is the nature of knowledge? (Epistemology)
10. What are the limits of knowledge?	What is the nature of knowledge? (Epistemology)
11. What is the relationship between cognition and knowledge?	What is the nature of knowledge? (Epistemology)
12. Are there certain moral or ethical values that are universal?	What is the nature of values? (Axiology—ethics)
13. How is beauty determined?	What is the nature of values? (Axiology—aesthetics)
14. What constitutes aesthetic value?	What is the nature of values? (Axiology—aesthetics)
15. Who determines what is right, just, or good?	What is the nature of values? (Axiology—ethics)

Wingo (1974) summarized how the mind and spirit constitute reality and the perfect order for the idealist:

> One part of the basic thesis of all idealism is that mind is prior; that when we seek what is ultimate in the world, when we push back behind the veil of immediate sense experience, we shall find that what is ultimate in the whole universe is of the nature of mind or spirit (the two words are interchangeable in most discussions of idealism)—just as it is mind that is ultimate in the inner world of personal experience. (p. 95)

If the mind is prior, in the sense that it is ultimate, then material things either do not exist (i.e., are not real), or if they do exist, their existence depends in some fashion on the mind. For example, an idealist would contend that there is no such thing as a chair, there is only the idea of a chair.

The idealist's concept of reality considers the self as one in mind, soul, and spirit. Such a nature is capable of emulating the Absolute or Supreme Mind.

Epistemology

Since idealism accepts a primarily mental explanation for its metaphysics or reality, it is not surprising that idealists also accept the premise that all knowledge includes a mental grasp of ideas and concepts. Deductive logic is heavily emphasized by idealism. Since the mind is the primary reality, the interpretation of perceptions and the unifying of ideas are the methods of knowledge. Thus it is important to master the science of logic. Logic is the tool by which our thinking can be examined and made consistent (Butler, 1966). While reason or logic is considered the primary way "to know" by idealists, especially traditional idealists, modern idealists also accept intuition as a dimension of knowing.

One of the most important considerations of knowledge to the idealist is its relationship to truth. Idealists accept the following propositions concerning knowledge and truth:

1. The universe is rational and orderly and therefore intelligible.

2. There is an objective body of truth that has its origin and existence in the Absolute Mind and that can be known, at least in part, by the human mind.

3. The art of knowing is essentially an act of reconstructing the data of awareness into intelligible ideas and systems of ideas.

4. The criterion for the truth of an idea is coherence; that is, an idea is true when it is consistent with the existing and accepted body of truth. (Wingo, 1974, p. 103)

Some idealists believe that it is not necessarily truth *per se* that is important, but rather the search for truth that is the ultimate challenge. Most idealists, however, believe that even though most of us resort to mere opinions about truth and may never reach what might be considered ultimate truth, there is a body of objective truth that can be known (Ozmon & Craver, 1990).

Axiology

Just as the idealists believe that order is an important element of reality, order is also considered a basic principle of values. Furthermore, values can be classified and ordered into a hierarchy or classification system. According to the educational philosopher Marler (1975), intuition is the means by which many idealists discover the presence of values and determine the hierarchy of those values.

Idealists believe that human behavior is inherently purposive and not merely the response to external stimuli. Rather, within the human self is an inherent urge for self-realization which provides the basic motivation for behavior. Since behavior is purposive, we cannot escape the need to value (or disvalue) the things and events that we experience (Wingo, 1974).

To the idealist values are rooted in existence and are part and parcel of reality. "We enjoy values . . . because the things we value are realities that have existence themselves and are rooted in the very structure of the cosmos" (Butler, 1966, p. 74).

Values also are absolute. The good, the true, and the beautiful basically do not change from generation to generation, or from society to society. They are not created by man but are part of the very nature and being of the universe (Kneller, 1971). They are, in fact, reflections of the Absolute Good, the Absolute Truth, the Absolute Beauty—God. Figure 6.4 provides an overview of idealism.

Leading Proponents

As noted in Chapter 3, the Greek philosopher Plato, the disciple of Socrates, is considered the father of idealism. In his famous "Allegory of the Cave," found in *The Republic,* Plato inferred that each of us lives in a cave of shadow, doubts, and distortions about reality. However, through education and enlightenment, the real world of pure ideas can be substituted for those distorted shadows and doubts.

Judaism and Christianity were both influenced by the philosophy of idealism in a different way. Judeo-Christian teaching suggested that ultimate reality could be found in God through the soul. A prominent theologian of the fourth and fifth century and one who applied a number of Plato's assumptions to Christian thought was St. Augustine (354–430). Plato's assumptions, as applied by St. Augustine, provided the rationale for the religious idealism that influenced Western thought for centuries (Ozmon & Craver, 1990).

Idealist thought influenced the writings of a number of major philosophers, including René Descartes, Immanuel Kant, and Georg Wilhelm Friedrich Hegel. The French philosopher Descartes (1596–1650), in his famous dictum, "*Cogito, ergo sum*—I think, therefore I am," declared that as humans we may doubt everything, but we cannot doubt our own existence. The concept of existence is further interpreted by Wingo (1974):

> I may succeed in doubting the existence of everything else, one thing is certain: every time I think, I exist. The primary and ultimate fact of my experience is

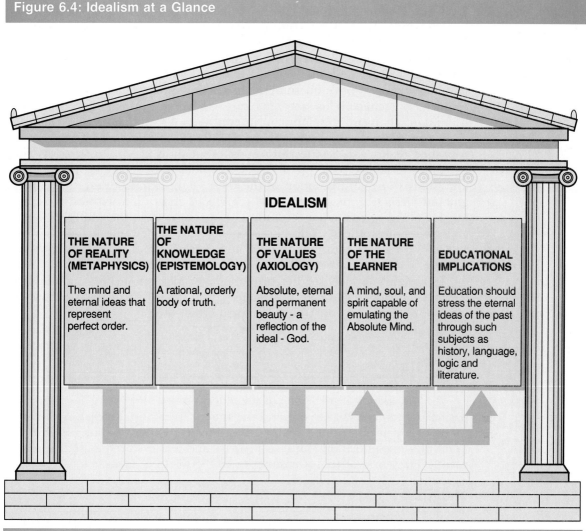

Figure 6.4: Idealism at a Glance

IDEALISM

THE NATURE OF REALITY (METAPHYSICS)	THE NATURE OF KNOWLEDGE (EPISTEMOLOGY)	THE NATURE OF VALUES (AXIOLOGY)	THE NATURE OF THE LEARNER	EDUCATIONAL IMPLICATIONS
The mind and eternal ideas that represent perfect order.	A rational, orderly body of truth.	Absolute, eternal and permanent beauty - a reflection of the ideal - God.	A mind, soul, and spirit capable of emulating the Absolute Mind.	Education should stress the eternal ideas of the past through such subjects as history, language, logic and literature.

mind and consciousness. It is not my physical body of members and organs that is necessarily real, for it is possible to believe that my body does not exist. The ultimate reality in my experience is my mind. It alone can be known to be real. (p. 95)

Descartes not only accepted the place of the finite mind and ideas as advanced by Plato, but determined that all ideas, save one, depend on other ideas. The only idea that does not depend on any idea other than itself is the idea of Perfect Being or God. The process used by Descartes, later known as the *Cartesian method*, involved the derivation of axioms upon which theories could be based by the purposeful and progressive elimination of all interpretations of experience except those that are absolutely certain. This method came to influence a number of fields of inquiry, including the sciences (Ozmon & Craver, 1990).

Can you think of other examples of categorical imperatives that might be espoused by idealists and that would be relevant to education?

Immanuel Kant (1724–1804), recognized as one of the world's greatest philosophers, also incorporated the major tenets of idealism into his thinking. Kant believed there were certain universal moral laws known as *categorical imperatives* which guide our actions or behaviors. One of Kant's categorical imperatives was "above all things, obedience is an essential feature in the character of a child." This moral maxim has become a primary basis for moral training or character development in education (Ozmon & Craver, 1990).

The German philosopher Hegel (1770–1831) was an idealist who approached reality as a "contest of opposites" such as life and death, love and hate, individual and society. For Hegel, each idea (thesis) had its own opposite (antithesis). The confrontation of the thesis (e.g., man is an end in himself) and antithesis (e.g., man cannot be merely an end to himself—he must also live for others) produces a resolution or synthesis (e.g., man fulfills his true end by serving others). This synthesis becomes a new thesis, which when crossed with a new antithesis forms a new synthesis, and so on (Morris & Pai, 1976).

In addition to Hegel, other proponents of idealism include such leading literary figures as Samuel Coleridge (1772–1834), William Wordsworth (1770–1850), and Ralph Waldo Emerson (1803–1882).

Realism

Realism, like idealism, is one of the oldest philosophies of Western culture, dating back to ancient Greece and the time of Aristotle. Realism is the antithesis of idealism. For the realists, the universe exists whether the human mind perceives it or not. Matter is primary and is considered an independent reality. The world of things is superior to the world of ideas.

Metaphysics

Realism stresses the world of nature or physical things and our experiences and perceptions of those things. Morris and Pai (1976) describe the role of human beings in relation to the world of nature.

> What are human beings, then, say the Realist, but tiny spectators of an enormous machine, the cosmos. They stand before it as fleas before an electronic computer, but with one advantage: intelligence. Gradually, piece by piece, they can come to a wider and fuller understanding of their world. And this is possible because this world, like any machine, is not a haphazard, fortuitous collection of atoms and molecules, but a structure built according to plan and endowed (as is the automobile engine) with predetermined and necessary movements. (p. 54)

For the realist, then, reality is composed of both matter (body) and form (mind). Matter can only "become" (be shaped or organized into being) by the

Today's students follow the precepts of Aristotle by formulating, testing, and discovering knowledge through the scientific method.

mind. Moreover, the interaction of matter and form is governed not by God but by scientific, natural laws.

As to the nature of self, the realist considers the person a sensing and rational being capable of understanding the world of things. The person, like all matter and form, has evolved from and is subject to nature and its laws.

Epistemology

There are several methods of discovering knowledge that realists perceive to be important. For some realists, the objects of our knowledge are presented directly in consciousness with no intervening mental construct or mental state and with none needed to account for our knowledge of the external world. That is, we know by direct sensing. For other realists, knowledge is established by the *scientific method,* that is, by the systematic reporting and analysis of what is observed and the testing of hypotheses formulated from the observations. To these realists, the purpose of inquiry is to discover the real character of the processes of nature. To know the truth means literally to discover that which is already there (Wingo, 1974). In essence, a logical, systematic approach to the discovery of knowledge is fundamental to the realist.

Consider yourself a realist. To what extent might you use the scientific method as a basis of inquiry in a beginning music class? In a class of preschoolers?

Axiology

In the axiology of realism, values are derived from nature. In the area of ethics, natural law or moral law are the major determinants of what is good; that which is good is dependent on leading a virtuous life, one in keeping with these natural or moral laws.

Although realism does not adhere to any hard and fast set of rules, realists believe that deviating from moral truth will cause injury both to persons and to society. Thus, certain codes of conduct or social law are written or are distilled in social tradition and must be followed to protect the common good (Power, 1982).

Figure 6.5: Realism at a Glance

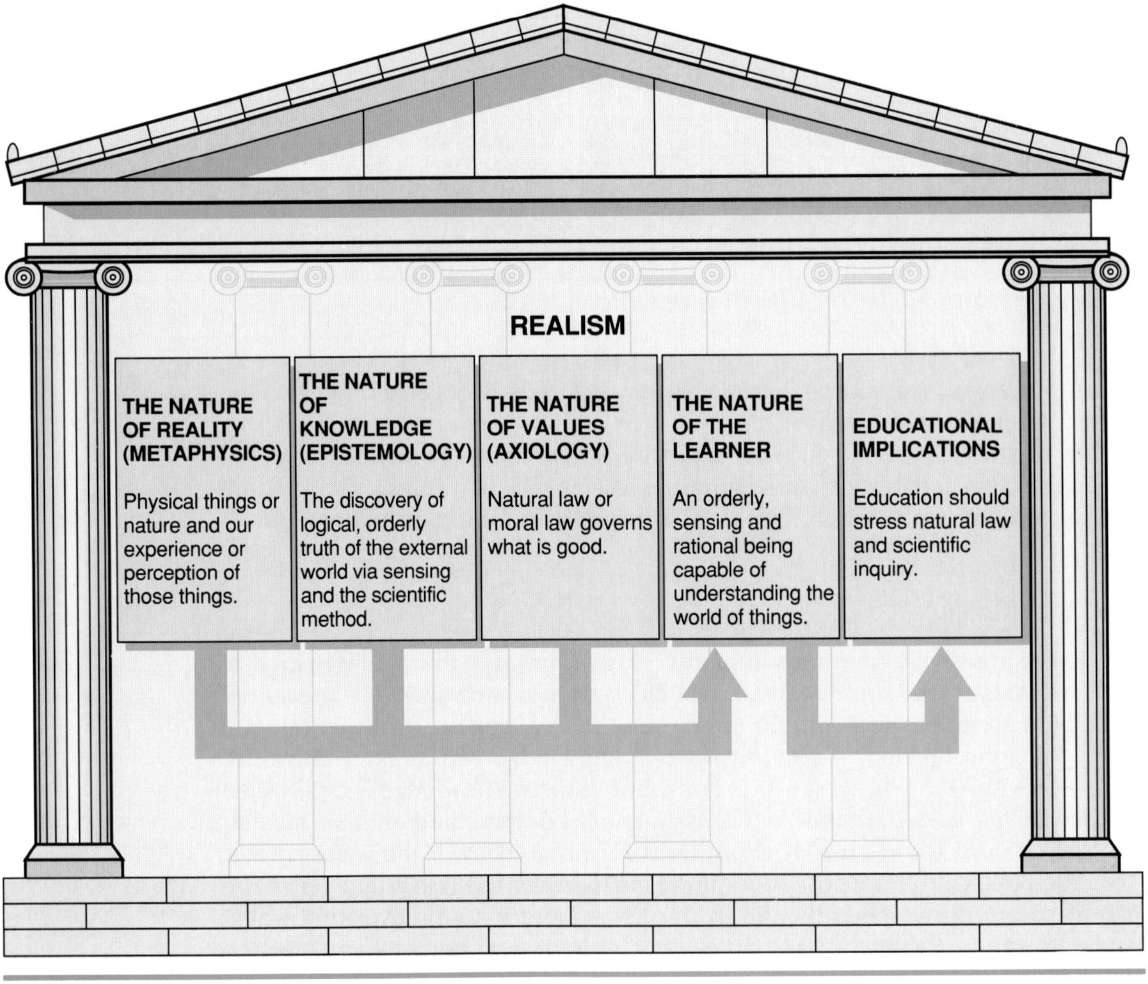

REALISM

THE NATURE OF REALITY (METAPHYSICS)	THE NATURE OF KNOWLEDGE (EPISTEMOLOGY)	THE NATURE OF VALUES (AXIOLOGY)	THE NATURE OF THE LEARNER	EDUCATIONAL IMPLICATIONS
Physical things or nature and our experience or perception of those things.	The discovery of logical, orderly truth of the external world via sensing and the scientific method.	Natural law or moral law governs what is good.	An orderly, sensing and rational being capable of understanding the world of things.	Education should stress natural law and scientific inquiry.

For the realist, aesthetics is the reflection of nature. What is valued is that which reflects the orderliness and rationality of nature. Figure 6.5 provides an overview of realism.

Leading Proponents

As discussed in Chapter 3, Aristotle, a pupil of Plato, is considered the father of realism. Aristotle disagreed with Plato's premise that only ideas are real. For Aristotle, reality, knowledge, and value exist independently of the mind and their existence is not predicated by our perception. According to Aristotle, material things exist in space and time. They have existed before our knowledge of them and they will exist after we are gone (Power, 1982).

Two other representatives of realism, also mentioned in Chapter 3, were Francis Bacon and John Locke. Bacon, both a philosopher and a politician, advanced a scientific form of realism that depended on the inductive method of inquiry. Following a similar path, Locke's advocacy of realism stemmed from his study of human knowledge. One of Locke's major notions, the *tabula rasa* concept, has gained wide acceptance. As explained in Chapter 3, according to this concept there are no such things as innate ideas. We come into the world with a mind like a blank sheet of paper. Knowledge is acquired from sources independent of the mind as a result of sensation and reflection (Ozmon & Craver, 1990).

Other major philosophers who contributed to realism as a scientific inquiry include the English mathematicians and philosophers Alfred North Whitehead (1861–1947) and Bertrand Russell (1872–1970).

Neo-Thomism

The third of the traditional philosophies is *neo-Thomism*. Neo-Thomism, or its antecedent, Thomism, dates to the time of St. Thomas Aquinas in the thirteenth century. As noted in Chapter 3, Aquinas attempted to bridge the dualism of idealism and realism which had separated philosophic thought up to his time. For the neo-Thomist, God exists and can be known by both faith and reason.

Metaphysics

Neo-Thomists believe that it is God who gives meaning and purpose to the universe. God is the Pure Being that represents the coming together of essence and existence. Things exist independently of ideas; however, both physical objects and human beings, including minds and ideas, are created by God. Thus, while both physical objects and God are real, God is preeminent. Neo-Thomists conceive of the essential nature of human beings as rational beings with souls, modeled after God, the Perfect Being.

Epistemology

Although some philosophies believe that one can come to know God only through faith or intuition, neo-Thomism believes that it is through both faith and our capacity to reason that we come to know God. What makes neo-Thomism unique in comparison to other traditional philosophies is the belief that both the so-called truths of revelation accepted on faith and the truths of science arrived at by rational observation can be accepted as equally unchangeable and "true." If there is a conflict between the two, it is not in their essence, but is a result of faulty reasoning.

To the neo-Thomist there is a hierarchy of knowing. At the lowest level is scientific or synthetic knowing. At the second level there is analytic or intuitive knowing. And at the highest level there is mystical or revelatory knowing (Morris & Pai, 1976).

Axiology

For the neo-Thomist, ethically speaking, goodness follows reason. That is, values are unchanging moral laws established by God, which can be discerned by reason. As a corollary, ignorance is the source of evil. If people do not know what is right, they cannot be expected to do what is right. If, on the other hand, people do know what is right, they can be held morally responsible for what they do. In terms of aesthetics, the reason or intellect is also the perceiver of beauty. That which is valued as beautiful is also found pleasing to the intellect (Morris & Pai, 1976). Figure 6.6 provides an overview of neo-Thomism.

Leading Proponents

Have you ever attended or known anyone who attended a parochial school? How did that experience compare with attendance at a public institution?

Thomas Aquinas, a theologian of the thirteenth century from whom the philosophy takes its name, is credited with interfacing the secular ideas of Aristotle and the Christian teachings of St. Augustine to form what has been termed "religious realism" or neo-Thomism. Both Aristotle and Aquinas viewed reality via reason and sensation. Aquinas believed God created matter out of nothing and gave meaning and purpose to the universe. In his most noted work, *Summa Theologica,* he used the rational approach suggested by Aristotle to answer various religious questions. As a result, many of the supporting arguments of Christian beliefs rely on Thomas Aquinas, and Roman Catholicism considers Thomism its leading philosophy (Ozmon & Craver, 1990).

Experimentalism

Experimentalism or pragmatism, as a philosophy, focuses on the things that work. Primarily viewed as a philosophy of the twentieth century developed by Americans such as John Dewey (see Chapter 5), experimentalism has its roots

Figure 6.6: Neo-Thomism at a Glance

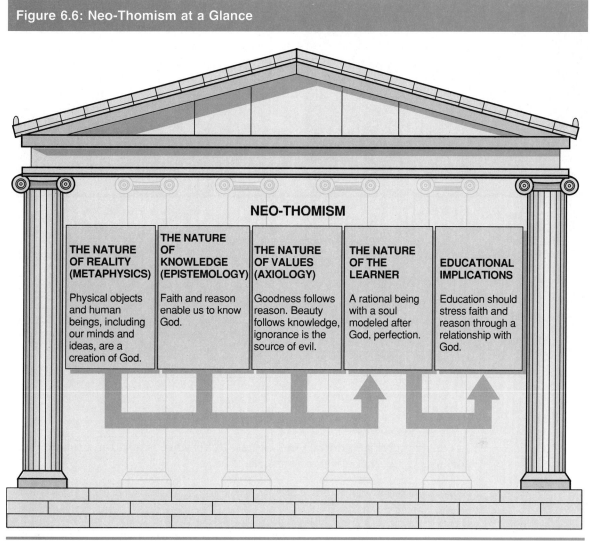

NEO-THOMISM

THE NATURE OF REALITY (METAPHYSICS)	THE NATURE OF KNOWLEDGE (EPISTEMOLOGY)	THE NATURE OF VALUES (AXIOLOGY)	THE NATURE OF THE LEARNER	EDUCATIONAL IMPLICATIONS
Physical objects and human beings, including our minds and ideas, are a creation of God.	Faith and reason enable us to know God.	Goodness follows reason. Beauty follows knowledge, ignorance is the source of evil.	A rational being with a soul modeled after God, perfection.	Education should stress faith and reason through a relationship with God.

in British, European, and ancient Greek tradition (Ozmon & Craver, 1990). For the experimentalist, the world of experience is central.

Metaphysics

The concept of reality for the experimentalist is somewhat vague. It can best be described as synonymous with "experience." Unlike the traditional theories, metaphysics to the experimentalist is a process rather than a substantive "something." Idealists, realists, and Thomists view reality as a thing—either material or intangible. But to an experimentalist, reality is an event, a process; in other words, experience (Morris & Pai, 1976). As such, it is subject

The teaching of Dewey is evident in classrooms where children actively participate in projects and social activities.

to constant change and lacks absolutes. Experience is also the ultimate basis for human existence.

Epistemology

Unlike the traditional philosophies, which promulgated truth as absolute, experimentalism's theory of knowledge accepts no truth as absolute, but rather advocates the idea that truth is determined by function. In fact, experimentalists shun the use of the word "truth" and will at best speak of a "tentative truth" that will serve the purpose until experience evolves a new truth. Knowledge is arrived at by the scientific method—testing, questioning, and retesting—and is never conclusive.

Axiology

Where the traditional philosophers concentrated primarily on metaphysics and epistemology, the experimentalist has focused primarily on axiology or values. As with truths, to the experimentalist values are only tentative. They are constructed from experience and are subject to testing, questioning, and retesting. For the experimentalist, that which is ethically or morally good is that which works, that which leads to desirable consequences. The focus on consequences is not to imply that the experimentalist is only concerned with what works for the self. In fact, the experimentalist is concerned with social consequences. "What works" is what works for the larger community, not just the self. The focus on consequences is in effect the application of the scientific method to questions of ethics.

Consequences are also the basis for aesthetic values. What is beautiful is not determined by some objective ideal but by what we experience when we see, hear, or touch. Figure 6.7 presents an overview of experimentalism.

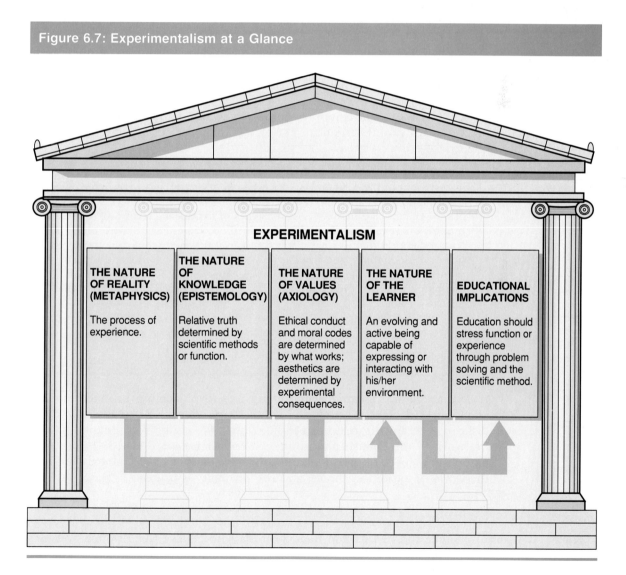

Figure 6.7: Experimentalism at a Glance

EXPERIMENTALISM

THE NATURE OF REALITY (METAPHYSICS)	THE NATURE OF KNOWLEDGE (EPISTEMOLOGY)	THE NATURE OF VALUES (AXIOLOGY)	THE NATURE OF THE LEARNER	EDUCATIONAL IMPLICATIONS
The process of experience.	Relative truth determined by scientific methods or function.	Ethical conduct and moral codes are determined by what works; aesthetics are determined by experimental consequences.	An evolving and active being capable of expressing or interacting with his/her environment.	Education should stress function or experience through problem solving and the scientific method.

Leading Proponents

An 80-year-old woman who is dying of cancer has requested assistance from her son, husband, physician, and the Hemlock Society to aid her in the design of her own suicide. How might an experimentalist deal with this ethical dilemma?

Although there are a number of British and European philosophers who supported the experimentalist philosophy, such as Jean-Jacques Rousseau (see Chapter 3), Auguste Comte (1798–1857), and Charles Darwin (1809–1882), experimentalism or pragmatism has received its major impetus from American philosophers such as Charles Sanders Peirce (1839–1914), William James (1842–1910), and John Dewey (1859–1952).

Peirce believed that true knowledge depends on verification of ideas through experience. Ideas are merely hypotheses until tested by experience. Although Peirce's philosophy was very complicated and included the concepts of the nature of God, immortality, and the self, his premise of verification by experience was the major influence on experimentalism or pragmatism (Ozmon & Craver, 1990).

William James incorporated his views of pragmatism or experimentalism in both philosophy and psychology. James also emphasized the centrality of experience. To James there were no absolutes, no universals, only an ever-changing universe.

It was James's contemporary, John Dewey, who had the greatest influence on American experimentalism. For Dewey, experience, thought, and consequence were interrelated:

> Thought or reflection, as we have already seen virtually if not explicitly, is the discernment of the relation between what we try to do and what happens in consequence. No experience having a meaning is possible without some element of thought. But we may contrast two types of experience according to the proportion of reflection found in them. All our experiences have a phase of "cut and try" in them—what psychologists call the method of trial and error. We simply do something, and when it fails, we do something else, and keep on trying until we hit upon something which works, and then we adopt that method as a rule of thumb measure in subsequent procedures (Dewey, 1916, pp. 169–170).

Existentialism

Existentialism appeared a century ago as a revolt against the mathematical, scientific, and objective philosophies that preceded it. Existentialism voiced disfavor with any effort toward social control or subjugation. Beginning with the work of the Danish philosopher Soren Kierkegaard (1813–1855), existentialism focused on personal and subjective existence. For the existentialist, the world of existence, choice, and responsibility is primary.

Metaphysics

Unlike the realists and neo-Thomists who believe that essence precedes existence, the existentialists believe that existence precedes essence. For the

The search for meaning, purpose in life, and individual existence continues to challenge contemporary youth as it challenged Kierkegaard in the nineteenth century.

existentialist there is neither meaning nor purpose to the physical universe. We are born into the universe by chance. Moreover, according to the existentialists, since there is no world order or natural scheme of things into which we are born, we owe nothing to nature but our existence (Kneller, 1971).

In addition to existence, the concept of choice is central to the metaphysics of existentialism. To decide who and what we are is to decide what reality is. Is it God? Reason? Nature? Science? By our choices we determine reality.

Epistemology

Similar to their position concerning reality, the existentialists believe that the way we come to know truth is by choice. The individual self must ultimately make the decision as to what is true and how we know. Whether we choose logic, intuition, scientific proof, or revelation is irrelevant; what matters is that we must eventually choose. The freedom to choose carries with it a tremendous burden of responsibility that we cannot escape. Because there are no absolutes, no authorities, and no single or correct way to the truth, the only authority is the authority of the self.

Axiology

For the existentialist, choice is imperative not only for determining reality and knowledge but also for determining value. Van Cleve Morris (1966) explains that concerning values, authenticity and choice are key:

> And who is the authentic? The individual whose example is perhaps beyond the reach of most of us; the individual who is free and who knows it, who knows that every deed and word is a choice and hence an act of value creation, and, finally and perhaps decisively, who knows that he is the author of his own life and must be held personally responsible for the values on behalf of which he has chosen to live it, and that these values can never be justified by referring to something or somebody outside himself. (p. 48)

How would an existentialist respond to the schools' attempts to influence students' choice in matters such as birth control and substance use?

Whether we are discussing ethics or aesthetics, we cannot escape our freedom to choose or our freedom to value. And here is the dilemma, say the existentialists. Since there are no norms, no standards, and no assurances that we have chosen correctly or rightly, choice is frustrating and exasperating at times. It is often much easier to be able to look to a standard or benchmark to determine what is right, just, or of value than to take responsibility for the choices we have made. Yet this is a very small price we pay for our free will. Figure 6.8 presents an overview of existentialism.

Leading Proponents

The leading proponent, indeed the "father of existentialism," was Soren Kierkegaard. Kierkegaard renounced scientific objectivity for subjectivity and personal choice. He was concerned with individual existence and attacked Hegelian philosophy on the grounds that it depersonalized the individual. He believed that we must understand our souls and destinies, and that we must take complete responsibility for the choices we make. He also believed in the reality of God (Ozmon & Craver, 1990).

Another nineteenth/twentieth-century expositor of existentialism was Martin Buber (1878–1965). Buber, a Jewish philosopher-theologian, advocated an "I-Thou" relationship whereby each individual recognizes the other's personal meaning and reality. Buber suggested that both the divine and human are related, and by one's personal relationship with the other one can enhance one's spiritual life and one's relationship with God. Buber's humanistic existentialist views had a profound impact, not only on philosophy and theology but on psychology, psychiatry, literature, and education (Ozmon & Craver, 1990).

Influenced by the philosophy of Immanuel Kant and Edmund Husserl (1859–1938), who developed a philosophical method called *phenomenology* or the study of phenomena, Martin Heidegger (1889–1976) expanded and revised phenomenology to another philosophical method known as *hermeneutics* or the interpretation of lived experience (Ozmon & Craver, 1990). The major thesis of Heidegger's numerous writings was the search for meaning. For Heidegger, metaphysical reality had to include such emotional phenomena as dread, anguish, concern, and sensitivity.

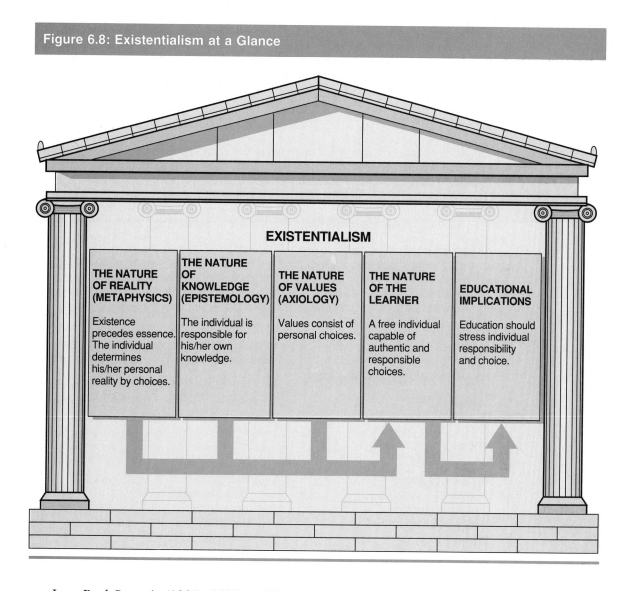

Figure 6.8: Existentialism at a Glance

EXISTENTIALISM

THE NATURE OF REALITY (METAPHYSICS)

Existence precedes essence. The individual determines his/her personal reality by choices.

THE NATURE OF KNOWLEDGE (EPISTEMOLOGY)

The individual is responsible for his/her own knowledge.

THE NATURE OF VALUES (AXIOLOGY)

Values consist of personal choices.

THE NATURE OF THE LEARNER

A free individual capable of authentic and responsible choices.

EDUCATIONAL IMPLICATIONS

Education should stress individual responsibility and choice.

Jean-Paul Sartre's (1905–1980) public appeal exceeded that of Kierkegaard and Heidegger and many devotees of existentialism considered Sartre the spokesman for the human condition. Sartre claimed that free choice implies total responsibility for one's own existence. There are no antecedent principles or purposes that shape our destiny. Responsibility for our existence extends to situations of the gravest consequence, including the choice to commit suicide (Kneller, 1958). Sartre's major philosophic work, *Being and Nothingness* (1943), is considered one of the most original philosophic treatises of the twentieth century.

Other proponents of existentialism include the French writers and philosophers Albert Camus (1913–1960), Gabriel Marcel (1889–1973), Maurice

Merleau-Ponty (1908–1961), the philosopher-theologian Paul Tillich (1886–1965), and a number of playwrights who espouse the Theater of the Absurd (e.g., Eugene Ionesco, Samuel Beckett, and Edward Albee).

Summary

The study of philosophy enables us to better understand our philosophy of life, while the study of theories of education enables us to better understand our philosophy of education. One of the most effective methods of developing a philosophy of life is to respond to three basic questions: What is the nature of reality? What is the nature of knowledge? What is the nature of values? These three questions and their accompanying responses comprise the branches of philosophy.

The philosophies of idealism, realism, and neo-Thomism are considered the classical or traditional philosophies, while experimentalism and existentialism represent the contemporary or modern philosophies. The traditional philosophies are more concerned with truths and absolutes; the contemporary or modern philosophies are more concerned with the present and future and the tentativeness and open-endedness of concepts.

In the next chapter, we will see how these basic philosophic views have led to a number of theories of education. We will also see the impact of these theories on educational programs and practices.

Key Terms

Aesthetics
Apparent reality
Axiology
Cartesian method
Categorical imperatives
Cosmology
Deductive logic
Epistemology
Ethics
Existentialism
Experimentalism

Hermeneutics
Idealism
Inductive logic
Metaphysics
Neo-Thomism
Ontology
Phenomenology
Philosophy of education
Real reality
Realism
Scientific method

Discussion Questions

1. Which of the philosophies discussed in this chapter is most like your own? In what ways? Which is the most unlike your own? In what ways?

2. List all the ways of knowing. Does what is to be known (i.e., the subject matter) dictate the approach to knowing? Explain.

3. How would representatives of each of the philosophies discussed in this chapter respond to the following statement? "Concepts such as understanding, insight, appreciation, and interest have no place in the curriculum since they cannot be observed."

4. Construct an argument using deductive reasoning to explain the following statement: "Teaching does not imply education and education does not imply learning."

5. Which of the major philosophies would be most apt to use the following fundamental principles: justice, freedom, truthfulness, should or "ought," and honesty?

6. The following metaphor, "learning is essentially growing," depicts which philosophy? Name three other metaphors that depict three other major philosophies.

7. Consider the vignette at the beginning of this chapter. Which philosophy would you ascribe to Ms. Jenkins? To Mr. Rhodes? Explain.

8. Rewrite the opening vignette by portraying Ms. Jenkins as a neo-Thomist and Mr. Rhodes as an experimentalist.

References

Butler, J. D. (1966). *Idealism in education.* New York: Harper & Row.

Dewey, J. (1916). *Democracy and education: An introduction to the philosophy of education.* New York: Macmillan.

Kneller, G. F. (1958). *Existentialism and education.* New York: John Wiley & Sons.

Kneller, G. F. (1971). *Introduction to the philosophy of education.* New York: John Wiley & Sons.

Kneller, G. F. (1984). *Movements of thought in modern education.* New York: John Wiley & Sons.

Marler, C. D. (1975). *Philosophy and schooling.* Boston: Allyn & Bacon.

Morris, V. C. (1966). *Existentialism in education.* New York: Harper & Row.

Morris, V. C., & Pai, Y. (1976). *Philosophy and the American school.* Boston: Houghton Mifflin.

Ozmon, H. A., & Craver, S. M. (1990). *Philosophical foundations of education.* Columbus, OH: Merrill.

Plato (1958). *The Republic* (F. Carnford, Trans.). New York: Oxford University Press.

Power, E. J. (1982). *Philosophy of education: Studies in philosophies, schooling and educational policies.* Englewood Cliffs, NJ: Prentice-Hall.

Soltis, J. F. (1978). *An introduction to the analysis of educational concepts.* Reading, MA: Addison-Wesley.

Wingo, G. M. (1974). *Philosophies of education: An introduction.* Lexington, MA: D. C. Heath.

Chapter 7

The Impact of Educational Theories on Educational Practice

The roots of education are bitter, but the fruit is sweet.

Aristotle, 4th century B.C.

During a typical microteaching session as part of a methods class, six prospective teachers had just finished presenting a 20-minute lesson in their subject field using an instructional technique of their choice. What was surprising to the instructor was that no two students used the same technique.

Jim, a physical education major, had chosen demonstration as the major technique for his 20-minute lesson on chipping in golf. Beth, an art major, had used the group project as the technique for her lesson on basic design, and Sam, a history major, used lecture as the principal instructional technique to teach about the Spanish-American War. During the class critique, all three students expressed how well prepared they felt they all had been and how appropriate each of their instructional techniques were. The rest of

the class concurred with their evaluation. Then, in a surprise move, Beth turned to Sam and added, "You know, even though I felt that your lesson on the Spanish-American War was excellent and your minilecture held my attention, I could not feel comfortable giving a lecture to my art class."

"What do you mean?" asked Sam, rather flabbergasted at her comment.

"Just what I said, Sam," Beth replied. "Maybe it's the subject matter of art or maybe it's just me. It just doesn't fit with basic design!"

Do you agree with Beth? What is the relationship between the preferred method or instructional technique used by the teacher and his or her philosophy of education?

It is not a surprise that Beth, or any other students in preprofessional teacher education programs, would be unclear about the relationship between her preferred method or instructional technique and her philosophy of education. One explanation for this lack of understanding is that much of the subject matter or pedagogy of teacher education is taught in a fragmented fashion with little or no explanation of its philosophic roots. As a result, the student or novice teacher sees little relationship between the study of philosophy, in particular educational philosophy, and the preprofessional coursework.

As you study the educational theories outlined in this chapter, you will be encouraged to formulate your own philosophy of education. Information regarding the impact of six major educational theories on curriculum, teaching methods, classroom management, instruction, and the teacher will also be presented. Last, the analytic approach to the study of philosophy will be described, along with its application to educational practice. To help you as you study these important concepts, consider the following outcome objectives:

- Define an educational theory and explain its relationship to philosophy as a discipline.

- Identify the various underlying protests that led to the establishment of the theories of perennialism, progressivism, behaviorism, essentialism, reconstructionism, and existentialism.

- Compare the curricula of perennialism, progressivism, behaviorism, essentialism, reconstructionism, and existentialism.

- Compare the teaching methods that characterize perennialism, progressivism, behaviorism, essentialism, reconstructionism, and existentialism.

- Compare the preferred classroom management of perennialism, progressivism, behaviorism, essentialism, reconstructionism, and existentialism.

- Compare the evaluation techniques of the perennialist, progressivist, behaviorist, essentialist, reconstructionist, and existentialist.

- Describe the perennialist, progressivist, behaviorist, essentialist, reconstructionist, and existentialist teacher.

- Explain philosophic analysis in education.

- Contrast philosophical analysis with the descriptive study of philosophy.

- Identify your philosophy of education.

Having examined the assumptions that underlie the major philosophies, it is now appropriate to examine how these basic assumptions translate to educational theories and practice. The major traditional and contemporary philosophies that were discussed in Chapter 6 each have a corollary educational theory. It is the combination of philosophy and theory that will enable us to frame our own philosophy of education.

Theories of Education

Theory may be defined in two ways. First, a theory may be defined as a hypothesis or set of hypotheses that have been verified by observation or experiment. Second, a theory is defined as a general synonym for systematic thinking or a set of coherent thoughts. Thus a *theory of education* is a composite of systematic thinking or generalizations about schooling (Kneller, 1971).

A well-thought-out theory of education is important, for it helps to explain our educational behavior and allows us to defend our position with respect to how we manage learning. In short, a theory of education enables the teacher to explain what he or she is doing and why. It provides academic accountability.

The major theories of education to be examined in this chapter include six schools of thought: perennialism, progressivism, behaviorism, essentialism, reconstructionism, and existentialism. Each theory was developed as a protest against the prevailing social and educational climate of the time. After examining the educational theories, you may think that perennialism, behaviorism, and essentialism represent the more conservative or traditional views of education, while progressivism, reconstructionism, and existentialism represent the more modern or liberal views. In truth, such a simple dichotomy actually clouds the issue and masks the real reasons behind the various protests that led to the development of each theory. For example, the protest culminating in perennialism was not against those educational theories that might be construed as modern or liberal. Rather, it was a protest against secularization and the excessive focus on science and technology at the expense of reason that dominated society and its educational institutions at the time.

As you review each educational theory, keep in mind the similarities and differences among the theories and the reasons or rationales behind the protests.

Perennialism

Eternal or perennial truths, permanence, order, certainty, rationality, and logic constitute the ideal for the perennialist. The philosophies of neo-Thomism and realism are embedded in the perennialist theory of education. Kneller (1971) described six basic principles of *perennialism*:

1. Despite differing environments, human nature remains the same everywhere; hence, education should be the same for everyone.

2. Since rationality is man's highest attribute, he must use it to direct his instinctual nature in accordance with deliberately chosen ends.

3. It is education's task to import knowledge of eternal truth.

4. Education is not an imitation of life, but a preparation for it.

5. The student should be taught certain basic subjects that will aquaint him with the world's permanencies.

6. Students should study the great works of literature, philosophy, history, and science in which men through the ages have revealed their greatest aspirations and achievements. (pp. 42–45)

The educational focus of perennialism is on the need to return to the past, namely, to universal truths and such absolutes as reason and faith. The views of Thomas Aquinas best personify this educational theory. (The Historical Note on page 202 gives a brief look at Aquinas' life.) Although perennialism has been associated historically with the teachings of the Roman Catholic Church, as a theory of education it has received widespread support from lay educators. Aristotle's views best represent this group of perennialists. Whether one is an ecclesiastical (Thomist) or a lay (neo-Thomist) perennialist, one would envision the purpose of the school to be to cultivate the rational intellect and to search for the truth.

Curriculum

For the ecclesiastical perennialist, Christian doctrine is an important aspect of the curriculum. The holy scriptures, the catechism, and the teaching of Christian dogma play a significant role. Wherever possible, theistic works would take precedence over purely secular works (Morris & Pai, 1976).

The curriculum of the perennialist education emphasizes a concern for subject matter. The cognitive subjects of mathematics, especially algebra and geometry, history, languages, logic, literature (in particular the *Great Books*), and science would occupy a central position in the perennialist curriculum since they epitomize Absolute Truth. Mastery of these subjects is considered necessary for the training of the intellect. In addition, the perennialist would contend that character training and moral development have an appropriate place in the design of the curriculum.

More recently, perennialists such as Mortimer Adler have placed less emphasis on subject matter. Rather, they view it as the context for developing

Consider yourself a perennialist. Choose 10 Great Books that you believe best represent absolute truth. At what grade level would you introduce these Great Books?

Historical Note:
St. Thomas Aquinas

St. Thomas Aquinas was born of a noble family in Roccasecca, Italy, in 1224. From 1239 to 1244 he attended the University of Naples, where he came in contact with the Dominican order. Against the violent opposition of his parents, Thomas became a Dominican friar in 1244. During the years 1245 to 1252, he studied philosophy and theology under the tutelage of the German theologian St. Albertus Magnus. From 1252 to 1259 and again from 1269 to 1272 he taught at the University of Paris where he was known as "The Angelic Doctor." In between he taught at the Papal Curia in Italy.

Aquinas' two most influential works were the *Summa Contra Gentiles*, which expressed the doctrine of scholasticism or Christian philosophy, and his most important work, *Summa Theologica*. In the latter work Thomas attempted to explain the truth of Christian theology and advanced the proposition that conflict need not exist between reason and faith.

Thomas believed that the government had a moral responsibility to assist the individual to lead a virtuous life. He further postulated that governments must not violate human rights, including the right to life, education, religion, and reproduction. Laws passed by human beings must be in concert with divine laws. He died in 1274.

In 1323, Pope John XXII canonized Aquinas and since then his philosophy has become the official doctrine of the Roman Catholic Church. In 1567, Pope St. Pius V proclaimed him a doctor of the Church. He has also been proclaimed the patron saint of all Catholic schools, colleges, and universities.

intellectual skills, including reading, writing, speaking, listening, observing, computing, measuring, estimating, and problem solving.

Teaching Methods

Perennialists maintain that education involves confronting the problems and questions that have challenged people over the centuries. The teaching methods deemed most appropriate for this confrontation are discussion, debate, and dialogue. Since the aim of the curriculum is to foster an intellectual and liberal approach to learning, any technique or strategy that would emphasize the laws of reasoning and the canons of induction would be chosen, as well as those that promote memory, drill and practice, recitation, and computation. Additionally, before studying the great works of literature, philosophy, history, and science, students would be taught methods of critical thinking and questioning strategies to prepare them to engage in "dialogue" with the classical writers.

For the ecclesiastical perennialists the highest goal of education is union with God. For these perennialists any type of teaching method that brings the learner into direct contact with the pure Spirit would be encouraged.

Classroom Management

In addition to training the intellect, perennialists believe that the teacher has the obligation to discipline in order to train the will. They would consider the most appropriate classroom environment for training the will to be one that is characterized as rigid and structured. A formal classroom that reinforces time on task, precision, and order best describes the learning environment of perennialism. In addition to orderliness and regularity, for the ecclesiastical perennialists the learning environment would also reflect an appreciation for prayer and contemplation.

Evaluation

Since perennialists place such a heavy emphasis on discipline, mental training, the development of reason, and the development of the will, the evaluation methods they would use assess those goals. Accordingly, the standardized, objective examination would be favored as an evaluation tool. In addition, because the study of the classical tradition of the Great Books promotes an exchange of ideas and insights, the essay examination would also be utilized.

The Perennialist Teacher

Perennialists view the teacher who is well educated in the liberal arts as the authority figure, the instrument that provides for the dissemination of truth. And if the teacher is the disseminator, then the student is the receptacle for learning. The metaphor "director of mental calisthenics" has been used to describe the perennialist teacher (Morris & Pai, 1976).

Another metaphor that describes the perennialist teacher is "the demonstrator or scientist." The perennialist teacher must be a model of intellectual and rational powers. He or she must be capable of logical analysis, comfortable with the scientific method, well versed in the classics, have a good memory, and be capable of the highest forms of mental reasoning. In short, he or she must be a scholar in the most literal sense.

Leading Educational Proponents

Jacques Maritain (1882–1973), a French Catholic philosopher who served as ambassador to the Holy See and who was a prominent figure in the United Nations Educational, Scientific and Cultural Organization (UNESCO), is perhaps the best spokesperson for the ecclesiastical perennialist position. According to Maritain (1941), intelligence alone is not sufficient to comprehend the universe fully. One's relationship to a Spiritual Being is necessary to understand the cosmos or universe. Robert M. Hutchins (1899–1977), former chancellor of the University of Chicago and founder of the Center on the Study of Democratic Institutions, was a noted spokesperson for the lay perennialist perspective. Hutchins (1936) argued that the ideal education was one that is designed to develop the mind. This can be done best by a curriculum that concentrates on the Great Books of western civilization.

The work of Mortimer Adler in the 1980s represents a resurgence of perennialism. In *The Paideia Proposal: An Educational Manifesto* (1982), Adler

Both Robert Hutchins (left) and Mortimer Adler (right) advocated the Great Books and the enduring lessons from the past.

advocated a curriculum that would be appropriate for all students. Adler, as well as Hutchins, opposed differential curricula (e.g., vocational vs. academic) and contended that all students in a democratic society should have access to the same high-quality education. This education is characterized by a curriculum that includes language, literature, mathematics, natural sciences, fine arts, history, geography, and social studies. Like Hutchins, Adler favors the Great Books tradition and maintains that by studying the great works of the past, one can learn enduring lessons about life that are relevant today.

Recently Allan Bloom, another perennialist, has referred to the crisis of liberal education, particularly in the university, as an intellectual crisis. In Bloom's book *The Closing of the American Mind* (1987) he refers to cultural illiteracy as the crisis of our civilization. Like Hutchins and Adler, Bloom advocates teaching and learning about the Great Books.

The curriculum of St. John's College at Annapolis, Maryland and Santa Fe, New Mexico, which emphasizes the importance of studying the Great Books tradition, is an excellent example of the perennialist curriculum. Overall, there are few examples of perennialism in education today. Figure 7.1 presents an overview of perennialism.

As a response to Allan Bloom's perceived "crisis in our civilization," what suggestions would you make for revamping the general studies curriculum at the university level?

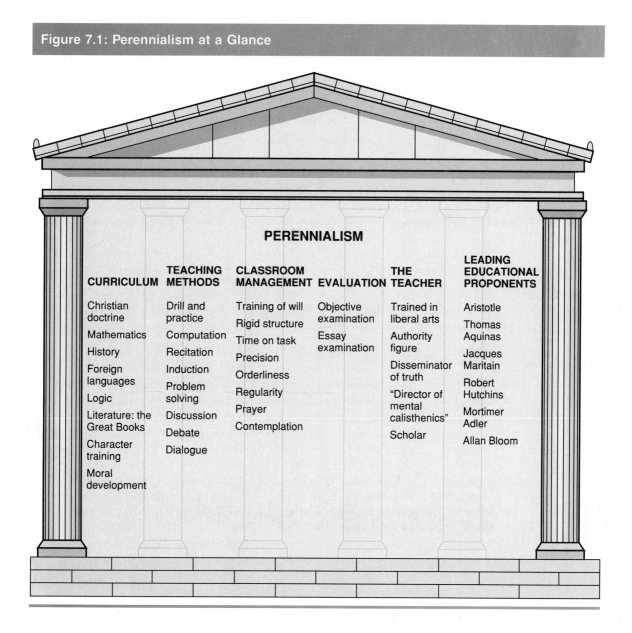

Figure 7.1: Perennialism at a Glance

PERENNIALISM

CURRICULUM	TEACHING METHODS	CLASSROOM MANAGEMENT	EVALUATION	THE TEACHER	LEADING EDUCATIONAL PROPONENTS
Christian doctrine	Drill and practice	Training of will	Objective examination	Trained in liberal arts	Aristotle
Mathematics	Computation	Rigid structure	Essay examination	Authority figure	Thomas Aquinas
History	Recitation	Time on task		Disseminator of truth	Jacques Maritain
Foreign languages	Induction	Precision		"Director of mental calisthenics"	Robert Hutchins
Logic	Problem solving	Orderliness			Mortimer Adler
Literature: the Great Books	Discussion	Regularity		Scholar	Allan Bloom
Character training	Debate	Prayer			
Moral development	Dialogue	Contemplation			

Progressivism

There are a variety of opinions concerning whether it is most appropriate to describe the educational theory that follows as pragmatism, instrumentalism, or *progressivism*. Regardless of the terminology used, what is common to any description of these terms is an educational theory that embraces the notion that the child is an experiencing organism who is capable of "learning by doing." The authors of this text believe that the term progressivism best describes this educational theory. The philosophy of experimentalism is embedded in the progressivist theory of education.

Kneller (1971) summarized six basic principles of the educational theory of progressivism.

1. Education should be life itself, not a preparation for living.

2. Learning should be directly related to the interests of the child.

3. Learning through problem-solving should take precedence over the inculcating of subject matter.

4. The teacher's role is not to direct but to advise.

5. The school should encourage cooperation rather than competition.

6. Only democracy permits—indeed encourages—the free interplay of ideas and personalities that is a necessary condition of true growth. (pp. 48–52)

This view of education is grounded in the scientific method of inductive reasoning. As an educational theory, it encourages the learner to seek out those processes that work and to do those things that best achieve desirable ends.

Curriculum

If one were to choose a description that best characterizes the progressivist curriculum, it would be problem solving and experience-centered. Such a curriculum would not consist of a given set of predetermined facts or truths to be mastered, but rather a series of experiences to be gained. For the progressivist, the subject matter or content to be studied would not be as important as the educative process itself, and that educative process would be the scientific method. Thus, it is not as important whether we study geography, history, or mathematics; what really matters is that all subjects begin with the experience of the individual. According to the progressivist, the subject matter of the curriculum would include any type of experience that would be meaningful and educational to the student. Such a curriculum would not reflect universal truths, a particular body of knowledge, or a core of courses *per se*. Rather, it would be responsive to the needs and experiences of the individual, which would vary from situation to situation.

Another important consideration in the design of the progressivist curriculum is relevance. Any materials that are used in the curriculum are chosen because of their relevance. The progressivist is not interested in the study of the past, but is governed by the present. Unlike the perennialist or essentialist who advocates the importance of the cultural and historic roots of the past, the progressivist advocates that which is meaningful and relevant to the student today.

Teaching Methods

For the progressivist, since there is no rigid subject matter content and since there is no absolute standard for what constitutes knowledge, the most appropriate teaching method is the project method. The experience-centered or problem-solving curriculum lends itself to cooperative group activities whereby students can learn to work together on units or projects that have relevance for their own lives. The indispensable instructional strategy that would be used along with the project method is the scientific method. However, unlike the perennialist or essentialist who views the scientific method as a means of verifying truth, the progressivist views scientific investigation as a means of verifying experience. What makes the outcomes of certain hypotheses true for the progressivist is that they work and that they are related to the individual's experience.

Since the progressivist curriculum is not a static curriculum but rather an emerging one, any teaching method that would foster individual and group initiative, spontaneity of expression, and creative new ideas would be used. Classroom activities in critical thinking, problem solving, decision making, networking, data collecting, and experimental inquiry are examples of some of the methods that would be incorporated in the curriculum.

Classroom Management

Progressivism views learning as educating "the whole child," including the physical, emotional and social aspects of the individual. As a result of this holistic view of education, the environment is considered fundamental to the child's nature.

How can a subject-oriented secondary school teacher justify a holistic view of education?

The type of classroom management that would appeal to a progressivist would be an environment that stimulates or invites participation, involvement, and the democratic process. Such an environment would not only be child-centered or student-centered but also community-centered. It would feature an open environment in which students would spend considerable time in direct contact with the community or cultural surroundings beyond the confines of the classroom or school. Students would experience the arts by frequenting museums and theaters. They would experience social studies by interacting with individuals from diverse social groups and social conditions. They would experience science by exploring their immediate physical world.

The progressivist teacher would foster a classroom environment that practices democracy. Students and parents would be encouraged to form their own councils and organizations within the school to address educational issues and advance social change.

With students deciding on appropriate rules and content to be studied, the teacher would manage groups of students engaged in a variety of simultaneous classroom tasks. Being able to distinguish between instructional and disruptive noise, to cope with a number of distractions, and to plan for the problems that emerge from a student-centered classroom are a few of the daily challenges that confront the progressivist teacher.

Evaluation

Since progressivism supports the group process, collaborative decision making, and democratic participation in the total educational experience, its

What type of process-oriented evaluation would you be most comfortable using in your teaching?

approach to evaluation differs from the more traditional approach. For example, the progressivist would engage in *formative evaluation*, which is process oriented and concerned with ongoing feedback about the activity underway rather than the measurement of outcomes. Monitoring what the students are doing, appraising what skills they still need to develop, and resolving unexpected problems as they occur would be typical of this type of evaluation used by the progressivist.

The Progressivist Teacher

The metaphor of the "teacher as facilitator" or "director of learning" might best describe the progressivist teacher. Such a teacher is not considered to be the authority or disseminator of knowledge or truth like the perennialist or essentialist teacher. Rather, he or she serves more as a guide or supervisor who facilitates learning by assisting the student to sample direct experience. Although the teacher is always interested in the individual development of each student, the progressivist instructor would envision his or her role as focusing beyond the individual. Progressivism by its very nature is socially oriented; thus the teacher would be a collaborative partner in making group decisions, keeping in mind their ultimate consequences for the students.

Leading Educational Proponents

Progressivism had its impetus in the first decades of the twentieth century at a time when many liberal thinkers alleged that American schools were out of touch with the advances that were being made in the physical and social sciences and technology (see Chapter 5). It is John Dewey who, perhaps more than any other American educator, is credited with having advanced progressivism. Dewey's approach to progressivism differed from earlier progressive educators in that rather than emphasize the individual learner, Dewey emphasized the importance of the teacher/student interaction and the importance of education as a social function.

One of the most important principles of Dewey's educational theory was the connection between education and personal experience. For Dewey, experience was the basis of education. However, he cautioned (1938) that not all experiences are equal:

> The belief that all genuine education comes about through experience does not mean that all experiences are genuinely or equally educative. Experience and education cannot be directly equated to each other. For some experiences are mis-educative. Any experience is mis-education that has the effect of arresting or distorting the growth of further experience. (p. 25)

John Dewey's establishment of the University Laboratory School at the University of Chicago provided the clinical testing ground for his educational theory. His leadership at the University of Chicago and his subsequent work at Teachers College, Columbia left a legacy to American education. Although some educators would argue that progressivism in education is no longer accepted as the leading philosophy of the 1990s, its profound impact on American education through the 1960s and 1970s is without debate. In fact, its critics contend that progressivism was the major cause of the decline in student performance in the 1960s and 1970s. Vestiges of progressivism can be found in *nongraded schools*, *alternative schools*, the *whole-child movement*, *humanistic education*, bilingual education, and some of the "open" educational arrangements. Figure 7.2 presents an overview of progressivism.

What do you see as the advantages and disadvantages of a nongraded school?

Figure 7.2: Progressivism at a Glance

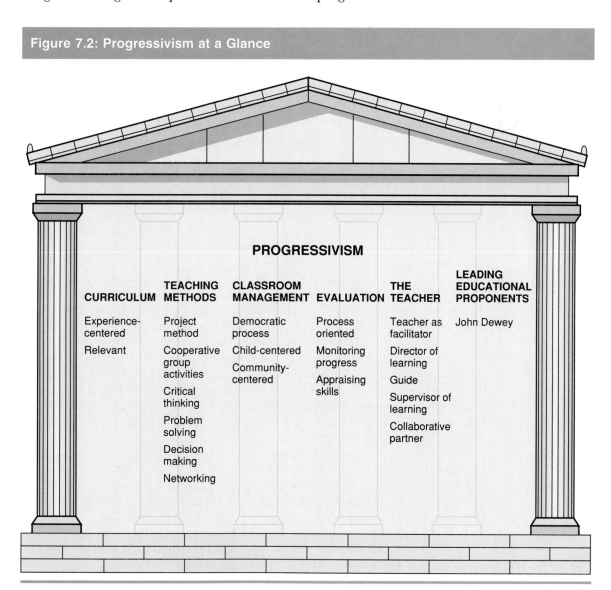

PROGRESSIVISM

CURRICULUM	TEACHING METHODS	CLASSROOM MANAGEMENT	EVALUATION	THE TEACHER	LEADING EDUCATIONAL PROPONENTS
Experience-centered	Project method	Democratic process	Process oriented	Teacher as facilitator	John Dewey
Relevant	Cooperative group activities	Child-centered	Monitoring progress	Director of learning	
	Critical thinking	Community-centered	Appraising skills	Guide	
	Problem solving			Supervisor of learning	
	Decision making			Collaborative partner	
	Networking				

Behaviorism

Behaviorism or behavioral engineering is an educational theory that is predicated on the belief that human behavior can be explained in terms of responses to external stimuli. The basic principle of behaviorism is that education can best be achieved by modifying or changing student behaviors in a socially acceptable manner through the arrangement of the conditions for learning. For the behaviorist, the predictability and control of human behavior are paramount concepts. The control is obtained not by manipulating the individual but by manipulating the environment.

The basic principles of the theory of behaviorism are as follows:

1. All behaviors are both objective and observable.

2. All behaviors are caused.

3. As natural organisms we seek positive reinforcement and avoid punishment.

4. The teacher should arrange conditions under which learning can occur.

5. Technology makes it possible for teachers to teach beyond their knowledge of content or subject matter.

6. Students will learn best by the use of carefully planned schedules of reinforcement.

There are two major types of behaviorism: (1) *classical conditioning* or stimulus substitution behaviorism, and (2) *operant conditioning* or response reinforcement behaviorism (Phillips & Soltis, 1985). Classical conditioning, based on the work of the Russian physiologist Ivan Pavlov (1849–1936) and the American experimental psychologist John B. Watson (1878–1958), demonstrates that a natural stimulus that produces a certain type of response can be replaced by a conditioned stimulus. For example, Pavlov found that in laboratory experiments with dogs the natural stimulus such as food will produce a natural response such as salivation. However, when Pavlov paired the natural stimulus (food) with a conditioned stimulus (bell), he found that eventually the conditioned stimulus (bell) produced a conditioned response (salivation). Watson eventually used Pavlov's classical conditioning model to explain all human learning.

The operant conditioning model can best be described by the work of psychologists E. L. Thorndike (1874–1949) and B. F. Skinner (1904–1990). Both Thorndike and Skinner suggested that any response to any stimulus can be conditioned by immediate reinforcement or reward. Skinner later determined that an action or response does not have to be rewarded each time it occurs. In fact, Skinner found that random reward or intermittent reinforcement was a more effective method for learning than continuous reward. Skinner also discovered that behavior could be shaped by the appropriate use of rewards.

As a theory of education, behaviorism was a protest against the importance placed on mental processes that could not be observed (e.g., thinking or motivation). Today, behaviorism has taken a more moderate stance and has adopted a cognitive-behaviorial approach which attempts to change the individual's cognitions or perceptions of the world and his or her self.

Curriculum

Unlike the curriculum of perennialism and essentialism, which advocate a prescribed subject matter, the behaviorist curriculum is not interested in subject matter *per se*, but is interested in environmental variables such as teaching materials, teaching methods, and teacher-classroom behaviors, since they directly influence the learner's behavior (Wittrock, 1987). The behaviorist curriculum includes cognitive problem-solving activities whereby students learn about their belief systems, recognize their power to influence their environment, and employ critical-thinking skills.

As a teacher, how could you help your students learn about their belief systems or values?

Teaching Methods

Behaviorist theory is primarily concerned with the process of providing contingencies of reinforcement as the basis for any strategy or method. If there are appropriate opportunities for the learner to respond and appropriate reinforcers that are readily available, learning will take place, say the behaviorists. Skinner supported the use of the teaching machine or *programmed instruction* as an effective teaching method. Programmed instruction enables individual students to answer questions about a unit of study at their own rate, checking their own answers and advancing only after answering correctly. A chief advantage of the teaching machine or programmed instruction is the immediate reinforcement that it provides. Today, computers have replaced the teaching machine. A wide variety of computer-assisted instruction, including interactive multimedia, has become a favored teaching method of many educators, in particular the behaviorists.

Classroom Management

For the behaviorist, classroom management is an integral part of the process of learning. Emmer (1987) described two general principles that guide the behaviorist teacher in classroom management:

1. Identify expected student behavior. This implies that teachers must have a clear idea of what behaviors are appropriate and are not appropriate in advance of instruction.

2. Translate expectations into procedures and routines. Part of the process of translating expectations into procedures is to formulate some general rules governing conduct. (pp. 438–439)

Other components of good management include careful monitoring or observation of classroom events; prompt and appropriate handling of inappropriate behavior; using reward systems, penalties, and other consequences; establishing accountability for completion of assignments; and maintaining lesson or activity flow (Emmer, 1987). Behaviorism is widely used in special education and mainstreamed classroom environments.

Evaluation

Measurement and evaluation are central to the behaviorist. Specified *behavioral objectives* (e.g., the behaviors or knowledge that students are expected to demonstrate or learn) serve not only as guides to learning for the student, but as standards for evaluating the teaching-learning process. For the behaviorist, only those aspects of behavior that are observable and preferably measurable are of interest to the teacher. Advocates of behavioral objectives claim that if teachers know exactly what they want students to learn and how they want them to learn, using behavioral objectives can be an efficient method for gauging how much learning has occurred. Measurement and evaluation also provide a method for obtaining accountability from teachers since they are pivotal to the learning process. Two other types of evaluation used by the behaviorist teacher include performance contracting and teaching students to record their own progress.

The Behaviorist Teacher

Since education as behavioral engineering entails a variety of technical and observational skills, the behaviorist teacher must be skilled in a variety of these techniques. Moreover, since behavioral engineering depends on psychological principles, the teacher must be knowledgeable about psychology, in particular educational psychology that emphasizes learning. Also, since behaviorism focuses on empirical verification, the teacher must be well versed in the scientific method.

What type of reinforcer would be most apt to motivate you to learn?

The behaviorist teacher is very concerned about the consequences of classroom behavior. Therefore, the teacher must be able to recognize which reinforcers are most appropriate. In addition, the behaviorist teacher must be skilled in using a variety of schedules of reinforcement that are effective and efficient in shaping and maintaining desired responses.

To establish the behaviors that will be most beneficial to the learner, behaviorist teachers are most concerned with the student's achieving specific objectives or competencies. For this reason the teacher must be capable of planning and using behavioral objectives, designing and using programmed instruction, using computers, and utilizing performance contracting. Two of the most appropriate metaphors for describing the behaviorist teacher are "the controller of behavior" and "the arranger of contingencies."

Leading Educational Proponents

As previously noted, classical conditioning had its beginnings with Pavlov and Watson. Both maintained that classical conditioning was the key mechanism underlying all human learning. The behaviorists Thorndike and Skinner are known for the concept of operant conditioning, which suggests that reinforcement of responses (operant behavior) underlies all types of learning.

Another noted behaviorist, psychologist David Premack, determined that organisms often freely choose to engage in certain behaviors rather than other behaviors. Consequently, providing access to the preferred activities can serve as a reinforcement for not engaging in nonpreferred activities. To apply the *Premack principle* in the classroom, the teacher first must observe and carefully record the behavior that students more often freely choose to perform and the relative frequency of competing behaviors (Bates, 1987). Figure 7.3 provides an overview of behaviorism.

Figure 7.3: Behaviorism at a Glance

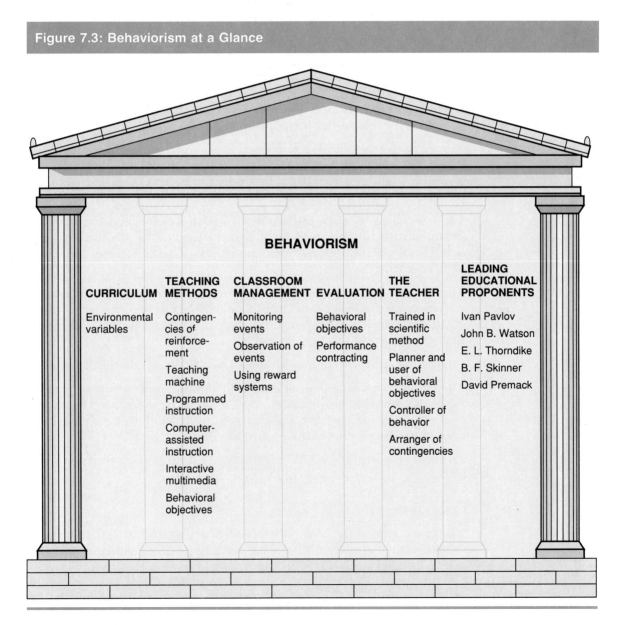

BEHAVIORISM

CURRICULUM	TEACHING METHODS	CLASSROOM MANAGEMENT	EVALUATION	THE TEACHER	LEADING EDUCATIONAL PROPONENTS
Environmental variables	Contingencies of reinforcement	Monitoring events	Behavioral objectives	Trained in scientific method	Ivan Pavlov
	Teaching machine	Observation of events	Performance contracting	Planner and user of behavioral objectives	John B. Watson
	Programmed instruction	Using reward systems		Controller of behavior	E. L. Thorndike
	Computer-assisted instruction			Arranger of contingencies	B. F. Skinner
	Interactive multimedia				David Premack
	Behavioral objectives				

Essentialism

Historically, there have been a variety of opinions concerning whether essentialism is a true educational theory. A number of scholars have suggested that essentialism is actually perennialism in disguise. If one were to choose a single adjective that best describes essentialism, it would probably be "eclectic." The philosophies of idealism and realism are embedded in the essentialist theory of education. Protesting against progressivism, essentialists believe that pragmatism or progressivism has had a negative impact on American education and that there is a need to return to the traditional or conservative educational goals.

Wingo (1974) described six basic tenets of essentialism:

1. Americans largely have lost sight of the true purpose of education, which is intellectual training. We tend to confuse education with all kinds of social, psychological, and vocational services that often are lumped together under the rubric "life adjustment."

2. The rigor of our educational programs and teaching methods has been declining steadily for several decades. This is true in some measure of every level of the school system from the kindergarten to the university, but the condition is particularly acute in the elementary and secondary schools.

3. We have failed to provide for the education of our brightest children because instruction has been pitched at the level of the mediocre student and the ablest have been systematically deprived in the name of "equality" and "democracy."

4. The curricula of our schools have been diluted by the introduction of courses consisting largely of "life adjustment" trivia, and these worthless substitutes have crowded out the historic disciplines that are the core of the true education.

5. Intellectual achievement has declined steadily among American students.

6. The schools are failing to meet their obligations to American youth and to American society. They are not only failing in the intellectual task, they also are failing in their responsibility to transmit those values that are the basis of the American tradition. (pp. 51–52)

Like the perennialists, essentialists believe that the best preparation for life is learning the culture and traditions of the past.

Curriculum

The curriculum of the essentialist school is a basic education that includes instruction in the "essentials," including reading, writing, and computing at the primary grades and history, geography, natural sciences, and foreign languages at the upper elementary grades. At the secondary level, the curriculum would place a major emphasis on the common core that all students should complete. Such a core would normally include four years of English, three or four years of social studies, a course in American government, and a year of natural science and general mathematics or algebra (Conant, 1959).Such a common core represents the comprehensive high school that was most popular during the 1950s. Some essentialists believe that the educational curriculum should not be limited only to the academic disciplines. They suggest that the physical and emotional well-being of the child is important (Wingo, 1974). Overall, essentialists maintain that the educational program should not permit any "frivolous" subjects, but rather should adhere strictly to sound academic standards.

What subjects might be construed as "frivolous" by an essentialist?

Teaching Methods

If the basic disciplines or basic subjects are at the heart of the school curriculum, then the methods of instruction that are to support such a curriculum include the more traditional instructional strategies such as lecture, recitation, discussion, and the Socratic dialogue. Written and oral communication occupy a prominent place in the instructional milieu of the essentialist school. Like perennialists, essentialists view books as an appropriate medium for instruction. Probably more than the other educational theories, essentialism deplores the lack of educational standards or the so-called "soft pedagogy."

Generally, essentialist educators have found educational technology to be congruent with their educational theory. They prefer instructional materials that are paced and sequenced in such a way that students know what they are expected to master. Detailed syllabi, lesson plans, learning by objectives, competency-based instruction, computer-assisted instruction, and audio-tutorial laboratory methods are other examples of teaching strategies that would be acceptable to the modern-day essentialist.

Classroom Management

Like the perennialists, who advocate intellectual discipline as well as moral discipline, the essentialists maintain that character training deserves an important place in the school. For the essentialist, students attend school to learn how to participate in society, not to manage the course of their own instruction. They prepare for life by being exposed to essential truths and values, as well as by exercising discipline. Thus, the essentialist teacher would take great pains in designing and controlling a classroom environment that creates an aura of certainty, an emphasis on regularity and uniformity, and a reverence for what is morally right.

Evaluation

Of all the theories of education, essentialism is perhaps most comfortable with testing. In fact, the entire essentialist curriculum reflects the influence of the testing movement. Extensive use of IQ tests, standardized achievement tests, diagnostic tests, and performance-based competency tests are examples of the widespread application of measurement techniques. Competency, accountability, mastery learning (see Chapter 16), and performance-based instruction have gained increasing acceptance by many educators as a result of the essentialists' influence on educational practice.

The Essentialist Teacher

The essentialist teacher, like the perennialist teacher, is an educator who has faith in the accumulated wisdom of the past. Rather than having majored in educational pedagogy, the essentialist teacher would have majored in a subject matter discipline, preferably in the liberal arts, science, or the humanities. The essentialist educator is viewed as either a link to the so-called "literary intellectual inheritance" (idealism) or as a demonstrator of the world model (realism). To be an essentialist teacher is to be well versed in the liberal arts, to be a respected member of the intellectual community, to be technically skilled in all forms of communication, and to be equipped with superior pedagogical skills to ensure competent instruction.

Contemporary essentialists such as Delattre (1984) have been critical of the preprofessional training of teachers since they believe that their training falls short of what is demanded of teachers today:

> Many have been subjected to too many textbooks and not enough original books: some have never read basic and profound works on learning, knowing, and teaching—have never been exposed to Deuteronomy, works by Plato, Aristotle, Loyola, Milton, Agassiz, Hadas, or Highet, not to mention Augustine and the intellectual predecessors of Dewey. That is, some cannot teach themselves in any systematic program of study because they do not know enough to design one, and their own teachers are not always qualified to do so for them. (p. 159)

Leading Educational Proponents

Although essentialism can be traced to Plato and Aristotle, its greatest popularity has emerged in the twentieth century. As noted in Chapter 5, in the 1930s and 1940s William C. Bagley, Arthur E. Bestor, and Herman H. Horne (1874–1946) led the essentialist criticism of the progressivism of Dewey and his followers. They formed the Essentialist Committee for the Advancement of American Education. In the 1950s, Admiral Hyman G. Rickover (1900–1986) became the spokesperson for the essentialists. According to Rickover (1963), the quality of American education declined considerably as a result of "watered-down" courses and "fads and frills." He called for a return to the basics, with particular emphasis on mathematics and science.

If you were an essentialist, would you raise the academic standards at the university? In what ways?

A major revival of essentialism has been evidenced by the *back-to-basics movement* that gained support in the 1970s and has been echoed in the education reform reports of the 1980s. For example, *A Nation at Risk* (National Commission on Excellence in Education, 1983), the premier of these reports, recommended a core of *new basics*: English, mathematics, science, social studies, and computer sciences, and for the college-bound a foreign language.

Many of the other reports not only proposed similar cores, but called for improvement in their content and increased rigor in their standards (see Chapter 15). The success of the essentialist position is evidenced by the steps taken in a number of states to mandate curricula, strengthen graduation requirements, and increase student testing and evaluation. Essentialism is the dominant philosophy in our schools today. Figure 7.4 presents an overview of essentialism.

Figure 7.4: Essentialism at a Glance

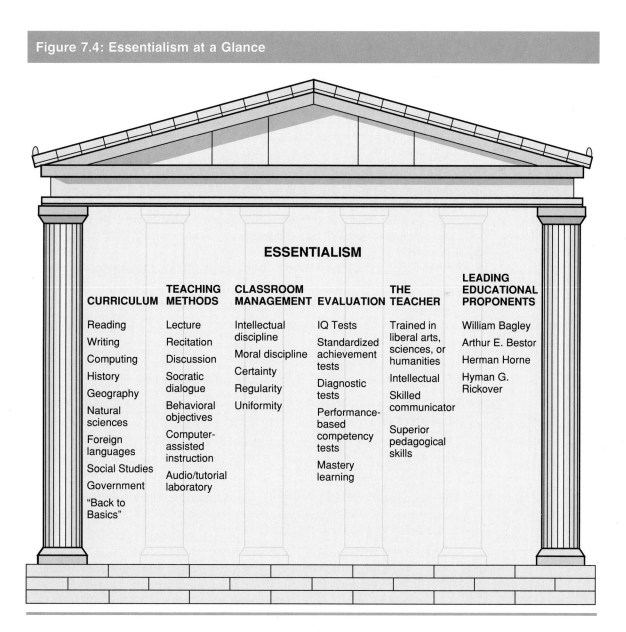

ESSENTIALISM

CURRICULUM	TEACHING METHODS	CLASSROOM MANAGEMENT	EVALUATION	THE TEACHER	LEADING EDUCATIONAL PROPONENTS
Reading	Lecture	Intellectual discipline	IQ Tests	Trained in liberal arts, sciences, or humanities	William Bagley
Writing	Recitation	Moral discipline	Standardized achievement tests		Arthur E. Bestor
Computing	Discussion	Certainty			Herman Horne
History	Socratic dialogue	Regularity	Diagnostic tests	Intellectual	Hyman G. Rickover
Geography		Uniformity		Skilled communicator	
Natural sciences	Behavioral objectives		Performance-based competency tests		
Foreign languages	Computer-assisted instruction			Superior pedagogical skills	
Social Studies	Audio/tutorial laboratory		Mastery learning		
Government					
"Back to Basics"					

Reconstructionism

Throughout history there have been reconstructionists who have aspired to improve, change, or reform society, including its educational institutions. Certainly Plato, who advocated a design for a future state in the *Republic*, could be considered a reconstructionist, as could the Christian philosopher Augustine, who sought to create an ideal Christian state. Likewise, Karl Marx (1818–1883), who decried the alienation and dehumanization of the worker and envisioned a reconstructed world based on international communism, could be considered a reconstructionist (Ozmon & Craver, 1990). Each of these individuals advocated far-reaching changes that anticipated radical social and educational reforms.

The educational theory of reconstructionism (referred to in Chapter 5 as social reconstructionism) has two predominant themes: (1) society is in need of change or reconstruction, and (2) education must take the lead in the reconstruction of society. It was John Dewey who suggested the term "reconstructionism" by the title of his book, *Reconstruction in Philosophy* (1920). Shortly thereafter, in the early 1930s, a group known as the "Frontier Thinkers" looked to the schools for leadership in creating a "new" and "more equitable" society (Kneller, 1971). These educational reformers advocated changes beyond what Dewey envisioned in his theory of progressivism. His emphasis was on the democratic social experience, theirs was on social reform.

Kneller (1971) described the main theses of reconstructionism as follows:

1. Education must commit itself here and now to the creation of a new social order that will fulfill the basic values of our culture and at the same time harmonize with the underlying social and economic forces of the modern world.

2. The new society must be a genuine democracy, whose major institutions and resources are controlled by the people themselves.

3. The child, the school, and education itself are conditioned inexorably by social and cultural forces.

4. The teacher must convince his pupils of the validity and urgency of the reconstructionist solution, but he must do so with scrupulous regard for democratic procedures.

5. The means and ends of education must be completely refashioned to meet the demands of the present cultural crisis and to accord with the findings of the behavioral sciences. (pp. 61–64)

Modern reconstructionism has been called "a theory of vision," "a theory of education-as-politics," "a theory of transformation," and "a theory of social reform." For the reconstructionist, the school should be an agency of social change, a participant in the construction of a society free of all forms of discrimination and concerned with issues of global welfare.

Social reconstructionists aspire to improve, change, or reform society.

Curriculum

Since the majority of reconstructionists believe in the importance of democracy and the proposition that the school is the fundamental institution in modern society, the curriculum of the reconstructionist school would reflect those democratic ideals. The emphasis would be on cultural pluralism, human relations, group dynamics, problem solving, and the politics of change. And since reconstructionists emphasize insights from the social and behavioral sciences, the curriculum would include economics, political science, anthropology, sociology, and psychology (in particular, social psychology and organizational psychology). The study of these subjects provides the tools and insights necessary to engage in a critical examination of society and to design its reconstruction—a primary function of the educational process.

Since the school should be viewed as an instrument for change, say the reconstructionists, one of the most effective methods for initiating change would be by studying the future. Accordingly, the study of the thinking of various futurists would occupy a central place in the curriculum of the reconstructionist school. In addition to the future, reconstructionists believe that students should be engaged in learning about other cultures, other mores, and other languages. At the heart of the reconstructionist curriculum would be activism and reform. Students would be encouraged to become involved in the social problems that confront the community and society. For example, rather than simply reading and studying about the problems of the poor or deinstitutionalization of the chronically mentally ill, students would spend time in the community becoming acquainted with and involved in these problems and their possible remedies or solutions. Reconstructionists favor learning in real life beyond the classroom or the school.

Teaching Methods

Like the progressivists, reconstructionists consider the most appropriate teaching methods to be those that promote problem solving, critical thinking, creative thinking, decision making, group process, and networking. Since the thrust of the curriculum of the reconstructionist school is planning for change, the teaching methods of simulation, gaming, role-playing, internships, and work-study experiences would be used. And since the goal of reform necessitates change-oriented teaching strategies, the "training of trainers" method would be considered another appropriate teaching strategy. Embedded in such a strategy would be a process whereby the trained change agent (student) trains other prospective change agents (interns or apprentice-students) in the art of reform.

Classroom Management

Can you name one or two so-called "Utopian thinkers"? How successful were they in achieving their ideal world?

The classroom environment for the reconstructionist would be a creative environment that questions the assumptions of the status quo and examines societal issues and future trends. Reconstructionists have a penchant for utopian thinking and alternative solutions. Therefore, the environment of the classroom might take on a "think tank" or problem-solving atmosphere in which students would be encouraged to take on new roles and experiment with the ideal world.

The teacher responsible for a reconstructionist classroom would model optimism and hope for the future. An atmosphere that promotes analysis, assessment, and evaluation would best describe this type of classroom environment. Conflict resolution and differences in world views would be encouraged and reinforced. The classroom in the school and life experience in the larger society would become the stage for experimentation and imaginative problem solving. Individuals, groups, and teams of students would become engaged in a variety of creative problem-solving activities. The underlying goals of these activities would be to develop conceptual flexibility and the willingness to question assumptions. Such an environment would condone a new respect for "expecting the unexpected."

Evaluation

The type of evaluation that would be appropriate for both the student and the teacher in a reconstructionist school would be formative evaluation that would entail a cooperative effort between student and teacher, student and student, teacher and administrator or supervisor, and community and teacher. The objectives of the evaluation would be developed cooperatively by all the parties concerned and progress would be monitored according to an agreed-upon plan. Information would be shared regularly during periodic formal and informal conferences and the student or teacher being evaluated would be an active participant in the process. Evaluation in an environment that promotes change would include ongoing feedback to students and teachers concerning their performance, strengths, deficiencies, and any corrective steps that should be taken to improve the situation. Although the reconstructionist educator would consider the needs of the individual as well as the needs of the organization, conflict would not be viewed as failure nor would the lack of consensus be considered problematic.

The Reconstructionist Teacher

The metaphors "shaper of a new society," "transformational leader," and "change agent" aptly describe the reconstructionist teacher. George S. Counts (1933) described the teacher and his or her responsibilities for reform in the following way:

> To teach the ideal in its historic form, without the illumination that comes from an effort to apply it to contemporary society, is an extreme evidence of intellectual dishonesty. It constitutes an attempt to educate the youth for life in a world that does not exist. Teachers, therefore, cannot evade the responsibility of participating actively in the task of reconstituting the democratic tradition and of thus working positively toward a new society. (p. 19)

The reconstructionist teacher also must be willing to engage in ongoing renewal of his or her personal and professional life, must have a high tolerance for ambiguity, and must be comfortable with constant change. As an educational reformer, such a teacher detests the status quo and views the school as a particular culture in evolution. Moreover, he or she views the larger society as an experiment that always will be unfinished and in flux.

The reconstructionist teacher should have excellent interpersonal communication skills and have command of languages. He or she should have a background in conflict management, organizational theory, organizational development, program evaluation, strategic planning (see Chapter 14), and the politics of change. The teacher must be open to diversity and view education from a global perspective.

Leading Educational Proponents

George S. Counts, Theodore Brameld (1904–1987), Harold Rugg, John Childs, and W. H. Kilpatrick were perhaps the best known of the American reconstructionists who, in the early part of this century, attempted to bring about major educational reform. Each of these individuals advocated the transformation of society and envisioned an ideal and more equitable world. Two contemporary spokespersons for the reconstructionist theory of education are Ivan Illich and Paulo Freire.

Ivan Illich (left) and Paulo Freire (right) found new approaches to education that revolutionized schooling.

Illich (1974), in his *Deschooling Society*, maintained that since schools have corrupted society, one can create a better society only by abolishing schools altogether and finding new approaches to education. Illich called for a total political and educational revolution. Freire, who was born, educated, and taught in Latin America, proposed that education be drawn from the everyday life experiences of the learners. From his students, the illiterate and oppressed peasants of Brazil and Chile, he drew his theory of educational reconstructionism. In his *Pedagogy of the Oppressed* (1973), Freire maintained that students should not be manipulated or controlled but should be involved in their own learning. According to Freire, by exchanging and examining their experiences with peers and mentors, students who are socially, economically, and politically disadvantaged can plan, initiate, and take action for their own lives. As with any learners, the key to working with these disadvantaged individuals is a teacher who respects and cares about his or her students. Figure 7.5 presents an overview of reconstructionism.

Figure 7.5: Reconstructionism at a Glance

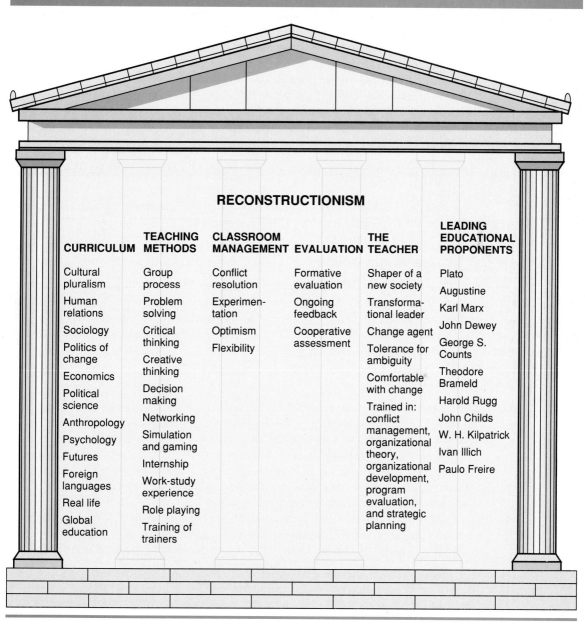

RECONSTRUCTIONISM

CURRICULUM	TEACHING METHODS	CLASSROOM MANAGEMENT	EVALUATION	THE TEACHER	LEADING EDUCATIONAL PROPONENTS
Cultural pluralism	Group process	Conflict resolution	Formative evaluation	Shaper of a new society	Plato
Human relations	Problem solving	Experimentation	Ongoing feedback	Transformational leader	Augustine
Sociology	Critical thinking	Optimism	Cooperative assessment	Change agent	Karl Marx
Politics of change	Creative thinking	Flexibility		Tolerance for ambiguity	John Dewey
Economics	Decision making			Comfortable with change	George S. Counts
Political science	Networking			Trained in: conflict management, organizational theory, organizational development, program evaluation, and strategic planning	Theodore Brameld
Anthropology	Simulation and gaming				Harold Rugg
Psychology	Internship				John Childs
Futures	Work-study experience				W. H. Kilpatrick
Foreign languages	Role playing				Ivan Illich
Real life	Training of trainers				Paulo Freire
Global education					

Existentialism

Freedom, responsibility, choice, anxiety, authenticity, alienation, paradox, and human subjectivity are the hallmarks of existentialism. Existentialist philosophy represents a protest against the earlier efforts of Western philosophy to reduce the human being to an essence or universal—to an abstraction (Wingo, 1974). For the existentialist, to reduce human life to such an abstraction is to deny the individual his or her existence. The philosophy of existentialism is embedded in the existentialist theory of education. Kneller (1971) described some of the basic principles of the educational theory of existentialism:

1. Students should be urged to take responsibility for and to deal with the results of their actions.

2. Teachers should not simply impose discipline on their students but rather should demonstrate the value of discipline.

3. Students should be helped to discover that true freedom implies communion, not self-interest.

Describe how you might demonstrate the value of discipline rather than impose discipline in your classroom.

For the existentialist, the child or student has a "right to live the extreme choice, the right to change, and the right to spontaneous self-realization" (Barnes, 1968, p. 296). The purpose of education is to foster self-discovery and consciousness of the freedom of choice, as well as the responsibility for making choices.

Curriculum

Like that of progressivism, the curriculum of the existentialist school evolves around the student's needs and interests. However, unlike progressivism, which emphasizes group learning, existentialism emphasizes the individual and views learning as a private and personal matter. It is a student-centered curriculum of individual choice. The main objective of such a curriculum is to immerse the student in a variety of existential situations that authenticate his or her own experience.

Although there are no universals in such a curriculum, there is a favored subject matter: the humanities. For the existentialist, the humanities offer visible evidence of the suffering that accompanies the human condition:

> Above all, it is the spiritual power of the humanities and the essential urge for affirmation inherent in all forms of art that attract the existentialist. To read and see how men in history have struggled with their conscience, labored with fate, rebelled against existing orders and absolutes and poured life-blood into their creations becomes a source of inspiration for the existentialist in his approach to learning. (Kneller, 1958, p. 125)

The essence of the curriculum is to stress the awareness of "being" and the awareness of "nothingness." The assumption made by the existentialist is that by dwelling on the unpleasant idea of meaninglessness or nothingness and its accompanying anxiety and absurdity, we ultimately create an affirmation of self and find a purpose in life. The curriculum, then, awakens a fundamental awareness in the learner. Such a subjective awareness has been called "the existential moment" (Marler, 1975; Morris, 1966) which marks the beginning of taking responsibility for assigning meaning to one's own life.

Have you ever experienced "the existential moment"? Describe the experience.

Teaching Methods

Since existentialists view the greatest obstacles to authenticity to be fear and conformity (Kneller, 1984), the teaching methods they use would be those methods that would not reinforce fear or conformity but would value what they refer to as "existential anxiety," which is the anxiety associated with the freedom to choose. Existential anxiety is a prerequisite to growth and as such is considered to be probably the most powerful experience that a student can have. It breaks down defenses, questions values and beliefs, and reveals the person as he or she really is. The best methods for encouraging and nourishing a certain amount of existential anxiety are those that teach decision making or choosing among alternatives. Any activities that develop the process of valuing or decision making would be supported by the existentialist educator.

The so-called "affective" approaches to values education, which engage students in cognitive discussions along with affective experiences, would be a favored teaching method of the existentialist teacher. In addition, the Socratic dialogue, which includes asking questions, refining answers, and asking further questions until a conclusion is reached, would be another important instructional strategy because it produces self-knowledge. Furthermore, the existentialist teacher would provide time for self-reflection and privacy because the questions of human existence are best addressed in the quietude of private time and space.

Classroom Management

The most appropriate metaphor for the classroom environment of an existential school is an *open classroom* (i.e., an open instructional space or "classroom without walls") where students enjoy the freedom to move about. Within such an environment, learning is dedicated to self-discovery and individual choice. Such a classroom invites participatory decision making and does not view the teacher as the authority figure. Rather, the teacher is considered a mediator who permits students to exercise freedom within a nonpunitive, democratic community.

Evaluation

Because authenticity and authentic teaching reflect the uniqueness of the individual teacher, the existential teacher spurns the use of standardized tests, rejects the notion of accountability, and stresses a more subjective form of appraisal or evaluation. The school is viewed as a place for experiencing life and making meaning out of nonmeaning, a place where students come to grips with their own values. The source of those values is inconsequential.

What matters most is that there is a personal endorsement for valuing and choosing. Within this paradigm of choice, the teacher is not viewed as an evaluator, monitor, or critic but rather as a subjective or reflective enabler who is committed to helping students fulfill their personal goals.

The Existentialist Teacher

With the overriding concern for the individual as the ultimate chooser, the existentialist teacher would model valuing, decision making, and choosing. Such a teacher would pose moral and ethical as well as intellectual questions to his or her students. The teacher's job would be to awaken students to the ultimate responsibility that they must bear for the decisions that they make. The teacher who would be most comfortable with the tenets of existentialism is typically one who is flexible, nondirective, and impervious to the type of noise and disorder that often accompanies an informal, open class atmosphere (Kneller, 1984).

The existentialist teacher attempts to become an excellent example of authenticity for students. By incorporating a humanistic approach to teaching, the existentialist educator would encourage a more personal and interactive teacher-student relationship. The whole child or student would be viewed as primary and the existentialist would be concerned with the cognitive as well as affective components of the student's development. Furthermore, since the thrust of existentialism is the search for meaning and purpose, the teacher would be an individual who is comfortable with being introspective and reflective.

Last, the existentialist teacher is an advocate of self-education and academic freedom. The teacher would encourage students to take responsibility for their own learning and education. Teaching, says the existentialist, is neither a science nor a technology, but an art.

Leading Educational Proponents

Perhaps the most well-known educational existentialists are A. S. Neill (1883–1973), Carl Rogers (1902–1987), and John Holt (1923–1985), as well as contemporary writers Charles Silberman and Jonathan Kozol. Neill, who founded Summerhill School outside London shortly after World War I, offered an educational experience built on the principle of learning by discovery in an atmosphere of unrestrained freedom. He contended that learning will evolve from the student's interest. According to Neill (1960), regardless of their age or maturity level, students are capable of self-discipline and can be responsible for their own learning. A similar institution established in 1968 and still in operation today in Framingham, Massachusetts is Sudbury Valley School, which operates on the existential principles that foster individual choice, democracy, and personal responsibility. Long and Ihle (1988) described the basic components of the school:

> Sudbury Valley operates on the principle that children's natural tendencies toward wanting to grow up, to be competent, to model older children and

Individual choice, democracy, and personal responsibility are key ingredients of Sudbury Valley School.

adults, and to fantasize, should be the foundation for education. Consequently, the school has set no curriculum and no activity takes place unless a student asks for it. Instead, the school offers a wide variety of educational options, including instruction in standard subjects in both group and tutorial formats: field trips to Boston, New York, and the nearby mountains, and seacoast; and facilities that include a laboratory, a woodworking shop, a computer room, a kitchen, a darkroom, an art room, and a number of music rooms. (p. 449)

Carl Rogers (1969), in his *Freedom to Learn*, asserted that the only things that one person can teach another person are those that are relatively inconsequential and of little or no significance. Only learning that is self-discovered, self-appropriated through experience can significantly influence behavior.

John Holt (1981), Charles Silberman (1970), and Jonathan Kozol (1972) were supporters of the so-called open schools, free schools, or alternative schools which flourished during the mid-1960s. Similar to Summerhill or Sudbury Valley, these nontraditional schools emphasized a permissive or a humanistic education that abhorred any type of rigidity or structure. In spite of the appeal of the humanistic education movement, its heyday was very short-lived and it was eventually replaced by the back-to-basics movement of the 1970s. Figure 7.6 presents an overview of existentialism.

If you had the opportunity to attend a school like Summerhill or Sudbury Valley, how different would your elementary education have been from the one you received?

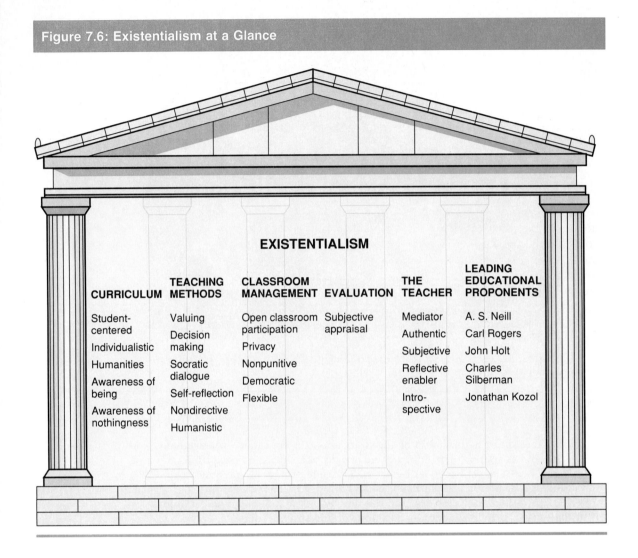

Figure 7.6: Existentialism at a Glance

EXISTENTIALISM

CURRICULUM	TEACHING METHODS	CLASSROOM MANAGEMENT	EVALUATION	THE TEACHER	LEADING EDUCATIONAL PROPONENTS
Student-centered	Valuing	Open classroom participation	Subjective appraisal	Mediator	A. S. Neill
Individualistic	Decision making	Privacy		Authentic	Carl Rogers
Humanities	Socratic dialogue	Nonpunitive		Subjective	John Holt
Awareness of being	Self-reflection	Democratic		Reflective enabler	Charles Silberman
Awareness of nothingness	Nondirective	Flexible		Intro-spective	Jonathan Kozol
	Humanistic				

Analytic Philosophy of Education

As we study the major philosophies and their corollary educational theo-ries, it becomes evident that these traditional schools of thought, or "isms" as they are often called, are very broad in their aims, are quite eclectic, and at times appear to lack clarity. For these reasons a number of philosophers of education began to move away from traditional thinking about philosophy and theory as disciplines and began to focus their attention on analysis or clarification of the language, concepts, and methods that philosophers and educators use (Ozmon & Craver, 1990; Partelli, 1987). The so-called "analytic movement" that resulted was less concerned with the underlying assumptions about reality, truth, and values addressed by the formal schools of thought than with clarification, definition, and the meaning of language.

One contemporary analytic philosopher is Jonas Soltis. Soltis (1978) pointed out the importance of philosophical analysis for teachers:

> We must be clear about its intent [language of education] and meaning and not be swayed by its imagery and poetry. The analytic temperament and techniques should prove very useful to all practicing educators in getting them to think through with care and precision just what it is they are buying from theorists, and more importantly, just what it is they're after and how best that might be achieved. (p. 88)

Analysis in philosophy began in the post–World War I era when a group of European natural scientists and social scientists formed what became known as the Vienna Circle. These scholars were particularly concerned about the alienation between philosophy and science that existed at that time. One of the major outcomes of the work of the Vienna Circle was that it clarified the joint roles of both science and philosophy. For example, it was determined that if the testing of hypotheses through experimentation and observation were to be the purview or charge of science, then the proper role of philosophy should be the analysis of the logical syntax of scientific language (Magee, 1971).

The concept of *logical positivism* or *logical empiricism* grew out of the thinking of the Vienna Circle. Logical positivism or logical empiricism suggests that the language of science consists of two types of expressions: logical and empirical. Eventually, the concept of logical positivism became associated with the "principle of verification." This principle asserts that no proposition should be accepted as meaningful unless it can be verified on formal grounds, logical or empirical (Magee, 1971).

One of the most important logical positivists was Ludwig Wittgenstein (1889–1951). Wittgenstein (1953) argued that the role of the sciences should be to discover true propositions and true facts while the role of philosophy should be to resolve confusion and clarify ideas.

The assumptions that were made by logical positivists became so rigid and restrictive that their popularity began to wane. Today, very few individuals identify themselves as logical positivists.

Another leading spokesperson for the analytic philosophy movement in education was Israel Scheffler (b. 1923). In his first major work, *The Language of Education* (1960), Scheffler focused attention on how philosophical analysis can help teachers formulate their beliefs, arguments, and assumptions about topics that are particularly important to the teaching and learning process. Both Scheffler and later Magee (1971) suggested that one of the best ways for teachers to do this is by answering the types of questions that analytic philosophers pose. Some of these questions might be:

1. What are teaching, learning and education?

2. What is the meaning of authority in education?

How would you answer each of these questions?

3. What is the relationship between the concept of excellence and the concept of equality in a democratic educational system?

4. What is moral education? (Magee, 1971, p. 42)

Maxine Greene (1981), a leading contemporary existentialist philosopher, summarized the importance of subjecting one's ideas to the analytic process:

> To do philosophy in this fashion is to pose distinctive critical questions: questions that provoke reflection on the knowledge gathered in the several fields of inquiry, questions that lead to examination of underlying assumptions and disclosures of major premises. Equally important are questions that lead to the framing of conceptual frameworks, perspectives through which the field in its interrelationships can be seen. It is important to note that these are not questions susceptible of ordinary answers. (p. 34)

Each prospective teacher should learn the art or science of *philosophical analysis*. One of the first steps in learning this process is to raise questions about the assumptions we make, the values we hold, the theories we propose, the procedures we use, and the methods we trust. In short, philosophical analysis confronts the language of education and forces the educator to translate his or her professional expression into parsimonious and meaningful terms. Without this clarity, many of our important assertions about education may become nothing more than today's favorite cliché or tomorrow's empty words.

Identifying Your Philosophy of Education

Identifying your philosophy of education is one of the best exercises in philosophical analysis for it affords you an opportunity to subject your thinking about numerous educational concepts to close scrutiny. Preparing your educational philosophy will enable you to clarify your own thinking about the learner, the teacher, and the school.

Philosophy of education influences educational theory, which has a strong impact on educational practice. A visit to any classroom provides ample evidence of the influence of educational theory on educational practice. Educational philosophies and theories do not remain static, but constantly change depending on the social, economic, and political climate at the time. After visiting more than a single classroom it quickly becomes evident that a variety of philosophies and theories of education can coexist in the same school. Furthermore, few teachers operate from a single philosophical or theoretical perspective. Most educators are eclectic; they find themselves sampling a variety of ideas, propositions, principles, or axioms that represent a smorgasbord of philosophical and theoretical views.

Identifying and developing your personal philosophy of education at this time may appear to be an awesome task. Yet it is one of the most important tasks that you will probably be asked to perform as a prospective teacher. It is not uncommon to be asked to articulate your philosophy of education on job

Ask Yourself:
What Is My Philosophy of Education?

To assess your preference for an educational philosophy, answer the following questions.

1. Are students intrinsically motivated to learn?

2. Should education be the same for everyone?

3. Are there certain universal truths that should be taught?

4. What determines morality?

5. What is the ideal curriculum?

6. What is the purpose of schooling?

7. If you were to choose one method or instructional strategy, what would it be?

8. What type of classroom environment is most conducive to learning?

9. How do you know when your students have learned?

10. What is the most important role of the teacher?

11. What is the role of the student?

12. How should prospective teachers be prepared?

---

applications or in job interviews. School districts may require that you express your philosophical ideas and compare them to the philosophy or mission of the school district.

In Chapter 6 you were asked to respond to a series of questions that reflected your personal philosophy of life. You also were advised that the answers to those questions reflect some of the assumptions you hold about teaching and learning. The time has come to combine philosophy, theory, and practice in constructing your philosophy of education. Your responses to the basic theoretical questions listed above reflect your philosophy of education. As you ask yourself these questions, recall the importance of clarity and meaning in the language you choose. The response you develop now may change before you enter the teaching profession, and may change one or more times during the course of your career. However, it is vitally important that you begin self-inquiry at this stage in your career.

Summary

The study of the theories of education provides a rationale for explaining how learning occurs. Each theory developed as a protest against the social and educational climate of its time.

There are six major theories of education: perennialism, progressivism, behaviorism, essentialism, reconstructionism, and existentialism. Educational theories influence educational practice by their impact on curriculum, teaching methods, classroom management, evaluation, and the teacher.

Although the theories of education provide a mechanism for translating basic philosophic tenets into educational practice, they are quite restrictive in that they are often too broad in their aims and seem to lack clarity. Today, many educators believe that a more effective way to study education is by philosophical analysis, which is concerned with clarifying the language we use to describe our educational concepts and assumptions.

In the next chapter, we will leave the philosophies and theories of education and concentrate on the school and society, examining the school as a socializing agent.

Key Terms

Alternative schools
Back-to-basics movement
Behavioral objectives
Behaviorism
Classical conditioning
Formative evaluation
Great Books
Humanistic education
Logical positivism (logical empiricism)
New basics
Nongraded schools

Open classroom
Operant conditioning
Perennialism
Philosophical analysis
Premack principle
Programmed instruction
Progressivism
Theory
Theory of education
Whole-child movement

Discussion Questions

1. Describe the relationship among philosophy of life, educational theory, and philosophy of education.

2. Which of the theories of education presented in this chapter is most similar to your theory of education? In what ways is it similar?

3. B. F. Skinner and other advocates of operant conditioning have been criticized for their emphasis on control. Are freedom and control incompatible concepts in the classroom?

4. Of the six educational theories presented, which theory best exemplifies clarity and meaning in the language used? Why?

5. As a reconstructionist, list five major changes that you would propose for education and schooling in the twenty-first century. Should teachers and students be involved in promoting these changes? Why? Why not?

6. Compare and contrast the teaching methods advocated by the essentialist and the existentialist.

7. Describe the classroom management strategies advocated by the perennialist. How do they differ from those of the behaviorist?

8. Choose a leading educational proponent of essentialism and, using his or her theories, construct a letter to the editor of a newspaper suggesting how the training of teachers today could be reformed.

9. Reflect on the vignette at the beginning of this chapter. Which theory of education would you ascribe to Jim? To Beth? To Sam? Explain.

10. Choose three basic educational concepts that are important to your philosophy of education. Describe the process you would go through in analyzing the language used to ensure that its meaning was clear and concise.

References

Adler, M. (1982). *The Paideia proposal: An educational manifesto*. New York: Macmillan.

Barnes, H. E. (1968). *An existentialist ethics*. New York: Alfred A. Knopf.

Bates, J. A. (1987). Reinforcement. In M. J. Dunkin (Ed.), *The international encyclopedia of teaching and teacher education* (pp. 349–358). New York: Pergamon Books.

Bloom, A. (1987). *The closing of the American mind*. New York: Simon and Schuster.

Brameld, T. (1971). *Patterns of educational philosophy*. New York: Holt, Rinehart, and Winston.

Conant, J. B. (1959). *The American high school today*. New York: McGraw-Hill.

Counts, G. S. (1933). *A call to the teachers of America*. New York: John Day Co.

Delattre, E. J. (1984). *The intellectual lives of teachers*. In C. E. Finn, D. Ravitch, & R. T. Fancher (Eds.), *Against mediocrity* (pp. 154–171). New York: Holmes & Meier.

Dewey, J. (1920). *Reconstruction in philosophy*. New York: H. Holt.

Dewey, J. (1938). *Experience and education*. New York: Macmillan.

Emmer, E. T. (1987). Classroom management. In M. J. Dunkin (Ed.), *The international encyclopedia of teaching and teacher education* (pp. 437–446). New York: Pergamon.

Freire, P. (1973). *Pedagogy of the oppressed*. New York: Seabury Press.

Greene, M. (1981). Contexts, corrections and consequences: The matter of philosophical and psychological foundations. *Journal of Teacher Education, 32*(4), 31–37.

Holt, J. (1981). *Teach your own*. New York: Delacorte/Seymour Laurence.

Hutchins, R. M. (1936). *The higher learning in America*. New Haven, CT: Yale University Press.

Illich, I. (1974). *Deschooling society*. New York: Harper & Row.

Kneller, G. F. (1958). *Existentialism and education*. New York: John Wiley & Sons.

Kneller, G. F. (1971). *Introduction to the philosophy of education*. New York: John Wiley & Sons.

Kneller, G. F. (1984). *Movements of thought in modern education*. New York: John Wiley & Sons.

Kozol, J. (1972). *Free schools*. Boston: Houghton Mifflin.

Long, L., & Ihle, E. (1988). Philosophy of education. In M. P. Sadker & D. M. Sadker, *Teachers, schools, and society* (pp. 422–459). New York: Random House.

Magee, J. B. (1971). *Philosophical analysis in education*. New York: Harper & Row.

Maritain, J. (1941). *Scholasticism and politics*. New York: Macmillan.

Marler, C. D. (1975). *Philosophy and schooling*. Boston: Gillyn & Bacon.

Morris, V. C. (1966). *Existentialism in education*. New York: Harper & Row.

Morris, V. C., & Pai, Y. (1976). *Philosophy in the American school*. Boston: Houghton Mifflin.

National Commission on Excellence in Education. (1983). *A nation at risk: The imperative for educational reform*. Washington, DC: U.S. Government Printing Office.

Neill, A. S. (1960). *Summerhill: A radical approach to child rearing*. New York: Hart.

Ozmon, H. A., & Craver, S. M. (1990). *Philosophical foundations of education*. Columbus, OH: Merrill.

Partelli, J. P. (1987). Analytic philosophy of education: Development and misconceptions. *Journal of Educational Thought, 21*(1), 20–24.

Phillips, D. C., & Soltis, J. F. (1985). *Perspectives on learning*. New York: Teachers College Press, Columbia University.

Rickover, H. G. (1963). *Education and freedom*. New York: New American Library.

Rogers, C. R. (1969). *Freedom to learn*. Columbus, OH: Merrill.

Scheffler, I. (1960). *The language of education*. Springfield, IL: Charles C. Thomas.

Silberman, C. (1970). *Crisis in the classroom*. New York: Random House.

Soltis, J. F. (1978). *An introduction to the analysis of educational concepts*. Reading, MA: Addison-Wesley.

Wingo, G. M. (1974). *Philosophies of education: An introduction*. Lexington, MA: D.C. Heath and Co.

Wittgenstein, L. (1953). *Philosophical investigations*. New York: Macmillan.

Wittrock, M. C. (1987). Models of heuristic teaching. In M. J. Dunkin (Ed.), *The international encyclopedia of teaching and teacher education* (pp. 68–76). New York: Pergamon Books.

Part Four

The Schools and Society

School and Society **Chapter 8**

Achieving Equity in Education **Chapter 9**

Students at Risk **Chapter 10**

Chapter 8
School and Society

In teaching there should be no class distinctions.

Confucius
(551–478 B.C.)

It was almost midnight and Ms. Cohen had one more term paper to read before retiring. It was an exhausting time before finals. Each semester she vowed that she would not assign a 20-page term paper to her senior social studies honors class. But, each semester she made the same assignment. And each semester she was glad that she did.

This semester she seemed to have an exceptionally gifted class. Of her 25 honors students, at least 75% had received admission and scholarships to more than one college or university. She glanced at her grade book and noticed some of the titles of the students' term papers. They read like a list of college theses, she thought, as she picked up the last term paper. It was David Marshall's paper and she smiled as she read his title: "Equal Educational Opportunity and the American Dream: You've Got To Be Kidding!"

As she turned to his introduction, Ms. Cohen was struck by the thoughtful perceptions and insights of this young 17-year-old. His introduction read as follows:

> To assume that the school as an institution can rectify the problems and concerns of the poor is either naivete or sheer ignorance. The truth of the matter is that schools not only reflect the classes within the society, but they do everything they can to reinforce those divisions. Until we recognize that the basic concept of society must be reconceptualized and that social classes must be eliminated, the goal of equal educational opportunity will continue to be, at best, a fantasy or myth.

If David Marshall had written such an introduction to a term paper for your class, how might you have responded? To what extent do you agree or disagree with David's assumptions about equal educational opportunity? About social class? Why or why not?

The issues that David Marshall has raised are central to any discussion of the relationship between the schools and society. In this chapter various dimensions of the relationship are explored. First, the concepts of culture, subculture, society, socialization, and acculturation are examined. Then the purposes and expectations of schooling are described and education and inequality are discussed. Last, educational attainment and achievement in relation to social class, ethnicity, race, and gender are examined. As you study this material, keep in mind these objectives:

- Define the basic concepts of culture, subculture, society, socialization, and acculturation.

- Explain how the family, the peer group, and the media socialize children and youth.

- Outline the role of the school in the cultural socialization of youth, its contribution to economic development, and its response to cultural diversity.

- Compare the social selection and social mobility purposes of education.

- Identify the major issues related to the inequality of educational opportunity.

- Describe the social class system in the United States.

- Compare the educational attainment and achievement of social class groups, ethnic and racial groups, and males and females.

- Evaluate the causes of differences in educational attainment and achievement among social class groups, ethnic and racial groups, and between males and females.

Some Basic Concepts

Before we can fully comprehend the relationship between the school and society, it is important to understand the concepts of culture and subculture. *Culture* may be defined as the behavioral patterns, ideas, values, religions and moral beliefs, customs, laws, language, institutions, art and all other material things and artifacts characteristic of a given people at a given period of time. Every culture passes on, or transmits, its patterns and products of learned behavior to the young, patterns that reflect its cultural values and norms, artifacts and symbols.

Complex societies such as the United States, in addition to having an overall culture, include a variety of subcultures. A *subculture* is a group of people distinguished by its ethnic, racial, religious, geographic, social, economic, or lifestyle traits. Most of us are members of a variety of subcultures.

Describe the cultures, subcultures, and societies to which you currently belong.

In addition to understanding the concepts of culture and subculture, it is also important to understand the concept of society. A *society* refers to a group of persons who share a common culture, government, institutions, land, or a set of social relationships. A person may be a member of several societies at the same time: a religious society, a professional society, and a social society. Each of these societies also will have its own culture or subculture. *Socialization* is the process by which persons are conditioned to the customs or patterns of a particular culture.

The concept of education is very similar to the concept of socialization, since both aim to preserve, inculcate, or transmit the cultural heritage of the society (Cave & Chesler, 1974). In addition, both socialization and education take place not only in school, but in a variety of institutions outside the school, such as the family, the peer group, and the media. These institutions or agents of socialization will be examined in the sections that follow.

Agents of Socialization

The Family

What were the child-rearing practices in your home during your formative years? How were sex roles perceived?

Although the organization of the family varies from culture to culture and from one period of history to the next, there are certain basic functions that all families serve. One of those is its socialization function. Children are born into families and, for a significant period in their life, in particular their early years, the family is the only world that the children know. Thus the family is the major socializing agent for the young. It is the family that first introduces the child to the world at large, and it is the family that transmits the culture's values to the young. Parents pass on their perceptions, values, beliefs, attitudes, experiences, and understandings to their children. These primary impressions are long-lasting and very difficult to modify or change. They also have significant impact on children's later educational development and success in school. The home and family environment, including parent/child interactions, the use of language in the home, child-rearing practices, and how sex roles are perceived in the home are a few of the many influences that are associated with the child's later educational attainment or achievement (Webb & Sherman, 1989).

Although traditionally the family has been the major instrument of socialization for the young, in the last quarter-century more and more of the responsibility for the socialization has been transferred to the school or other institutions. The major reason why the school and other institutions have taken on a greater role as a socializing agent is the change in the structure of the family.

Extended families in many cultures play a major role in the socialization of children.

The Changing Family

How has your family configuration changed over the past two decades?

Since World War II, the family configuration has changed dramatically. Demographic, economic, and cultural changes have altered the very definition of "family" as we perceive it today. The "traditional" or nuclear family of two or more school-age children, with a father who works and a mother who stays home to care for the children, is no longer the norm. In 1955, approximately 60% of the nation's families fit this model, but by 1986 only about 4% of American families were considered "traditional" families ("Traditional Families," 1986). Dual-career families, single-parent families, ethnically and linguistically different families, and blended families with previously divorced fathers and mothers living together with children from previous marriages and often children from the present marriage have become the norm rather than the exception.

The following highlights describe the families and households of today:

- The average household size is 2.63 persons.

- The number of unmarried couple-households increased 63%, from one-half million in 1970 to 2.6 million in 1988.

- Three out of every four mothers with children aged 6–17 are employed.

- Twenty-four percent of children under age 18 live in single parent homes.

- More than 50% of couples have no children.

Socialization Responsibility Shifts

Today, families spend less time together than they did in the past. Too often, what time they do spend together is spent watching television. Little interaction occurs and less time is given to teaching children acceptable values and behaviors. As a result, the school has taken on the function of teaching certain subjects that were once considered the purview of the family. For example, sex education and values education, domains that were traditionally considered the responsibility of the family and church, have been transferred to the school.

The schools also have become involved in other functions that historically were considered family responsibilities. For example, schools provide breakfast and lunch for needy children, offer counseling and mental health services, make referrals for medical and psychological needs, and offer parent education in after-school programs. These changes have left the family with fewer social roles and have diminished the family's socialization function.

Every indication is that the American family will continue to change. The percentage of childless couples will increase, and so will the number of unmarried mothers and the number of women with school-aged children employed outside the home. As the number of two-income families continues to grow, the contact time between parents and children will continue to decrease. The school will become increasingly responsible not only for the education of the child, but the socialization of the child. The school may have to expand its curriculum to include education about child development and parenting, and the teaching of "proper behavior" and acceptable discipline (Connecticut ASCD, 1989).

The Peer Group

The peer group is one of the most significant institutions for socializing the child or adolescent. Each peer group has its own set of rules and regulations, its own social organization, its own customs, and in some cases its own rituals and language. Although the peer group relationship may be transitory in nature, its influence can be profound. Unlike the family influence, which tends to lessen with time, the peer group becomes more influential (Levine & Havighurst, 1989).

Children develop friendship patterns at an early age. According to Selakovich (1984), "usually by the time children reach the sixth or seventh grade, these groups are fairly well defined and they constitute a sort of subculture within the schools, with each group having its own rules of initiation, often its own language, and its own acceptable pattern of behavior" (p. 162).

As a socializing agency, the peer group reflects and reinforces the values of the adult society, e.g., competition, cooperation, honesty, and responsibility. The peer group communicates what constitutes appropriate sex roles and appropriate social behavior in the culture. The peer group also legitimizes and prioritizes the value of information received from a variety of sources (Levine & Havighurst, 1989).

The peer group also serves as a reference group for the young. A reference group is a kind of barometer. That is, the child or adolescent learns to judge himself or herself against the attitudes, values, and aspirations of his or her peers and learns to act in accord with those values (Levine & Havighurst, 1989).

In addition to peer groups within the school, peer groups outside the school serve as agents of socialization for children and adolescents. These peer groups consist of organized social groups such as the Boy Scouts, Girl Scouts, and Little League. Like the peer groups within the school, these social groups offer opportunities for learning rules, cooperation, and the spirit of equity while developing friendship patterns.

Describe the peer groups in your early life that served as an agent of socialization for you.

The Media

"The media" is a term commonly used to refer to the television, radio, newspaper, and magazine industries. Of these, the one that has the most influence on children is television. In fact, increasingly it is acknowledged that the socialization effect of television is almost as strong as the home, school, and neighborhood in influencing children's development and behavior.

Time Watching Television

According to a recent report, 42% of the children surveyed watched television four or more hours a day on school days, and 12% watched television eight or more hours. As seen in Table 8.1, of those watching eight or more hours of television on school days, males are proportionally more represented than females, blacks and Hispanics more than whites, and urban children

Table 8.1: The Relationship between TV Watching on School Days and Selected Characteristics of Students

Student Characteristics	Number of Students	Percent Who Watch TV 8 Hours or More on School Days
Sex		
Male	1,307	14
Female	1,429	11
School level		
Elementary (4–6)	978	21
Junior high (7–9)	775	11
High school (10–12)	983	5
Father's education		
Less than high school	300	12
High school	776	10
Some college	356	7
College graduate/above	764	11
Mother's education		
Less than high school	304	14
High school	944	11
Some college	375	7
College graduate/above	712	12
Ethnicity		
White	1,752	7
Black	302	27
Hispanic	214	19
Population density		
Urban	755	16
Suburban	972	12
Rural	1,013	9
Frequency of conversations with parents about school		
2–3 times weekly or more	1,761	11
Once a week	330	9
Once a month	173	13
Rarely	458	18
Frequency of conversations with parents about homework		
2–3 times weekly or more	1,128	13
Once a week	452	7
Once a month	288	9
Rarely	855	14
Extent of school problems		
Very serious	438	7
Somewhat serious	1,000	11
Not serious	1,298	14
TOTAL	2,736	12

Source: Louis Harris and Associates, Inc. (1988). *The Metropolitan Life survey of the American teacher, 1988: Strengthening the relationship between teachers and students* (pp. 106–107). New York: Metropolitan Life Insurance Company. Reprinted with permission.

more than rural children. Perhaps not surprising, those children who rarely talked with their parents about school were also proportionately more represented.

It has been estimated that by the time the average child graduates from high school he or she will have spent significantly more time in front of the television than in school (Pearl, 1987). Given that "observational learning and incorporation of social messages from television are a well-established phenomenon" (Anderson & Collins, 1988, p. 70), the potential effects of this much exposure to television are significant.

Effects of Television Viewing

Although the positive effect of television in broadening our experiences and shrinking our world has been tremendous, in recent years increasing concerns have been raised regarding the negative effects of:

● the transmission of violent and antisocial behavior

● the transmission of inappropriate sexual values

● the transmission of unrealistic attitudes toward drugs and alcohol

● the promotion of irrational and superstitious beliefs

● the devaluation of work

● the underrepresentation of women and members of various races, ethnic backgrounds, and cultures

● a neglect of reading (Radeki, 1989)

Of these, perhaps the greatest concern is the effect of television (and film) violence on children. Considerable evidence has been found to indicate that exposure to television programming laden with violence and antisocial behavior increases both aggression and antisocial behavior in children. For example, a large-scale longitudinal study of middle-class children in upstate New York found that children with the heaviest diet of violent entertainment were convicted of criminal offenses 150% more than children from the same classroom with the lightest diets of violent viewing (Eron, Huesmann, Dubow, et al., cited in Radeki, 1989).

Also of concern is the message that the depiction of acts of violence communicates about the rules, power distribution, and conventional norms of the social order. While portraying the reality that our social system is one that includes aggressive acts, the pattern of television violence is one in which society's dominant groups consistently are depicted as triumphing over those of lesser status and power (Turiel, 1987).

Television and School Achievement

The relationship between television viewing and school achievement is also a matter of concern. Except for limited evidence that television viewing may increase vocabulary, most studies that have examined the relationship between television viewing and school achievement have found a negative correlation between amount of viewing and level of achievement, especially at the higher levels of viewing (Anderson & Collins, 1988; Beentjes & Van der Voort, 1988; Ritchie, Price, & Roberts, 1987). Many teachers also complain that increased television viewing shortens attention spans, interferes with homework, and creates in children an expectation that they must be entertained.

Since television is here to stay and its impact on children is so profound, the challenge for parents and educators is to find ways to make it a positive educational tool and to mitigate against its negative influence. This can be done by reinforcing the positive messages and values communicated through television. Research has shown that the influence of television is greatest when its messages are confirmed by other social agents or when the influence of other institutions is declining. Thus, if the schools can combine the positive messages of television with other prosocial teachings, the television message may be kept in perspective. The reality is that it may be easier to develop students' critical viewing skills than to regulate television programming (Webb & Sherman, 1989).

The Purposes and Expectations of Schooling

The purposes and expectations of schooling have varied over time with the aims of society. However, in spite of the different expectations of the school that have been promoted by the larger society or any of its subsets, several expectations are always found. Among these are cultural socialization; contribution to economic growth and development; social selection or social mobility; and responding to diversity.

Cultural Socialization

One of the major purposes of schooling is to socialize the young in the norms and values of society. The school trains children for responsible citizenship and socializes them for their future adult role. Through the curriculum, classroom rules, and interactions with teachers and other adults, children learn the symbols and rituals of patriotism and the values of our democratic society. They also learn the behaviors that are necessary to support the system and those that are valued by the system. They come to understand that to be a "good boy" or a "good girl" means to obey and to succeed. To be bad is to disobey or to fail. Competition is valued, as is "working well together," "cooperating nicely," or "being a team player."

Think back to your elementary school experience. Which teachers had the most impact on you? Why?

Within the culture of the school, teachers exercise significant control over how the culture is transmitted to the young. It is the teacher who ultimately determines what subject matter will be taught and the manner in which the subject matter will be conveyed. As a result of that control, teachers are one of the central figures in the socialization process. The teacher is the symbol of authority to the child. Within the social system and reward structure created by teachers in their classrooms, children learn the beliefs, values, and expectations of the larger society.

The schools also play an important role in the moral training of children. This was an explicit expectation of the schools throughout much of America's history. The textbooks and curriculum of the school were directed toward the development of character and moral behavior. Although the continued push for separation of church and state has greatly eliminated the religious involvement that was the vehicle for much of this training, the emphasis on values education underscores the continued expectation that schools be involved in the development of morals.

The teacher also serves as a role model for children in the development of morals and values. As the family has relinquished more and more of its role as "model for morality," the teacher has taken on this function. Teachers are expected not only to exhibit high ethical and moral principles, but to teach those principles to their students.

In fulfilling its socialization role, the school is constantly challenged to assume a major role in either (1) inculcating or reinforcing the past or present values of the social order or (2) encouraging the adoption of new and emerging values for the culture. Often, the school is called on to reinforce and transmit the common values of the past and at the same time to implement social change. However, in spite of the significant changes that have taken place within the family and neighborhood since World War II, relatively few major changes have taken place in the school itself. The school still tends to reflect or mirror the society and has traditionally played a minor role as an agent of change.

Contribution to Economic Growth and Development

One of the most important purposes of education is to advance economic growth and development. Education contributes to economic growth and development primarily through its effect on productivity, influencing productivity by upgrading the skills of the labor force. In addition, research has shown that more educated workers (1) are less likely to lose time because of unemployment and illness; (2) are more likely to be aware of and receptive to new ideas and knowledge; (3) produce better goods and render services with greater skill; and (4) produce more goods and services in a given period of time because of their skill, dexterity, and knowledge (Webb, McCarthy, & Thomas, 1988). In addition, schooling prepares children to support the economic system by enhancing the development of personal attributes compatible with the industrial workplace as it provides them with the credentials required for the practice of various occupations and careers. The school also socializes the future worker for industry through the "hidden curriculum" (see Chapter 15), which emphasizes the need for planning, time on task, competition, individualism, independence, and obeying rules (Ogbu, 1986).

A recognition of the importance of education to the economic survival of our nation served as a major impetus for the reappraisal of education by the reform reports of the 1980s. The report makers asserted that the United States was losing in the competition with other industrialized nations, particularly Japan and West Germany. They praised the educational systems of these countries and attributed their economic success to the success of their schools. As the National Commission on Excellence in Education (1983) clearly pronounced:

> Our Nation is at risk. Our once unchallenged preeminence in commerce, industry, science, and technological innovation is being overtaken by competitors throughout the world. . . . If only to keep and improve on the slim competitive edge we still retain in world markets, we must dedicate ourselves to the reform of our educational system for the benefit of all. (pp. 5, 7)

Social Selection or Social Mobility

The question of whether the schools promote social selection or social mobility is one of the most controversial issues in American education. One of the primary positions on this issue is the one shared by Marxists, neo-Marxists, and revisionists, which states that the schools serve a *social selection* purpose. According to this group, the schools essentially serve the wealthy and power-ful at the expense of the poor. The schools, they contend, serve the upper classes by socializing the multitudes to conform to the values and beliefs that are necessary to maintain the existing social order. Revisionist scholars such as Michael Apple and Henry Giroux argue that the classroom, with its extrinsic reward system and hierarchical relationship between teacher and student, is like a miniature factory system. Through the hidden curriculum (see Chapter 15), students are taught the goals and ideology of the capitalist system. They further contend that the real purpose of schooling, which they point out is controlled by the elite, is to train the workers needed for business and industry, not to promote the movement of disadvantaged, lower class youth into the upper classes (Apple, 1979, 1982; Bowles & Gintis, 1976; Giroux & Purpel, 1983; Illich, 1970; Spring, 1976, 1988).

Do you believe that schools promote social selection or social mobility?

An opposing point of view is that one of the purposes of the school is to advance *social mobility*. This position, often called the meritocratic position, recognizes that a class system does exist but also recognizes that such a class system is not rigid; that school achievement and years of schooling attained, as well as other evidence of individual merit (ability and effort), significantly contribute to an improvement in social status. Those who espouse the merit-ocratic position maintain that social class and a class society do not prevent individuals from improving their social status. Rather, they argue that indi-viduals fail to improve their social class or social prestige because of a host of other factors, including genetic inferiority, the organizational structure of the school, the attitudes and values of the educational staff, individual aspirations, and family environment (Selakovich, 1984).

Responding to Diversity

There are at least four schools of thought concerning the purpose of schooling in regard to responding to diversity: (1) assimilation; (2) amalgam-ation; (3) cultural pluralism; and (4) separatism (Thomas, 1973). The *assimi-lation* view supports what Thomas refers to as the "Dick and Jane culture."

According to Thomas (1973), "assimilation requires conformity to a single model which was largely defined by traditional British political, social, cultural, and religious institutions" (p. 50). The *amalgamation* view supports the "melting pot" notion, which envisions American culture as emerging from the best elements of many cultures. In contrast, the *cultural pluralism* view supports the idea of the strength of multiple cultures in the larger society. Last, the *separatism* view suggests that by maintaining a separatist position, at least on a temporary basis, certain minority groups can build strength, maintain their identity, and gain power. Examples of groups that support the cultural separatist view are the Amish, the Seventh Day Adventists, and the Black Muslims. To some extent, these groups not only maintain a separate lifestyle and separate social or ethnic identity, but a separate system of schooling (Thomas, 1973).

Historically, the most favored response of the American schools to cultural diversity has been assimilation (see discussion of multicultural education in Chapter 9). Since the mid-1960s, however, the role of the school in promoting cultural pluralism has been popularized. Yet assimilation continues to be perceived as an important goal of schooling (Levine & Havighurst, 1989).

The Inequality of Educational Opportunity

Notwithstanding the popular rhetoric that schools advance economic growth, economic productivity, and social mobility, the goal of equal educational opportunity for all has never been fully achieved in the United States. One of the most widely published critics of the myth of equal educational opportunity has been James S. Coleman, noted researcher and professor of sociology and education. In his early writing, Coleman (1966) described some of the basic elements that traditionally have been considered in the concept of equal educational opportunity:

- Providing a free education up to the level that constitutes the principal entry point to the labor force.

- Providing a common curriculum for all children, regardless of background.

- Providing for children from diverse backgrounds to attend the same school.

- Providing equality of financial expenditures within a given locality.

However, Coleman asserted, providing the above elements, although meritorious, does not ensure equal educational opportunity. For example, providing a free education up to a certain level does not mean that children will stay in school to take advantage of it. Moreover, providing the education really only means exposure to a given curriculum; it does not ensure equality of achievement.

Neither does a common curriculum assume equal educational opportunity. In fact, the change in the secondary school curriculum in the early twentieth century from a classical curriculum appropriate for the college bound to a nonclassical curriculum that supposedly was more fitting for the new majority, namely those adolescents seeking a terminal education, created a form of tracking that defined a certain expectation for the child's future. As the child is matched with the curriculum path (vocational vs. higher education), certain decisions and explicit assumptions are made about the child's future attainment and career goals.

The idea that equal educational opportunity will be accomplished if children from diverse backgrounds are allowed to attend the same school also was challenged by Coleman. The fact that children of different races and backgrounds attend the same schools does not ensure equality of various intangibles (e.g., that they bring the same interest in learning, arouse the same expectations from teachers) nor equality of results.

Last, providing equality of expenditures within a given locality via local taxes does not lead automatically to equal educational opportunity. Here Coleman referred to his own research as well as that of others, which demonstrated that expenditures have very little impact on educational attainment when compared to family characteristics and home environment.

The myth of equal educational opportunity is evident particularly when one examines certain subgroups in the society and their educational attainment and achievement. In this section the educational attainment and achievement of the following subgroups will be examined: social class groups, ethnic groups, racial groups, and gender differences.

Social Class Differences and School Achievement and Attainment

When asked to which social class they belong, the vast majority of Americans identify themselves as being middle class. Despite this single class self-identification, however, ours is not a classless society. Sociologists maintain that a number of social classes exist within most societies, distinguishable by great differences in wealth, prestige, and power. (See the Historical Note on page 249 for a review of the concept of social class.)

Social Classes in the United States

Identify your current social class and indicate what impact your socioeconomic status has had on your educational achievement and attainment.

The *social class* system in the United States is often described in terms of five classes: upper class, upper-middle class, lower-middle class, working class, and lower class. The *upper class* comprises 1–3% of American society and includes those individuals who control great wealth and wield great power and influence. Most have a family history of wealth and power. Members of the *upper-middle class* do not have the family background of the upper class. They are generally leading professionals, high-level managers, or corporate executives. They are well educated and financially well off. The *lower-middle class* consists of middle-income business people, white-collar professionals, and some semiprofessionals. The *working class* is made up largely of blue-collar

Historical Note:
The Concept of Social Class

The concept of social class and social stratification can be found as early as the time of Plato (427–347 B.C.) and Aristotle (384–322 B.C.). Although Plato and Aristotle did not attempt to advance any particular theory to explain the causes and consequences of such stratification, they did recognize the different classes that existed in their social structures. Both Plato and Aristotle discussed social class distinctions in the ideal society. Plato envisioned a utopian society that was divided into three social classes—guardians, auxiliaries, and workers. According to Plato, the guardians would be a disinterested ruling elite. Aristotle acknowledged three social classes including the very wealthy, the very poor, and the middle class. According to Aristotle, in the ideal political system the middle class would be the dominant or ruling class.

By the seventeenth and eighteenth centuries, the concept of social class was an important subject for discussion. During this period, John Locke (1632–1704) developed a theory of social class

that identified two separate classes: property owners and laborers. In 1755 the French philosopher Jean-Jacques Rousseau recognized the existence of social classes by describing what he referred to as natural inequalities and those inequities that resulted from the social order.

Perhaps more than any other political philosopher, Karl Marx (1818–1883) was able to demonstrate the relationship between social class and the political economy. For Marx, what distinguishes one type of society from another is the mode of production (i.e., technology and the division of labor). Marx hypothesized that each mode of production creates a particular class system whereby one class controls the process of production and the other class or classes become the producers or service providers for the dominant/ruling class. Marx was primarily concerned with modern capitalist society. He envisioned a successful working class revolution and the birth of a new classless society.

workers in skilled, semiskilled, and unskilled jobs. Some lower-level white-collar workers also are considered working class. The *lower class* is composed of individuals with incomes at or below the poverty level, usually poorly educated, and often unemployed. An overview of these five classes in terms of income, occupation, wealth, status, family life, personal satisfaction, mental health, life expectancy, education, and political persuasion and participation is given in Table 8.2.

The socioeconomic distinctions among the social classes affect not only lifestyles, patterns of association, and friendships, but patterns of school attainment and achievement. In fact, the preponderance of evidence from all over the world suggests that socioeconomic status affects school attainment and achievement more than any other variable, including race (Brody, 1989).

Social Class and School Achievement

One of the first and best known studies in the United States to address the relationship between achievement and socioeconomic variables was that conducted by James Coleman and his associates, who analyzed data from more than 645,000 students and about 4,000 schools (Coleman, 1966). Their report, *Equality of Educational Opportunity,* documented the relationship between

Class (and approximate percentage of population)	Income	Occupation (responsibilities)	Wealth	Status
1 Upper class (1 to 3%)	Very high income	Executives of big business, large-scale banking (makers of large-scale, long-term policies; goal setters)	Great inherited wealth increased via investments and added earnings	High inherited status
				High earned status
II Upper-middle class (10 to 15%)	High income	Professionals, high-ranking business executives, military officers, civil servants (second-level decision makers, determiners of means not ends)	Some inherited wealth (usually after death of parents), but largely accumulated wealth via savings and investments	
	Comfortable income			Middle status
III Lower-middle class, white-collar workers (30 to 35%)		Owners of small businesses, low-level professionals and semiprofessionals, sales workers (few decisions; narrow range of responsibilities), clerical workers	Little, if any, inherited wealth	
	Moderate income		Some savings	
IV Working class blue-collar workers (40 to 45%)	Low income	Skilled workers, semiskilled and service workers, unskilled workers		Low status
			No savings	
V Lower class (10 to 20%)	Poverty income	High unemployment		Stigma of poverty status

Family Life	Personal Satisfaction, Mental Health, Life Expectancy	Education	Political Persuasion and Participation
Stable	Good mental and physical health, high life expectancy, reported satisfaction with work and life	College education, liberal arts major, elite schools	High participation, Republican, seldom run for office
Stable; some sex-role differentiation	Autonomous, good mental and physical health, long life expectancy, reported satisfaction with work and life	Graduate training, often at elite schools	High participation, conservative Republican (some "professional liberals"), may run for office
Higher incidence of women working; generally stable, but higher incidence of divorce; sharing of family duties	Higher stress, higher incidence of illness and job-related hazards, lower life expectancy, less reported satisfaction with life and work	College Some college	Votes less frequently; Democrat, sometimes votes Republican
Unstable family life	Higher stress, higher incidence of illness and job-related hazards, lower life expectancy, less reported satisfaction with life and work	Junior college training, postsecondary vocational training, high school, some high school, grade school	Doesn't run for office, Democrat, conservative on some issues
Highest incidence of divorce, separation, and desertion	Poorer physical and mental health, lowest life expectancy, lowest reported satisfaction with life and work	Some high school, grade school, highest incidence of functional illiteracy	Seldom participates; Democrat

Source: Reprinted by permission of Macmillan Publishing Company from *Schooling and Society* (2nd Ed.) by Rodman B. Webb and Robert R. Sherman. Copyright © 1989 by Macmillan Publishing Company.

test scores, ethnic and racial status, various socioeconomic characteristics of the student's family and peers, and various teacher and school characteristics (e.g., facilities, expenditures per pupil, number of library books, and class size). The findings showed that the single most important variable accounting for differences in test scores was the educational and social class background of the family. The second most important variable was the educational and social class background of the other children in the school. The Coleman report generated considerable discussion regarding whether and to what extent schools do make a difference. Although the methodology was subject to criticism, reanalysis of this data by Jencks et al. (1972), as well as hundreds of other studies since, have yielded the same result: Socioeconomic status is the major determinant of school success.

A number of indicators of school success have been linked to various indicators of *socioeconomic status*. The *National Assessment of Educational Progress (NAEP),* by congressional mandate, periodically tests a national representative sample of students in public and private schools in certain subject and skill areas. As indicated in Table 8.3, mathematics and reading achievement on the NAEP have been related to parental education, an indicator of socioeconomic status. Proficiency scores at each age level consistently increased as level of parental education increased.

Additional documentation of the relationship between educational achievement and socioeconomic status comes from the National Longitudinal Studies of senior high school students. These studies revealed that students who represented the higher socioeconomic categories received better mean scores on tests that measured vocabulary, associative memory, reading, inductive reasoning, mathematical skills, and perceptual speed, while the lowest mean scores were achieved by those in the lowest socioeconomic class. Simi-

Table 8.3: National Assessment of Educational Progress (NAEP) 1982 Mathematics and 1984 Reading Proficiency Scores and Socioeconomic Status

	Parental Education		
	Not High School Graduate	Graduate High School	Post High School
Mathematics scores:			
Age 9	197.1	211.4	224.3
Age 13	241.5	253.8	268.4
Age 17	269.5	280.6	300.0
Reading scores:			
Age 9	49.2	57.1	58.9
Age 13	52.4	58.8	63.7
Age 17	50.3	58.2	63.1

Source: U.S. Department of Education, National Center for Education Statistics. (1989). *The condition of education 1989* (pp. 102, 106). Washington, DC: U.S. Government Printing Office.

larly, high school students from the highest socioeconomic groups achieved the highest grade point averages (g.p.a.). For example, high school seniors from the highest socioeconomic level had a mean g.p.a. of 3.07, as compared to 2.85 for seniors from the middle class and 2.68 for those from lower socioeconomic levels (Parelius & Parelius, 1987).

Social Class and Educational Attainment

The relationship between social class and educational attainment is evidenced by differences in dropout rates and continuation beyond high school. Regardless of race or ethnicity, students from impoverished families are three to four times more likely to drop out of school than their more affluent peers (Children's Defense Fund, 1987). And, while 60% of the high school graduates from the highest socioeconomic strata continue their education at baccalaureate-granting institutions, only 20% of those from the lowest strata matriculate at baccalaureate institutions (U.S. Department of Education, 1988).

Contributing Factors

The condition of poverty seems to be the major socioeconomic indicator affecting educational achievement and attainment. In 1989, nearly 40 million people lived in families below the poverty level. In fact, more people live in poverty today than before the War on Poverty. During the decade of the 1980s, while the number of U.S. billionaires quintupled, child poverty jumped by 23% (Reed & Sautter, 1990). Almost 20% of America's children still grow up poor; often sick, hungry, and illiterate; deprived of safe and adequate housing and special learning assistance. As a result, many poor children are condemned to physical and psychological deficiencies for life. As a special report in *The Phi Delta Kappan* grimly noted:

> When these children wake each day, they face little prospect that the economic plight of their families will improve enough to make their lives better. Often they internalize the bleakness of their situation and blame themselves for it. Their lives become bitter and humorless or filled with anxiety and fear. Of course, many poor children retain their dignity, and their character is tempered by the Spartan battle for subsistence. But millions of others, permanently damaged, are unable to recover and fall victim to the vicious social pathology of poverty. . . .
>
> Some American youngsters will never even have the chance to see the turn of the century. As has happened in other wars, they will perish. More than 10,000 children in the U.S. die each year as a direct result of the poverty they endure. (Reed & Sautter, 1990, p. K3)

The effects of poverty are seen early in the child's development and academic career. A study by the U.S. Department of Education showed that poverty's adverse effects on achievement could be seen as early as the first grade. The achievement differences appear to become greater as the child progresses through school (Saks, 1988/89). In addition, it is estimated that 11% of children end up in special education classes because of cognitive and developmental problems, many of which could have been prevented if even the most simple and inexpensive prenatal health care had been available to their mothers (Reed & Sautter, 1990).

While the effects of poverty appear to be obvious, how do you explain why it has become increasingly more difficult to convince legislators that we either pay now or pay later for programs aimed at the disadvantaged?

The factors that seem to perpetuate poverty also seem to be related to education, and in the end a low education/poverty/low education cycle is created. That is, low educational attainment can lead to poverty and poverty, in turn, has an impact on children's educational attainment and achievement.

The problem of low attainment among the children of the poor is made worse by the fact that the typical school serving these children faces a number of problems including high rates of student mobility, high incidence of severe behavioral and emotional problems among students, large numbers of students with limited English proficiency, low staff morale, poor facilities, and inadequate resources (Knapp & Shields, 1990). The results are graphically seen in Table 8.4, which shows the average NAEP reading proficiency scores of students from disadvantaged urban areas to be significantly below those from advantaged urban areas. By the eleventh grade, students from disadvantaged areas scored below the grade 7 level for students from advantaged urban communities. These results are even more distressing when one considers that, by grade 11, most of the low achieving students have already dropped out. Dropout rates in many urban schools range from 40 to 60% and as high as 80% in schools enrolling predominantly students from the lowest socioeconomic class (Hahn, Panzerger, & Lykavitz, 1987).

Perhaps the greatest challenge facing America today is to provide the programs and services necessary to ensure the educational success of these children and free them from the cycle of poverty. As the National Commission on Excellence in Education (1983) so succinctly pronounced in *A Nation at Risk:* "All, regardless of race or class or economic status, are entitled to a fair chance" (p. 4).

Ethnic Differences and School Achievement and Attainment

Ethnic groups are subgroups of the population that are distinguished by having a common cultural heritage (language, customs, history, etc.). Significant differences in educational achievement and attainment are found among different ethnic groups in this country. The Hispanic population (22.4 million) is the largest and second–fastest-growing ethnic group in this country, representing 9% of the entire population (U.S. Bureau of the Census, 1991). It is a diverse group made up of 60% Mexican-Americans, 14% Puerto Ricans, 6% Cubans, and 20% other Hispanics (U.S. Bureau of the Census, 1983). Each of these subgroups is unique and has had a distinct pattern of immigration and settlement in this country (Baratz-Snowden, Rock, Pollack, & Wilder, 1988).

Hispanics and School Achievement

Hispanics are the most undereducated group in America. This group has the highest dropout rate of all the major ethnic groups, tends to be overrepresented in remedial and vocational programs, is the most highly segregated,

Over 40 million people of all ages live in families with income below the poverty level.

and exhibits overall low academic achievement (Hyland, 1989). For example, the most recent NAEP results (see Table 8.4) indicate that Hispanic children's reading skills were substantially lower than their Anglo counterparts and slightly lower than their black counterparts at grades 3, 7, and 11.

NAEP mathematics and science assessments results across the 13-year period 1973 to 1986 by race and ethnicity are depicted in Figures 8.1 (p. 257) and 8.2 (p. 258). Hispanic students showed improvement in proficiency scores at all grade levels in both mathematics and science. Because the scores of white students did not improve significantly over the 13-year period, the improvements shown by Hispanic students narrowed the performance differences

Table 8.4: Average Reading Proficiency Score of Students in Grades 3, 7, and 11 on the National Assessment of Educational Progress, by Selected Characteristics, 1986

Characteristics	Average Reading Proficiency Score		
	Grade 3	Grade 7	Grade 11
Total	38.1	48.9	56.1
Race/ethnicity			
White	39.8	50.3	57.3
Black	33.4	45.2	51.5
Hispanic	33.2	44.4	51.3
Asian[1]		52.5	
Native American[1]		43.9	
Region			
Northeast	39.1	50.7	57.4
Southeast	37.2	48.1	54.8
Central	39.3	49.0	56.5
West	36.9	48.0	55.4
Type of community			
Disadvantaged urban	31.9	43.8	51.2
Advantaged urban	41.2	51.6	59.5
Gender			
Male	37.3	47.5	54.5
Female	38.9	50.3	57.7

Source: U.S. Department of Education, National Center for Education Statistics. (1989). *The condition of education 1989*. Washington, DC: U.S. Government Printing Office.

[1]Only seventh grade reading scores available from Baratz-Snowden, J., Rock, D., Pollack, J., and Wilder, G. (1988). *The educational progress of language minority children: Findings from the NAEP 1985–86 special study*. Princeton, NJ: National Assessment of Educational Progress/Educational Testing Service.

between the two groups. Nonetheless, the performance of Hispanic students remained well below that of white students.

Studies also have shown that Hispanic students are less likely to receive *A*s and more likely to receive *D*s or *F*s than white students. They also take fewer college preparatory courses than white or black students and more vocational offerings (Hyland, 1989).

Hispanics and Educational Attainment

Ethnic differences also have been shown to be related to educational attainment. By the time Hispanics reach high school age, approximately 25% are two or more years overage for their grade level, a condition that may place them at risk for dropping out. It is estimated that approximately 40% of all Hispanics who drop out of school do so before they reach the tenth grade (Hispanic Policy Development Project, 1987). In 1988, 77.7% of whites 25 years old and older had completed secondary school, compared to 51% of Hispanics of the same age group (see Figure 8.3). Perhaps more disturbing,

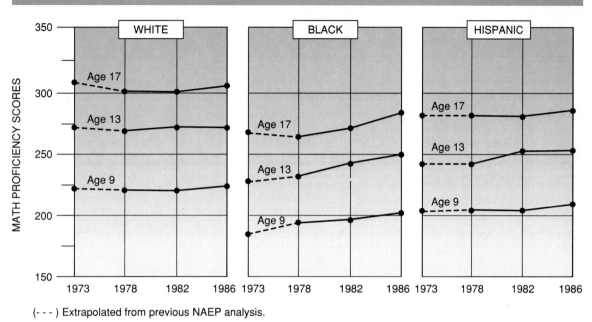

Figure 8.1: Trends in Average Mathematics Proficiency for 9-, 13-, and 17-Year-Olds by Race/Ethnicity, 1973–1986

(- - -) Extrapolated from previous NAEP analysis.

Source: National Assessment of Educational Progress. (1988). *The mathematics report card: Are we measuring up?* (pp. 22–23). Princeton, NJ: Educational Testing Service.

the high school completion rates for Hispanics age 18–24 has actually dropped in recent years, from 62.8% in 1985 to 56% in 1989 (Carter & Wilson, 1990).

In the attainment of a higher education, Hispanics also lag behind the non-Hispanic population. In 1988 approximately 10% of Hispanics who were 25 years of age or older had completed four or more years of college, compared to 21% of whites.

Contributing Factors

The lower educational achievement of many Hispanic youth is no doubt associated with socioeconomic status. Approximately 25.8% of Hispanic families are below the poverty level, as compared to 8% for whites. In general, Hispanics experience higher unemployment and lower income than non-Hispanics. In 1988, the Hispanic unemployment rate was 8.5%, compared to the unemployment rate of 5.8% for non-Hispanics, and the median Hispanic family income in 1987 was $20,310 or approximately $11,000 less than for non-Hispanic families (U.S. Bureau of the Census, 1989).

A number of studies have looked beyond the family and targeted the inferior schools that many Hispanic children attend as a primary factor in their underachievement and alienation. Studies have found that a large per-

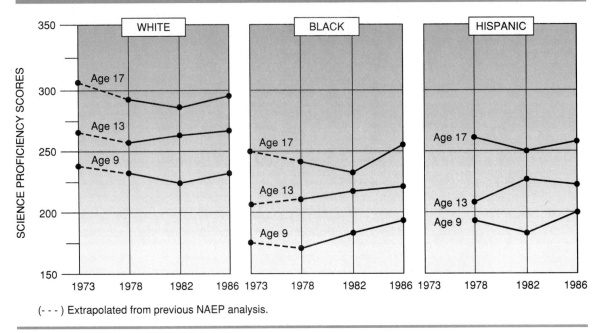

Figure 8.2: Trends in Average Science Proficiency for 9-, 13-, and 17-Year-Olds by Race/Ethnicity, 1973–1986

(- - -) Extrapolated from previous NAEP analysis.

Source: National Assessment of Educational Progress. (1988). *The science report card: Elements of risk and discovery* (pp. 28–29). Princeton, NJ: Educational Testing Service.

What implications do the estimates regarding the increase in the Hispanic population have for you as an individual? For you as a prospective teacher?

centage of Mexican-American students attend segregated schools that are understaffed, poorly equipped, and poorly funded (Orfield, 1987).

A major explanation for the poorer performance of Hispanic children is their linguistic minority background. The term *linguistic minority* includes the growing population of nonnative English speakers, as well as other student populations who are native speakers of English but who have been exposed to some other language in the home since birth (O'Conner, 1989). A 1985–86 NAEP survey of Hispanic children whose primary language was not English indicated that these children experienced many more academic difficulties than their English-speaking counterparts.

It is also estimated that by the year 2020 the Hispanic population will be equal to or greater than the black population and that one in four children will be Hispanic. If the relationship between ethnic group identity and poverty continues, one can expect an even greater number of ethnic minority children, in particular Hispanic children, to be educationally disadvantaged (Pallas, Natriello, & McDill, 1989). These children's needs require that teachers and schools modify their approaches to teaching and educating to ensure that these children, too, can use the public schools as their springboard to the American Dream (Hyland, 1989).

Figure 8.3: High School and College Graduates by Race, 1970, 1980, and 1988 (percentage of persons 25 years and over)

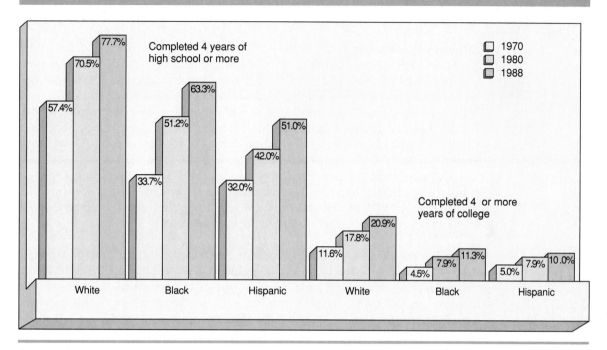

Source: U.S. Bureau of the Census. (1988). *Educational attainment in the United States: March 1987 and 1986,* Current Population Reports, Series P-20, No. 428, Table 12; and U.S. Bureau of the Census. (1989). *Population profile of the United States 1989,* Special Studies, Series P-23, No. 159, Figures 20, 36. Washington, D.C.: U.S. Government Printing Office.

Racial Differences and School Achievement and Attainment

Black Americans

School Achievement. The 30 million blacks in the U.S. make up 12.1% of the population (U.S. Bureau of the Census, 1991). Black students, like Hispanic students, have shown overall improvement in achievement during the past two or three decades, but still perform below the level of white students. For example, as was shown in Table 8.4, in grades 3, 7, and 11 black students' performance was below that of white students but slightly above that of Hispanics in terms of the 1986 National Assessment for Educational Progress reading proficiency scores. In regard to the NAEP mathematics assessment (Figure 8.1), black students consistently score below both white and Hispanic students at each age level. The same is true for NAEP science proficiency scores (Figure 8.2), where the gap between blacks and whites, and blacks and Hispanics, is even greater. However, the overall improvement by black students during the period depicted has narrowed the performance gap between white and black students.

Racial differences also are found in the results of other standardized tests, in program enrollments, and in grades earned in school. For example, in 1989 white students taking the Scholastic Aptitude Test (SAT) averaged 200 points higher than black students (Mitgang, 1989). Black students, like Hispanics, also are more likely to be enrolled in general and vocational programs and are less likely to be enrolled in academic programs than their white counterparts.

Educational Attainment.   Another indicator of racial differences can be found in high school completion. As shown in Figure 8.3, while the proportion of blacks 25 years of age and older who have completed high school has increased since 1970, the rate of high school completion for blacks (76%) in 1989 was still somewhat behind that of whites (82%) (Carter & Wilson, 1990). Blacks also tend to complete high school at an older age than whites, reflecting the fact that blacks are more likely than whites to fail and repeat one or more grades.

The percentage of persons 25 years of age and older who have completed college also differs by race. For example, as shown in Figure 8.3, in 1988 approximately 11% of blacks 25 years of age and older had completed four or more years of college, as compared to 21% of whites.

Contributing Factors.   As in the case of Hispanics, explanations for achievement differences between blacks and whites are to be found in the lower socioeconomic status of blacks and the social milieu of black families. For example, in 1988, 43% of black families were headed by a female householder with no husband present. About 33% of black families in 1988 lived below the poverty level, three times the rate for white families. The unemployment rate for blacks (13%) was more than twice as high as that for whites (5.3%). The median family income for blacks was $18,100, compared to $20,310 for Hispanics and $32,270 for whites (U.S. Bureau of the Census, 1989).

During the past decade it has become more apparent that one of the major reasons why black children do not achieve as well as white children is because the public schools are not meeting the needs of poor children in general. Also, it is suggested that many black children may bring to school skills, attitudes, and achievement orientations that differ from their white middle-class peers. Too often, these differences are perceived as fixed deficits by teachers, counselors, and administrators who, rather than provide for these differences, often relegate black children to a permanently inferior position in the school and the self-fulfilling prophecy continues (Bock & Moore, 1986; Haskins, Walden, & Ramey, 1983; Rist, 1973).

Asian-Americans
School Achievement.   Although their percentage of the U.S. population is relatively small (2.9%), the 7.3 million Asian-Americans in the United States are the fastest growing racial group in America, increasing by 108% since 1980 (U.S. Bureau of the Census, 1991). Of its more than 20 subgroups, the Chinese (23%), Filipino (23%), Japanese (21%), Asian-Indian (11%), Korean (10%), and Vietnamese (7%) are the largest (U.S. Bureau of the Census, 1983). In the past two decades many of the new Asian immigrants have come from Laos and Cambodia. Research on the achievement of Asian-Americans

has been limited, a condition that has been justified by the fact that their achievement is generally greater than that of other racial and ethnic groups (see Table 8.4). For example, on the 1989 American College Test (ACT), with a score of 20.0, Asian-Americans outscored whites (19.6) and all other groups. On the SAT that same year, Asian-Americans "blew away the math component with an average score that was 34 points higher than the next closest score" (Pitzi, 1989, p. B12).

Educational Attainment. Asian-Americans complete high school at a much higher rate than other racial and ethnic groups. The 1980 census data showed that almost 80% of Asian-American men and 70% of Asian-American women had completed high school. Chinese-Americans and Japanese-Americans did better than Southeast Asian and Filipino Americans (Carter & Wilson, 1990).

Contributing Factors. Much of the research that has been done on Asian-American students' achievement has concentrated on the factors contributing to their success. Cultural factors have been found to be among the most important variables. Among the cultural variables noted by Baratz-Snowden et al. (1988) are:

> high expectations of parents and teachers, and a home learning structure that is perceived to be supportive of academic success. . . . Asian-American parents place a high value on education for self-improvement and family honor. These high expectations are transmitted to children and, further, to teachers. Teachers' high expectations are reinforced because they have positive attitudes towards Asian cultural chracteristics, which in turn reciprocally reinforces children's expectations and performance. (p. 9; citations omitted)

There is also considerable evidence that Asian-Americans consider education to be an effective strategy in offsetting discrimination and achieving social mobility (Tsang, 1983).

To what do you attribute the proportional overrepresentation of Asian-Americans in the sciences as opposed to fields such as education or social work?

Native Americans

Even more limited than the research on Asian-American educational achievement is the research on the achievement and attainment of Native Americans. Demography may be one reason for this lack of visibility: The 1.2 million Native Americans make up only a little over one-half of 1% of the population (U.S. Bureau of the Census, 1991). However, they are a diverse population of more than 500 tribes and native groups, 206 languages, and vast differences in customs and economic development (Reeves, 1989).

School Achievement. Such information as does exist about the achievement of Native American children suggests achievement deficits (e.g., NAEP reading proficiency scores, Table 8.4, and low ACT scores, 14.7 for 1989) and low attainment. According to Witthuhn (1982):

> three-quarters of all Indian children are at least one grade level behind for their age; over one-half of Indian students drop out of school; and, on the average, Indian students fall further and further behind as they progress

through school until finally they are three to four years behind in school achievement by graduation. (cited by Baratz-Snowden et al., 1988, p. 10)

High Dropout Rate.   The dropout rate for Native Americans is higher than that of any racial or ethnic group in the United States— 29%, according to one U.S. Department of Education study. Additionally, other studies have shown that Native American students drop out much earlier than other groups, often in the elementary grades (Reeves, 1989). The causes of such high dropout rates vary; some stem from the family and some from the school. Often parents and students distrust the purposes and payoffs of education. Some parents fear that their children will lose their culture and therefore keep them at home. A number of experts say that Native American children who leave school are not dropouts, but are "pushed" out of schools that have failed to motivate them or recognize their unique needs (McDonald, 1989).

Contributing Factors.   One possible explanation for the poor achievement of Native American students suggests that their cultural values promote a learning style that inhibits interaction with adults or in new situations, and creates a reluctance to volunteer to ask or answer questions (Baratz-Snowden et al., 1988). Other evidence suggests that Native American parents do not have as high expectations for the educational achievements of their children as do other minority parents. According to a 1988 report by the Bureau of Indian Affairs, only about 50% of Native American parents thought their high school child should go to college. This compares to about 70% for black parents (Reeves, 1989).

Other explanations for the underachievement of Native American students are the same as those advanced for the underachievement of other minority children. That is, many Native American children come from disadvantaged homes in which parents have lower levels of educational attainment and lower socioeconomic status. According to a report by the U.S. Department of the Interior, male unemployment on reservations is 58% and the poverty rate is almost 50%. Forty percent of Native American households are single-parent families. And in no other racial or ethnic group are as many children living with neither parent (Reeves, 1989).

Gender Differences and School Achievement and Attainment

Although sex-based differences in school achievement appear to be declining, differences still remain. On most tests of verbal ability females achieve at higher levels than males. For example, as shown in Table 8.4, 1986 NAEP reading proficiency scores are slightly higher for females than males at each grade level.

Math and Science Differences

The reverse is true in science and mathematics, where males commonly score higher than females. For example, on the 1986 NAEP science assessment, the scores of females were behind those of males, particularly at age 17, continuing the pattern of previous assessments (see Figure 8.4). Although the greatest difference in 1986 scores was for 17-year-olds, the disparity between 17-year-old males and females actually has lessened over time, while the disparity for 9- and 11-year-olds appears to have increased during the period under review.

In mathematics the 1986 assessments showed no gender differences at age 9 and only minimal differences at ages 13 and 17 (see Figure 8.5). Past assessments showed a similar pattern with the greater (though marginal) gender difference being for the 17-year-olds.

A recent synthesis of research on gender differences in science and mathematics achievement has indicated that gender differences are declining, particularly in spatial ability, an ability thought to be closely associated with mathematics and science performance. Spatial ability relates to tasks such as locating a single object or figure embedded within a more complex figure and mentally rotating an object as quickly as possible. The same study also con-

Figure 8.4: Trends in Average Science Proficiency for 9-, 13-, and 17-Year-Olds by Gender, 1973–1986

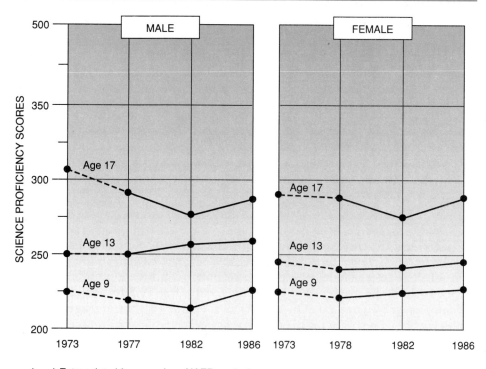

(- - -) Extrapolated from previous NAEP analysis.

Source: National Assessment of Educational Progress. (1988). *The science report card: Elements of risk and discovery* (p. 30). Princeton, NJ: Educational Testing Service.

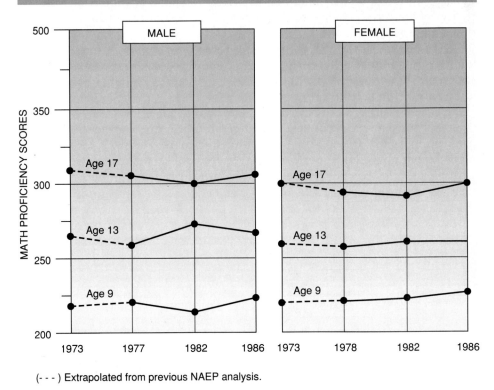

Figure 8.5: Trends in Average Mathematics Proficiency for 9-, 13-, and 17-Year-Olds by Gender, 1973–1986

(- - -) Extrapolated from previous NAEP analysis.

Source: National Assessment of Educational Progress. (1988). *The mathematics report card: Are we measuring up?* (p. 25). Princeton, NJ: Educational Testing Service.

cluded that differences in spatial ability that do exist are responsive to training (Linn & Hyde, 1989).

ACT and SAT Differences

Have you ever taken either the ACT or the SAT? Do you feel your score was affected by your race, gender, or social class?

Gender differences are also found in the scores of high school seniors on the American College Test (ACT) and the SAT, particularly on the math sections of these tests. The most recent data show a continuation of these differences. In 1989 the average composite ACT score was 19.3 for males and 18.0 for females (see Figure 8.6). On the SAT in the same year the average score for males was 934, one point higher than a year earlier, while the average score for females was 875, two points lower than the previous year (Mitgang, 1989).

In 1987 the Educational Testing Service, the developer of the SAT, initiated a study to determine the causes of the gender differences in test scores. The study found that when the variables of family income, ethnic group, high school courses, and choice of college major were controlled, the differences in males' and females' scores disappeared (Landers, 1989).

Gender differences in mathematics continue to decline.

Gender and Educational Attainment

Sex differences are also evident in educational attainment. Although in 1988 the proportion of males and females 25 years of age and older who had completed high school was not significantly different, both around 76%, the proportion who completed four or more years of college are somewhat different: 24% of males and 17% of females. Completion rates also varied by age group. Figure 8.7 illustrates the percentage of college graduates by age and gender in 1988.

Sex differences in college completion rates favoring males should disappear within the next decade as women's college enrollment rate surpasses men's. It is estimated that throughout the 1990s women will earn more bachelor's and master's degrees than men, and by the year 2001, women will lead in doctorates awarded (Gerald & Hussar, 1990).

Contributing Factors. A number of hypotheses have been offered as to why males and females achieve differently. The most common explanation is that the differences are largely attributable to sex-role stereotyping. As summarized by Fennema (1987):

> Boys and girls have different educational experiences. Teachers interact differently with girls and with boys, and girls and boys choose to participate in different learning and social behavior. These differences develop because perceived sex role acts as a mediator influencing what boys and girls do and, as a consequence, what they learn. Teachers, students, and the entire educational

For Future Reference:
Strategies for Eliminating Sex-Related Differences in Outcomes

1. Talk about sex-role stereotyping in society so that both girls and boys become aware of it.

2. Be sure all learners recognize the importance of all content areas to their future life.

3. Be sure your expectations of learning are high for all students.

4. Ensure that both girls and boys learn to be self-reliant and to value independence.

5. Be sure that instructional materials are non-biased.

Source: Fennema, E. (1987). Sex-related differences in education: Myths, realities, and interventions. In V. Richardson-Koehler (Ed.), *Educators' handbook: A research perspective* (p. 345). New York: Longman.

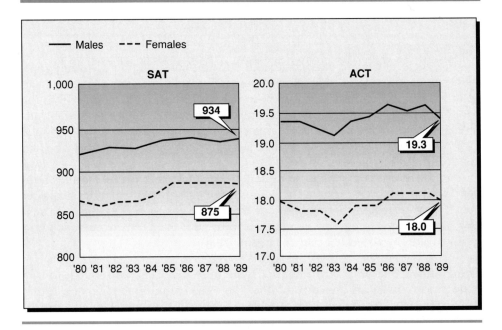

Figure 8.6: National SAT and ACT Scores for Males and Females over the Past 10 Years

Source: Mitgang, L. (1989, September 12). College-admission scores slip. *Arizona Republic,* A1. Reprinted with permission.

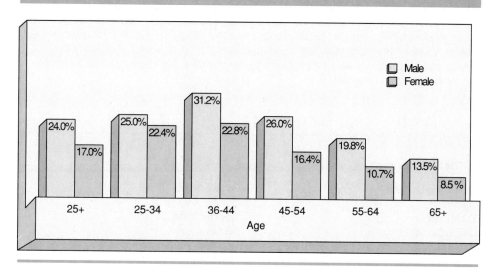

Figure 8.7: College Graduates by Age and Sex, 1988 (percentages)

Source: U.S. Bureau of the Census (1989). *Population profile of the United States* (Current population reports, Series P-23, No. 159) (p. 39). Washington, DC: U.S. Government Printing Office.

community hold beliefs about appropriate roles for females and males. Part of that belief includes stereotyping learning in specific areas as masculine or feminine. When a central area such as reading is stereotyped as being feminine . . . or masculine (mathematics), it is more difficult for boys and girls to achieve equally. (p. 341)

Concerned parents and teachers can do much to eliminate gender differences in educational outcomes. Some of the things you might do as a teacher are listed on page 266.

Summary

In this chapter the definitions of culture, subculture, society, socialization, and acculturation were presented. The family, the peer group, and the media were examined as agents of socialization. Of these institutions, the family has undergone the most significant changes since World War II. As a result of those changes, many of the earlier functions of the family have now been transferred to the school. At the same time, as children spend more time viewing television, its influence on children's behavior and school achievement has increased.

Cultural socialization, contributing to the economic development of the nation, social selection or social mobility, and responding to diversity continue to be the major purposes and expectations of schooling. Of these, the debate as to whether the schools promote social selection or social mobility remains one of controversy in American education.

Many would agree that there are numerous opportunities for education, but most believe that equal educational opportunity is more a myth than a fact in the American educational system. The myth of equal educational opportunity is particularly evident as one examines differences in the educational attainment and achievement of social class groups, ethnic groups, racial groups, and the sexes. In the next chapter, we will look at some of the strategies that have been employed to increase equality of educational opportunity and ameliorate against the effects of economic and cultural deprivation and discrimination.

Key Terms

Amalgamation
Assimilation
Cultural pluralism
Culture
Ethnic group
Linguistic minority
National Assessment of Educational Progress (NAEP)

Separatism
Social class
Social mobility
Social selection
Socialization
Society
Socioeconomic status
Subculture

Discussion Questions

1. How would a social reconstructionist respond to David Marshall's position as presented in the opening vignette of this chapter?

2. How could you as a teacher attempt to mitigate against the negative influence of television on children's aggressive behavior? What suggestions would you make to parents?

3. Reflect on the high school from which you graduated. To what extent did it promote upward social mobility? In what ways did it resemble a miniature factory system?

4. Discuss what is meant by the cycle of poverty. What can the schools do to break this cycle?

5. Discuss the impact of differing cultural values on school achievement and attainment. Give specific examples.

6. Discuss the common factors contributing to the underachievement of Hispanics, blacks, and Native Americans.

7. What are the levels of educational attainment of the females in your family? The males? What factors account for any differences that may exist between the two groups? To what extent are the factors evident today?

References

Anderson, D. R., & Collins, P. A. (1988). *The impact of children's education: Television's influence on cognitive development.* Washington, DC: U.S. Department of Education, Office of Educational Research and Improvement.

Apple, M. W. (1979). *Ideology and the curriculum.* London: Routledge & Kegan Paul.

Apple, M. W. (1982). *Education and power.* New York: Routledge, Chapman, & Hall.

Baratz-Snowden, J., Rock, D., Pollack, J., & Wilder, G. (1988). *The educational progress of language minority children: Funding from the NAEP 1985–86 special study.* Princeton, NJ: National Assessment of Educational Progress/Educational Testing Service.

Beentjes, J. W. J., & Van der Voort, T. H. A. (1988). Television's impact on children's reading skills: A review of research. *Reading Research Quarterly, 23,* 389–413.

Bickers, P. M. (1987). *Indicators of future school enrollments.* Arlington, VA: Educational Research Service.

Bock, R. D., & Moore, E. G. L. (1986). *Advantage and disadvantage: A profile of America's youth.* Hillsdale, NJ: Lawrence Erlbaum Associates.

Bowles, S., & Gintis, H. (1976). *Schooling in capitalist America.* New York: Basic Books.

Brody, J. (1989). Minority achievement. *Educational Vital Signs, IV,* A9.

Carter, D., & Wilson, R. (1990). *Ninth annual status report on minorities in higher education.* Washington, DC: American Council on Education.

Cave, W. M., & Chesler, M. A. (1974). The societal context of education. In W. M. Cave & M. A. Chesler (Eds.), *Sociology of education: An anthology of issues and problems* (pp. 1–18). New York: Macmillan.

Children's Defense Fund. (1987). *Opportunities for prevention.* Washington, DC: Author.

Coleman, J. S. (1968). The concept of equality of educational opportunity. *Harvard Educational Review, 38,* 7–22.

Coleman, J. S., et al. (1966). *Equality of educational opportunity.* Washington, DC: U.S. Government Printing Office.

Connecticut ASCD (1989). *Curriculum for the new millennium: Trends shaping our schools.* Fairfield, CT: CASCD.

Fennema, E. (1987). Sex-related differences in education: Myths, realities, and intervention. In V. Richardson-Koehler (Ed.), *Educators' handbook: A research perspective* (pp. 329–347). New York: Longman.

Gerald, D. E., & Hussar, W. J. (1990). *Projections of education statistics to 2001: An update.* Washington, DC: U.S. Department of Education, Center for Education Statistics.

Giroux, H. A., & Purpel, D. (Eds.). (1983). *The hidden curriculum and moral education.* Berkeley, CA: McCutchan.

Hahn, A., Panzerger, J., & Lykavitz, B. (1987). *Dropouts in America.* Washington, DC: Institute for Educational Leadership.

Haskins, R., Walden, T., & Ramey, C. T. (1983). Teacher and student behavior in high and low ability groups. *Journal of Educational Psychology, 75,* 865–876.

Hispanic Policy Development Project (1987). Policy remedies. *The Research Bulletin, 1*(2), 9.

Hyland, C. R. (1989). What we know about the fast growing minority population: Hispanic Americans. *Educational Horizons, 67,* 131–35.

Illich, I. (1970). *Deschooling society.* New York: Harper & Row.

Jencks, C., Smith, M., Arland, H., Bane, M. J., Cohen, D., Gintis, H., Heyns, B., & Michelson, S. (1972). *Inequality: A reassessment of the effect of family and schooling in America.* New York: Basic Books.

Landers, S. (1989). New York: Scholarship awards are ruled discriminatory. *The American Psychological Association Monitor, 20*(4), 14.

Levine, D. U., & Havighurst, R. J. (1989). *Society and education* (7th ed.). Boston, MA: Allyn & Bacon.

Linn, M. C., & Hyde, J. S. (1989). Gender, mathematics, and science. *Educational Researcher, 18*(8), 17–27.

Knapp, M. S., & Shields, P. M. (1990). Reconceiving academic instruction for the children of poverty. *Phi Delta Kappan, 71,* 753–758.

McDonald, D. M. (1989, August 2). Education: The first condition. *Education Week,* 5–7.

Mitgang, L. (1989, September 12). College-admission scores slip. *Arizona Republic,* A1, A7.

National Commission on Excellence in Education. (1983). *A nation at risk: The imperative for educational reform.* Washington, DC: U.S. Government Printing Office.

O'Conner, M. C. (1989). Aspects of differential performance by minorities on standardized tests: Linguistic and sociocultural factors. In B. R. Gifford (Ed.), *Test policy and test performance: Education, language, and culture.* (pp. 129–181). Boston, MA: Kleewer.

Ogbu, J. U. (1986). Structural constraints in school desegregation. In J. Prager, D. Longshore, & M. Seeman (Eds.), *School desegregation research: New directions in situational analysis* (pp. 21–45). New York: Plenum Press.

Orfield, G. (1987). *School segregation in the 1980s: Trends in the states and metropolitan areas.* Report to the Joint Center for Political Studies. Chicago, IL: National School Desegregation Project.

Pallas, A. M., Natriello, G., & McDill, E. L. (1989). The changing nature of the disadvantaged population: Current dimensions and future trends. *Educational Researcher, 18*(5), 15–22.

Parelius, R. J., & Parelius, A. P. (1987). *The sociology of education* (2nd ed.). Englewood Cliffs, NJ: Prentice-Hall.

Pearl, D. (1987). Familial, peer, and television influences on aggressive and violent behavior. In D. H. Crowell, I. M. Evans, & C. R. O'Donnell (Eds.), *Childhood aggression and violence* (pp. 231–247). New York: Plenum Press.

Pitzi, M. J. (1989, September 17). Test drop microscopic. *Arizona Republic,* B1, B12.

Radeki, T. (1989). Television and film entertainment. *Mothering, 50,* 54.

Reed, S., & Sautter, R. C. (1990). Children of poverty: The status of 12 million young Americans. *Phi Delta Kappan, 71,* K1–K12.

Reeves, M. S. (1989, August 2). The high cost of endurance. *Education Week,* 2–4.

Rist, R. C. (1973). *The urban school as a factory for failure.* Cambridge, MA: M.I.T. Press.

Ritchie, D., Price, V., & Roberts, D. F. (1987). Television, reading, and reading achievement. *Communications Research, 14,* 292–314.

Saks, J. B. (1988/89). Minority achievement. *Education Vital Signs, IV,* A9–A12.

Selakovich, D. (1984). *Schooling in America: Social foundations of education.* New York: Longman.

Spring, J. (1976). *The sorting machine.* New York: McKay.

Spring, J. (1988). *Conflicts of interests: The politics of American education.* New York: Longman.

Thomas, D. R. (1973). *The schools next time.* New York: McGraw-Hill.

Traditional families: A dying breed. (1986, May 14). *Education Week,* 22.

Tsang, S. L. (1983). *Asian Americans and mathematics education.* Oakland, CA: ARC Associates, cited in Baratz-Snowden, J., Rock, D., Pollack, J., & Wilder, G. (1988), *The educational progress of language minority children: Funding from the NAEP 1985–86 special study.* Princeton, NJ: National Assessment of Educational Progress/Educational Testing Service.

Turiel, E. (1987). Potential relations between the development of social reasoning and childhood aggression. In D. H. Crowell, I. M. Evans, & C. R. O'Donnell (Eds.), *Childhood aggression and violence* (pp. 231–247). New York: Plenum Press.

U. S. Bureau of the Census. (1983). *1980 census of population, general social economic characteristics.* Washington, DC: U.S. Government Printing Office.

U. S. Bureau of the Census. (1989). *Population profile of the United States* (Current Population Reports, Series P–23, No. 159). Washington, DC: U.S. Government Printing Office.

U. S. Bureau of the Census. (1991). *1990 census of population: Population characteristics* (Current Population Reports, Series P–20). Washington, DC: U.S. Government Printing Office.

U. S. Department of Education, National Center for Education Statistics (1984). *Two years in high school: The status of 1980 sophomores in 1982.* Washington, DC: U.S. Government Printing Office.

U. S. Department of Education (1988). *National assessment of vocational education,* Second Interim Report to Congress. Washington, DC: U.S. Government Printing Office.

Webb, L. D., McCarthy, M. M., & Thomas, S. (1988). *Financing elementary and secondary education.* Columbus, OH: Merrill.

Webb, R. B., & Sherman, R. R. (1989). *Schooling and society.* New York: Macmillan.

Chapter 9
Achieving Equity in Education

As the son of a tenant farmer, I know that education is the only valid passport from poverty. As a former teacher—and I hope a future one—I have great expectations of what this law will mean for all of our young people. . . . I believe deeply no law I have signed or will ever sign means more to the future of America.

President Lyndon Johnson
Upon signing the Elementary and Secondary Education Bill, April 1, 1965

At the end of the second week of school a student, Linda Wilson, comes to the counseling office with a problem. She complains that she has been the subject of harassment by the teacher and students in the auto mechanics class. According to Linda the boys refuse to work with her on small group projects, ignore her when she talks to them, and on various occasions have hidden her tools or put grease in her book. One day when she went to her car she found all the air let out of her tires with a note on the windshield saying "do it yourself if you're such a red-hot mechanic." She says she knows Mr. Thompson, the teacher, is aware of the students' behavior but just ignores it. According

to Linda, Mr. Thompson acts as if she's stupid when she asks a question, always refers to the class as "you men," and when discussing employment opportunities makes it clear auto mechanics is for men only. Linda says she's really interested in auto mechanics, but under the circumstances wants to drop the course.

Do you agree with Linda that she should drop the course? Why or why not? What other options would you suggest to Linda? What evidence is there of sex bias, sex stereotyping, or sex discrimination in this example?

As we have seen in previous chapters of this text, a variety of circumstances have combined in society and the schools to restrict the educational opportunities of many students, including students such as Linda Wilson. This chapter presents a number of strategies for combating inequity and inequality in education. As you review these strategies, consider the following learning objectives:

- List the major court decisions concerning segregation and their impact on local school districts.

- Discuss the possible effects of desegregation on the academic achievement and self-esteem of minority students and on community integration.

- Outline the principles inherent in P. L. 94–142 and their impact on American education.

- Describe the major compensatory education programs and their current status.

- Differentiate the concepts of multiculturalism, multiethnic education, English as a second language, cultural pluralism, and bilingual education.

- Describe current issues in the education of Native Americans.

- Discuss the progress of sex equity in education and the process for its attainment.

- Evaluate the role of adult education in overcoming illiteracy.

- Outline the major secondary vocational education programs and comment on the reform movement's impact on them.

The burden of eliminating social inequality rests not with the schools but with social action programs and the enforcement of legal prohibitions against inequality; however, the schools do have a role in providing opportunities that foster social equality and in removing barriers that make it difficult for children and adults to take maximum advantage of educational opportunities (Cameron, 1987). Beginning in the 1960s with the civil rights movement and the federal government's War on Poverty, numerous federal programs were initiated to promote educational opportunity. In addition to the federal initiatives, state governments, professional organizations, and the private sector have introduced strategies to combat inequity in education. In this chapter the following strategies are discussed: desegregation, education of the handicapped, compensatory education, multicultural and bilingual education, Indian education, promotion of sex equity, adult and continuing education, and vocational education.

Desegregation

School *desegregation* is a complex and controversial issue. It is multidimensional in that it has personal, political, social, legal, and educational aspects. Historically, children and youth in the United States generally have attended socially segregated schools, a reflection of a segregated society. They also have attended socioeconomically segregated schools. This is particularly true for black children, but it is also true for other social and ethnic minority groups. School segregation also extends to teachers. Black teachers typically are concentrated in schools that primarily serve black students, while white teachers tend to be concentrated in schools that primarily serve white students.

The First Phase

Desegregation is a strategy for realizing constitutional protection and equality of educational opportunity. Desegregation became a major issue in American education with the landmark Supreme Court case of *Brown v. Board of Education* (1954). This case involved elementary school students in Topeka, Kansas, who filed suit challenging a Kansas law that sanctioned racially separate schools. The Court ruled that segregation has a detrimental effect and concluded that the doctrine of "separate but equal" has no place in public education. Recognizing the importance of any order they might make and the uniqueness of each community, the Court ordered that schools must desegregate "with all deliberate speed." Local school districts were charged with the responsibility of creating desegregation plans under the supervision of the closest federal district court.

Desegregation Techniques

The design of any specific desegregation plan is determined by the extent of the segregation, geographic considerations, demographic trends, community support and, of course, the law. Desegregation plans employ a variety of techniques that may be classified as voluntary or involuntary, depending on whether students are allowed to choose the school they attend. Figure 9.1 presents a summary of the most common desegregation techniques.

In the early years of school desegregation, attention was focused on the *de jure* segregated districts in the southern states. Initially, districts attempted to accomplish desegregation by adopting freedom of choice plans. In most instances, these plans had little impact on the level of segregation, and a decade after *Brown* little progress toward integration had been made. In *Green v. County School Board of New Kent County* (1968), the Supreme Court ruled that

Figure 9.1: Desegregation Plans

Voluntary

1. *Freedom of choice* (open enrollment) allows students to attend the school of their choice.
2. *Controlled choice* allows parents to indicate a school preference, then the school system assigns students so that each school is racially balanced. Few mandatory assignments are made.
3. *Magnet plans* may involve an entire school focusing on a particular education program (dedicated magnets) or only part of the school curriculum having a special focus (minimagnets or part schools). Magnet programs at the elementary level typically offer special learning environments (e.g., basic skills or accelerated learning); magnets at the secondary level offer a specialized curriculum (e.g., vocational education, performing arts, science, or a "traditional" curriculum).
4. *Majority-to-minority transfers and one-way transfers.* Majority-to-minority transfers allow students to transfer from a school where they are in the majority to a school where they are in the minority, or in some cases to schools where they are less in the majority. One-way transfers allow minority students attending predominantly minority schools to transfer to designated receiver schools within the district or, if involved in the plan, to suburban districts.

Involuntary

1. Assigning students to schools according to *neighborhood attendance zones*. This technique was employed in dual systems to stop the practice of sending students to segregated schools outside their neighborhood.
2. *Rezoning* or changing attendance zones to improve the racial balance between two or more schools.
3. *Pairing and clustering*, which involves reassigning students of two or more schools, usually according to grade. For example, a predominantly white elementary school and a predominantly black elementary school may be paired by converting one to a lower elementary school (grades 1–3) and the other to an upper elementary school (grades 4–6). Pairing and clustering plans usually involve busing, but they also normally have a greater desegregative effect than other plan types.

Source: Harrington-Lueker, D. (1989). The courts step in where school people fail to tread. *Executive Educator, 11* (10), 27; and Welch, F., Light, A., Dong, F., & Ross, J. M. (1987). *New evidence on school desegregation.* Los Angeles, CA: Unicorn Research Corporation.

if freedom of choice plans were not working, other means *must* be used. These means could include forced busing, as established in *Swann v. Charlotte-Mecklenburg Board of Education* (1971), when the Court endorsed the use of reasonable student busing as well as pairing schools, consolidating schools, altering attendance zones, reassigning teachers, and using racial quotas. Following *Swann*, the courts exercised broad powers in ordering remedies and substantial desegregation was attained in southern school districts (McCarthy & McCabe, 1987). Table 9.1 lists some important Supreme Court desegregation cases related to public schools.

The Second Phase

The second phase of desegregation moved beyond the *de jure* segregation in the South to the *de facto* segregation that existed in many communities

Table 9.1: Selected U.S. Supreme Court Desegregation Cases Related to the Public Schools	
Case	**Decision**
Brown v. Board of Education of Topeka (1954)	The doctrine of separate but equal in education is a violation of the Fourteenth Amendment.
Green v. County School Board of New Kent County (1968)	Local school boards should immediately take whatever steps are necessary to achieve a unitary system.
Swann v. Charlotte-Mecklenburg Board of Education (1971)	Transportation of students to opposite-race schools is permissible to achieve desegregation.
Keyes v. School District No. 1 (Denver) (1973)	Proof of intent to segregate in one part of a district is sufficient to find the district to be segregated and to warrant a districtwide remedy. For purposes of defining a segregated school, blacks and Hispanics may be considered together.
Milliken v. Bradley (1974)	In devising judicial remedies for desegregation, the scope of the desegregation remedy cannot exceed the scope of the violation.
Washington v. Davis (1976)	The mere existence of segregation is not sufficient evidence to warrant judicial intervention; there must be evidence of intentional discrimination.
Dayton Board of Education v. Brinkman (1977)	Judicially mandated desegregation plans cannot exceed the impact of the segregatory practices.

outside the South. In these communities, state law did not explicitly mandate segregation, but local zoning ordinances, housing restrictions, attendance zones, gerrymandering, or other deliberate official actions were designed to segregate blacks. In 1972, 46% of all black students in the South attended schools where whites were in the majority, as compared to only 28% in the North and West (Webb & Sherman, 1989). The next year, in a case involving Denver, Colorado, *Keyes v. School District No. 1* (1973), the Supreme Court held that when official actions had a segregative intent, they were just as illegal as *de jure* segregation. In subsequent cases, the Court clarified that the mere existence of segregation was not sufficient evidence to warrant court action (*Washington v. Davis*, 1976) and that the scope of the remedy could not exceed the scope of the violation (*Milliken v. Bradley*, 1974) or the impact of the segregatory practices (*Dayton Board of Education v. Brinkman*, 1977). Any concern that the Court might be retreating from the desegregation arena was satisfied by two 1979 decisions involving Detroit, Michigan and Columbus, Ohio where the Court ruled that:

> if school officials are unable to refute that intentional school segregation existed in 1954, their post-1954 acts must be assessed in light of their *continuing affirmative duty* to eliminate the effects of such segregation. Racially neutral actions cannot satisfy this duty; school officials must take affirmative steps to eradicate school segregation until unitary status is attained. (McCarthy & McCabe, 1987, p. 490)

The Current Struggle

During the 1980s, numerous school districts continued to be involved in desegregation struggles. However, during this decade the Supreme Court declined to review most such cases and more recently has not issued any substantive ruling in the area of desegregation. Many districts have adopted *magnet school* programs to complement or replace their zoning and pairing and clustering plans (Welch, Light, Dong, & Ross, 1987), and large urban districts have become increasingly segregated as middle and upper class whites have fled to the suburbs. Increasingly, poor black students are segregated in neighborhoods and schools with other poor students. Hispanic students are even more likely to experience segregation. The result of urban segregation is that the students most in need of and most likely to benefit from an integrated educational experience are the ones least likely to have it (Webb & Sherman, 1989). One of the major fears of those who oppose parental choice plans (see discussion on page 279) is that they will lead to further ethnic and racial segregation. At this time, such choice programs as are in place are too new to determine if this fear will be realized.

What types of magnet schools have proven to be most successful in achieving integration? What made them attractive?

Effects of School Desegregation

Of the numerous possible effects of desegregation, the most attention has been focused on three: the effect on the academic achievement of minority students, the effect on self-esteem of minority students, and the effect on community integration.

Busing as a strategy to achieve school desegregation has met with mixed results.

Effect on Academic Achievement

The voluminous body of research regarding the effects of desegregation on academic achievement has yielded mixed results. However, the evidence seems to suggest some small though positive effect on student achievement. These gains have taken place during a period when the academic achievement of white students was declining. Perhaps more important, the research also indicates that desegregation is a complex situation; to try to assess its effects without recognizing the interacting variables results in oversimplification. For example, the level of integration appears to be an important variable in how much positive gain is realized. The research suggests that desegregation is most effective when minority enrollment reaches 20 to 30%. At very small

Controversial Issues:
Parental Public School Choice

One of the most popular proposals of the emerging restructuring movement is the proposal to let parents choose the public school their children will attend. President Bush and, according to the Gallup Poll, 60% of Americans favor public school choice, but a number of educational groups as well as many in the lay public oppose choice plans. The reasons stated by proponents of each side include the following:

Arguments For

1. Breaks the monopoly of the public schools and makes them more responsible to the forces of the marketplace.

2. Competition will promote efficiency and excellence in operation.

3. Encourages diversity in programs.

4. Students achieve better in schools they have chosen to attend.

5. Parents are more satisfied with and committed to the schools when they have a choice.

6. Teacher satisfaction and morale is higher in schools of choice.

Arguments Against

1. Will lead to ethnic, racial and socioeconomic segregation.

2. Conditions will worsen in poorest districts as students leave and take their per-pupil state aid with them.

3. Transportation costs will be dramatically increased.

4. Potential for fluctuations in enrollments make planning for staffing and budgeting difficult.

5. Most parents would not be able to make an informed choice among the alternative schools.

What, if any, support for parental choice is there in your state? How has it been evidenced? What is your position on parental public school choice?

---

numbers, minority children are likely to feel isolated or stereotyped. At large percentages of minority student enrollments, majority withdrawals increase, resulting in resegregation (Yinger, 1986).

Other factors that affect achievement results are the age of the student when entering the desegregated school, preschool preparation, teacher and staff preparedness for the desegregated situation, and the extent of tracking in the classroom (Yinger, 1986). There is substantial evidence that tracking results in increased segregation in the classroom and that segregated classrooms have a negative effect on achievement.

Effects on Self-Esteem of Minority Students

The research on the effects of integration on the self-esteem of minority students also has yielded mixed results. A number of studies have shown that minority children's self-esteem is lowered by desegregation. In desegregated schools, they are more likely to experience prejudice than in segregated schools. They are also more likely to perform less well academically than their white peers in the integrated school and to recognize their lower socioeconomic status—all potentially damaging to their self-esteem (Rosenberg, 1986). The majority of the studies, however, show that while in the short term there is no effect or a slight lowering of self-esteem, the longer the minority student remains in the integrated school, the higher his or her self-esteem becomes (Webb & Sherman, 1989). However, it is not clear whether the higher self-esteem noted in the longitudinal studies can be attributed to the effects of desegregation or to changed self-attitudes generated by the black pride movement.

Effect on Assimilation

Were you involved in any school desegregation programs? What were the advantages? Disadvantages?

A major goal of education in this country has always been the assimilation of minorities. Supporters of desegregation argue that it is a major strategy in the attainment of this goal. In fact, according to Jencks, the case for school desegregation should not be argued in terms of academic achievement but of a desegregated society (Jencks et al., 1972). The evidence does support the contention that school desegregation contributes to community desegregation. This is especially true in relatively small districts and in districts where minority enrollment is not more than one-third (Yinger, 1986).

White flight.   School desegregation has resulted in resegregation in some urban areas because of the *white flight* of middle and upper class whites to the suburbs. White enrollment losses usually are greatest in the year of plan implementation, tapering off in the years following. Plans that involve busing are associated with larger losses in white enrollment than other plans. Those using voluntary techniques experience the smallest losses (Welch et al., 1987).

Integration in the community, higher education, and the workplace.

Despite the white flight phenomenon, a growing body of research documents the fact that education in integrated public schools promotes integration in the community, in higher education, and in the workplace. Among the research findings are the following:

1. Black students from majority white public schools are more likely to enroll and succeed in majority white colleges.

2. Blacks and whites from integrated public schools are more likely to work in desegregated firms than students from segregated schools.

3. Blacks from predominantly white colleges are more likely to work in integrated firms than those from predominantly black colleges.

4. Blacks from integrated public schools are more likely to have white social contacts and live in integrated neighborhoods than those from segregated schools.

5. Communities with communitywide school desegregation have more integrated housing and less "racial steering" by real estate agents.

6. Large cities with integrated schools have more integration than cities with segregated schools. (Braddock, Crain, & McPartland, 1984)

Although the desegregation efforts of the last quarter century have not brought about the changes in the schools or in the communities they serve that many envisioned, there is no question that desegregated schools are a condition of a desegregated society. In the past, the courts have been a major instrument for achieving desegregation. Their retreat from the foreground places responsibility on our political leaders. Unless a commitment to the desegregation of our schools is made by the political leadership of the nation, the states, and local communities, equality of educational opportunity for children of every race will remain a dream.

Education of Children with Disabilities

Special education for children with mental and physical disabilities is a relatively recent provision of most state and local school systems. In fact, prior to the 1970s most state laws allowed the expulsion or absolute exclusion from school of children who were deemed uneducable, untrainable, or otherwise unable to benefit from the regular education program. It was not until two important federal court decisions in the early 1970s (*Pennsylvania Association of Retarded Citizens v. Commonwealth of Pennsylvania*, 1972 and *Mills v. Board of Education*, 1972) that the right of children with disabilities to an education was recognized by most states and school districts.

Individuals with Disabilities Education Act

These decisions, combined with intense lobbying by special education professionals, interest groups, and parents of handicapped children, led Congress in 1975 to pass the Education of the Handicapped Act (Public Law 94–142). In 1990, the legislation reauthorizing the bill also renamed it, calling it the Individuals with Disabilities Education Act. The act, often referred to as the Bill of Rights for Handicapped Children, has served not only to guarantee the rights of children with disabilities but to define and expand the rights of all children.

P. L. 94–142 introduced a number of principles that have had a great impact on American education. These principles, which have been expanded through subsequent litigation and legislation, are summarized below.

Right to an Education

Perhaps the most fundamental and important principle of P. L. 94–142 is that "*all* handicapped children have available to them . . . a free appropriate education and related services designed to meet their unique needs." This provision of the law means that *no* children, regardless of the nature or severity of their disability, can be denied a public education. P. L. 94–142 applied to children with disabilities aged 5 to 18, but in 1986 it was amended (P. L. 99–457) to extend the right to an education to disabled children aged 3 through 5. In addition, P. L. 99–457 offers financial and technical assistance to school districts in developing preschool programs for disabled children from birth to age 3.

For Future Reference:
Mainstreaming Strategies for Students with Behavioral Problems

Most teachers at some time or another will have students with mild behavioral problems mainstreamed into their classes. Some proven classroom strategies you might consider using with these children are presented below:

1. No matter what kind of activity you are engaged in, visually scan the room every two or three minutes. This is an effective strategy for controlling student behavior.

2. Explain expected behaviors and the consequences of undesirable behaviors.

3. Explain classroom rules in positive rather than negative terms (e.g., "we walk" as opposed to "we don't run").

4. Be consistent in enforcing your classroom management plan—students need to know you mean what you say.

5. Make the punishment fit the infraction. A minor infraction should not be followed by a major punishment.

6. Call attention to the type of behavior you want in the classroom, thereby establishing models of appropriate behavior, rather than calling attention to inappropriate behavior.

7. When not working directly with students, walk about the classroom. This allows you to move close to students who need to control their behavior and to assist those who need help with their lessons.

8. When giving directions, first alert students to the fact that you are going to say something they should carefully attend to, then give clear and simple directions, making sure to use only words the children can understand.

Source: Adapted from Hart, V. (1981). *Mainstreaming children with special needs.* New York: Longman.

Nondiscriminatory Education

This provision requires that each child must receive a comprehensive evaluation before being placed in any special education program. Placement cannot be made on the basis of a single test, but on multiple instruments and procedures. Additionally, whatever evaluation mechanisms are used must be nondiscriminatory in terms of culture, race, and language and must be designed for assessment with specific handicaps (e.g., tests for non-English speakers or tests for the visually impaired).

Individualized Educational Program

The concept of the IEP has met with success for special education needs. How might the IEP be used with all students?

P. L. 94–142 and P. L. 99–457 require that an *individualized education program (IEP)* be prepared for each child who is to receive special education services. The IEP is "the backbone of the special education process . . . the formal mechanism by which the goal of an appropriate education is to be realized" (Shore, 1986, p. 6). Designed to meet the unique needs of the child for whom it is developed, the IEP is prepared by a team of educators, parents, and, if appropriate, the student. The IEP includes a description of present performance, a statement of annual goals, including short-term objectives, a statement of services to be provided and their duration, and evaluation criteria and procedures to determine if the objectives are being achieved. IEPs are reviewed annually and provide the means for ensuring parent involvement in the educational decisions affecting their children, the means for accountability for the delivery of services, and a record of progress.

Least Restrictive Environment

The regulations implementing P. L. 94–142 mandate that children with disabilities are to be educated in the *least restrictive environment* possible. This requirement has encouraged the practice of *mainstreaming* children with disabilities, to the maximum extent possible and feasible, into the regular classroom where they have contact with nondisabled children. It is possible that you will have special education students mainstreamed in your classes when you begin teaching. The list on page 282 offers some things you might do to help such students in your classes.

One reason for the decline in institutional placements in the last decade was the desire to move disabled students to less restrictive environments and to cease the unnecessary isolation of these children. In keeping with the least restrictive environment principle, a disabled child cannot be moved from the regular classroom without a due process hearing, and schools have been required to provide supplemental services in the regular classroom before moving the disabled child to a more restrictive environment.

The least restrictive environment principle does not require mainstreaming; in fact, P. L. 94–142 does not mention mainstreaming. What the principle does call for is the careful consideration of all possible placement alternatives for each disabled child before a final placement is made (Peterson, 1988). In the end it may be necessary to place the child in a segregated setting in order to provide him or her with the most appropriate education or in order to prevent the disruption of the educational process for other students. See Figure 9.2 for the continuum of special education placements.

How would you respond to having a student with a severe physical disability mainstreamed into your classroom?

Due Process

The extensive procedural requirements of P. L. 94–142 are designed to ensure the rights of children with disabilities to receive a free appropriate education and to protect them from improper evaluation, classification, and placement. As shown in Figure 9.3, parents have the right to obtain an individual evaluation of their child in addition to that conducted by the school district and to be involved in every stage of the evaluation, placement, and educational process. Parents must be informed of the IEP conference and encouraged to attend. In addition, the school district must inform parents in writing or in a format understandable by them before it initiates, changes, or refuses to initiate or change the identification, evaluation, or educational placement of the child. Parents also have the right to a due process hearing to challenge the district's decision on any of these matters and to examine all records pertaining to their children.

Figure 9.2: Continuum of Special Education Placements

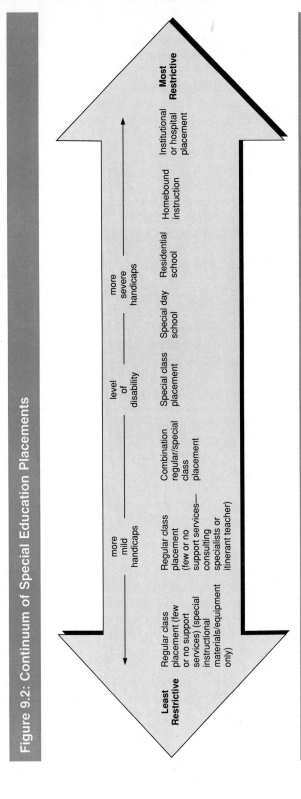

Source: Peterson, N. L. (1988). *Early intervention for handicapped and at-risk children* (p. 337). Denver, CO: Love Publishing Company. Reprinted with permission.

Figure 9.3: The Special Education Process

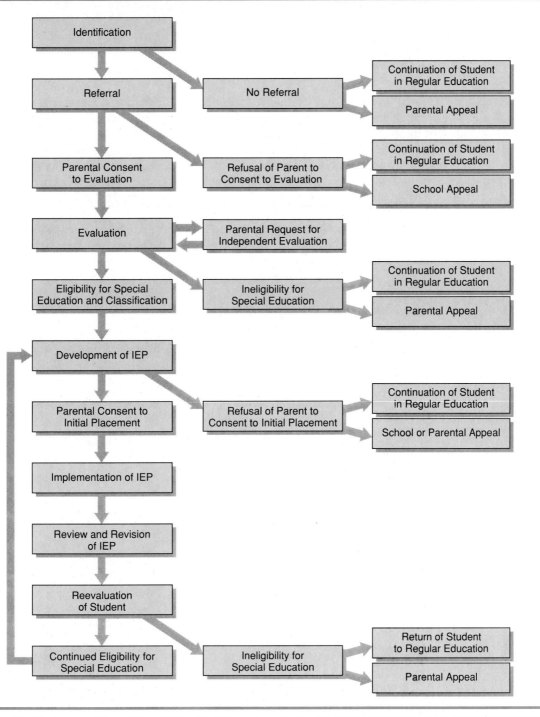

Source: Reprinted by permission of the publisher from Shore, Kenneth, *The Special Education Handbook*. (New York: Teachers' College Press, © 1986 by Teachers College, Columbia University. All rights reserved.), pages 16 and 17.

Current Enrollments and Issues of Minority Placements

Since P. L. 94–142 was implemented in 1978, the number of children enrolled in federally supported education programs has risen steadily (see Table 9.2). This is due primarily to the growth in the numbers of students classified as having a *learning disability*, that is, having a disorder or delayed development in one or more of the processes of thinking, speaking, reading, writing, listening, or doing arithmetic operations. Currently, almost one-half of all students served in special education are classified as learning disabled. This figure would not be of particular concern were it not for the fact that there appears to be a disproportionate representation of minority students in classes for the learning disabled, as well as in those for the mentally retarded. During the 1970s the courts expressed concern about the misdiagnosis and inappropriate placement of Hispanics and other minority groups (e.g., *Diana v. California State Board of Education*, 1970 and *Larry P. v. Wilson Riles*, 1979). Concerns continue, and the unresolved issues of accurate assessment labeling and disproportionate representation "have only begun to be researched in the last few years" (Ochoa, Pacheco, & Omark, 1988, p. 257).

The "Appropriate" Services Debate

Over the years perhaps the most controversial and still unresolved issue in the implementation of P. L. 94–142 has been in regard to what is meant by a

Table 9.2: Number of Elementary and Secondary Students Served in Federally Supported Education Programs for the Disabled and Number as a Percentage of Total Enrollment, by Type of Disability, School Year Ending 1978, 1983, 1988 (number served in thousands)

Type of Disability	1978 Number Served	1978 Percent of Total	1983 Number Served	1983 Percent of Total	1988 Number Served	1988 Percent of Total
Learning disabled	964	2.21	1,741	4.39	1,928	4.82
Speech impaired	1,223	2.81	1,131	2.85	953	2.38
Mentally retarded	933	2.14	757	1.91	582	1.45
Seriously emotionally disturbed	288	.66	352	.89	373	.93
Hard of hearing and deaf	85	.20	73	.18	56	.14
Orthopedically disabled	87	.20	57	.14	47	.12
Other health disabled	135	.31	50	.13	45	.11
Visually impaired	35	.08	28	.07	22	.06
Multiple disabled	-	-	63	.16	77	.19
Deaf-blind	-	-	2	.01	1	<.005
Preschool	-	-	-	-	363	.91
Total	3,751	8.61	4,255	10.73	4,446	11.10

Source: U.S. Department of Education, National Center for Education Statistics. (1989). *The condition of education*, Vol. 1 (Table 1:23-1). Washington, DC: U.S. Government Printing Office.

"free appropriate public education." Because the act does not specify what programs and services must be provided to satisfy this guarantee, the provision of services has often been debated on a case-by-case basis. In *Board of Education v. Rowley* (1982) the Supreme Court stated that a free appropriate public education did not mean "an opportunity to achieve full potential commensurate with the opportunity provided to other children," but rather, "*access* to specialized instruction and related services which are designed to provide educational benefit to the handicapped child." This ruling left many educators and supporters of children with disabilities with the fear that the court had sacrificed the very heart of P. L. 94–142. Almost any program, no matter how ill conceived, might have *some* benefit. However, this fear has not been realized. In the approximately 100 cases handed down by lower courts since *Rowley*, the courts have continued to support parents in their attempts to expand services to their disabled children, including year-round services, health services, and private residential placements (Gallegos, 1989). Nonetheless, cases are still determined on an individual basis and the courts do tend to accept the most *reasonable* program rather than require the *best* possible program.

P. L. 94–142 was supplemented in 1986 by P. L. 99–372, the Handicapped Children's Protection Act, which allows the court to award attorneys' fees to parents who are successful in their challenge of district action(s). Challenges based on the Education of the Handicapped Act, Section 504, and related state statutes constitute the most active area of school law today.

Compensatory Education

Compensatory education programs designed to overcome the deficiencies associated with educational and socioeconomic disadvantages have been an important part of federal educational policy and funding since the Elementary and Secondary Education Act was passed in 1965. Title I of that act, which directed one billion dollars the first year to supplement state and local funds for the education of disadvantaged children, was the flagship of President Lyndon Johnson's Great Society education program (Elmore & McLaughlin, 1988). As a weapon in the War on Poverty, the intent of Title I was to "enhance the education of disadvantaged children, improve their achievement, and hence redistribute economic and social opportunities in society" (Durbin, 1989, p. 27). Federal funds were allocated to states to be reallocated to local school districts based on the number of low-income families, which was viewed as an indicator of student educational need. At the local level, services were provided to eligible students in schools with high concentrations of disadvantaged students. Both disadvantaged public and nonpublic schools could receive services.

Chapter 1

In 1981 Title I was converted into Chapter 1 of the Education Consolidation and Improvement Act. Chapter 1 retained essentially the same features as Title I, the major change being a reduction in federal regulations, placing greater responsibility for monitoring local programs on the states. In 1989, over four billion dollars, almost one-fifth of the Department of Education's total budget, was appropriated to support Chapter 1 programs. These programs operate in 90% of the nation's 16,000 school districts and include 70% of the nation's elementary schools (Savage, 1987). In addition, 28 states also provide state funds to support compensatory education programs (Salmon, Dawson, Lawton, & Johns, 1988).

Types of Programs

Compensatory education programs encompass a variety of educational services delivered primarily in program-eligible schools during school hours. The most common types of programs are:

1. Early childhood readiness programs such as Head Start, which takes children between the ages of three and five and gets them ready for school.

2. Enrichment programs in subject areas. Almost all (94%) Chapter 1 districts offer programs in reading, 64% offer math, and 25% offer programs in other language arts.

3. Programs for handicapped students. Almost three-fourths of the districts provide Chapter 1 services to mentally handicapped students. In most districts, these students must be eligible for Chapter 1 to receive services.

4. English as a second language (ESL). ESL instruction is offered to students with limited English proficiency in 8% of the districts. Again, normally the students must be eligible for Chapter 1 to receive services.

5. Programs for migrant students. Most commonly found in larger districts, these programs are offered by 14% of Chapter 1 districts. (Williams, Thorne, Michie, & Hamar, 1987)

What are the disadvantages of pulling students out of the regular class to receive compensatory instruction?

Most Chapter 1 instruction is provided through the "pullout" method, in which eligible students are removed from the regular classroom to receive additional instruction. Instruction is delivered in smaller classes by separately hired "Chapter 1 teachers," often with the assistance of aides and often with more equipment and materials than are available in the regular classroom. Even though there is some criticism of pullout models, they are popular with school districts because they are the safest way of meeting the requirement that Chapter 1 funds be spent only on students eligible for Chapter 1.

Program Effectiveness

The effectiveness of compensatory education has been the subject of some controversy, especially in the early years. Studies from the late 1960s did not show Title I to be very effective in achieving lasting or long-term improvement in student achievement. More recent longitudinal studies indicate that compensatory education programs do have a positive effect on achievement, which is mostly observable in the early grades and is strongest in mathematics

(Ralph, 1989). These studies also show compensatory education programs to be a factor in reducing special education placements and dropout rates (Schweinhart & Weikart, 1985). However, one troubling finding is that Chapter 1 programs are most effective with marginal students, who often make rapid improvements and are then transferred out of the program, rather than with the weakest students, who remain in the program year after year (Ralph, 1989). Another troubling result is that the positive gains observed in the early grades often are not sustained, but disappear by the middle grades, when most Chapter 1 services end.

Meeting the Needs

To address these and other perceived shortcomings of current compensatory education policies, the suggestion has been made that Chapter 1 services be extended into the high school and be expanded to include all eligible students. Fewer than 20% of districts operating Chapter 1 programs serve prekindergarten or grades 10, 11, and 12 (Williams et al., 1987). Head Start, one of the programs that appears to have the most positive results, currently serves only about one in five of all eligible 3- to 5-year-olds. Overall, Chapter 1 serves only about half of those eligible to receive remedial help (William T. Grant Foundation, 1988). Although it would require at least a doubling of current Chapter 1 funding to extend and expand the program, thoughtful policy makers and educators realize that this is what is required if President Johnson's dream of breaking the cycle of poverty is to be realized.

What types of compensatory education programs should be operated at the secondary level?

At this time, increased federal funding for at least one of the major compensatory education programs does seem likely. The 1990 reauthorization of Head Start proposed to triple funding from 1991 to 1994 from $2.4 billion to $7.7 billion, presumed to be enough to serve all eligible children. If these funds are not subsequently appropriated, it may well be that the amount of state resources spent on disadvantaged students will be the ultimate measure of the success of compensatory education.

Multicultural and Bilingual Education

Multicultural education is a relatively new phenomenon in the United States, in spite of the fact that we have always been a pluralistic nation. Many believe that our cultural and ethnic diversity is what makes our nation and society strong. This view has helped to foster the current support for multicultural and bilingual education, an interest that has prevailed for the past two decades.

Growth of Minority Populations

Some racial and ethnic groups in the U.S. are growing at a faster rate than other groups. For example, during the 1980s, Asians and Pacific Islanders had growth rates much higher than those for blacks and whites. Nonetheless, the black population grew at a faster rate between 1980 and 1987 than the total population, increasing by 11.4%, compared to a 5.7% growth for whites and a 7.4% growth for the total population. The Hispanic population, which numbered about 19.1 million or 7.9% of the population in 1987, increased 31% since the 1980 census. Higher than average fertility rates, a low death rate due to a youthful age group, and high levels of immigration (legal and illegal) all have contributed to the rapid growth of the Hispanic population (U.S. Bureau of the Census, 1989).

Multicultural Education

Students who represent these varied backgrounds often find their school culture to be alien to their home environment. In recent years, research has suggested that when students' acculturation prepares them for a social context that differs from the social context of the school, alienation may result.

Multicultural education is a strategy for addressing this alienation by providing educational opportunities for those students whose cultural and linguistic backgrounds may prevent them from succeeding in the traditional school setting that historically reflects the dominant Anglo-Saxon culture. Specifically, multicultural education includes a number of educational efforts that (1) promote positive multiethnic and multiracial relationships among students, faculty, and staff; (2) provide for differences in cognitive learning styles; and (3) recognize the similarities and differences among all cultures.

Historical Framework

As discussed in Chapter 8, historically society has considered one of the roles of the American schools to be the assimilation of racial and ethnic groups. The emphasis on assimilation dates from the colonial period and was particularly favored during the period from 1880 to 1945 when countless numbers of immigrants came to America from eastern and southern European nations. During this period, "military-style" assimilation was advocated, meaning the rapid assimilation of immigrant children, by force if necessary. Military-style assimilation encouraged English-only classrooms, the Anglicization of immigrants' names and of the school community, and no use of the native language, even outside the school environment. Since the Anglocentric curriculum was considered as standard, any other culture was viewed as substandard (Stein, 1986).

From 1945 to 1968, assimilation continued; however, it was "missionary-style." This type of assimilation reflected the cultural deprivation theory, an environmentalist theory that blamed poor school achievement on deficiencies in the minority culture rather than on inheritance of low intelligence. It also reflected the "melting pot" idea that contended that not to assimilate would be to preordain the immigrants to poverty and exclude them from the mainstream. The solution adopted by many school districts during this period was to attempt to replace parental and community values with the values of the Anglo middle class (Stein, 1986).

Programs were also initiated to overcome the so-called "language disability." *English as a second language (ESL)* programs flourished. ESL had been

Did you or any of your ancestors come to America as immigrants? What was your or their assimilation experience?

designed in the 1930s, primarily for instruction of foreign diplomats, business people, and government officials, but by 1950 ESL programs were introduced in many southwestern and eastern school districts to instruct poor Hispanic children. The ESL programs provided instruction in English-only classes. Students from a variety of language backgrounds participated in the same ESL class for the purpose of English language acquisition. The most common ESL program was a pullout program, which removed students from their regular classes daily or several times a week. These ESL programs were not particularly successful with Hispanic children and did not equip them with sufficient English to succeed in their content classes. The pullout method also exacerbated the problem by requiring the children to miss some of their content instruction, thereby causing them to fall behind and having to repeat a grade or grades (Stein, 1986).

Many believe that the cultural deprivation theory led to lowered expectations and a self-fulfilling prophecy of failure, particularly for Hispanics. Unfortunately, the concept of cultural deprivation became the operative theory behind the War on Poverty during the 1960s and eventually provided the theoretical basis for the use of bilingual education as a compensatory or remedial program (Stein, 1986).

Cultural Pluralism

In spite of the rhetoric concerning the importance of uniformity, patriotism, and the Anglo-Saxon tradition, by the 1960s it was quite clear that the assimilation approach had many shortcomings. Blacks, Hispanics, Native Americans, and other racial and ethnic groups continued to experience discrimination, and attempts to increase upward mobility of children from poor families were generally unsuccessful. Thus, during the 1960s, concurrent with the civil rights movement, the concept of cultural pluralism replaced the assimilation concept. As noted previously, cultural pluralism emphasizes the unique strength in diversity and recognizes the positive contributions of numerous cultures.

One way that school districts have endorsed cultural pluralism is by recognizing differences in learning or cognitive styles that stem from differences in socialization and then accommodating these different styles by using different instructional approaches. For example, in terms of learning styles, some students respond better to learning environments that encourage cooperative learning activities; others may be more comfortable with an independent learning approach; and others may be more successful in an environment that stresses competitive learning.

Differences in *cognitive styles* may be found between those who are characterized as field-independent analytic thinkers and those who are characterized as field-dependent descriptive thinkers. An individual with a field-independent style will tend to organize his or her environment and approach tasks objectively using an analytic style, while an individual with a field-dependent style will be characterized by using a more descriptive approach and will more likely attend to global features and be more self-centered in his or her orientation to reality. Research has shown that differences in learning

How would you describe your learning and cognitive styles?

Teachers need to recognize the variety of learning styles related to ethnic and social differences.

and cognitive styles are related to ethnic and racial differences. For example, there is some evidence that individuals who are reported to be global, field-dependent, relational, and concrete in their cognitive styles are found primarily in certain subcultures including women, Mexican-Americans, and blacks. The teacher's task is to observe differences and offer a variety of alternatives for classroom learning (Casanova, 1987).

Bilingual Education

Bilingual education is instruction of core or required subjects such as mathematics, science, and language arts in the student's native language while he or she learns or masters English (Ovando & Collier, 1985). Bilingual education includes a broad range of programs and provides instruction for limited-English-proficient as well as non-English-proficient students. The current debate over the provision of bilingual education is highly controversial.

Lau v. Nichols

Federal support for bilingual education programs began in 1968 through an amendment to the Elementary and Secondary Education Act of 1965 entitled the Title VII Bilingual Education Program, also referred to as the Bilingual Education Act (BEA). However, while the BEA prompted school districts to design and implement programs for language minority students, it was the Supreme Court decision in *Lau v. Nichols* (1974) that provided the major impetus for federal involvement in the education of children with English language deficiencies. In the *Lau* case, the court relied on Title VI of the Civil Rights Act of 1964 and concluded that school districts are obligated to provide assistance for all children with English language deficiencies. The Supreme Court ruled that:

> there is no equality of treatment merely by providing students with the same facilities, textbooks, teachers, and curriculum; for students who do not understand English are effectively foreclosed from any meaningful education. Basic English skills are at the very core of what these public schools teach. Imposition of a requirement that, before a child can effectively participate in the educational program, he must already have acquired those basic skills is to make a mockery of public education. We know that those who do not understand English are certain to find their classroom experiences wholly incomprehensible and in no way meaningful. (p. 566)

Although the court mandated that the schools provide assistance for children with English language deficiencies, it did not require a specific type of instructional model for language minority education. That is, the court did not specify whether Title VII requires bilingual education, English as a second language, or any nonbilingual education approach. As a result, each state and territory has defined its own approach to the education of language minority students. State legislative provisions may also mandate the criteria for program eligibility and for the type of program to be offered. However, in most states school districts are allowed a great deal of latitude in determining the manner in which they incorporate the native language of the student.

Bilingual Program Options

There is considerable controversy surrounding the most effective language minority program. August and Garcia (1988) describe some of the possible program options:

- *Submersion.* Students with limited English proficiency are placed in regular classrooms where English is the primary mode of instruction.

- *English as a second language.* A combination of English instruction and submersion.

- *Immersion or sheltered English.* English is used in instruction and the native or home language is used in a limited way to enhance classroom communication.

- *Transitional bilingual education.* The student's native language is used as a transition or bridge to the total use of English.

- *Bilingual maintenance.* Students representing two groups are given instruction in both languages. For students whose native language is not English, special attention is focused on the acquisition of English while developing the native language. For students whose native language is English, emphasis is on developing the second language.

1988 Bilingual Education Act Amendments

In 1988, the Bilingual Education Act was amended to specify that a percentage of the funds be distributed for certain types of educational programs, such as transitional bilingual education programs, special alternative instruction programs, developmental bilingual education programs, programs of academic excellence, family English literacy programs, and programs for special populations. This bill authorized $200 million for fiscal year 1989 and such sums as necessary for each remaining year through fiscal year 1993 (August & Garcia, 1988).

The English Only Movement

What position has your state government taken in regard to the English Only movement?

At the same time that both the federal and many state governments have acknowledged the need for education services for limited-English-proficient students, almost all states have considered "English Only" amendments, which declare English to be the official language of the state and the only language to be used in conducting public affairs. Sixteen states have passed such legislation to date: Arizona, Arkansas, California, Colorado, Florida, Georgia, Illinois, Indiana, Kentucky, Mississippi, Nebraska, North Carolina, North Dakota, South Carolina, Tennessee, and Virginia. One of the major controversies surrounding the English Only movement is that the restricted language legislation appears to be targeted at the Hispanic and Asian communities and the legislation is contradictory to the goals of bilingual education (Arias, 1989). However, a significant segment of society remains highly critical of the idea of allocating scarce resources to teaching immigrant students in a language other than English.

Indian Education

Indian education is the term used by most states and the federal government to refer to educational programs specifically directed at Native American children and adults. The education of Native Americans has a unique history in this country because the federal government was obligated by various treaties to provide for the education of Native American children. The course of this federal involvement, which was detailed in earlier chapters, was largely one of dictating educational policy and practice. It was not until the self-determination movement gained strength in the late 1960s that a serious commitment was made in federal policy to increase the involvement of Native Americans in the management of their own affairs, including education.

The Self-Determination Movement

The commitment to increase participation was actualized in the Indian Education Act of 1972 and its successor, the Indian Self-Determination and Education Assistance Act of 1975, and the Indian Education Amendments of 1988, all of which mandate increased participation and decision making by Native Americans. The results have been significant. A number of tribes have opted to operate schools under contract with the federal government, rather than leave their operation to the Bureau of Indian Affairs (BIA). Funding is provided by the BIA, but the schools have elected Indian school boards. More Native American parents than ever before are involved actively in the education of their children, serve on school boards or special committees, or are otherwise involved in providing direction to the schools serving Native American children.

The Problem of Parental Noninvolvement

However, even with this progress, the noninvolvement of parents is of concern to Native American educators. Yet they also recognize that these parents are not prepared for involvement because of the long history of Native American parents not being welcomed or invited to be involved in the education of their children. That is, many Native American parents don't know how to be involved, don't know what kind of involvement is expected, or what kind of involvement would be most helpful. What is needed, say noted Native American educators, is a large-scale educational process "to inform parents of the importance of involvement, provide them with basic program information, and develop their skills to impact schools" (Tippeconnic & Gipp, 1982, p. 127).

Enrollments

More than 85% of Native American school children (about 350,000) attend public schools (see Figure 9.4). Of those enrolled in the public schools, one-half attend public schools located on or near reservations and most of the other half are enrolled in urban and inner city schools. There, they are likely to encounter "the same kinds of pressures and problems faced by black and Hispanic students—with the additional burden of a sometimes fierce battle of cultures" (Reeves, 1989, p. 4).

Federal Support

Public schools enrolling Native American students receive federal assistance under several programs (see Figure 9.4). Public school districts that include federal, nontaxable Indian reservations receive federal impact aid as a substitute for lost tax revenues. Funds are also provided under Title IV of the 1972 Education Amendments for culturally relevant programs (including curriculum projects) for Native American students. In addition, Native American students in both BIA-supported and public schools receive special services if they are disadvantaged, have limited English proficiency, have a handicapping condition, or are enrolled in vocational education.

Curriculum Issues

The question of the most appropriate and effective curriculum for Native American students remains controversial. The Native American community itself is divided on the kind of education it wants for its youth, and support can be found for a number of positions, including the extremes of assimilation and

Figure 9.4: Overview of Indian Education

Federal Indian Program	FY 1986 Appropriation	Purpose
Impact Aid (Education Department)	$221.2 million	Alleviate local tax burden for public-school districts that include nontaxable reservation lands
Title IV (Education Department)	$62 million	Supplemental instruction for Indian students in public schools
Johnson-O'Malley (Bureau of Indian Affairs)	$22.1 million	Supplemental programs in public schools, including participation costs for Indian students and parents
B.I.A. Schools (Bureau of Indian Affairs)	$259.1 million	Operation, maintenance, and construction of B.I.A. schools
Miscellaneous	$55 million	Bilingual education, special education, and vocational education in public and B.I.A. schools

Ten Reservations with the Largest Number of American Indians: 1980

Number	Reservation
104,517	Navajo, Ariz., N.M., Utah
11,868	Pine Ridge, S.D.
6,906	Gila River, Ariz.
6,870	Fort Apache, Ariz.
6,772	Tohono O'Odham, Ariz.
6,592	Hopi, Ariz.
5,973	Zuni Pueblo, N.M.
5,795	San Carlos, Ariz.
5,643	Rosebud, S.D.
5,529	Blackfeet, Mont.

Indian Student Enrollments

	Number	Percent
In B.I.A. Schools:		
Operated by the B.I.A.	26,000	6.4
Operated by Indian communities	12,000	2.9
In Public Schools:		
On reservations	70,000	17.2
Near reservations*	105,000	25.7
Distant from reservations	175,000	42.9
In Private and Parochial Schools	20,000	4.9
Total Indian Students Nationwide	408,000	100.0

* Both students living on and those living off reservations.

Source: McDonald, D. (1989, August 2). From "no power" to local power? *Education Week,* 11. Compiled from data from U.S. Bureau of Indian Affairs, U.S. Education Department, U.S. Census Bureau, and ERIC/CRESS, a clearinghouse for rural-education statistics. Reprinted with permission.

separatism (Levine & Havighurst, 1989). And in spite of the emphasis on self-determination, the BIA-supported schools tend to have an externally defined curriculum that doesn't differ that much from that found in the schools of, for example, Los Angeles. The emphasis is on the replacement of native languages and values with those of the larger society. The result is often a failure to prepare Native American children for full participation in their bicultural environment and the creation of value conflicts that leave the children feeling alienated from both tribal and mainstream life (McCarthy, Wallace, & Lynch, 1989). In schools where attention has been given to cultural maintenance, there are often major differences of opinion as to what is culturally relevant instruction. Even when there is agreement, finding adequate instructional materials is a problem (McDonald, 1989).

Adding to the problems of the curriculum is the fact that very few children are taught by Native American teachers or by teachers able to provide native language instruction or who have an understanding of Native American language and culture. It also represents a shortage of positive adult Native American role models.

Current Issues

Although many improvements in Indian education have taken place in the almost two decades since the passage of the Indian Education Act in 1972 and the creation of the Office of Indian Education, the "vital signs" do not appear to have changed significantly. Dropout rates are still alarmingly high. Achievement differentials between Native American children and majority children have not shown any appreciable change, and proportionate to population increases, college continuation and completion rates are virtually unchanged (Red Horse, 1986).

The educational reform movement has also sparked concern among Native American leaders that the movement's emphasis on basics, increased high school graduation requirements, and stiffer college admission standards may have serious repercussions for Native American students. What is needed, say some Indian education experts, are dramatic shifts in education designed to align Indian education with effective schooling methodologies and to provide bilingual models that recognize the "unalterable circumstances" of language and culture that affect the school performance of Native American children. Unless this occurs, "Indian students may move from the category of an at-risk population to an endangered species" (Red Horse, 1986, p. 42).

Promotion of Sex Equity

In education, the term *sex equity* refers to "the concepts of equal treatment and equal opportunity for all students, regardless of their sex" (Carelli, 1988, p. xiii). In the 1970s, national attention was focused on sex equity in education, which it was hoped would be achieved with the passage of Title IX in

1972 (and its implementing regulations in 1975) prohibiting sex discrimination in access to courses, extracurricular programs, instructional materials, counseling and counseling materials, employment, and any other policies and regulations governing the treatment of students and employees. And, indeed, Title IX did result in some significant changes.

Title IX's Unfilled Promise

Yet almost two decades after the passage of Title IX, sex equity in education is far from being achieved. According to one women's rights group, there is blatant sex segregation in vocational education; dropout prevention programs often focus their attention on boys although significant numbers of girls also drop out of school; and women are denied scholarships because of low SAT scores, a test that "underpredicts the grades women can expect to earn in college" (Sex Discrimination, 1987). Nationwide, women occupy only 5% of the superintendencies, 10% of the high school principalships, and 32% of the elementary school principalships (Leadership, 1989/1990).

Sex Equity and the Reform Movement

Moreover, the reform movement has all but ignored issues of gender. One analysis of the first wave of reform reports and books found that Title IX was not mentioned even when other nondiscriminatory legislation was discussed. In fact, the word gender was missing even when other attributes such as race, ethnicity, or social class were discussed (Tetreault & Schmuck, 1985). A later review of articles dealing with reform also found that "in the professional dialogue about educational reform, gender equity received the silent treatment" (Sadker, Sadker, & Steindam, 1989, p. 45). Furthermore, a national survey of teachers and administrators revealed that practitioners do not believe the reform movement has done much to promote educational opportunities for females (and minorities) (Sadker et al., 1989).

The Process for Attaining Sex Equity

Have you experienced sex bias in your education? Sex discrimination?

If sex equity is to become a reality in our schools, not rhetoric, more must be done than ensuring that boys and girls are taught in the same classroom or have the same right to enroll in courses or participate in extracurricular activities (Fennema, 1987). The attainment of sex equity requires the elimination of three forms of limitations by sex: sex role stereotyping, sex bias, and sex discrimination. *Sex role stereotyping* is the attribution of specific behaviors, abilities, personality characteristics, and interests to one sex. *Sex bias* is the biased behavior that results from believing in the sex role stereotypes. *Sex discrimination* is any action that denies opportunities, privileges, or rewards to a person or persons because of their sex, in violation of the law (Carelli, 1988). Figure 9.5 provides two examples of the interrelationships of sex role stereotyping, sex bias, and sex discrimination.

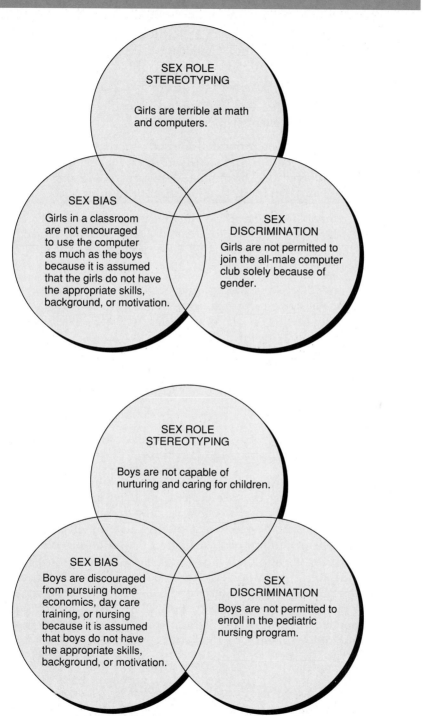

SEX ROLE
STEREOTYPING

Girls are terrible at math
and computers.

SEX BIAS

Girls in a classroom
are not encouraged
to use the computer
as much as the boys
because it is assumed
that the girls do not have
the appropriate skills,
background, or motivation.

SEX
DISCRIMINATION

Girls are not permitted to
join the all-male computer
club solely because of
gender.

SEX ROLE
STEREOTYPING

Boys are not capable of
nurturing and caring for children.

SEX BIAS

Boys are discouraged
from pursuing home
economics, day care
training, or nursing
because it is assumed
that boys do not have
the appropriate skills,
background, or motivation.

SEX
DISCRIMINATION

Boys are not permitted to
enroll in the pediatric
nursing program.

Source: From A. O. Carelli (Ed.), *Sex Equity in Education: Readings and Strategies* (pp. xvi–xvii), 1988. Courtesy of Charles C Thomas, Publisher, Springfield, Illinois.

The promotion of sex equity in education is a process that involves the following broad steps:

1. Educators must understand the need for all students to have the opportunity to become self-fulfilled and their right to experience the full range of educational opportunities.

2. Educators must realize that maintaining an equitable school climate is an integral part of excellent schooling.

3. Sex equity must be incorporated into all aspects of the school program. Educators must examine and modify instructional materials and their own attitudes and behaviors to eliminate sex stereotyping and unintentionally biased behavior so that all students *experience* equity.

4. Educators must understand that students and colleagues are continuously and strongly affected by equity-related factors outside the schools (e.g., the increase in teenage pregnancy, lack of child care, decline of the nuclear family, etc.). (Carelli, 1988)

The attainment of sex equity should be a primary goal of all educational institutions. As we strive to prepare our citizens for the twenty-first century and to remain competitive in the world markets, Plato's words of 2,500 years ago seem remarkably relevant:

> Nothing can be more absurd than the practice . . . of men and women not following the same pursuits with all their strength and with one mind, for thus the state . . . is reduced to a half. (*Laws*, VII, 805)

Adult and Continuing Education

Adult education is instruction provided to individuals beyond the age of compulsory attendance who have either completed or interrupted their formal education. In this country workers' reading groups, mechanics' institutes, literary societies and the lyceums were among the local self-help study groups that preceded the institution of formal adult education programming. Major public support for the adult education movement came in the 1960s with the passage of the Adult Education Act and other social legislation that required some form of education or training. In 1986, a record 3.1 million adults were enrolled in programs included under the Adult Education Act. Of the $405 million expended on these programs, approximately one-fourth was provided by the federal government (National Advisory Council on Adult Education, 1987).

Adult and Continuing Education Defined

The terms adult education and *continuing education* are often used interchangeably, although some educators limit discussion of adult education to the so-called entitlement programs for disadvantaged adults funded under Title I

Adult learners comprise a growing segment of today's population.

of the Education Amendments of 1984: adult basic education (ABE), high school equivalency (general education diploma or GED), and English as a second language (ESL). Continuing education is considered to be a much broader concept, including not only compensatory education programs for adults but career development programs, degree programs, and vocational offerings.

Adult Education Providers

Adult education providers include public and private schools; vocational, trade, and business schools; two- and four-year colleges and universities; religious and civic organizations; community and governmental agencies; the military; and professional organizations. Although educational institutions are the primary providers of adult education, business and industry providers have increased their offerings significantly in recent years.

Distance Education

Adult education is offered in a variety of formats, including formal courses, television courses, workshops, seminars, lectures, institutes, correspondence courses, and demonstrations. One delivery system that is growing in importance is distance education. *Distance education* is characterized by a separation in space and time for the majority of teaching and learning activities. Teaching takes place to a large extent through audio, video, computer, and print technologies and learning generally is on an individual basis through independent study in the student's home or workplace (Kaye, 1989). Correspondence courses are perhaps the oldest form of distance education. Now, not only print materials are transmitted through the mails, but audio and video tapes and computer disks.

How might distance education be used to provide professional development for teachers?

Perhaps the leading example of distance education is the British Open University, which provides a variety of courses through British public radio and television to between 150,000 and 200,000 students each year. Another notable example is a general education diploma (GED) telecourse produced by Kentucky Educational Television and used by several other states to reach thousands of students annually.

Adult Education, Illiteracy, and Economic Development

In recent years, adult education has been viewed as a major weapon in the battle against illiteracy and as a means of economic development. An estimated 23 to 25 million Americans are functionally illiterate and another 25 to 30 million function at the fifth to eighth grade level.

Recognizing the magnitude of the illiteracy problem and its impact on economic development, in 1983 President Reagan announced a National Adult Education Initiative. In the years immediately following, a number of major initiatives were launched, including B. Dalton Bookseller's National Literacy Initiative and Project Literacy U.S. (PLUS), a campaign of national outreach sponsored by the American Broadcasting Company and the Public Broadcasting Service. As a result of the PLUS campaign, millions of calls have been received at local and national hotlines from potential volunteers and students, and a major teleconference was held involving the American Association of Community and Junior Colleges and IBM, among others, who announced their goal to be "conquering illiteracy by the year 2000." In 1987, the first National Adult Literacy Congress was held in Philadelphia as a part of the We The People Bicentennial Celebration of the Constitution. In 1990, international attention was focused on illiteracy by the International Literacy Year sponsored by UNESCO (Costa, 1988).

As discussed in the preceding chapter, higher levels of education are associated with higher socioeconomic status. Thus, supporters of adult education have generally stated that one of its functions is to promote greater social equity. Consequently, it is of growing concern to adult educators that they are unable to attract many of those most in need, primarily undereducated minorities (Reed, 1988).

Each year billions of dollars are spent on adult education. Millions of adults commit even more millions of hours to adult education activities. This monetary and time expenditure represents a significant involvement in education that is not part of the formal educational system, but is part of a changing concept of education, one in which education does not end with high school or college graduation but is a lifelong process (U.S. Department of Education, 1987).

Vocational Education

The majority of high school graduates do not go on to college; they enter the world of work. *Vocational education* is designed to provide an alternative to college preparation and to prepare students for employment in all occupations except those requiring at least a baccalaureate degree. Vocational education is intended to address the needs of the student as well as the labor market. It begins in high school and may continue into the two-year postsecondary school.

Types of Programs

There are three major types of vocational education: (1) consumer and homemaking education, (2) general vocational education, and (3) occupationally specific vocational education in certain subjects (agriculture, business, marketing and distribution, health, occupational home economics, trade and industry, and technical and communications). A comprehensive vocational education delivery system is described as:

> a continuum of planned, coordinated, articulated and sequential educational experiences that are designed to prepare students for successful future participation in their community, home and work. It encompasses the development of a career awareness, exploration of jobs, vocational guidance and counseling, the establishment of career and life goals, and the development of employability and job skills. (Cowan, 1987, p. 22)

Enrollment Profile

In 1987 some 7.4 million students were reported to be enrolled in vocational education classes. Students who expect to terminate their education at the end of high school are the largest consumers of vocational education (an

*Have you
participated in
any vocational
education
program? How
has it benefited
you in your
college career?*

average of 6.02 credits per student) but, surprisingly, college-bound students also take significant amounts of vocational education (an average of 4.55 credits for those who plan to attend some college and 3.17 credits for those who plan to graduate) (Wirt, Muraskin, Goodwin, & Meyer, 1989). Although approximately one-fourth of all high school seniors are enrolled in vocational education programs, minority students and students from lower socioeconomic backgrounds are proportionately more represented in vocational education than white students or students from higher socioeconomic levels.

Federal Support

The largest source of federal assistance to vocational education is the Carl D. Perkins Vocational Education Act of 1984 (VEA). In 1989, the VEA provided approximately $900 million to the states to make vocational education programs accessible to all persons, including special needs populations such as the disadvantaged, the disabled, single parents, homemakers, participants in programs designed to reduce sex bias and stereotyping, and the incarcerated. This level of funding represents a decrease of approximately 10% since 1980 (U.S. Department of Education, 1989). In 1989, state and local governments provided 90% of the total spending for vocational education, approximately $2 billion.

Impact of the Reform Movement

Since the beginning of the reform movement in 1983, enrollments in vocational education in more than half the states have declined or failed to keep pace with increases in the high school student population. Areas hardest hit have been agriculture, health occupations, and trade and industrial programs (Frantz, Strickland, & Elson, 1988). This decline has been attributed to the increased academic graduation requirements that have been enacted by a number of states. To provide for the required increase in academic courses within their budgetary limits, some high schools have had to reduce their vocational educational offerings.

Rather than sacrifice vocational education to academic courses, an increasing number of states and school districts are reaffirming vocational education's place in the secondary school; providing ways, whenever appropriate, for vocational education courses to satisfy academic graduation requirements; and adopting strategies (e.g., extending the school day) that make time for vocational education (Moffett, 1987). Vocational education has a vital function in providing non-college-bound youth with preparation for participation in the work force, in reducing the dropout rate, and in supplying the trained manpower needed by our increasingly industrial, technological, and service-oriented society. The choice should not be between academic, general, or vocational education. Schools must provide for the postgraduation needs of all students, regardless of their career goals. The goal of the reform movement, to ensure that high school graduates are adequately prepared to succeed in the marketplace, contribute as literate citizens to our democratic society, and fully participate in the cultural, ethical, and political life of our society, is a goal that is shared and reinforced by vocational education.

Summary

Desegregation is one of many strategies for realizing equality of educational opportunity. It is also a strategy based on constitutionally guaranteed protections. Educating children with disabilities and language minority students and ensuring sex equity are other strategies similarly based. Although the financial support afforded these programs is not guaranteed, unless the Supreme Court reverses current law and decisions, their existence is. Other strategies—compensatory education, Indian education, adult education, and vocational education—are solely creations of statute and rely entirely on state and federal statutes for their existence.

The presence of each of these strategies in the American educational system has served to expand not only the educational opportunities of the targeted populations, but of all students. It is largely through the efforts of those asserting their rights under the constitutionally based programs that the rights of all students have been expanded. The success of our educational system and, indeed, our economic and social structure depends on the full participation of all children. This chapter focused attention on strategies for increasing equality of educational opportunity. The next chapter turns to strategies directed at specific populations of "at-risk" youth.

Key Terms

Adult education
Bilingual education
Cognitive styles
Compensatory education
Continuing education
Desegregation
Distance education
English as a Second Language (ESL)
Indian Education
Individualized Education Program (IEP)
Learning disability

Least restrictive environment
Magnet school
Mainstreaming
Multicultural education
Sex bias
Sex discrimination
Sex equity
Sex role stereotyping
Vocational education
White flight

Discussion Questions

1. What responsibilities does a counselor have in the Linda Wilson situation described in the opening scenario? A principal?

2. What do you see as the major obstacles to racial and ethnic integration in the schools?

3. Discuss ways in which the Individuals with Disabilities Education Act has benefited all children.

4. What economic benefits can the nation hope to gain from significantly increased funding of compensatory education?

5. Describe the bilingual education program in a school district with which you are familiar. What evidence exists that it has improved the academic performance of participants? Is it viewed as helping or hindering progress toward racial or ethnic integration?

6. Compare the treatment of males and females in the schools with their treatment in other institutions.

7. How do the missions of adult education, bilingual education, special education, vocational education, and sex equity in education complement each other?

References

Arias, M. B. (1989). English is Arizona's official language: Constitutional amendment XXVIII. *El Portavoz, 1,* 1–2.

August, D., & Garcia, E. E. (1988). *Language minority education in the United States.* Springfield, IL: Charles C. Thomas.

Board of Education v. Rowley, 458 U.S. 175 (1982).

Braddock, J. H., II, Crain, R. L., & McPartland, J. M. (1984). A long-term view of school desegregation: Some recent studies of graduates as adults. *Phi Delta Kappan, 66,* 259–264.

Brown v. Board of Education, 347 U.S. 483 (1954).

Cameron, C. E. (1987). Adult education as a force toward social equity. *Adult Education Quarterly, 37,* 173–177.

Carelli, A. O. (Ed.) (1988). *Sex equity in education: Reading and strategies.* Springfield, IL: Charles C. Thomas.

Casanova, U. (1987). Ethnic and cultural differences. In V. Richardson-Koehler (Ed.), *Educator's handbook: A research perspective* (pp. 370–393). New York: Longman.

Costa, M. (1988). *Adult literacy/illiteracy in the United States: A handbook for reference and research.* Santa Barbara, CA: ABC-CLIO.

Cowan, J. (1987). Vocational education's place in the secondary schools. *Thrust, 17,* 22.

Dayton Board of Education v. Brinkman, 433 U.S. 406 (1977).

Diana v. California State Board of Education, 1970.

Durbin, J. (1989). *Assessment of the vertical equity of state supported compensatory education programs in Arizona.* Unpublished doctoral dissertation, Arizona State University, Tempe.

Elmore, R. F., & McLaughlin, M. W. (1988). *Steady work: Policy, practice, and the reform of American education.* Santa Monica, CA: The Rand Corporation.

Fennema, E. (1987). Sex-related differences in education: Myths, realities, and interventions. In V. Richardson-Koehler (Ed.), *Educator's handbook: A research perspective* (pp. 329–347). New York: Longman.

Frantz, N. R., Jr., Strickland, D. C., & Elson, D. E. (1988). Is secondary vocational education at risk? *Vocational Education, 63,* 34–37.

Gallegos, E. M. (1989). Beyond *Board of Education v. Rowley:* Education benefit for the handicapped. *American Journal of Education, 97,* 258–288.

Green v. County School Board of New Kent County, 391 U.S. 430 (1968).

Jarvis, P. (1985). *The sociology of adult and continuing education.* Dover, NH: Crown Helm.

Jencks, C., Smith, M., Arland, H., Bane, M. J., Cohen, D., Gintis, H., Heyns, B., & Michelson, S. (1972). *Inequality: A reassessment of the effect of family and schooling in America.* New York: Basic Books.

Kaye, A. (1989). Computer-mediated communication and distance education. In R. Mason & A. Kaye (Eds.), *Mindweave: Communications, computers, and distance education* (pp. 3–21). New York: Pergamon Press.

Keyes v. School District No. 1, 413 U.S. 189 (1973).

Kozol, J. (1985). *Illiterate America.* Garden City, NY: Doubleday.

Larry P. v. Wilson Riles, 495 R. Supp. 926 (N.D. Cal. 1979).

Lau v. Nichols, 414 U.S. 563 (1974).

Leadership (1989/1990). *Education Vital Signs,* V, A7.

Levine, D. U., & Havighurst, R. J. (1989). *Society and education* (7th ed.). Boston: Allyn & Bacon.

McCarthy, M. M., & McCabe, N. H. (1987). *Public school law* (2nd ed.). Boston: Allyn & Bacon.

McCarthy, T. L., Wallace, S., & Lynch, R. H. (1989). Inquiry-based curriculum development in a Navajo school. *Educational Leadership, 46,* 66–71.

McDonald, D. (August 2, 1989). Indian people just want to be themselves. *Education Week,* 12–16.

Milliken v. Bradley, 418 U.S. 717 (1974).

Mills v. Board of Education of the District of Columbia, 348 F. Supp. 866 D.D.C. (1972).

Moffett, W. (1987). Academic credit—Pros and cons for vocational education. *Thrust, 17,*(2), 18–20.

National Advisory Council on Adult Education (NACAE) (1987). *Annual report FY 1987.* Washington, DC: NACAE.

Ochoa, A. M., Pacheco, R., & Omark, D. R. (1988). Addressing the learning disability needs of limited-English proficient students: Beyond language and race issues. *Learning Disability Quarterly, 11,* 257–264.

Ogbu, J. U. (1985). Minority education and costs. In N. R. Yetman & C. H. Steele (Eds.), *Majority and minority: The dynamics of race and ethnicity in American life* (3rd ed.), (pp. 426–439). Boston: Allyn & Bacon.

Ovando, C., & Collier, V. (1985). *Bilingual and ESL classrooms: Teaching in multicultural contexts.* New York: McGraw-Hill.

Pennsylvania Association of Retarded Citizens v. Commonwealth of Pennsylvania, 343 R. Supp. 279 (E. D. Pa. 1972).

Peterson, N. L. (1988). *Early intervention for handicapped and at-risk children.* Denver, CO: Love Publishing Company.

Ralph, J. (1989). Improving education for the disadvantaged: Do we know whom to help? *Phi Delta Kappan, 70,* 395–401.

Red Horse, J. (1986). Educational commentary: Education reform. *Journal of American Indian Education, 25,* 40–44.

Reed, H. B. (1988). Programmatic adult education in the context of lifelong learning. *Adult Education Quarterly, 38,* 172–181.

Reeves, M. S. (August 2, 1989). The high cost of endurance. *Education Week,* 2–4.

Rosenberg, M. (1986). Self-esteem research: A phenomenological corrective. In J. Prager, D. Longshore, & M. Seeman (Eds.), *School desegregation research* (pp. 175–203). New York: Plenum Press.

Sadker, M., Sadker, D., & Steindam, S. (1989). Gender equity and education reform. *Educational Leadership, 46,* 45.

Salmon, R., Dawson, C., Lawton, S., & Johns, T. (1988). *Public school finance programs of the United States and Canada.* Blacksburg, VA: American Education Finance Association.

Savage, D. G. (1987). Why Chapter I hasn't made much difference. *Phi Delta Kappan, 68,* 581–584.

Schweinhart, L., & Weikart, D. (1985). Evidence that good early childhood programs work. *Phi Delta Kappan, 66,* 565.

Selakovich, D. (1984). *Schooling in America: Social foundation of education.* New York: Longman.

Sex discrimination remains in education, rights group charges. (September 12, 1987). *Arizona Republic,* 87.

Shore, K. (1986). *The special education handbook.* New York: Teachers College Press, Columbia University.

Stein, C. B., Jr. (1986). *Sink or swim: The politics of bilingual education.* New York: Praeger.

Swann v. Charlotte-Mecklenburg Board of Education, 402 U.S. 1 (1971).

Tetreault, M. K., & Schmuck, P. (1985). Equity, educational reform, and gender. *Issues in Education, 3,* 50.

Tippeconnic, J. W., III, & Gipp, G. E. (1982). American Indian education. In H. E. Mitzel, J. H. Best, & W. Rubinowitz (Eds.), *Encyclopedia of educational research* (pp. 125–128). New York: The Free Press.

U.S. Bureau of the Census. (1989). *Population profile of the United States 1989.* Washington, DC: U.S. Government Printing Office.

U.S. Department of Education, National Center for Education Statistics. (1987). *Trends in adult education 1969–1984.* Washington, DC: U.S. Government Printing Office.

U.S. Department of Education, National Center for Education Statistics. (1989). *Digest of education statistics 1989.* Washington, DC: U.S. Government Printing Office.

Washburn, J. S., & McEwen, T. (1989). Fifteen ways to make time for vocational education. *Vocational Education Journal, 64,* 42–43.

Washington v. Davis, 426 U.S. 229 (1976).

Webb, R. B., & Sherman, R. R. (1989). *Schooling and society.* New York: Macmillan.

Welch, F., Light, A., Dong, F., & Ross, J. M. (1987). *New evidence on school desegregation.* Los Angeles, CA: Unicorn Research Corporation.

The William T. Grant Foundation Commission on Work, Family and Citizenship. (1988). The forgotten half: Non-college-bound youth in America. *Phi Delta Kappan, 69,* 409–414.

Williams, B. I., Thorne, J. M., Michie, J. S., & Hamar, R. (1987). *The district survey: A study of local implementation of ECIA Chapter I.* Chapel Hill, NC: Research and Evaluation.

Wirt, J. G., Muraskin, L. D., Goodwin, D. A., & Meyer, R. H. (1989). *Final report volume I: Summary of findings and recommendations.* Washington, DC: U.S. Department of Education, National Assessment of Vocational Education.

Yinger, J. M. (1986). The research agenda: New directions for desegregation studies. In J. Prager, D. Longshore, & M. Seeman (Eds.), *School desegregation research* (pp. 229–254). New York: Plenum Press.

Chapter 10

Students at Risk

Child abuse casts a shadow the length of a lifetime.

Herbert Ward, 1985

It was twilight when Tom Wright finished packing the last box in his apartment. The movers had already taken the furniture. All that remained were a few boxes. As Tom lifted one of the boxes, an old photograph fell to the floor. He picked it up and smiled as he recognized the photo of his eighth grade graduating class.

Twelve years had passed since that photo was taken. It seemed more like an eternity. He studied the photo for long moments. He immediately identified one of his best boyhood friends. Whatever happened to Jake Nash? He and Jake began kindergarten together and were like brothers for the entire eight years of elementary school. The last time he saw Jake was the summer after the photo was taken. Tom went on to Springview High School, but Jake moved away. It was so sudden, Tom remembered. He and Jake planned for high

school together. But that summer Jake's life turned upside down. Jake's mother and father divorced and shortly afterward his younger sister, Karen, attempted suicide. By August Jake, his mother, and his sister moved to Michigan to be near his grandparents. He and Tom promised that they would see each other often. But that never happened. They exchanged letters and telephone calls for the first year or so and then they grew apart. Tom was horrified and shocked when he learned from a former neighbor that Jake had dropped out of high school in his senior year and had been indicted on drug trafficking charges on his twenty-first birthday.

What, if any, clues indicated that Jake was at risk for dropping out of school? For substance use or abuse? For suicide?

Jake is typical of millions of youth in and out of our schools whose life experiences and situations place them at risk for educational, emotional, mental, and physical problems. In this chapter at-risk children and youth are described. In addition, methods of identifying a number of at-risk conditions and behaviors are suggested and prevention and intervention strategies that are used successfully in the schools are presented. The following objectives should guide you in your study of at-risk populations:

- Identify the predictors of being at risk.

- Describe the conditions or behavior associated with substance abuse.

- Discuss prevention and intervention strategies aimed at reducing the occurrence of substance use and abuse in children and adolescents.

- Indicate the extent of the problem of cult participation by youth, the

properties of a cult, and intervention strategies.

- Identify the suicidal child or adolescent.

- Review strategies for suicide prevention and intervention.

- Consider the incidence and consequences of dropping out of school and adolescent pregnancy.

- Describe successful pregnancy prevention and intervention programs.

- Suggest reasons why certain adolescents are at high risk for AIDS, pregnancy, and running away.

- Name the common signs or indicators of child abuse and sexual abuse.

- Detail the problem of runaways and homelessness among youth.

- Review the extent of the problem of crime, violence, and gangs in the schools.

At-Risk Children and Youth

A variety of terms have been used to describe children and adolescents who are in need of special treatment or special services. We are not referring here to the special education student, but to that group of students described as *at risk:* children and adolescents who are already achieving below grade level or are likely to experience educational problems in the future. The term also is used to describe children and adolescents who are already or are likely to experience physical and mental health problems.

Frymier and Gansneder (1989) describe the severity of being at risk as a function of the negative experiences or events that happen to a child or youth, the severity and frequency of these experiences or events, and other intervening variables in the child's or adolescent's immediate environment that either help or hinder the youngster's ability to cope. They offer the following example.

> A pregnant 14-year-old is at risk. But a pregnant 14-year-old who uses drugs is even more at risk. And a pregnant 14-year-old who uses drugs, has been retained in grade, has missed 30 days of school, and has a low sense of self-esteem is still more seriously at risk. (p. 142)

To be at risk is not solely a phenomenon of adolescence. Children at any age who are victims of abuse—sexual, physical, or emotional—are at risk. Children as young as five or six can be at risk. For example, a child whose parents are in the process of finalizing a divorce and who is failing in school is definitely at risk. So is a seven-year-old whose older sister just committed suicide, or a preschooler whose mother is an alcoholic and whose father has been cited for sexually abusing his teenage daughter. All of these youngsters are at risk not only for academic underachievement but mental health problems.

Identifying the At-Risk Student

Early identification is the key to developing and implementing effective educational programs for at-risk students. The Council of Chief State School Officers (1987) has identified 67 possible behaviors or factors that identify the at-risk student; Frymier & Gansneder (1989) identified approximately 45 risk factors. Among the most prominent were underachievement, retention in grade, discipline problems, dropping out of school, low parental support, physical problems, using and abusing drugs or alcohol, and contemplating or attempting suicide. Other researchers have reported additional risk factors: being born to or raised by a mentally ill parent; suffering from the loss of a significant other; having experienced perinatal trauma or poor health status at birth; having been born to a teenage mother; having been abused or physically or emotionally neglected; being from a poor family; and living in an abject environment such as being homeless (Gersten & Shamis, 1988).

The research also indicates that a disproportionate number of ethnic/minority children, in particular black, Hispanic, and Native American children, non-English-speaking children, and children of single-parent families are represented among the at-risk population. These groups have a high incidence for certain at-risk behaviors, including low achievement, dropping out of school, and teen pregnancy (Robertson & Frymier, 1989).

The following sections of this chapter describe a number of at-risk conditions or behaviors and discuss how they might be identified. In addition, for each at-risk condition or behavior, prevention and intervention strategies are discussed. The conditions or behaviors to be discussed include drug and alcohol use and abuse, cult participation, suicide, dropping out of school, teenage pregnancy, AIDS, physical and sexual abuse, running away and homelessness, and delinquency and violence.

Are you familiar with the term "at risk"? Could you, a member of your family, or a close friend be classified as at risk? Why?

Drug and Alcohol Use and Abuse

The use and abuse of chemical substances and alcohol by children and adolescents is one of the most challenging problems facing schools today. Children and teenagers use alcohol, cigarettes, and a wide assortment of illicit chemical substances including marijuana; stimulants (e.g., amphetamines, cocaine, "crack," "rock," and "uppers"); inhalants (e.g., solvents, aerosols, and nitrites); dissociative anesthetics (e.g., PCP [Phencyclidine] or "angel dust"); anabolic steroids; depressants (e.g., barbiturates, "ludes," tranquilizers or "downers"); hallucinogens (e.g., LSD, mescaline, and STP); and narcotics (e.g., opium, morphine, heroin, codeine and methadone).

The Effects of Abuse

The abuse of these and other substances often is associated with harmful and deleterious effects on both the individual and society. On an individual level, drug and alcohol abuse interfere with cognitive development and academic achievement. On a societal level, neighborhoods near schools often become the target of drug dealers, many of whom are students themselves. Additionally, crimes of violence often are associated with substance abuse, particularly among teenage gang members. Research also suggests that teenage drug abuse is a contributing factor to personal, social, and occupational maladjustment in later young adulthood. For example, it has been found that habitual use of marijuana and hard drugs as a teen are predictive of later job instability, emotional turmoil, and early divorce. It has also been found that use of hard drugs (hypnotics, stimulants, cocaine, inhalants, and narcotics) as a teenager appears to contribute to deterioration in social relationships, increased loneliness, and suicidal ideation as an adult (Newcomb & Bentler, 1988).

Trends in Use

Has the decline in the abuse of drugs and alcohol among high school students also been evidenced among college students? Among your age cohort?

Although the level of drug and alcohol use among teens remains alarmingly high, recent statistics show some decline. A 1988 survey for the National Institute on Drug Abuse found declining drug use among high school seniors, continuing a trend that was first evident in 1986 (U.S. Department of Health and Human Services, 1989). In fact, the use of cocaine, marijuana, and other drugs were found to be at their lowest levels in more than a decade. Between 1986 and 1988, the proportion of seniors reporting any cocaine use in the prior 12 months dropped from 13% to 8%. The use of crack cocaine, a highly addictive, smokeable form of cocaine, also declined for the first time.

There also were signs of a decline in alcohol consumption. The survey found that the proportion of seniors who might be considered "current drinkers" (those who had one or more drinks in the past 30 days) declined from 66% to 64%. Similarly, the proportion who reported consuming five or more drinks in a row during the prior two weeks had declined from 38% to 35%, down from an all-time high of 41% in 1983. The findings regarding cigarette smoking, however, were disappointing. The proportion of seniors who were current smokers was 29%, while 18% smoked daily. Teenage cigarette smoking has remained stable since the class of 1984. Figure 10.1 displays the trends in the use of drugs and alcohol by high school seniors for the years 1975–1988.

The evidence concerning alcohol use by younger children does not seem as promising as that for older children. Research has shown that the average age of first use of alcohol is approximately 12.3 years. By age 13, approximately 30% of boys and 22% of girls drink alcohol on a regular basis. Thirty percent report that they experienced peer pressure to consume alcohol as early as age nine or ten. The use of alcohol by the very young is particularly distressing because the research has suggested that alcohol, tobacco, and marijuana are truly *gateway drugs* for the very young child, whose early and frequent use of these substances can be a stepping-stone to later use of hard drugs (MacDonald, 1984; Welte & Barnes, 1985).

Identifying Alcohol and Drug Use

Parents, teachers, counselors, and administrators are better prepared to provide early intervention when they recognize the difference between normal childhood and adolescent behavior and behavior that may indicate substance use or abuse. Figure 10.2 identifies some of the behaviors that have been found to be associated with substance abuse.

The differences between so-called normal behavior and behavior that may reflect substance use or abuse often are a matter of degree. For example, it is normal for a child or adolescent to desire to spend time alone, but it may not be normal to exhibit sudden, almost complete withdrawal from family or friends. A pattern of changes, not any single behavior, best predicts possible substance abuse (Dorman, Geldof, & Scarborough, 1982).

Figure 10.1: Trends in the Use of Drugs and Alcohol by High School Seniors, 1975–1988.

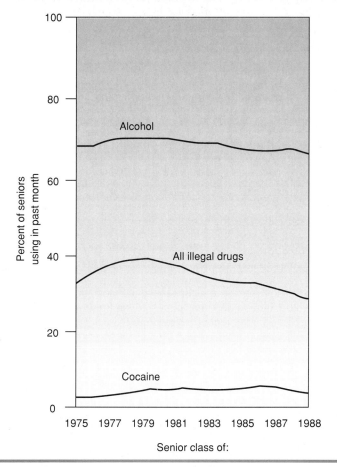

Source: U.S. Department of Health & Human Services, Alcohol, Drug Abuse & Mental Health Administration, National Institute on Drug Abuse. (1989). *Drug use among American high school students, college students, and other young adults.* Washington, DC: U.S. Government Printing Office.

Prevention Strategies

Prevention strategies include those programs, activities, and services that help reduce the occurrence of substance use and abuse in children and adolescents. In 1986, the federal government passed the Drug Free Schools and Communities Act to assist states in establishing new drug prevention programs or supplementing existing programs. With the assistance provided by federal funds under this act, a number of states have developed substance-abuse prevention programs and provided training for educators. In a number of locales, mental health agencies have collaborated with school districts to

What programs are available in your community to discourage drug and alcohol abuse among young children?

Figure 10.2: Behavioral Characteristics Associated with Substance Abuse

- Abrupt changes in work or school attendance, quality of work, work output, grades, discipline

- General attitude changes and/or irritability

- Withdrawal from responsibility

- Deterioration of physical appearance and grooming

- Impaired performance on the job or in the classroom

- Wearing of sunglasses at inappropriate times (to hide dilated or constricted pupils)

- Continual wearing of long-sleeved garments (to hide injection marks), particularly in hot weather or reluctance to wear short-sleeved attire when appropriate

- Association with known substance abusers

- Unusual borrowing of money from friends, co-workers, or parents

- Stealing small items from employer, home, or school

- Secretive behavior regarding actions and possessions; poorly concealed attempts to avoid attention and suspicion such as frequent trips to storage rooms, closets, restrooms, basements (to use drugs)

Source: Pharmaceutical Manufacturers Association. (1987). *Substance abuse: Signs and symptoms.* Washington, DC: Author. Reprinted with the permission of: The Pharmaceutical Manufacturers Association, 1100 Fifteenth Street, NW, Washington, DC 20005.

develop and implement substance-abuse prevention curricula that emphasize problem solving, assertion training, decision making, wellness, and health awareness.

Although the developmental level of the child will determine the specific design of the drug and alcohol prevention curriculum, certain themes should be present at all grade levels. The U.S. Department of Education (1988) recommends the following themes:

- A clear and consistent message that the use of alcohol, tobacco, and other illicit drugs is unhealthy and harmful.

- Knowledge of all types of drugs, including what medicines are, why they are used, and who should (or should not) administer them.

- The social consequences of substance abuse.

- Respect for the laws and values of society.

- Promotion of healthy, safe, and responsible attitudes and behaviors by correcting mistaken beliefs and assumptions, disarming the sense of per-

Early prevention efforts are a key to combating this serious problem that affects adolescents of all cultures and socioeconomic classes.

sonal invulnerability, and building resistance to influences that encourage substance abuse.

- Strategies to involve parents, family members, and the community in the effort to prevent use of illicit substances.

- Appropriate information on intervention and referral services, plus similar information on contacting responsible adults when help is needed in emergencies.

- Sensitivity to the specific needs of the local school and community in terms of cultural appropriateness and local substance abuse problems. (p. 10)

It is also important that parental involvement be a component of any substance abuse prevention curricula.

Community-based organizations also have become increasingly involved in alcohol and drug abuse prevention activities. Examples of these community efforts include Mothers Against Drunk Driving (MADD), which has influenced the drunk-driving laws; the "Chemical People" campaign on public television, which spearheaded local drug abuse prevention task forces in at least 10,000 communities; and Project DARE (Drug Abuse Resistance Education), offered in the schools by law enforcement agencies. Similarly, a number of major community organizations such as the Lions Club International, National 4-H, the Association of Junior Leagues, the National PTA, and the American Association of School Administrators (AASA) have formed the National Coalition for the Prevention of Drug and Alcohol Abuse (Buscemi, 1985).

Intervention Strategies

School-sponsored *intervention programs* are aimed at providing assistance to those children and adolescents who are already using or abusing drugs or alcohol. Among the more widely used intervention strategies are referral to mental health agencies and psychiatric hospitals for treatment; peer counseling programs aimed at teens helping teens; school-based individual and group counseling; mental health consultation whereby community health agencies offer psychological services to school districts; and community practitioners, educators, and former substance abusers who monitor and treat children and teens who have drug and alcohol problems (Salzman & Salzman, 1989).

Chemical dependency has serious implications for the schools. Practically every teacher at all grade levels from middle school on will be confronted by a sizable number of students who are engaging in regular use of drugs and/or alcohol. Beginning teachers need to become familiar with the educational prevention programs offered by their district and their school. They also need to become acquainted with the treatment programs available in the community for children and adolescents. The school counselor, social worker, or psychologist will be an invaluable resource to the beginning teacher who may feel unprepared to deal with this particular type of problem.

Cult Participation

The term *cult* has been defined in a variety of ways. The most common definition is that a cult is a group bound together by devotion to a person, belief system, or set of practices. Not all cults are harmful and some may have a positive purpose or goal that is beneficial to its members. However, certain cults are considered to be destructive. A destructive cult is one in which a group of individuals is under the control of an authoritative leader or group of leaders. Such a group may or may not be religious in nature. The leader or leaders of such a group often resort to deception and indirect techniques of persuasion and manipulation to promote their own power, wealth, or vanity (Cult Awareness Network, 1985).

Classifications of Cults

Cult groups may be classified as neo-Christian–based cults; Hindu and Eastern religion–based groups; occult, satanic, and witchcraft movements; spiritualistic groups; Zen-based assemblies; race-based cults; flying saucer–based cliques; psychological movements; political cults; and communal living groups (Singer & West, 1980). Depending on one's definition of a cult, there are approximately 2,500 to 3,000 cults in the United States, many of which appeal to youth.

The recent upsurge of cults in the United States began in the late 1960s. However, it was not until the tragic mass suicide-murders of almost 1,000 American followers of Jim Jones in Guyana in 1978 that the American public began to recognize the powerful influence of cult leaders. By the mid-1970s, cults were a highly visible phenomenon. It has been estimated that approximately two to three million young adults have participated in cult activities in the past decade.

Have you or anyone you know been involved in a cult movement? What were the positive effects of membership? Negative effects?

Identifying Cults and Cult Participation

Since cults are known to have a deleterious effect on members and their families, it is imperative that educators, mental health professionals, and parents be able to identify the basic characteristics of a cult and the signs that a child may be involved in such a movement. Figure 10.3 lists a number of characteristics of destructive cults and their leadership.

The particular signals that may indicate that a child or adolescent is involved in a cult are these: a sudden personality change; a change in life goals, such as dropping out of school or leaving a job; sudden attempts to transfer funds or personal possessions; or a sudden disappearance (Addis, Schulman-Miller, & Lightman, 1984).

Prevention and Intervention Strategies

The best strategy for preventing cult participation is education and training. Unfortunately, few schools include information on cults in their regular curriculum. The most effective intervention strategies are counseling and therapy. Although in some cases the counseling may be provided by the school, in most instances these services are outside the domain of the school. Cult clinics have been established to offer counseling and educational services to families who have lost a child to cults.

One of the most controversial intervention strategies used with youngsters who are cult members is deprogramming. Deprogrammers argue that their intervention methods are designed to help cult members leave the cult life and once again make free, rational choices. The American Civil Liberties Union (ACLU) has argued that deprogramming is a violation of the rights of freedom of religion, association, and privacy. The debate concerning the legality of deprogramming continues.

Figure 10.3: Characteristics of a Destructive Cult and Its Leadership

1. Cult leaders are often charismatic and claim divinity or special expertise while demanding unquestioning obedience.

2. Cults tend to use deception in their recruiting and fundraising activities.

3. Exclusivity, elitism, secrecy, and vagueness describe many cults.

4. Financial, physical, and psychological exploitation characterize a number of cults.

5. Cults tend to emphasize a totalitarian view of the world that fosters group goals over individual goals.

6. Members can become alienated or separated from their families, friends, and society. There appears to be a noticeable change in values and eventually the group/cult becomes the substituted "new family."

7. Members can experience severe fatigue as a result of extended working hours and repetition of hypnotic practices including meditating, pseudo-speaking in tongues, chanting, classes and/or training sessions.

8. In order to inhibit the ability to question, there is an interference with private contemplation, independent thought, and privacy.

9. Fear and guilt are prevalent, and sometimes sexual abuse, child abuse with accompanying punishment, and other exploitation occur.

10. Some cult groups approve violence or criminal activity under the guise of goodness.

11. Some of the techniques of mind control used by the cults include group pressure or "love bombing"; isolation or separation; hypnosis; creation of confusion, fear, and guilt; rejection of old values; sleep deprivation; and absolutism.

Source: Cult Awareness Network (1991). 2421 West Pratt Blvd., Suite 1173, Chicago, IL 60645.

Postvention Strategies

For the individual who chooses to leave cult life, the emotional problems can be profound. Research has suggested that many former cult members experience severe emotional problems including depression, loneliness, indecisiveness, slipping into altered states, blurring of mental acuity, and fear of retaliation. For some, the emotional problems are severe enough to warrant hospitalization (Singer, 1979).

Destructive cults are a major social problem that demand a response from a variety of institutions, including the schools. If this type of problem is not addressed, the potential long-term psychological effects on the young cult member and his or her family may be irreversible.

Teachers need to be sensitive to the unique problems associated with cult membership and cult participation. Like the other at-risk behaviors or conditions mentioned in this chapter, cult participation has far-reaching psychological effects on youth. Often the cult membership or involvement may not be obvious to the teacher or parent. As a result, the youngster who associates with a cult movement may become deeply involved before anyone notices any signs or symptoms.

Suicide

Extent of the Problem

During the past 30 years, the number of adolescents who have committed suicide has increased by 300% and the number of suicide attempts has increased between 350 and 700% (Frymier, 1988). Suicide is the second leading cause of death among youth 15 to 24 years of age; only accidents and homicides rank higher. It is estimated that suicide accounts for more than 5,000 deaths each year for this age group. A recent survey by the Gallup Organization found that 6 in 100 teenagers aged 13 to 19 have attempted suicide, and 20 in 100,000 actually complete suicide. And for each completed suicide it is estimated there are 300 attempts (Lawton, 1991). In 1988 the national suicide rate for 15–24-year-olds was 12.8 per 100,000, while the suicide rate for children 10–14 years of age was 2.0 per 100,000 (Mrela, 1989). Yet, these data probably do not reflect the magnitude of the problem, since many suicides and suicide attempts go undetected or unreported. It has been predicted that in the average high school approximately 35–60 students will attempt suicide every year and at least one student will commit suicide every five years (Phi Delta Kappa, 1988).

Although suicide is considered rare in children under the age of 12, thoughts of suicide (*suicide ideation*), suicidal threats and gestures, and suicide attempts are common even among young children (Strother, 1986). A strong association has been found between depression and severe suicidal behaviors in these children (Pfeffer, 1986).

Group Differences

Gender, racial differences, and locale differences have been found in suicide rates among teens and younger children. For example, boys are more apt to *commit* suicide, girls are more apt to *attempt* suicide. The difference in rate may be explained by the methods used. Boys are more apt to use violent means such as firearms to commit suicide; girls tend to use less lethal means such as injecting drugs or slashing wrists. The rate of suicide for black youth is approximately one-fifth that of whites, while Native Americans are 10 times more likely to commit suicide than their white peers. Rural youth tend to resort to self-destructive behavior more than do urban youth (Frymier, 1988).

Identifying the Suicidal Child or Adolescent

What suicide messages are there in rock music? To what extent do they influence children and adolescents?

Many of the symptoms of suicidal thoughts or actions are similar to the symptoms of depression. Parents, teachers, and counselors should be aware of the warning signs or indications that a child or adolescent may be suicidal. Table 10.1 presents the major indicators of possible childhood or adolescent suicidal behavior. Of these indicators, substance abuse, stressful life events, and *clinical depression* deserve mention because of their particular importance in predicting self-destructive behavior. In addition, those children who tend to be preoccupied with death, who know a teenager who has attempted suicide, or who have a family member who exhibited suicidal tendencies have been found to be more at risk for self-destructive behavior.

The research suggests that substance abuse is linked closely to suicide and that drugs or alcohol may temper the fear of death. Similarly, the child or adolescent who experiences a significant number of stressful life events such as death of a parent, separation or divorce of parents, marriage of a parent, or birth of a sibling may also be at risk for self-destructive behavior (Ferguson, 1981; Johnson & McCutcheon, 1980; Yeaworth, York, Hussey, Ingle, & Goodwin, 1980). Suicidal children also are more likely to have alcoholic parents, experience parental suicide, and experience illness as well as the loss of a loved one such as a grandparent (Cohen-Sandler, Berman, & King, 1982).

Signs of Depression

The clinically depressed child or youth is likely to exhibit signs of hopelessness, a change in eating and sleeping habits, withdrawal from family and friends, substance abuse, persistent boredom, loss of interest in pleasurable activities, neglect of personal appearance, violent or rebellious behavior, and frequent complaints about physical symptoms. In early adolescence, the depression is often masked by acting out or delinquent behavior. Older adolescents are more apt to resort to drugs, alcohol, and sex rather than face their pain (Greuling & DeBlassie, 1980).

All children and youth may experience some depression with its highs and lows, but the clinically depressed youngster experiences a more serious depression with persistent symptoms that typically last for at least two or more weeks. It is the clinically depressed child who is most at risk for suicide (Fra-

Table 10.1: Indicators of Childhood or Adolescent Suicide

Psychosocial	Familial	Psychiatric	Situational
1. Poor self-esteem and feelings of inadequacy.	1. Disintegrating family relationships.	1. Prior suicide attempt.	1. Stressful life events.
2. Hypersensitivity and suggestibility.	2. Economic difficulties and family stresses.	2. Verbalization of suicide or talk of self-harm.	
3. Perfectionism.	3. Child and adolescent abuse.	3. Preoccupation with death.	
4. Sudden change in social behavior.	4. Ambivalence concerning dependence v. independence.	4. Repeated suicide ideation.	
5. Academic deterioration.	5. Running away.	5. Daredevil or self-abusive behavior.	
6. Underachievement and learning disabilities.	6. Unrealistic parental demands.	6. Mental illness such as delusions or hallucinations in schizophrenia.	
	7. Family history of suicide.	7. Overwhelming sense of guilt.	
		8. Obsessional self-doubt.	
		9. Phobic anxiety.	
		10. Clinical depression.	
		11. Substance abuse.	

Source: Adapted from Metha, A., & Dunham, H. M. (1988). Behavioral indicators. In Capuzzi, D., & Golden, L. *Preventing adolescent suicide* (pp. 49–86). Muncie, IN: Accelerated Development Inc. Reprinted with permission.

zier, 1985). The period when the depression appears to subside is the most vulnerable time, for that is when the child has the psychic energy to become acutely suicidal (Hipple & Cimbolic, 1979).

Although most children and youth will exhibit a number of verbal and nonverbal warning signs and clues of possible suicidal behavior, the majority will not be suicidal. However, it behooves every parent and educator to be sensitive to any one of the signs or clues, since it may be the youngster's last desperate plea for understanding and help. If one or more of these signs is observed, the parent or educator should talk to the child about his or her concerns and seek professional help if those concerns or problems continue to persist. If we fail to recognize the child's pain, fear, doubt and confusion, we may have missed an opportunity to save a life.

Controversial Issues:
The School's Role in Suicide Prevention

The school's role in suicide prevention was a controversial issue of the 1980s and probably will continue to be debated during the 1990s. The extent to which the schools should assume this role is debated by educators, school boards, and parents. The reasons often given in favor or against suicide prevention in the school are:

Arguments For

1. Suicide prevention programs can help students cope with the various stresses they experience in their school and personal lives.

2. The suicide prevention programs usually include a curricula that teaches coping, problem solving, and survival skills which are valuable life skills for all students.

3. Suicide prevention programs help teachers and students recognize the warning signs of the suicidal child or adolescent, enabling them to make a timely referral if necessary.

4. Suicide prevention programs offer training in peer counseling, which has been an invaluable strategy for identifying the suicidal child or adolescent.

5. The alarming statistics concerning suicide among children and adolescents require that schools take a proactive step in addressing the problem.

Arguments Against

1. School counselors, teachers, and other professional staff do not have the time or training to deal effectively with the suicidal youngster.

2. There is little research evidence that confirms that suicide prevention programs lessen suicidal behavior.

3. The liability of the school is unclear concerning suicide prevention programming.

4. Recent research on imitative and modeling behavior raises serious questions about offering suicide prevention programs in the schools, i.e., teaching about suicide will trigger a suicide, since children and youth are so suggestible.

What is your view of suicide prevention in the school? What types of program(s) exist in a school with which you are familiar?

Prevention Strategies

The focus of suicide prevention programs is on identification or detection. The majority of prevention programs in the schools emphasize strategies that focus on building self-esteem, decision making, communication, listening and coping skills, problem solving, nutrition, and physical exercise. In recent years a number of states have passed legislation requiring the department of public instruction to develop a suicide prevention curriculum. Impetus for developing suicide prevention programs in the schools has also come from the courts. A decision of the Ninth Circuit Court of Appeals in *Kelson v. The City of Springfield* (1985) held that the parents of a deceased child may bring action against the school if the death allegedly resulted because of the lack of a suicide prevention program. On page 324 are arguments for and against the schools taking a role in suicide prevention.

What is your position on the enactment of gun control laws as a suicide prevention measure?

Intervention Strategies

The most common suicide intervention program is the *crisis intervention team* approach. The typical crisis intervention team is composed of volunteer teachers, counselors, administrators, social workers, school nurses and school psychologists. The members of the crisis team meet regularly and participate in training workshops conducted by local community mental health agencies. The role of crisis team members is to network with each other and identify the youngster who appears to be overwhelmed by stress or displays a *suicide gesture* or *suicide threat*. Problems often are solved at the team level; however, the crisis team may refer a student to a community mental health agency or hospital for emergency care. Other intervention strategies include individual and group counseling, peer counseling, and referral to a suicide hotline for students who are in crisis when school is not in session.

Postvention Strategies

In addition to prevention and intervention strategies a *postvention program* also is important for the school. The purpose of a postvention program is to help the school return to normal in the aftermath of a suicide and to prevent *cluster suicides*. Grief counseling, support groups, interacting with the media, and follow-up care are examples of postvention strategies facilitated by the crisis intervention team.

Schools are in a better position to respond to suicidal concerns if they have prevention, intervention, and postvention policies and procedures in place. The worst time to plan for a crisis such as a suicide or attempted suicide is during the crisis.

Today, no school is immune to the loss of a child or adolescent by suicide. Parents and teachers are often the last to recognize that the child or adolescent is at risk for taking his or her own life. The peer group will probably be the first to know that the child is in need of immediate help. Teachers need to be able to establish a trust relationship with students so that the students will come forward to seek the help they need to respond to a suicidal friend. Many beginning teachers feel very inadequate and fearful of handling a suicidal student for fear that their actions may precipitate an actual suicide or suicide attempt. The truth is that talking about suicidal tendencies will not exacerbate a suicide or suicide attempt. Most youngsters at risk for suicide are relieved to be able to articulate their fears and concerns to an adult who will listen. The worst response is no response.

Dropping Out of School

The majority of states and school districts define the *dropout* as a pupil who leaves school for any reason before graduation or completion of a program of study without transferring to another school or institution (Ascher & Schwartz, 1987). The statistics on dropouts are alarming. The latest available data showed that in 1987, 2.7 million males and 2.3 million females between the ages of 16 and 24 were not enrolled in high school and had not completed a high school diploma (U.S. Department of Education, 1989). In any given year, approximately 682,000 American teens drop out of school, an average of 3,789 each day (U.S. Department of Education, 1987).

In a study entitled *Dropout Rates in the United States: 1988*, Frase (1989) reported the following:

● The dropout problem is particularly serious among Hispanics, and the rate is not declining.

● Differences between dropout rates for blacks and whites have decreased significantly in the past decade as the dropout rate for blacks has declined.

● Dropout rates for whites and blacks are similar when individual and family background are taken into account, i.e., dropout rates for blacks and whites living in central cities are comparable, as are rates for blacks and whites living in suburbs.

● Dropout rates are higher in the South and West. (p. 2)

In 1988, approximately 13% of all 16- to 24-year-olds were not in school and had not completed school, down from 16% in 1968. Figure 10.4 depicts the trend in the percentage of dropouts for persons aged 16–24 by race, ethnicity, and gender for the period 1968 to 1988.

Economic Consequences

The dropout problem has profound economic implications. It has been estimated that $228 billion in earnings and $68 billion in local, state, and federal tax revenues are lost over the lifetime of the total number of dropouts each year. Moreover, if the costs for unemployment, welfare, and other social services for dropouts and their families are considered, the combined lost tax revenues escalate to approximately $75 billion per year (Greene, 1986).

Identifying the Potential Dropout

Although not every student who leaves school prior to graduation will possess these characteristics, Grossnickle (1986) lists the following as the most common signs of a potential dropout: poor attendance; absenteeism; tardiness; underachievement; lack of basic skills, in particular reading; problems at home; poor communication between home and school; poorly developed organizational skills; a history of school transfers and family moves; poor social adjustment; failure to foresee the importance of an education; inability to

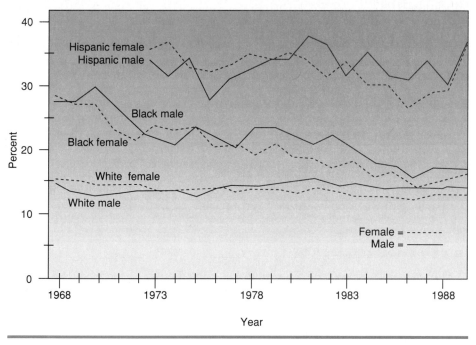

Figure 10.4: Percentage of High School Dropouts Among Persons Age 16–24 by Race, Ethnicity, and Gender, 1968–1988

Source: U.S. Department of Education, National Center for Education Statistics. (September, 1989). *Dropout rates in the United States: 1988* (p. xv). Washington, DC: U.S. Government Printing Office.

relate to authority figures; having a parent or older sibling who is a dropout; and low self-esteem. Other research has found that dropouts often are over-age students who have been retained at earlier grade levels; those who have a lengthy history of law violations; those who are drug or alcohol abusers; or those who are pregnant (Bialo & Sivin, 1989; Natriello, 1987).

Prevention Strategies

As with other at-risk behaviors, timely identification of the potential dropout is very important. The earlier the student is identified, the more likely it is that prevention efforts will be successful. And since research indicates that the effects of dropping out are more devastating for females than males in terms of academic and economic implications, prevention programs should be especially sensitive to the needs of females. Mentoring programs and programs that expose students to nontraditional occupations are two examples of positive prevention strategies (Hayes, 1987).

Monitoring students' progress is another successful prevention strategy. For example, the Dade County, Florida public schools (the fourth largest school district in the nation) have used computers to identify students at risk

Why would dropping out of school have a more deleterious effect on females than on males?

for dropping out. Once identified, grades and standardized test scores are tracked, along with parent-teacher conferences notes, meetings with counselors, attendance information, and any legal problems (U.S. Department of Education, 1987).

Other examples of prevention programs include:

- A New Orleans school district program that reimburses teachers and tutors to work with at-risk students after school and on Saturdays, providing special help in language and mathematics.

- The Los Angeles Unified School District's Adopt-A-Student Program, which operates at a high school that has a 60% attrition rate. Some 125 at-risk youngsters work closely with teachers, counselors, and staff personnel, who are available to offer special assistance and help.

- A program at Kansas City's Northeast Junior High School for seventh graders who have been absent from school 30% of the time. Students participate in weekly support groups. (U.S. Department of Education, 1987).

Intervention Strategies

Do you advocate the "dropouts don't drive law" as an intervention strategy? Why or why not?

Of all intervention strategies, mandatory suspension of a driver's license is currently the most controversial. Known as the "dropouts don't drive law," this strategy is intended to keep teens in school by revoking their driver's license if they drop out of school. To date, Florida and West Virginia have passed such legislation, but it is still too soon to make any judgments about their success (McGarrahan & Brecher, 1989).

All teachers have an obligation to try to prevent students from dropping out of school. School districts must improve their efforts at identifying the potential dropout and must find effective methods to work with the families of students who are at risk of leaving school.

Teenage Pregnancy

It is estimated that one out of ten, or more than one million American teens, will become pregnant each year. Of these teens, some 500,000 will give birth, and approximately 30,000 of the new mothers will be girls younger than 15 years (Bonjean & Rittenmeyer, 1987). While the birth rate of adolescent mothers aged 15–19 appears to be declining, the birth rate for teens aged 14 or younger is increasing. Perhaps the most discouraging data is that the younger a teen gives birth, the more likely she is to repeat the cycle of pregnancy. In fact, 19% of births to teens are actually second births, while as many as 4% are the third birth or more (Lachance, 1985).

A general myth surrounding the teenage pregnancy problem is that it affects primarily minority teens. In reality, teen pregnancy affects all ethnic and socioeconomic groups. A profile of girls who become pregnant shows that many tend to perform below average in school subjects and on academic achievement tests prior to giving birth, and that they tend to display a lack of motivation for an education, a vocation, or a career (Hayes & Cryer, 1987).

Consequences of Adolescent Pregnancy

Adolescent parenthood has profound implications for health care and social services, for poverty and crime, for family relationships, and for the institution of the school. Since so many teenage parents often lack sufficient health care insurance and the necessary funds for the delivery, they must resort to outside subsidies to meet their financial commitments. In addition, they often lack proper prenatal care, one of the major prerequisites of a healthy delivery. This, coupled with inadequate diet (a problem for countless teens whether pregnant or not), has resulted in a significant number of premature deliveries with accompanying low birth weight. Unfortunately, premature infants often are at risk for a host of serious health problems at a later date. The mortality rate for teenage mothers also is higher than for any age group. Because teen mothers experience so many health problems before and after the birth, they place heavy demands on the accompanying social service agencies, which accentuates the costs for the teen, her family, and society.

Pregnant teens are at high risk for dropping out of school.

Economic Consequences

Teenage pregnancy has other, more serious economic consequences. Approximately 4 in 10 teen mothers under the age of 15 fail to complete the eighth grade, and 8 in 10 do not graduate from high school (Morrison & Jensen, 1982). Nationally, only 50% of adolescent parents graduate from high school, and a high school education is a major factor in earning potential. The mean family income of white adolescent girls who give birth before the age of 16 is approximately one-half the income earned had they delayed the birth until young adulthood (Alan Guttmacher Institute, 1981). Families headed by teen mothers are 7 times more likely to be poor than their nonchildbearing peers (Wallace, Weeks, & Medina, 1982).

Prevention Strategies

The major aim of pregnancy prevention programs is to keep teens from conceiving. School district policies and practices vary widely on this and other controversial issues, so it is important that teachers be aware of the policies of their district. Some prevention programs in the schools encourage adolescents to abstain from sexual activity, others provide birth control information, and a few provide contraceptive devices. The majority limit their prevention strategies to critical thinking and communication skills, family life planning, or some form of reproductive health curriculum.

Of all prevention strategies, in-school health clinics appear to be the most successful. School-based clinics are designed to provide contraceptive counseling and related health services to adolescents. Typically sponsored by a combination of organizations, including hospitals, medical centers, departments of public health, community health agencies, and the school district, these clinics offer a wide range of services including counseling, physical examinations, and immunization, in addition to reproductive health services and sex education. A survey by the Center for Population Options found that 52% of school-based health clinics prescribed contraceptives, 28% dispensed contraceptives, and 20% referred the students to other community agencies (Bonjean & Rittenmeyer, 1987).

To what extent should the school bear the cost and responsibility for providing a pregnancy prevention and intervention program?

An example of a successful state-sponsored pregnancy prevention program is the Illinois "Parents Too Soon" project, which uses a media campaign to help reduce the incidence of teen pregnancy. Using public service announcements, billboards, posters, and bus advertisements, messages such as "Being a teenage parent is 24 hours a day, every day" have been disseminated statewide. As a result of the media blitz, the Illinois program's statewide hotline received almost 10,000 calls (mostly from teens) requesting pregnancy-related information in a single year (Rosauer, 1987).

Intervention Strategies

The major goals of most intervention strategies are to provide prenatal care, parenting skills, and vocational and personal counseling to adolescent mothers in an effort to reduce the cycle of repeated pregnancies, welfare dependency, and potential child abuse (The Flinn Foundation, 1989). Parent resource centers have proven to be a promising intervention strategy. Typically, such parent resource centers provide the pregnant and parenting student a wide range of health, educational, and social services. A case management team that includes a social worker, teacher, and nurse interacts with the students' parents and closely monitors the academic progress, attendance, and health of each girl.

Since it is estimated that approximately 50 to 67% of adolescent girls who drop out of high school do so because of pregnancy, the educational implications of teenage pregnancy are profound (Phipps-Yonas, 1980). However, the school's problems are not over if the teen mother drops out. Many of the children of teen mothers are at risk educationally and psychologically and often are overrepresented in classes for the learning disabled and emotionally disturbed (Bonjean & Rittenmeyer, 1987). These "children of children" very often become adolescent parents themselves, repeating the cycle and worsening the problem.

AIDS

Acquired immune deficiency syndrome (AIDS) is a serious disease caused by a virus that destroys the immune system and leaves the body susceptible to infection. Two diseases identified in AIDS patients are *Pneumocystis carinii* pneumonia, an infection of the lungs, and a rare form of cancer, Kaposi's sarcoma, both of which can cause death.

About 1.5 million Americans have been infected with the AIDS virus. Since a cure has not yet been found for AIDS, it is estimated that at least 20 to 30% of these individuals will develop AIDS within five years. It is estimated further that by the year 1991, some 270,000 individuals in the United States will contract AIDS and approximately 179,000 of them probably will die (American Council of Life Insurance, 1987).

Vulnerability of Teens and Youth

Only about 1% of AIDS cases occur in individuals under the age of 20, but there is growing evidence that teens and young adults are increasingly at risk for contracting the disease (Yarber, 1987). The reasons why this group is at high risk for AIDS are that:

- A significant number of adolescents are sexually active, which increases their risk of exposure to the AIDS virus. Research indicates that by age 19, approximately 63% of females and 78% of males have had at least one coital experience, and approximately 28% of youngsters 12 to 17 are sexually active (National Research Council, 1987).

- Approximately five million teenagers are intravenous drug users (Yarber, 1987), and sharing of needles by drug users greatly increases the risk of infection of the AIDS virus.

- Approximately 50% of the cases of sexually transmitted diseases (STDs) (AIDS is one example of an STD) occur in persons 25 years of age or younger (Yarber, 1987).

- As many as 80% of teenage runaways eventually become involved in prostitution, which places them at high risk for AIDS (Community Update, cited in AIDS, and Teens, 1987).

Identifying AIDS

The following are some of the more common symptoms of AIDS or a less severe condition known as AIDS-Related Complex (ARC): (1) low energy, easy fatigue, or generalized weakness; (2) fevers or night sweats; (3) weight loss; (4) persistent cough; (5) persistent diarrhea; (6) depression or anxiety; (7) lack of concentration or forgetfulness; and (8) headache, nausea, and vomiting (Social Security Administration, 1989).

Prevention Strategies

Since AIDS is a serious public health problem that has far-reaching implications for our society, the schools have an obligation to offer prevention or educational strategies that address this problem. However, there is considerable controversy among school officials, health educators, and governmental officials regarding the most effective approach to AIDS education. The federal government has taken the position that is should not mandate a specific AIDS curriculum, but should leave such a curriculum up to the local school districts (Yarber, 1987).

What type of AIDS educational curriculum would be best suited for the elementary school?

A number of vocal community and religious groups have argued that sexual abstinence and marital fidelity should be the only prevention method emphasized in the AIDS educational program. Although the majority of school curricula do suggest that sexual abstinence is the most effective prevention strategy, a significant number of the schools also suggest that the educational curricula should include information on such topics as using condoms, restricting sex to monogamous relationships, and not sharing IV drug needles and syringes (Yarber, 1987).

Most communities do support AIDS education in the schools; however, a number of communities have requested that parental consent should be obtained before any student participates in such an education program. A study of AIDS education in the schools indicated that of the 73 largest school districts in the country, approximately 45% of them did require parental permission (U.S. Conference of Mayors, 1987).

Intervention Strategies

In 1985, the Center for Disease Control issued guidelines to assist schools in developing policies and procedures for individuals with AIDS in the school environment. These guidelines recommend that students who have developed AIDS or are infected with the AIDS virus should not be excluded from school attendance except under certain circumstances (see discussion in Chapter 12).

It behooves each school district to develop an AIDS education curriculum and establish policies and procedures concerning how the institution will respond to those who already have AIDS or are carrying the AIDS virus. To do less would be negligent.

Today's teacher cannot ignore the reality of AIDS or ARC. With the increasing number of adolescents who are sexually active, are intravenous drug users, or are runaways who become involved in prostitution, unfortunately, most teachers will probably encounter a student with the AIDS virus at some time in their professional career.

Child Abuse and Sexual Abuse

Child abuse is the repeated mistreatment or neglect of a child which can result in physical, emotional, verbal, or sexual injury or harm (Bete, 1990). More than 1.5 million cases of child abuse or child neglect are reported annually to local child protective agencies (Distad, 1987). *Sexual abuse* of children is defined as:

> contact or interaction between a child and an adult when the child is being used for the sexual stimulation of the perpetrator or another person. Sexual abuse may also be committed by a person under the age of 18 when that person is either significantly older than the victim or when the perpetrator is in a position of power or control over another child. (U.S. Department of Health and Human Services, 1979, p. 1)

Sexual abuse is classified as nonincestuous or incestuous. Father-daughter incest is the most frequently reported, accounting for approximately 75% of all reported cases (Pettis & Hughes, 1985). More recently, a growing number of extrafamilial sexual abuse cases have been reported involving teens who are stepsiblings of the opposite sex (Finkelhor, 1979).

The Extent of the Problem of Sexual Abuse

It is estimated that approximately 5.5 children per 10,000 enrolled in day care facilities are sexually abused each year. Furthermore, it is estimated that 8.9 children per 10,000 who are under the age of six years are sexually abused in their homes (Report Addresses, 1989). In total, approximately 336,000 children are sexually abused every year in the United States. Although this number may seem to be astonishingly large, it has been suggested that the reported cases constitute only 9% of all child sexual abuse cases (Jones, 1982).

According to the National Committee for the Prevention of Child Abuse, the reported cases of sexual abuse have increased considerably during the past few years. Research indicates that in the United States, approximately 25% of adult women and 8% of adult men were sexually abused as children. In 85% of the reported cases, the children were abused by someone they knew (Herman, 1985). The average age of victims of sexual abuse is approximately 8.5 years (Dezseran & Myerson-Katz, 1985). The majority of victims are female

(80% or more), while the majority of perpetrators are male (90%) (Pettis & Hughes, 1985).

Identifying Child Abuse and Sexual Abuse

Some of the common signs or indicators of child abuse include repeated physical injuries such as bruises, cuts, burns, missing hair, etc. The abused child will often exhibit a variety of behavior changes including aggressive or withdrawn behavior, neglected appearance, anxiety or fear, attention seeking behavior, fatigue, and frequent tardiness or absence from school. The adult abuser may appear super-critical, seem unconcerned about the child's welfare, and become defensive when questioned about the child's health or safety (Bete, 1990). Some of the indicators of sexual abuse you should be on the alert for as a teacher are listed on page 335. While these indicators may or may not point to sexual molestation, if two or more of them appear the matter should be investigated and, if warranted, reported to the appropriate authority.

What are the procedures for reporting child abuse in your state?

As discussed in Chapter 12, state child abuse statutes require that child abuse, including child molestation, be reported by school counselors, school psychologists, social workers, teachers, nurses, or administrators to the local child protective agency, department of welfare, or law enforcement agency. It is important that prospective and practicing teachers be familiar with the applicable statutes in their state.

Prevention Strategies

Since 1980, a number of child abuse and sexual abuse prevention programs have been introduced. The majority of these programs serve the following objectives: (1) to increase the child's and teen's knowledge about sexual abuse; (2) to enhance the child's and teen's awareness of the risk of sexual molestation; and (3) to identify children and adolescents who are in abusive situations (Graham & Harris-Hart, 1988). Many school districts have incorporated the prevention program content into the health education curriculum in order to keep it outside the controversial sex education domain. The use of humor and entertainment also have been used with all grade levels to transmit information about sexual abuse through theater performances, art, role playing, play therapy, puppets, coloring books, *bibliotherapy,* and so forth. Bibliotherapy includes the use of selected reading materials as a therapeutic prevention technique.

Intervention Strategies

The most important intervention strategy, particularly for the child or teen who suffers from physical injury, malnutrition, or neglect, is immediate treatment. Support services and counseling also are important interventions for the victim. Crisis intervention centers, self-help groups, crisis hotlines, and law enforcement agencies all have contributed to intervention efforts for the abused child or adolescent and his or her family. Of all the prevention and

For Future Reference:
Indicators of Sexual Abuse

The following are some behavioral indicators of sexual abuse that you are in a position to observe as a teacher:

- personality change

- change from being outgoing to clingy

- regression in toilet-training habits

- signs of being uncomfortable with someone formerly trusted

- withdrawal into self

- sophisticated sexual knowledge, beyond what is expected for age group

- moodiness, excessive crying

- changes in eating, sleeping habits

- increased activity

- behavior problems

- unusual shyness

- sudden, unfounded fears

- unusual need for reassurance, needing to be told "you're okay"

- unnatural interest in own or other's genitals

- poor peer relations or absence of friends

- gender role confusion

- consistently leaving early for school and arriving late

- inappropriate sexual self-consciousness

Source: Herman, P. (1985). Educating children about sexual abuse. *Childhood Education, 61,* 174. Reprinted by permission of the Association for Childhood Education International, 11141 Georgia Avenue, Suite 200, Wheaton, MD. Copyright © 1985 by the Association.

---

early intervention efforts, strengthening the family is probably the best hope for preventing any future child abuse, sexual molestation, or neglect.

Since child abuse and sexual abuse are prevalent in all socioeconomic classes and ethnic and racial groups, it is possible that you will be confronted with this problem during your teaching career. When this happens, it is important to remember not only your legal obligations but your obligations to your students. Although these are normally delicate and emotionally charged situations, avoidance is not the appropriate response. If you are in error, better that it be on the side of the child's welfare. Remember, you are protected from civil or criminal liability for reporting the alleged abuse.

Running Away and Homelessness

The U.S. House Select Committee on Children, Youth, and Families in its 1989 report, *No Place to Call Home: Discarded Children in America,* estimated that by 1995 almost one million children will no longer be living with their parents and will cause serious problems for the schools. Some of these children will be in foster homes, some in mental health facilities, and others will be runaways. Other estimates are that 220,000 school-aged children are homeless, another 186,000 are "precariously housed," living on the verge of homelessness, and 65,000 of the homeless children do not attend school (Reed & Sautter, 1990).

Profile of Runaway and Homeless Youth

There are no typical runaways—children or youth under the age of 18 who are away from home at least overnight without permission from a parent or guardian. Research indicates that 36% run from physical and sexual abuse; 44% run from dysfunctional families with drug abusing or alcoholic parents; and 20% run from divorce, illness, death of a loved one, and school-related problems (Hersch, 1988).

Many runaway youth experience severe emotional problems. One study found that as many as 30% of the runaways in youth shelters in New York City could be categorized as depressed, 18% as antisocial, and 41% as both depressed and antisocial. Furthermore, 25% had attempted suicide and another 25% had seriously contemplated suicide (Hersch, 1988).

Significant numbers of these runaway and homeless adolescents suffer from a wide range of infectious diseases, including tuberculosis and whooping cough (Reed & Sautter, 1990). Many also are placed in extraordinary danger of contracting AIDS since they resort to drug use, drug dealing, and prostitution for income.

A study by the University of California at Berkeley's Alcohol Research Group found that 79% of homeless teens had been homeless more than once, and 57% had lived part of their lives in a foster or group home. The study also found that many of the homeless suffered from alcohol and other substance abuse, as well as depression. Nearly half had attempted suicide more than once. Additionally, approximately 44% of the females reported one or more pregnancies, with one-quarter being pregnant at the time of the study (Landers, 1989).

Identifying Potential Runaway and Homeless Youth

As with other conditions for which youth are at risk, experience and research have revealed certain warning signs that may be used in identification and prevention efforts. Among these are:

- discipline problems at school
- alcohol and other substance abuse
- increased sleeping or a desire to be alone
- poor school performance or an unusual drop in grades
- repeated truancy
- abrupt mood swings
- increased breaking of rules (Bete, 1989, p. 6)

The majority of youth who exhibit some of the above symptoms probably never will run away. However, these signs may help identify a potential runaway youngster who is in need of professional help.

Prevention Strategies

Parents and teachers are in a key position in regard to preventing their children and students from running away. Some recommended prevention efforts include providing accurate information about drugs, alcohol, and sex; encouraging responsible decision making; building self-esteem; making learning a positive experience; getting professional help where necessary; setting up rules and regulations that are fair and appropriate for youth; being honest with one's feelings; and being a good listener (Bete, 1989).

Intervention Strategies

Intervention strategies are normally outside the domain of the schools. Runaway shelters, runaway hotlines, and a host of other outreach projects designed to provide emergency help in the form of counseling, temporary housing, and medical care are the major intervention strategies used with runaway and homeless youth. Reaching the runaway youngster will continue to be a challenge through the 1990s.

The number of runaway children and youth is staggering, as is the serious nature of the many problems faced by these children and teens. The estimates of homeless youth are equally overwhelming. Tomorrow's teacher cannot afford to be ill prepared to meet the challenge of working with these at-risk groups.

What type of shelters are available in your community for runaway and homeless youth? Has there been community resistance to the location of these shelters?

Delinquency and Teen Violence

There are varied definitions of *delinquency* or delinquency-prone adolescents. In defining delinquency, Bortner (1988) distinguishes between juveniles who are accused of committing adultlike crimes and those who allegedly are involved in status offenses. According to Bortner, those juveniles who are accused of committing adultlike crimes are defined as "delinquents," while those who allegedly are involved in status offenses are referred to as "youths in need of supervision."

Delinquent acts range from misdemeanors such as shoplifting, disturbing the peace, or minor theft to felonies including murder, rape, robbery, arson, or motor vehicle theft. Status offenses by their very nature are acts for which only juveniles can be arrested. They include possession of alcohol, running away, truancy, incorrigibility, or curfew violation (Bortner, 1988).

Identification of Youth Gang Members

There are a variety of identifiable symbols of gang membership. For example, graffiti is a popular form of written expression. Dress, use of specific colors in clothing, and hair style also may indicate gang presence or gang identification. Gang members use hand signals as well as their own secret verbal and nonverbal language to communicate with each other.

Skinheads

What gangs are active in your community? To what extent have they been associated with youth violence?

Recently, a new subculture has infiltrated gangs—the so-called neo-Nazis or *skinheads*. Skinheads participate in virtually every type of hate movement rally, march, or meeting. It is estimated that these specific youth gang members are increasing their membership more rapidly than any other subgroup. Their presence is currently felt in at least one-half the states.

Prevention Strategies

The primary goal of gang or delinquency prevention programs is to identify juveniles who are at risk of becoming delinquents. With the increased number of gangs and gang-related crimes, a number of school districts have established gang prevention programs. For example, the Los Angeles Unified

Skinheads tend to identify with hate movements and are a growing subculture.

School District has introduced a special program aimed at building self-esteem, identifying alternative social activities, and focusing on the negative outcomes of gang membership. This particular prevention program is aimed at the younger elementary age student (Vican, 1988). Another prevention program is the controversial documentary film shown in many schools, *Scared Straight,* which emphasizes the negative consequences of crime. Similarly, the Juvenile Awareness Project conducted at the New Jersey Rahway State Prison provides confrontation sessions between youth and adult prisoners (Bortner, 1988).

Intervention Strategies

Examples of intervention strategies include traditional probation as well as programs such as "halfway houses" designed for juveniles while they participate in educational or treatment programs in the community. The employment of gang members or gang leaders within the community, community support groups for juvenile offenders, and incarceration for the small group of violent juveniles who are a threat to public safety represent the range of intervention possibilities.

Impact on the Schools

Crime and violence in our public schools has been a major problem of the past decade and is likely to continue unless major changes occur. The crimes perpetrated in the schools are similar to the crimes committed in the streets and neighborhoods of our cities and include extortion, gambling, stabbings, rapes, murders, and assaults on teachers and students (David & David, 1980).

With the increased number of adolescents carrying and using firearms, our nation's schools are beset with a serious problem. According to the U.S. Department of Justice, more than 27,000 youths between the ages of 12 and 15 were handgun victims in one year (Hackett, Sandza, Gibney, & Gareiss, 1988).

Gangs and gang violence have transformed many of our nation's schools into campuses where fear, intimidation, and crime prevail. Drug trafficking, vandalism, extortion, arson, theft, assault, and murder are a few of the negative consequences of gangs in schools. What was once considered a phenomenon of large inner city populations has become a problem of even the so-called suburban or "bedroom" communities. It is estimated that Chicago has at least 125 gangs, with a membership of approximately 15,000 (Haddock, 1988), and Los Angeles has approximately 430 gangs with a membership of 50,000 (Vican, 1988).

The schools are in a critical position to prevent delinquency or gang membership before it occurs by identifying the potential at-risk populations. Inner city, minority, and poor male juveniles tend to be at the highest risk for juvenile offenses. Teachers, counselors, social workers, nurses, and administrators need to be aware of the student's family environment, neighborhood environment, and past record of crime and delinquency so that they can identify the potential youth offender and recommend the most appropriate services and programs within the school and community. Unfortunately, far too many juvenile offenders drop out of school before they are identified or before they receive the appropriate help.

Summary

At-risk children and youth are a particular challenge for school personnel and mental health professionals. There are, however, a number of predictors for identifying the at-risk student. Because of their association with students, teachers play a vital role in identifying at-risk students.

Prevention and intervention programs for a variety of at-risk behaviors have become the combined responsibility of schools, social service agencies, religious organizations, parent groups, and law enforcement agencies. Although for each at-risk behavior a number of prevention and intervention strategies and programs have been devised, growing evidence supports the primacy of early identification and treatment, reinforcing both the opportunity and the responsibility of teachers and other educators in the success of prevention and intervention efforts.

In Chapter 12 we will expand our discussion of the responsibilities of teachers. In that chapter we will also consider their legal rights, as well as those of their students. But first we will explore the legal basis for public education and the legal issues surrounding the church-state relationship in education in Chapter 11.

Key Terms

Acquired immune deficiency syndrome (AIDS)
At risk
Bibliotherapy
Child abuse
Clinical depression
Cluster suicides
Crisis intervention team
Cult
Delinquency

Dropout
Gateway drugs
Intervention programs
Postvention programs
Prevention programs
Sexual abuse
Skinheads
Suicide gesture
Suicide ideation
Suicide threat

Discussion Questions

1. How can the school help in combating teen pregnancy? AIDS? How comfortable would you be in discussing "safe sex" with students in the middle grades?

2. How does peer pressure contribute to adolescent substance abuse and youth violence? How can teachers use the power of peer influence to combat these same problems?

3. Compare the behavioral indicators of substance abuse with those of child abuse and sexual abuse.

4. How does a destructive cult differ from other youth groups?

5. If a student approached you, the teacher, and indicated that he or she had a plan for committing suicide, how would you respond?

6. A popular television advertisement states that society will either "pay now, or pay later." Discuss this message in relation to investments in educational programs to combat the dropout problem.

7. What is the relationship between being at risk for becoming a runaway and other at-risk conditions? What are the common identifying characteristics?

References

Addis, M., Schulman-Miller, J., & Lightman, M. (1984). The cult clinic helps families in crisis. *Social Casework, 65,* 515–522.

AIDS, and teens and sex and drugs. (July/August, 1987). *Chemical People Newsletter.*

Alan Guttmacher Institute (1981). *Teenage pregnancy: The problem that hasn't gone away.* New York: Author.

American Council of Life Insurance and Health Insurance Association of America (1987). *Teens & AIDS: Playing it safe.* Washington, DC: American Council of Life Insurance.

Ascher, C., & Schwartz, W. (1987). *Keeping track of at risk students.* New York: ERIC Clearinghouse on Urban Education.

Barrett, T. C. (1989, November 22). Evaluation of suicide-prevention programs. *Education Week,* 36.

Bete, C. L. (1989). *About youth runaways.* South Deerfield, MA: Channing L. Bete Co.

Bete, C. L. (1990). *About child abuse.* South Deerfield, MA: Channing L. Bete Co.

Bialo, E. R., & Sivin, J. P. (1989). Computers and at-risk youth: A partial solution to a complex problem. *Classroom Computer Learning, 9*(5), 48–52.

Bonjean, L. M., & Rittenmeyer, D. C. (1987). *Teenage parenthood: The school's response.* Bloomington, IN: Phi Delta Kappa Educational Foundation.

Bortner, M. A. (1988). *Delinquency and justice: An age of crisis.* New York: McGraw-Hill.

Buscemi, M. (1985). What schools are doing to prevent alcohol and drug abuse. *The School Administrator, 42*(9), 11–14.

Cohen-Sandler, R., Berman, A. L., & King, R. A. (1982). Life-stress and symptomatology: Determinants of suicidal behavior in children. *Journal of the American Academy of Child Psychiatry, 21,* 178–186.

Council of Chief State School Officers. (1987). *Characteristics of at-risk students.* Washington, DC: Author.

Cult Awareness Network. (1985). *A handbook for newcomers.* New York: Citizens Freedom Foundation.

David, L., & David, I. (1980). *Violence in our schools.* New York: Public Affairs Pamphlet.

Dezseran, C., & Myerson-Katz, B. (1985). Theatre-in-education and child sexual abuse: A descriptive study. *Children's Theatre Review, 34*(4), 7–13.

Distad, L. (1987). A personal legacy. *Phi Delta Kappan, 68,* 744–745.

Dorman, G., Geldof, D., & Scarborough, B. (1982). *Living with 10-to-15-year-olds: A parent education curriculum.* Carrboro, NC: Center for Early Adolescence, University of North Carolina-Chapel Hill.

Ferguson, W. E. (1981). Gifted adolescents, stress, and life changes. *Adolescence, 16,* 973–985.

Finkelhor, D. (1979). *Sexually victimized children.* New York: Free Press.

The Flinn Foundation. (1989). *An occasional report about the ongoing work of grantees of the Flinn Foundation.* Phoenix, AZ: Author.

Frase, M. J. (September, 1989). *Dropout rates in the United States: 1988.* Washington, DC: U.S. Department of Education, National Center for Educational Statistics, 2.

Frazier, S. H. (June, 1985). *Task force on youth suicide.* Paper presented at the meeting of the National Conference on Youth Suicide, Washington, DC.

Frymier, J. (1988). Understanding and preventing teen suicide: An interview with Barry Garfinkle. *Phi Delta Kappan, 70,* 290–293.

Frymier, J., & Gansneder, B. (1989). The Phi Delta Kappa study of students at risk. *Phi Delta Kappan, 71,* 142–146.

Gersten, J. C., & Shamis, S. (1988). Review of risk factors for children's mental health problems. *Children at risk.* Tempe, AZ: Arizona State University, 1–96.

Graham, L., & Harris-Hart, M. (1988). Meeting the challenge of child sexual abuse. *Journal of School Health, 58,* 292–294.

Greene, B. Z. (September, 1986). Lower the risk for "at risk" students. *Updating School Board Policies, 17*(8), 1–3.

Greuling, J. W., & DeBlassie, R. R. (1980). Adolescent suicide. *Adolescence, 15,* 589–601.

Grossnickle, D. R. (1986). *High school dropouts: Causes, consequences, and cure.* Bloomington, IN: Phi Delta Kappa Educational Foundation, 1–26.

Hackett, G., Sandza, R., Gibney, F., & Gareiss, R. (1988). Kids: deadly force. *Newsweek, 3*(2), 18–19.

Haddock, V. (December 6, 1988). California: Days late dollars short. *San Francisco Examiner,* E3.

Hayes, L. (September 24, 1987). Dropout problem attracts widespread attention. *Guidepost.* Washington, DC: American Association for Counseling and Development, *30*(4), 10.

Hayes, R. L., & Cryer, N. (1987). Urban adolescents give birth to children: A developmental approach to the issue of teen pregnancy. *Counseling and Human Development, 20*(1), 1–12.

Herman, P. (1985). Educating children about sexual abuse. *Childhood Education: The Teacher's Responsibility, 61,* 169–174.

Hersch, P. (1988). Coming of age on city streets. *Psychology Today, 22*(1), 28–37.

Hipple, J., & Cimbolic, P. (1979). *The counselor and suicidal crisis.* Springfield, IL: Charles C. Thomas.

Johnson, J. H., & McCutcheon, S. M. (1980). Assessing life stress in older children and adolescents: Preliminary findings with the life events checklist. In I. G. Sarason & C. D. Spielberger (Eds.), *Stress and anxiety.* Washington, DC: Hemisphere.

Jones, J. G. (1982). Sexual abuse of children. *American Journal of Diseases of Children, 136*(2), 142–146.

Kelson v. The City of Springfield, 767F 2d. 651 (1985), *aff'd.* 823F 2d. 554.

Lachance, L. (1985). *Teen pregnancy: An ERIC/CAPS fact sheet.* Ann Arbor, MI: ERIC Clearinghouse on Counseling & Personnel Services.

Landers, S. (1989). For runaway youth, a homeless existence. *The APA Monitor, 20*(11), 27.

Lawton, M. (1991, April 10). More than a third of teens surveyed say they have contemplated suicide. *Education Week,* p. 5.

MacDonald, D. I. (1984). Drugs, drinking, and adolescence. *American Journal of Drug Counseling, 138,* 117–125.

McGarrahan, E., & Brecher, E. J. (December 19, 1989). Pulling driving rights of dropouts triggers an outburst of yawns. *The Arizona Republic,* A6.

Morrison, J. R., & Jensen, S. (1982). Teenage pregnancy: Special counseling considerations. *The Clearinghouse, 56*(2), 74–77.

Mrela, C. (1989). *Suicide mortality: Arizona, 1983–1988.* Phoenix, AZ: Arizona Department of Health Services.

National Research Council. (1987). *Risking the future: Adolescent sexuality, pregnancy, and childbearing.* Washington, DC: National Academy Press.

Natriello, G. (Ed.). (1987). *School dropouts: Patterns and policies.* New York: Teachers College Press.

Newcomb, M. D., & Bentler, P. M. (1988). *Consequences of adolescent drug use.* Beverly Hills, CA: Sage.

Pettis, K. W., & Hughes, R. D. (1985). Sexual victimization of children: A current perspective. *Behavioral Disorders, 10,* 136–144.

Pfeffer, C. (1986). *The suicidal child.* New York: Guilford Press.

Phi Delta Kappa. (September, 1988). Current issues memo: Responding to student suicide—The first 48 hours. Bloomington, IN: Author.

Phipps-Yonas, S. (1980). Teenage pregnancy and motherhood: A review of the literature. *American Journal of Orthopsychiatry, 50,* 403–431.

Reed, S., & Sautter, R. C. (1990). Children of poverty: The status report of 12 million young Americans. *Phi Delta Kappan, 71,* K1–K12.

Report addresses child sexual abuse in day care. (January/February, 1989), *The Police News of New Jersey,* 56.

Robertson, N., & Frymier, J. (1989). *Developing a measure of at-riskness.* Unpublished paper. Bloomington, IN: Phi Delta Kappa.

Rosauer, R. (1987). Teen pregnancy. *The ECS survey of state initiatives for youth at risk.* Denver, CO: The Education Commission of the States.

Ruof, S. R., & Harris, J. M. (1989). The school corner, school suicide prevention programs: Legal issues. *Newslink.* Denver, CO: American Association of Suicidology, *14*(2), 8.

Salzman, K. P., & Salzman, S. A. (1989). *Characteristics of adolescents at risk for psychological dysfunction and school failure.* Paper presented at the Annual Convention of the American Educational Research Association, San Francisco, CA.

Sherman, J. D. (December, 1987). *Dropping out of school: Executive summary.* Washington, DC: Pelavin Associates.

Singer, M. T. (1979). Coming out of the cults. *Psychology Today, 12*(1), 72–82.

Singer, M. & West, L. J. (1980). Cults, quacks, and non-professional psychotherapies. In H. Kaplain, A. Freedman, & B. Sadock (Eds.), *Comprehensive textbook of psychiatry III.* Baltimore, MD: Williams & Wilkins.

Social Security Administration. (April, 1989). *Providing medical evidence for individuals with AIDS and ARC: A guide for health professionals.* Washington, DC: U.S. Government Printing Office.

Spano, J. (October 27, 1988). Threat from skinhead gangs reported on rise. *Los Angeles Times,* G10.

Stark, E. (1986). Young, innocent and pregnant. *Psychology Today, 20*(10), 28–30.

Strother, D. B. (1986). Practical applications of research: Suicide among the young. *Phi Delta Kappan, 67,* 756–759.

U.S. Conference of Mayors. (January, 1987). *Local school districts active in AIDS education: AIDS information exchange.*

U.S. Department of Education, National Center for Education Statistics. (1989). *Digest of education statistics 1989.* Washington, DC: U.S. Government Printing Office.

U.S. Department of Education, Office of Educational Research and Improvement. (November, 1987). *Dealing with dropouts: The urban superintendents' call to action.* Washington, DC: U.S. Government Printing Office.

U.S. Department of Education, Office of Educational Research and Improvement. (1988). *Drug prevention curricula: A guide to selection and implementation.* Washington, DC: U.S. Government Printing Office.

U.S. Department of Health and Human Services. (1979). *Child sexual abuse: Incest, assault, and sexual exploitation.* Special report from the National Center on Child Abuse and Neglect. Washington, DC: U.S. Government Printing Office.

U.S. Department of Health and Human Services, National Institute on Drug Abuse. (1989). *Drug use among American high school students, college students, and other young adults.* Washington, DC: U.S. Government Printing Office.

Vican, L. (1988). The growing threat of gang violence. *School and College, 27*(4), 25–26, 28–29.

Wallace, H. W., Weeks, J., & Medina, A. (1982). Services for the needs of pregnant teenagers in large cities of the United States, 1979–1980. *Public Health Reports, 97,* 583–588.

Welte, J. W., & Barnes, G. M. (1985). Alcohol: The gateway to other drug use among secondary-school students. *Journal of Youth and Adolescence, 14,* 487–498.

Yarber, W. L. (1987). *AIDS education: Curriculum and health policy.* Bloomington, IN: Phi Delta Kappa Educational Foundation.

Yeaworth, C. R., York, J., Hussey, M. A., Ingle, M. E., & Goodwin, T. (1980). The development of an adolescent life change event scale. *Adolescence, 15,* 91–98.

Part Five

Legal and Political Control and Financial Support

Legal Framework for the Public Schools **Chapter 11**
Teachers, Students, and the Law **Chapter 12**
Organizing and Administering Elementary and Secondary Schools **Chapter 13**
Financing Public Education **Chapter 14**

Chapter 11

Legal Framework for the Public Schools

The Law is the true embodiment
Of everything that's excellent.

W. S. Gilbert (1836–1911)

During the lunch recess, a teacher at Oceanview High School discovered two girls smoking in the lavatory. Because smoking in the lavatory was a violation of a school rule, the teacher took the two girls to the office of the principal, Harold Rose. In response to questioning by Mr. Rose, one of the girls admitted smoking, while the second girl, Susan Kramer, denied that she had been smoking and claimed that she did not smoke at all.

Mr. Rose then demanded to see Susan's purse. Opening the purse he found a pack of cigarettes. As he reached into the purse for the cigarettes he also noticed a package of cigarette rolling papers. Knowing that such papers were often used for smoking marijuana, Mr. Rose suspected that a closer examination of the purse might yield evidence of drug use. A thorough search of the purse did, indeed, yield a small amount of marijuana, a pipe, several empty plastic bags, a large number of one dollar bills, and an index card that appeared to be a record of students who owed Susan money. Confronted with this evidence, Susan confessed that she had been selling marijuana at the high school.

What should Mr. Rose do now? What federal constitutional amendments are involved in the case? How would you have handled the case if you had been the teacher? The principal? What would you do if you were Susan's parent or guardian?

School officials such as Mr. Rose exercise considerable authority in the control of public education. The basis for that authority is grounded in the law. The basis for Susan's right to be free from unreasonable search and seizure is also found in the law. The *law* may be defined as "a body of rules of action or conduct prescribed by controlling authority, and having binding legal force" (Black, 1983, p. 457). It is within the rules of action or conduct provided by federal and state constitutional provisions, federal and state statutory law, regulations and decisions of administrative agencies, court decisions, and attorney general opinions that the framework is established for the operation of the public schools. Before going into the specifics of the law as they affect students' and teachers' rights, this chapter provides a brief overview of the major sources of school law, the federal and state court systems, and their interrelationship in forming the legal basis for public education. After reading this chapter you should be able to:

- Identify federal constitutional provisions affecting education.

- Discuss the importance of state constitutional provisions affecting education.

- Compare statutory law, common law, and administrative law.

- Describe the levels of the federal court system and those of a typical state court system.

- Explain how challenges under the establishment clause are evaluated.

- Give the current posture of the courts in regard to prayer and Bible reading, student devotional activities, compulsory attendance, and private and home schooling.

- Distinguish between permissible and impermissible state aid to nonpublic education.

Federal Constitutional Provisions Affecting Education

Written contracts for the establishment of governments, known as *constitutions*, are uniquely American (Collins, 1969). Constitutions are the highest level of law. They are the fundamental laws of the people of a state or nation, establishing the very character and concept of their government, its organization and officers, its sovereign powers and the limitations of its power. Constitutions are written broadly so as to endure changing times and circumstances. While constitutions can be changed by amendment, the process is normally difficult and is seldom utilized. The Constitution of the United States, written over two hundred years ago, has served the needs of a fledgling nation and a world power, with only 26 amendments.

Education, though, is not mentioned in the United States Constitution. It is therefore considered to be one of the powers reserved to the states by the Tenth Amendment, which states, "The powers not delegated to the United States by the Constitution, nor prohibited by it to the States, are reserved to the states respectively, or to the people." Although the provision of education is considered one of the powers of the state, the supremacy clause of the Constitution (Article VI, Section 2) declares that the Constitution and the laws enacted by the United States Congress are the supreme law of the land. Thus the states, in exercising their authority, may not enact any laws that violate any provisions of the federal Constitution.

Several important sections of the federal Constitution have an impact on the schools (see Figure 11.1). Among these are Article I, Section 8; Article I, Section 10; and the First, Fourth, Fifth, Eighth, Ninth, Tenth, and Fourteenth Amendments. These constitutional provisions serve as the basis for education-related cases being brought to federal courts.

General Welfare Clause

In what ways does federal support of education contribute to the "common defense" of the United States?

Article I, Section 8, known as the general welfare clause, gives Congress the power to tax and to "provide for the common defense and general welfare of the United States." Over the years, the Supreme Court has interpreted the general welfare clause as authorizing Congress to tax and spend money for a variety of activities, education among them, that were construed as being in the general welfare. However, the general welfare clause does not give Congress the authority to do anything it pleases to provide for the general welfare, only to tax for that purpose. In regard to education, this means that while Congress may levy taxes to provide support for education, it may not legislate control of education. However, in recent years the Supreme Court has ruled that the federal government can attach conditions to the use of federal funds which, if not complied with, may result in the denial or withdrawal of the funds.

Exercising its authority under the general welfare clause, Congress has enacted a massive body of legislation that has provided direct federal support

Figure 11.1: Laws Affecting the Schools

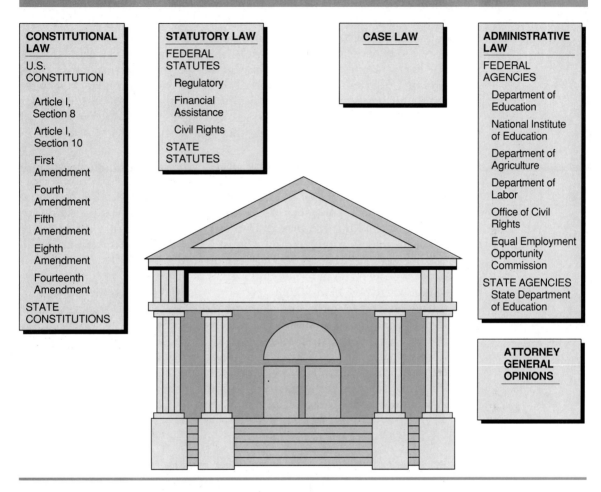

CONSTITUTIONAL LAW

U.S. CONSTITUTION

Article I, Section 8

Article I, Section 10

First Amendment

Fourth Amendment

Fifth Amendment

Eighth Amendment

Fourteenth Amendment

STATE CONSTITUTIONS

STATUTORY LAW

FEDERAL STATUTES

Regulatory

Financial Assistance

Civil Rights

STATE STATUTES

CASE LAW

ADMINISTRATIVE LAW

FEDERAL AGENCIES

Department of Education

National Institute of Education

Department of Agriculture

Department of Labor

Office of Civil Rights

Equal Employment Opportunity Commission

STATE AGENCIES
State Department of Education

ATTORNEY GENERAL OPINIONS

for a variety of instructional programs (e.g., foreign language education, math education, science education, adult education, career education, vocational and technical education), as well as providing services and programs for identified special need students (e.g., free and reduced-cost food programs, special education, bilingual education) and financial assistance to prospective teachers. Article I, Section 8 has also served as the authority for the federal government to establish the U.S. military academies (Air Force, Army, Coast Guard, and Navy), operate overseas schools for dependents of military and civilian personnel, and establish schools on Indian reservations, in the U.S. territories, and in the District of Columbia. In addition, Congress may operate libraries, such as the Library of Congress, and conduct a variety of other activities and operations deemed educational in nature.

Obligations of Contracts Clause

Article I, Section 10, the obligations of contracts clause, declares: "No state shall . . . pass any Bill of Attainder, *ex post facto* law, or law impairing the obligation of Contracts." This provision of the Constitution prohibits a state legislature from passing a law relative to teacher tenure or retirement that would be to the detriment of teachers who had acquired a contractive status under existing statutes. The obligation of contracts clause also protects school personnel who have contracts from arbitrary dismissals. That is, a teacher who has a contract cannot be dismissed during the term of that contract without a showing of cause and without due process (see discussion in Chapter 12).

The obligation of contracts clause protects both the school board and those businesses and individuals with whom it does business from nonperformance relative to the terms of the contract. For example, a Louisiana school district entered into a contract for the building of a junior high school to replace one that had burned down. The contract provided that the building was to be substantially completed by August 1. According to the contract, the school board was to be paid $200 for every day after August 1 that the building was not completed. When the building was not completed until September 4 the school board withheld $6,600 from the final payment to the contractor. The contractor sued for recovery, claiming that the delay was excused under a clause in the contract that allowed for extensions caused by adverse weather conditions. The school board's action was upheld on appeal because the contractor did not present proof that the rain and cold weather experienced was in excess of what an experienced contractor should have taken into account in estimating time for weather losses when bidding on contracts that have a term for performance (*S. J. Lemoine v. St. Landry Parrish School*, 1988).

First Amendment

The First Amendment addresses several basic personal freedoms. It provides that:

> Congress shall make no law respecting an establishment of religion, or prohibiting the free exercise thereof; or abridging the freedom of speech or of the press; or of the right of the people peaceably to assemble, and to petition the Government for a redress of grievances.

Increasingly, the first clause of the First Amendment, the establishment and free exercise of religion clause, has become the focus of litigation in education. The schools have become a battleground for some of the most volatile disputes over the appropriate governmental relationship vis-à-vis religion (McCarthy & Cambron-McCabe, 1987). As discussed later in this chapter, these cases have dealt with numerous issues surrounding: (1) school practices objected to on the basis of promoting or inhibiting religion (e.g., released time, prayer, and Bible reading), (2) curriculum content, and (3) public funds used to provide support to nonpublic schools or to students or parents of students attending nonpublic schools.

The second clause of the First Amendment, that dealing with the freedom of speech and press, has also been the subject of a growing number of education cases in recent years. Both teachers and students have increasingly protested abridgements of their rights to express themselves—from wearing of long hair to publicly criticizing school board practices. Teachers have also become more concerned with what they consider attempts to infringe upon their academic freedom to select textbooks and other teaching materials and to practice certain teaching methodologies.

The third clause of the First Amendment, which deals with the rights of citizens to assemble, has also been called into question in a number of education cases concerning the freedom of association. Both students and teachers have become more assertive of their right to belong to various organizations including those that may have goals contrary to that of the school system. The question of freedom of association has also been at issue in a number of cases dealing with teachers' associations or unions. Questions of non-school-sponsored student assemblies are usually not addressed under this clause but under the freedom of religion (if that is their purpose) or freedom of expression clauses.

Fourth Amendment

The Fourth Amendment provides that the right of the people to be "secure in their persons, houses, papers, and effects, against unreasonable searches and seizures, shall not be violated and no warrants shall issue, but upon probable cause." The growing problem of student possession of drugs and other contraband has led to an increasing number of student searches. As we will see in the next chapter, the Fourth Amendment has served as the basis for a number of student challenges to warrantless searches of their automobiles, lockers, or persons by school officials and others. A few cases involving searches of teachers' desks or other personal belongings have also been heard.

Fifth Amendment

According to the provisions of the Fifth Amendment, no person shall be "compelled in any criminal case to be a witness against himself, nor be deprived of life, liberty, or property, without due process of law; nor shall private property be taken for public use, without just compensation." The first clause of the Fifth Amendment, the self-incrimination clause, permits individuals to refuse to answer questions, the answers to which might be used against them or might subject them to prosecution by the state. In education cases, this clause has been invoked by teachers in refusing to answer questions about their affiliations and activities outside the school. However, the courts have ruled that teachers may not use the Fifth Amendment to avoid answering questions about their activities outside the classroom that relate to their qualifications or fitness to teach (*Beilan v. Board of Public Education*, 1958).

The due process protection of the Fifth Amendment is not usually involved in education cases. Rather, the due process clause of the Fourteenth Amendment is used because it relates directly to the states.

School officials have both the right and the duty to search a student's locker if reasonable suspicion exists that it contains something illegal.

The last clause of the Fifth Amendment is relevant in those few cases where the state or school system is seeking to obtain private property for school purposes in the exercise of the government's right of *eminent domain*, the right to take private property for public use. Thus a school district attempting to gain property to enlarge a school may find it necessary to exercise its power of eminent domain (if such power has been given it by the state) if it has not been able to negotiate a voluntary purchase of the needed property. Whenever the power of eminent domain is exercised, just compensation must be given to the owners of the property that is taken.

Eighth Amendment

The Eighth Amendment, in part, provides protection against "cruel and unusual punishments." This amendment on occasion has been involved in challenging the practice or use of corporal punishment in schools. The Supreme Court has held, however, that disciplinary corporal punishment *per se* is not cruel and unusual punishment as anticipated by the Eighth Amendment (*Ingraham v. Wright,* 1977). This does not mean, however, that corporal punishment may not be prohibited by state or school district regulations or that punishment can be excessive. In fact, if the punishment causes physical harm it may be grounds for a civil action for assault and battery.

How have society's views regarding corporal punishment in the schools changed since you began school?

Fourteenth Amendment

The Fourteenth Amendment is the federal constitutional provision most often involved in education-related cases because it pertains specifically to state actions and, as previously stated, education is a state function. The Fourteenth Amendment states:

> No State shall make or enforce any law which shall abridge the privileges or immunities of citizens of the United States; nor shall any State deprive any person of life, liberty, or property, without due process of law; nor deny to any person within its jurisdiction the equal protection of the laws.

The due process clause of the Fourteenth Amendment has proved to be of great importance to students in disciplinary actions and to teachers in negative personnel actions, and has been invoked in a wide array of issues involving student and teacher rights. As discussed in the next chapter, the equal protection clause has served as the basis for numerous cases involving discrimination on the basis of race, sex, handicapping condition, or other classifications used in the schools.

State Constitutional Provisions Affecting Education

Like the federal Constitution, state constitutions have provided the foundation for the enactment of subsequent innumerable statutes that govern the activities of the state and its citizens. However, unlike the federal Constitution which contains no reference to education, every state constitution includes a provision for education, and all but one expressly provides for the establishment of a system of public schools. These provisions range from very general to very specific but their overall intent is to ensure that schools and education be encouraged and that a uniform system of schools be established. For example, Article X, Section 3 (as amended, April 1972) of the Wisconsin constitution provides:

> The Legislature shall provide by law for the establishment of district schools, which shall be as nearly uniform as practical; and such schools shall be free and without charge for tuition to all children between the ages of 4 and 20 years.

The constitutions of 45 states provide for the establishment of "common schools" (see Chapter 4 for history of common schools), and 35 states establish specific methods for financial support (Collins, 1969). The constitutions of 30 states expressly prohibit the use of public funds for the use of religious schools and the constitution of every state except Maine and North Carolina contains a provision prohibiting religious instruction in the public schools. In addition, some state constitutions also specifically prohibit both religious and political requirements for admission. For example, Article XI, Section 7 of the Arizona constitution provides:

> No sectarian instruction shall be imparted in any school or State educational institution and no religious or political test or qualification shall ever be required as a condition of admission into any public educational institution of the State, as teacher, student, or pupil.

The wording of the state constitutional provision for education has proven to be very important to the courts in determining whether particular legislative enactments were constitutionally permissible or required. For example, a Court of Appeals ruled that the constitutional requirements that the state legislature provide for a system of free common schools did not require that free textbooks be provided to high school students (*Carpio v. Tucson High School District No. 1,* 1974). The basis for the court's decision was its interpretation of common schools as consisting only of grades one through eight.

Regardless of the particular provisions related to education contained in a state's constitution, the state constitution does not grant unlimited power to the state legislature in providing for the public schools. Rather, it establishes the boundaries within which the legislature may operate. The legislature may not then enact legislation exceeding these parameters or violate any provisions of the federal Constitution, which is the supreme law of the land.

Statutory Law

Statutory law is that body of law consisting of the written enactments of a legislative body. These written enactments, called statutes, constitute the second highest level of law, following constitutions. Where constitutions provide broad statements of policy, statutes establish the specifics of operation. Both the U.S. Congress and state legislatures have enacted innumerable statutes affecting the provision of education in this country. These statutes are continually reviewed and often revised or supplemented by successive legislatures. They are also subject to review by the courts to determine their intent and to determine if they are in violation of the constitution. If they do not violate constitutional limitations, they are binding on all citizens and agencies (Valente, 1987).

Despite the federal constitutional silence on education, during each session the U.S. Congress enacts or renews numerous statutes that affect the public schools. Some of these, such as the Occupational Safety and Health Act (OSHA), which requires employers to furnish a safe working environment, although not directed specifically at school districts, do affect their operation. Many of the statutes enacted by Congress are related to the provision of financial assistance to the schools for a variety of special instructional programs, research, or programs for needy children. Yet another finance bill, the Servicemen's Readjustment Act, popularly known as the G.I. Bill, provides aid to veterans to complete their education, including those who want to complete a regular high school program.

In addition to federal statutes providing financial assistance, federal civil rights statutes also have had a considerable impact on educational programs and personnel. An overview of the major civil rights statutes affecting schools is provided in Table 11.1. They are discussed in more detail in relevant sections of this text.

State Statutes

Most of the statutory laws affecting the public schools are enacted by state legislatures. The power of the state legislature is *plenary*, or absolute; it may enact any legislation that is not contrary to federal and the state constitutions. Although the principle is challenged every year by local school districts, the courts have clearly established that education is a function of the state, not an inherent function of the local school district, and that the local district has only those powers delegated to it by the state legislature. The courts have also affirmed the authority of the state to regulate such matters as certification, powers of school boards, accreditation, curriculum, the school calendar, graduation requirements, facilities construction and operation, and raising and spending of monies. In fact, the courts have made it clear that school districts have no inherent right to exist; they exist only at the will of the legislature and can be created, reorganized, or abolished by legislative prerogative.

Although the state legislature has in fact delegated the actual operation of the majority of the schools to the local school districts (state governments often retain operation of certain types of specialized schools, such as schools for the deaf and blind), the legislature still must pass legislation to administer the system as a whole and to provide for its financing and operation. Consequently, numerous education statutes exist in every state and in every legislative session new statutes will be enacted that affect education.

What laws or statutes have recently been passed in your state that affect education?

Case Law

Distinct from statutes, regulations, or other sources of law is that body of law originating with historical usages and customs, including court decisions. This body of law is referred to as case law or common law. Case law is based on the doctrine of *stare decisis*, which means "let the decision stand." The doctrine requires that once a court has laid down a principle of law as applicable to a certain set of facts, it will apply it to all future cases where the facts are substantially the same and other courts of equal or lesser rank will similarly apply the principle (Black, 1983). However, adherence to the doctrine of *stare decisis* does not mean that all previous decisions may never be challenged or overturned. On numerous occasions a higher or subsequent court has

Table 11.1: Major Civil Rights Laws Affecting Schools

Statute	Groups Protected	Interests Protected	Schools Covered
Sec. 1981, 1982; acts of 1866, 1870	Race	Right to make contracts	Public and private if they solicit clients
Sec. 1983; act of 1871	All groups; general civil rights	Constitutional rights	Public and private if they operate "under color of law"
Sec. 1985 (3) (Conspiracy)	All groups; general civil rights	Equal protection of law	Any conspiracy by any persons
Sec. 1988; acts of 1866, as amended	All groups	Federal court proceedings if civil rights are violated	According to the law violated
Equal Pay Act	Sex	Salaries and wages	All who are subject to the Fair Labor Standards Act
Civil Rights Act of 1964, Title VI	Race, color, or national origin	All benefits under federally aided programs	All, in federally supported activities
Civil Rights Act of 1964, Title VII	Race, color, national origin, religion, sex	Employment benefits	All with 15 or more employees
Education Amendments of 1972, Title IX	Sex	Educational benefits that are federally supported	All, in federally supported activities
Family Rights and Privacy Act of 1974	All students	Access to records and confidentiality of records	All, in federally supported activities
Rehabilitation Act of 1963 (sec. 504)	All handicapped persons	All benefits under federally aided programs	All, in federally supported activities
Education of all Handicapped Children Act of 1975	All handicapped children	Educational benefits under federally aided programs	All, in federally supported activities
Bilingual Education Act	All children of limited-English-speaking proficiency	Educational benefits under federally supported programs	All, in federally supported activities
Equal Access Act of 1984	All students	Equal access for student groups to conduct extracurricular meetings on school premises	Public secondary schools receiving federal funds

Source: From *Teachers and the Law* by Louis Fischer, David Schimmel, and Cynthia Kelly. Copyright © 1987 by Longman Publishing Group. Reprinted with permission from Longman Publishing Group.

rejected the reasoning of a lower or earlier court or constitutional or statutory changes, in effect, have overturned the previous decision.

Administrative Law

Administrative law consists of the formal regulations and decisions of those state or federal agencies that are authorized by law to regulate public functions. These regulations carry the force of law, are subject to judicial review, and will stand as law unless found to be in conflict with federal or state constitutional provisions, statutes, or court decisions.

The U.S. Department of Education and the National Institute of Education (NIE) are the federal agencies most directly concerned with education. The secretary of education and the director of the National Institute of Education are both appointed by the president. The regulations issued by the Office of Civil Rights of the Department of Education in regard to the implementation of Title IX are a prime example of the profound impact that administrative law can have on the operations of the schools.

Among the other federal agencies that have significant interaction with schools are the Department of Agriculture, which administers the National School Lunch Act; the Department of the Interior, Bureau of Indian Affairs, which administers numerous programs aimed at improving the education of Native Americans and the Department of Labor, which administers the Occupational Safety and Health Act. In addition, both the Office of Civil Rights of the Department of Education and another federal agency, the Equal Employment Opportunity Commission (EEOC), are charged with enforcement of civil rights and nondiscrimination legislation.

The state agency that has the most direct control and responsibility over education is the state department of education. A large body of administrative law is generated by this agency as a result of the promulgation of numerous rules and regulations relating to such areas as certification of teachers, accreditation of schools, adoption of textbooks, courses of study, minimum standards for specified areas, and distribution of state funds.

Attorney General Opinions

Yet another source of education law is the opinions of the state attorney general. The *attorney general* is the chief legal officer of the state and acts as legal advisor to state agencies. The attorney general is normally required to furnish written opinions concerning an interpretation of law to the governor and other state and local officials (i.e., not to private citizens or school personnel such as teachers or even principals, but to officials such as the chairperson of the school board). State attorney generals are often called on to interpret the state's education law, school board policies, and the pronouncements and actions of school administrators and teachers (Hudgins & Vacca, 1985). For example, in a 1988 opinion to the executive secretary-treasurer of the Georgia Teachers' Retirement System, the Georgia attorney general concluded that the same period of military service could not be counted for credit for both military retirement and state retirement. To do so would constitute "double dipping" (Ga. Op. Atty. Gen., 1988).

Powers and Organization of the Courts

According to our system of government a separation of power exists between the executive, legislative, and judicial branches of the government. In school-related matters, the courts have generally taken the position that they will not intervene in a dispute unless all internal appeals have been exhausted. For example, where school board policy provides teachers with the right of direct appeal to the board in cases involving involuntary teacher transfers, this avenue of appeal must be exhausted before the courts will hear the appeal. The exceptions to this provision are those cases involving an alleged violation of a constitutionally protected right.

Courts cannot become involved in education cases of their own initiative. A case must be brought to the court for resolution. The most common type of school case brought to the court is one that requires the court to interpret laws within its jurisdiction. Another common type of school case requires the court to determine the constitutionality of legislative or administrative enactments.

Federal courts generally are involved in only two kinds of issues: those involving questions of interpretations of the federal Constitution or federal statutes and those involving parties of different states. Sometimes a case will involve questions of both federal and state law. When this occurs, the federal court can decide on the state issue, but it must do so according to the rules governing the courts of that state. Most education cases that come to federal courts involve alleged violations of constitutionally protected rights or interpretations of federal statutes.

The Federal Court System

The federal court system consists of three levels of courts of general jurisdiction: a supreme court, district courts, and courts of appeals. In addition, the federal court system includes courts of special jurisdiction, such as the Customs Court or the Tax Court. These courts would normally not be involved in education cases (see Figure 11.2).

How many district courts are in your state? What is the name of the district court in the area in which you reside?

District Courts

The lowest level federal courts are district courts. There are more than 90 district courts: at least one in each state and in the more populated states, such as California, New York, and Texas, as many as four. Federal district courts are given names reflective of the geographic area they serve; for example, S.D. Ohio indicates the Southern District of Ohio. District courts are the courts of

Figure 11.2: Federal Court System

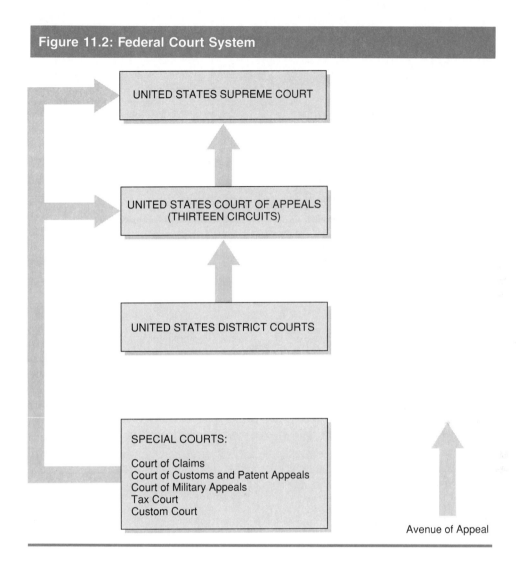

UNITED STATES SUPREME COURT

UNITED STATES COURT OF APPEALS
(THIRTEEN CIRCUITS)

UNITED STATES DISTRICT COURTS

SPECIAL COURTS:

Court of Claims
Court of Customs and Patent Appeals
Court of Military Appeals
Tax Court
Custom Court

Avenue of Appeal

initiation or original jurisdiction for most cases filed in the federal court system, including most education cases. They are trial courts, meaning a jury hears the case. The decisions of federal district courts have an automatic right of appeal to the next level of federal courts—U.S. Circuit Courts of Appeals.

Circuit Courts

There are 13 circuit courts of appeals in the federal system. Like the district courts, each court of appeals has jurisdiction over a specific geographic area (see Figure 11.3). The circuit court carries the name of the geographic circuit it serves (e.g., the Sixth Circuit, abbreviated as 6th Cir.). A circuit court hears appeals from the decisions of district courts and certain federal administrative agencies. It hears arguments from attorneys, but it does not retry the

Figure 11.3: The Thirteen Federal Judicial Circuits

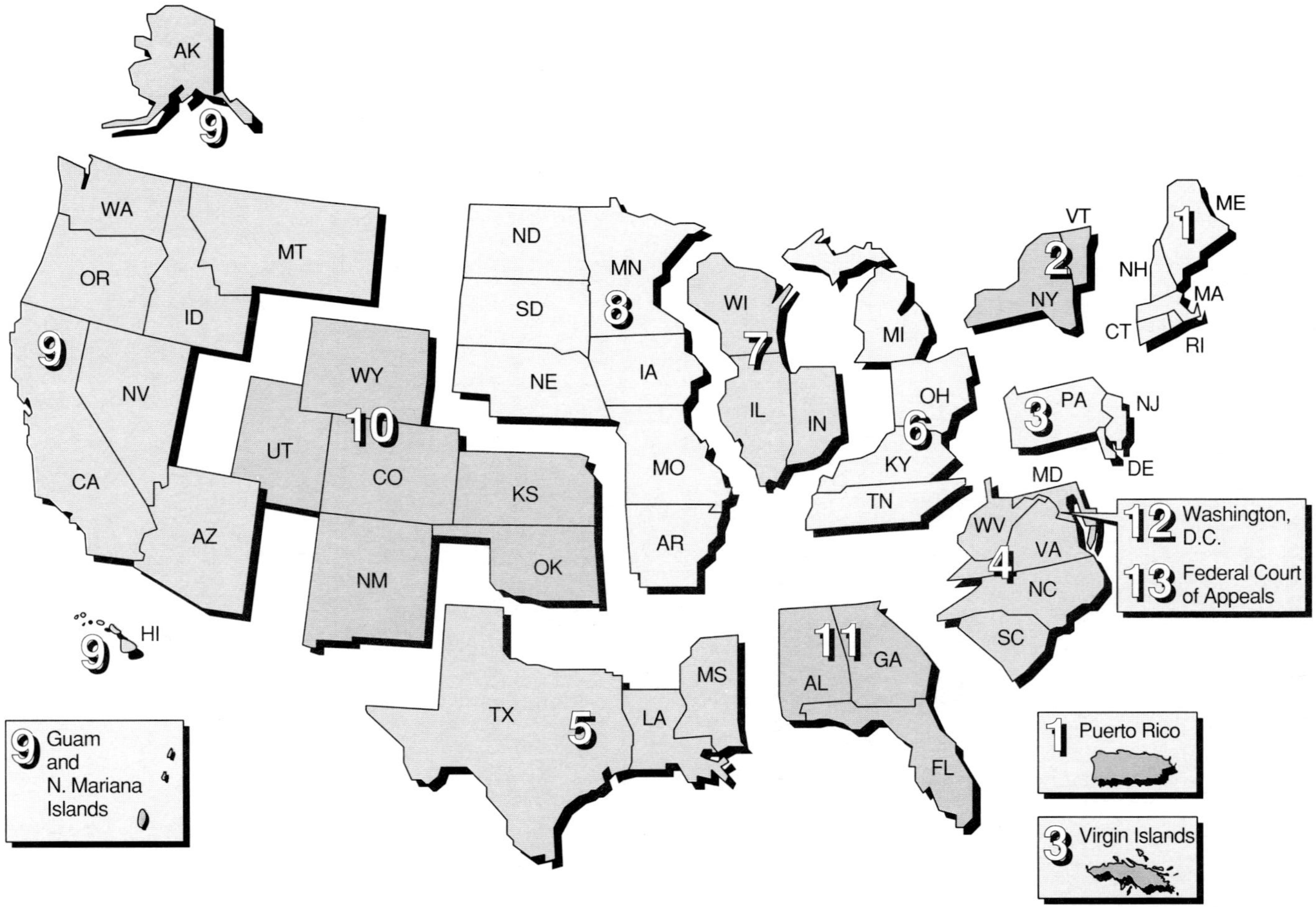

case. There is no jury. A panel of judges, usually three, hears the case and can affirm, reverse, or modify the decision of the lower court, or remand the case back to the lower court for modifications or retrial.

The decision of a federal circuit court is binding only on federal district courts within its geographic jurisdiction. Circuit courts have no power over state courts and do not hear appeals from them, nor does the decision of one circuit court bind other circuit courts or the district courts in other circuits. Thus it is possible, and indeed it happens quite often, that one circuit court will rule one way, for example that the wearing of long hair is constitutionally protected, while another circuit court will rule in the reverse.

U.S. Supreme Court

The highest federal appeals court, indeed the highest court in the land, is the United States Supreme Court. Decisions of the Supreme Court are absolute: there is no appeal. If Congress or citizens do not agree with a decision of the Supreme Court, the only ways they can mediate against the effect of the decision are to pass a law or to get the court to reconsider the issue in a later case. Both of these events happen with some regularity. A notable example in education of the Supreme Court reversing itself on reconsideration is the case of *Brown v. Board of Education of Topeka* (1954). In *Plessey v. Ferguson* (1896), the Supreme Court had said "separate but equal" public facilities for blacks and whites were constitutionally permissible. But in 1954 in the *Brown* decision the court reversed this position and ruled that separate educational facilities for blacks and whites were inherently unequal.

The Supreme Court hears cases on appeal from lower federal courts or from state supreme courts if the state case involves questions of federal law. While thousands of cases are appealed to the Supreme Court each year, only a small number are heard. However, in recent years the number of education cases being appealed to the Supreme Court and heard by it has increased.

The State Court Systems

Since most education cases do not involve the federal Constitution or federal statutes, they are handled by state courts rather than federal courts. Like the federal court system, the state court system is created by the state constitution and subsequent legislative enactments. Although the specific structure of the court system and the names given to courts vary from state to state, there are sufficient commonalities to permit a description of the general structure for state courts as shown in Figure 11.4.

Most states have courts that are designated as courts of limited or special jurisdiction. The limitation may be related to the types of cases they may handle (e.g., probate courts or juvenile courts) or the amount in controversy (e.g., small claims courts or traffic courts). Generally, state court systems do not permit appeal of the decisions of courts of limited jurisdiction.

All states have courts of general jurisdiction. Courts of general jurisdiction are generally trial courts and as such hear witnesses, admit evidence, and, when appropriate, conduct jury trials. Depending on the state, courts of

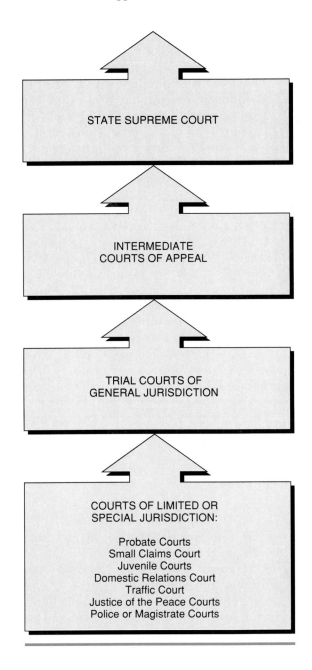

Figure 11.4: State Court Systems

STATE SUPREME COURT

INTERMEDIATE
COURTS OF APPEAL

TRIAL COURTS OF
GENERAL JURISDICTION

COURTS OF LIMITED OR
SPECIAL JURISDICTION:

Probate Courts
Small Claims Court
Juvenile Courts
Domestic Relations Court
Traffic Court
Justice of the Peace Courts
Police or Magistrate Courts

eral jurisdiction may be referred to as district courts, county courts, circuit courts, superior courts, or supreme court (in New York State).

Appeals from the decisions of courts of general jurisdiction are made to state appellate courts, often referred to as courts of appeals. Appellate courts are found in all state court systems. Normally they are organized by geographic area. Like the federal appellate courts, state appellate courts do not

Historical Note:
U.S. Supreme Court Justices

John Marshall served longer than any other justice, over 34 years. Four other justices also served over 30 years: William J. Brennan (33 years), Stephen J. Field (34 years), John McLean (32 years), and Joseph Story (34 years).

While a number of justices were said to be able sportsmen, perhaps the one who demonstrated this most visibly was Byron R. White, who played three seasons in the National Football League.

Several justices resigned to assume other public offices. James F. Brynes left in 1942 to become director of the Office of War Mobilization. Arthur Goldberg became U.S. ambassador to the United Nations, and John Rutledge became chief justice of the South Carolina Supreme Court. Rutledge later returned to the Court and served as chief justice *pro tem* for one year, but his apparent insanity led the Senate to reject his nomination. Charles Evans Hughes resigned to run unsuccessfully as the Republican candidate for the presidency in 1916. In 1930, upon nomination by President Herbert Hoover, he returned to the Court as its chief justice.

Some justices have done double duty. While serving as chief justice, John Jay also served as ambassador to Great Britain; and while serving on the Court, Robert Jackson became chief counsel to the U.S. at the Nuremberg war crimes trials.

---

retry cases but sit as a panel of judges (usually three) to review the record of the trial court and hear attorneys' arguments.

The final appeal in state court systems is to the state supreme court, the final authority on questions related to the state constitution or state law. If the case involves federal issues, however, appeal may be taken from the state supreme court to the United States Supreme Court.

Church-State Relations

The issue of the appropriate relationship between religion and the state has been one of the most controversial in American legal history. The first clause of the First Amendment, the "establishment and free exercise" clause, states that "Congress shall make no law respecting an establishment of religion or prohibiting the free exercise thereof." The experience of the nation's founders with state control of education prompted a desire to erect what Jefferson called "a wall of separation between Church and State." Although the clause makes reference only to actions of the federal government (Congress), it is made applicable to the states by the Fourteenth Amendment which prohibits state actions that violate the constitutional rights of citizens.

Maintaining the wall of separation without being "hostile to religion" has been the challenge faced by policy makers at every level of government, as well as by public school teachers and administrators. Often they find their actions challenged in the courts, and a few cases have reached the U.S. Supreme Court (see Table 11.2). The issues most often contested can be categorized

Table 11.2: Overview of Selected U.S. Supreme Court Cases Affecting Church-School Relations

Case	Decision
Pierce v. Society of Sisters (1925)	Parents have the right to educate their children in private schools.
Cochran v. Louisiana State Board of Education (1930)	States may provide secular textbooks to children attending sectarian schools.
West Virginia State Board of Education v. Barnette (1943)	Public schools may not require the salute to the flag.
Everson v. Board of Education (1947)	States may use public funds to provide for transportation of children to and from private, sectarian schools where state constitution permits it.
Illinois ex rel. McCollum v. Board of Education (1948)	Released time program whereby instruction is provided during school hours on school grounds is unconstitutional.
Zorach v. Clauson (1952)	Released time program whereby students are released to go off campus to receive instruction and where no state support is provided is constitutional.
Engel v. Vitale (1962)	Public schools may not require the recitation of prayers.
School District of Abington Township v. Schempp (1963)	State may not promote Bible readings and prayers, even when participation is not compulsory.
Epperson v. Arkansas (1968)	State law forbidding the teaching of evolution is unconstitutional.
Lemon v. Kurtzman (1971)	State support to nonpublic schools, their personnel, and their students is unconstitutional if it (1) has a primarily religious purpose, (2) either advances or inhibits religion, or (3) creates an excessive entanglement between church and state.
Muller v. Allen (1983)	State may provide income tax deduction for educational expenses of nonpublic school parents if also available to public school parents.
Wallace v. Jaffree (1985)	State laws authorizing silent meditation or prayer are unconstitutional.
Witters v. Washington Department of Services for the Blind (1986)	Student financial aid provided by the state can be used at a sectarian institution.
Edwards v. Aguiilard (1987)	Public schools may not be required to teach creationism.
Board of Education of Westside Community Schools v. Mergens (1990)	Schools must provide access to student-sponsored religious groups if access is provided to other student groups not directly related to the school's curriculum.

into three broad areas: religious activities, curriculum bias, and public support. Other areas of importance, if not as litigious, involve compulsory attendance and private and home schooling.

Religious Activities

Released Time

Traditionally, a not uncommon practice in American public schools was the releasing of children during the school day for religious instruction. The first case to reach the Supreme Court, *McCollum v. Board of Education* (1948), resulted in a ruling that the released time program violated the establishment clause of the First Amendment. In this case, students were excused from regular classes to attend private religious instruction in another part of the building. Four years later the court upheld a program in which, by parental request, children were permitted to leave the public school to receive religious instruction (*Zorach v. Clauson*, 1952). As in *McCollum*, the instructors were not paid by the school. The distinction made by the court between *Zorach* and *McCollum* was that public school facilities were not involved in *Zorach*.

Since *Zorach*, the court has adopted a tripartite test to evaluate claims under the establishment clause, including those related to released time. The test, often called the *Lemon test* (from the case in which it was developed, *Lemon v. Kurtzman*, 1971), asks three questions, all of which must be answered in the negative if the policy or action is to be judged constitutional: (1) Does the policy or action have a primarily religious purpose? (2) Does the policy or action have the primary effect of advancing or inhibiting religion? (3) Does the policy or action foster an excessive entanglement between the state and religion?

In applying the test to a case in Utah that involved instruction of high school students at a Mormon seminary, the Tenth Circuit Court of Appeals found the program unconstitutional in two areas that created "excessive entanglements." First, it involved sending a public school student to the school to gather attendance slips (as opposed to *Zorach* where attendance was sent to the public school by the religious school); second, credit toward graduation was awarded for successful completion of the seminary studies. The court maintained that the assessment and monitoring of the course content to assess whether the course content was mainly denominational would necessitate the state being too involved with the church (*Lanner v. Wimmer*, 1981).

Prayer and Bible Reading

Two of the most controversial rulings ever made by the U.S. Supreme Court involved compulsory flag salute and prayer in the public schools. In *West Virginia State Board of Education v. Barnette* (1943), the Court ruled that the compulsory flag salute violated the religious freedom of Jehovah's Witnesses. In *Engel v. Vitale* (1962), parents challenged the use of a prayer composed by the New York Board of Regents as part of morning exercises. The denominationally neutral prayer read: "Almighty God, we acknowledge our dependence upon thee, and we beg thy blessings upon us, our parents, our teachers,

Prayer and Bible reading, once openly and legally practiced in the public schools but now unconstitutional, are favored by the majority of Americans.

Do you recall being involved in any religious activities in a public school situation? If you attended a private school, was religion an important part of your day?

and our country." The Court held that "it is no part of the business of government to impose official prayers for any group of American people" and to do so constituted a violation of the establishment clause.

The following year, the Supreme Court rendered another significant decision affecting school prayer. In *School District of Abington Township v. Schempp* (1963), the Court declared unconstitutional Pennsylvania and Maryland statutes that required daily Bible reading and recitation of the Lord's Prayer (optional in Pennsylvania). Although children could be exempted from participation in the Maryland case upon request by their parents, the Court held that such activities, held in public school buildings under the supervision of public school personnel, served to advance religion in violation of the establishment clause of the First Amendment. While prohibiting Bible readings as a religious exercise, the Court in *Schempp* did specifically note that its opinion did not prevent studying the Bible as literature and studying *about* religion. A Supreme Court decision 20 years later overturned a Kentucky statute that required every public school classroom to have one portion of the Bible—the Ten Commandments—posted on the wall (*Stone v. Graham,* 1983).

Not only are state-imposed prayers and Bible readings constitutionally impermissible, so too are voluntary prayers and Bible readings, whether given by teachers or students, or even if requested by students. The courts have found little to distinguish these from state-imposed prayers in that both are sanctioned by the school (*Collins v. Chandler Unified School District*, 1981; *Jaffree v. Wallace*, 1985; *Karen B. v. Treen*, 1982). Likewise, the courts have in recent years shown a reluctance to accept the stated nonsectarian purpose of periods of silent meditation (or silent prayer). In the lead U.S. Supreme Court decision, the court in *Wallace v. Jaffree* (1985) concluded that the intent of the 1981 Alabama statutes providing for a period of silent meditation or prayer was clearly to encourage and/or accommodate prayer and thus violated the establishment clause. However, the court did indicate in *Jaffree* that statutes providing for periods of silence that did not demonstrate legislative intent to encourage prayers would probably be upheld. Currently, "moment of silence" laws are in effect in about half the states and the legality of each is subject to determination on a state-by-state basis.

Prayers held outside the classroom but at school-sponsored activities are also the subject of some controversy. Traditionally, the courts have been less inclined to find establishment clause violations in connection with baccalaureate services and prayers at graduation ceremonies, judging them to be more ceremonial in nature with no intent to indoctrinate (McCarthy & Cambron-McCabe, 1987). However, some more recent decisions have invalidated such practices as violations of the establishment clause. As articulated by the Oregon Court of Appeals, "prayer by its very nature is religious; accordingly, the purpose for which a prayer is given necessarily must be religious" (*Kay v. David Douglas School District*, 1986).

The courts also have shown increasing disfavor toward prayers at other school-sponsored events. For example, the Supreme Court recently let stand an Eleventh Circuit Court of Appeals ruling that banned organized prayers before high school football games (*Jager v. Douglas County School District*, 1989). Again, the Court reasoned that such prayers violate the establishment clause in that they promote religion.

In spite of the U.S. Supreme Court's ruling on prayers and Bible readings, these practices continue in schools across the nation in open defiance of the Court. Public opinion surveys indicate that 68% of the American people favor prayer in the schools (Gallup & Clark, 1987). Additionally, various amendments to the Constitution to authorize prayers or Bible reading in the public schools have been proposed. However, until such an amendment is ratified, both prayers and Bible reading are considered unconstitutional under the establishment clause of the First Amendment.

Equal Access for Student Devotional Meetings

Partially in response to public sentiment that prayer and other devotional activities should not be banned from the school grounds, in 1984 Congress passed the Equal Access Act (20 U.S.C., sections 4071–73). The act specified that if a federally assisted public secondary school provides a *limited open forum* to noncurriculum student groups to meet on school premises during noninstructional time, "equal access" to that forum cannot be denied because of the "religious, political, philosophical, or other content of the speech at such meetings."

In the years after its adoption, there were judicial contradictions as to the application of the law and as to whether the Equal Access Act (EAA) violated the establishment clause. For example, several circuit courts and several district courts ruled that student devotional meetings held at a time closely associated with the school day and under the supervision of public school personnel implied recognition of the religious activities and served to advance religion, in violation of the establishment clause. In *Garnett v. Renton School District No. 403* (1989) the Ninth Circuit Court of Appeals upheld the school district in denying a student group's request to use a classroom to meet before school to discuss religious and moral issues, read the Bible, and pray. The district denied the request because the club was not curriculum related.

The next year, however, the U.S. Supreme Court ruled on the constitutionality question and asserted that secondary students are mature enough to understand that a school does not endorse or support a particular speech just because it permits it on a nondiscriminatory basis (*Board of Education of Westside Community Schools v. Mergens*, 1990). In this case, the Court also attempted to clarify the meaning and scope of "curriculum related" under the EAA. According to the Court, a noncurriculum related student group is:

> any student group that does not *directly* relate to the body of courses offered by the school . . . (and) a student group directly relates to a school's curriculum if the subject matter of the group is actually taught, or will soon be taught, in a regularly offered course; if the subject matter of the group concerns the body of courses as a whole; if participation in the group is required for a particular course; or if participation in the group results in academic credit.
> (pp. 4723–24)

In light of the Supreme Court decision in Mergens, *should school districts attempt to eliminate all noncurriculum-related student clubs or seek to accommodate a plethora of such clubs?*

While the Court acknowledged that whether a specific group is "noncurriculum related" would depend on a particular school's curriculum, if even one noncurriculum-related student club is allowed, the school has opened a limited open forum and cannot discriminate against students based on the content of the student's speech at the club's meetings. Central to the Court's decision upholding the request by students to form a Christian Bible Study Club in *Mergens* was the finding that the school's existing student clubs included one or more other noncurriculum-related clubs (e.g., a club for students interested in scuba diving, a chess club, a philosophy club, etc.). The result of the *Mergens* decision will undoubtedly be an increase in the number and types of clubs seeking to gain access to school facilities.

Curriculum Bias

Challenges to the curriculum traditionally have been brought by parents attempting to eliminate specific courses, activities, or materials thought to be advancing religion. Recent challenges brought with this same goal have raised the complex question as to what constitutes "religion." Increasingly, fundamentalist parents contend that certain courses, materials, and practices in the curriculum promote the "religion" of *secular humanism*, allegedly a faith that denies God, deifies man, and glorifies reason. The fundamentalists demand that the influences of secular humanism be removed from the curriculum or that religion be inserted in the curriculum to bring balance.

In the majority of cases thus far, the courts have rejected the secular humanism argument and reaffirmed the position of the Supreme Court in *Epperson v. Arkansas* (1968), in which the Court struck down an Arkansas law forbidding instruction in evolution. The Court said: "The state has no legitimate interest in protecting any or all religions from views distasteful to them." For example, the courts have not been convinced that the teaching of sex education promotes the "religion" of secular humanism. The courts consistently have found that sex education courses present public health information that promotes legitimate educational objectives and that the establishment clause prevents the state from barring such instruction simply to conform to the religious beliefs of some parents (McCarthy & Cambron-McCabe, 1987).

The teaching of evolution is another area that has been targeted as advancing secular humanism. Prior to *Epperson,* some states had attempted to prevent the teaching of evolution by state law. With the declaration of *Epperson* that evolution is a science, not a secular religion, and that states cannot restrict student access to such information to satisfy religious preferences, attempts were made in a number of states to secure "balanced treatment" or "equal time" statutes. However, these too have been invalidated (*Edwards v. Aguillard,* 1987).

Other curriculum challenges have involved the use of specific curriculum materials. (To help you examine your position on censorship, think about the questions on page 370.) A group of fundamentalist parents in Tennessee brought suit against the school district claiming that the required use of the 1983 Holt, Rinehart, and Winston basic reading series violated their rights by exposing their children to beliefs that were offensive to their religious beliefs. The parents maintained that after reading the series, a child might adopt the views of "a feminist, a humanist, a pacifist, an anti-Christian, a vegetarian, or an advocate of the 'one-world government.' " On appeal, the Sixth Circuit Court of Appeals concluded that exposure to concepts does not constitute promotion of the concepts, and that no evidence existed that students were asked to affirm or deny any religious beliefs, to engage in activity forbidden by their religious beliefs, or to refrain from engaging in any action required by their religious beliefs. Accordingly, no constitutional violations were found (*Mozert v. Hawkins County Public Schools,* 1987).

Secular humanism was acknowledged as a religion by a district court in an Alabama case challenging 44 home economics, history, and social studies books on the state-approved textbook list. The district court noted, as has the U.S. Supreme Court in cases involving conscientious objectors (*United States v. Seeger,* 1965; *Welsh v. United States,* 1970), that a religion need not have a belief in a Supreme Being. The district court ruled that the 44 textbooks did advance the religion of secular humanism and inhibited theistic faiths in violation of the establishment clause.

Censorship is defined as "any act intended to keep students from reading, seeing, or hearing any materials that some person deems objectionable" (Jenkinson, 1986, p. 17). Although censorship has been practiced throughout our history, in recent years members of certain fundamental religious groups appear to be more vocal in their efforts to censor materials and methods in the schools. Sooner or later in your teaching career you will probably encounter a situation in which students, parents, or others attempt to censor some aspect of your class material or presentation. The following questions are designed to encourage you to examine your position on censorship:

1. Do parents have the right to keep their children from being exposed to materials and methods to which they are opposed?

2. Do school personnel have an obligation to protect children from inaccurate and unsuitable material and methods?

3. What effect does censorship have on the academic climate and the quality of education?

4. Do schools themselves practice censorship in selecting materials?

5. Can censorship really work, or does it only increase the attractiveness of censored materials to students who then obtain them by other avenues?

6. To what extent does the average high school student have the intellectual and emotional maturity to engage in a free exchange of ideas?

7. Is censorship a violation of the academic freedom of teachers?

Many of the curricular materials being objected to have been used for 20 years or more with limited objection (e.g., Huckleberry Finn, Catcher in the Rye, Of Mice and Men). *To what do you attribute the recent objections to such material?)*

The circuit court reversed the ruling and spoke directly to the demand by many fundamentalists that religion be given equal time with secular humanism in the curriculum. According to the appellate court what the establishment clause requires is not the comprehensive identification of the state with religion, but the *separation* of the state from religion. Separation requires that there be no fusing of government functions and religious sects, not merely that the state treat them all equally (*Smith v. Board of School Commissioners,* 1987).

Public Support of Nonpublic Schools

As noted in Chapter 14, nonpublic schools educate a significant number of children in the United States. In recognition of the role that they play in the educational system and of the financial burden placed on parents who pay property taxes to support the public schools as well as tuition at nonpublic schools, legislatures have regularly attempted to provide some type of public support to these schools or their clients. The legal issue involved in these attempts is whether the assistance violates the First Amendment prohibition against governmental actions that promote the establishment of religion.

Student Support

The courts have recognized that direct subsidies to nonpublic schools violate the establishment clause. Most state constitutions also forbid state aid to religious schools. However, the courts have relied on the *child benefit theory* to provide several types of assistance that primarily benefit the private school child rather than the private school itself. This theory was first articulated by the U.S. Supreme Court in *Cochran v. Louisiana State Board of Education* (1930). The court upheld a Louisiana law that provided textbooks directly to children attending nonpublic schools.

The same rationale was applied in another Supreme Court decision, *Everson v. Board of Education* (1947), which supported a New Jersey law reimbursing parents for the cost of bus transportation for children attending both public and nonpublic schools. However, the fact that the U.S. Supreme Court has said that transportation, textbooks, or the provision of other services is permissible under the federal Constitution does not mean that states *must* provide this assistance, or that such assistance may not be invalidated by state laws or constitutions.

Since 1970, the courts have applied the *Lemon* test in determining the constitutionality of various state aid programs. The results have been inconsistent, illogical, and controversial (Strahan & Turner, 1987). In *Wolman v. Walter* (1977), the court ruled on an Ohio statute that sought to provide broad support for nonpublic schools. The court found the following aid to be constitutional:

1. the purchase or loan of secular textbooks

2. the provision and scoring of such standardized tests as are available in the public schools of the state

3. speech, hearing, and psychological diagnostic services provided at the nonpublic schools by employees of the public schools

4. therapeutic and remedial services provided by employees of the public schools so long as they are off the premises of the nonpublic school

Ruled unconstitutional were:

1. the purchase or loan of instructional materials and audiovisual equipment (science kits, maps, globes, and charts)

2. providing funds for field trips

In other decisions, the Court has approved support for the cost of testing and record-keeping required by the state (*Committee for Public Education and Religious Liberty v. Regan*, 1980), but disallowed support for teacher-prepared tests (*Levitt v. Committee for Public Education and Religious Liberty*, 1973) and salary reimbursement or supplements for parochial school teachers (*Lemon v. Kurtzman*, 1971).

In recent years, the courts have shown a greater receptivity to various types of aid directed at providing services to students. However, the very

The courts have shown increasing favor toward state aid programs directed to parochial school students, as opposed to the schools they attend.

monitoring of the services to ensure that they are not advancing religion can create an excessive entanglement (*Aguilar v. Felton*, 1985; *Meek v. Pittenger*, 1975). In the absence of clear judicial guidance distinguishing permissible from impermissible aid to nonpublic schools, states will undoubtedly continue to attempt to provide various forms of aid and challenges will be resolved on a case-by-case basis.

Vouchers

In addition to assistance to nonpublic school students, proposals have been made to reduce the fiscal burden on parents of nonpublic school children through *voucher* systems and *tax benefits*. The last decade saw increasing approval for the voucher concept and this will undoubtedly continue given the government's current support of parental choice in education. Additional support for experimentation with voucher plans was provided by the Supreme Court decision in *Witters v. Washington Department of Services for the Blind* (1986). In this case, the court said that the use of financial aid available under a state vocational rehabilitation assistance program by a blind student to pursue a Bible studies degree at a Christian college would not be an "impermissible direct subsidy" to the sectarian institution, since the aid went directly to the student, not the institution. The decision in this case strengthens the likelihood that voucher plans could withstand an establishment clause challenge, and it appears likely that various proposals will be tried during the next decade (Webb, McCarthy, & Thomas, 1988).

Tax Benefits

Various tax deduction and tax credit proposals have been introduced to the U.S. Congress, as well as in almost every state legislature. They have invariably invoked challenges on establishment clause grounds. Two have reached the U.S. Supreme Court. In *Committee for Public Education and Religious Liberty v. Nyquist* (1973), the Court overturned a New York statute that allowed state income tax credits for parents of nonpublic school students. Although the plan aided parents rather than the schools, the court said it was nonetheless an aid to religion in violation of the establishment clause.

In the decade after *Nyquist,* various other tax relief measures were struck down by the courts. Then, in *Mueller v. Allen* (1983), the Supreme Court upheld a Minnesota statute that permitted a state income tax deduction to parents of both public and nonpublic school students for expenses for tuition, books, and transportation. The Court distinguished this case from *Nyquist* in that the New York statute provided the tax benefits only to parents of nonpublic school students. Here, the Court said, a secular purpose was served in providing financial assistance to a "broad spectrum" of the states' citizens. Following *Mueller,* a number of states considered similar tax benefit packages, but only Iowa passed legislation. However, public opinion continues to support tuition tax credits and advocates undoubtedly will continue to lobby for their passage.

What effect might the reduction in income tax collections resulting from tax benefit proposals have on the financing of the public schools? How should replacement tax revenues be generated?

Compulsory Attendance

Each of the fifty states has legislation requiring school attendance—at a public, private, or parochial school—by children of a certain age range residing within the state. The age range is normally from 6 or 7 to 16 or 18.

Although attendance is compulsory, attendance in a particular school district normally requires that the parents or legal guardian be a resident of the district. Additionally, attendance at a specific school within the district may legally be restricted to those residing within a certain attendance zone or may be determined by voluntary or court-ordered desegregation remedies.

The residency requirement is not the same as a citizenship requirement. The U.S. Supreme Court in *Plyler v. Doe* (1982) upheld the right of children of illegal aliens to attend school in the district of their residence. According to the court, the state's interest in deterring illegal entry was insufficient to justify the creation and perpetuation of a subclass of illiterates within our borders.

Although it is clearly established that compulsory attendance laws are not unconstitutional, the courts have placed some limits on the right of the state to compel school attendance. In 1972, in *Wisconsin v. Yoder,* the U.S. Supreme Court recognized the interests of the Amish people in preserving their two-hundred-year-old established way of life from the teaching of the values and worldly knowledge found in the public high schools. While these values and knowledge are deemed necessary for success outside the Amish community, the Court recognized that they were inconsistent with Amish religious beliefs. The Amish are a traditional, pacifist religious group that has rejected modern dress, modern conveniences, and other aspects of modern life. Within the Amish community, children are given continued education beyond elementary education through vocational training. The U.S. Supreme Court, examining the successful existence of the Amish way of life, found it to be, in effect, an alternative to formal secondary education that did fulfill the state's stated goals in compelling school attendance—to prepare children to be productive and contributing members of society.

The exception given to the Amish is not likely to be extended to other religious groups. The Court emphasized that the long history of the Amish way of life was important to its decision and that other groups "claiming to have recently discovered some other 'progressive' or more enlightened process for rearing children for modern life" would not qualify for similar exemptions.

Private and Home Schooling

The states' right to mandate school attendance does not extend to requiring that schooling take place in the public schools. In 1925, in *Pierce v. Society of Sisters,* the Supreme Court recognized the right of parents to educate their children in private schools. However, the decision also recognized the right of the state to regulate private schools, including requiring that their teachers be certified and that their curricula comply with established state guidelines.

What are the statutory provisions related to home schooling in your state?

Home schooling as a form of private schooling is another alternative to attendance in the public schools. The interest in home schooling has increased in the last two decades as many parents, primarily members of fundamentalist religious sects, have objected to the instruction provided in the public schools. Thirty-two states have adopted home school statutes or regulations (Richardson, 1989).

Although each of these statutes vary in its wording, in most states where home schooling is recognized as an alternative to school attendance the home school must meet certain criteria: (1) instruction must essentially be equivalent to that taught in the public schools and include the subjects required by state law, (2) the parent or other adult providing the instruction must be qualified (not necessarily certified) to teach, (3) some systematic reporting must be made to local school authorities, and (4) a minimum number of hours of instruction per day must be provided. In 15 states and the District of Columbia, home schools must be approved by the local school board. And in 25 states, students in home schools must participate in standardized testing or evaluation (Richardson, 1989).

Summary

The legal foundation of education derives from state and federal constitutional provisions, the laws of state and federal legislatures, the enactments of state and federal agencies, court decisions, and state attorney general opinions. Every state constitution includes a provision for education and the wording of the provision has proved important in determining the obligation of the state in providing for education and the constitutionality of legislative action. Although the federal constitution does not mention education, a number of its provisions affect education and afford protections to school personnel, pupils, and patrons.

The interaction of the institutions of religion and education has become the source of increasing legal controversy in recent years. A tension exists between the efforts of the schools to accommodate religion and yet maintain the wall of separation between church and state required by the First Amendment. Thus far the courts have been generally consistent in their decisions keeping religious practices and proselytizing efforts out of the schools. However, the recent decision of the U.S. Supreme Court in *Mergens* to allow student prayer and worship groups access to school property represents not only a potential crack in the wall of separation between church and state, but the growing conservative thrust of the Court. In the next chapter other constitutional rights of teachers and students are explored. Generally the courts have tended to constrain expressions of religion in the schools, as we will see, but these same courts have expanded the rights of teachers and students in a number of other areas.

Key Terms

Administrative law	*Lemon* test
Attorney general	Limited open forum
Child benefit theory	Plenary
Constitution	Secular humanism
Eminent domain	*Stare decisis*
Ex post facto law	Statutory law
Home schooling	Tax benefits
Law	Voucher

Discussion Questions

1. What action, if any, should the school or school board take in regard to any of the parties in the opening vignette of this chapter? What might be done to prevent similar occurrences?

2. What are the provisions of your state constitution regarding education?

3. Describe the levels and types of state courts in your state.

4. What is your school (or school system) policy on silent meditation? Is there support for prayer or Bible reading? On what grounds?

5. What is meant by the *Lemon* test? How effective has it been in distinguishing permissible and impermissible aid to nonpublic school students?

6. How does the child benefit theory serve to justify educational vouchers? How does it operate in the school systems in your area? Are textbooks provided? Is bus transportation provided?

7. What First Amendment issues are currently being debated in the schools in your area?

References

Aguilar v. Felton, 105 S. Ct. 3232 (1985).

Beilan v. Board of Public Education of Philadelphia, 357 U.S. 399 (1958).

Black, H. C. (1983). *Black's law dictionary.* St. Paul, MN: West Publishing Co.

Board of Education of Westside Community Schools v. Mergens, 58 L.W. 4720 (1990).

Brown v. Board of Education of Topeka, 347 U.S. 483 (1954).

Carpio v. Tucson High School District No. 1 of Pima County, 517 P. 2d 1288 (1974).

Cochran v. Louisiana State Board of Education, 281 U.S. 370 (1930).

Collins, G. J. (1969). Constitutional and legal basis for state action. In E. Fuller & J. B. Pearon (Eds.), *Education in the states: Nationwide development since 1900.* Washington, D.C.: National Education Association.

Collins v. Chandler Unified School District, 644 F. 2d 759 (9th Cir. 1981), *cert. denied,* 454 U.S. 863 (1981).

Committee for Public Education and Religious Liberty v. Nyquist, 413 U.S. 756 (1973).

Committee for Public Education and Religious Liberty v. Regan, 444 U.S. 646 (1980).

Edwards v. Aguillard, 107 S. Ct. 2573 (1987).

Engel v. Vitale, 370 U.S. 421 (1962).

Epperson v. Arkansas, 393 U.S. 97 (1968).

Everson v. Board of Education, 330 U.S. 1 (1947).

Ga. Op. Atty. Gen. 1988, No. 18, p. 52.

Gallup, A. M., & Clark, D. L. (1987). The 19th annual Gallup Poll of the public's attitudes toward the public schools. *Phi Delta Kappan, 69,* 24.

Garnett v. Renton School District No. 403, 865 F. 2d 1121 (9th Cir. 1989).

Hudgins, Jr., H. C., & Vacca, R. S. (1985). *Law and education: Contemporary issues and court decisions.* Charlottesville, VA: The Michie Co.

Ingraham v. Wright, 430 U.S. 651 (1977).

Jaffree v. Wallace, 472 U.S. 38 (1985).

Jager v. Douglas County School District, 862 F. 2d 824 (11th Cir. 1989), *cert. denied* (1989).

Jenkinson, E. B. (1986). *The schoolbook protest movement.* Bloomington, IN: Phi Delta Kappa Educational Foundation.

Karen B. v. Treen, 653 F. 2d 897 (5th Cir. 1981), *aff'd mem.,* 455 U.S. 913 (1982).

Kay v. David Douglas School District, 719 P. 2d 875 (Or. App. 1986).

Lanner v. Wimmer, 662 F. 2d 1349 (10th Cir. 1981).

Lemon v. Kurtzman, 93 S. Ct. 1463 (1971).

Levitt v. Committee for Public Education and Religious Liberty, 413 U.S. 472 (1973).

McCarthy, M., & Cambron-McCabe, N. (1987). *Public school law: Teachers and students rights* (2nd ed.). Boston: Allyn and Bacon.

McCollum v. Board of Education of School District No. 71, 68 S. Ct. 461 (1948).

Meek v. Pittenger, 421 U.S. 349 (1975).

Mozert v. Hawkins County Public Schools, 827 F. 2d 1058 (6th Cir. 1987).

Mueller v. Allen, 103 S. Ct. 3062 (1983).

Pierce v. Society of Sisters, 268 U.S. 510 (1925).

Plessey v. Ferguson, 16 S. Ct. 1138 (1896).

Plyler v. Doe, 457 U.S. 202 (1982).

Richardson, S. N. (1989). Home schooling. *NOLPE Notes, 24*(6), 6.

School District of Abington Township v. Schempp, 374 U.S. 203 (1963).

S. J. Lemoine v. St. Landry Parish School, 527 So. 2d 1150 (La. App. 3 Cir. 1988).

Smith v. Board of School Commissioners of Mobile County, 827 F. 2d 684 (11th Cir. 1987).

Stone v. Graham, 449 U.S. 39 (1983).

Strahan, R. D., & Turner, D. L. (1987). *The courts and the schools.* New York: Longman.

United States v. Seeger, 380 U.S. 163 (1965).

Valente, W. D. (1987). *Law in the schools* (2nd ed.). Columbus, OH: Merrill.

Wallace v. Jaffree, 105 S. Ct. 2479 (1985).

Webb, L. D., McCarthy, M. M., & Thomas, S. T. (1988). *Financing elementary and secondary education.* Columbus, OH: Merrill.

Welsh v. United States, 398 U.S. 333 (1970).

West Virginia State Board of Education v. Barnette, 319 U.S. 624(1943).

Witters v. Washington Department of Services for the Blind, 106 S. Ct. 748 (1986).

Wisconsin v. Yoder, 406 U.S. 205 (1972).

Wolman v. Walter, 433 U.S. 229 (1977).

Zorach v. Clauson, 72 S. Ct. 679 (1952).

Chapter 12

Teachers, Students, and the Law

If there is any principle of the Constitution that more imperatively calls for attachment than any other it is the principle of free thought—not free thought for those who agree with us, but freedom for the thought that we hate.

Justice Oliver Wendell Holmes, Jr.
(1841–1935)

Ms. Przanowski is a third grade teacher. It is the first day of the school year. After making a writing assignment, she walks around the room. The children are bent over their desks busily writing "What I Did on My Summer Vacation." Stopping at Johnny Avery's desk, she notices scratch marks on his neck. When asked how he got the marks, Johnny says his cat scratched him. After school, however, Marty Robinson, who was sitting near him when Ms. Przanowski asked the question and heard his reply, comes to her and volunteers that "Johnny has marks all over his back. I saw them during gym."

The next day when Ms. Przanowski again asks Johnny how he got the marks on his neck, she also asks him if he has any marks on his back and if she can see his back. Johnny continues to say that the marks came from his cat, but refuses to let Ms. Przanowski see his back.

What should Ms. Przanowski do now? What are the consequences for the teacher if she fails to report the incident and subsequent child abuse occurs and is confirmed? What are the consequences if she reports her suspicions and subsequent examination proves no further injury?

Like Ms. Przanowski, every day teachers must make decisions that affect the rights of students, their own rights, and their professional lives. It is therefore imperative that teachers be knowledgeable about applicable state and federal legislation, school board policies, and court decisions. After completing this chapter, you will be able to:

- Identify the personal and professional requirements for employment of prospective teachers.

- Describe teachers' employment rights as derived from the employment contract and tenure status.

- Discuss the teacher's responsibility in reporting child abuse and using copyrighted materials.

- Outline the legal requirements for dismissing a teacher.

- Provide an overview of teachers' rights, inside and outside the classroom.

- Define the elements of negligence.

- Compare discrimination, equal opportunity, and affirmative action.

- Contrast the procedural requirements for suspension, expulsion, and corporal punishment.

- Trace the development of student rights in the area of search and seizure.

- Explain the restraints that may be placed on student expression and personal appearance.

- Discuss how the Buckley Amendment has expanded parental and student rights in regard to student records.

- Summarize the response of the courts and school districts to school attendance by AIDS victims.

Teacher Rights and Responsibilities

Although school personnel are not expected to be legal experts, it is imperative that they understand their rights and obligations under the law and that these rights and obligations be translated into everyday practices in the schools. In this chapter the basic concepts of law are presented as they relate to terms and conditions of employment; teacher dismissal; teacher rights outside the classroom; tort liability; and discrimination, equal opportunity, and affirmative action. Although there is some variation in the application of these legal concepts from one state or locality to another, certain topics and issues are of sufficient importance and similarity to warrant consideration. Some of these topics are also discussed in other chapters of this text. Here, attention is given to the legal considerations of these topics.

Terms and Conditions of Employment

As emphasized in the previous chapter, within the framework provided by state and federal constitutional and statutory protections, the state has complete power to conduct and regulate public education. Accordingly, through its legislature, state board of education, state department of education, and local school boards the state promulgates the rules and regulations for the operation of the schools. Among these rules and regulations are those establishing the terms and conditions of employment. The areas most often covered by state statutory and regulatory provisions are those dealing with certification, teacher competency testing, loyalty oaths, citizenship and residency requirements, health and physical requirements, contracts, and tenure.

Certification

As noted in Chapter 1, to qualify for most professional teaching, administrative, and other positions in the public schools, an individual must acquire a valid certificate or license. The certificate does not constitute a contract or guarantee of employment; it only makes the holder eligible for employment.

Does certification ensure a quality teaching force? How have certification standards changed in the state in which you plan to teach since the education reform movement began a decade ago?

All states have established certification requirements for prospective teachers. These requirements may include a college degree with minimum credit hours in various curricular areas, evidence of specific job experience, "good moral character," a specified age, United States citizenship, the signing of a loyalty oath, good health, and a minimum score on a job-related exam. Where specified certification requirements exist, failure to meet the requirements can result in dismissal of the employee and nonpayment.

Competency Testing

Teacher testing is not a new phenomenon. Prior to the growth of teacher education programs, the testing of prospective teachers by the state, county, or school district was common. Depending on the test results, the prospective teacher could get a one-year, two-year, five-year, or life certificate to teach. However, until the last decade only a few states required teachers to pass an examination prior to certification. Beginning in the early 1980s the number of states that tested teachers increased dramatically.

The use of competency tests as either a prerequisite to certification or in the evaluation of practicing educators has generated substantial controversy and has raised questions regarding the legality of basing employment decisions on the results of specific tests (McCarthy, 1985). The legal question is not whether tests can be used; in fact, the U.S. Supreme Court has specifically approved teacher testing (*United States v. South Carolina*, 1978). Rather, the primary issues involve questions of discrimination and unreasonableness in violation of the equal protection clause of the Fourteenth Amendment.

The concern arises as a result of the fact that in most instances where tests have been used in employment decisions, their use has disqualified proportionately more minorities than whites. At the same time, in a number of instances the tests have been shown not to be significantly related to successful job performance. As a result, the judiciary has become more stringent in its requirement that tests be validated for job relatedness and serve a legitimate state purpose. These standards have not been impossible to meet. In the lead case in education, *United States v. South Carolina* (1978), the state conducted content validation studies, pilot tested the test, and submitted test items to a panel of expert reviewers. When the test was administered, a disproportionate number of blacks, especially those educated in predominantly black institutions, fell short of the minimum score. The U.S. Supreme Court ruled that the validation procedure was sufficient and that the test was rationally related to a legitimate state purpose: that of ensuring that certified teachers possess the minimum level of knowledge necessary for effective teaching.

The most recent focus of litigation about teacher testing is on the testing of practicing educators. This testing has been challenged in Arkansas and Texas, two of the three states that have such programs. The Texas testing program required that both teachers and administrators pass an examination as a condition of recertification. The Supreme Court of Texas upheld the requirements, finding that (1) because the teaching certificate is not a contract, the constitutional prohibition against impairment of contracts is not violated, and (2) teacher testing is a rational means of achieving a legitimate state purpose, namely, maintaining competent teachers in the public schools (*State of Texas v. Project Principle, Inc.*, 1987).

Loyalty Oaths

Although there has been increased opposition to loyalty oaths in the last quarter century, they still are required by most states and many school districts as a requirement for certification or as a condition of employment. The courts have said that school employees can be required to sign an oath pledging support for the United States Constitution or an individual state constitution (*Mitchell v. King*, 1975). However, oaths that require employees to disavow *membership* in an allegedly subversive organization are not allowed (*Keyishian v. Board of Regents*, 1967). The courts have held such oaths to be

Does your state require a competency test for certification? Do you feel this type of test is necessary for those who have graduated from a state-approved teacher preparation program?

Most states now require that prospective teachers pass a specified test prior to certification.

unconstitutionally vague and an infringement on the First Amendment right of association.

Citizenship and Residency Requirements

The courts have upheld both citizenship and residency requirements for certification and/or as a condition of employment. With regard to the citizenship requirement, the U.S. Supreme Court has held that education is among those governmental functions that is "so bound up with the operation of the state as a governmental entity as to permit the exclusion from those functions of all persons who have not become part of the process of self-government" (*Ambach v. Norwick*, 1979, pp. 73–74).

Requirements that teachers reside within the district where they are employed have been upheld when there is a rational basis for the requirements. For example, the Sixth Circuit Court of Appeals upheld the residency requirement of the Cincinnati school district because it agreed with the district's stated purposes for the requirement, namely, that teachers would be more committed to urban education, more likely to vote for district taxes, less likely to engage in illegal strikes or to refuse to support tax levies, more likely to be involved in school and community activities bringing them in contact with parents and community leaders, and more likely to gain sympathy and understanding for the racial, social, economic, and urban problems of the children they teach (*Wardwell v. Board of Education of Cincinnati*, 1976).

Health and Physical Requirements

Most states and school boards have adopted health and physical requirements for teachers. The courts have recognized that such requirements are necessary to protect the health and welfare of students and other employees. However, such requirements may not be arbitrarily applied or violate state and federal laws intended to protect the rights of the handicapped (McCarthy & Cambron-McCabe, 1987). For example, Section 504 of the Rehabilitation Act of 1973, which protects otherwise qualified handicapped individuals from discrimination, served as the basis for a 1987 U.S. Supreme Court ruling that overturned the dismissal of an Arkansas teacher with tuberculosis, a contagious disease (*School Board of Nassau County v. Arline*, 1987). The court concluded that persons suffering from the contagious disease of tuberculosis had a physical impairment that justified their being considered handicapped persons within the meaning of the Rehabilitation Act. Accordingly, discrimination based solely on fear of contamination is to be considered discrimination against the handicapped. Thus, the district could not dismiss the teacher without proof that the teacher was otherwise not qualified to teach.

The decision in *Arline* has been relied on by plaintiff teachers in cases involving AIDS. In the lead case, Vincent Chalk, a California teacher of hearing-impaired children, was excluded from the classroom and given an administrative assignment after having been diagnosed as having AIDS. Chalk sought an injunction ordering the school district to restore him to his classroom duties (*Chalk v. U.S. District Court Cent. Dist. of California*, 1988). The U.S. District Court, in granting the injunction, relied heavily on the standard articulated in *Arline* for determining when a contagious disease would prevent an individual from being "otherwise qualified"—that a person who poses a significant risk of communicating an infectious disease to others will not be "otherwise qualified" if reasonable accommodation will not eliminate that risk. In applying the "significant risk of communicating" standard in this instance the court found that the overwhelming consensus of medical and scientific opinion regarding the nature and transmission of AIDS did not support a conclusion that Chalk posed a "significant" risk of communicating the disease to children or others through casual social contact.

How would you respond to being assigned to team teach with a colleague who has a contagious disease?

The Employment Contract

The general principles of contract law apply to the teacher employment contract. That is, in order for the contract to be valid, it must contain the basic elements of: (1) offer and acceptance, (2) legally competent parties, (3) consideration (compensation), (4) legal subject matter, and (5) agreement in form required by law. In addition, the employment contract must meet the specific requirement of applicable state law.

The authority to contract lies exclusively with the school board. Although the superintendent or other officials may screen candidates and recommend employment, only the school board is authorized to enter into contracts, and only when it is a legally constituted body. That is, contracts issued when a quorum of the board is not present or at an illegally called meeting of the board (e.g., adequate notice is not given) are not valid.

In order to be enforceable, a contract must pertain to a legal subject matter (i.e., a contract for the purchase of illegal substances or the performance of illegal services is not enforceable). Also, the contract must be in the proper form required by law.

The employee's rights and obligations of employment are derived from the contract. The courts have held that all valid rules and regulations of the school board, as well as all applicable state statutes, are part of the contract, even if not specifically included. Accordingly, employees may be required to perform certain tasks incidental to classroom activities, regardless of whether the contract specifically mentions them. These have included such activities as field trips, playground and cafeteria duty, supervision of extracurricular activities, and club sponsorship. Teachers cannot, however, be required to drive a bus, perform janitorial duties, or perform duties unrelated to the school program.

Tenure

Tenure is "the status conferred upon teachers who have served a period . . . which then guarantees them continual employment, until retirement, subject to the requirements of good behavior and financial necessity" (Gee & Sperry, 1978, p. T–7). Tenure is a creation of statute designed to maintain permanent and qualified instructional personnel. Most states statutes specify the requirements and procedures for obtaining tenure, which normally include the satisfactory completion of a probationary period of three years. Satisfactory completion of the probationary period does not guarantee tenure, however. In some states tenure is automatically awarded at the end of the probationary period, in others official action of the school board is necessary.

Tenure statutes also normally specify the grounds for dismissal of a tenured teacher and the procedures that must be followed in the dismissal. The dismissal protection afforded tenured teachers is perhaps the major benefit of obtaining tenure. Tenure status gives teachers the security of practicing their profession without threat of removal for arbitrary, capricious, or political motivations. In fact, the courts have said that the granting of tenure in effect awards the teacher with a *property right* to continued employment that cannot be taken away without due process of law.

Does a tenure system protect incompetent teachers? What is your response to proposals that the tenure system be abolished?

However, the awarding of tenure does not guarantee permanent employment. The teacher may be dismissed for disciplinary reasons or because of declining enrollments or financial exigencies. Nor does the granting of tenure guarantee the right to teach in a particular school, grade, or subject area. Subject to due process requirements, teachers may be reassigned to any position for which they are certified.

Other Employment Requirements

In addition to the terms and conditions of employment disclosed in the preceding section, other requirements may be made as a condition of teacher employment as long as they do not violate teacher rights or state or federal law. Some requirements, such as those related to providing reasonable care and maintaining discipline, are discussed later in this chapter. Requirements related to two topics, reporting child abuse and use of copyrighted materials, are discussed here. These topics have become increasingly important to educators in the last decade.

Reporting Child Abuse

As discussed in Chapter 10, teachers are among those professionals named in state statutes as being required to report suspected child abuse. Under most such statutes, failure to report abuse may result in the teacher being found criminally liable with penalties as high as a year in jail and a fine of $1,000 (Fischer, Schimmel, & Kelly, 1987). A civil suit claiming negligence also may be brought against the teacher for failure to report child abuse. Because of the serious consequences of failure to report child abuse, both to the child and to the teacher (and possibly the district), most school boards also have adopted policies affirming the responsibility of district employees to report child abuse and detailing the procedures to be followed when abuse is suspected.

State statutes that require teachers to report suspected child abuse do not demand that reporters be absolutely sure that the child has been abused, only that there be "reasonable cause to believe." All states grant immunity from civil and criminal liability to reporters if the report was made in good faith (McCarthy & Cambron-McCabe, 1987).

Use of Copyrighted Materials

Copyright laws are designed to protect the author or originator of an original work from unauthorized reproduction or use of the work. Because of their widespread use of print and nonprint material in the classroom, it is important that teachers be knowledgeable about and comply with federal copyright laws. Some guidelines that will give you some direction in determining what constitutes fair use of copyright material for classroom use are presented on page 386.

The increasing use of instructional technology has brought to light a number of issues related to use of copyrighted nonprint materials, namely, television programs, videotapes, and computer software. In 1981 Congress issued Guidelines for Off-the-Air Recording of Broadcast Programming for Educational Purposes. The guidelines provide that a nonprofit educational institution may tape television programs for classroom use if requested by an individual teacher. Programs also may be taped at home by the teacher. All copies must include the copyright notice on the program. During the first 10 days after taping, the material may be shown once by the individual teacher and may be repeated only once for purposes of instructional reinforcement. Additional use is limited to viewing for evaluating the program. After 45 days the tape must be erased or destroyed.

The copying of copyrighted computer software became a major area of copyright infringement in the 1980s. The 1980 amendments to the copyright law permit one archival or backup copy to be made of the master program; making multiple copies, even for educational purposes, would be a violation of

For Future Reference:
Guidelines for Classroom Copying

1. A single copy may be made of any of the following for your own scholarly research or use in teaching:

   A. A chapter from a book;

   B. An article from a periodical or newspaper;

   C. A short story, short essay or short poem;

   D. A chart, graph, diagram, drawing, cartoon or picture from a book, periodical, or newspaper.

2. Multiple copies (not to exceed in any event more than one copy per pupil in a course) may be made for classroom use or discussion, provided that each copy includes a notice of copyright and that the following tests are met:

   A. Brevity Test

      (i) Poetry: (a) a complete poem if less than 250 words and if printed on not more than two pages, or (b) from a longer poem, an excerpt of not more than 250 words.

      (ii) Prose: (a) Either a complete article, story or essay of less than 2,500 words, or (b) an excerpt from any prose work of not more than 1,000 words or 10 percent of the work, whichever is less, but in any event a minimum of 500 words.

      (iii) Illustration: One chart, graph, diagram, drawing, cartoon or picture per book or per periodical issue.

      (iv) "Special" works in poetry, prose or in "poetic prose" which combine language with illustrations and are less than 2,500 words in their entirety may not be reproduced in their entirety; however, an excerpt of not more than two of the published pages of such special work and containing not more than 10 percent of the words may be reproduced.

   B. Spontaneity Test

      (i) The copying is at your instance and inspiration, and

      (ii) The inspiration and decision to use the work and the moment of its use for maximum teaching effectiveness are so close in time that it would be unreasonable to expect you would receive a timely reply to a request for permission.

   C. Cumulative Effect Test

      (i) The copying of the material is for only one course in the school in which the copies are made.
      (ii) Not more than one short poem, article, story, essay or two excerpts may be copied from the same author, nor more than three from the same collective work or periodical volume during one class term.
      (iii) There cannot be more than nine instances of multiple copying for one course during one class term.

   [These limitations do not apply to current news periodicals and newspapers and current news sections of other periodicals].

3. Copying cannot be used to create or to replace or substitute for anthologies, compilations or collective works.

4. There can be no copying of, or from, "consumable" works (e.g., workbooks, exercises, standardized tests and test booklets and answer sheets).

5. Copying cannot substitute for the purchase of books, publishers' reprints or periodicals.

6. Copying cannot be directed by a higher authority.

7. You cannot copy the same item from term to term.

8. No charge can be made to the student beyond the actual cost of the photocopying.

Source: Excerpt from Report of the House Committee on the Judiciary (House Report No. 94–1476).

Teachers are responsible for prohibiting unauthorized use of copyrighted computer software in their classes.

the fair use principle. Not as clear a violation of the copyright law but probably a violation of most license agreements is multiple use of a single master program (e.g., loading it onto a number of computers in a laboratory for simultaneous use or using it in a computer network) unless the program is specifically a network-compatible version or unless such use is covered by a site license agreement. In the use of copyrighted software, as in the use of any copyrighted material, teachers are required to obey both the letter and the spirit of copyright laws and adhere to any relevant school board policies or guidelines.

Teacher Dismissal

Teacher dismissal actions take several forms. Among them are dismissal for cause, reduction in force, and nonrenewal of contract. The legal requirements for dismissal vary not only among the states but with the form of dismissal and the status (tenured or nontenured) of the teacher. In this section, broad legal concepts applicable to these three forms are discussed.

Dismissal for Cause

All states have some statutory provisions regarding teacher dismissal for cause. The reasons specified for dismissal vary from the very general (e.g., "good cause") to the very specific. The reasons most frequently cited in statutes are immorality, incompetency, and insubordination. Among the other commonly mentioned reasons are neglect of duty, unprofessional conduct, unfitness to teach, and the catchall "other good and just cause."

Immorality.   Although immorality is the most frequently cited ground for dismissal, state statutes normally do not define the term or discuss its application to specific conduct. However, dismissals related to immorality generally have been based on one or more of the following: sexual misconduct with students, sexual misconduct with nonstudents, homosexuality, drug or alcohol abuse, criminal misconduct, and dishonesty.

Should teachers be held to a higher standard of conduct than other professionals? Why or why not?

In reviewing cases alleging immorality the courts have applied certain standards. First is the exemplar standard. That is, the courts recognize that "a teacher serves as a role model for his student" (*Ambach v. Norwick*, 1979) and thus is required to meet a higher standard of conduct than that required of a noneducator. Second, there must be a connection between the out-of-school conduct of the teacher and the teacher's ability to teach, or the conduct must have an adverse effect on the school or be the subject of notoriety. About the only offenses not requiring the establishment of a connection between conduct and fitness to teach are sexual misconduct with students and conviction of certain crimes (Delon, 1982).

Most cases involving alleged immorality must be decided on a case-by-case basis, balancing the teacher's personal freedom against the school board's interest in maintaining a proper educational environment and taking into consideration the size of the community, its values, and when and where the conduct took place. The courts have provided guidance on some issues, however. For example, most courts have not supported the dismissal of pregnant, unwed teachers (see, e.g., *Eckmann v. Board of Education*, 1986) or the dismissal of teachers for consenting sexual relationships out of wedlock (see, e.g., *Littlejohn v. Rose*, 1985), unless it can be shown that the teacher's effectiveness has been impaired by his or her action.

The courts also have held that conviction of a felony or misdemeanor, including possession of illegal drugs, does not necessarily, in and of itself, serve as grounds for dismissal. Again, the circumstances of each case are important, especially the effect on the school, students, and co-workers. For example, courts might not uphold the dismissal of a teacher solely because he or she once was indicted for possession of a small amount of marijuana. But they probably would support a firing based on evidence of a widely publicized conviction, combined with testimony that the teacher's criminal behavior would undermine his or her effectiveness as a teacher (Fischer, Schimmel, & Kelly, 1987).

The exceptions to the principle that to sustain a sanction the behavior must affect teaching performance or become the subject of notoriety have been made most often in regard to notoriously illegal or immoral behavior, including sexual misconduct with minors and homosexual conduct. In some states, engaging in certain homosexual activity is a violation of state sodomy laws and a conviction of such a violation could serve as the basis for dismissal. In states other than California the courts have upheld the dismissal of homosexual and bisexual teachers based only on their private conduct, when no conviction of law had taken place. In Washington, a high school teacher was dismissed after admitting to his assistant principal that he was a homosexual. Although it was not the teacher but school officials who then publicized his homosexual status, the court accepted the officials' testimony that his continued presence would interfere with the orderly operation of the school (*Gaylord v. Tacoma School District No. 10*, 1977).

The Supreme Court refused to review the *Gaylord* case. The high court also refused to review the case of a guidance counselor who was not rehired after sharing with several co-workers that she was bisexual and had a female lover (*Rowland v. Mad River Local School District*, 1984). Since the Supreme Court has not recognized a privacy right to engage in homosexual conduct, a range of interpretations among lower courts regarding homosexual teachers' rights seems likely to continue (McCarthy & Cambron-McCabe, 1987).

Incompetency.   Those conditions or behaviors that have been sustained most successfully as constituting *incompetence* fall into four general categories: (1) inadequate teaching; (2) poor discipline; (3) physical or mental incapacity; and (4) counterproductive personality traits. As with other attempted dismissals, in dismissals for incompetence the courts require that there be an established relationship between the employee's conduct and the operation of the school. Additionally, the standard against which the teacher is measured must be one used for other teachers in a similar position, not some hypothetical standard of perfection, and the conduct must not be an isolated incident but a demonstrated *pattern* of incompetence. Most jurisdictions also require that before termination a determination be made whether the behavior in question is remedial and that, in jurisdictions where remediation is required, a reasonable period for remediation be provided (Landauer, Spanfer, & Van Horn, 1983).

Insubordination.   Regardless of whether or not it is specified in statute, *insubordination* is an acceptable cause for dismissal in all states. Insubordination involves the *persistent* and *willful* violation of a reasonable rule or direct order from a recognized authority. Among the actions that have been held to constitute insubordination are absence from duty without official authority; refusal to follow established procedures; use of corporal punishment in violation of school policies; encouraging students to disobey or disrespect school authority;

and disrupting school harmony by improper criticism of authority (Valente, 1987).

Reduction in Force (RIF)

Declining enrollments, school consolidations, financial shortfalls, curriculum changes and other occurrences often result in a *reduction in force (RIF)*, i.e., reduction of the total number of employees needed by the district and the release of excess employees. Normally, neither tenured nor nontenured teachers released because of position abolition are entitled to a hearing unless it is required by statute. The courts generally consider these dismissals to be impersonal, in no way impugning the teacher and therefore outside the scope of teacher termination statutes. However, the reasons articulated by the district must be real, reasonable, and supported by substantial evidence (Valente, 1987).

The majority of litigation related to RIF has been concerned with questions of preference, i.e., who was selected for release from employment. State statutes and school board policies often specify the order of release in terms of tenure, seniority, or other criteria. When statutes or policies are silent or ambiguous about order of release, the courts have tended to give qualified tenured teachers priority over nontenured teachers in similar positions. Certification has been the major but not the exclusive criterion considered by the courts in determining "qualifiedness." Among tenured teachers holding similar positions, seniority has been the primary but not the exclusive factor in determining order of release. Seniority rights may be qualified by other factors such as performance evaluations, areas of need, affirmative action goals, or collective bargaining agreements.

In 1986 the U.S. Supreme Court addressed the circumstances under which seniority rights may be abrogated by an affirmative action plan. In *Wygant v. Jackson Board of Education*, the Supreme Court overturned a Michigan school district's collective bargaining agreement that released white employees with greater seniority than black employees in order to preserve the percentage of minority teachers employed prior to the layoffs. The court held that in the absence of convincing evidence supporting past discrimination in the district, the desire to remedy general societal discrimination was insufficient to give blacks preferential treatment. The court likewise rejected the role model argument—that the percentage of minority teachers should reflect the percentage of minority students—suggesting instead that the proper comparison is to the percentage of available minorities in the relevant labor market.

The order of recall of RIF employees, should vacancies arise for which they are qualified, is roughly the inverse of the order of release. That is, qualified tenured teachers would be called back before nontenured teachers in the order of seniority within each group.

Nonrenewal of Contract

The contracts of tenured teachers are renewed automatically unless they are dismissed for cause or declared excess. Nontenured teachers, however, have no such right. In the absence of state law to the contrary, school boards may terminate nontenured teachers without giving any statement of reasons or providing opportunity for a hearing or any due process, except perhaps timely notification of intent to nonrenew. However, if the nontenured teacher is dismissed before the expiration of the contract, the teacher is entitled to due process.

Procedural Due Process

In keeping with the Fourteenth Amendment, if the dismissal of a teacher involves a liberty or property right, procedural *due process* must be provided. As previously noted, tenured teachers have a property right to continued employment. Nontenured teachers do not have a property right claim to due process unless they are dismissed during the contract year or unless the dismissal action impairs a fundamental constitutional right, creates a stigma, or damages the employee's reputation to the extent that it forecloses other employment opportunities.

What do the statutes say in the state in which you plan to teach regarding the nonrenewal of contracts of nontenured teachers? What, if any, due process is required?

Once it has been established that a school district action requires procedural due process, the central issue becomes *what process is due.* In arriving at its decision the court will look to the procedural due process requirements in state statutes, state agency or school board regulations, or employment contracts to determine both their propriety and the extent to which they were followed.

Generally the courts have held that an employee facing a severe loss such as termination of employment must be ensured the following procedural elements:

1. notice of charges
2. adequate time to prepare a rebuttal to the charges
3. names of witnesses and access to evidence
4. a hearing before an impartial tribunal
5. the right to representation by legal counsel
6. the opportunity to introduce evidence and cross-examine witnesses
7. a decision based solely on the evidence presented
8. a transcript or record of the hearing
9. the right to appeal (Cambron-McCabe, 1983)

Notice must not merely be given, it must be timely (on or before an established date) and in sufficient specificity to enable the employee to attempt to remediate or to prepare an adequate defense. A formal hearing as practiced in courts is not required, but the hearing must provide the employee a full and fair opportunity to rebut all charges. Table 12.1 lists some Supreme Court cases affecting teachers' rights in matters of employment and in matters inside and outside the classroom.

Table 12.1: Selected U.S. Supreme Court Cases Affecting Teachers' Rights

Case	Decision
Indiana *ex rel.* Anderson v. Brand (1938)	Tenure statutes provide qualifying teachers with contractual rights that cannot be altered by the state without good cause.
Keyishian v. Board of Regents (1967)	Loyalty oaths that make mere membership in a subversive organization grounds for dismissal are unconstitutionally overbroad.
Pickering v. Board of Education (1968)	Absent proof of false statements knowingly or recklessly made, teachers may not be dismissed for exercising the freedom to speak on matters of public interest.
Board of Regents v. Roth (1972)	A nontenured teacher does not have a property right to continued employment and can be dismissed without a statement of cause or a hearing as long as the employee's reputation or future employment have not been impaired.
Perry v. Sindermann (1972)	Teachers may not be dismissed for public criticism of superiors on matters of public concern.
Hortonville Joint School District No. 1 v. Hortonville Education Association (1976)	A school board may serve as the impartial hearing body in a due process hearing.
Washington v. Davis (1976)	To sustain a claim of discrimination an employee must show that the employer's action was a deliberate attempt to discriminate, not just that the action resulted in a disproportionate impact.
Mount Healthy City School District v. Doyle (1977)	To prevail in a First Amendment dismissal case school district employees must show that the conduct was protected and was a substantial and motivating decision not to renew the contract and the school board must prove that it would have reached the same decision in the absence of the protected conduct.
United States v. South Carolina (1978)	Use of the National Teachers Examinations both as a requirement for certification and as a factor in salary determination serves a legitimate state purpose and is not unconstitutional despite its disparate racial impact.
Connick v. Myers (1983)	The First Amendment guarantee of freedom of expression does not extend to teachers' public comments on matters of personal interest (as opposed to matters of public concern).
Cleveland Board of Education v. Laudermill (1985)	A teacher who can be dismissed only for cause is entitled to an oral or written notice of charges, a statement of the evidence against him or her, and the opportunity to present his or her side prior to termination.
Garland Independent School District v. Texas State Teachers Association (1986)	Teachers can use the interschool mail system and school mailboxes to distribute union material.
Wygant v. Jackson Board of Education (1986)	Absent evidence that the school board has engaged in discrimination or that the preferred employees have been victims of discrimination, school board policies may not give preferential treatment based on race or ethnicity in layoff decisions.
School Board of Nassau County v. Arline (1987)	Persons suffering from contagious diseases are considered handicapped persons, and discrimination against them based solely on fear of contamination is considered unconstitutional discrimination against the handicapped.

Teacher Rights Outside the Classroom

Even in the twentieth century, school boards in this country considered it their right and indeed their responsibility to control the personal as well as the professional conduct of teachers. School boards sought to regulate teachers' dress, speech, religion, and association. As the twentieth century has progressed, teacher activism, court decisions, and enlightened legislators and school boards have greatly expanded the rights of teachers.

Freedom of Expression

In the landmark U.S. Supreme Court decision regarding freedom of expression in the public schools, *Tinker v. Des Moines* (1969), the Court ruled that neither teachers nor students shed their constitutional rights to freedom of speech or expression when they enter the schoolhouse gate. However, this does not mean that teachers or students are free to say or write anything they wish. Rather, in reviewing cases involving expression, the courts attempt to balance the rights of the individual against the harm caused to the schools.

In the lead case involving teachers' freedom of expression, Marvin Pickering, a high school teacher in Illinois, was terminated after writing a letter to the newspaper severely criticizing the superintendent and school board for their handling of school funds. On appeal the U.S. Supreme Court (*Pickering v. Board of Education*, 1968) overturned his dismissal and ruled that teachers, as citizens, do have the right to make critical public comments on matters of public concern. The court further held that unless the expression undermines (1) the effectiveness of the working relationship between the teacher and the immediate superior, (2) harmony among co-workers, (3) the proper performance of the teacher's duties in the classroom, or (4) the orderly operation of the schools, such expression may not furnish grounds for reprisal. Finding that the issue of school board spending is an issue of legitimate public concern and that Pickering's statements were not directed at people he normally worked with, nor that there was any undermining of the operation of the schools (in fact, the letter had been greeted with apathy by everyone but the board), the Supreme Court overturned Pickering's dismissal.

If, however, the public comment is not concerned with matters of public concern, it is not protected. The U.S. Supreme Court ruled in *Connick v. Myers* (1983) that free expression is not protected when a public employee "speaks not as a citizen upon matters of public concern, but instead as an employee upon matters only of personal interest" (p. 138). Thus public criticism or complaints about individual work assignments, conditions of employment, or relations with superiors generally have not been found to be matters of public concern (McCarthy & Cambron-McCabe, 1987).

Even if expression does involve a public issue, it still is not protected if it undermines the effectiveness of working relationships or the normal operation of the schools. For example, in an Alaska case (*Watts v. Seward School Board*, 1969) two teachers were dismissed for writing an open letter to the school board (which they also publicly distributed) that contained a number of false allegations against their immediate superior. Unlike the apathetic response to Pickering's letter, the response to the letter in this case was public controversy that lasted for more than a year. In upholding their dismissal, the Alaska Supreme Court found that the teachers' actions had in fact impaired the working relationship between the supervisor and the teachers and was detrimental to discipline and harmony in the schools.

Last, school employees do not have the right to make public statements about confidential matters related to the school district, its employees, or students. The courts have concluded that public disclosure of such matters can, in fact, "interfere with the orderly operation of the school system" (*Swilley v. Alexander*, 1978).

Right to Organize, Bargain Collectively, and Strike

The associational rights of teachers have been greatly expanded in the last quarter century. The courts have ruled that teachers have the right of free association, and unjustified interference with this right by school boards violates the Fourteenth Amendment. In fact, the Supreme Court has sanctioned the use of the school mail for dissemination of union literature, as well as the right to engage in discussion of union activities during nonclass time (*Texas State Teachers' Association v. Garland Independent School District*, 1986).

Although teachers have a right to form or join a union or professional association, whether they have a right to engage in collective bargaining depends on state law. About two-thirds of the states have passed laws permitting school boards to engage in collective bargaining with teacher groups. The collective bargaining laws vary widely. Some states require school boards only to "meet and confer" with the teacher organization. Other statutes are much more detailed, specifying the topics to be negotiated (typically, salary, leaves of absence, job benefits, transfers, and days and hours of employment) and the procedures to be followed if an impasse occurs in the negotiations (Fischer, Schimmel, & Kelly, 1987).

Should teachers be denied the right to strike? What would you do if your professional association called for a strike when state law forbids teachers to strike?

Despite the recognition of the right of teachers to organize, the right to strike has not been recognized by the courts and is denied by about half the states. In those states where strikes are allowed, they usually are allowed only after the requirements for impasse resolution have been met and only after the school board has been notified of the intent to strike. When teachers strike in violation of state law or without having met the requirements of the law, the school board may seek an injunction to prohibit the strike. Violation of a court order or an injunction ordering strikers back to work may result in a contempt of court decree and fine or imprisonment. Moreover, those who engage in illegal strikes may be subject to various economic sanctions (e.g., withholding of raises or fines) or disciplinary actions, including dismissal (*Hortonville Joint School District No. 1 v. Hortonville Education Association*, 1976).

Political Activity

Teachers have the right to engage in political activities and hold public office; however, restrictions may be placed on the exercise of this right. For example, teachers may discuss political issues and candidates in a nonpartisan manner in the classroom and even wear political buttons, badges, or armbands to class. However, they may not make campaign speeches in the classroom or otherwise take advantage of their position of authority over a captive audience to promote their own political views. Political activity in the schools that would cause divisiveness among the faculty or otherwise be disruptive also may be restricted if the school can demonstrate it is necessary to meet a compelling public need to protect efficiency and integrity in the school (McCarthy & Cambron-McCabe, 1987).

The authority of the school board to restrict teachers' political activities outside the school setting is far less than their authority to restrict activities in the schools. The courts have upheld teachers' right to support candidates of their choice, display political buttons and stickers, and participate in demonstrations. In addition, the courts generally have upheld the right of teachers to run for and hold public office. However, the courts also have indicated that if the time and activities associated with running for or holding office interferes with the performance of teaching duties, the teacher may be required to take a leave of absence or even resign. Also, the courts in some states have found the holding of certain political offices (e.g., school board member), to present a conflict of interest with employment in the schools and therefore forbid the joint occupancy of both positions.

Academic Freedom

Academic freedom refers to the teacher's freedom to discuss the subject matter discipline and to determine the most appropriate instructional materials and teaching strategies without unwarranted restrictions. Academic freedom is not without limits. For example, teachers do not have the ultimate right to determine course content or select textbooks; that authority belongs to the school board. Nor do teachers have the right to ignore prescribed content or to refuse to follow the designated scope and sequence of content or materials. In addition, teachers may be required to receive prior approval for the use of supplementary materials. Failure to follow prescribed policy may result in disciplinary action (*Fisher v. Fairbanks North Star Borough School District*, 1985).

Although teachers have limited freedom in determining the content of the curriculum, they have greater freedom in choosing the particular strategies to teach the prescribed content. In reviewing school board attempts to restrict teachers' methodologies, the courts consider a number of factors, including

> the adequacy of notice that use of specific teaching methodologies will result in disciplinary action, the relevance of the method to the course of study, the support for the strategy or materials by the teaching profession, and the threat of disruption posed by the method. The judiciary also has considered community standards in assessing challenges to various teaching methods. However, if a particular strategy is instructionally relevant and supported by the profession, it will probably survive judicial review even though it might offend some parents. (McCarthy, 1989, p. 260)

In a case in point, a Texas teacher was discharged for failure to obey a school board warning that she refrain from using a role-playing simulation to teach about post–Civil War American history (*Kingsville Independent School*

If you felt strongly that a particular candidate would be in the best interest of education in your community or state, how would you work for his or her election? Would you consider running for public office as an "education candidate" in order to improve education?

District v. Cooper, 1980). Parents had complained that the simulation aroused strong feelings about racial issues. When the teacher refused to obey the district's directive "not to discuss Blacks in American history" her contract was not renewed. The Fifth Circuit Court of Appeals reinstated the teacher and awarded back pay and attorney's fees, finding that the district violated her constitutional rights by basing the nonrenewal on classroom discussions that were protected by the First Amendment.

If, however, the teacher is discussing or distributing material that is not relevant or using a teaching method that is not supported by the profession, the teacher may be sanctioned. This was the case when a math teacher was dismissed for expressing his opinion on the inappropriateness of Army recruiters being at the school and urging students to take action against the recruiters to force them off campus. The court held his comments to be irrelevant to his math class and to divert time and attention from the prescribed curriculum and supported his dismissal (*Birdwell v. Hazelwood School District*, 1974).

Book Banning.   Currently, perhaps the most contested academic freedom issue involves attempts to censor the curriculum by excluding certain offerings (e.g., on evolution, sex education, and values clarification) or materials deemed vulgar, offensive, or that promote secular humanism. The courts typically have supported the school board in the face of parental attempts to censor the curriculum or ban certain books from the school library. However, when it is the school board itself that advocates censorship, judicial support is not as easily won. This is because the courts traditionally have recognized the authority of the school board to determine the curriculum, select texts, purchase books for the library, approve the use of supplementary materials, and perform a host of other curriculum-related activities. Nonetheless, in a number of instances the courts have found that specific censorship activities violated the teacher's right to academic freedom or students' First Amendment rights to have access to information. While acknowledging that the banning of books and materials on the basis of obscenity or educational unsuitability is permissible, the courts in these cases have held that censorship motivated primarily by the preferences of school board members or to suppress particular viewpoints or controversial ideas is not permissible.

The only U.S. Supreme Court decision dealing with curriculum censorship in the public schools offers little guidance. The case, *Board of Education, Island Trees Union Free School District No. 26 v. Pico* (1982), involved the removal of nine library books and one book in the curriculum of a twelfth grade literature course. The Supreme Court affirmed the appellate court's order for a trial to determine the board's motivation and the procedure followed in the removal of books, but it did not resolve the censorship issue. However, the case did provide a recognition by the highest judicial authority that arbitrary censorship activities by school boards can violate the First Amendment rights of students.

The controversy regarding who controls instructional and curricular matters, teachers or the school board, is likely to continue as are parental attempts to exert greater control over the curriculum. Until definitive guidance is provided by the Supreme Court, resolution will continue on a case-by-case basis, attempting to balance the teacher's interest in academic freedom against the school board's interest in promoting an appropriate educational environment.

Tort Liability of Teachers

A *tort* is defined as a civil wrong that leads to injury to another (criminal wrongs are not torts) and for which a court will provide a remedy in the form of an action for damages. Historically, school districts were protected from acts of tort liability by the doctrine of *sovereign immunity*, which prevents potential litigants from suing the government unless the government consents to the suit. Over the years, the doctrine has been weakened as over half the states have abandoned this protection. Even when the district has immunity, teachers and others do not. To protect both school district employees and school board members against financial loss resulting from a tort suit, many school districts purchase liability insurance. Many educators also participate in liability insurance programs through their professional organizations.

The most common category of torts in education is *negligence*. Basically, negligence can be defined as a failure to do (or not do) what a reasonable and prudent person would have done under the same or similar circumstances, resulting in injury to another. Before an educator can be found guilty of negligence, four elements must be proved:

1. The educator had a duty to provide an appropriate standard of care to another individual (student, co-worker, the public).

2. The educator failed in his or her duty to provide the reasonable standard of care.

3. There is a causal relationship between the negligent action and the resultant injury (i.e., the action was the *proximate cause* of the injury).

4. There is a physical or mental injury resulting in actual loss.

Standard of Care and Duty

Although teachers have the responsibility of providing an appropriate standard of care for their students, the standard of care expected is not the same for all teachers and all students. Teachers of younger children are held to a higher standard of care than teachers of more mature students. A higher standard of care also is required of teachers of the physically or mentally handicapped, as well as of physical education and vocational and industrial arts teachers because of the inherent dangers in the activities involved.

Reasonableness Doctrine. In determining whether the educator failed to provide the appropriate standard of care, the courts compare the teacher's actions with those of the hypothetical "reasonable and prudent" teacher—one with average intelligence and physical attributes, normal perception and memory, and possessing the same special knowledge and skills as others with his or her training and experience—not some "ideal" or "super" teacher.

Foreseeable Doctrine.   A related element is whether the hypothetical reasonable teacher could have foreseen and thus prevented the injury. The actions of the teacher are compared with those of the reasonable teacher to determine negligence.

Proximate Cause

Even in situations in which the teacher has failed in his or her recognized duty to provide a reasonable standard of care, liability will not be assessed unless it can be shown that the teacher's action was the proximate cause of the injury, that is, that the injury would not have occurred had it not been for the teacher's conduct. In some cases an intervening event, such as the negligent act of a third party, may relieve the teacher of liability.

What impact does the potential for negligence suits have on educational practice?

Because each case brings with it a set of circumstances distinct from all others, the determination of proximate cause must be made on a case-by-case basis. For example, when a six-year-old kindergarten student was injured by a rock thrown by a ten-year-old while both were waiting at a bus stop, the court found that not only was there no duty owed by the school district to prevent older students from mingling with younger students at the same bus stop, but that the "intervening unforeseeable" act of the older student was the "sole proximate cause" of the injury (*Fornaro v. Kerry*, 1988).

Educational Malpractice

Historically, most educational liability litigation has involved pupil injuries. In the last 15 years, however, a new topic of negligence litigation called educational *malpractice* has emerged and has become the focus of concerned discussion in both the educational and legal communities. As in medical malpractice, the term is concerned with some negligence on the part of the professional. In general there are two kinds of educational malpractice suits: (1) instructional malpractice, or suits involving students who have graduated from high school but are functionally illiterate, and (2) suits involving misdiagnosis and improper educational placement.

Thus far, each educational malpractice suit filed has been dismissed. In regard to the first kind of suit, the courts have continued to reject student claims that they have a right to a predetermined level of achievement in return for compulsory school attendance. In the seminal case in this area, *Peter W. v. San Francisco Unified School District* (1976), Peter W. was awarded a high school diploma even though he was functionally illiterate. Peter W. sued the district for negligence in allowing him to graduate. The courts dismissed the case, finding no certainty that a causal relationship existed between the defendants' conduct and Peter W.'s injuries. In *Peter W.* and a similar action in New York, *Donohue v. Copiague Union Free Schools* (1979), the courts noted that allowing such suits would require the courts to intervene in matters of

Some activities, such as physical education, require that teachers exercise a higher standard of care.

educational policy and to become entangled in educational questions—actions judged inappropriate for the courts and that would flood the courts with similar suits.

In the lead case concerned with placement malpractice, *Hoffman v. Board of Education of the City of New York* (1979), plaintiff Hoffman was examined by a school psychologist upon entry to kindergarten using the Stanford-Binet intelligence test, which, in part, requires verbal responses. Hoffman had a severe speech defect. The psychologist recommended that he be placed in a class for the mentally retarded, but also that he be reexamined in two years. No reexamination took place for 13 years, and then only at his mother's request. This examination showed him to be of normal intelligence. Hoffman sued and was awarded $750,000 in damages by the jury. A New York Court of Appeals later overturned the award, stating that it was unwilling to

> substitute its judgment for the professional judgment of the board of education as to the type of psychometric devices to be used and the frequency with which such tests are to be given. Such a decision would allow a court or a jury to second guess the determinations of each of the plaintiff teachers. To do so would open the door to an examination of the propriety of each of the procedures used in the education of every student in our school system. (p. 320)

Other cases involving alleged negligence in diagnosis and placement have been equally unsuccessful.

Discrimination, Equal Opportunity, and Affirmative Action

Discrimination

School districts and their employees are prohibited by the Fourteenth Amendment and numerous state and federal statutes (see Table 11.1) from engaging in practices that intentionally discriminate against employees or students on the basis of race, sex, age, religion, national origin, or handicapping condition. To be successful in a claim of *discrimination*, the employee must prove either that the district's action constituted a deliberate intent to discriminate, not just that the action resulted in a disproportionate impact (*Washington v. Davis*, 1976), or that the district's stated reason for the action could be accomplished by less discriminatory means.

However, even if the action has an adverse impact on an individual in a protected class, the court will not intervene if the district can show that its action was based on a legitimate, nondiscriminatory reason, such as following established criteria related to academic preparation or experience or evaluation of past performance. For example, a court upheld a district's decision not to rehire a woman who had held the position of assistant director of transportation prior to its abolishment for financial reasons when the position was reinstated three years later, because evidence presented related to her past performance indicated a serious lack of interpersonal skills (*Mira v. Monroe County School Board*, 1988).

Equal Opportunity

The legal principle of *equal opportunity*, whether equal employment opportunity or equal educational opportunity, is founded in antidiscrimination legislation. Equal opportunity requires that school districts and other agencies develop policies and procedures to ensure that the rights of employees and students are protected and that they are given equal treatment in employment practices, access to programs, or other educational opportunities.

Affirmative Action

Where does the primary responsibility reside for increasing the number of minorities in education? What should school districts do to increase the percentage of women in school administration?

Affirmative action goes beyond equal opportunity. The principle of affirmative action holds that ensuring nondiscrimination is not enough; what is needed are affirmative steps to recruit, hire, and retain individuals who are underrepresented in the workplace or the classroom. Many school districts have adopted affirmative action plans that set forth their intended goals in these areas and their intended actions to achieve these goals.

The U.S. Supreme Court in *Regents of the University of California v. Alan Bakke* (1978) ruled against the establishment of firm quotas that designate a predetermined number of "slots" only for minorities, resulting in so-called *reverse discrimination*. However, the court has upheld the voluntary adoption of goals designed to bring balance to the composition of the workforce or student body (see, e.g., *Kaiser Aluminum and Chemical Corporation v. Weber*, 1979). Nonetheless, as the U.S. Supreme Court ruled in the *Wygant* case previously discussed, as well as in a later noneducation case, *City of Richmond v. J. A. Croson Co.* (1989), affirmative action plans must be designed to remedy location-specific past discrimination, not general societal discrimination. That is, evidence must first exist that remedial action is necessary and, second, the plan must be "narrowly tailored" to remedy the past discrimination.

Student Rights and Responsibilities

Traditionally, it was accepted that school officials had considerable authority in controlling student conduct. Operating under the doctrine of *in loco parentis* (in place of a parent) school authorities exercised almost unlimited and usually unchallenged discretion in restricting the rights of students and in disciplining students. However, beginning in the late 1960s students increasingly challenged the authority and actions of school officials. Subsequent court decisions have broadened the scope of student rights and, at the same time, have attempted to maintain a balance between the rights of students and the responsibilities of school officials (see Figure 12.1 and the discussion of "no pass, no play" on p. 405).

Student Discipline

Although the *in loco parentis* doctrine has been weakened in recent years, school officials do have the authority—and in fact the duty—to establish reasonable rules of student conduct designed to protect students and employees, as well as rules necessary to establish and maintain a climate conducive to learning. The authority and responsibility to establish rules of conduct carries with it the authority to discipline students for violations of these rules. The severity of the violation will determine the nature of the discipline and the due process required. Because state compulsory attendance laws give students a property right to attend school, if disciplinary action involves exclusion from school or the removal of the student from the classroom for even a minimal period of time, some due process is required, even if in the latter instance it is only informally providing the student the opportunity to give his or her side of the story.

Suspensions and Expulsions

Short-term *suspensions* usually are defined as exclusions of students from school for periods of time of 10 days or less; *expulsions* (i.e., long-term suspensions) are for periods of time in excess of 10 days. While a teacher or administrator may initiate an expulsion proceeding, normally only the school board can expel the student. Because of the severity of expulsions, state statutes and school board regulations detail the procedures that must be followed. Such procedures usually include the right to:

1. a written notice specifying the charges, the time and place of the hearing, and the procedures to be followed at the hearing

2. a hearing before an impartial tribunal

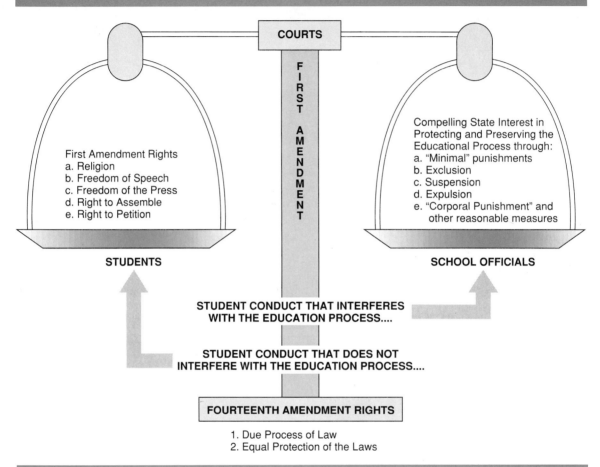

Figure 12.1: Balancing the Rights of Students and the Responsibilities of School Officials

Source: From *The Schools, the Courts, and the Public Interest* by J. C. Hogan. Copyright © 1974, 1985 by Lexington Books, an imprint of Macmillan, Inc.

3. cross-examine witnesses and present witnesses and evidence to refute adverse evidence

4. representation by counsel (usually only in the more serious disciplinary actions)

5. a written statement of the findings/recommendations of the hearing body

6. a written or taped record of the hearing if appeal is to be made

7. a clear statement of the right to appeal

In contrast to the detailed statutory guidelines pertaining to expulsions, state laws and school board policies traditionally did not address short-term suspensions; therefore, practices have varied across the country. In 1975, however, in *Goss v. Lopez*, the U.S. Supreme Court established the basic procedures that must be followed in short-term suspensions. The Court held that for suspensions of less than 10 days the student must be given oral or written notice of the charges, and if the student denies the charges, he or she must be given a hearing with the opportunity to rebut the charges before an objective decision maker and be given an explanation of the evidence against him or her. The Court in *Goss* also recognized that there might be situations that would require more detailed procedures, such as situations in which the facts are disputed and not easily resolved. While *Goss* specified only the basics of due process that must be followed for short-term suspensions, state laws may and often do require additional procedures.

One month after *Goss*, the Supreme Court handed down another decision that had further impact on student exclusion cases. In *Wood v. Strickland* (1975), the Court held that students may sue school board members for monetary damages under the Civil Rights Act of 1871 if their constitutional rights are violated. In this case, two girls were suspended from school without a hearing for spiking the punch at a school party. The Supreme Court clarified its *Wood* decision in *Carey v. Piphus* (1978). The Court said that in order to collect damages when their rights have been violated, students must show that they have sustained an actual injury. Otherwise, they are entitled to recover only the nominal damage amount of $1.

In a more recent decision, the Supreme Court has held that disruptive handicapped students can be expelled for up to 10 days but that they cannot be unilaterally expelled for disciplinary reasons (*Honig v. Doe*, 1988). Rather, they are to be retained in their current educational placement until the necessary procedural requirements under P.L. 94–142 have been satisfied and an alternative placement has been agreed upon.

What effect does the expansion of the due process rights of students have on the willingness of educators to discipline disobedient or disruptive students?

Corporal Punishment

Although the U.S. Supreme Court has said that corporal punishment is not a form of "cruel and unusual punishment" under the Eighth Amendment and that its administration does not require procedural due process (*Ingraham v. Wright*, 1977), if the punishment is excessive, the student may have an assault and battery claim and the administrator or teacher administering the punishment may be found liable for the injuries sustained. In addition, the Courts of Appeals for the Fourth and Tenth Circuits have acknowledged that grossly excessive corporal punishment might be a violation of the constitutional right to be "free of state intrusions into realms of personal privacy and bodily security" (*Garcia v. Miera*, 1987; *Hall v. Tawney*, 1980).

When corporal punishment is not prohibited by state law or school board policy, the teacher administering corporal punishment would be wise "(a) to have another adult present when administering corporal punishment, (b) to be sure that its use is reasonable in light of the student's age and circumstances necessitating the punishment, and (c) to administer the punishment without malice" (McCarthy, 1989).

Search and Seizure

The issues surrounding search and seizure of students have increased in recent years, along with the concern about drug use among school-age children. The Fourth Amendment protection against unreasonable search and seizure has been interpreted as requiring law enforcement officials to have probable cause that a crime has been committed and to obtain a search warrant before conducting a search. Prior to 1985, some courts held school officials to the same standard. However, in *New Jersey v. T.L.O.* (1985) the Supreme Court ruled that school officials' interest in maintaining discipline in the schools was sufficient to justify their being held to a lesser standard than probable cause. Rather, school officials may conduct searches based on a "reasonable suspicion" that the search will reveal evidence of a violation of the law or school rules. However, the lesser standard does not authorize school officials to go on "fishing expeditions" for evidence. In addition, the method of the search must be reasonably related to the objective of the search and may not be excessively intrusive in light of the student's characteristics (e.g., age and sex) and the nature of the alleged infraction.

In determining whether a particular search is reasonable, the courts have distinguished between school property such as lockers and personal property. The courts have held that while a student may have exclusive use of a locker in regard to other students, the possession is not exclusive in regard to school officials who retain control of the lockers. In fact, the courts have said that it is not only the right but the duty of school officials to search a locker if suspicion arises that something of an illegal nature may be concealed there (*People v. Overton*, 1969).

The use of drug-sniffing dogs is currently one of the most unsettled issues in the area of student searches. The Fifth Circuit Court (*Horton v. Goose Creek Independent School District*, 1982) and a federal district court (*Jones v. Latexo Independent School District*, 1980) have held the use of drug-detecting dogs an unconstitutional invasion of the student's privacy. Other courts have viewed the use of dogs as preliminary to the search itself and legal (*Doe v. Renfrow*, 1980). However, the drug-detecting dog must be used to sniff particular students, not all students or random groups. Drug-detecting dogs may be used to search lockers or cars.

What would be some examples of student conduct that would constitute "reasonable suspicion" for you to institute a search for firearms?

Strip searches, regardless of the reasonableness of the suspicion, have to date not been upheld by the courts (*Bellmer v. Lund*, 1977; *Doe v. Renfrow*, 1980). The courts have considered strip searches an inexcusable violation of privacy.

Perhaps the most controversial current issue in the area of student rights is drug testing of students. Thus far, the courts have invalidated blanket drug testing of the general student population on the basis of the individual suspicion standard (*Anable v. Ford*, 1985; *Odenheim v. Carlstadt-East Rutherford School District*, 1985). However, certain exceptions to this standard have been made. The random drug testing of interscholastic athletes and cheerleaders in grades 9–12 by the Tippecanoe (Indiana) School District was upheld by the Seventh Circuit Court of Appeals (*Schaill v. Tippecanoe Country School Corp.*, 1988). Those testing positive were not excluded from school, only from par-

Controversial Issues:
No Pass, No Play

In the search to find ways to curb declining academic achievement and failing grades, "no pass, no play" rules are being adopted by school districts across the country. Such rules require students to pass a minimum number of courses to be eligible to participate in cocurricular activities.

Arguments For

1. Students who do not perform in the classroom should not be allowed to perform on the athletic field, stage, etc.

2. Such rules are needed to ensure that students place the appropriate priority on academic achievement—the primary purpose of attending school.

3. Students enrolled in cocurricular activities fail fewer courses.

4. No pass, no play rules provide the impetus for students to improve their study skills, manage their time more wisely, and exercise self-discipline.

5. Maintaining only a passing grade is a minimum, not maximum, requirement.

6. Fosters success in later life.

Arguments Against

1. Students who might have stayed in school to participate in cocurricular activities drop out.

2. Such rules do nothing for students who do not participate in cocurricular activities—the students most at risk for dropping out.

3. Discourages students from participating in activities.

4. Participation in cocurricular activities should not be made subject to academic achievement. The implication is that the development of the intellect is more important than the development of other domains (social, physical, emotional).

5. Students are discouraged from taking more challenging courses for fear of losing their eligibility.

6. Rules discriminate against poor and minority students.

Should participation in cocurricular activities be made contingent upon academic achievement?

ticipation in the sport and any evidence obtained was not used for criminal prosecution but for prevention and rehabilitation. According to the court, individualized suspicion is not an absolute requirement to justify a search; suspicionless searches are more likely to be permissible in circumstances where a student has a diminished expectation of privacy, in particular in regard to urine testing. Student athletes who have a urinalysis as part of the general physical required for participation are among those who would have a diminished expectation of privacy in regard to urine testing. Although the court upheld the random testing of student athletes, it pointed out that this did not signal support for random testing of other student groups, such as "band members or the chess team." Table 12.2 lists some Supreme Court decisions affecting students' rights.

Table 12.2: Selected U.S. Supreme Court Decisions Affecting Students' Rights

Case	Decision
Tinker v. Des Moines (1969)	School officials cannot limit students' rights to free expression unless there is evidence of a material disruption or substantial disorder.
Goss v. Lopez (1975)	For suspensions of less than 10 days, the student must be given an oral or written notice of charges, an explanation of the evidence against him or her, and the opportunity to rebut the charges before an objective decision maker.
Wood v. Strickland (1975)	Students may sue school board members for monetary damages under the Civil Rights Act of 1871.
Ingraham v. Wright (1977)	Corporal punishment does not constitute cruel and unusual punishment under the Eighth Amendment and does not require due process prior to administration.
Board of Education, Island Trees Union Free School District v. Pico (1982)	Censorship by the school board acting in narrowly partisan or political manner violates the First Amendment rights of students.
Pyler v. Doe (1982)	The denial of a free public education to undocumented alien children violates the equal protection guarantees of the Fourteenth Amendment.
Bethel School District v. Fraser (1985)	School boards have the authority to determine what speech is inappropriate in the school and need not tolerate speech that is lewd or offensive.
New Jersey v. T.L.O. (1985)	School officials are not required to obtain a search warrant or show probable cause to search a student, only reasonable suspicion that the search will turn up evidence of a violation of the law or school rules.
Hazelwood School District v. Kuhlmier (1988)	School officials may limit school-sponsored student speech as long as their actions are related to a legitimate pedagogical concern.

Freedom of Expression

In 1965, several students in Des Moines, Iowa were suspended after wearing black armbands to school to demonstrate their opposition to the Vietnam War. The wearing of armbands was prohibited by a school district policy which had been adopted by Des Moines principals to prevent possible disturbances after they learned of the students' plan to wear the armbands. The suspended students filed suit and the decision by the Supreme Court (*Tinker v. Des Moines*, 1969) has become a landmark case not only in student expression, but in the broader area of student rights. In finding for the students, the court said that students have the freedom to express their views by speech or other forms of expression so long as the exercise of this freedom does not cause "material disruption," "substantial disorder," or invade the rights of others. According to the court:

In order for the State in the person of school officials to justify prohibition of a particular expression of opinion, it must be able to show that its action was caused by something more than a mere desire to avoid the discomfort and unpleasantness that always accompany an unpopular viewpoint . . . . undifferentiated fear or apprehension of disturbance is not enough to overcome the right to freedom of expression. (pp. 508–509)

The "material and substantive disruption" standard articulated in *Tinker* has been applied to numerous student expression cases in the more than two decades following the decision. Subsequent rulings have clarified that while the fear of disruption must be based on fact, not intuition (*Butts v. Dallas Independent School District*, 1971), school officials need not wait until a disruption has occurred to take action. If school officials possess sufficient evidence on which to base a "reasonable forecast" of disruption, action to restrict student expression is justified (*Dodd v. Rambis*, 1981).

Disruptive Speech

Freedom of expression does not include the right to use lewd and offensive speech, even if it does not cause disruption. At a high school assembly in Washington, Matthew Fraser nominated a classmate for a student council office using what the court described as "an elaborate, graphic, and explicit sexual metaphor," which provoked other students to disruptive behavior. Fraser was suspended for two days. Both the district court and the circuit court held his suspension to be a violation of his rights to free speech and stated that his speech was not disruptive under the *Tinker* guidelines. The U.S. Supreme Court, however, concluded that the school board has the authority to determine what speech in the classroom or in school assembly is inappropriate, and that "lewd, indecent, or offensive speech or conduct" need not be tolerated (*Bethel School District No. 403 v. Fraser*, 1986).

Student Publications

The area of student publications has generated considerable litigation in recent years. Although students have the right to publish and distribute literature published both on and off campus, school officials can enact reasonable rules as to the time, place, and manner of distribution. In addition, the courts have said school officials can interfere with the publication and distribution of material that is libelous, obscene, disruptive of school activities, or psychologically harmful. However, until recently the courts have been careful to emphasize that in cases where school policies require faculty or administrative approval before publication, censorship is only justified if the material is libelous, obscene, or likely to cause material and substantial disruption. In addition, the procedures and standards for review must be clearly articulated. Unpopular or controversial content or content critical of school officials was considered insufficient justification for restricting student expression. This standard was applied to school-sponsored as well as to nonsponsored publications.

In a 1988 case, however, the Supreme Court awarded significant discretion to school authorities in censoring school-sponsored publications. In this case, *Hazelwood School District v. Kuhlmeier*, a school principal deleted two articles from a school newspaper. One article dealt with pregnant students and contained comments about their sexual histories and use or nonuse of birth control. Although names were not used, because of the small number of pregnant students in the school, the principal judged that anonymity was not assured. The second article was on divorce and included quotes from a student condemning her father. The principal judged that this article did not meet standards of journalistic fairness because the father did not have the opportunity to defend himself. According to the principal, he was not concerned with the content of the articles, but felt that they were not well written by journalistic standards. Believing that there was not enough time before the publication deadline to make the needed changes in the articles, he deleted the two articles.

The Supreme Court decision said that school officials "do not offend the First Amendment by exercising editorial control over the style and content of student speech in school-sponsored expressive activities so long as their actions are reasonably related to legitimate pedagogical concerns." Such concerns were described as "speech that is ungrammatical, poorly written, inadequately researched, biased or prejudiced, vulgar or profane, or unsuitable for immature audiences."

In making its decision, the court made a distinction between personal expressions by students and those activities that students, parents, and the public might reasonably assume bear the "imprimatur of the school." In the latter category, the court included not only school-sponsored publications but "theatrical productions and other expressive activities."

The ultimate effect of the *Hazelwood* decision on the range of student free speech issues cannot yet be determined. It has become a "springboard" for censorship involving school-sponsored activities and some fear it could be extended to "student art shows, science fairs, debates, research projects, and even cheerleading or pep squads" (Pankratz, 1989, p. 1B).

Students' Appearance

Although attempts by school officials to regulate students' appearance have become less stringent over the years, students have become more assertive in expressing themselves through their appearance. The U.S. Supreme Court has not provided any guidance in the area of student appearance, but the majority of lower courts have recognized that students have either a liberty right or a right of expression that be violated by appearance regulations that are unduly vague or restrictive. As a general rule the courts will not uphold appearance regulations unless the district can show a compelling interest in having such a regulation, such as the disruptive effects of the appearance on the educational process or for health and safety reasons.

The courts also have held that dress and appearance requirements for extracurricular activities cannot be more restrictive than those for the classroom. However, schools have been successful in prohibiting dirty clothing, scant or revealing clothing, clothing displaying obscene pictures (*Gano v. School District No. 411 of Twin Falls*, 1987), clothing caricaturing school administrators as being drunk, loose clothing in shop areas, or other dress deemed likely to cause a material or substantial disruption to school operations. In one provocative case, the court upheld a school principal who refused to let two students (brother and sister) dressed in clothing of the opposite sex attend the prom (*Harper v. Edgewood Board of Education*, 1987). The plaintiffs claimed that they were denied the equal protection of the Fourteenth Amendment because the school district allowed female students to wear dresses and male students to wear tuxedos, but did not allow males to wear dresses and females tuxedos. The court denied this claim, finding that the school dress code did not differentiate based on sex, but required only that students dress in conformity with the acceptable standards of the community (and cross-sex dressing was not considered acceptable in that community).

Did the elementary and secondary schools you attended have dress codes or regulations regulating student appearance? How did you respond to them at the time? Do you now feel they served any educational purpose?

Student Records

For every student who attends the public schools a permanent record is kept by school authorities. Questions about the contents of this record and who has access to it have been the source of serious contention over the years. Until the passage of the Family Educational Rights and Privacy Act, also known as the Buckley Amendment, in 1974, parents often were denied access to these records, while they were open to various nonschool personnel (e.g., employers). The Buckley Amendment sought to redress this situation by:

1. Requiring school districts to establish procedures for accessing student records and informing parents, guardians, and eligible students (over 18 years old) of their rights under the law.

2. Requiring written permission from parents or eligible students before sharing the records with anyone other than educators in the same school who have a legitimate educational interest; officials of a school to which the student is transferring; persons who have obtained a court order; persons for whom the information is necessary "to protect the health or safety of the student or other individuals"; or in connection with financial aid for which the student has applied.

3. Providing a complaint and investigation mechanism for alleged violations.

4. Providing for the loss of federal funds to districts found not in compliance with the law.

When students become 18 years old or enroll in a postsecondary institution, they must be allowed to see the record if they so desire.

Although the Buckley Amendment guarantees parents and eligible students access to records, this does not mean that records must be produced anytime or anywhere on demand. School officials can adopt rules that specify reasonable time, place, and notice requirements for reviewing. Neither does this law give parents the right to review the personal notes of teachers and

What kind of information would you record in your personal notes that you would not record in a student's official record?

administrators if these records are in their sole possession and not shared with anyone except a substitute teacher.

Parental rights under the Buckley Amendment are not limited to custodial parents. Unless prohibited by court order, a separated parent who is not the custodial parent or guardian has the same right of access to the student's record as does the custodial parent.

After reviewing the record, if the parents (or the eligible student) believe that information contained in the record is inaccurate, misleading, or in violation of the rights of the student, they can request that the information be amended. If school officials refuse, the parents or eligible student must be advised of their right to a hearing. If the hearing officer also agrees that the record should not be amended, the parents or student are entitled to place a statement of explanation or objection in the record.

Students with AIDS

As of this writing, neither a cure nor a vaccine for AIDS has been discovered and medical researchers believe that it will be several years before either will be available. In the meantime, fear and prejudice are likely to continue (see Figure 12.2). As school districts wrestle with the question of how best to deliver schooling to children with AIDS, educators often find themselves placed squarely between the fears of parents and the rights of children with AIDS (Flygare, 1988).

The initial response by school districts to AIDS-infected children was to exclude them from the school setting and provide home instruction or separate facilities for their instruction. More recently, in part as a result of more information and education on how the disease is transmitted, there appears to be a growing belief that children with AIDS should be educated in the school environment if their health permits their attendance. A number of court decisions also have been instrumental in increasing access for AIDS victims. The courts have held that children infected with the AIDS virus are protected from discrimination by section 504 of the Rehabilitation Act. The courts have been unanimous in rejecting exclusion as the automatic answer to dealing with AIDS-infected students (see, e.g., *Doe v. Donton Elementary School District*, 1988; *Phipps v. Saddleback Valley Unified School District*, 1988). Rather, the courts now must consider the "significant risk of communicating standard" spelled out by the Supreme Court in *Arline*. Another important factor that the courts have looked at, when weighing the interests of the child against those of protecting the health and safety of other students, has been the potential effect of the exclusion or isolation on the social and emotional well-being of the child.

Application of the *Arline* standard has led to the exclusion of some students. In Florida, a federal trial court ordered that a trainable mentally handicapped (TMH) and AIDS-infected student (who was not toilet-trained and, with lesions in her mouth, habitually sucked on her fingers, leaving saliva on her hands) be placed in a small, separate, visually open and sound-equipped room within a TMH classroom with a full-time aide until such time as she was toilet-trained and no longer sucked her fingers (*Martinez v. School Board*, 1988).

Figure 12.2

Source: Center for Attitudinal Healing, Tiburon, CA. Reprinted with permission.

The widespread public concern over the spread of AIDS has prompted most states and school districts to adopt policies regarding the admission and instruction of infected children. These policies often are modeled after guidelines issued by the National Centers for Disease Control (CDC). Most of these policies state that such children should not be excluded automatically, but should be considered on a case-by-case basis by a team composed of health and educational personnel. Often, such policies also provide guidelines for handling body fluids and other procedures designed to protect fellow students and personnel in the school, as well as steps to protect the privacy of victims and to educate both school district personnel and parents.

Summary

The educational process takes place in an environment in which the rights of teachers and students are constantly being balanced against the rights and responsibilities of school officials to maintain a safe and orderly environment conducive to learning. Although the rights of both teachers and students have been greatly expanded in the last quarter century, they do not include the right to say, publish, or teach whatever one feels or believes. The courts continue to uphold the rights and responsibilities of school districts to limit teacher conduct that has a negative impact on performance in the classroom, that is unrelated to the course of study, or that is materially or substantially disruptive. Teachers also have the responsibility to comply with various statutory requirements related to terms of employment, copyright, and so on and to provide a reasonable standard of care for their students. When they do not comply with these statutory requirements or when they breach the standard of care, they can be subjected to a variety of disciplinary actions both within and outside the school system. While every situation is unique, certain legal principles have been established that can provide direction in many situations. It is imperative that teachers not only be knowledgeable about these principles, many of which are broadly discussed in this chapter, but that they become familiar with applicable law and school board policy in their state and district.

In the next chapter, we will discuss a topic that sometimes is not given sufficient attention in teacher preparation programs—the governance structure of the public schools. Yet, as you will see, the way schools are organized and administered has a vital impact on the teacher and the educational program.

Key Terms

Academic freedom	*In loco parentis*
Affirmative action	Incompetence
Discrimination	Insubordination
Due process	Malpractice
Equal opportunity	Negligence
Expulsion	Property right

Proximate cause   Suspension
Reduction in force (RIF)   Tenure
Reverse discrimination   Tort
Sovereign immunity

Discussion Questions

1. What action should be taken against Marty Robinson if an examination of Johnny Avery's back shows no marks? Should students be encouraged to "be on the lookout" for and report suspicions of physical and sexual abuse among their peers? How could they do this?

2. What limits can be placed on teachers' expressing themselves on political issues in the classroom? Outside the classroom?

3. Describe the "reasonable teacher" guideline as it relates to tort liability.

4. What should be the role of the schools in confronting the AIDS epidemic?

5. To what extent should teachers, administrators, and school board members be held liable for the education or lack of education received by the students under their control?

6. What are the statutory requirements in your state regarding student expulsions? Student suspensions?

7. How does the doctrine of *in loco parentis* serve to give students expectations about the care given them in the schools? How does the doctrine serve to define the teacher's right to control and supervise students?

References

Ambach v. Norwick, 441 U.S. 68 (1979).

Anable v. Ford, 653 F. Supp. 22 (W. D. Ark, 1985), *modified*, 663 F. Supp. 149 (W. D. Ark. 1985).

Bellmer v. Lund, 438 F. Supp. 47 (N.D.N.Y. 1977).

Bethel School District No. 403 v. Fraser, 106 St. Ct. 3159 (1986).

Birdwell v. Hazelwood School District, 491 F.2d 490 (8th Cir. 1974).

Board of Education, Island Trees Union Free School District No. 26 v. Pico, 457 U.S. 853 (1982).

Burch v. Baker, 861 F. 2d 1149 (9th Cir. 1988).

Butts v. Dallas Independent School District, 436 F.2d 728 (5th Cir. 1971).

Cambron-McCabe, N. H. (1983). Procedural due process. In J. Beckham & P. A. Zirkel (Eds.), *Legal issues in public school employment* (pp. 78–97). Bloomington, IN: Phi Delta Kappa.

Carey v. Piphus, 435 U.S. 247 (1978).

Chalk v. U.S. District Court Cent. Dist. of California, 840 F. 2d 701 (9th Cir. 1988).

City of Richmond v. J. A. Croson Co., 57 U.S.L.W. 4132 (1989).

Conners, E. T. (1981). *Educational tort liability and malpractice.* Bloomington, IN: Phi Delta Kappa.

Connick v. Myers, 461 U.S. 138 (1983).

Delon, F. G. (1982). *Legal issues in the dismissal of teachers for personal conduct.* Topeka, KS: National Organization on Legal Problems of Education.

Dodd v. Rambis, 535 F. Supp. 23 (S.D. Ind. 1981).

Doe v. Donton Elementary School District, 694 F. Supp. 440 (N.D. Ill. 1988).

Doe v. Renfrow, 631 F. 2d 91 (7th Cir. 1980), *cert. denied,* 451 U.S. 1022 (1981).

Donohue v. Copiague Union Free Schools, 407 N.Y.S. 2d 874 (App. Div. 1978), *aff'd,* 391 N.E. 1352 (N.Y. 1979).

Eckmann v. Board of Education, 630 f. Supp. (N.D. Ill. 1986).

Fischer, L., Schimmel, D., & Kelly, C. (1987). *Teachers and the law* (2nd ed.). New York: Longman.

Fisher v. Fairbanks North Star Borough School District, 704 P.2d 213 (Alaska 1985).

Flygare, T. J. (1988). Judge orders children with AIDS back into the classroom. *Phi Delta Kappan, 69,* 382.

Fornaro v. Kerry, 527 N.Y.S. 2d 61 (A.D. 2 Dept. 1988).

Gano v. School District No. 411 of Twin Falls, 674 F. Supp. 796 (D. Idaho 1987).

Garcia v. Miera, 817 F. 2d 650 (10th Cir. 1987).

Gaylord v. Tacoma School District No. 10, 559 P. 2d 1340 (Wash. 1977).

Gee, E. G., & Sperry, D. J. (1978). *Education law and the public schools: A compendium.* Boston: Allyn and Bacon.

Goss v. Lopez, 419 U.S. 565 (1975).

Hall v. Tawney, 621 F. 2d 607 (4th Cir. 1980).

Harper v. Edgewood Board of Education, 655 F. Supp. 1353 (S. D. Ohio 1987).

Hazelwood School District v. Kuhlmeier, 108 S. Ct. 562 (1988).

Hoffman v. Board of Education of the City of New York, 400 N.E. 2d 317 (1979).

Honig v. Doe, 198 S. Ct. 592 (1988).

Horton v. Goose Creek Independent School District, 677 f. 2d 471 (5th Cir. 1982).

Hortonville Joint School District No. 1 v. Hortonville Education Association, 225 N.W. 2d 658 (Wis. 1975), rev'd on other grounds and remained, 426 U.S. 482 (1976), aff'd, 274 N.W. 2nd 697 (Wis. 1979).

Ingraham v. Wright, 430 U.S. 651 (1977).

Jones v. Latexo Independent School District, 449 F. Supp. 223 (E.D. Tex. 1980).

Kaiser Aluminum and Chemical Corporation v. Weber, 443 U.S. 193 (1979).

Keyishian v. Board of Regents of University of State of New York, 385 U.S. 589 (1967).

Kingsville Independent School District v. Cooper, 611 F.2d 1109 (5th Cir. 1980).

Landauer, W. L., Spanfer, J. H., & Van Horn, Jr., B. F. (1983). Good cause dismissal of education employees. In J. Beckham & P. A. Zirkel (Eds.), *Legal issues in public school employment* (pp. 154–169). Bloomington, IN: Phi Delta Kappa.

Littlejohn v. Rose, 768 F.2d 765, 769 (6th Cir. 1985), *cert. denied,* 106 S. Ct. 1260 (1986).

Martinez v. School Board, 692 F. Supp. 1293 (M.D. Fla. 1988).

McCarthy, M. (1985, March). *Competency tests in public employment: A legal view.* Paper presented at the annual meeting of the American Education Research Association, Chicago, IL.

McCarthy, M. (1989). Legal rights and responsibilities of public school teachers. In M. C. Reynolds (Ed.), *Knowledge base for the beginning teacher* (pp. 255–266). New York: Pergamon Press.

McCarthy, M. M., & Cambron-McCabe, N. H. (1987). *Public school law: Teachers' and students' rights* (2nd ed.). Boston: Allyn and Bacon.

Mira v. Monroe County School Board, 687 F. Supp. 1538 (S.D. Fla. 1988).

Mitchell v. King, 363 A. 68 (Conn. 1975).

New Jersey, Petitioner v. T.L.O., 105 S. Ct. 733 (1985).

Odenheim v. Carlstadt-East Rutherford School District, 510 A. 2d 709 (N.J. Super. 1985).

Pankratz, H. (1989, May 4). Students believe rights declining. *Denver Post*, 1B, 10B.

People v. Overton, 249 N.E. 2d 366 (N.Y. 1969).

Peter W. v. San Francisco Unified School District, 131 Cal. Rptr. 854 (Cal. App. 1976).

Phipps v. Saddleback Valley Unified School District, 251 Cal. Rptr. 720 (Cal. Ct. App. 1988).

Pickering v. Board of Education, 391 U.S. 563 (1968).

Regents of the University of California v. Alan Bakke, 438 U.S. 265 (1978).

Ross v. Springfield School District No. 19, 691 P.2d 509 (Ore App. 1984).

Rowland v. Mad River Local School District Montgomery County, OH, 730 F. 2d 444 (6th Cir. 1984).

Schaill v. Tippecanoe County School Corp., 864 F. 2d 1309 (7th Cir. 1988).

School Board of Nassau County v. Arline 107 S. Ct. 1129 (1987).

Spears v. Board of Education of Pike County, Kentucky, 843 F. 2d 882 (6th Cir. 1988).

State of Texas v. Project Principle, Inc., 724 S.W. 2d 387 (Tex. 1987).

Swilley v. Alexander, 448 F. Supp. 702 (S.D. Ala. 1978).

Texas State Teachers' Association v. Garland Independent School District, 777 F.2d 1046 (5th Cir. 1985), *aff'd*, 107 S. Ct. 41 (1986).

Tinker v. Des Moines Independent Community School District, 393 U.S. 503 (1969).

United States v. South Carolina, 445 F. Supp. 1094 (D.S.C. 1977), *aff'd* 434 U.S. 1026 (1978).

Valente, W. D. (1987). *Law in the schools* (2nd ed.). Columbus, OH: Merrill.

Wardwell v. Board of Education of Cincinnati, 529 F. 2d 625 (6th Cir. 1976).

Washington v. Davis, 426 U.S. 229 (1976).

Watts v. Seward School Board, 454 P. 2d 732 (Alaska 1969), *cert. denied* 397 U.S. 921 (1970).

Wood v. Strickland, 420 U.S. 308 (1975).

Wygant v. Jackson Board of Education, 106 S. Ct. 1842 (1986).

Chapter 13

Organizing and Administering Elementary and Secondary Schools

In every complex school system there is always the two-sided question whether: (1) the responsibilities of the people working in the various positions are such that each works effectively and they all work cooperatively; (2) the geographical organization of schools into districts is accomplishing efficiently the work of the system.

Robert J. Havighurst, The Public Schools of Chicago, *1964*

A school board election is scheduled in a few months in the school district where you live and work as a teacher. You are attending a parent-teacher meeting at your school. A parent asks questions about the functions and desirable qualifications of school board members in your community. As a new teacher in the district, you are asked to be a panelist at a public forum on school board selection. Your assignment is to indicate why you decided to work in the district and what you think are some needs of the district.

How would you contrast your role as a teacher with that of a school board member? What levels of education and other qualifications should be required of school board members?

How active should teachers be in school board elections? Should the teachers' association endorse specific candidates? What are some possible implications of teachers endorsing candidates for the school board?

What information would you need about the school district to prepare for the meeting?

While you may not ever be asked to serve on a panel such as the one described above, it is important that you understand the organization and administration of public education, issues surrounding the governance of education, and ways in which the structure affects the work of teachers. To help you develop a better understanding of the relationships between educational organization and the life of the teacher, consider the following learning objectives:

- Discuss the role of the federal government in elementary and secondary education.

- Identify the effect of federal programs on local school district decisions about educational programs.

- Differentiate between the roles of the local school superintendent and the chief state school officer.

- Describe the role and function of intermediate educational service agencies.

- Determine the number and different types of local school districts in your state.

- Identify criteria that relate to the optimal size of school districts.

- Describe the roles of the local school board and the superintendent of schools.

- Discuss the impact that school site decision making might have on the roles and responsibilities of the classroom teacher.

- Discuss the role that private education has played in American elementary and secondary education.

The Context of the Public Schools

Contrary to governmental functions such as national defense, interstate commerce, and international relations, which have a heavy federal orientation, the governmental structure for the public schools has evolved as a combination of state and local powers and responsibilities. Rather than being the source of centralized educational *policies* and decisions about the operation of public elementary and secondary schools, the federal government has a very limited role. The decentralized governance system for education in America has been characterized as a local function, a state responsibility, and a federal concern. This construct has been reinforced by the various recommendations and actions associated with educational reform in the 1980s. In the quest for educational improvement, state legislative actions have resulted in increased duties, responsibilities, and expectations being placed on local school districts.

Consistent with the checks and balances inherent in the American governmental system, the governance system for public elementary and secondary education also has its checks and balances. The primary concerns of the federal government are the educational needs of special populations, funding for national research priorities, and data gathering and reporting. Each state establishes the governance system for its schools, provides for the funding of the schools, and establishes various minimum standards for school operation. The actual operation of schools is the responsibility of a series of local school districts governed by lay citizens who serve on school boards. Among the nations of the world, the United States is unique in the emphasis placed on local participation in the conduct of public elementary and secondary education.

This chapter provides an overview of the governance structure for public elementary and secondary education in the United States. Initial attention is given to the role of the federal government; then the discussion focuses on the structure of the public schools. States typically have created a three-level structure for delivering education as pictured in Figure 13.1. The structure consists of a state department of education, intermediate educational service agencies, and local school districts. The chapter concludes with a brief discussion of private education.

The Federal Government and Public Education

As noted in Chapter 4, the absence of mention of education in the federal Constitution and the reservation of this function to the states should not be interpreted as indicating a lack of interest in education by the nation's founders. When the Constitution was being written, several states already had provided for education in their state constitutions and leaders in those states did not want the federal government to interfere with those provisions. Private and church-related schools were numerous in some states and some persons may have supported this option for providing education. Questions

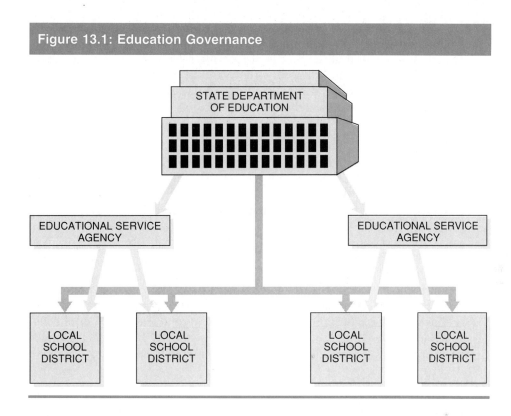

Figure 13.1: Education Governance

also may have been raised about the relative merits of educating the masses (Grieder, Pierce, & Jordan, 1969).

The federal government provides funds to support educational programs to serve students with special needs and awards grants for educational research. As noted in Chapter 11, the rationale for these programs can be traced to the general welfare clause of the Constitution that gives Congress the authority to take certain actions to provide for the general welfare of the citizens of the United States. This provision has served as the legal basis for numerous federal programs ranging from education of the handicapped and the disadvantaged to loans and grants for college students.

Department of Education

For more than 120 years, some type of federal agency for education has been in existence. Starting in 1867 with the creation of a Department of Education without cabinet status, various federal agencies have had responsibility for education. The chronology indicates an uncertainty in the federal commitment to education. For example, in 1869 the title was changed to Office of Education, in 1870 to Bureau of Education, and in 1929 back to Office of Education (Grieder, Pierce, & Jordan, 1969). That designation was retained until the second creation of the Department of Education in 1980 when education again was given cabinet status. Until the creation of the

Department of Education with a *secretary of education,* the various federal education agencies had been administered by a commissioner of education.

Those who questioned the merits of creating a Department of Education because of the fear of federal control have found that their fears were not justified. The level of federal involvement in education does not appear to have increased during the decade since the creation of the department.

Secretary of Education

The first secretary of education, Shirley Hufsteder, was a federal judge at the time of appointment. The second, Terrel Bell, was a former U.S. commissioner of education, chief state school officer in Utah, local superintendent, and college professor. Next was William Bennett, a former college professor appointed to the position from another federal position; after him, Lauro Cavazos, a university president at the time of appointment. In 1991, President Bush nominated Lamar Alexander, former governor of Tennessee, to succeed Cavazos as secretary of education.

Some secretaries of education have viewed the position as an opportunity to ensure that all students have access to educational programs and services. Others have tried to maintain and expand federal educational programs and services. Some have viewed the position as a "bully pulpit" from which to make pronouncements and admonitions designed to improve education.

Federal Role and Involvement

The federal interest in education has been influenced by the national and economic interests prevalent at the time of federal actions. For example, the Northwest Ordinances in the 1780s and the Morrill Act in 1862 can be perceived as responses to the interest in promoting the westward expansion of the nation (see Chapter 4). The Morrill Act was enabling legislation for the land grant college system. The enactment of federal funding for vocational education in 1917 was related to the need for trained workers on the assembly lines of the growing manufacturing establishment. Surplus agricultural commodities provided some of the impetus for the development of the federal school lunch program in the 1940s.

What current national issues might contribute to new federal initiatives?

These patterns also can be observed in recent federal education programs. As discussed in Chapter 5, the launch of Sputnik in the Soviet space program was an incentive for the enactment of the National Defense Education Act in 1958. National concerns about the economic effects of poverty and disadvantaged youth were major reasons for the enactment of the Elementary and Secondary Education Act in 1965. Programs for education of the handicapped in the 1970s came in response to court cases and concerns about the national neglect of handicapped youth. The 1981 consolidation of categorical educational programs under President Reagan reflected a desire to diminish the federal role in state and local governmental functions. As the federal role in education has evolved, the functions of the federal agency also have shifted.

Various proposals have been presented for the role of the federal education agency, but Congress has never given the agency responsibility for the actual operation of schools, even the service academies, which are operated by the related military services. With the creation of the Department of Education, a schedule was included for the department to assume operational responsibility for the overseas schools for dependents of United States military personnel operated by the Department of Defense. However, after considerable discussion and delay, the decision was made to leave operational responsibility for these schools with the Department of Defense.

Since the formation of the first Department of Education in 1867, the one constant and continuing role of the federal education agency has been data gathering. Even though education is a state function, there is an interest in national information about the educational enterprise. Congress has established the National Center for Educational Research and has provided for the center to be administered by a career administrator instead of a political appointee. Rather than each individual state gathering and reporting data in the state's format, it has been more cost-effective for the function to be performed by the federal education agency. Reporting consistency and comparability can be enhanced and information can be provided for international comparisons.

Since the Office of Education began funding the Cooperative Research Program in 1957, the federal education agency has funded educational research projects. The National Institute of Education was created in 1972, but was terminated with the creation of the Department of Education. Its functions now are assigned to an assistant secretary of education in charge of the Office of Educational Research and Information. The principal rationales for federal support of educational research are the same as those related to data gathering reporting. Cost-effectiveness will be greater by providing central funding of national research priorities and emphasizing the importance of this information for better informed educational decision making.

Emphases of Current Federal Education Programs

The emphases of current federal education programs are fourfold. First, the major portions of the funds are for programs and services for special populations; these include the handicapped, educationally disadvantaged, financially needy college students, and vocational education students. A second emphasis is on ways to get funds to schools with minimal restrictions. An example is the education block grant under Chapter 2 of the Education Consolidation and Improvement Act of 1981. A third focus is on specific programs that are administered as competitive special purpose grants. The fourth emphasis area is the previously mentioned educational statistics and research. Since the federal government has no responsibility for the operation of schools, state and local educational agencies conduct federal programs as a component of the educational delivery system.

State Educational Agencies

The legal principle of education being a state responsibility contributes to state educational agencies playing a key role in the development of the structure and delivery system for public elementary and secondary education. At the state level, each state has an administrative agency whose primary functions include:

- Setting broad policies for the operations of the state's public elementary and secondary schools.

- Monitoring the schools in accordance with legislative mandates.

- Providing technical assistance to the schools.

- Collecting data about the schools.

- Disbursing state funds for the operation of local school districts.

This state-level governance structure typically includes a *state board of education* as the policy-making body, a state administrative agency typically referred to as the *state department of education,* and a *chief state school officer* who serves as executive officer of the state board of education and as administrator of the state department of education. Figure 13.2 reflects the state-level administrative organization in many states.

State Boards of Education

What should be the qualifications for members of the state board of education?

State boards of education are charged with adopting regulations and monitoring local school districts to ensure implementation of the constitutional and statutory mandates related to the operation of the state system of schools. Most state boards are not responsible for the direct operation of any educational institutions or schools; rather, their concern is with the overall direction of the state's schools.

Responsibilities of State Boards of Education

State boards of education have various responsibilities. These boards adopt regulations and procedures that apply to local school boards in the operation of schools and receive monitoring reports about the operation of schools. Their directives and mandates are related to policy formulation and enforcement within the context of the state's statutory provisions. Examples include graduation requirements for high school students and mandated curricular offerings in elementary schools. Advisory functions are related to leadership, encouragement, and interactions with local school districts. Among the important state board functions are providing the state legislature with timely reports about the schools, proposing changes in statutes, serving as advocates for new initiatives and programs, and presenting and serving as an advocate for the budget for state support of schools.

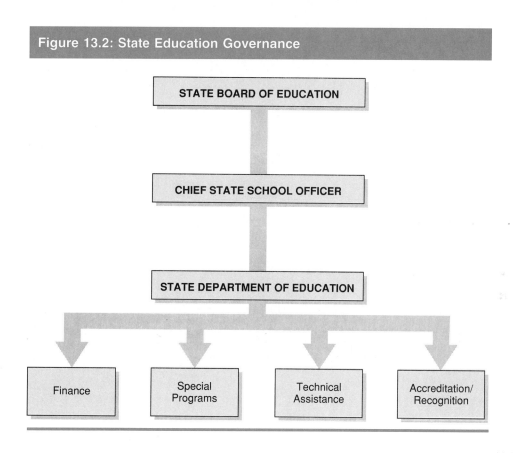

Figure 13.2: State Education Governance

Virtually all states have a state board of education, but they differ in composition, method of selection, relationship with the chief state school officer, and functions. For example, in Florida, the cabinet consisting of the state's elected officials also serves as the state board of education. The state superintendent of public instruction is elected and is a member of the cabinet. This is in contrast to Texas, where members of the state board are elected on a population-based district basis and the commissioner of education is appointed by the governor with the advice and consent of the state senate and serves as the executive officer of the state board of education. In other states, members are appointed by the governor, sometimes with the consent of the state legislature.

Chief State School Officer

Each state has either constitutional or statutory provisions for a chief state school officer; the person often is referred to as the superintendent of public instruction or the commissioner of education. In most instances, responsibilities are limited to elementary and secondary education, but in a few states the person also has responsibilities for higher education.

The state level of government has primary responsibility for public education; schools operate within the context of state legal provisions.

What should be the qualifications of the chief state school officer?

The professional status of the position is improving, but in several states required qualifications are either unstated or very broad. This is especially true in those states where the chief state school officer is elected on a statewide basis. In states where the chief state school officer is appointed, the tendency is to select a person with professional training and experience in educational administration.

Over 30 of the 50 chief state school officers are appointed either by the governor or the state board of education. The others are elected on a popular basis statewide (Campbell, Cunningham, Nystrand, & Usdan, 1985). Selection processes for the latter group resemble those for other elected statewide offices such as attorney general, secretary of state, secretary of agriculture, or state treasurer.

In some states, relationships between the chief state school officer and the state board of education are not clear. For example, the state legislature may assign certain duties and responsibilities directly to the chief state school officer and may assign others to the state board of education. To further complicate the issue, some state department of education employees may be selected by the chief without consultation or action of the state board of education. Then the state board of education must rely on the staff of the state department of education to implement legislative mandates or monitor local school district compliance.

State Secretaries of Education

A recent development in several states has been the adoption of the federal cabinet system with a secretary of education who is responsible to the governor. Usually, the statutory provisions related to the chief state school officer and the state board of education have not been altered by the creation of this cabinet position and the state department of education has remained in place. The primary duties of the secretary of education have been related to long-range planning and budgeting rather than to operating, administering, or monitoring the public schools.

State Department of Education

The operating arm for the administration of state education activities and functions is the state department of education; this agency usually has a mixture of professional and support staff with specific responsibilities. Since Congress enacted the Elementary and Secondary Education Act of 1965, state departments of education have grown in both size and influence. This movement can be attributed to Title V of this landmark legislation, which provided funds to strengthen state departments of education (Grieder, Pierce, & Jordan, 1969).

In addition to their state functions, these agencies are responsible for working with local school districts in the implementation and administration of a variety of federal programs related to the education of disadvantaged youth, instructional materials, and promotion of innovation in schools. These state agencies provide administrative guidance and have a liaison role between the federal government and local school districts.

Functions of State Departments of Education

The primary state-level functions of state departments of education are leadership, technical assistance, regulation, inspection, and data reporting. In an earlier era, state departments of education often operated schools or educational programs, but today, with the exception of pilot programs, these agencies seldom have responsibility for program operation.

The leadership function involves providing technical assistance to assist local school districts in improving their programs and implementing state mandates. The regulatory function involves monitoring local school districts to ensure compliance with statutes and regulations. Data gathering is emerging as an important function to provide the state legislature with accountability information about the progress that local school districts are making in meeting state goals.

Positions in the agency are now considered to provide desirable and satisfying professional careers with the opportunities for creative work and technical assistance to local school districts. Most of this work is done with small- and medium-size school districts; large school districts often do not call on the state department of education for assistance because these districts have full-time employees with equal qualifications. Local school districts also receive services and technical assistance through intermediate educational service agencies.

Intermediate Educational Service Agencies

The concept of the *intermediate educational service agency (IESA)* has been part of the organizational structure of public education in America for more than 150 years. About 40 states have some form of intermediate unit (Campbell, Cunningham, Nystrand, & Usdan, 1985). Many started as the office of the county superintendent of schools which served as a record keeper for the school districts in the county. The state department of education relied on the office to communicate with the local school districts and to submit various reports to the state. Eventually, in many states, these offices assumed additional duties and began to function as IESAs.

The recent interest in the creation and expansion of intermediate educational service agencies may be attributed to a variety of developments. The roles and functions of the IESAs have changed as local school districts have consolidated and become sufficiently large to assume responsibility for many of the original support services provided by the county superintendent. However, without some type of outside assistance, many small local school districts, with their varied enrollments and separate elementary and high school districts, would not be able to provide an adequate level of programs and services.

In some states, new functions have been assigned to IESAs in response to changes in programs and services for the education of the handicapped and specialized vocational education programs. Many local school districts have found that these programs are extremely expensive when only a few students are being served; therefore, in a quest for efficiency and better programs, districts are seeking alternative ways to provide their students with these programs. Other functions of IESAs include data processing, staff development, and fiscal management for special programs and services funded with state and federal funds.

Types of Intermediate Educational Service Agencies

IESAs appear to be evolving in three basic patterns—the special district, the regional education service agency of the state educational agency (SEA), and the cooperative intermediate agency. The discriminating differences among the three types of IESAs are related to their legal basis, programs and services, governance, and financing.

Special District

Typically, the special district is an agency established by the state legislature that functions between the SEA and a collection of local school districts.

The agencies provide various services to the SEA and also to a defined group of local school districts. Their strengths include a legal structure that defines roles and missions, a relatively stable financial base, and identifiable programs and services; their weaknesses are related to variations in the number of local school districts belonging to individual IESAs.

Regional Education Service Agency

These agencies are established by the SEA to deliver specific services to local school districts or conduct certain activities for the SEA. Some provide only administrative services, others provide specific educational programs or services, and still others provide both administrative services and educational programs or services. As arms of the SEA, the advantages of this structure are that, for organization and governance, the agencies are an extension of the SEA bureaucracy and their base of support is not dependent on the whims of the local school districts in their service area. The principal disadvantage is the difficulty that these agencies have in making an impact on local school educational programs. The regional service units in Texas originally functioned under this definition, but they have become a hybrid of all three types as programs have been expanded.

Cooperative Education Service Agency

In contrast to the "top-down" governance and program and service delivery system found in the two previously discussed types of IESAs, the functions and activities of the cooperative education service agency are determined by the local school districts in the cooperative. These agencies may be multipurpose or single purpose. The major strength of this type of agency is the extensive involvement of local education agencies in determining the programs and services to be provided. Weaknesses are related to the dependence of the agency on the preferences of the constituent local school districts and the potential fluctuations in both interest in various programs and services and level of funding for the agency. The special education and vocational education districts in Ohio are examples of this type of intermediate unit.

IESAs often were created to perform a specific function, but the responsibilities of the agencies have changed over time. The typical pattern appears to be that the agencies assume all three roles as they develop and respond to changes in federal programs, provide technical assistance and programmatic thrusts from the state education agency, and organize to respond to the needs of local school districts. For example, the IESAs in Texas began as regional service centers funded largely with federal funds. The Texas legislature and state board of education then began to assign them specific functions as regional offices of the SEA. As they have evolved over the past 25 years, a major portion of their funding and activities now can be classified under cooperative activities with local school districts.

An IESA may have had a narrow function when created, but the agency typically has expanded beyond its original purpose because of changes in state and federal programs and legislative or judicial mandates. However, this trend is not as evident with those IESAs that were created for the specific purpose of providing special education or vocational education programs and services. IESAs provide some instructional programs, but the primary responsibility for the delivery of educational programs resides with local school districts.

Local School Districts

Why should school boards rather than teachers make policy about school operation?

Responsibility for public education resides with the individual states. All states except Hawaii have formed local school districts that are responsible for the actual operation of schools. These local school districts are referred to as "creatures of the state" or extended arms of the state formed for the single purpose of operating elementary and secondary schools.

Local school districts and their governing bodies, local *school boards,* are often the targets of criticism, but they appear to be permanent features in the structure of American government. Citizens place a high value on this opportunity to participate in educational decision making. In a variety of ways, these citizens determine the direction that the schools will take.

The "Myth" of Local Control

Since their origin in colonial days, local school districts always have been subject to the control of state legislatures. Local school districts have two kinds of powers, stated and implied. Stated powers are explicit in actions of the state legislature or provisions of the state constitution. Implied powers are implicit, but are required to carry out the stated powers or the assigned functions. An example of these implied powers is the authority of the school district to purchase chalk and custodial cleaning materials. The likelihood of these items being mentioned specifically in state statutes is slim, but they fall under the category of implied powers because they are necessary for the effective operation of schools.

To illustrate the various ways in which the states have retained control over public education, local school districts only have the taxing powers that have been granted by the state. On the other hand, state legislatures have granted to state boards of education such powers as setting minimum standards for teacher licensing or certification, minimum graduation requirements, minimum length of school day, and minimum number of school days in a year.

The recent interest in education reform has resulted in state legislatures and boards of education imposing a variety of additional requirements on local school districts (Stedman & Jordan, 1986). Examples include graduation requirements and "no pass, no play" requirements for participants in high school interscholastic activities. However, these requirements typically are imposed as minimums; local schools have the authority to exceed the imposed minimums by local policy.

The public schools in all states except Hawaii are administered and operated by local school districts.

Limits on Powers of Local School Districts

In some states, additional limits have been placed on the power of local school districts. For example, in Maryland, North Carolina, and Virginia, local school districts do not have the authority to fix a tax rate or levy taxes. School districts in these states must submit their budgets to municipal or county governments who then levy the taxes required to support schools. Members of these elected county or city councils review the budgets and determine the level of funding that they will provide for schools. In this manner, these school districts are fiscally dependent on general governmental agencies. The alternative arrangement is one in which school districts adopt their budgets and levy the taxes required to fund the budget. About 85% of the nation's school districts are in this latter group and are considered to be fiscally independent (Salmon, Dawson, Lawton, & Johns, 1988).

Number of School Districts in the States

Among the states, the number of school districts varies greatly and is associated with differences in educational opportunity for students. The number of school districts in each state is shown in Table 13.1. As indicated in the

Table 13.1: Number of School Districts by State, 1987–88

50 states and D.C.	15,577	Missouri	544
Alabama	129	Montana	550
Alaska	55	Nebraska	891
Arizona	240	Nevada	17
Arkansas	331	New Hampshire	173
California	1,084	New Jersey	604
Colorado	177	New Mexico	88
Connecticut	166	New York	722
Delaware	19	North Carolina	140
District of Columbia	1	North Dakota	303
Florida	67	Ohio	703
Georgia	186	Oklahoma	611
Hawaii	1	Oregon	304
Idaho	115	Pennsylvania	501
Illinois	986	Rhode Island	40
Indiana	303	South Carolina	91
Iowa	436	South Dakota	194
Kansas	304	Tennessee	141
Kentucky	178	Texas	1,063
Louisiana	66	Utah	40
Maine	200	Vermont	275
Maryland	24	Virginia	136
Massachusetts	396	Washington	296
Michigan	563	West Virginia	55
Minnesota	436	Wisconsin	431
Mississippi	152	Wyoming	49

Source: U.S. Department of Education, National Center for Education Statistics. (1989). *Digest of education statistics.* Washington, DC: U.S. Department of Education.

table, excluding Hawaii and the District of Columbia, the number of school districts in a state ranges from 17 in Nevada, 19 in Delaware, and 24 in Maryland to about 1,000 in California, Illinois, and Texas. Other states with relatively few school districts include Florida, Louisiana, New Mexico, Utah, and West Virginia.

Data in the table indicate that the number of school districts in a state is not related to either the total enrollment or geographic size of the state. For example, California, Illinois, Nebraska, New York, and Texas all have large numbers of school districts, but Nebraska has a much lower total enrollment than the other states.

Southeastern states tend to have the fewest school districts. In several states, school districts are organized on a county unit basis where the county and school district have the same boundary. States in the Midwest and Great Plains have tended to have more districts because the civil township was a beginning point for their school districts. However, in the 1950s and 1960s, several of these states took action to consolidate small school districts so that educational opportunities for students would be enhanced. During this period, the number of school districts in the nation was reduced from 100,000 to 16,000. In the past two decades, little progress has been made in reducing the number of school districts; the number has remained constant at slightly less than 16,000.

The number of school districts also has little relationship to the number of schools in a state. For the nation, the number of public schools totals about 80,000. The number of schools in a school district may be the result of need for facilities, geographic conditions, or tradition. Some districts operate only one school; others may operate several hundred.

Types of School Districts

Among the states, the typical pattern of school district organization is the unit school district that provides educational programs for students in kindergarten through grade 12. However, a few states permit the operation of separate high school districts serving grades 9 through 12 (9–12) and elementary districts serving students in kindergarten through grade 8 (K–8). For example, Arizona, Illinois, and Montana operate high school districts that are superimposed over underlying elementary school districts. These three states and a few others permit the operation of three types of school districts: K–8, 9–12, and K–12.

The original rationale for separate high school and elementary districts may have been that this arrangement would increase the high school offerings available to students, but the benefits of unified school districts serving students in kindergarten through grade 12 seem to outweigh the disadvantages. Educational program planning and sequencing can be handled more efficiently and students can be assisted in making the transition from elementary to high school.

In addition to the costs associated with duplicate sets of administrators in separate districts for elementary schools and high schools, a more important consideration may be the lack of coordination between the elementary schools and the high schools. Courses and programs may not be coordinated between elementary and high school districts and students may experience difficulty in making the transition from grade 8 to grade 9. These conditions contribute to a situation in which neither the elementary nor the high school district is held accountable for the educational outcomes.

Optimal Enrollment for a School District

Rather than prescribing a maximum and minimum number of students who should be enrolled in a school district, the more critical consideration is how to provide the students with the best possible educational opportunities. Advancements in technology and telecommunication, changes in instructional methods, and the importance of ancillary support services have made previous enrollment standards for minimum and maximum school district size inadequate. If all the services and programs were to be provided by a single school district, the minimum number of students would be so great that the recommended size would be rejected by most educators and interested citizens.

Minimum School District Enrollments

Certain minimal educational services and programs should be provided by local school districts: services and programs for the handicapped, learning opportunities for gifted and talented students, and programs that will help graduates succeed in either the world of work or postsecondary education. A school district with only a few hundred students is unable to provide these services and programs.

Depending on the sparsity of population and geographical conditions, recommendations for the minimum enrollment of a school district have ranged from 10,000 to 50,000 students (Grieder, Pierce, & Jordan, 1969). For large cities and densely populated suburban areas these enrollment numbers may seem small, but many large districts are characterized as unresponsive and impersonal and often have administrative and instructional problems that limit the effectiveness of local schools. Concerns about the negative and impersonal effects of bigness can be alleviated by creating regional school districts, decentralizing control, and transferring some budgetary and educational planning authority to the school site.

To provide the desired programs and support services in rural areas, the state might authorize the creation of cooperative service units or intermediate educational service agencies. As discussed earlier in this chapter, these agencies can provide a variety of services to benefit both students and teachers. These "overlay" educational service units provide an economically efficient way to increase local school districts' access to educational program and support services.

Criteria for Determining Minimum School District Size

For effective operation, criteria other than the number of students also should be considered in determining school district size. One criterion is that each school district should provide education for students from kindergarten through grade 12. However, this does not imply that all students in a district would attend the same school. One of the common misconceptions in discussions of the minimum enrollments of school districts in rural areas is the assumption that a school district might have only one location with several schools on the site. Rather than having all schools on the same site, the district could have several elementary schools scattered throughout the district with a central high school.

What should be the criteria for the continued operation of school districts in your state?

Another criterion would be related to minimum enrollment; rather than being an absolute number in all situations, factors such as population sparsity and topography should be considered when selecting a minimum enrollment. In rural areas, the geographical size of a school district is not as critical as the availability and feasibility of an adequate pupil transportation program. Population sparsity may necessitate that school enrollments be smaller to keep transportation time within acceptable limits. For example, one hour is often stated as the maximum one-way time for a student to ride on a bus.

A third criterion for determining minimum school district size is the tax base of the school district. Given the reliance on local revenues from the property tax as the source of about 50% of the funding for schools, the capacity of a school district to raise funds by taxation is a major concern. In rural areas, application of this criterion might result in school districts that encompass an entire county. However, problems also exist in suburban areas because of low property wealth attributable to concentrations of low-cost housing and high property wealth resulting from locations of shopping centers, electrical generating plants, or capital-intensive industrial plants.

The problem may be more severe in suburban areas with a number of relatively low enrollment districts; these districts often vary greatly in taxable wealth per pupil as well as the educational and income level of their citizens. Districts with the lowest levels of taxable wealth often have disproportionate numbers of students with a need for special educational programs and services. Some of these latter problems can be alleviated if the state funding program recognizes both the special needs of students and the low tax-paying capacity of these districts.

Local School Boards

The ability of lay citizens to control public education through a system of local school boards is a unique feature of the American educational system. In principle, school boards represent all the people; members are chosen as stewards with a public trust. There is no time or place for personal agendas. Through the schools, these lay citizens help build the future of the nation (American Association of School Administrators, 1946).

As each state established its own system, a school district governing board comprised of lay citizens became a common element found in all the states. This pattern has continued. These local school boards are either appointed or elected. In most cases, there are no educational requirements for school board membership. Members come from all walks of life. People seek appointment or election to school boards for a variety of reasons. The only prerequisite may be that the board member be a resident of the school district.

What should be the qualifications for membership on a local school board?

Functions of Local School Boards

The primary function of the local school board is to set the policies under which the schools will operate. Before making decisions, the board has a responsibility to consider alternative courses of actions in terms of the beliefs, values, and traditions of the community. However, the board should seek and rely on the counsel and recommendations of the superintendent and the management team selected by the superintendent. In the process the board must work as a group, for board members only have power and authority when the board is in session (Orlosky, McCleary, Shapiro, & Webb, 1984).

Other functions of the school board include budget adoption, approval of expenditures, approval of the school's organizational pattern, employment of personnel, and issuance of contracts. These legal functions are in addition to the role of the school board in providing for community participation in school governance. This community participation is especially critical because of the role of the local property tax in financing schools in many states and the importance of maintaining a strong base of citizen support for the public schools.

Lay persons serving on local school boards play a critical role in the governance of American public education.

Local school boards have been a part of the governance system for America's schools longer than superintendents of schools. In rural areas, many local school districts consisted of a one-room school staffed by one teacher and governed by a three- to five-member school board. Thus, there were more school board members than teachers in some localities. In other instances, the school principal also functioned as the superintendent of schools. As enrollments increased and as school districts became more complex organizations, the need for full-time professional leadership and management became evident and the position of superintendent of schools became a full-time position. The typical administrative organization in many school districts is illustrated in Figure 13.3.

Superintendent of Schools

As the role and responsibilities of the *superintendent of schools* have evolved, the position has become that of the chief executive officer of the local school district. Typically, educational program and related responsibilities of the superintendent include planning, staffing, coordinating, budgeting, administering, evaluating, and reporting. A profile of an early superintendent of schools is presented in the Historical Note on page 436.

When compared with private business, in many ways the local school board functions like the board of directors of a corporation. The superintendent of schools, the counterpart of the chief executive officer of the corporation, is responsible for the day-to-day operation of the enterprise, the schools (Campbell, Cunningham, Nystrand, & Usdan, 1985).

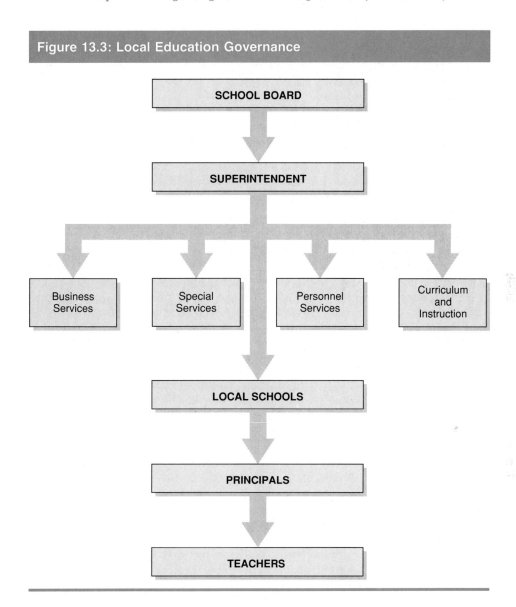

Figure 13.3: Local Education Governance

In contrast to an earlier time when the superintendent often was a part-time teacher and may have had only a bachelor's degree, today's superintendent has a full-time position, views the job as a career, and has advanced training in educational administration, often at the doctoral level. One of the primary responsibilities of the superintendent is to work with the local school board to improve educational programs in the district.

Career Patterns for Superintendents

The usual employment pattern has been for superintendents to come from the teaching ranks through roles as principals or assistant superintendents.

Historical Note:
Ella Flagg Young, Pioneer School Administrator

Ella Flagg Young served as a teacher, principal, and area superintendent of schools before receiving her doctorate from the University of Chicago. From 1899 to 1904, she was a professor of pedagogy at the University of Chicago and a colleague of John Dewey with whom she collaborated on several published works. She also served as supervisor of instruction at Dewey's laboratory school at the university.

Dewey regarded Ella Flagg Young as the "wisest person on school matters" with whom he had ever come in contact. According to Dewey, he was "constantly getting ideas from her. . . . More times than I could well say I didn't see the meaning or force of some favorite conception of my own until Mrs. Young had given it back to me." Dewey further confessed that "it was from her that I learned that freedom and respect for freedom mean regard for the inquiring and reflective processes of individuals."

In 1905, Ella Flagg Young returned to the Chicago public schools, became principal of Chicago Normal School, and from 1907 to 1915 served as the superintendent of schools for Chicago, the first woman to head a large city school system. In 1910, she was elected president of the National Education Association, the first woman to hold this office.

Throughout her career, Ella Flagg Young sought to improve the training and condition of teachers. She espoused democratic administration and organized teachers' councils to provide teachers with a greater voice in decision making. She worked for higher teachers' salaries and once resigned as superintendent because of the Board of Education's policies regarding teachers' organizations and salaries. At the outbreak of World War I, she became chairman of the Women's Liberty Loan Committee and, although over 70 years old, traveled throughout the country in its behalf. While on one trip, she became ill and died on October 18, 1918.

Ella Flagg Young's capable administration of both the National Education Association and Chicago's schools was a victory for all women educators. She inspired many women to seek positions of leadership and led many men (and women) to reconsider the capabilities of women for administration.

Should it be a requirement that superintendents and principals must have been successful teachers before becoming administrators?

Specialized training in educational administration beyond the master's degree is typically required for licensing or certification. Many states require the equivalent of two years of graduate work, and the trend is toward requiring the doctorate in educational administration for permanent certification (Report of the National Policy Board, 1989). However, among the states there appears to be some interest in nontraditional certification for persons with high leadership potential who have demonstrated in other fields that they possess the management and leadership skills required to be a successful superintendent of schools.

Administrative Council

Many school districts have a council of the school district's administrators that meets regularly to plan, hear reports, and make administrative decisions about the operation of the school district. One of the major benefits of the *administrative council* arrangement is the improvement of communication among the district's administrators and a reduction of the isolation of administrators with specialized functions. The superintendent typically chairs the administrative council. This group, often referred to as the management team of the school district, represents an effort by the superintendent to share decision-making responsibilities.

Membership on the administrative council varies according to district size and local management style. In some districts, building principals and central office administrators are members of the council; in others, membership is limited to central office administrators. Membership is a function of size as well as the preferences of the school district's leadership. If principals do not hold membership on the council, they may meet separately as a group for similar purposes. These meetings may be chaired by an assistant superintendent with administrative responsibility for the supervision of the schools and the principals.

Attendance Centers—The Local School

Just as local school districts are creations of state statutes and regulations, local schools are created by the policies and regulations of local school boards. As the smallest management unit of the school district, the local school is the most critical unit in the educational delivery system. The school reform movement of the 1980s placed strong emphasis on the important role of the local school and the leadership role of the principal in promoting school improvement (Stedman & Jordan, 1986).

Building Principal

Even though education is a state responsibility and a variety of state and school district requirements are imposed on local schools, the primary responsibility for the success or failure of the educational program in each local school resides with the *building principal*. Successful administration of a school requires that the principal exercise leadership as well as management skills.

Career Paths for Building Principals

Principals typically come from the ranks of teachers. Historically, some have viewed the principalship as a career and others have considered the job to be a stepping stone to a position such as assistant superintendent or superintendent. Recently, a new career pattern has emerged. At each level the principalship has come to be viewed as a career opportunity with a unique set of skills and professional opportunities. Preparation and licensing or certification programs usually involve the minimum of a master's degree and often a year of formal study after that. Proposals for reform of administrator preparation programs have advocated that a doctoral degree be a requirement for both superintendents and principals (Report of the National Policy Board, 1989). (Additional discussion on effective principals is found in Chapter 17.)

Decentralized Decision Making

One focus of the education reform movement in the 1980s was the emphasis on decentralized or school-site decision making as a way to increase teacher morale, improve the management of schools, and raise student performance. This casts the principal more in a leadership role, working with rather than directing faculty members. Models for involvement and decision making include school-site budgeting as well as school-level decision making. One potential problem with this management technique is the need to maintain open communications between the central office and the school site so that school-level personnel do not invest major amounts of time and energy and then find that their proposals have been ignored or re-jected. The principal concepts related to *site-based management* are outlined on page 439.

How much authority should teachers and parents have in operational decisions at the school level?

Central office decisions made by a single administrator without consulta-tion or school-site decisions made in the privacy of the principal's office with-out staff or community participation do not represent the management style anticipated by the advocates of decentralized decision making. An underlying assumption is that teachers should be heavily involved in planning, discussing, and making the final decisions. This process also is viewed as an opportunity to increase parental participation in schools by involving parents in critical aspects of school-site decision making.

In the previous discussion, the complexities of determining minimum enrollments of school districts were explored. As illustrated in the following discussion, similar complexities can be identified in efforts to determine the optimal number of students for an individual school.

Optimal School Enrollments

Enrollment standards for individual schools vary with grade level and program offerings. However, there appears to be consensus that an elemen-tary school should be sufficiently large for each grade to be in a separate room and that educational opportunities can be improved if the school has four sections of each grade. Using a class size of 25 students, that would result in a K−6 elementary school of 600−700 students. Educational opportunities can be enhanced in schools of this size by providing specialized facilities, special teachers, and a full-time principal. Population density and school-site plan-ning might justify larger elementary schools, but the challenge is to develop and maintain a positive educational environment.

At the junior and senior high levels, specification of optimal size ranges is more difficult. In the late 1950s, James Conant (1959) in *The American High School Today* recommended that a high school should have a minimum of 100 students in a graduating class, resulting in 400 students in a four-year high school. Rather than specifying a number of students, the more critical con-sideration is that the number of students be sufficiently large to enable the school district to provide the desired range of educational programs and ser-vices in a cost-effective manner. Operationally, this might mean a countywide

Controversial Issues:
Site- or School-Based Management?

The one-room schoolhouse was the ultimate in site-based management. In addition to teaching, the teacher often served as the custodian, principal, bookkeeper, and clerk for the school board. As schools were consolidated, management became more centralized and often detached from the classroom. This central-ization trend continued through the mid-1960s when interest in citizen involvement in schools began to develop. About two decades later, the school reform reports made multiple references to the potential benefits of increasing the authority of personnel at the school level. The concept of site-based management can have a significant impact on how individual schools are organized and how decisions are made.

Arguments For

1. Level of decision making is closer to the client, i.e., students.

2. Involvement of teachers and school patrons in-creases commitment to the goals of the school.

3. Resources are allocated according to the goals of the school.

4. Schools can adapt programs and allocate re-sources to meet local needs.

Arguments Against

1. Joint decision making takes teacher time away from instruction and increases the administra-tive paperwork burden on the principal.

2. Central office loses control over the curriculum and fiscal affairs.

3. Building level personnel do not have the exper-tise to develop and manage budgets.

4. Decentralized decision making can contribute to schools making decisions contrary to school district goals.

How would the role of the teacher in a school with site-based management be different from the role of a teacher in a school with centralized management? In which system would you prefer to teach?

---

high school in a district serving a rural area, multipurpose high schools in suburban districts, and special-purpose high schools in large urban districts.

Some of the negative effects of large enrollments in secondary schools can be reduced by operating on a "school-within-a-school" basis. When the school enrollment exceeds 2,500–3,000 students, the school can be divided into "houses" based on grade levels or program emphasis. Each "house" would have its own student body and its own teaching, administrative, and support staff. Programs and space can be allocated to the "house" so that students and staff develop a sense of community within the school.

Determining the desired size of a school is a matter of school board policy. Policies should be influenced by the types of programs to be provided, enroll-ment growth or decline, and the population configuration of the school dis-trict. The challenge is to develop and implement a school facility planning system that will maximize student access to educational programs and services.

In contrast to public education being provided through a range of school districts with multiple schools, private education typically is provided through a system of independent schools. A variety of motivations have contributed to their formation and continued operation.

Private Education

With the level of concern being raised about such issues as working/learning conditions and student performance in the public schools, interest in the private school alternative is being expressed by a wide variety of parents. The private school option is not new; it has provided an alternative to public education in the United States since the colonial period. However, these schools take different forms in response to parents who want their children to have broader educational opportunities, who seek a more rigorous or more restrictive environment for their children, or who desire a more permissive environment than can be provided in the public schools. This pattern of diverse aspirations has contributed to the development of private schools noted more for their differences than their similarities. They include traditional church-related schools, schools associated with evangelical groups, private traditional day schools, and "free" schools in which students can pursue individual interests.

Private School Enrollments

In 1989, about 5,700,000 students were enrolled in private schools, or about 12% of the total number of students enrolled in elementary and secondary schools. The vast majority (80%) of private schools are church-related, or *parochial schools*, and about half of those that are church-related are Roman Catholic. However, while overall enrollments in private elementary and secondary schools have remained relatively stable over the past 20 years, enrollments in Roman Catholic–affiliated schools have dropped considerably. And while the Catholic school enrollment has declined, the non-Catholic enrollment has increased, largely in schools operated by evangelical and fundamental Christian denominations (U.S. Department of Education, 1988a).

During the past two decades, minority enrollments in private schools have increased, particularly in Catholic-affiliated schools in urban areas. The percentage of minority enrollments in Catholic-affiliated schools more than doubled from 1970 – 71 to 1988–89, from 10.8% to 22.7% (Mahar, 1989). This trend takes on special significance, considering that achievement differences between white students and minority students are less in private schools than in public schools. Smaller differences in student achievement between white and minority students at all socioeconomic levels in type of program enrollments (e.g., college preparatory, vocational, and general education) have been found in the Catholic-affiliated schools. In addition, more than 85% of private school students graduate from high school as compared to 73% of public school students (Orstein, 1989). These observations suggest the need for a careful study of the differences between public and private schools and their student bodies to identify ways in which the success rates of all students might be improved (Hispanic Policy Development Project, 1987).

Proprietary Schools

Schools operated for profit make up a growing sector of the private school market. *Proprietary schools* have been an educational option since the colonization of America, but recently their numbers have been increasing. Their popularity has been attributed to the fact that parents are attracted to the high standards that many espouse, the extras (e.g., before and after school remediation and counseling and a wide variety of extracurricular activities), in-depth education, and smaller class size. Although proprietary schools represent only 1% of all elementary and secondary schools, the National Education Association (NEA) has referred to privatization as a threat to America's public schools. The NEA has expressed concern about the lack of accountability (i.e., many do not have governing boards) and the equity implications of an educational option that essentially is available only to upper-income families. Additional concerns are related to the need for regulations. The attention of educators and policy makers to these issues likely will increase if the number of proprietary schools continues to grow (Bridgman, 1988).

In spite of the recent growth in new Christian schools, projections suggest that the overall percentage of American students enrolled in private elementary and secondary schools will remain stable for the next several years. However, if states and/or the federal government provide public funds for the general operation of private schools, the percentage of students enrolled in private schools might increase dramatically.

What controls should the state have over the operation of private schools?

Summary

The organizational structure of American education is constantly undergoing changes. The balance between school site decision making and uniform state standards for school performance likely will be one of the focal points for discussion in the 1990s. As pressures for accountability increase, reporting and monitoring requirements likely will increase.

The governmental structures and organization of schools differ in some ways, but the general pattern is consistent among the states. As discussed in the following chapter, patterns of financing schools also differ among the states with a wide range in the proportion of funds that come from state and local revenue sources.

Key Terms

Administrative council
Building principal
Chief state school officer
Intermediate education service agency
  (IESA)
Parochial school
Policies

Proprietary school
School board
Secretary of education
Site-based management
State board of education
State department of education
Superintendent of schools

Discussion Questions

1. How could local control of schools be increased without the state abdicating its responsibilities to students?

2. What qualifications should a person have to hold membership on a local school board?

3. In making decisions and setting school policy, what would be the advantages and disadvantages of replacing the school board with professional educators?

4. What are the advantages and disadvantages of requiring that a superintendent of schools have successful experience as a teacher? A principal?

5. What kinds of responsibilities should teachers have in the administration of an individual school?

6. How can intermediate educational service units improve overall educational opportunities?

7. What should be the relationship between the chief state school officer and the state board of education?

8. What are the advantages and disadvantages of electing or appointing the chief state school officer?

9. What would be the merits of restricting the role of the federal government in education to gathering and reporting data and funding educational research?

10. In what ways are private schools and their students different from public schools and their students?

References

American Association of School Administrators. (1946). *School boards in action,* 24th yearbook. Arlington, VA: American Association of School Administrators.

Bridgman, A. (1988). Private, for-profit schools: Where they stand. *Education Digest, 23*(6), 10–13.

Campbell, R. F., Cunningham, L. L., Nystrand, R. O., & Usdan, M. D. (1985). *The organization and control of American schools* (5th ed.) Columbus, OH: Merrill.

Conant, J. B. (1959). *The American high school today.* New York: McGraw-Hill.

Conant, J. B. (1961). *Slums and suburbs.* New York: McGraw-Hill.

Cubberley, E. P. (1929). *Public school administration.* Boston: Houghton Mifflin Co.

Grieder, C., Pierce, T. M., & Jordan, K. F. (1969). *Public school administration.* New York: Ronald Press.

Hispanic Policy Development Project. (1987). Policy remedies. *The Research Bulletin, 1*(2), 9.

Mahar, M. (Ed.) (1989). *Catholic schools in America: 1989* (17th ed.). Montrose, CO: Fisher Publishing Co.

Orlosky, D. E., McCleary, L. E., Shapiro, A., & Webb, L. D. (1984). *Educational administration today.* Columbus, OH: Merrill.

Orstein, A. C. (1989). The growing non-public school movement. *Educational Horizons, 67*(71), 74.

Report of the National Policy Board. (1989). Charlottesville, VA: Curry School of Education, University of Virginia.

Salmon, R., Dawson, C., Lawton, S., & Johns, T. (1988). *State school finance programs 1986–87.* Blacksburg, VA: American Educational Finance Association, Virginia Polytechnic Institute and State University.

Stedman, J. B., & Jordan, K. F. (1986). *Education reform reports: Content and impact.* Washington, DC: Congressional Research Service, Library of Congress.

U.S. Department of Education, National Center for Education Statistics. (1988a). *Digest of education statistics.* Washington, DC: U.S. Department of Education.

U.S. Department of Education, National Center for Education Statistics. (1988b). *The condition of education 1988.* Washington, DC: U.S. Government Printing Office.

U.S. Department of Education, National Center for Education Statistics. (1989). *The condition of education 1989.* Washington, DC: U.S. Government Printing Office.

Chapter 14

Financing Public Education

We may have reached the time when the public will not grant us more money for public instruction unless we can show greater efficiency in spending the dollars which have already been voted for school use.

NASSP Fifth Yearbook (1921)

You find yourself employed in a state where funding for the public schools has not kept pace with rising costs. Average per pupil expenditures in the state are below the national average, but the per capita personal income is above the national average—indicating a low level of tax effort for education. Teachers' salaries in your district are lower than in neighboring school districts and nearby states. The state's educational organizations are supporting a statewide initiative to secure additional funds for the public schools. Taxpayers' groups are opposing the effort. The business community is calling for a greater emphasis on the basic skills so that high school graduates can perform well on the job. Interested citizens are questioning whether the additional funds will "make a difference."

What arguments can be given for increased funding? What kinds of information should be provided to justify the need for additional funds? Should the new funds be targeted for a specific purpose? How can the schools demonstrate that they will be accountable in the use of the new funds? What role should citizens and patrons play in making these decisions?

The material presented in this chapter is intended to increase your understanding of how schools are financed and the issues related to that financing. Whether or not you become employed in a state that matches the one described above, throughout your career as an educator you will be asked to justify educational funding and the way funds are expended. As an employee in the nation's largest industry with the largest public expenditure except for defense, you should not feel the public's interest to be unexpected or unwarranted. As you read and discuss this chapter and undertake the related activities, consider the following objectives and their impact upon you in your future role as a teacher. After reading the chapter, you should be able to:

- Discuss the perception of education as an investment.

- Describe the five goals of school finance programs.

- Compare the goals of the six school finance programs.

- Identify the criteria used to evaluate a tax structure.

- Identify the major local, state, and federal revenue sources.

- Discuss future funding challenges.

Financing the Schools

Public interest in education is high, and one of the concerns is the level of funding that should be provided for the schools. Concerns include the ability of graduates to do their jobs in the workplace and the competition for public funds from other public services such as health care, mental health, programs for the elderly, and law enforcement.

Support for elementary and secondary education is the largest single item in the budgets of many state and local governments. Expenditures for public elementary and secondary schools will exceed $200 billion annually in the early 1990s. While funds come from a combination of local, state, and federal sources, the great majority of the money will be from state and local taxes. Federal funds are targeted for special programs or conditions rather than designed to provide a significant portion of the general funding. Figure 14.1 shows the degree of participation of the three levels of government in the financing of education.

The complexity of the educational enterprise is awesome. For example, one person in four either attends or is employed in the nation's public elementary and secondary schools. Rather than a single system of schools like a large corporation, the American educational delivery system operates through 50 separate state educational agencies with instruction being provided by 16,000 local school districts in about 80,000 schools. Operational policies are set by governors, state legislatures, and local school boards. Governors and legislators not only face the public policy challenge of determining the funding system for the schools, but also are expected to provide adequate and equitable financing for this system of schools.

Figure 14.1: Sources of Educational Funding for Elementary and Secondary Public Schools, 1986–87

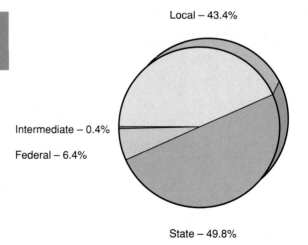

Local – 43.4%

Intermediate – 0.4%

Federal – 6.4%

State – 49.8%

Source: National Center for Education Statistics, U.S. Department of Education (1988). *E.D. TABS* (November, CS 89–043, table 2, p.8). Washington, DC: U.S. Government Printing Office.

Methods of financing public elementary and secondary schools differ in a variety of ways both within and among states; so do funding levels per pupil. However, two basic legal principles guide the financing of the public schools in the United States. First, education is a responsibility of the state level of government. Second, in the design and implementation of the state school finance program, the state has an equal responsibility to each pupil. Adhering to these principles has been difficult because the states have chosen to let the local school districts, with their wide differences in enrollment, taxable wealth, and citizen aspirations, administer and deliver education.

How many school districts are in your state? What is their range of enrollment?

Education—An Expense or an Investment?

One of the continuing questions about any public service is whether the activity should be viewed as a public expense or a societal investment. The general consensus is that sufficient funding for a quality education should not be viewed as an expense, but as an investment in the future of the nation. The failure of a nation to educate its populace results in an expense for both society and individuals. The Committee for Economic Development (1987) has estimated that each year's class of dropouts will cost the nation $240 billion in lost earnings and unpaid taxes over their lifetime. This projection does not include the billions more for crime control, welfare, health care, and other social services that this undereducated group will cost the nation. Increasing attention is being given to ways in which states can fund programs and services for at-risk youth. (See Chapter 10 for a discussion of the costs associated with various categories of at-risk youth.)

Potential problems resulting from inadequate funding for schools are especially severe in those states with projections of above-average growth in the number of youth who are likely to be educationally disadvantaged because of English language deficiencies and economic poverty. (See Chapter 8.) Educational interventions to address these problems not only can increase the productivity of the state's youth, they also can reduce the long-term social burden associated with poverty, welfare, and crime. Providing these youth with a quality education requires lower pupil-teacher ratios and special instructional materials. Rather than assuming that these problems can be addressed by reallocation and more efficient use of current resources, the Committee for Economic Development (1987) stated that any plan for improving the education of disadvantaged youth is doomed to failure if it does not recognize the need for additional resources over a sustained period. Businesses have become especially interested in the quality of America's educational system because of the important role that a well-educated and well-qualified work force has in maintaining and improving the nation's, or a state's, competitive position.

The contributions of education to the economy occur in different ways. As discussed in Chapter 8, well-educated workers increase productivity and are needed to help industry compete internationally. In addition, literate workers can make informed choices and become contributing citizens. The assumption is that these workers will have the income required to support the economy through their purchase of consumer goods. Current concerns about both the fairness and responsiveness of the current educational system are related to the on-the-job performance of the graduates of the educational system and their capacity to be informed and discriminating consumers of goods and services.

Public Policy Goals in School Finance

The world of financing schools is imperfect and full of educational and political compromises. Public policy decisions about how schools should be financed are made with five goals in mind: equity, choice, adequacy, account-ability, and efficiency. Of these goals, equity usually is the most important. The problem with equity is that the majority may not be able to agree that equity has been attained, but they can agree that equity has *not* been attained as long as large disparities in per pupil expenditures exist.

Equity

The concept of *equity* refers to the equal treatment of persons in equal circumstances. For students, this means an equal opportunity for education. The problem is that equity may not result in sufficient funds for schools; it may only result in equal treatment.

Horizontal equity assumes that students who are alike should be treated the same way. *Vertical equity* assumes that groups that have different needs should be treated differently and also that those within each group should be treated in the same way. Some of the issues related to the concept of equity are raised on page 449. Use them to explore the concept in greater depth.

Choice

In the 1990s, the term *choice* is being used to refer to two different goals. One is local control of funding decisions. Traditionally, local school officials have been permitted to choose the level of funding for the schools. In some cases, equity and choice have come into conflict because a district's freedom to choose the level of funding has resulted in unequal treatment of taxpayers and students. The more recent definition of choice refers to the power of parents to select schools. There have not been enough experiences with this type of choice to indicate the impact on equity to either students or taxpayers.

What is the range from high to low in per pupil expenditures among the school districts in your state?

Adequacy

Adequacy refers to the extent to which funding for programs and learning opportunities is sufficient. Factors affecting adequacy include staff, materials, and skill levels of teachers.

Ask Yourself:
Issues of Equity

In the process of funding education, questions are raised about the relative amounts of funds that should come from local, state, and federal sources and the procedures that should be used in allocating funds to local school districts and schools. The concept of equity refers to equal treatment of persons in equal circumstances. Equity is a commonly accepted goal in the financing of elementary and secondary schools. As you consider how schools should be financed, ask yourself the following questions.

- *Federal responsibilities.* To what extent should the federal government assume responsibility for funding public education? What kinds of programs should be supported with federal funds? Should the federal government equalize spending per pupil among the states?

- *State responsibilities.* Should the state guarantee that the same funds are provided for each pupil? Does this meet the standard for treating pupils in an equitable manner? What kinds of differences among pupils should the state recognize in the allocation of funds? What kinds of differences among school districts should the state recognize in the allocation of funds?

- *Local responsibilities.* Should the same amount of money be spent on each student? Does this meet the standard for treating pupils in an equitable manner? What kinds of differences among pupils should the local school district recognize in the allocation of funds to individual schools? What kinds of differences among individual schools should local school districts recognize in the allocation of funds to schools?

Accountability

Increased attention is being given to *accountability,* with the focus on the responsibility of the schools to accomplish expressed educational goals. Although those held accountable are generally students, teachers, administrators, and parents, the concept can be extended to the responsibilities of taxpayers, school board members, and legislators.

Efficiency

The term *efficiency* refers to ways in which administrative or operational decisions can lead to increased productivity without increased funding. Examples of these decisions include making reductions in administrative costs, promoting increased use of educational technology, setting higher standards for pupils, making changes in teacher education programs, and putting greater emphasis on basic skills instruction.

Which of the school finance goals would you consider to be most important? Least important?

The Courts and School Finance

Since 1970, state programs for financing the public schools have been challenged in about 35 states (LaMorte, 1989). Litigation has been initiated in both federal and state courts. The issues are related to contentions that the state is failing to provide "equal protection" for students because the state system for financing education has resulted in unequal levels of spending among school districts and the differences in spending are related to differences in wealth among districts. In this context, wealth refers to assessed value of taxable real property per student.

Following the rejection by the United States Supreme Court in *San Antonio v. Rodriguez* (1973) of the argument that education is a constitutionally protected right and that equal treatment is required in the providing of education, some observers thought that the amount of legal actions would diminish, but the number of cases in state courts suggests a continuing interest in challenging state school finance programs. The effect of *Rodriguez* was to base challenges of existing state school finance programs on the technical provisions of the state constitutions rather than provisions in the federal Constitution.

These legal challenges have been initiated because of the interaction of two conditions—the use of the local property tax as a major source of revenue for schools and the wide differences in taxable wealth per pupil among local school districts. As a result of these conditions, tax rates to provide an equal level of funding for education vary among school districts. This condition is viewed as being unfair to both taxpayers and students; depending on the district, taxpayers must be taxed at different rates to provide the same level of

Schools and students often are funded unequally because of the differences in the value of local taxable property.

support. The result is that students in poor districts are at a disadvantage relative to students in other districts with greater wealth or higher tax rates.

Trends in the court decisions are difficult to determine. Of the decisions that have been issued by state supreme courts, ten have upheld the provisions of the state school finance system, and eight have held the system to be unconstitutional. In the decisions that have upheld the existing funding systems, education has been viewed as an important government service, but not a fundamental right under which each student in the state would be guaranteed equal treatment. In some instances, the courts have been critical of the financing systems but have indicated that the problem should be resolved by legislative actions rather than judicial decisions (LaMorte, 1989).

In the decisions that have thrown out state school finance programs, the courts have held that the current system was unconstitutional on the grounds of unfairness to both taxpayers and students. Unequal tax burdens were considered to be in violation of the equal protection provisions of the state constitutions, and differences in expenditures per pupil were found to be in violation of the equal protection provisions of the state constitutions or the technical provisions of the state constitution pertaining to education (LaMorte, 1989).

The 1989 actions of the highest state court in Kentucky illustrate how the courts can affect the schools. The state's entire system of education was found to be in violation of the state constitution because of unequal spending per pupil and low student achievement in low spending/low wealth districts. In 1990, the state legislature responded to the court decision by enacting legislation to meet the requirements of the court decision. If the legislature had not acted, Kentucky's entire system of education would have been dissolved. The legislative reform covers the organization of local school districts, school-site decision making, the state board of education, and the state department of education as well as the state financing system (Walker, 1989). This is the most dramatic court decision that has been issued, and the resulting reforms in the schools will be interesting to observe.

State School Finance Equalization Programs

Commonly used state school finance programs can be divided into six models or funding approaches. Three are equalization models: equalized foundation grants, equalized reward for tax effort, and full state funding. The other models are flat grants, categorical funding, and competitive grants. The equalization models were developed in the early decades of the twentieth century; prior to that time, state funds were limited and typically were distributed on a flat grant basis irrespective of differences in local wealth or educational need.

These equalization models generally have been modified by state legislators to accommodate specific state needs. The most frequently used approach is a version of the equalized foundation grants.

Although state school finance laws were originally developed to assist schools in the poorer rural areas, it is the urban school districts that now require additional help. They have two types of additional burdens. One is *educational overburden,* which refers to the relatively larger number of pupils in city schools who require high-cost educational programs and the higher costs of instructional goods and services. A related problem is *municipal overburden,* which is caused by the need for a greater range of social services in urban areas that must be paid for by the same taxpayers who support the schools.

Foundation Programs

What kind of school finance program does your state use to fund elementary and secondary schools?

The major state school finance programs are described in Figure 14.2. The Strayer-Haig model, typically referred to as the *foundation plan,* provides the difference between a fixed amount per pupil and the amount the district can collect locally through a uniform tax rate (Strayer & Haig, 1923). For example, if the foundation plan provides for $4,000 per pupil and the uniform local tax rate for a school district raises $2,500 per pupil, the state payment would be $1,500 per pupil. If the uniform local tax rate raises $1,000 per pupil, the state payment would be $3,000 per pupil. However, if the uniform local tax rate raises $5,000 per pupil, the state would make no payment to the local school district. The different amounts of state payments illustrate the ways in which equalization can be operationalized so that state and local revenues provide a foundation of funds. In terms of the previously discussed school finance goals, equity and adequacy can be achieved if the foundation amount per pupil is sufficiently high.

Some form of the equalized foundation program of allocating funds to local school districts is used in over half the states (Salmon, Dawson, Lawton, & Johns, 1988). This program has been criticized because it keeps funding at a minimum level, one insufficient to support an adequate educational program. This has a stifling effect because the state typically does not participate in local tax efforts to provide funds beyond the minimum level.

Power Equalization Programs

Under *power equalization* formulas, local school officials choose the level of funding they desire for their schools. Revenues raised by taxes in the district are "equalized" by state allocations (Updegraff, 1922). This differs from the foundation plan in which the state sets the target amount per pupil or per teacher. In the late 1980s, about one-third of the states were using some modification of the power equalization concept.

Under power equalization funding programs the local school board sets a tax rate and the state then guarantees a specified amount per unit of tax rate (Coons, Clune, & Sugarman, 1970). For example, if the state guarantees $50 per pupil per penny of tax rate and a penny in district A raises $30 per pupil, the state would provide $20 per pupil per penny of tax rate. If a one-penny tax rate raises $10 in district B, the state would provide $40 per pupil per penny of tax rate. Under this option, the state does not provide a foundation funding level, but allocates funds in relation to the tax rates selected in local

Figure 14.2: Current Funding Approaches

Description	Who Uses It?	Problems
Strayer-Haig Equalization Funding Model (foundation plan)		
Developed in 1920s by George D. Strayer and Robert M. Haig at Columbia University.	Used in some form in over half the states.	Keeps funding at a minimum level; insufficient to support an adequate educational program.
Provides difference between district's need and amount collectible locally.		State does not participate in efforts to provide funds beyond minimum.
Uniform tax rate applied to assessed value of property in school district.		
Entitlement based on funds required to ensure a minimum per pupil or per teacher; minimum determined by legislature.		
Adjusted to recognize additional funds needed for concentration of pupils with special needs.		
Power Equalization (effort oriented)		
Developed in 1922 by Harlan Updegraff at University of Pennsylvania.	About ⅓ of states used it in some form in the late 1980s.	No state was recapturing all "excess" funds in late 1980s.
Local school officials choose level of funding.		No assurance of funding at an adequate level.
Tax revenues in district "equalized" by state allocations.		
Any excess raised in a district sent to state treasury.		
Full State Funding		
No local taxes collected.	Used only in Hawaii.	No local choice permitted.
Flat grants		
State provides uniform amount per student; funds available for any legal educational purpose.	Originally most common form of state support.	Funds do not generally go to area of greatest need.
	May be used with an equalization program to ensure that wealthy school districts receive some funds.	
Categorical Funding		
State funds are allocated for specific purpose (e.g., bilingual education, in-service programs for teachers, instructional materials, etc.).	Often used to encourage specific programs that are not mandated by state law.	Typically allocated irrespective of district's wealth.
Discretionary Competitive Grants		
Districts compete for limited funds through an application process.	Often used to support demonstration projects or to fund specific research.	Likely to go to either urban school districts, or districts with skilled grant proposal writers.

school districts. In terms of the previously discussed school finance goals, equity and local district choice can be achieved, but there is no assurance that the level of funding will be adequate or sufficient.

Full State Funding

Full state funding for public schools occurs when no local tax revenues are collected for support of schools. All funds for schools come from state-level taxes (Morrison, 1930). This model is used only in Hawaii, which has just one school district for administrative management of all state schools. A single teacher's salary schedule is in effect for all schools on the islands.

Flat Grants

Originally the most common form of state payment to school districts, *flat grants* have now been replaced by foundation or equalization programs. Under the flat grant program, states provided a uniform amount per student and the funds could be used for any legal educational purpose (Cubberley, 1905). Several states still include a low-level flat grant program when enacting an equalization program to ensure that high-wealth schools that might not receive funds under the equalization program do receive some state funds.

Categorical Funding

Categorical funding means that state funds are allocated for a specific educational purpose, e.g., bilingual education, education of handicapped pupils, pupil transportation, in-service programs for teachers, or instructional materials. Most states have some type of categorical funding for special programs, but this is not the principal method for funding schools.

Competitive Grants

Under the *competitive grants* program districts compete for limited funds through an application process. This approach often is used to support demonstration projects or to fund specific research activities. One of the common criticisms of this funding approach is that school districts with good grant writers often are recipients even though their need for the funds may be no greater than other districts' needs.

What are the sources of revenues for all governmental services in your state? What is the proportion from each source?

Sources of Tax Revenue for Schools

The principal sources of funds for public elementary and secondary schools are the various types of taxes levied by local, state, and federal governments. As indicated previously, the relative proportion of revenues from each source varies both among and within states. In this section we present criteria for evaluating a tax system and discuss the major tax sources in terms of these criteria.

Criteria for Evaluating Taxes

Taxation systems have effects beyond the raising of revenues. They must be evaluated in terms of their impact on overall social, political, and economic conditions. The criteria of economic distortions, equity, compliance, and revenue elasticity are used to evaluate the tax structure of a governmental unit.

Economic Distortions

A tax should not cause *economic distortions*. That is, a tax should not alter consumer spending patterns, create business preferences for particular geographic areas, or affect the willingness of a person or a business to be part of the local, state, or national economy.

Equity

A tax should be equitable. Persons in the same relative circumstances should share the tax burden equally. When those with greater incomes pay a higher tax rate, the tax is called progressive. If persons with greater incomes pay a smaller proportion in taxes, the tax is called regressive.

Compliance

The rate of compliance should be high. This means there will be a minimum cost for enforcement, a reasonable cost for collection, and no loopholes to allow persons to evade the tax.

Revenue Elasticity

The revenues generated by the taxing system should respond to the economy. *Revenue elasticity* occurs when the yield from taxation increases during inflation and declines during a recession. Funds for schools come from a limited number of revenue sources, and the relative merits of each can be evaluated in terms of the four general criteria.

Local Revenue Sources—Property Tax

The principal source of local revenue for schools is the ad valorem tax on real property, which includes land, residences, apartment buildings, commercial buildings, railroads, and utilities. On average, over 90% of the local tax revenues for schools comes from taxes on real property.

The property tax fails to meet some of the criteria used in evaluating a taxation system. Variations in property wealth and resulting differences in tax rates among taxing jurisdictions tend to create economic distortions. Businesses may choose to locate in areas with lower property taxes, resulting in citizens who reside in one area having easier access to the business than those who live in others. Residences in a low tax area may sell more easily than those in a high tax area. However, the property tax is considered to be a desirable tax because it discourages the hoarding of property and the concentration of wealth in the hands of a few citizens.

The equity of the property tax has been subject to the following criticisms:

1. The burden of payment has the heaviest impact on fixed-income taxpayers whose residences are increasing in value at a rate greater than their income from which taxes must be paid. In such cases, the property tax is considered to be regressive.

2. Various types of property often are assessed at different rates for taxpaying purposes. The rates are set by the state legislature, and the action results in favored treatment for certain types of property or taxpayers.

3. The property tax has a potential punitive effect because failure to pay can result in forfeit of the property. This action may be taken even if the property is not generating income and the person is unable to pay the taxes.

4. The costs of administering and collecting the property tax are much higher than for sales or income taxes. A more extensive administrative bureaucracy is required for the maintenance of records related to the ownership of property and payment of taxes.

5. Assessment is a major administrative cost. Assessors must be trained and their assessments have to be verified to ensure accuracy. In addition, provision must be made for taxpayers to appeal the assessment decision.

The property tax does not fare well on the criterion related to a minimum cost for enforcement and a reasonable cost for collection. But it has the advantage of being more stable than other taxes, such as sales and income. Property tax receipts can be projected with reasonable accuracy for a budget year. In contrast, sales tax receipts are immediately responsive to economic shifts, and income taxes are only slightly more stable.

State Revenue Sources—Sales and Income Taxes

The principal sources of state revenues for schools are taxes on retail sales and on personal and business income. In 1986–87, sales tax revenues accounted for 49% of state revenues. Statewide personal and corporate income tax revenues accounted for 39% of total state revenues (U.S. Department of Commerce, 1988). As shown in the following discussion, both sales and income taxes fail to meet several criteria used in evaluating a taxation system.

All states have either sales or income taxes and many have both. The resulting choices of where to live and to purchase goods and services tend to create economic distortions. Individuals may choose to locate in states without personal income taxes. For example, people may work in Boston and live in New Hampshire, a state without a personal income tax. Oregon has an income tax but no sales tax, and Washington has a sales tax but no income tax. Similarly, different levels of sales taxes or the absence of a sales tax may result in persons electing to make their purchases across the state boundary to escape some or all of the sales tax payments.

Sales Tax

The sales tax is considered to be inequitable unless exemptions are granted for such necessities as groceries, essential basic clothing, and medical prescriptions. In this sense, the sales tax is considered to be regressive, or less equitable, because it has the strongest impact on those least able to pay. For example, a low-income person will pay a larger percent of actual income in the form of sales taxes than a high-income person.

Compliance with the sales tax can be more easily monitored because payments are made at the point of purchase and retail establishments can be identified and policed. Even though both sales and income taxes require an administrative bureaucracy, the costs of administering and collecting either tax are much less than for the property tax. Enforcement problems may be encountered, but both taxes do fare well on the criteria related to a minimum cost for enforcement and a reasonable cost for collection.

Income Tax

The scenario for the income tax is quite different. Most state income taxes include a rate structure in which the rate increases with income. Thus, the person with the highest income pays a higher rate. In these instances, the income tax is considered to be more equitable because the tax is progressive.

Compliance rates for payment of state income and sales taxes are subject to interpretation. State income tax systems often utilize the administrative system of the federal income tax, and questions have been raised about the overall compliance rates for the federal income tax. When significant changes are made in the federal income tax structure, states often find it necessary to adjust their systems because of the linkages between exemptions and rates in state and federal income taxes.

Both sales and income taxes are quickly responsive to changes in the economy. Thus, they may not have the level of stability desired to permit sound fiscal planning because revenue receipts can shift within a tax year if economic predictions are not correct. This is different from the property tax which is a more stable source of revenue. The combination of sales and income with property taxes has considerable merit; the joint system has a mix of the desired qualities of stability and responsiveness.

A majority of the states raise some amount of revenues through lotteries. The proceeds typically become a part of the state's general fund, but education often benefits. (See the Historical Note on page 460.)

What kinds of state taxes are levied in your state?

Federal Revenue Sources—Income Tax

Federal funding for elementary and secondary education has been limited, but the principal source of federal revenue for education is the federal income tax. In 1986–87, about 88% of the revenues of the federal government came from corporate and personal income taxes (U.S. Department of Commerce, 1988).

A major advantage of the federal income tax is that it relies on the entire nation as the taxpaying base. Because the tax is collected throughout the nation, the possibility of creating economic distortions through collections is minimized. However, economic distortions can be created through the tax's exemption rate structure. Exemptions can be used to discourage or encourage certain economic behavior by taxpayers, e.g., deductions for interest charges associated with installment purchases.

The federal income tax is considered to be equitable because of its progressive rate structure, but in the 1984 reform of the tax the level of progressivity was reduced. However, rates continue to increase as a person's income increases, and those with high incomes pay a higher rate.

Compliance rates for payment of the federal income tax are matters of concern, but the Internal Revenue Service has established a complex system of reporting to increase collections and ease enforcement. Even though the federal income tax has a large administrative bureaucracy, the costs of administering and collecting this tax have been estimated to be much less than for any other tax. The federal income tax fares well on the compliance criterion because of its relatively low cost for enforcement and collection.

The federal income tax is more stable than state sales and income taxes because of the national economic base. However, revenues from the tax respond to changes in the economy. Thus federal income tax receipts provide the additional revenues required for orderly fiscal planning as revenue receipts shift in a pattern consistent with economic conditions. The federal income tax ranks second to the property tax as a stable source of revenue, but it has greater elasticity.

This discussion illustrates that no single tax is the perfect solution to providing funds for schools. The optimal taxation system consists of a balance between stability and responsiveness with a progressive effect. In addition, the taxing system should not place an unfair or confiscatory burden on any group of taxpayers or encourage undesirable economic behavior.

Local School District Planning and Budgeting

Public elementary and secondary schools are labor-intensive endeavors. Personnel costs represent the majority of expenditures in local school budgets. About 75% of the typical school district's personnel costs are for teachers' salaries and fringe benefits. Additional funds are spent for administrator salaries at both the central office and the building level; however, they account for less than 10% of the total. Figure 14.3 shows the percentage of the budget allocated for various functions in the typical local school district.

Strategic Planning

The concept of *strategic planning* has become part of the vocabulary of the program planning and funding decisions of local school districts. Starting with the school district's or the school's mission statement supported by goals and objectives, funding priorities are linked to resource allocations to ensure that budgetary decisions are compatible with program priorities.

Figure 14.3: Typical School District Expenditures by Category

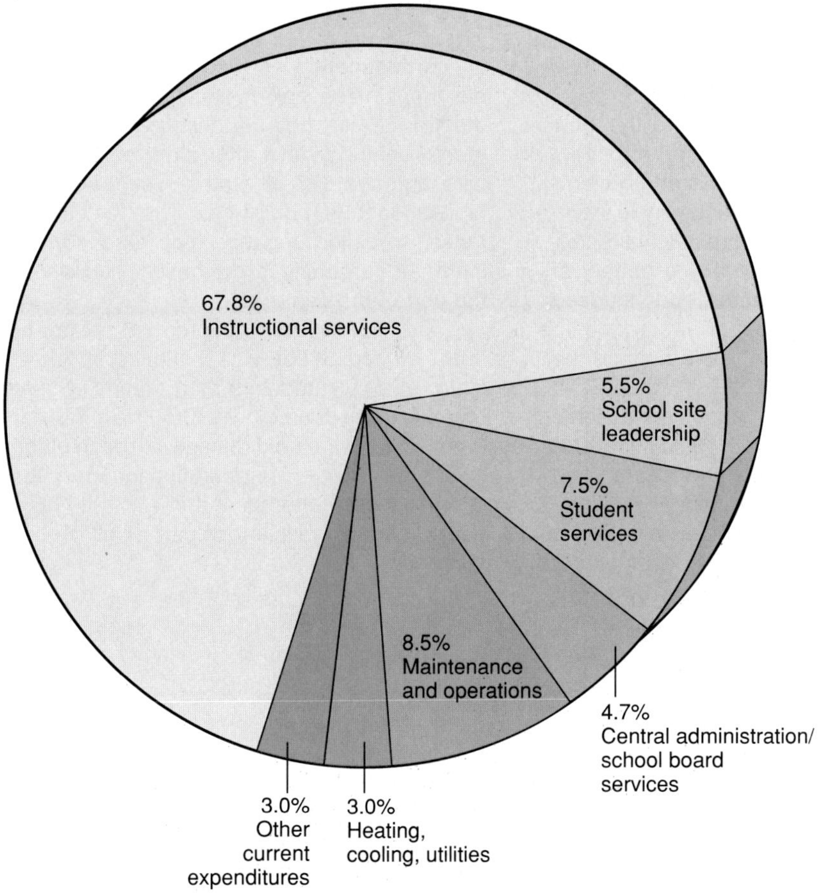

67.8%
Instructional services

5.5%
School site
leadership

7.5%
Student
services

8.5%
Maintenance
and operations

4.7%
Central administration/
school board
services

3.0%
Other
current
expenditures

3.0%
Heating,
cooling, utilities

Source: Robinson, G. E., & Protheroe, N. (1990). Local school budget profiles study. *School Business Affairs, 56* (9), 8–17. Reprinted with permission.

Note: Percents do not total 100 because of rounding.

However, it would be incorrect to assume that use of strategic planning by a school district will result in participative decision making. If the planning process is to be from the bottom up, teachers will be active participants. They will be members of the school working committee and possibly also of various subcommittees. However, if the planning process is to be top down, opportunities for broad-based teacher participation will be limited.

School-Site Decision Making

Several school reform reports in the mid-1980s advocated decentralized decision making and greater teacher participation in operational decisions at

Historical Note:
The Lotteries and Education

The use of lotteries, both for settling disputes and as games of chance, has been traced to 3500 B.C. When the English colonists came to the New World, they brought with them a tradition of private and public lotteries. Colonial churches and governments made use of the lottery. Benjamin Franklin and other leading citizens of Philadelphia sponsored a lottery to raise money to buy a battery of cannon for the city. The Continental Congress used a lottery to generate funds to support the troops. In the 1790s, lotteries were used to help finance the construction and improvement of Washington, D.C.

Lotteries were also used by various educational institutions. Dartmouth, Harvard, Kings College (Columbia University), Pennsylvania, Princeton, and William and Mary are among the colonial colleges that benefited from lotteries. From the signing of the Constitution to the Civil War, some 300 elementary and secondary schools and 47 colleges were beneficiaries of lotteries (Ezell, 1960).

Unfortunately, as the use of lotteries grew, so did the abuses and irregularities associated with them. In the second and third quarters of the nineteenth century, state after state passed antilottery bills, and by 1878 all states except Louisiana prohibited lotteries. Louisiana's "Golden Octopus" lotteries, so called because they reached into every state and large city in the nation, had also died by the end of the century.

The first modern government-operated lottery in the United States was instituted in 1964 by the state of New Hampshire as a means of generating revenues for education. In 1967, New York started a lottery. Within the next decade, a dozen other states joined the list of those operating lotteries. Today, 30 states operate lotteries and in about 20 states, education is a beneficiary of part or all of the lottery proceeds.

---

the individual school level. These recommendations have been operationalized as school-site decision making. Complete decentralization in decision making is not possible because local schools, as part of a school district within a state educational agency, are subject to statutes, policies, and regulations from the school district and the state. However, there seems to be a consensus that schools are more successful when teachers have a voice in decisions about their working conditions and the operation of the local school.

Nontax Sources for School Revenues

An interesting effect of the recent court cases seeking greater equity in school funding has been the development of greater reliance on nontax sources of funding for schools. The pressures for greater equity have been countered by local citizens' creativity in finding other sources of funding for schools, including participation or user fees for school activities, formation of nonprofit educational foundations at the school or school district level, and local profit-making activities.

The school reform recommendations have called for teachers to have a greater role in making operational decisions at the school level.

Participation Fees

Increased reliance on fees as a condition for participation in school activities appears to conflict with the court cases that were seeking greater equity in funding and equality of access to educational programs and services. For example, athletes are being required to purchase their equipment, which can be expensive. In some instances, local school officials provide waivers for those students unable to pay the fees, but the effect is that poor children will have less opportunity to participate in many school activities. The basic question may be whether the activity is considered to be a necessary part of the school program or a truly extracurricular activity being provided under the sponsorship of the school. If the activity is a basic part of the school program, charging a participation fee might be considered to be discriminatory because a poor student is denied access to the program.

Educational Foundations

Some school districts have created nonprofit educational foundations to provide funds for programs and services that cannot be supported from tax funds. As a result of state restrictions on local school spending and court actions seeking greater equity in funding for public education, schools have been forced to curtail programs and services. In an effort to find alternative ways to fund and maintain programs, some local schools have formed educational foundations that can receive tax-deductible gifts from parents, interested citizens, and businesses.

For-Profit Enterprises

The concept of school districts initiating profit-making activities is somewhat different from the previous two examples of efforts to secure more funds for school operation. An enterprise activity refers to the involvement of the schools in some type of profit-making venture to enhance funding. Enterprise ventures might include development of a catering service that uses the school's bulk food preparation facilities, for example. Public resistance to such ventures might be minimal, but the involvement of the school in a profit-making activity in direct competition with local businesses might be challenged. Such activities would be subject to criticism because school districts are public agencies with limited powers, and the activity might be questioned if it were not related to the primary mission of the schools.

Federal Aid for Elementary and Secondary Schools

Should federal funds be targeted to programs to serve special populations or used as general aid to support the education of all youth?

Consistent with the concept that education is a state responsibility and a local function, the federal government has played a limited role in the financing of elementary and secondary education. As noted previously, somewhat less than 10% of the total expenditures for elementary and secondary education comes from federal revenue sources. Even though its role has been limited, the federal government's involvement in education has been a matter of recurring controversy.

Federal spending in education has generally been as a response to a perceived national problem. As the need for trained workers grew after World War I, for example, the government began funding vocational training. When the veterans of World War II needed job training, the G.I. Bill was passed. When the nation needed to compete with the Soviets in space in the late 1950s, the National Defense Education Act was enacted. Federal programs were devised to address the social problems of the nation in the 1960s. Rather than providing funds for the general support of education, the federal government has tended to respond to identified needs by providing funds for target populations of students or specific activities.

Since 1965, the federal role in education has expanded with the enactment of a variety of elementary and secondary education programs as well as higher education student assistance programs. Programs have included funds for instructional materials, locally oriented programs to encourage innovation, regional research and development centers, and improvement of state education agencies.

Education of Disadvantaged Youth

Of the continuing elementary and secondary education programs, the largest is Chapter 1 of the Education Consolidated and Improvement Act for the education of disadvantaged pupils. The funding level for this program was about $4 billion annually by 1990 for programs in local school districts (Irwin,

Improvement of educational opportunities for disadvantaged youth is a major federal program.

1989). As discussed in Chapter 9, the intent of the program is to improve educational programs for disadvantaged pupils from low-income homes. These programs are funded completely by the federal government and would not be continued if the federal funds were terminated.

Education of Students with Disabilities

Federal funds and regulations for education of the handicapped under Public Law 94–142 represent a different type of major federal initiative. Under the statute and resulting regulations, local school districts have to provide eligible handicapped pupils with a free and appropriate education irrespective of the level of federal funds. (See Chapter 9 for a more detailed discussion of P.L. 94–142.)

About 7% of the total school-age population has been classified as disabled and in need of special education programs and services. Funds for this federal program reached about $1.5 billion in 1990 (Irwin, 1989). While this seems to be a significant amount, this funding level as well as the $4 billion in federal funds for the education of disadvantaged pupils should be placed in the context of the more than $200 billion in annual funding from all revenue sources for public elementary and secondary education.

Education Block Grants

In addition to funding for these target populations, the federal government allocates about $500 million annually (Irwin, 1989) in *block grants* to states and local school districts. Rather than being limited to a narrow purpose, the funds may be used for one or more broad purposes including purchasing instructional materials, advancing staff development, or supporting special programs. The assumption is that educational needs differ among states and local school districts. However, support for this federal policy appears to have been reduced with the reauthorization of elementary and secondary education programs in 1988. At that time, funding for competitive and discretionary categorical programs for special populations such as at-risk and gifted pupils was increased.

Vocational Education

Federal funds have been provided for vocational education since the enactment of the Smith Hughes Act in 1917. This program was started in response to the need for trained workers following World War I. Since that time, the emphasis of vocational education has shifted as the nation's economy and job needs have changed. As noted in Chapter 9, in 1989 the federal government provided about $900 million to support vocational education, representing about 10% of the total spending for public school vocational education programs (Irwin, 1989).

Educational Research and Assessment

As the federal government has provided more funds for elementary and secondary education programs, interest in federal funds for a national research program has increased. The most visible major effort was the creation of the National Institute for Education under the former U.S. Office of Education. Typically, the actual research has not been conducted by these federal agencies but has been contracted to institutions of higher education and private research firms.

Currently, federal research funds for education are administered through the Office for Educational Research and Improvement in the Department of Education. In 1990, the Department of Education was projected to spend over $80 million dollars on research (Irwin, 1989). The actual level of federal funding for educational research efforts is difficult to determine because various programs are funded under the rubric of research in a variety of federal agencies including the National Science Foundation and the Department of Defense.

Research, Development, and Dissemination

In the Department of Education, research, development, and dissemination programs are conducted through regional research laboratories and centers, and funds are provided for the administration of the National Assessment of Educational Progress (NAEP). The laboratories and centers conduct educational research and seek to find ways to improve the nation's schools.

NAEP consists of a series of tests that are given to a sample of students throughout the nation. The purpose is to provide information about the general level of performance of elementary and secondary school students. State-by-state comparisons and comparisons by race, ethnicity, and gender are available. (See Chapter 8.) However, results of the testing administration are not designed to provide detailed information about the performance of students in a particular school. The intent is to provide national or state summary information rather than give direction to efforts to revise a school district's or a school's curriculum. This program was first administered on contract by the Education Commission of the States and later by the Educational Testing Service. State and national educational leaders have been concerned about NAEP because of the potential implications of developing a national curriculum solely to ensure that students performed well on the NAEP tests.

Data Gathering

Over the years, one aspect of the federal role in education has been relatively constant: data gathering. Under the National Center for Education Statistics, the Department of Education maintains an extensive data-reporting system. This emphasis has contributed to the development of compatible data reporting systems among the states.

Differences Among the States

The proportion of funds from local, state, and federal revenue sources varies greatly both among and within states. Differences in proportions among the states are the result of a combination of tradition, values, school district organizational patterns, concentrations of students from low-income families, federal ownership of land within the state, and differences in state economies. The exceptions to this principle are Hawaii and the District of Columbia which have no local school districts or local taxing units.

Expenditure and Enrollment Differences

In fiscal year 1987, among the 50 states and the District of Columbia, per pupil expenditures for current operation (excluding school construction and retirement of debt) ranged from $7,122 in Alaska to $2,242 in Utah. The 1987 national average was $3,680 per pupil (National Center for Education Statistics, 1988). Data for each state are presented in Table 14.1.

Among the 50 states, the estimated number of pupils in 1987 ranged from 4,377,989 in California and 3,207,515 in Texas to 94,410 in Delaware and 92,112 in Vermont. The 10 states with more than 1,000,000 pupils accounted for over 55% of the total of slightly less than 40 million pupils (National Center for Education Statistics, 1988).

Table 14.1: Current Expenditures per Pupil in Membership, Fiscal Year 1987

	Membership	Current Expenditures
50 states and D.C.	39,837,450	$3,680
Alabama	733,735	2,420
Alaska	107,973	7,122
Arizona	534,538	3,436
Arkansas	437,438	2,558
California	4,377,989	3,772
Colorado	558,415	3,814
Connecticut	468,847	5,150
Delaware	94,410	4,429
District of Columbia	85,612	5,153
Florida	1,607,320	3,515
Georgia	1,096,425	3,148
Hawaii	164,640	3,503
Idaho	208,391	2,462
Illinois	1,825,185	3,541
Indiana	966,780	3,213
Iowa	481,286	3,585
Kansas	416,091	3,573
Kentucky	642,778	2,483
Louisiana	795,188	2,843
Maine	211,752	3,591
Maryland	675,747	4,211
Massachusetts	833,918	4,490
Michigan	1,681,880	3,822
Minnesota	711,134	3,963
Mississippi	498,639	2,231

Differences in Sources of Revenue

In fiscal year 1987, excluding Hawaii and the District of Columbia, the percentage of the total revenues for schools that came from local tax sources ranged from 90.7% in New Hampshire to 12.7% in New Mexico. The percentage from state tax sources ranged from 72.4% in Washington to 5.9% in New Hampshire. The percentage from the federal government ranged from 12.2% in New Mexico to 3.4% in New Hampshire. The national average was 43.4% from local sources, 0.4% from intermediate levels of government, 49.8% from state sources, and 6.4% from federal sources. Data for each state are presented in Table 14.2.

School Finance Issues of the 1990s

Concerns about the role of education in the development of youth and the importance of an educated populace in a democracy may not be sufficient to

Table 14.1: *continued*

	Membership	Current Expenditures
Missouri	800,606	$3,142
Montana	153,327	3,808
Nebraska	267,139	3,549
Nevada	161,239	3,182
New Hampshire	163,717	3,603
New Jersey	1,107,487	5,508
New Mexico	281,943	3,071
New York	2,607,719	5,647
North Carolina	1,085,248	2,942
North Dakota	118,703	3,159
Ohio	1,793,508	3,408
Oklahoma	593,183	2,878
Oregon	449,307	3,888
Pennsylvania	1,674,161	4,287
Rhode Island	134,126	4,535
South Carolina	611,629	2,988
South Dakota	125,458	2,935
Tennessee	818,073	2,649
Texas	3,209,515	3,163
Utah	415,994	2,242
Vermont	92,112	4,107
Virginia	975,135	3,533
Washington	761,428	3,689
West Virginia	351,837	3,493
Wisconsin	787,819	4,020
Wyoming	100,955	4,852

Source: National Center for Education Statistics, U.S. Department of Education (1988). *E.D. TABS* (November, CS 89–043, table 6, p. 12). Washington, DC: U.S. Government Printing Office.

generate public support for the funds required to provide quality education in the 1990s. Providing adequate financing for public elementary and secondary schools is becoming more difficult because of a series of interactive social and economic developments.

Changes in the Population

The American population is becoming younger and older at the same time; that is, both the proportion of the population that is of school age and the proportion that is elderly or retired are increasing. Further, youth who comprise the increases in the school-age population tend to be educationally disadvantaged because they often live in urban areas, are poor, and come to school with limited English-speaking ability. Consequently, providing these youth with an adequate education requires more funds.

Table 14.2: Percentage Distribution of Revenues by Source, Fiscal Year 1987				
	Local	Intermediate	State	Federal
50 states and D.C.	43.4	0.4	49.8	6.4
Alabama	21.4	0.6	66.3	11.7
Alaska	24.7	0.0	63.7	11.7
Arizona	38.0	4.7	48.3	9.0
Arkansas	33.5	0.2	54.8	11.5
California	23.4	0.1	69.5	7.1
Colorado	56.0	0.1	39.0	4.9
Connecticut	55.6	0.0	40.0	4.4
Delaware	23.1	0.0	69.2	7.7
District of Columbia	88.4	0.7	0.6	10.3
Florida	38.6	0.0	54.2	7.2
Georgia	33.2	0.0	59.7	7.1
Hawaii	0.1	0.0	88.1	11.8
Idaho	28.3	0.0	62.9	8.9
Illinois	56.5	0.0	39.1	4.3
Indiana	36.8	0.2	58.1	4.9
Iowa	50.4	0.0	44.5	5.1
Kansas	48.4	6.4	42.4	4.8
Kentucky	23.8	0.0	64.5	11.6
Louisiana	33.4	0.0	55.1	11.5
Maine	43.4	0.0	50.2	6.4
Maryland	56.4	0.0	38.5	5.1
Massachusetts	50.0	0.0	45.1	4.9
Michigan	59.2	0.1	34.9	5.9
Minnesota	38.4	0.4	56.9	4.2
Mississippi	24.3	0.0	65.2	10.5

Special Needs Students

The great debate of the 1990s may be over the proportion of funds that should be spent for special needs students as contrasted to funds for the education of regular students or for social services. In addition to the need for more funds to support education, competition for scarce public funds will come from the elderly population that is in need of a variety of services including better health care. Many of the elderly are on fixed incomes and must have some type of public assistance for medical and other essential social services. Reconciling these two social pressures will be a formidable challenge to public policy makers.

State Funding Systems

A continuing issue is the extent to which a state's school funding system should reduce the disparities in educational opportunity for pupils among districts and move the state toward providing an adequate program for all

Table 14.2: *continued*

	Local	Intermediate	State	Federal
Missouri	49.4	3.1	41.2	6.3
Montana	34.0	9.6	47.8	8.5
Nebraska	70.2	1.1	22.5	6.1
Nevada	56.0	0.0	39.5	4.4
New Hampshire	90.7	0.0	5.9	3.4
New Jersey	52.5	0.0	43.0	4.4
New Mexico	12.7	0.0	75.1	12.2
New York	52.7	0.0	42.4	4.8
North Carolina	26.0	0.0	66.0	7.9
North Dakota	37.8	2.0	50.8	9.4
Ohio	44.8	0.0	49.6	5.5
Oklahoma	28.1	2.8	63.5	5.6
Oregon	63.4	2.0	28.0	6.6
Pennsylvania	48.3	0.3	46.3	5.1
Rhode Island	52.9	0.0	42.6	4.5
South Carolina	34.0	1.2	56.0	8.9
South Dakota	59.5	1.6	27.2	11.8
Tennessee	44.4	0.0	44.5	11.1
Texas	45.5	0.3	47.1	7.1
Utah	39.6	0.0	54.4	6.1
Vermont	60.6	0.0	34.4	5.1
Virginia	n/r	n/r	n/r	n/r
Washington	21.2	0.1	72.4	6.3
West Virginia	22.6	0.0	69.8	7.5
Wisconsin	60.7	0.0	34.5	4.7
Wyoming	44.6	8.7	43.0	3.7

Source: National Center for Education Statistics, U.S. Department of Education (1988). *E.D. TABS* (November, CS 89–043, table 2, p. 8). Washington, DC: U.S. Government Printing Office.

pupils. Local school officials seek predictable and relatively stable levels of funding for schools to facilitate orderly budgetary and educational planning. Taxpayers seek stability in their tax rates so that they can plan their businesses.

From a different perspective, local school officials seek a state system for financing schools that will respond to changing economic and demographic conditions. As the number of pupils increases and as costs for services and materials increase, the state school finance system should provide additional funds for school operations.

Accountability

Concerns also are being expressed about accountability in terms of the performance and responsiveness of schools. Some have advocated that funding for schools be based on pupil performance. However, local school officials seek a level of stability in funding that might be threatened if performance

If funding for schools is based on student performance, how might this affect your job as a teacher?

fluctuates. Caution has been advocated because reducing state aid to an underachieving school district would mean that the district would have less to spend on programs even though its need would be greater.

Urban/Suburban/Rural Tensions

Given the concentration of the potential school enrollment growth in the urban areas, adequate funding for education becomes more complex. Many of the nation's large cities are confronted with a declining tax base, an aging infrastructure, and expanding social needs. Even though the social needs are great, relief from state legislatures may not be forthcoming because frequently the majority coalition in state legislatures has been developed from suburban and rural interests. The possibility of meaningful responses from either state or local governments has been reduced further because of citizen support for revenue or expenditure limitations such as Proposition 13 in California and Proposition 2½ in Massachusetts.

Education Reform

The 1980s were characterized by broad-based calls for reform of public elementary and secondary education. Many reform recommendations are additive, i.e., they call for increased requirements for graduation, longer school days and years, and higher teacher salaries (Stedman & Jordan, 1986), and they will require additional funds. Justification for school reforms has been based on the need to improve America's competitive position in the world economy. However, state legislatures have not provided significant funding to implement the reforms (Jordan & McKeown, 1989).

Competition for Funds

During a period of reduced economic growth at the national and state levels, demands are being made for increased social services in areas other than education. The unanswered question is whether policy makers will view funds for education as an expenditure to be curtailed as the economy slows or as a necessary investment to improve the nation's economic position.

Summary

The cost of education, the largest item in many state and local budgets, will exceed $200 billion in the early 1990s. This outlay is viewed as an investment because education contributes trained workers who support the economy through the purchase of consumer goods. The challenge is to find the funds needed and to distribute them in an equitable manner.

In terms of state provision for education, one challenge will be to develop school finance programs that provide for an acceptable balance between the conflicting goals of equity, choice, adequacy, accountability, and efficiency. A second challenge will be to raise the revenues for the programs in a fair and equitable manner.

Providing adequate funds for education will become more difficult. More older citizens and an increased number of educationally disadvantaged students will be competing for scarce public funds. While state programs look for stability in funding, local school officials seek a system that will respond to changes. The responses will depend on whether policy makers view funds for education as an expenditure or an investment.

With this background on school finance and the previous chapter on school organization and administration, you have a context in which to place the discussion of school curriculum in the following chapter.

Key Terms

Accountability

Adequacy

Block grants

Categorical funding

Choice

Competitive grants

Economic distortions

Educational overburden

Efficiency

Equity

Flat grants

Foundation plan

Full state funding

Horizontal equity

Municipal overburden

Power equalization

Revenue elasticity

Strategic planning

Vertical equity

Discussion Questions

1. How does the per pupil funding level for schools in your state compare with the level in other states?

2. In what ways does education represent an investment in the future of the nation rather than an expenditure?

3. In comparing school finance policy goals, which ones likely would be supported by which types of school districts?

4. What types of school districts are most likely to initiate legal action challenging the system for financing schools in a state?

5. As a teacher, what features would you like to have included in the state school finance program?

6. What are the implications of relying on various types of taxes for the support of schools?

7. What programs should the federal government finance?

8. Given the shortage of funds for public services, what should be the priority, funding for education or health care for the elderly? Funding for children with special needs or for regular children?

9. What actions should advocates for the public schools take to secure additional funding for schools?

References

Committee for Economic Development. (1987). *Children in need: Investment strategies for the educationally disadvantaged.* New York: Committee for Economic Development.

Coons, J. E., Clune, W. H., III, & Sugarman, S. D. (1970). *Private wealth and public education.* Cambridge, MA: Belknap Press.

Cubberley, E. P. (1905). *School funds and their apportionment.* New York: Teachers College, Columbia University.

Due, J. F. (1970). Alternative tax sources for education. In R. L. Johns, I. J. Goffman, K. Alexander, & D. H. Strollar (Eds.), *Economic factors affecting the financing of education* (pp. 291–328). Gainesville, FL: National Educational Finance Project.

Ezell, J. S. (1960). *Fortune's merry wheel, the lottery in America.* Cambridge, MA: Harvard University Press.

Friedman, M. (1955). The role of government in education. In R. A. Solo (Ed.), *Economics and the public interest* (pp. 123–144). New Brunswick, NJ: Rutgers University Press.

Irwin, P. M. (1989). *U.S. Department of Education: Major program trends, fiscal years 1980–1990* (89–144 EPW). Washington, DC: Congressional Research Service, Library of Congress.

Jordan, K. F., & Cambron-McCabe, N. H. (Eds.). (1981). *Perspectives in state school support programs.* Cambridge, MA: Ballinger.

Jordan, K. F., & McKeown, M. P. (1980). Equity in financing public elementary and secondary schools. In J. W. Guthrie (Ed.), *School finance policies and practices* (pp. 79–129). Cambridge, MA: Ballinger.

Jordan, K. F., & McKeown, M. P. (1989). State fiscal policy and education reform. In J. Murphy (Ed.), *The educational reform movement of the 1980s: Perspectives and cases* (pp. 97–120). Berkeley: McCutchan.

LaMorte, M. W. (1989). Courts continue to address the wealth disparity issue. *Educational Evaluation and Policy Analysis, 11*(1):3–16.

Morrison, H. C. (1930). *School revenue.* Chicago: University of Chicago Press.

Mort, P. R. (1933). *State support for public education.* Washington, DC: American Council on Education.

National Center for Education Statistics, U.S. Department of Education. (1988). *E.D. TABS* (November, CS 89–043). Washington, DC: U.S. Government Printing Office.

Robinson, G. E., & Protheroe N. (1990). Local school budget profiles study. *School Business Affairs, 56*(9):8–17.

Salmon, R., Dawson, C., Lawton, S., & Johns, T. (1988). *State school finance programs 1986–87.* Blacksburg, VA: American Education Finance Association, Virginia Polytechnic Institute and State University.

San Antonio Independent School District v. Rodriguez (1973). 411 U.S. 1.

Snider, W. (1989). Iowa, Arkansas enact "choice"; Proposals gain in other states. *Education Week, 8*(25)1, 19.

Stedman, J. B., & Jordan, K. F. (1986). *Education reform reports: Content and impact* (86–56 EPW). Washington, DC: Congressional Research Service, Library of Congress.

Strayer, G. D., & Haig, R. M. (1923). *The financing of education in the state of New York.* Report of the Educational Finance Commission 1. New York: Macmillan.

Updegraff, H. (1922). *Rural school survey in New York state: Financial support.* Ithaca, NY: author.

U.S. Department of Commerce, Bureau of the Census. (1988). *Government finances in 1986–87* (GF–87–5). Washington, DC: U.S. Government Printing Office.

Walker, R. (1989). Lawmakers floating "radical" ideas to shift control of Kentucky schools. *Education Week, 9*(1):1–20.

Part Six

Curriculum and Instruction

The School Curriculum: Development and Design **Chapter 15**
Instructional Practices in Today's Schools **Chapter 16**
Effective Schools and Teachers **Chapter 17**

Chapter 15
The School Curriculum: Development and Design

The young man taught all he knew and more;
The middle-aged man taught all he knew;
The old man taught all that his students could understand.

Arnold Ross

Lauren Cook, newly elected president of the United States, had just left the platform at the National Education Association Annual Convention after delivering an address, "Policy, Politics, and the U.S. Educational System." She was quickly escorted to a nearby room for a meeting with the press. The first question came from Tom White, who represented Cable News Network. "Madam President, what did you mean when you said that the curriculum of the schools has become the major political issue of the 1990s?" The sec-

ond question came from Sarah Mullins of the Denver Register. "Madam President, what role should the federal government play in setting a curriculum agenda?" A third question was shouted out by Eric Greely of CBS News. "Do you support the establishment of national standards?"

If you were President Cook, how would you respond to Tom White's question? To Sarah Mullins's? To Eric Greely's?

As was forecast by "President Cook," we have entered a period of widespread public debate over what should be taught in the schools and who should control the curriculum. Curriculum issues have increasingly become issues of class, race, ethnicity, gender, and religion. In this chapter the concept of curriculum is explored from its many perspectives, ranging from curriculum as content to curriculum as experiences. This chapter provides information to help you to:

● Review the sociopolitical forces that influence curriculum policy making and design.

● Contrast the technical production process of curriculum development with the critical theorist process of curriculum development.

● Compare the subject-centered and student-centered patterns of curriculum organization.

● Describe the hidden curriculum and its effects on schooling.

The term *curriculum* is a complex and evasive notion. Curriculum theorists do not agree on any one definition. Broadly defined, curriculum is said to be all the educational experiences of students that take place in the school. A 1973 study identified 119 different definitions of curriculum (Rule, cited in Portelli, 1987). Another two or three dozen could probably be added today. Yet how we conceive of curriculum is important because our conception of curriculum reflects and shapes how we think about, study, and act on the education provided to students (Cornbleth, 1988).

In this chapter, various concepts of the curriculum will be examined. First, the influence of a number of sociopolitical forces on curriculum policy making and design will be reviewed. Next, the curriculum development process will be summarized. Last, the major patterns of intended curricular organization or design will be described, followed by a discussion of the unintended or hidden curriculum.

Forces Influencing the Curriculum

Decisions about the curriculum are not made in a vacuum by teachers, administrators, and curriculum specialists. They take place in the context of a particular community, state, and nation at a particular point in time. At different times various professional, political, social, economic, and religious forces have attempted to influence the curriculum. Their motives, methods, strengths, and successes have varied. In this section, the influence of the following forces on curriculum are briefly reviewed: parent and community groups, the federal government, state governments, local school boards, professional organizations, national committees and reports, national testing, and textbooks.

Parent and Community Groups

Should parents be the ultimate deciders of what their children are taught? Why or why not?

Because of their vested interest in the local school and their proximity to local decision makers, parents and community groups have the potential for exercising tremendous influence on the curriculum. For example, in recent years parent groups active in the areas of special education and gifted education have had great success in encouraging educational programs for these groups. Parents often serve on textbook adoption committees or education committees at the local, state, or national level. Parent Teacher Associations, band boosters, and other special interest groups are often active in supporting special programs or influencing legislation and the outcome of tax or spending referenda. Still other groups have brought pressure on school boards and school officials to include or not include curriculum material on sex education, substance abuse, suicide, ethnic or women's studies, and religion. Currently, fundamentalist groups of the New Right are bringing unrelenting pressure on local school boards, state boards of education, political decision makers, and the textbook industry to rid our schools of all material and teaching that promotes secular humanism and ignores religion (see Chapter 11).

The Federal Government

The federal government's influence over the curriculum does not come from mandating that certain courses or programs of study be taught, but from providing support for specific initiatives. For example, as noted in previous chapters, when the launching of the Sputnik spacecraft by the Soviet Union in 1957 caused fear that we were falling behind in the space race, the federal government did not respond by mandating more mathematics or science offerings, or higher graduation requirements, but by passing the National Defense Education Act. This act provided financial encouragement to schools to upgrade their mathematics, science, and foreign language offerings. In later years, the National Science Foundation became instrumental in curricular revision in mathematics.

Vocational education is an area that has been heavily influenced by federal legislation. In fact, it was federal legislation that often set the course for or at least stimulated state action, and state programs often paralleled federal programs in vocational education. Federal legislation in other areas, including compensatory education, bilingual education, sex equity, career education, and adult education has also tended to direct attention in the curriculum to areas deemed necessary at the federal level. The federal government also influences curriculum development by virtue of the support given to research in certain areas, which has the effect of promoting curriculum reform in these areas.

Parent and community groups have increasingly contested curriculum and textbook content.

State Governments

Has the state in which you plan to teach changed the subject area requirements since 1984? What changes have been made?

The growing involvement of the state in the financing of education has led to increased involvement in curricular matters. The state's influence over the curriculum is exercised in several ways. First, state statutes often mandate that certain subjects be included in the curriculum. Some states also specify what cannot be taught (e.g., communism). The state's impact on the curriculum has been particularly evident in the aftermath of the reform reports of the 1980s. A major recommendation of many of the reform reports was that students be required to take an increased number of basic courses in English, social studies, mathematics, and science (see Table 15.1, pp. 482–483). In response, virtually every state increased minimum high school graduation requirements. In the period 1980 to 1987, mathematics requirements were increased in 42 states, science requirements in 36 states, English/language arts in 18 states, and social studies in 29 states (Common Measures, 1989). Figure 15.1

Figure 15.1: Minimum High School Graduation Requirements, 1980 and 1987

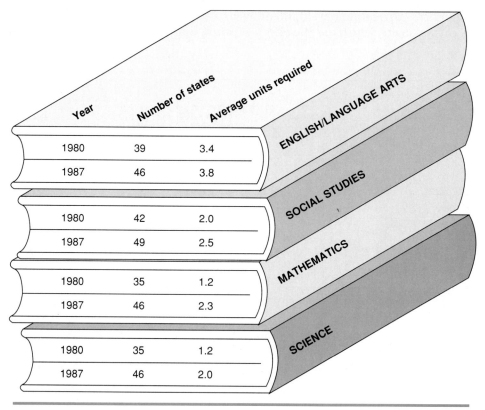

Year	Number of states	Average units required
ENGLISH/LANGUAGE ARTS		
1980	39	3.4
1987	46	3.8
SOCIAL STUDIES		
1980	42	2.0
1987	49	2.5
MATHEMATICS		
1980	35	1.2
1987	46	2.3
SCIENCE		
1980	35	1.2
1987	46	2.0

provides a comparison of the number of states with specific subject area requirements for graduation and the average number of units required in 1980 and 1987. Despite the increase in graduation requirements, the majority of the states still do not require as many credits as recommended by the first, and perhaps the foremost reform report, *A Nation at Risk*, which recommended a minimum of four credits of English and three credits each of social studies, mathematics, and science.

Accompanying the movement to increase graduation requirements, a number of states have imposed a minimum competency test that must be passed before a diploma will be awarded. In 1988, 19 states had such a requirement.

In addition to statutory requirements, the state influences the curriculum through the state board of education which, in many states, is authorized to decide upon curriculum requirements, review curriculum proposals, promulgate curricular guidelines, and establish teacher certification requirements. Yet another state entity, the state department of education, also influences the curriculum through leadership, instructional resources and support, and curriculum guides provided to local school districts. State curriculum guides often detail the goals and objectives, competencies, and instructional activities for every subject at every grade level. (See Chapter 13 for a discussion of the roles and responsibilities of state boards and departments of education.)

Another important way in which the state influences the curriculum is through the textbook adoption and selection process. In many states, local school districts cannot purchase textbooks unless they are on a state adoption list. Books are adopted on the basis of state-mandated criteria. In some states, such as California, the state adoption committee determines the approach and perspective a text must have in order to be approved.

Local School Boards

Local school boards make a host of curriculum decisions. Within the limits of state authority local boards decide what electives will be offered, which textbooks and other instructional material will be purchased, which curriculum guides are to be followed, what teachers will be hired, how the budget will be spent, and innumerable other issues that directly or indirectly influence the curriculum. It is the local school board that most often feels the pressure of parents and special interest groups, for it is the local school board that decides such matters as whether a new program will be piloted, whether such courses as sex education will be offered, or whether a program for the hearing-impaired will be offered by the district.

In recent years, increasing concern has been expressed regarding the extent to which the local school board represents all constituencies in the community. One concern is that local boards are too much influenced by small but vocal groups of parents or concerned citizens. Another concern is the elitist composition of boards of education. Except for rural school boards, most school boards tend to be composed of a disproportionate number of upper income males who are college educated and have high-status occupations

What is the composition of the school board in the district in which you live? How representative are the board members of the local community?

Table 15.1: Curriculum Recommendations from Selected Education Reform Reports

Reform Report	Recommendations
A Nation at Risk (The National Commission on Excellence in Education)	• Significantly more time should be devoted to learning the "new basics"—English, mathematics, science, social studies, computer science, and, for the college-bound, a foreign language. • Elementary schools should provide a sound base in English language development and writing, computational and problem-solving skills, science, social studies, foreign language, and the arts. • Foreign languages should be started in the elementary grades. • All students seeking a diploma should be required to complete four years of English; three years each of mathematics, science, and social studies; and one-half year of computer science.
Making the Grade (Twentieth Century Fund Task Force)	• The federal government should clearly state that the most important objective of elementary and secondary education in the United States is the development of literacy in the English language. • A common core should include the basic skills of reading, writing, and calculating; technical capability in computers; training in science and foreign languages; and knowledge of civics.
Action for Excellence (Education Commission of the States Task Force on Education for Economic Growth)	• The academic experience should be more intense and more productive. Courses in all disciplines must be enlivened and improved. The goal should be both richer substance and greater motivational power—elimination of "soft," nonessential courses, more enthusiastic involvement of students in learning, encouragement of mastery of skills beyond the basics, e.g., problem-solving, analysis, interpretation, and persuasive writing. • Educators, business and labor leaders, and other interested parties should clearly identify the skills that the schools are expected to impart to students for effective employment and citizenship.

(Spring, 1989). It is also not uncommon to find board members sending their own children to private schools, rather than the schools of the district they govern.

National Committees and Reports

As was discussed in several other sections of this text, it has been a practice in this country throughout this century for select national committees to be formed to study and make recommendations regarding some aspect of education. The curriculum impact of some of these committees has been profound. For example, the *Cardinal Principles of Secondary Education*, issued by the NEA Commission on the Reorganization of Secondary Education in 1918, played a major role in the establishment of the comprehensive high school.

Table 15.1: *continued*

Reform Report	Recommendations
American High School Study (Ernest L. Boyer, Carnegie Foundation)	• In elementary schools, the focus should be on communication skills. All high school students should complete a basic English course with an emphasis on writing. The high school core should stress the spoken word. • Required courses in the student's core should be increased from one-half to two-thirds of the total required for graduation. The core would include three units of English; two and a half units of history; two units each of science, mathematics, and foreign language; one unit of civics; one-half unit each of technology and health; a seminar on work; and a senior independent social issues project. • In the last two years of high school, students should enroll in a cluster of electives and explore career options. • A service requirement involving school or community volunteer work should be added.
A Place Called School (John Goodlad)	• There should be a better balance in the curriculum of the school and the student. The individual curriculum should be devoted to up to 18% language and literature, up to 18% mathematics and science, up to 15% each to society and social studies, the arts, and the vocations, and the remaining 10% to guided individual choice.
The Paideia Proposal (Mortimer Adler)	• There should be a common curriculum for all students involving: (a) acquisition of knowledge through didactic instruction in three subject areas: language, literature, and fine arts; mathematics and natural sciences; history, geography, and social sciences; (b) the development of intellectual skills in linguistics, mathematics, and science through coaching, exercise, and practice; and (c) the enlargement of understanding, insight, and aesthetic appreciation through the Socratic discussion of books and other works of art and participation in artistic activities such as music, drama, and the visual arts. • The only elective in the 12 years of school should be for a second language.

The most recent series of national committees and reports contain a number of observations and recommendations directed at the curriculum. The first wave of these reports tended to look at a number of things that were alleged to be "wrong" with the nation's schools, the curriculum being one of them. Required courses, their number and content, and minimum skills and competencies are all addressed by the reports. A second wave of reports, appearing at the end of the 1980s, focused more directly on specific academic components of the curriculum and are noted in the next section. The curriculum recommendations of the major reports in the first wave are summarized in Table 15.1.

Although it is still too early to measure the total impact of these reports, in some areas, such as the increased emphasis on the "new basics," their effect

North Kansas City, Missouri has followed Boyer's suggestion and has piloted a program requiring 36 hours of community service for graduation. What are the advantages and disadvantages of such a requirement?

can already be seen. They can also be credited with the increased attention given to homework, mastery learning, and competency testing. Some of the recommendations, such as merit pay, the extended day, and the extended year have not seen widespread adoption. It is safe to say, however, that these reports have received more publicity and have been the subject of more discussion by professional educators, educational decision makers, and lay citizens than any educational event in the past quarter century.

Professional Organizations

In addition to their individual influence, educators have influence over the curriculum through their collective association in professional organizations. Both the National Education Association and the American Federation of Teachers, the two largest organizations, attempt to influence the curriculum through full-time lobbying efforts directed at the state and national legislatures. These and other influential professional organizations, such as the National Council of Social Studies, the International Reading Association, the Association for Supervision and Curriculum Development, and the American Association of School Administrators influence the profile and direction of the school curriculum as they set national agenda and goals and raise their collective voices.

The second wave of school reform reports, concerned with curriculum and emanating primarily from these professional organizations, is the most recent example of their involvement and attempt to provide direction for the school curriculum. Directed at the core subjects of mathematics, science, language arts and social studies, these reports have focused on essential knowledge and skills, called for more rigorous content, and encouraged the development of critical thinking skills (Lewis, 1990). Among the more widely publicized of these curriculum reports are:

- National Council of Teachers of Mathematics—*Curriculum and Evaluation Standards for School Mathematics* (1989)

- National Science Teachers Association—*Essential Changes in Secondary Science: Scope, Sequence, and Coordination* (1989)

- American Association for the Advancement of Science—*Science for All Americans* (1989)

- National Research Council—*Everybody Counts: A Report to the Nation on the Future of Mathematics Education* (1989)

- National Council of Teachers of English—*The English Coalition Conference: Democracy Through Language* (1989)

- National Commission on Social Studies in the Schools—*Charting a Course: Social Studies for the 21st Century* (1989)

National Testing

The impact of national standardized tests on the entire educational enterprise in the last two decades has been nothing short of overwhelming.

Many educators are concerned that a national standardized test will result in a national curriculum.

Students, schools, and school districts are praised or prodded based on test results. Students are admitted to postsecondary institutions, private elementary and secondary schools, and specialized programs in the public schools based on their test results. Many scholarships are based all or in part on test results. Teachers, programs, and schools are considered more or less effective based on test results. The admission of prospective teachers and administrators into degree or certification programs, or their later certification, is determined by test results. Practicing teachers and administrators are tested in some states. Many accountability or merit pay plans include test results as output indicators.

To a large extent, these tests function as "gatekeepers of knowledge" (Spring, 1989). The knowledge tested is that which is considered the most worthy by test developers. Although within any discipline there is usually considerable debate as to what knowledge is of most worth, in the end it is often the viewpoint of the test makers that gives direction to the curriculum. While not necessarily advocating "teaching to the test," school boards, administrators, and teachers themselves seek to ensure that the schools' curriculum "prepare[s] students to do well on the test." If test scores are down in a certain curriculum area, district resources and instruction may be redirected to that area. Increasingly, individual students and their families invest in tutorial books, computer software, and seminars in an attempt to raise test scores.

Standardized tests can play an important role in providing standards and data needed for curriculum assessment, but their limits must be recognized.

What desired outputs of the learning experience cannot be measured with a test?

Educators, policy makers, and parents should keep in mind that the only thing that most of the tests measure is *achievement;* they do not measure other desired outputs of the learning experience. Nor do they measure whether individual teachers or schools are achieving their own instructional goals. Thus, to allow the concern about national standardized tests to dictate the curriculum would be a serious error.

This is particularly true in light of the concerns expressed by many educators and psychologists that some tests are biased against females, minorities, and those from lower socioeconomic strata. Although the testing industry has taken steps to rid tests of their blatant white, male, middle-class bias, test analyses continue to reveal content that discriminates against certain populations. An overreliance on items involving sports contexts and items that assume experiences or knowledge not common to certain racial and ethnic groups are examples of the type of content that causes test bias. Although the decision to administer most tests is not within the authority of teachers, they can play a role in examining tests for bias and in ensuring that results are properly interpreted, communicated, and utilized.

Textbooks

In the course of his or her educational career a student may be exposed to hundreds of textbooks. In the classroom, students spend at least two-thirds of their time using textbooks. Teachers rely heavily on textbooks for instructional content, organization, and evaluation. Without question, textbooks and other instructional material influence what is learned in the classroom. By virtue of what material is included and how it is portrayed, textbooks have an impact on not only the knowledge base of students, but their attitudes and beliefs. It is because they recognize the powerful influence of textbooks that religious and other special interest groups have been so vocal and persistent in their attempts to influence not only textbook adoption decisions but the textbook industry itself.

In addition to the previously discussed concerns about context expressed by some religious groups, textbooks have also been criticized for being too "soft" on communism, too "hard" on American institutions and activities, and for their portrayal of women, minorities, and other groups. That is, women and minorities are often portrayed in traditional and lower status roles or are given limited coverage. The elderly and handicapped often are excluded from narrative discussion or pictures and illustrations.

Does your state have a textbook adoption process? What prohibitions are placed on textbook selection (e.g., most states have a prohibition against subversive books)?

Given the potential influence of textbooks and the unresolved concerns about their content, it is important that teachers be sensitive to cultural diversity, gender differences, and special populations. Teachers should actively participate in the textbook selection process. Unfortunately, far too often teachers have not received training in the evaluation of instructional material or are not given sufficient time to thoroughly review the textbooks under consideration. Ultimately, the influence that textbooks have on the curriculum is determined by the care taken in their selection and how they are used in the classroom.

Curriculum Development

The curriculum development and planning literature is replete with models, paradigms, and "steps," which all can be categorized according to two perspectives: the technical production perspective and the critical perspective. The technical production perspective has dominated thought on curriculum planning for 40 years. The newer critical perspective takes issue with the very assumptions underlying the technical production perspective and advocates critical reflection on all assumptions in discussions about the curriculum (Posner, 1988).

Technical Production Prospective

The technical production perspective views curriculum planning as a rational and technical process that can be accomplished by objective decision making. Further, curriculum planning is presumed to be a production-oriented enterprise in which the planner objectively and, if possible, scientifically establishes the means to obtain the desired educational outcomes. The technical production model has been popular for so long because it is congruent with the prevailing assumption that education is a production process in which individual learning is the primary product (Posner, 1988).

The technical production perspective is best represented by the work of Ralph Tyler (1949). Tyler's rationale for curriculum planning is organized around four steps. First, the planners must determine what educational purposes (aims and objectives) the school(s) should pursue. As discussed in Chapters 6 and 7, there are widely varying schools of thought about the purpose of education, and these are translated into curriculum and instructional practice.

After deciding on the educational objectives, planners must decide what learning experiences can be provided that are likely to attain these purposes. (Some practical hints for preparing and stating appropriate learning experiences, which you as a teacher might find helpful, are given on page 490.) Once developed, possible experiences must be checked to see if they give students the opportunity to acquire the behavior stated in the objectives and if they lead to the effect intended (Walker & Soltis, 1986).

In the next step, planners must decide how the learning experiences can be organized effectively. Here attention must be given to the *continuity* and *sequence* of experiences. Consistent with Piaget's theory that cognitive development is gradual (progressing through four levels) and that any subject can be taught in some form to any child at any stage of development, continuity is concerned with the reiteration of major curriculum elements so that skills can be practiced and developed. Sequencing aims at ensuring that successive experiences build on preceding ones. The concepts of continuity and sequence, which Tyler refers to as vertical organizational dimensions, also correspond to Bruner's concept of the spiral curriculum, which, as explained in Chapter 5, proposes that concepts and topics be treated at progressive grade levels in increasing complexity and detail.

The effective organization of experiences also involves the *integration* of skills and knowledge across disciplines. Tyler refers to integration as the horizontal dimension of curriculum organization. As the last step in the Tyler model, the planner must develop a means of evaluating whether the stated purposes are being attained by the selected learning experiences.

Tyler (1949) viewed curriculum planning as a continuous process whereby:

> as materials and procedures are developed, they are tried out, their results appraised, their inadequacies identified, suggested improvements indicated; there is replanning, redevelopment and then reappraisal; and in this kind of continuing cycle, it is possible for the curriculum and instructional program to be continuously improved over the years. (p. 123)

Figure 15.2 provides a graphic depiction of Tyler's curriculum planning cycle.

Critical Perspective

In sharp contrast to the technical production perspective is the critical perspective, which rejects the notion that curriculum planning can be an objective, value-free process. Rather, this perspective argues that curriculum decisions are essentially ideological and sociopolitical. As some critical theorists point out, the very decisions about what the objectives should be, what knowledge is of most value, how the curriculum will be organized and delivered, to whom it will be delivered, and how it will be evaluated involve assumptions and values that reinforce the existing power and social structure. For example, because of the relationship between evaluators and employers, if it were known to an evaluator that the administration of a district had been active in initiating a particular curriculum and had fought hard to secure financial support for the program, the evaluator would probably feel great pressure to discover results not unfavorable to the program.

Which do you have most developed, technique or curriculum conscience? How can each be improved?

Each of these perspectives is important in curriculum development. Knowing how to develop a curriculum involves technique. Being able to identify the assumptions underlying curriculum discussions requires a curriculum conscience. Curriculum planning without technique is incompetent and without curriculum conscience is ungrounded (Posner, 1988).

Patterns of Curriculum Organization

Decisions about how the curriculum should be organized involve choices about what subjects to study and how these subjects will be presented to the students. Although there are many different structures that reflect alternative perspectives about the nature of the curriculum, these alternatives can be classified as being either subject-centered or student-centered. The subject-centered perspective is the oldest, more traditional, and most common. It views the curriculum as a program of studies or collection of courses that

Figure 15.2: The Tyler Planning Cycle

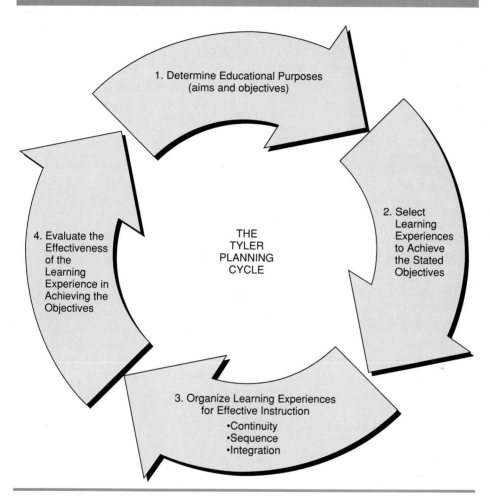

1. Determine Educational Purposes (aims and objectives)

2. Select Learning Experiences to Achieve the Stated Objectives

3. Organize Learning Experiences for Effective Instruction
   •Continuity
   •Sequence
   •Integration

4. Evaluate the Effectiveness of the Learning Experience in Achieving the Objectives

THE TYLER PLANNING CYCLE

represent what students should know. The second perspective focuses on the needs and interests of the child and the process by which learning takes place.

The subject-centered and student-centered perspectives are the two ends of a continuum of curricular design. In this section six alternative curriculum designs along this continuum are examined: subject-area design, integrated design, core curriculum design, child-centered design, social reconstruction design, and deschooling design.

The Subject-Area Design

The *subject-area curriculum* design is the oldest and most common organization plan for the curriculum. This design views the curriculum as a group of

For Future Reference:
Practical Hints for Preparing and Stating Learning Objectives

1. If you are going to describe learning experiences at all, spell them out in sufficient detail to make them understandable.

2. Know the purpose or function of each experience within your curriculum plan.

3. If possible, have each experience serve more than one of your objectives. For instance, a single experience can easily serve a cognitive objective and also an affective one.

4. Try to organize each experience within a hierarchy of experiences. For example, move from the concrete and experientially close to the abstract and experientially remote, or from the easy to the difficult.

5. Make increments in experiencing "bite size." Instead of providing substantially bigger bites for bright pupils, try preparing alternative experiences for them.

6. Try rotating *types* of experiences, like the following:

   a. Experiences for intake

   b. Experiences for expression

   c. Experiences for assimilation of big ideas and concepts, through planned practice

   d. Experiences for accommodation or restructuring of big ideas and concepts, through making them functional in real situations

   e. Experiences to sensitize or to otherwise develop feeling

   f. Experiences to stimulate intellectual growth, including gaming, puzzles, and simulation

   g. Experiences to interrelate mind and physical movement, as in sophisticated practice in sports

7. Use within the experiences varied ways of learning, including reading, writing, observing, analyzing, dramatizing, making products in the arts, working individually, working in groups, and making maps and charts. Keep a master list of possibilities like these.

Source: Ronald C. Doll, *Curriculum Improvement: Decision Making and Process,* Seventh Edition. Copyright © 1989 by Allyn & Bacon. Reprinted with permission.

---

subjects or body of subject matter. The subject matter to be included in the curriculum is that which has survived the test of time. It is also that which is perceived to be of most value in the development of the intellect—said by supporters to be the primary purpose of education. The subject-area curriculum is consistent with the essentialist philosophy of education.

The subject area design has its roots in classical Greece. In this country William T. Harris, superintendent of schools in St. Louis, Missouri in the 1870s and U.S. commissioner of education from 1886 to 1906, is credited with establishing this design, which has been the dominant curriculum organization for over a century. Harris viewed the curriculum as the means by which the child is introduced to the essential knowledge and values of society and transformed into a reasoning and responsible citizen. The curriculum of the elementary school was to include the fundamentals, which Harris called the "five windows of the soul": mathematics, geography, literature and art, grammar, and history. In the high school, concentration was on the classics, languages, and mathematics (Cremin, 1962). Electives in languages, fine arts, and industrial arts were to be used to develop specific skills or meet special interests (Ellis, Mackey, & Glenn, 1988).

Modern spokespersons for the subject-area curriculum include Arthur Bestor, Mortimer Adler, and Robert Hutchins. They have been joined in their call for a return to fundamentals and a curriculum of basic studies by supporters of the back-to-basics movement and the Moral Majority group. The back-to-basics movement grew out of parents' and educators' disappointment with the level of knowledge and skills learned by students and declining student test scores. The Moral Majority is opposed to all humanistic, child-centered curriculum (Pulliam, 1987).

What impact has the back-to-basics movement had on your discipline? What impact has the Moral Majority had on your field of study?

Criticism of the Subject-Area Design

Those who criticize the subject-area curriculum claim that it ignores the needs, interests, and experiences of students and discourages creativity on the part of both students and teachers. Another major criticism of the subject-area curriculum is that it is fragmented and compartmentalized. The subject-area curriculum is also faulted for failing to adequately consider both individual differences and contemporary social issues. The primary teaching methods of the subject-area curriculum are lecture and discussion. Rote memorization and recitation are required of students.

Popularity of the Subject-Area Design

The subject-area curriculum has remained the most popular and dominant curriculum design for four basic reasons. First, most teachers, especially secondary school teachers, are trained in the subject areas. Secondary school teachers usually think of themselves as American history teachers, biology teachers, English teachers, or whatever. Second, organizing the school by subject matter makes it easy for parents and other adults to understand children's education since most adults attended schools that were organized by subject matter. Third, the subject-area organization makes it easy for teachers to develop curriculum and goals: the content provides the organization and focus needed in planning. Finally, textbooks and other instructional materials are usually developed for subject-area use (Ellis, Mackey, & Glenn, 1988). Because the subject-area design has been so dominant in this country, it is possible to go into schools from Seattle to Key West and find much the same curriculum.

The Integrated Design

The *integrated curriculum* design emerged as a response to the multiplication of courses resulting from the subject-centered design. In this design emphasis remains on subjects, but in place of separate courses in history, geography, economics, political science, anthropology and sociology, for example, an integrated course in social studies might be offered. By this approach, it is claimed, knowledge is integrated in a way that makes it more meaningful to the learner. The integrated design also provides greater flexibility to the teacher in choosing subject matter.

Among the more common integrated courses are language arts, which has taken the place of separate courses in reading, writing, spelling, speaking, grammar, drama, and literature; mathematics, which integrates arithmetic, geometry, and algebra; general science, which includes botany, biology, chemistry, and geology or earth science; and the previously mentioned social studies. Although the integrated design usually combines separate subjects within the same discipline, in some instances content from two or more branches of study have been integrated into a new field of study. Futuristics, which integrates knowledge from mathematics, sociology, statistics, political science, economics, education, and a number of other fields, is one such new field of study. Multicultural education, which integrates knowledge from sociology, psychology, history, and anthropology, is another relatively new area (Ornstein & Hunkins, 1988).

The integrated curriculum has been widely accepted at the elementary level. Where once a number of separate subjects were taught for shorter periods of time, the typical elementary curriculum is now more likely to integrate these subjects into "subject areas" that are taught in longer blocks of time. At the secondary level, the integrated curriculum has experienced limited success. A few integrated courses can be found (e.g., Problems of American Democracy), but as previously noted, the subject-area design dominates secondary school curricula. However, recent efforts in reading and writing across the curriculum are an attempt to respond to reform recommendations that the curriculum not be presented in such discrete, independent blocks and that students be provided greater opportunity to synthesize and integrate knowledge and skills. A major criticism of the integrated curriculum is that in providing breadth, it provides only a cursory knowledge of any subject. While depth may not be considered necessary at the elementary level, the bias towards discipline mastery remains at the secondary level.

The Core Curriculum Design

The definition of a *core curriculum* has changed significantly since it was first advanced in the 1930s. Originally, the core curriculum was proposed as an interdisciplinary approach of relating one subject to another in the study of everyday situations of interest and value to students. The content of the core was taught in an extended block of time and centered around defining and solving problems of concern to all students. Attention was directed to the study of culture and fundamental social values. Typical core courses dealt with how to earn a living, social relations, or life adjustment. As described at the time, the core curriculum was said to be:

> made up of those educational experiences which are thought to be important for each citizen in our democracy. Students and teachers do not consider subject matter to be important in itself. It becomes meaningful only as it helps the group to solve the problems which have been selected for study.
> (MacConnell et al., cited in Goodlad, 1987, p. 10)

Different interpretations of the core concept have emerged in the last decade, primarily as a result of the national reports of the early 1980s. Alternately, the concept of a core curriculum is used to refer to the required minimum "subjects and topics within subjects that all students in a given system are required to or expected to learn" (Skilbeck, 1989, p. 198) or, more broadly, "the comprehensive body of common learnings deemed necessary for all" (Goodlad, 1987, p. 11).

The support for the "new core" came from the same disillusionment with American education that fed the back-to-basics movement that began in the 1970s. The curriculum was said to be lacking in rigor, to contain too many "frills" and soft courses, and to inadequately prepare students to effectively participate and contribute to our increasingly technological and global society. Serious deficits in mathematics, science, and languages also were noted.

The response of some of the national studies was to recommend a core of subjects to be taken by all students. As seen in Table 15.1, the National Commission on Excellence recommended 13.5 units in "the Five New Basics," Boyer proposed a "core of common learning" consisting of 14.5 units, and others wanted less specific but still identifiable cores. To others the concept of a core is more reminiscent of the core curriculum espoused by the progressive educators of the 1930s, '40s, and early '50s. For example, although Goodlad in *A Place Called School* "deliberately and reluctantly" defined a core in conventional terms, he subsequently has joined that body of educators who recognize that increasingly the expectations of schooling are broad and transcend mere academic outcomes. What is needed is not a core of subjects to be taken by all students but a core curriculum consisting of the domains of human experience and thought that should be encountered by all students. The American Association for Supervision and Curriculum Development (ASCD), like Boyer, refers to a core of common learning to help ensure that "all students are provided the curriculum content and learning experiences most appropriate to their future lives" (Cawelti, 1989, p. 33). The ASCD also makes the broad proposal that the core curriculum should center around "fundamental concerns such as global interdependence, civic responsibility, ecology, economic productivity, and world peace" (Cawelti, 1989, p. 33).

Yet many educators are concerned that it is not possible to have a core curriculum for all students and still maintain quality. Others are concerned about the impact of a universal core requirement on the schools' ability to meet the needs of different populations, including those interested in vocational preparation. Probably all agree that the task of defining the proper core will be among the most challenging professional tasks of the 1990s.

The Child-Centered Design

The concept of the *child-centered curriculum* has its roots in the efforts of Rousseau, Pestalozzi, and Froebel (see Chapter 4). In the United States, the concept was revived by the progressive education movement. There are a number of variations of the child-centered curriculum, including the experience- and activity-centered curriculum and the humanistic curriculum.

Creative expression is central to the child-centered curriculum.

The emphasis of all child-centered curricula is on the child's freedom to learn and on activities and creative self-expression.

Where the traditional curriculum is organized around the teaching of discrete subject matter, in the child-centered curriculum children come to the subject matter out of their own needs and interests. The child-centered curriculum focuses on the individual learner and the development of the whole child. The scope of the child-centered curriculum is as broad as all of human life and society. The goal of the curriculum is to motivate and interest the child in the learning process. To achieve this goal, the curriculum encompasses a wide range of activities, including field geography, nature study, number concepts, games, drama, storytelling, music, art, handicrafts, other creative and expressive activities, physical education, and community involvement projects.

Child-centered designs are often criticized for being too broad and for being so inclusive as to be nonfunctional (Portelli, 1987). They are also criticized for being too permissive and for their lack of attention to subject matter mastery. Modern proponents (e.g., John Holt, Herbert Kohl, and Elliot Eisner) counter that the child-centered curriculum enhances learning because it is based on the needs and interests of the learner. Child-centered curricula have operated in numerous districts and schools throughout this century, primarily at the elementary level. However, they have never been seriously considered at the secondary level.

The Social Reconstruction Design

The *social reconstruction curriculum* design is based on the belief that through the curriculum the school can and should effect social change and create a more equitable society. As discussed in Chapter 5, the social reconstruction movement in education emerged in the 1930s and had its origin in the progressive education movement. In 1932, in his book, *Dare the Schools Build a New Social Order?*, George Counts (1969) proposed that the schools involve students in a curriculum designed to reconstruct society. Modern reconstructionists such as Theodore Bramald continue to advocate that the schools become the agents of social change and improvement.

The major assumption underlying the social reconstruction curriculum is that the future is not fixed, but is amenable to modification and improvement. Accordingly, the social reconstruction curriculum seeks "to equip students with tools to deal with the forces about them and to manage conditions as they meet them. . . . (and) to alert students to social issues and choices and to equip them with attitudes and habits of action" (Wiles & Bondi, 1989, p. 354). The primary goal of the curriculum according to the social reconstructionist view is to engage students in a critical analysis of society at every level so that they can improve it.

The social reconstruction design combines classroom learning with application outside the school. Teachers and students join in inquiry. Instruction is often carried on in a problem-solving or inquiry format (Wiles & Bondi, 1989).

What kinds of materials would be used in the social reconstruction curriculum? How difficult would it be to obtain a variety of such materials?

The Deschooling Design

Supporters of the *deschooling curriculum* design seek to disestablish formal schooling because they believe that the values promoted by formal educational institutions are unhealthy and harmful. Unlike the school reconstructionists, who are willing to attempt a reformation of the present structure, the deschooling critics do not believe reformation is possible and call for an end to the public school system. According to this view's chief spokesperson, Ivan Illich (1973), compulsory attendance in government-sponsored schools, along with the requirements for academic certificates, actually inhibits the learner's "private initiative to decide what he will learn and his inalienable right to learn what he likes rather than what is useful to somebody else" (p. 2). Schools, say Illich, operate for the benefit of a few and function as a screening device for the gifted few or "to justify the existence of high schools and colleges for the children of the wealthy and powerful." According to Illich, the disadvantaged are hurt by the formal system of schooling because they not only do not receive an education of value, but are further discriminated against by a system that makes them dependent upon its credentials for the opportunity to advance. In fact, government-sponsored schools, by their very nature, are incapable of meeting the needs of the disadvantaged and compensating for racial and ethnic differences.

The best examples of deschooling design are to be found in the private *free schools* and, to a lesser extent, the private and public alternative schools, which received national attention in the late 1960s and early 1970s. Although not representing a complete deschooling of education, they did "lend support to the fast growing assumption that out-of-school activities were equal in educational value, and perhaps actually superior, to in-school activities" (Ravitch, 1983, p. 238). The free schools and alternative schools sought to release students from the institutional oppression of the traditional school by providing travel-learn programs, work and apprenticeship programs, and affective experiences, as well as the opportunity for volunteer service and informal study in the community (Glatthorn, 1975). In the free schools emphasis was placed on children discovering for themselves what they want to learn and on the abolishment of the authority relationship between the teacher and the student.

Although the free school movement has declined and the disestablishment of the formal educational system in this country does not seem likely, efforts to break the monopoly of the formal educational system continue. Deschooling designs are likely to appear again in the future (Apple, 1979).

Which of the curriculum designs summarized in Figure 15.3 best fits your concept of the curriculum?

Curriculum Contrasts

In practice, most schools do not adopt a strictly subject-centered or student-centered design, but use variations of both in their curriculum organization. Historically, elementary schools have tended to be more student-centered in their orientation and secondary schools more subject-centered. Ultimately, the choice of curriculum design reflects philosophical orientation. The major arguments in support of the subject-centered and student-centered curricula are summarized on page 498.

The Hidden Curriculum

Perhaps even more important than the formal curriculum is the *hidden curriculum*. This concept was briefly mentioned in Chapter 8 in regard to the socialization role of the school. In contrast to the formal curriculum which is designed to produce intended effects, the hidden curriculum involves the unintended effects of schooling, or what Apple (1979) terms "incidental learn-

Figure 15.3: Patterns of Curriculum Organization			
Curriculum Design	**Philosophical Orientation**	**Curriculum Focus**	**Proponents**
Subject-centered	Essentialism	A group of subjects or subject matter that represent the essential knowledge and values of society that have survived the test of time.	Bestor Adler Hutchins
Integrated	Experimentalism	The integration of two or more subjects, both within and across disciplines, into an integrated course.	Broudy Silberman Sarason
Core curriculum	Perennialism	A common body of curriculum content and learning experience that should be encountered by all students; the Great Books.	Goodlad Boyer
Child-centered	Progressivism	Learning activities centered around the interests and needs of the child, designed to motivate and interest the child in the learning process.	Dewey Holt Kohl Eisner
Social reconstructionist	Social reconstructionism	Critical analysis of the political, social, and economic problems facing society; future trends; social action projects designed to bring about social change.	Counts Rugg Bramald Shane
Deschooling	Social reconstructionism	In-school experiences, primarily in the social sciences, designed to develop the child's sense of freedom from the domination of the political, social, and economic systems; out-of-school experiences of equal value.	Illich Goodman Friedenberg Friere

ing." According to Apple (1988), the hidden curriculum includes three areas. One is the hidden social messages present in textbooks and other curriculum materials. A second includes the norms and values taught by the rules, regulations, rituals, school structure, and interactions that are part of the everyday life of the school. Through the hidden curriculum students learn how to cope with power, praise, reward, and authority in the classroom (Apple, 1979), how to move through both social and physical spaces (Bowers, 1984), and the value of competition, obedience, the proper use of time, and seriousness of purpose.

The third area Apple included in the hidden curriculum is the knowledge or information that is not included in the overt curriculum, or what Eisner (1985) has termed the *null curriculum*. The null curriculum, which is potentially

Controversial Issues:
The Subject-Centered and Student-Centered Curricula

The debate between the essentialists and others who support the subject-centered curriculum and the progressives and others who support a child-centered curriculum has continued unabated for almost a decade and appears likely to continue into the next century. Among the arguments the proponents of each orientation give are the following:

Arguments for the Subject-Centered Curriculum	Arguments for the Student-Centered Curriculum
1. Introduces learners to the cultural heritage.	1. Releases the teacher from the pressure to follow a prescribed scope and sequence that invariably does not meet all learners' needs.
2. Gives teachers a sense of security by specifying what their responsibilities are for developing given skills and knowledge.	2. Has a positive influence on learners as they find that instruction is varied to meet individual needs and purposes.
3. Reduces repetition or overlap between grade levels or different sections of the same class.	3. Encourages teacher judgment in selecting the content deemed most suitable for a group of learners.
4. Increases the likelihood that learners will be exposed to knowledge and develop skills in an orderly manner.	4. Increases the likelihood that content has relevance to learners.
5. Permits methodical assessment of pupil progress; assumes that knowledge is the only measurable outcome of learning experiences.	5. Modifies instruction to accommodate developmental changes and behavioral tasks as individual differences are identified and monitored.
6. Facilitates cooperative group planning by educators in allocating the scope and sequence of learning experiences.	6. Allows much more latitude for creative planning by the individual teacher.

What other arguments can you think of for the subject-centered or student-centered curriculum?

Source: Shane, H. G., & Tabler, M. B. (1981). *Educating for a new millennium* (pp. 79–80). Bloomington, IN: Phi Delta Kappa. Reprinted with permission.

---

infinite, refers to those things that are consciously excluded because of their controversial nature, because they represent different values, or because of a lack of time, or that cannot be included because of a lack of resources. It also includes those things that are unintentionally excluded because educators are uninformed or because relevant materials are nonexistent.

The null curriculum, like all areas of the hidden curriculum, does not have the same impact on all students. That is, not only are different values and norms stressed with different social classes or different sexes, but differences are also found even within the same school or classroom in what students have the opportunity to learn.

Historically, what is now called the hidden curriculum was not hidden because the schools explicitly served a social control function in unifying a diverse population, advancing a common culture, and preparing individuals economically for their place in society. In fact, the hidden curriculum did not become hidden until the end of the nineteenth century "when the education system shifted from one that provided uniform experience for the good of society to a system that was concerned with individual and personal advancement" (King, 1988, p. 86).

In recent years increasing attention has been focused on the hidden curriculum as more has been learned about the strength of its influence. Particular concern exists about its negative influence. For example, the lessons of the hidden curriculum tend to promote conformity and in the process may stifle creativity and discourage independent thinking. The hidden curriculum also teaches children to avoid conflict and change and to support the dominant orientation at all costs (Apple, 1979). Through the hidden curriculum bias and stereotyping of race, gender, and class are reproduced and reinforced.

Teachers affect the hidden curriculum through their own personalities, values, interests, strengths, and weaknesses which they communicate as they teach the overt curriculum, establish and maintain order and discipline, and attend to their other responsibilities (McCutcheon, 1988). For this reason it is important that teachers understand their own philosophy of education (see Chapter 7). The important role of teachers in relation to the hidden curriculum is to become more conscious of it, to examine the social and political assumptions within the materials and practices they employ (Apple, 1988), and to find ways to take advantage of this important opportunity for learning. By doing this teachers can reinforce the positive lessons of the hidden curriculum, ameliorate the negative lessons, and make the hidden curriculum more visible.

The Curriculum Cycle

Throughout the twentieth century, the curriculum in America's schools has shifted between a subject-centered orientation and student-centered orientation (see Figure 15.4). The first two decades of the century were dominated by the progressive movement and its child-centeredness. In the wake of World War I came a more conservative political posture and a renewal of interest in a more orderly academic curriculum. Out of the social upheaval of the Great Depression emerged a more liberal voice that championed concern for the individual. In the 1950s, Conant's study of secondary schools, which underscored the need for greater attention to academic studies, was reinforced by the Soviet launching of Sputnik, and a curriculum reform movement was initiated aimed at strengthening mathematics, science, and foreign language offerings and providing greater rigor in all disciplines. The Great Society of the 1960s drove the cycle in the opposite direction. The open school and alternative school movements were the most visible reflections of the increased attention

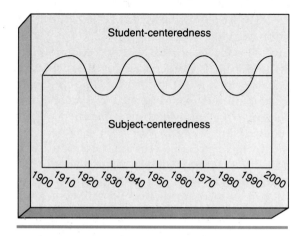

Figure 15.4: Cycle of Curriculum Orientation, 1900–2000

being focused on students. By the late 1970s many of the curricular innovations of the previous decade had disappeared, and again a call was heard for a return to the basic academic subjects and an elimination of the frills. This mood dominated the 1980s.

As we begin the 1990s, we anticipate that the cycle will once again move in the direction of a concern for students and student issues. Curricular reforms will probably focus on values education, decision making and critical thinking skills, the development of students' self-esteem, and the individuality of students. Those who do not applaud this shift should bear in mind that the curriculum cycle is short (McDaniel, 1989).

Summary

The decade of the 1990s has seen the school reform movement focus its attention on the curriculum in an effort to achieve what increasing core requirements and expenditures had not been able to do—increase student performance. The increased attention on the curriculum has served not only to highlight the controversy about various curriculum orientations, but to emphasize the sociopolitical context within which curriculum decisions are made.

The beginning of the 1990s also sees a shift in the dominant curriculum orientation. The conservative, subject-centered approach that was emphasized by the first wave of reform reports is giving way to a more balanced approach that incorporates greater concern for critical thinking and student issues. The involvement of various professional educational associations and the nation's governors into the reform arena should bring new force to curriculum change.

A curriculum standing alone is of little value. Not until it is implemented does it take on meaning. The process by which it is implemented, termed instruction, is discussed in the following chapter, along with the emerging issues and trends in curriculum and instruction.

Key Terms

Child-centered curriculum
Continuity
Core curriculum
Curriculum
Deschooling curriculum
Free schools
Hidden curriculum

Integrated curriculum
Integration
Null curriculum
Sequence
Social reconstruction curriculum
Subject-area curriculum

Discussion Questions

1. How would you define the terms "curriculum" and "hidden curriculum"? Should the lessons of the hidden curriculum be incorporated into the formal curriculum? If not, how can they be dealt with by the teacher? Should they be dealt with?

2. Which of the agencies or groups discussed in this chapter has had the most influence on the curriculum in your district in the last five years?

3. Who should have the most input on textbook content? The author? The publisher? The user?

4. Which of the curricular designs discussed in this chapter is most consistent with your philosophy of education as identified in Chapters 6 and 7?

5. Describe the curriculum that would best prepare students for the twenty-first century.

References

Apple, M. W. (1979). *Ideology and curriculum.* Boston, MA: Routledge & Kegan Paul.

Apple, M. W. (1988). Hidden curriculum. In R. A. Gorton, G. T. Schneider, & J. C. Fisher (Eds.), *Encyclopedia of school administration* (p. 137). Phoenix, AZ: The Oryx Press.

Bowers, C. A. (1984). *The promise of theory: Education and the politics of cultural change.* New York: Longman.

Cawelti, G. (1989). Designing high schools for the future. *Educational Leadership, 47*(1), 33.

Common measures. *Education vital signs.* (1988–89). IV.

Cornbleth, C. (1988). Curriculum in and out of context. *Journal of Curriculum and Supervision, 3,* 85–96.

Counts, G. S. (1969). *Dare the schools build a new social order?* New York: John Dey.

Cremin, L. A. (1962). *The transformation of the school.* New York: Alfred A. Knopf.

Eisner, E. (1985). *The educational imagination* (2nd ed.). New York: Macmillan.

Ellis, A. K., Mackey, J. A., & Glenn, A. D. (1988). *The school curriculum.* Boston, MA: Allyn and Bacon.

Glatthorn, A. (1975). *Alternatives in education: Schools and programs.* New York: Dodd, Mead.

Goodlad, J. I. (1987). A new look at an old idea: Core curriculum. *Educational Leadership, 44*(4), 10.

Illich, I. (1973). After deschooling, what? In A. Gartner, C. Greer, & F. Riessman (Eds.), *After deschooling, what?* New York: Perennial Library.

King, S. E. (1988). Inquiring into the hidden curriculum. *Journal of Curriculum and Supervision, 2,* 86.

Lewis, A. C. (1990). Getting unstuck: Curriculum as a tool of reform. *Phi Delta Kappan, 71,* 534–538.

McCutcheon, G. (1988). Curriculum and the work of teachers. In L. E. Beyer & M. W. Apple (Eds.), *The Curriculum: Problems, politics, and possibilities* (pp. 191–203). Albany, NY: State University of New York.

McDaniel, T. R. (1989). Demilitarizing public education: School reform in the era of George Bush. *Phi Delta Kappan, 71,* 15–18.

Ornstein, A. C., & Hunkins, F. P. (1988). *Curriculum: Foundations, principles, and issues.* Englewood Cliffs, NY: Prentice Hall.

Portelli, J. P. (1987). On defining curriculum. *Journal of Curriculum and Supervision, 2,* 354–367.

Posner, G. J. (1988). Models of curriculum planning. In L. E. Beyer & M. W. Apple (Eds.), *The curriculum: Problems, politics and possibilities* (pp. 77–97). Albany, NY: State University of New York.

Pulliam, J. D. (1987). *History of education in America* (4th ed.). Columbus, OH: Merrill.

Ravitch, D. (1983). *The troubled crusade.* New York: Basic Books.

Skilbeck, M. (1989). Revitalizing the core curriculum. *Journal of Curriculum and Supervision, 4,* 198.

Spring, J. (1989). *American education: An introduction to social and political aspects,* (4th ed.). New York: Longman.

Tyler, R. W. (1949). *Basic principles of curriculum and instruction.* Chicago: University of Chicago Press.

Walker, D. E., & Soltis, J. F. (1986). *Curriculum and aims.* New York: Teachers College Press, Columbia University.

Wiles, J., & Bondi, J. (1989). *Curriculum development* (3d ed.). Columbus, OH: Merrill.

Chapter 16

Instructional Practices in Today's Schools

All education is a continuous dialogue—questions and answers that pursue every problem to the horizon.

William O. Douglas
Wisdom, *October 1956*

You have been appointed to a school district task force whose charge is to develop a plan for the district to choose goals for the school program. Several members of the task force have indicated that they do not think that the planned system of goals, objectives, and outcomes will affect the ways in which they organize their classes and work with students. You have been asked to indicate how the role of the teacher might be different under the various ways in which schools and classrooms might be organized.

Students differ among the schools in the district. How can teachers determine if certain strategies would be more appropriate with particular groups of students? The superintendent is advocating more extensive use of educational technology in the classroom. How would that affect the role of the teacher? How can the teacher use technology to improve instruction and student performance?

Not only do instructional practices differ among schools, but exciting discussions are underway about the goals and objectives of education and the ways in which teachers and students interact. The following objectives should guide you as you study, observe, and analyze the variety of instructional practices found in today's classrooms:

- Describe the difference between educational goals and instructional objectives.

- Relate the ways in which district goals, objectives, and outcomes will affect how a teacher organizes instruction and works with students.

- Discuss methods of organizing for instruction.

- Identify the components of mastery learning.

- Compare and contrast four different teaching strategies.

- Discuss the effect of technology on instruction.

- Describe the current issues in curriculum and instruction.

Schools for All

The organization of America's schools and the ways that teachers work with students in the classroom are extensions of the overarching goals of American education. The schools and the classrooms are the arena in which the goal of free public instruction for all citizens is achieved.

How can a teacher demonstrate the use of democratic principles in the classroom?

This chapter reviews various instructional practices associated with good teaching. Rather than advocating a particular approach, the focus is on different techniques and approaches that teachers may use for different purposes with different groups of students. First, attention is given to the importance of instructional goals and objectives in schools. The second section contains a discussion of how schools may be organized for instruction. Teaching strategies are discussed in the third section, followed by an overview of the concept of mastery learning. Next, we focus on some of the implications of technological developments on the instructional process. The chapter concludes with a discussion of issues and trends in curriculum and instruction.

Instructional Goals and Objectives

An overarching goal of American public education, and thus of states, school districts, and individual schools, has been to provide free public instruction for all citizens. This goal together with more specific educational and instructional goals should guide school districts and schools as they select educational and instructional objectives. The interaction between educational goals and objectives is discussed in the following paragraphs.

Educational Goals

In making decisions about education, the first issue is to decide what to teach. To make that decision, educators and policy makers need clearly defined goals and objectives for instruction and information about the roles and responsibilities of learners in relation to the specific goals and objectives.

Educational goals are broad general statements of desired learning outcomes (Kourilsky & Quaranta, 1987). Examples of goal statements are:

The learner will develop:
- basic math skills

- an appreciation of poetry

- an understanding of World War II

"Educational goals are changes in students toward which we want learning outcomes to lead" (Brookover, 1980). Rather than identifying specific skills, educational goals describe characteristics or attributes of what society considers to be a well-educated person. Goals are to be the result or cumulative effect of a series of learnings. Obviously, as defined, goals designate the desired outcome of instruction but lack the specificity to actually implement an instructional sequence (Kourilsky & Quaranta, 1987). That is where educational objectives come into play.

Educational Objectives

An *educational objective* is a clearly defined, observable, and measurable student behavior which indicates learner progress toward the achievement of a particular educational goal. Educational objectives also are referred to as instructional or behavioral objectives. An educational objective should meet the criteria listed in Figure 16.1.

Educational or instructional objectives are used to operationalize educational goals. Reference is often made to a more specific term, "behavioral objectives." Unlike other types of educational objectives, behavioral objectives force the teacher to describe the learning outcomes from the learner's viewpoint. Behavioral objectives answer the questions "How do you know the learner has learned?" and "What is the learner to do to prove he/she has learned?" (Burn, 1977). Examples of behavioral objectives are shown in Figure 16.2.

How precise should an educational objective be to be effective?

Taxonomies of Educational Objectives

In the development of educational objectives, a taxonomy or classification system is needed. Benjamin S. Bloom has developed a widely used hierarchy of levels of intellectual behavior referred to in the literature as *Bloom's Taxonomy of Educational Objectives* (Bloom, 1956). The levels are listed in Figure 16.3. This hierarchy is helpful in delineating the increasingly complex levels of the intellectual process. It is also important when planning instruction to incorporate activities from the full range of levels in students' learning experiences to stimulate and develop their intellectual skills. This is especially true relative to helping students master what is popularly referred to as higher order

---

Figure 16.1: Criteria for Educational Objectives

1. The place or condition for learning is established. Specific references should be made to the activity in which the goal is to be attained, i.e., test, game, laboratory experiment, recital, or report on an activity.

2. The learner's behavior is stated in measurable and observable terms. The types of evidence need to be stated clearly, i.e., completion of a specific test or experiment, completion of a recital, or submission of a written report.

3. The minimally acceptable level of performance is stated. Examples include the desired percentage of correct responses on the test, the maximum number of permissible errors in the recital, and the desired length of the report and number of permissible grammatical errors.

Source: Kourilsky, M., & Quaranta, L. (1987). *Effective teaching: Principles and practice.* Glenview, IL: Scott, Foresman.

Figure 16.2: Examples of Educational or Behavioral Objectives

1. The student provides the correct answer for 90% or more of the items on the test.

2. The student places 50% or more of the arrows within six inches of the center of the target.

3. The student dissects the frog and correctly identifies and labels each part of the frog stipulated in the exercise.

4. The student is present for all rehearsals, arrives on time for the recital, and is error-free in the recital.

5. The student prepares a 10-page report on an activity with five or fewer spelling errors and no incomplete sentences.

Figure 16.3: Levels of Bloom's Taxonomy

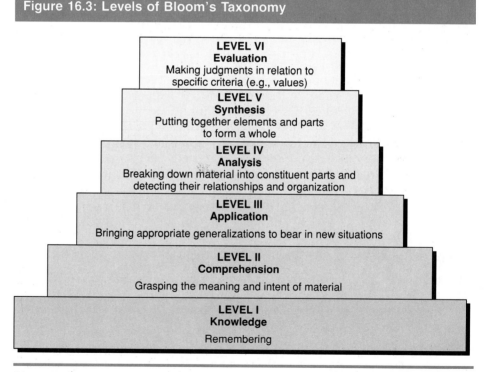

Source: Kourilsky, M., & Quaranta, L. (1987). *Effective Teaching: Principles and practice.* Glenview, IL: Scott, Foresman.

thinking skills (HOTS). The higher order thinking skills in Bloom's Taxonomy are analysis, synthesis, and evaluation.

Goals and objectives become the structure that schools and teachers use in determining how they will organize for instruction. As indicated in the following section, several different approaches are used.

Organizing for Instruction

Teachers and principals can be creative in organizing schools and students. Typically, students are treated as members of a group, but the group does not have to include the entire class; students may be clustered into smaller groups with similar interests or instructional needs. An alternative to group instruction is cooperative learning in which the teacher encourages students to work together in addressing problems; the teacher provides the initial leadership in defining the activity and functions as a resource person for the process. Another alternative is individualized instruction in which the teacher works with each student on a one-to-one basis diagnosing, prescribing, and evaluating progress. Independent learning can be viewed as an extension of individualized instruction, but the responsibility of the student is increased and the teacher is not as closely involved with the student. Additional descriptions of each of these types of instruction are found in the following discussion. Figure 16.4 summarizes the principal types of instruction with brief information about the teacher's role and an example of a typical activity. The description of the Montessori Method in the Historical Note on page 510 provides brief background information about a learning environment that focuses on sensory training and physical exercises.

How can a teacher individualize instruction in a group?

Group Instruction

Much classroom teaching can be classified as *group instruction*. The teacher either views all students in the room as members of a single group or divides

Figure 16.4: Types of Instruction		
Type of Instruction	**Teacher's Role**	**Typical Activity**
Group instruction	Provides formal instruction Monitors class activity	American history: Teacher gives formal lecture on historical facts.
Cooperative learning	Sets the stage for learning Facilitates groups of students Organizes the structure of the classroom	U.S. presidents: Class is divided into teams of three or four students. Each team is responsible for conducting research on one U.S. president.
Individualized instruction	Acts as resource person Guides and monitors student's learning	Reading: Each student is assigned a different short story according to his/her reading ability.
Independent instruction	Negotiates topics and assignments with students Consults and advises students Evaluates student's learning activities	English: Each student consults individually with the teacher and is given a special essay topic.
Mastery learning	Provides formal instruction Administers formative tests Provides feedback to students	Math: Students work progressively through the basic math facts (e.g., addition before subtraction).

Historical Note:
Maria Montessori and the Montessori Method

Maria Montessori was the first woman in Italy to receive a medical degree. Her early career involved working with retarded children at the University of Rome psychiatric clinic and pedagogical school that prepared teachers of the mentally retarded and emotionally disturbed. The methods she developed were extended to normal children at her first Casa dei Bambino (Children's House), opened in 1907 in a Roman slum area. This gave her an opportunity to test and perfect ideas, methods, and materials. The school proved so successful that other Montessori schools were established in Rome and other cities.

The Montessori Method, as it came to be called, emphasizes sensory training using a set of materials and physical exercises developed by Montessori. Intent and motivation are at the heart of the method. Materials are intended to arouse the student's interest, and interest provides the motiva-tion for learning. Instruction is highly individualized and is designed to develop self-discipline and self-confidence.

Through numerous lectures and extensive writings, Dr. Montessori disseminated her ideas, and educators from throughout the world came to Italy to observe her program and be trained in her approach. By 1915, almost 100 Montessori schools were in operation in the United States. In 1929, the International Montessori Association was formed. Montessori fled fascist Italy for Spain in 1934, and worked in several places in Europe and Asia before her death in 1952. Although the Montessori Method has been considered controversial by many educators since its inception, today thousands of Montessori schools operate in virtually every country in the world.

---

the class into subgroups. In the first instance, the setting is teacher dominated. Various instructional strategies may be used, but individualization often is sacrificed in an effort to accommodate the needs and interests of the group.

When subgroups are used the role of the teacher changes. Major portions of the teacher's time are spent planning, coordinating, and monitoring the activities of the subgroups. For the groups to function, students must assume more responsibility for their learning. The capacity of the group to teach itself is enhanced because students typically are assigned to subgroups on the basis of special needs or interests.

A major challenge for the teacher in group instruction is to develop ways to organize teaching/learning activities for the entire group, while at the same time recognizing individual differences among students. Thus, in planning the group activities, the teacher also must be sensitive to the needs of individual students.

Cooperative Learning

In *cooperative learning*, the class consists of students working in small groups rather than as individuals. The groups often are considered to be heterogeneous in terms of contribution and/or classroom performance, and students have the opportunity to learn from their peers. The result of this interaction is a higher noise level in the classroom, sometimes referred to as

Student learning is an active process in which the teacher often assumes a variety of roles.

the "busy hum of learning." Peers are rewarded for helping one another. Rather than being in competition with each other, students experience a sense of interdependence; they have a reduced likelihood of failure and an increased probability of success because of the combined resources of the group. Depending on the specific content, teachers can vary their instructional approach. The teacher still has responsibility for setting the stage and working with students, but students work in groups rather than as individuals (Brandt, 1989).

The positive effects of cooperative learning in elementary and secondary schools appear to be associated with two essential elements—group goals and individual accountability (Slavin, 1989b). By working together, students have the opportunity to exercise leadership and also reap the benefits of other indicators of group success. As individuals, they are responsible for their personal performance and achievement. Peer tutors and support groups can be especially useful in breaking down some of the barriers found in multicultural schools.

For several reasons, the use of cooperative learning as the organizing scheme in the classroom is likely to increase. First, research findings are

*How do the
different methods
of organizing for
instruction affect
the role of the
teacher?*

positive. Students who have had good experiences in cooperative learning are more willing to participate in the instructional approach and will have a higher level of confidence as they become involved. Second, the likelihood of cooperative learning becoming more commonplace also is enhanced because this approach is frequently employed in preservice and in-service education for teachers. Last, and possibly most important, students and teachers seem to enjoy this method of organizing the classroom for instruction (Slavin, 1989b).

Individualized Instruction

Individualizing instruction for each student is a worthy but difficult goal. Traditionally, schools have been organized to provide instruction for groups of students. When the group approach is not successful in addressing the specific instructional needs of a few students, *individualized instruction* often is used as an alternative. The teacher assumes the role of a resource person who guides and monitors the student's learning rather than providing formal instruction in a traditional class setting.

Individualized instruction also may be used to cope with teaching and/or learning differences in the classroom. The approach can be especially effective as teachers work with gifted and talented students or slow learners in the same classroom.

Independent Learning

In this organizational option, topics or assignments are negotiated between the student and the teacher on an individual basis. Then students assume personal responsibility for their learning; the role of the teacher is to facilitate the process. The teacher functions first as a consultant/adviser to the student and later as an evaluator of the student's learning activities.

Rather than being an option restricted to gifted and talented students, *independent learning* can be used with most students. As they work independently, students learn to set goals, plan their learning, and assume personal responsibility for their programs. Students thus assume an increased level of responsibility for their own schooling. The teacher's responsibilities are different with different students. Success is measured by the extent to which the student completes the topics or assignments in a timely manner at the predetermined level of quality.

Mastery Learning

Mastery learning is more than an organizational option; it is a process for teaching and learning. Benjamin S. Bloom of the University of Chicago is the person most commonly associated with mastery learning. The two basic assumptions of mastery learning are that (a) most learning units are sequential; thus, the concepts from one unit are built upon and extended by the next unit; and (b) all students can learn at the mastery level if the learning units are small enough. Mastery learning is generally taught through group instruction and, therefore, is primarily teacher centered. Table 16.1 shows the major differences between mastery learning and other systems of instruction (Guskey, 1985).

The mastery learning instructional format assumes that the teacher presents the learning unit and then administers what is called the first formative test. The purpose of the test is to check learning progress and provide the students with feedback and suggestions to help them overcome any difficulties they are experiencing. Following the test, students who have not mastered the material are provided corrective work for a few class periods. Then a second parallel test is administered to ensure that the students have achieved mastery before the class moves on to the next learning unit. Students who demonstrated mastery on the first formative test are given enrichment activities during the corrective phase of instruction. Figure 16.5 illustrates the mastery learning instructional process.

Mastery learning as a process has been especially popular with researchers involved in effective schools research. The concept enables the teacher to address the special needs of students in multicultural environments. Critics, however, assert that the process has been oversimplified, that mastery of the individual units does not necessarily transfer to future learning, and that students cannot be expected to learn and achieve at the mastery level indefinitely.

Table 16.1: Major Differences Between Mastery Learning and Personalized Systems of Instruction

	Model	
Characteristic	Mastery Learning	Personalized Systems of Instruction
Basis of instruction	Group	Individual
Pace of instruction	Teacher determined	Student determined
Primary source of instruction	Teacher, supplemented by materials	Materials, supplemented by the teacher
Standard of mastery	80–90%	100%
Number of retake tests per unit	One	As many as needed for mastery
Correctives	New and different approach	Repetition of original material
Major applications	Elementary and secondary levels	College level

Figure 16.5: The Mastery Learning Instructional Process: (a) Instructional Sequence and (b) Achievement Distribution Curve in a Mastery Learning Classroom

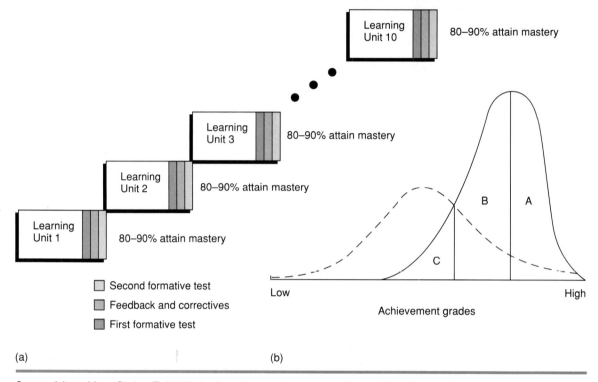

(a)   (b)

Source: Adapted from Guskey, T. (1985). *Implementing mastery learning.* Belmont, CA: Wadsworth.

Teaching Strategies

What criteria should the teacher use in determining which teaching method to use with different subject matter or learning objectives?

Effective teachers use different strategies, tactics, or methods depending on their personal talents, the content to be taught, and the interests and abilities of the students. As discussed in Chapter 1, teaching is often described as an art. This does not imply that teachers operate without design or planning; rather, it underscores the need for teachers to understand and be able to use a variety of strategies as they work with students.

Teaching has also been described as a craft or an applied science (Tom, 1984). In fact, it may be inappropriate to assume that teaching should take a single form. Adler (1984) refers to three types of teaching—didactic instruction, coaching, and Socratic questioning. In didactic teaching, students acquire knowledge by becoming actively engaged in instruction through question and answer strategies. Coaching calls on the teacher to prepare the student for exhibiting a skill in public. Socratic questioning does not assume that the teacher or the student knows all the answers; the goal is to develop an understanding of ideas and values. Adler's ideal teacher possesses a blend of instructional skills, judgment about student understanding of the material, expertise on the subject matter, and the capacity to communicate effectively with individuals and groups (Duke, 1984).

Models of instruction may be grouped into five categories: expository, demonstration, inquiry or discovery, critical thinking, and independent learning. Rather than selecting a single method of instruction, the effective teacher should be familiar with and understand how to use a variety of methods in response to different teaching/learning opportunities. Summary information on the models of instruction is presented in Figure 16.6.

Expository Instruction

Expository instruction, a teacher-centered method, gets its name from exposition, which is the discourse designed to convey information. The most common forms of expository instruction are formal lecture, informal lecture, and teacher-led discussion. Expository instruction is considered appropriate when (a) all students need to know an essential body of knowledge and (b) the students are relatively homogeneous in their ability and knowledge of the topic.

Teacher Role

In expository instruction, the teacher controls and directs the learning process and determines the methods of presentation, the pace of instruction, the quantity of supervised practice or reinforcement, and the form of student evaluation. The role of the student is to "follow the leader." The student is expected to listen, read, and answer questions as the teacher directs.

Resources

Appropriate instructional resources for expository instruction include filmstrips, films, slides, videotapes, and guest speakers. These resources are used to summarize and reinforce information or skills already provided through teacher-centered instruction. The most common forms of evaluation are standardized tests or teacher-written criterion-referenced tests.

Potential Problems

Expository instruction works effectively in small segments. Several weaknesses emerge when this method is the primary method of instruction. First, expository or lecture instruction can result in the teacher being especially vulnerable to manipulation by students. For example, if the teacher is diverted, instruction ceases. Another weakness of expository teaching is that the second assumption associated with the method—homogeneity of the students—is seldom met.

The principles underlying this method are not consistent with the current emphasis on individualizing instruction to meet the diverse needs of students and to stem the tide of student dropouts. Causes of and solutions for the dropout problem are complex, but the consensus appears to be that overde-

Figure 16.6: Models of Instruction

	Teacher's Role	Student's Role	Strengths
Expository instruction	• Teacher–centered • Controls and directs the learning process • Determines methods of presentation	• Follow the leader • Listens, reads, and answers teacher-directed questions	• Best method for students grouped homogeneously by ability
Demonstration instruction	• Plans, organizes, and conducts the demonstration	• Observes, listens, and participates as directed	• Retention is enhanced by active participation
Inquiry or discovery instruction	• Guides the learning process • Stimulates and challenges learners	• Student-centered activities • Self-directed critical thinking and problem solving	• Encourages higher order thinking skills • Challenges gifted/talented students
Critical thinking	• Facilitates the learning process • "Nondirected" • Stimulates and challenges learners • Empowers students	• Finds out information for themselves • Asks questions, rather than being asked questions	• Encourages higher order thinking skills and problem solving
Independent instruction	• Provides the stage for learning • Provides resources • Provides individual instruction	• Exercises initiative and responsibility • Reports progress to teacher • Establishes own learning pace	• Frees teacher to work individually with students

pendence on teacher-centered and teacher-dominated instruction contributes to students dropping out of school. One of the reasons is that expository teaching assumes that the student has a level of preknowledge that often is not present. Thus, the student is quickly frustrated and feels lost. These feelings compound themselves until the learner simply gives up and drops out of school at the first opportunity (Barone, 1989; Cuban, 1989).

In elementary and secondary schools expository instruction can be effective. However, the teacher who uses the method should keep in mind that students differ in their levels of competence and that expository instruction requires more extensive and detailed daily lesson planning. Some would contend that lectures virtually need to be scripted. The structure and direction of the lecture or discussion should be obvious to the learner. Further, even with extensive preparation and a quality presentation, the teacher must realize that portions of the information contained in a lecture will have to be repeated or retaught.

Weaknesses	Resources	Evaluation
● Principles not consistent with meeting the needs of individual students	● Filmstrips ● Films ● Slides ● Videotapes ● Guest speakers	● Standardized tests ● Teacher-written criterion-referenced tests
● Students must have prior knowledge to benefit from demonstration	● Science labs ● Computer labs ● Drama classrooms ● Specialized materials	● Written exams ● Student products (e.g., lab reports, computer programs, discussion, etc.)
● Takes a sophisticated learner to really be effective	● Topics and ideas for exploration ● Research tools	● Oral and written student reports ● Standardized tests that focus on higher order thinking skills and problem solving
● Many teachers find this method difficult	● Topics and ideas for exploration ● Research tools	● Standardized tests that focus on higher order thinking skills and problem solving ● Open-ended questions
● Difficult to orient students to work independently	● Learning packets ● Teaching kits ● Reading machines ● Computers	● Written exams ● Student products ● Oral and written student reports

Demonstration Instruction

In *demonstration instruction*, the student learns through doing and/or observing. This method includes laboratory experiments, dramatizations, constructions, recitations, and exhibitions. Demonstration instruction is assumed appropriate when (a) the student's level of understanding will be enhanced by observing or working with a functioning model or guide, and (b) the student has sufficient background and maturity to understand the value or relevance of the demonstration.

Teacher Role

The teacher's role is to plan, organize, and in most cases conduct the demonstration. Additional responsibilities include emphasizing and clarifying those portions of the demonstration activity especially related to the desired learning outcomes. For example, the teacher demonstrates to students how to dissect a frog. The student's role is to observe, listen, and participate as directed. Usually, the teacher will supervise closely the first cut with a scalpel. Then, after the demonstration and the initial supervised activity, the student becomes more independent. The merits of this method are that retention is enhanced if the student, in addition to observing, is able to become actively involved in the teaching/learning activity.

Resources

The required resources for demonstration instruction generally make this method relatively expensive. Fully equipped science laboratories, computer laboratories, and drama classrooms all require specialized equipment and instructional materials. Evaluation may be by written examination; however, it may be more appropriate to evaluate students' products in the form of laboratory reports, computer programs, discussion, or recitation because students can model what has been demonstrated.

Potential Problems

Properly conducted and supervised, this methodology can be most effective; however, the learner must have sufficient prior knowledge to benefit from the demonstration. For this reason, demonstration instruction is often preceded by expository instruction. The teacher's ability to teach skills is critical to the effectiveness of this methodology. The teacher must be capable of conducting the demonstration effectively. For example, the teacher who "cannot carry a tune" is not the teacher who should sing the scale in a vocal music class. The demonstration should relate directly to the specific instructional objectives; if it does not, the demonstration may be merely an effort to entertain students.

Inquiry Instruction

Inquiry instruction was first made popular in America by John Dewey at the beginning of this century. (See Chapter 5 for additional discussion.) Subsequently, other authors have referred to this method of instruction as problem solving, the inductive method, creative thinking, the scientific method, or conceptual learning. Irrespective of the title, the essential elements of each approach are basically the same as those identified by Dewey.

Reflective thinking or inquiry takes place when a person is faced with a problem or forced choice. The five phases of reflective thinking are (a) suggestion (selection of topic), (b) intellectualization (exploratory discussion), (c) hypothesis (educated or informed guess about the outcome), (d) reasoning (drawing of inferences or conclusions based on facts), and (e) testing of the hypothesis (Massialas & Zevin, 1983). Each phase is part of a well-designed *inquiry instruction*. The activity is student centered. The most common forms are oral and written student reports and nonmathematical problem-solving activities.

In contrast to other forms of instruction or teaching, the "transmission of the accumulated knowledge and wisdom of a culture" is not the primary role of inquiry instruction (Skinner, 1965). Rather, the focus of inquiry instruction is to teach the learner to be a self-directed critical thinker and problem solver. Given this philosophy, inquiry instruction is assumed appropriate if (a) students have the tools needed, i.e., sufficient reading ability to follow the directions and successfully complete the lesson; (b) students are self-directed enough to enjoy the process and not be frustrated; (c) the activity is student-centered and thus gives additional responsibility to the student; and (d) students are sufficiently sophisticated in higher order thinking skills to progress from one inductive level to another.

How will you as a teacher select the instructional strategy that you will use in the classroom?

Critical Thinking Instruction

With the development of *critical thinking* as the instructional goal, the student becomes more active and responsible and the teacher becomes less dominant. The teacher organizes and provides direction for student learning, but the student is an active rather than passive participant.

Analytic or higher order thinking skills are the central elements in the process of critical thinking. Students who become critical thinkers can view problems in different dimensions and consider problems in a larger context. They seek maximum information before deciding on a course of action. Rather than finding quick and simple solutions to complex problems, critical thinkers not only examine the particular problem as an individual issue but also consider it in the larger dimension of related issues (Ellis, Mackey & Glenn, 1988). Teachers and students become active in identifying and seeking solutions to problems. The process of critical thinking is illustrated in Figure 16.7.

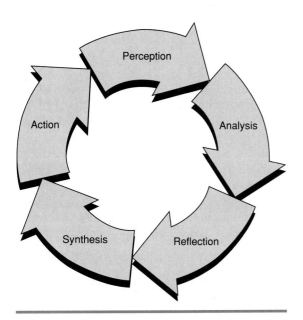

Figure 16.7: The Process of Critical Thinking

Teacher Role

The teacher is no longer the center of activity. In the critical thinking or inquiry model, the teacher is a guide, facilitator, stimulator, even a cheerleader who challenges learners. In essence, the teacher abdicates his/her position and empowers students. By empowering students, the teacher no longer monopolizes the learning process; thus, the term "nondirected" is often applied to the teacher's role. To an extent this is a misnomer, for the teacher does direct, but in a less visible manner. The teacher must plan carefully the topics and ideas the class will explore, organize and time the various activities, and arrange to make available the resources the students will use. The teacher often assumes the role of devil's advocate; students are usually forced to defend and explain their positions. A self-evaluation checklist for critical thinkers is presented in "Ask Yourself" on page 522.

At the conclusion of the activity, the teacher summarizes, recaps, and asks students for clarification. Students are the focus of inquiry instruction; they take the initiative to find out for themselves, and they ask questions rather than being asked. Students are free to explore. Evaluation focuses on the students' ability to internalize and apply content to other situations. Options for evaluation include standardized tests that focus on higher order thinking skills, problem solving, and critical thinking as well as open-ended questions.

Potential Problems

The problems associated with this mode of instruction are primarily an outgrowth of teachers' experiences as students; teachers tend to do as they were taught. For this reason, teachers often have difficulty adapting to change. Most teachers were taught by expository instruction; to teach and help students learn differently requires a totally new orientation. Modeling of critical thinking or inquiry instruction is something few teachers have observed, let alone experienced as a method of learning.

Independent Learning

As a teacher, can you vary the instructional strategy depending on the subject matter content and the interests and abilities of students?

A range of student-centered teaching methodologies may be used in independent learning. They include programmed instruction, self-paced instruction, contract learning, and performance-based instruction, which are often collectively labeled personalized systems of instruction (PSI). These methodologies are individually based, student-paced instructional models in which students learn independently of their classmates. A PSI may be an appropriate mode of instruction if the following assumptions are held by the teacher: (a) students are not homogeneous; (b) as they mature, students' heterogeneity increases; and (c) most students will learn best if allowed to learn at their own pace.

Teacher Role

The teacher's role is to provide the stage for learning. This includes providing both the various instructional materials and a stress-free environment. Much as in inquiry instruction, the teacher using PSI assumes the role of

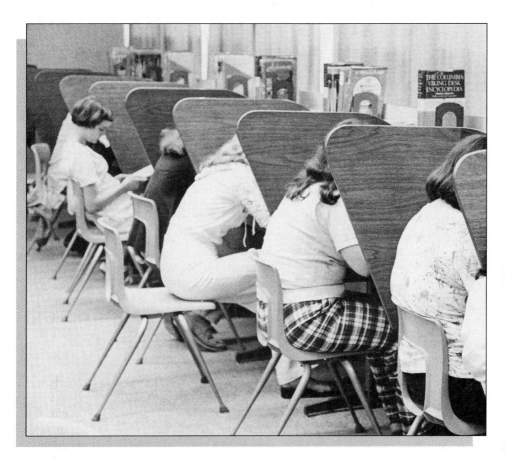

Independent learning provides an opportunity for students to work at their own pace.

learning facilitator, stimulator, and informational resource. The primary role of the teacher in a PSI classroom is to provide individual instruction. Whole class presentations are usually informational rather than an opportunity for instruction (Guskey, 1985). Optimally, the teacher sets goals and, with individual students, establishes the criteria and means for evaluating each student's learning. The student's role is crucial; the student must exercise initiative and responsibility. The student reports progress to the teacher at prescribed, regular intervals and establishes his/her own learning pace.

Resources

Instructional materials for PSI vary greatly. They include teacher-written learning packets, sophisticated programmed teaching kits, the spectrum of reading machines, and computer-programmed or assisted instruction. Ideally, a PSI classroom would resemble a mini instructional media center more than a classroom.

Ask Yourself:
A Checklist for Critical Thinkers

A critical thinker has the ability to deal reasonably and reflectively with questions about beliefs or actions. How do you rate yourself as a critical thinker on the following criteria?

- Clearly states the thesis or question.

- Seeks reasons.

- Is well informed.

- Uses and refers to credible sources.

- Takes the total context/culture into account.

- Keeps focused on the primary issue.

- Looks for alternatives.

- Is sensitive to the feelings, level of knowledge, and degree of sophistication of others.

- Is open-minded, i.e., considers the positions of others.

- Takes a position when the evidence and reasons are sufficient to do so.

- Seeks as much precision as the subject permits.

- Deals in an orderly manner with the parts of a complex whole.

Which areas gave you the most concern? What could you do to improve your critical thinking skills? How would you model critical thinking in the classroom? How would you help your students become critical thinkers?

Potential Problems

Evaluation under most forms of PSI bears little resemblance to traditional forms of evaluation because the focus of instruction is on how well the students use the tools of learning—reading, writing, and speaking—to solve problems and think critically. The PSI setting may provide reward systems for purposes of providing motivation, feedback, and discipline (Womack, 1989).

A classroom operating exclusively under a PSI format is a rarity. One of the largest potential problems with the PSI format is that, once established, the system can run so smoothly that teachers feel they have nothing to do and so end up behind their desks. Rightfully, under this mode of instruction, the teacher is liberated to work individually with students. Another potential problem is that administrators accustomed to the more traditional teacher-centered forms of instruction have difficulty evaluating PSI instruction and the teacher using the methodology. A final problem is how to orient students effectively so that they can work independently and sustain their self-motivation.

Technology and Instruction

Recent and projected technological developments provide immense opportunities to expand the instructional capacities of teachers and learning opportunities for students. (See Chapter 18 for a discussion of emerging and future technologies.) Educators and policy makers face a series of opportunities and challenges as they search for effective uses of technology in learning and instruction.

One challenge is to become informed and discriminating users of technology in the schools rather than captives of the latest fad. A second challenge is to use technology as a tool to improve learning for all students rather than for a select few who may be eligible for federal programs, have access to technology, or are considered to be gifted and talented. A further admonition is that the human element should not be displaced by technology, but rather that human relations should be enhanced by the use of technology. Finally, technological tools are only as good as the humans who have developed the software. Installation of instructional technology in a school is expensive in terms of both dollars and staff time; therefore, decisions to acquire this technology should be made only after sufficient time has been provided for study and analysis (Apple, 1988).

As a new teacher, what kinds of training and experiences will you need to make effective use of technology in the classroom?

Technology has the potential for expanding curricular opportunities and affecting classrooms in a variety of ways. Various national efforts have been made to expand the use of technology. Instructional television via satellite transmission brings outstanding instructors into classrooms in isolated areas. Both teachers and students have the opportunity to learn through this activity. Media such as videotapes may be used repeatedly to enhance the understanding of complex concepts. Significant advancements have been made in information retrieval systems through telephone linkages between computers. For example, a teacher can access research information (e.g., the ERIC system) related to the improvement of teaching and learning.

Classroom Uses of Computers

Progress has been made in providing students with access to computers. Teachers are using them in a variety of ways: for drill and practice, tutorial programs, and simulation (Streibel, 1988).

Drill and Practice

The assumptions for *drill and practice* are that students have already received basic instruction and that the computer can be used for mastery learning. Students learn at different rates, and the computer provides the opportunity for individualized, self-paced learning.

Tutorial Programs

Tutorial programs are an extension of drill and practice in that they are interactive with the student. Though limited by the instructions used in the program, tutorial programs provide an artificial person who responds to the student. The goal is to maximize the student's educational performance. One of the limitations is that typical tutorial programs assume an orderly progression in learning and have difficulty with the quantum leaps and reflective thinking of some students.

Simulation

Simulation provides the student with the potential to maximize the computer's capabilities and expand learning opportunities. Rather than being restricted by programs prepared by others, the student writes the instructions and uses the computer to solve problems. The student becomes involved in the orderly progression of steps involved in addressing a problem. A major benefit of simulation is that efforts to address problems are made in a safe and artificial setting. The results of the simulation can then be used in determining the options to be considered in real-life situations.

Issues and Trends in Curriculum and Instruction

Schools are being confronted with multiple social and educational expectations as they prepare students for the twenty-first century. A variety of issues and trends relating to curriculum and instruction in the schools are listed in Figure 16.8 and discussed below.

Grouping of Students

For decades, one of the debates in education has been whether students with similar abilities and interests should be grouped together in classes (i.e., homogeneous grouping) or whether students with differing abilities and interests should be in the same class (i.e., heterogeneous grouping). Criticisms of homogeneous grouping of similar students have been that this arrangement promotes an attitude of elitism, that it deprives students of the opportunity to be in classes with students of differing abilities and interests, and that this arrangement does not provide students with the interactions they will face in real-world situations.

How does grouping differ from individualized or small group instruction?

Concerns about heterogeneous grouping of students with different abilities and interests include the abilities of teachers to identify and address the individual needs and interests of students, the range of materials and supplies required in each classroom to meet the instructional needs of a diverse group

---

Figure 16.8: Issues in Curriculum and Instruction

- Should all students be educated together? Or should students with similar interests and talents be educated separately?

- Are students (and the general population of our country) culturally illiterate?

- How can schools make the best use of new technological developments?

- Should there be national performance standards for students?

- How can we best educate students for a future in which state and national interests are secondary to global interests?

of students, and the loss of efficiency in classroom instruction because of the various needs and interests of students. However, students can benefit from being in classes in which their peers are progressing at different rates and have diverse abilities and interests.

Even though questions of efficiency have been raised, experiences with mainstreaming special education students into regular classes suggest that students do benefit from interacting with those who are different. If one function of schooling is to prepare students for life, heterogeneous grouping of students with different abilities and interests appears to achieve this goal.

Cultural Literacy

Recently, considerable attention has been focused on defining *cultural literacy* and agreeing on what evidence should be used to indicate that a person is culturally literate. Hirsch (1987) startled the nation in the 1980s with his book *Cultural Literacy: What Every American Needs to Know*. The book contained a list of about 5,000 items that Hirsch maintained the literate American should know. The question is to what extent schools should be responsible for providing students with what some feel are the essentials of cultural literacy.

Even though few questions were raised about the importance of Hirsch's individual items, questions have been raised about the accuracy and validity of his general assertions about cultural literacy and the potential implications for schooling and teaching. For example, is the ability to memorize, recall, and state facts or define terms sufficient evidence of a learned or culturally literate person, or should a person also demonstrate the capacity to apply facts and concepts in addressing real-life problems (Estes, Gutman, & Harrison, 1988)?

Hirsch responded to these questions by indicating that high literacy was a key to educational progress, and that high literacy enabled students to assimilate new information through the use of analogies. In the absence of a national curriculum, cultural literacy becomes even more important to Americans' ability to share knowledge (Hirsch, 1988). A counter position is that schools should strive for a more effective integration of knowledge and process so that students can engage in thoughtful behavior. The goal, then, is not only for students to be culturally literate but also to be culturally thoughtful (Worsham, 1988).

The discussion about cultural literacy again raises the issue of whether the appropriate role of schools is to transmit the culture's accumulated values and knowledge or to foster reflective thinking, or both. Attempting to do both may pose problems if the process of reflective thinking leads to serious challenges of some of the basic premises of the culture.

Impact of Technological Developments

Given the pace at which knowledge about information processing and retrieval is expanding, the challenge for both teachers and students will not be to learn specific subject content, but to learn how to learn. By the time schools identify what technical information or skills to teach, the content often is obsolete. When confronted with a problem in the technological age, the stu-

What skills will the teacher need to make the most effective use of technology in the classroom?

Computers can be a valuable tool in the teaching/learning process.

dent will not be expected to recall from memory the necessary information; rather, the student will secure the desired information by utilizing various data retrieval systems. Instead of teaching students what they will need to know in life, the challenge for the schools will be to help students become (1) literate in a variety of media, (2) more objective and critical consumers of information, and (3) able to draw upon a diverse knowledge base to solve problems (Buckley, 1989).

Technology has the potential of linking content in different subject matter areas so that teachers and students can understand interrelationships. By using tools and information from multiple fields, attention can be focused on finding solutions for real-world problems rather than on subjects and disciplines, which has been the traditional emphasis (Dede, 1989).

National Goals and Standards

In the 1990s, increased attention is being given to national goals and standards for education. The desire to improve the schools because of declining student performance, increased international competition, and low overall quality of the schools has become so great that less importance is being given to traditional anxieties about the emergence of a national curriculum and the potential loss of local control over schools.

Questions often are raised about the appropriateness of national goals and standards for public elementary and secondary education. The concept of national goals and standards appears to conflict with the traditional position that education is a local function, state responsibility, and national concern. However, various writers have emphasized that the goals and standards are "national" in terms of being important to the nation's citizens rather than "federal" in terms of being a responsibility of the federal government.

Advocates for national goals and standards contend that students are not learning enough to get and keep good jobs or to be good citizens, that education is more than the memorizing of facts, and that a national curriculum already exists in the form of nationally marketed textbooks (Brandt, 1988; Chira, 1989). The intent of the national goals movement is to develop a national consensus about the core of knowledge and skills that a high school graduate should possess (Finn, 1989). In most of the discussions, goals are generally aspirational statements; standards provide the measures that can be used to determine the extent to which the schools have attained the goals.

What impact might national educational goals have on the role of the teacher in the classroom?

Phi Delta Kappa Gallup Poll

In the 1989 Phi Delta Kappa Gallup Poll national survey, strong support was expressed for national standards and goals for public schools; 70% of the respondents favored national goals, a national testing program, and a national curriculum. Supporters of national goals indicated that they had considerable confidence in having professional educators establish the national goals (Elam & Gallup, 1989). This annual poll is a rich resource of information about the public's opinions concerning the schools.

National Education Association

The National Education Association (NEA) has viewed national educational goals from a different dimension (Geiger, 1989). Rather than focusing on such output goals as test performance, citizenship, postschool employment, mathematical skills, expository writing, and analytical skills, the NEA has stressed the importance of every child being well fed and emotionally, intellectually, and socially ready to learn.

In terms of specific programs, the NEA has proposed expansion of prenatal care, nutritional support, health screening, and child care programs. The contention is that current programs in these areas reach only a small proportion of the children who need assistance.

Other goals call for a reduction in the dropout rate and an end to adult illiteracy. More general goals call for school programs and funding practices that ensure all students access to a quality education. In contrast to the previously discussed perspective on national output goals, the NEA goals also include specific programs and services to which students should have access if they and the schools are to be held accountable for reaching the standards associated with the national output goals.

National Governors Association

The adoption of national education goals by the president and the nation's governors is the first time that political leaders have made a comprehensive formal statement about goals for the public schools. As listed in Chapter 5, the goals focus on readiness for school, retention of students in school, student performance, good citizenship, adult literacy, and a safe, drug-free environment for teaching and learning. Lacking the authority to take formal action, the National Governors Association adopted a resolution calling for state-by-state discussion of these goals (National Governors Association, 1990).

Governors, other state officials, and the general public have expressed support for national goals and standards (Chira, 1989). However, responsibility for identifying solutions and sources of funding resides with state and local school officials, and responsibility for adopting and implementing policies in the operation of schools resides with the 16,000 local school boards.

Assessment of National Goals

One critical concern with national goals and related educational outcomes is the method of assessment. Much of the discussion focuses on observable behaviors and levels of student performance. Many public policy figures appear to have great confidence in the ability of tests to measure the desired outcomes. However, some members of the educational community have expressed reservations about the capacity of available tests to support the emphasis on higher order thinking skills in the curriculum (Resnick & Klopfer, 1989).

Nickerson (1989) identified a series of issues about the capacity of tests and the uses of test results. One is the extent to which higher order cognitive ability can be measured by current testing technologies. A related issue is the degree to which tests can indicate that the student understands the concepts, principles, relationships, and processes in a course of study. Another issue is whether tests can determine the extent to which an individual is capable of applying knowledge in addressing problems outside the classroom. The capacity of the testing process can be enhanced through greater utilization of technology-based testing procedures, but the development costs for the tests and the procedures will be high. The challenge for educational policy makers may be to increase the use of testing and evaluation results in instructional decision making without sacrificing local community values and interests.

Educational Governance

The attention given to national goals and standards suggests rather dramatic changes in the governance of education. Local school boards have lost some of their traditional power as states have assumed an increasing level of responsibility for education in the areas of finance, regulations, student performance, requirements, and procedures. Now, the national goals and standards issue suggests that states will find their educational efforts viewed in terms of national goals and objectives. Also, the recognized linkages between education and economic productivity and competitiveness suggest that national concerns about the educational performance of America's youth require some type of national solution (Finn, 1989).

Reservations about National Goals

There are four general reservations about the potential impact of national goals and standards (Chira, 1989):

1. What level of government will pay for the cost of developing the types of tests needed to assess the desired outcomes?

2. What role will those most directly involved in education—teachers and local school officials—have in setting goals and standards?

3. To what extent will the diversity among states be recognized and accommodated in the national goals and objectives?

4. Will politicians and the public be willing to provide teachers and administrators with the funds and administrative flexibility to respond to these increased expectations?

Global Education

As our nation plans for the twenty-first century, we no longer have the luxury of feeling isolated from other nations. International economic competition, international politics, and the interaction among peoples and nations emphasize the importance of students being informed about the world.

The National Council for the Social Studies (Kneip, 1986) has proposed that students should study the following essential areas:

1. Human values, including those that are common across groups and those that differ among groups

2. Global economic, political, ecological, and technical systems

3. Global issues and problems

4. Global history

Global issues change over time with the expansion of knowledge, changes in political alignments, and advancements in transportation and communication. Rather than consisting of a set of accepted premises, instruction should emphasize different points of view, comparisons of different times, geographical areas, and cultures, and the possible impact of alternative actions. A critical consideration in this area is to balance the presentation of different frames of reference and points of view (Global Education, 1987).

Different approaches may be used in selecting materials and working with students in these areas. Issues and concepts often overlap. Continuing attention needs to be given to refinement of materials and processes of instruction. Few would question the critical importance of students having a broader perspective of the world, but the wide differences in the values of different cultures present a challenge for the teacher in organizing and presenting materials (Vocke, 1988).

These issues and trends illustrate the range of social and technological forces that influence curricular choices. The challenge for professional educators and educational policy makers is to develop a rational system for reviewing curricular options and making choices about what is to be taught.

Summary

The overall goal of education, free public instruction for all, is attained through the selection of educational goals and the implementation of instructional objectives for meeting the goals. These goals and objectives help teachers to determine how to organize for instruction. Teachers may use a variety of organizational options as they work with students and often vary the strategies to recognize differences in students. Technology has the potential to provide teachers and students with opportunities to increase instruction capacity, but effective utilization of technology requires knowledgeable implementation.

Schools are being confronted with a variety of issues and trends as they prepare students for the future. The grouping of students, the role of schools in teaching cultural literacy, changes caused by advances in technology, the possibility of a national curriculum, and global education are all factors that require careful consideration. The challenge is to develop a system for reviewing options for future education.

In the next chapter, the focus is on effective schools and teachers. The principal concern is how schools and teachers can organize to serve an increasingly diverse and multicultural pupil population.

Key Terms

Bloom's Taxonomy of Educational
   Objectives
Cooperative learning
Critical thinking
Cultural literacy
Demonstration instruction
Drill and practice
Educational goals
Educational objectives

Expository instruction
Group instruction
Independent learning
Individualized instruction
Inquiry instruction
Mastery learning
Reflective thinking
Simulation
Tutorial programs

Discussion Questions

1. What are the most important goals of American public education?

2. How will a well-designed system of goals, objectives, and outcomes affect the ways in which a teacher organizes instruction and works with students?

3. How does the role of the teacher change in the various ways in which schools and classrooms may be organized for instruction?

4. How can the teacher determine if certain strategies would be more appropriate with particular subjects or groups of students?

5. How has technology affected the role of the teacher? How can the teacher use technology to improve instruction and student performance?

6. How will the interest in national goals and standards for American education affect the daily activities of teachers in the classroom?

References

Adler M. (1984). *The Paideia program.* New York: Macmillan.

Apple, M W. (1988). Teaching and technology: The hidden effects of computers on teachers and students. In L. E. Beyer and M. W. Apple (Eds.), *The curriculum: Problems, politics, and possibilities* (pp. 289–311). Albany, NY: State University of New York Press.

Barone, T. (1989). Ways of being at-risk: The case of Billy Charles Barnett. *Phi Delta Kappan, 71,* 147–151.

Bloom, B. (1956). *Taxonomy of educational objectives 1: Cognitive domain.* New York: David McKay.

Brandt, R. (1988). On the high school curriculum. *Educational Leadership, 46*(1), 4–9.

Brandt, R. (1989). On cooperative learning: A conversation with Spencer Kagan. *Educational leadership, 47*(4), 8–11.

Brookover, W. (1980). *Measuring and attaining the goals of education.* Alexandria, VA: Association for Supervision and Curriculum Development (ASCD) Committee on Research and Theory.

Buckley, B. (1989). A good question: What curriculum for the information age? *Educational Researcher, 18*(1), 46.

Burns, R. (1977). *New approaches to behavioral objectives.* Dubuque, IA: Wm. C. Brown.

Chira, S. (December 26, 1989). National standards for schools gain. *The New York Times National,* 10.

Cuban, L. (1989). The "at-risk" label and the problem of school reform. *Phi Delta Kappan, 70,* 780–784.

Dede, C. (1989). The evolution of information technology: Implications for curriculum. *Educational Leadership, 47*(1), 23–26.

Duke, D. L. (1984). *Teaching: The imperiled profession.* Albany, NY: State University of New York.

Elam, S., & Gallup, A. (1989). The 21st annual Gallup Poll of the public's attitudes toward the public schools. *Phi Delta Kappan, 71*(1), 41–57.

Ellis, A. K., Mackey, J. A., & Glenn, A. D. (1988). *The school curriculum.* Boston, MA: Allyn and Bacon.

Estes, T., Gutman, C. J., & Harrison, E. K. (1988). Cultural literacy: What every educator needs to know? *Educational Leadership, 46*(1), 14–17.

Finn, C. (1989). National standards for American education: A symposium. *Teachers College Record, 91*(1), 3–29.

Geiger, K. (December 25–31, 1989). An immodest proposal. *The Washington Post National Weekly Edition*, 22.

Global Education: In bounds or out? (1987). *Social Education*, 51, 342–349.

Guskey, T. (1985). *Implementing mastery learning*. Belmont, CA: Wadsworth Publishing Co.

Hirsch, E. D. (1987). *Cultural literacy: What every American needs to know*. Boston, MA: Houghton Mifflin.

Hirsch, E. D. (1988). Hirsch responds: The best answer to a caricature is a practical program. *Educational Leadership*, 46(1), 18–19.

Kneip, W. (1986). Defining global education by its content. *Social Education*, 50(6), 437–446.

Kourilsky, M., & Quaranta, L. (1987). *Effective teaching: Principles and practice*. Glenview, IL: Scott, Foresman.

Lipman, M. (1988). Critical thinking—What can it be? *Educational Leadership*, 46(1), 38–43.

Massialas, B., & Zevin, J. (1983). *Teaching creatively: Learning through discovery*. Malabar, FL: Robert E. Krieger.

National Governors Association. (1990). *National education goals*. Washington, DC: National Governors Association.

Nickerson, R. (1989). New directions in educational assessment. *Educational Researcher*, 18(9), 3–7.

Resnick, L., & Klopfer, L. (1989). Toward the thinking curriculum: Concluding remarks. In *Toward the thinking curriculum: Current cognitive research*. 1989 Yearbook of the Association for Curriculum Development. Alexandria, VA: ACD.

Skinner, B. (1965). Why teachers fail. *Saturday Review*, 67, 101.

Slavin, R. (1989a). Here to stay—or gone tomorrow? *Educational Leadership*, 47(4), 3.

Slavin, R. (1989b). Research on cooperative learning: Consensus and controversy. *Educational Leadership*, 47(4), 52–54.

Streibel, M. (1988). A critical analysis of three approaches to the use of computers in education. In L. E. Beyer & M. W. Apple (Eds.), *The curriculum: Problems, politics, and possibilities* (pp. 259–288). Albany, NY: State University of New York Press.

Tom, A. (1984). *Teaching as a moral craft*. New York: Longman.

Vocke, D. (1988). Those varying perspectives on global education. *The Social Studies*, 18–20.

Womack, S. (1989). Mode of instruction. *The Clearing House*, 62, 205–210.

Worsham, T. (1988). From cultural literacy to cultural thoughtfulness. *Educational Leadership*, 46(1), 20–21.

Chapter 17
Effective Schools and Teachers

The schools will be little better and little worse than the aspirations and expectations of the citizens in the local community.

Lyons & McDonough, 1990

During a work session of the Pineville School Board, one of the board members asked how they could improve their schools. After board members spent an hour criticizing current conditions, Donna Knight, an assistant superintendent, volunteered to review the research on how to improve schools and make a presentation at the next meeting of the school board. At that meeting, Dr. Knight presented a report on research findings about the characteristics of schools in which students were achieving higher than expected, student attendance was up, student disciplinary problems were down, and teachers were excited about the school.

The school board directed the superintendent to work with central office staff and building principals to develop a plan for implementing the research findings in one elementary school in the district. As the plan was being developed, it be-came evident that the principal and teachers in the school were the keys to having an effective school; they would have to implement any plan. The principal worked with the school staff in developing a plan that included a focus on the basic skills, the standards for student success, and changes needed in the school to bring about the desired goals. Contacts were made with local businesses and organizations to seek their assistance in improving the school.

Is this approach consistent with the literature and research about school improvement? What should be the criteria for determining if a school is effective? What steps need to be taken to ensure that the school's actions are consistent with district procedures and goals? How are these actions related to the concepts of teacher empowerment and school-site decision making?

The school reform movement of the 1980s and the general concern about declining student performance contributed to school boards such as Pineville's becoming increasingly interested in ways to make schools more effective. School board members and the general public are raising their expectations for the schools. As citizens become more knowledgeable about educational research, the expectations of the schools likely will rise. The material in this chapter addresses some of the basic issues and concerns about ways to improve the effectiveness of schools. After reading and discussing this chapter, you should be able to:

- Describe the characteristics of effective schools.

- Discuss the criticisms of the effective schools concept.

- Identify characteristics of effective teachers and principals.

- Discuss the conflicts that emerge as teachers seek to balance the attention they give to managerial activities with the time needed for instructional strategies.

- Identify the various ways that teachers and students can interact to enhance the teaching/learning process.

- Describe the current status of business–education partnerships.

Impact of Schools on Student Learning

For more than 25 years, experts have wondered whether schools or family background have the greater effect on student achievement. Current doubts concerning the contributions of schools can be traced to the *Equality of Educational Opportunity Report,* popularly referred to as the Coleman Report (discussed in Chapter 8). The study found a strong association between family background and pupil performance. The findings of the Coleman Report were overgeneralized; they were interpreted as indicating that schools can do little to overcome the educational disadvantages produced by minority group status and poverty. The findings also resulted in questioning the effect on student learning of factors such as:

- facilities

- laboratories

- special personnel

- curricular offerings

- instructional materials (Cohen, 1982).

The response of the educational research community to the criticisms of the schools was to direct multiple research efforts toward providing evidence to show that schools can make a difference. Rather than focusing research on the effects of the factors listed above, Edmonds (1982) studied a series of schools and found that positive changes in student performance were associated with:

- leadership in the school

- positive climate and working conditions

- strong focus for the school

- high expectations from students and teachers

- periodic assessment

Additional research confirmed Edmonds's findings that schools can be organized to enhance instructional effectiveness (Cohen, 1982). This research found the critical factors leading to effective schools to be:

- working conditions that support the efforts of teachers to address the specific problems of their students

- positive teacher expectations about students

- an environment that is conducive to teaching and learning

Teachers in schools that meet the effective schools criteria discussed later in this chapter find that the frustrations of teaching are balanced by the rewards. Principals of these schools devote their energies to protecting teachers' time so that teachers can devote their efforts to improving student learning, monitoring academic progress, and working with fellow teachers to improve the learning environment (Rosenholtz, 1985). Specific findings about effective schools, their teachers, and their principals are discussed in the following sections.

Effective Schools

Considerable research efforts in the 1980s were devoted to a search for the characteristics of an effective school. In this context, *school effectiveness* refers to the level at which students are performing in the basic skills. Although this search ended successfully with the identification of some characteristics of effective schools, the literature on effective schools also met with criticism. One additional outcome was that the *culture of the school* (i.e., the values, beliefs, and interactions of the faculty and staff) were associated with student achievement.

Characteristics of Effective Schools

Starting with the work of Ron Edmonds (1979), a number of studies have reexamined the results of the Coleman Report and found differences in effectiveness among schools. The findings are summarized in Figure 17.1 and are discussed in the following sections.

Strong Administrative Leadership

Schools appear to be most effective when the principal and the instructional staff:

- Are in agreement about what they are doing.

- Believe that they can accomplish their objectives.

- Are committed to providing an environment in which they can accomplish the task.

- Show a willingness to monitor and assess their effectiveness and adjust their performance based on information.

This type of cohesiveness takes place when the school principal shows strong administrative leadership.

Another dimension of strong administrative leadership might be called power sharing. Many effective schools have developed ways to increase administrator/teacher participation in decision making about such matters as instructional materials, techniques, and policies. By participating in the management of the school, the teacher implies acceptance of the school's goals and willingness to participate in the decision-making process about the future of the school. Throughout the nation, many school districts have decentralized their management process and initiated school-site decision making to provide for greater teacher involvement and participation in decisions about the daily

What kinds of decisions would you like to be able to make in the school in which you will be teaching?

Figure 17.1: Characteristics of an Effective School

Strong administrative leadership
- Principal has a clear vision about the desired direction for the school.
- Principal has a commitment to the improvement of instruction.

Safe and orderly environment
- Working conditions support the efforts of teachers to address specific problems of their students.
- Environment is conducive to teaching and learning.

Emphasis on instruction in the basic skills
- Commitment to the basic skills as instructional goals.
- Basic skills are the foundation for higher order thinking skills.

High teacher expectations of students
- Teachers set high performance standards for students.
- Teachers use clear and appropriate rewards to recognize student work.

Monitoring and reporting student performance
- Systematic assessment of student progress.
- Curriculum alignment.
- Curriculum, desired outcomes, and the assessment activities all match.

Necessary resources to meet objectives
- Sufficient personnel and materials.
- Sufficient time for instructional planning, staff development, and adapting new innovations.
- Opportunities provided for professional growth.

operation of schools. This is being done, for example, in Dade County, Florida; Hammond, Indiana; Adams County, Colorado; and Santa Fe, New Mexico.

Safe and Orderly Environment

Schools with an orderly and safe environment provide the setting in which teachers and students can devote their time and energies to teaching and learning the basic skills. Teachers and students should not be diverted from their primary mission by disruptions or outside interference. One of the functions of the principal is to ensure the safety of the school, but the principal is only one person. Teachers and students also have responsibilities in maintaining a safe and orderly school environment.

Emphasis on Basic Skills

Research findings at both the classroom and the school level support the importance of commitment to basic skills as instructional goals. The assumption is that students must master the basic skills before they can succeed with higher order thinking skills or be successful at higher levels of education. The basic skills are the foundation that enables students to be more effective in abstract learning and critical thinking and to become discriminating consumers of knowledge and information.

High Expectations of Students

Successful instruction also is related to the beliefs of teachers that they and their students can be successful. With this attitude, a climate is provided in which success rather than failure becomes the expectation. This requires teachers to be sensitive to students' individual differences and the various teaching approaches and materials that are most effective with different students.

Monitoring and Reporting of Student Progress

Monitoring and reporting student progress involves several elements. First, the systematic assessment of students allows teachers to gauge their success in working with students and gives students critical information about their progress.

A second consideration related to student assessment is *curriculum alignment,* the effort to ensure that what is assessed during the evaluation was both planned and taught. Significant amounts of classroom time are consumed by the administration of standardized tests to students. For these assessment activities to be relevant, either of two conditions should be met:

1. The test has been created to assess the curriculum that has been selected to produce the desired outcomes.

2. The curriculum has been created to teach the things on the test that have been selected to assess attainment of the desired outcomes. (Berliner, 1985)

The critical element in both of these statements is that what is tested should have been taught. Teachers and administrators of effective schools make every effort to ensure that curriculum, desired outcomes, and assessment activities are carefully matched.

Necessary Resources

Resources also are critical considerations for effective schools. The number of personnel in the school must be sufficient to provide teachers with time for staff development and to plan new activities. Rather than having all of their time scheduled for necessary activities, teachers need some *slack time* during which they have some independence. They must have opportunities to experiment and invent or adapt innovations, which is not possible in settings where efficiency has a higher priority than flexibility and creativity.

What conditions in a school have encouraged you to increase your performance as a student?

Many of the characteristics of effective schools are supported by conventional wisdom and experience, but the movement is not without its critics. In fact, several of the basic assumptions have been questioned by respected researchers.

Criticisms of the Effective Schools Concept

Criticisms of the concept of effective schools focus on a variety of issues, including basic skills, role of the principal, assessment measures, generalizability of research findings, and culture of the school. These major points are summarized in Figure 17.2 and discussed below.

Narrow Focus of the Basic Skills

One concern has been that the effective schools concept has focused on a single dimension of school effectiveness—basic skills outcomes (Rowan, 1983). The contention is that the basic skills focus is too narrow and that other factors or conditions also should be considered in measuring school effectiveness. These factors include administrative effectiveness, social progress of students, and evidence of emotional stability of students (Tikunoff et al., 1981). Measures of effectiveness that focus solely on instruction do not capture these additional dimensions.

Increased Supervisory Duties for Principals

Questions also have been raised about the implications of the principal devoting increasing amounts of time to supervising classroom instruction. Studies indicate that principals spend major portions of their day on noninstructional tasks that are viewed as essential for successful school operation (Dwyer et al., 1982). If the principal changes behaviors and devotes major portions of time to working with teachers to improve classroom instruction,

What kinds of support and assistance would you expect from the building principal?

- Who will assume the noninstructional tasks?

- What will be the consequences of this shift in administrative attention?

The effectiveness of classroom instruction depends on the quality of administrative tasks performed as well as instructional support. Reducing the emphasis on one to increase the attention to the other might not be productive.

Figure 17.2: Criticisms of the Effective Schools Concept

- The focus of the effective schools concept has been on only one dimension— student test performance.

- Adding supervisory duties would decrease the effectiveness of the principal's performance of administrative tasks.

- Current testing programs prevent low-income schools from being classified as "effective."

- The degree to which research findings can be generalized is unknown.

- The emphasis placed on leadership fails to recognize the influence of the culture of the school on student performance.

Effective schools are stimulating environments in which students are active learners.

Assessment Measures for Effectiveness

Concerns also have been expressed about the measures used to assess instructional effectiveness. Teachers and principals are confronted with a range of choices. Options include the following:

- Measuring student performance on normed tests.

- Comparing trends in student performance over a period of years.

- Analyzing scores for groups of students.

- Developing predicted scores that will indicate whether average achievement is above or below what can be expected in terms of the school's demographic composition.

Measuring student performance on normed tests may appear to be a logical choice, but this approach has certain limitations. Schools with high percentages of students from low socioeconomic backgrounds likely will have difficulty attaining "effective" levels of achievement when compared with national norms. Similar concerns are related to assessing effectiveness on the basis of trends in student performance over a period of years. If the composition of the student body is different from that used in the development of the national norms, these assessment approaches may not be appropriate. As an alternative, scores for groups of students can be predicted based on the school's demographic composition. Students can be considered to be performing better than predicted even when their actual scores are below average.

Generalizability of Research Findings

Another criticism addresses the degree to which research findings can be generalized. What works in one community may not work in another. In addition, the relationships between cause and effect are not known. For example, does the effective principal create an effective school, or does the effective school become a positive influence on the performance of the principal (Murphy, n.d.)?

Importance of the Culture of the School

Perhaps the most comprehensive criticism of the effective schools movement has been the failure to recognize the importance of the entire culture of the school in creating an effective school; it cannot be created through leadership alone. The culture of the school, in turn, is a result of both content and process. Content refers to the information in the curriculum as well as the structure, norms, values, and instructional techniques used in the school. Process refers to the political and social relationships that develop in a school.

In terms of the potential importance to school improvement, the culture of the school can be influential in different ways. It can be a supportive environment in which teachers cooperate and assist each other or a competitive environment in which interaction and cooperative activities are limited to those that are required. School cultures also differ in the extent to which they are rule-oriented or laissez-faire. Acceptance of the premise that the culture of the school is influential assumes that human attitudes and behaviors and the administrative structure influence the extent to which the school is effective (Purkey & Smith, 1982).

How would you describe the culture of your high school? How did it differ from the culture of your elementary school?

The culture of the school can be improved by changing the attitudes and behaviors of the school staff as well as changing the school's organization and norms. Leadership is considered to be important, but consensus is considered to be more important than overt control. Positive changes are more likely to continue if they have become part of the culture of the school and its value system rather than being imposed by administrative edict. Under the culture of the school premise, the effective school is distinguished by the ways in which its structure, process, values, and norms channel staff and students toward successful teaching and learning (Purkey & Smith, 1982).

Differences in the underlying assumptions about the characteristics of effective schools appear to be minor, but opinions differ about how to achieve the goal. Some assume that schools can be changed from the top down. Others view the school as a social system in which incremental progress is made toward improvement in all schools rather than in a few with outstanding leaders or special conditions.

Ask Yourself:
How Will Adoption of the Effective Schools
Concept Affect You as a Teacher?

1. Will the strong emphasis on teaching basic skills result in a neglect of higher order thinking skills?

2. As a teacher in a school implementing the effective school concepts, do you feel that student performance on nationally standardized tests is an adequate indicator of how well the school, or the teacher, is doing?

3. As a new teacher, what kinds of assistance would you expect from the building principal? How can the principal help you to be a good teacher? Should the principal be an expert in all subject matter areas in the school?

4. What impact do my expectations as a teacher have on student learning? How will I respond when students are unable to keep pace with their peers?

5. How do the premises of the effective schools research affect my role as a teacher? Will I lose my right to exercise academic freedom? Will teachers be permitted to adapt the curriculum to the needs of their students?

The effective schools movement was a major force in education during the 1980s. Supporters of the movement were able to provide new hope for the capacity of the schools to educate disadvantaged youth. Even though various researchers raised serious questions about some of the movement's claims, the basic assumptions continued to receive support. The importance of having strong building-level leadership and educational standards with accountability were still recognized as important. Perhaps most critical was acceptance of the premise that schools can make a difference in the future of the disadvantaged. Even though many contended that education is more than the mastery of the basic skills, the effective schools movement has brought renewed attention to the importance of mastery of the basic skills for success in education.

Characteristics of Effective Teachers

The Northwest Regional Educational Laboratory has identified a series of characteristics and practices associated with effective schools and improved student achievement (*Effective Schooling Practices*, n.d.). Effective teacher behaviors include those listed in Figure 17.3. In general, the behaviors associated with effective teachers include time allocation, teaching styles, and the expectations that teachers have for students. Effective teachers have been characterized as those who exhibit hard work, commitment, and involvement in the school (Rosenholtz, 1985). They help students achieve the desired outcomes. The single most important factor in determining whether or not a teacher is effective is whether the curriculum being delivered to the students is logically or empirically related to the desired outcomes (Berliner, 1985).

How have your teachers exhibited the characteristics of an effective teacher?

Figure 17.3: Behaviors of Effective Teachers

- They set high standards for students, inform them of the standards, and expect the students to perform well on examinations.

- They assume responsibility for getting students ready to learn.

- They preview their lessons, give clear written and verbal instructions, and repeat key points and instructions.

- They ask clear questions to ensure that students understand the concepts.

- They select problems and other activities that are well matched to lesson content to enhance student success rates.

- They assign homework that students can complete; homework is checked and students are given quick feedback.

- They monitor student learning and hold students accountable for their academic work.

- They use assessment results to evaluate students and to diagnose problems as well as to determine if teaching methods are working.

- They reteach priority lesson content to ensure student mastery.

- They review key concepts and skills to verify and strengthen student retention.

- They follow a system of priorities in the use of class time.

- They maintain a brisk pace of instruction.

- They introduce new concepts and skills through whole group instruction.

- They review and adjust the composition of student groups, moving students when achievement levels change.

- They inform students about the high standards of behavior in the classroom.

- They stop student disruptions quickly and try to avoid disrupting the entire class.

- They focus disciplinary actions on the inappropriate behavior rather than on the penalty.

- They exhibit a concern for student interests, problems, and accomplishments.

- They define excellence by objective standards rather than by peer comparisons.

- They reward specific student achievements.

- They take steps to inform parents of student progress.

Members of the School Team

Teachers also function as part of a school team. They share desired outcomes for particular grades and courses and knowledge of the school district's curriculum goals. This information is sustained by high levels of interaction with various personnel in the school and the school district.

Teacher/Student Interactions

Effective teachers assume responsibility for informing students about the school's expectations and providing them with the opportunity to learn. To meet this responsibility, teachers must have a clear understanding about the desired outcomes of a class or a course. Outcomes may be identified in a variety of ways; the administrative staff is responsible for communicating them to teachers. The teacher's task is to ensure that students engage in classroom activities that will lead to achievement of the outcomes (Berliner, 1985).

Berliner (1985) also identified a limited number of characteristics of teacher/student interaction. One is that the good teacher spends major portions of time monitoring students by moving among and interacting with them. As students work on an individual basis, the teacher checks student progress, asks substantive questions, and gives students feedback. Students progress at different speeds, and teachers should adapt their classroom/teaching behavior to recognize the differences. In their efforts to adjust to the interests and abilities of students, effective teachers:

- Spend time discussing goals or structures of the lesson.

- Give students instructions.

- Recognize students' ability differences.

- Select the optimal pace that should be used in covering the content.

When adjustments have been made for differences in students, research suggests that the faster the pace and the more content covered, the higher the achievement of students.

Peer Support Networks

In terms of their contacts with peers, effective teachers tend to cooperate rather than compete. Teachers often work together in the development of school policies and in curriculum planning. This lets teachers feel that their views are respected and presented to those who make decisions. Rather than being independent of the administration of the school, cooperative group activities often are coordinated by the school principal (Berliner, 1985). Thus, teachers have an opportunity to influence the direction of school policies and administrative decisions.

Group Activities for Students

Consistent with teachers becoming involved in cooperative ventures is the involvement of students in group activities. In classes and related activities with goals of cooperative behavior, students are given the opportunity to work together and solve problems in creative ways. In this context, the effective teacher emphasizes cooperative behavior rather than competition. Since some of these desired student behaviors may not be easily measured by traditional

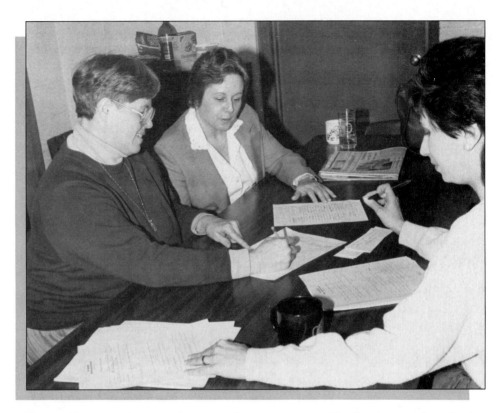

By working together, teachers can become more effective in meeting the individual needs of students.

assessment techniques, teachers need to use recorded observations to document the change.

Effective teachers engage their students in high levels of task-oriented activities (Westbrook, 1982). Research indicates that *time on task* is positively correlated with increases in student achievement. Of course, the assumption underlying the importance of time on task is that quality instruction and learning are taking place. An additional assumption is that the instruction conforms with accepted principles about effective teaching practices.

Teacher Use of Time

How many different teaching strategies have you observed in a classroom?

The practical application of the time on task concept is found in the teacher's daily activities. Typically, the teacher's activities can be divided into two distinct groups: the managerial activities that keep the classroom functioning in an orderly manner and the instructional strategies employed by the teacher. For the teacher, the challenge is to minimize the time and attention given to managerial activities and to maximize the time used to implement instructional strategies.

Student Use of Time

The extent to which classroom *instructional time* (IT) is spent on a specific teaching/learning activity can be observed and measured; research indicates that the amount of IT time is related to student learning. *Academic learning time* (ALT) refers to the amount of *engaged time* (ET) during which students work with materials or activities, which results in a high success rate (Berliner, 1985). For an illustration of the concepts of instructional time, engaged time, and academic learning time, see Figure 17.4.

The extent to which students are actively engaged in academic learning can be used as an indicator of the teacher's effectiveness. However, consideration also must be given to the ways in which time interacts with the effort put

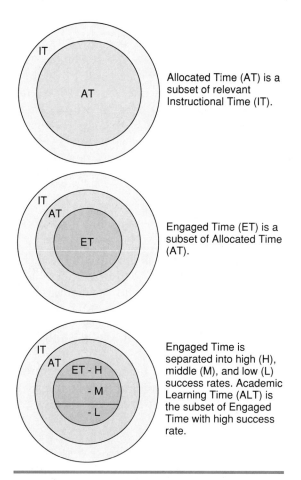

Figure 17.4: How Time Is Used in the Classroom

Allocated Time (AT) is a subset of relevant Instructional Time (IT).

Engaged Time (ET) is a subset of Allocated Time (AT).

Engaged Time is separated into high (H), middle (M), and low (L) success rates. Academic Learning Time (ALT) is the subset of Engaged Time with high success rate.

Source: Based on Berliner, D. (1985). Effective classroom teaching: The necessary but not sufficient condition for developing exemplary schools. In G. R. Austin & H. Garber (Eds.), *Research in exemplary schools* (pp. 136–138). New York: Academic Press.

forth by the student, the student's capacity to learn, and the quality of resources available to help the student learn (Levin, 1984).

For example, the level of difficulty of the task and the required cognitive style of work have an effect on the time–capacity relationship. The time–effort relationship is affected by the quality of instruction, the student's health and fatigue level, and the student's motivation. Student learning also is influenced by resources such as qualified teachers, sufficient materials, appropriate curriculum, and an environment conducive to learning. This suggests that rather than simply increasing the length of the school day, the total learning environment should be reviewed with the goal of improving situational variables and school resources. One of the principal concerns is the extent to which an increase in resources may be a better investment than an increase in time (Levin, 1984).

In-Service Training for Teacher Effectiveness

Teacher effectiveness can be increased with training. The Program for Effective Teaching (PET) (n.d.) in Arkansas provides an example of the utilization of effective schools research to improve practice. Over 300 school districts with 1,000 schools participate in the voluntary in-service program designed to increase student achievement and teacher effectiveness. The program assumes that the following strategies are related to teacher effectiveness:

- selection of learning objectives
- teaching to the objective
- maintaining the student's focus on the objective
- monitoring student progress

In the PET project, teachers are expected to develop their questioning techniques and improve their skills in helping students become more competent in the following four components of learning: motivation, reinforcement, retention, and transfer. Additional information about the four components of learning is given in Figure 17.5.

The previous discussion has focused on teacher attitudes, behaviors, and expectations. The next section reviews various characteristics of effective principals as they work with teachers to improve the instructional climate in the schools. Principals use a variety of leadership styles in their efforts to improve schools, but research indicates that similar characteristics are associated with effective principals.

Effective Principals

The leadership role of the principal in developing and maintaining an effective school is a common theme in the literature. Effective principals are self-confident and persuasive. They articulate a clear vision about the desired

Figure 17.5: Four Components of Learning

Motivation
- The intention to learn something.
- Controlled by five variables:
  - anxiety
  - success
  - knowledge of results
  - interest
  - feeling tone

Retention
- Ability to retrieve learned information from the memory bank.
- Dependent on five controllable variables:
  1. degree of original learning
  2. feeling tone
  3. practice
  4. meaning
  5. transfer

Reinforcement
- Positive—strengthens behavior because the reinforcer is desired.
- Negative—temporarily stops behavior because the reinforcer is not desired.

Transfer
- Ability to learn in one situation and then use the learning in other appropriate situations.
- Linking old learning to new learning.

---

direction for the school and they have the power to integrate their personal/professional aspirations with those of others (Nelson, 1986).

Formula for the Successful Instructional Leader

Different principals have different personal administrative behaviors, and the community and school board expectations of the principal also vary with the school and the setting. Behaviors that succeed in one school may not succeed in another. Irrespective of the setting, however, the formula in Figure 17.6 has emerged as one for the successful instructional leader (Cawelti, 1987).

Clear Goals

Having clear goals would seem to be obvious, but administrators find themselves confronted with conflicting priorities from school board members, teachers, students, and parents. Reaching consensus on goals and priorities is a significant challenge, but agreement on how to test them is even more difficult. These goals also include clear expectations in terms of rules, procedures, and penalties (Rosenholtz, 1985).

What different types of leadership behaviors have you observed in building principals?

Strong Incentives

Most school districts do not provide incentives for principals to take the risks associated with leadership for school improvement. However, lack of incentive does not relieve the principal of the inherent responsibility to strive for school improvement. The challenge for local school district policy makers is to create a climate that will encourage principals to promote school improvement activities.

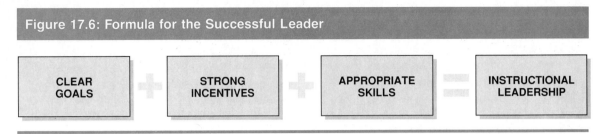

Figure 17.6: Formula for the Successful Leader

CLEAR GOALS + STRONG INCENTIVES + APPROPRIATE SKILLS = INSTRUCTIONAL LEADERSHIP

Source: Adapted from Cawelti, G. (1987). Why instructional leaders are so scarce. *Educational Leadership, 45*(1), 3.

Appropriate Skills

The concept of appropriate skills encompasses technical, conceptual, and human relations skills. Technical skills are required to meet the reporting and management requirements of the job. Conceptual skills are needed to provide the level of vision and leadership needed to work with staff for school improvement. Human relations skills are critical because successful principals must deal with a variety of persons in the school and community. The Historical Note on page 551 discusses the responsibilities of the principal.

Roles of the Principal

After reviewing the research on educational leadership as it applies to the school principal, researchers at the Northwest Regional Educational Laboratory divided the different roles of the effective principal into an interrelated set of content strands (Blum, Butler, & Olson, 1987):

- *Building a vision.* Clear statement of direction for the school and integration of that vision with the direction being pursued by the school district. (The school has a philosophy or mission statement, and this document guides the operation of the school.)

- *Creating a positive school climate and culture.* An atmosphere conducive to teaching and learning with high staff morale by promoting collegiality and cooperative decision making. (The principal uses informal conversations, working committees, and well-organized faculty meetings to create a positive school climate.)

- *Implementing the curriculum.* Establishment and maintenance of the focus on the goals and objectives with an emphasis on ensuring alignment of curricular elements with efforts to increase student achievement of the priority goals. (The principal guides the development of goals with strategies that are used in implementing the school's curriculum.)

- *Improving instruction.* Use of state-of-the-art instructional practices, strategies, and techniques in working with staff to improve teaching. (The

Historical Note:
The Effective Principal

The critical role of the principal in developing and maintaining an effective school has been recognized for decades. Almost 40 years ago, research indicated that the building principal plays a key leadership role in the efforts to provide a good learning environment for children and productive working conditions for teachers.

Then, as today, teachers evaluated the school principal's performance on a daily basis. In a 1950 study of the behaviors of effective principals, critical behaviors listed in order of frequency by teachers were:

1. The principal provides leadership for teachers by:

   a. Building teacher morale and unity.

   b. Evaluating teacher performance to upgrade and generally give help to teachers.

   c. Sharing decisions and responsibilities with teachers.

   d. Maintaining firm but constructive control of the faculty so there is adherence to school regulations.

   e. Planning and using faculty meetings to provide leadership, giving consideration to frequency, length, topics, and teacher participation.

2. The principal works with and for children by:

   a. Maintaining discipline in the school, working with parents on the solution of discipline problems, and maintaining dignity and consistency.

   b. Demonstrating a personal interest in children.

   c. Making special provisions for atypical children.

3. The principal maintains constructive relationships with the community by:

   a. Coping with parental pressures, determining the extent of the influence that parents as individuals in groups should have on school policy or routines.

   b. Encouraging and promoting parent groups or organizations.

4. The principal provides for effective administration of the school program by:

   a. Establishing administrative devices and procedures that systematize routine operations and delegate responsibility.

   b. Resolving emergencies that arise in the school, particularly those involving children, and taking steps to prevent them in the future.

5. The principal works effectively with individual parents by:

   a. Dealing with irate parents with skill and calmness.

   b. Gathering all the facts before making judgments or handling complaints from parents.

Source: Administrator's Notebook (September, 1955). Chicago: Midwest Administrative Center, University of Chicago.

principal provides staff as a group with a *continuing education program* of professional development and encourages individual staff members to have a personal professional growth program.)

● *Monitoring school performance.* Resources and procedures for determining school performance and using this information to enhance performance and improve school practices. (The principal works with teachers to develop a school report card as well as pupil report cards to provide the community and the school administration with school performance information.)

This perception of the role of the principal is very similar to the school management productivity model developed for principals in Pasco County, Florida (Snyder & Giella, 1987). As shown in Figure 17.7, the model views the role of the principal as consisting of four phases: organizational planning, staff development, program development, and assessment of school productivity. The model consists of 10 management competencies that are related to

Figure 17.7: A School Management Productivity Model

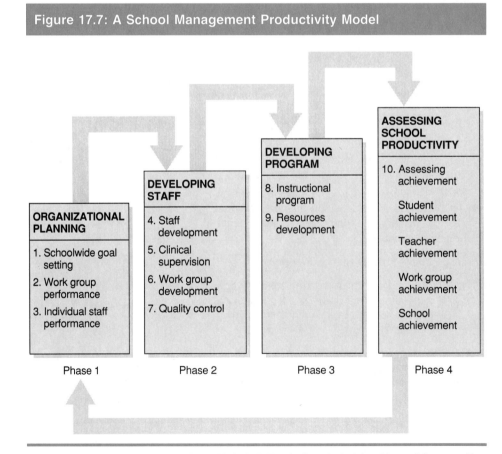

Phase 1 | Phase 2 | Phase 3 | Phase 4

ORGANIZATIONAL PLANNING

1. Schoolwide goal setting
2. Work group performance
3. Individual staff performance

DEVELOPING STAFF

4. Staff development
5. Clinical supervision
6. Work group development
7. Quality control

DEVELOPING PROGRAM

8. Instructional program
9. Resources development

ASSESSING SCHOOL PRODUCTIVITY

10. Assessing achievement

Student achievement

Teacher achievement

Work group achievement

School achievement

Source: Adapted from Snyder, K., & Giella, M. (1987). Developing principals' problem-solving capacities. *Educational Leadership, 45*(1), 39.

the management tasks needed to develop a productive school. Rather than working in isolation, the Pasco County principals are encouraged to share their experiences and forge networks to develop the concepts and skills needed for management competencies. This concept of networking has become an integral part of the continuing staff development program for principals and is especially appropriate for principals working in isolated areas (Donaldson, 1987).

One of the principal's most important roles is to serve as a buffer for teachers. In this role, the principal stands between the teacher and various outside influences such as parents and other school staff. The teacher is then free to perform the primary task—helping students learn. The proportion of time devoted to the primary responsibility (i.e., teaching) increases the likelihood of producing the desired student outcome (i.e., learning). This buffering by the principal also includes minimizing such classroom interruptions as announcements and assemblies (Rosenholtz, 1985).

The effective principal assumes a variety of roles. Providing leadership and monitoring teacher performance and student progress are major responsibilities. However, perhaps the most important and understated responsibility is to ensure that the school is a safe place. Without this security, students and teachers are unable to pursue learning without fear of interference.

Business–Education Partnerships

Renewed interest is being expressed in finding ways in which businesses and organizations can facilitate school improvement and provide additional support for schools. Presidents Reagan and Bush have both advocated stronger ties between the schools and businesses. The same theme also was expressed in the recommendations of several of the education reform reports of the 1980s. The entire report of the Business–Higher Education Forum (1983) was focused on the development of new partnerships between business and higher education with the emphasis on the education and training of America's workforce. The Education Commission of the States (1983) called for new alliances between educators and groups such as business leaders, legislators, labor leaders, parents, and colleges and universities. In the report *High School: A Report on Secondary Education in America,* Boyer (1983) chastised corporate America for its aloofness and suggested a number of ways that corporations could become involved with school improvement. Boyer's suggestions included "adopt-a-school" partnerships, tutoring programs for disadvantaged students, summer employment for teachers, support for in-service education, minigrants for innovative projects, and management and leadership training for school personnel.

What are some of the potential hazards for the schools in business–education partnerships?

Partnerships and School Improvement/Reform

Business–education partnerships have had mixed results as a strategy for school improvement and reform. Mann (1987) suggested that the major reason why business has not had a significant influence on school reform is because the business community lacks the necessary authority or expertise to carry out school reforms. However, even though business–education partnerships have not been able to bring about broad-based educational reform, businesses have helped many local public schools in practical ways. Reports indicate that more than 100,000 business–school partnerships have been formed in local schools since 1983 (Domaine, 1990). Although similar to past collaborations between schools and civic organizations, the recent partnership projects involve many more corporate representatives than in the past. Another development is the greater number of structured and long-term coordinated efforts being implemented (Mann, 1987).

Business Interest in Education

It is not surprising that businesses have become interested in improving the quality of the nation's schools. The American economy needs a well-trained and knowledgeable workforce to maintain an international competitive position. It also needs customers with sufficient income and education to be active, intelligent consumers. The unanswered question is whether business firms are sufficiently interested in education to provide the funds needed to bring about meaningful and sustained change. Some skeptical observers contend that there is no evidence of businesses' commitment to provide the re-

Businesses and schools are working together to improve learning opportunities for students.

sources needed to tackle a single national educational concern like the dropout problem, which affects about 700,000 students a year, more than the entire student population of Minnesota.

More optimistic persons believe that corporate America definitely wants to play a role in fixing what is often referred to as a "system failure" in public elementary and secondary education. These persons contend that businesses not only are willing to "tinker" with isolated projects, but also will contribute funds for the development of strategies designed to address a number of educational problems (Mann, 1987). Ultimately, the response of the business community in the next few years will define the role that the private sector will play in efforts to improve the nation's schools and will set the parameters for the business–education relationship.

Summary

Research and observations about effective schools have contributed to a change in attitude about the capacity of schools to affect the performance of disadvantaged students. Results show that effective schools have strong leadership, high standards, shared expectations, and a safe, orderly environment.

The effective schools movement has been criticized for its focus on a single dimension, student scores. Other concerns derive from the feasibility of suggestions and the interpretation of causality.

The effective teacher is an active person in the classroom who delivers a curriculum related to school outcomes. His or her students are engaged in high levels of task-oriented activities. In addition, the effective teacher is involved in the policy-making process that affects the classroom.

Good leadership at the building level is viewed as critical in the development of an effective school. Effective principals have a clear vision of the desired direction for the school, the motivation to make changes, and the skills to bring about these changes.

An added dimension to the school reform movement has been the encouragement of business partnerships. A number of projects have been initiated, but the results have been mixed and these efforts have not been a source of significant revenue for education.

Several of the developments discussed in this chapter have implications for the future developments in education that are projected in the following chapter.

Key Terms

Academic learning time (ALT)
Continuing education program
Culture of the school
Curriculum alignment
Engaged time (ET)

Instructional time (IT)
School effectiveness
Slack time
Time on task

Discussion Questions

1. How can the characteristics of an effective school be made relevant in both suburban or rural schools and in inner-city schools?

2. In what ways have the criticisms of the effective schools concept contributed to a better understanding of what makes a good school?

3. How have schools changed in their day-to-day operation and decision-making styles compared to the early days in American education discussed in Chapter 4?

4. If teachers are to become involved in school-site decision making, what types of activities are most appropriate? What additional skills will teachers need?

5. Given the importance of building-level leadership in developing an effective school, what action can teachers take when the principal fails to provide active instructional leadership for the school?

6. What specific kinds of business–education cooperative programs exist in your community? If none exist, what kinds of programs would you like to see initiated?

References

Berliner, D. (1985). Effective classroom teaching: The necessary but not sufficient condition for developing exemplary schools. In G. R. Austin & H. Garber (Eds.), *Research in exemplary schools* (pp. 127–154). New York: Academic Press.

Blum, R., Butler, J., & Olson, N. (1987). Leadership for excellence: Research-based training for principals. *Educational Leadership, 45*(1), 25–29.

Boyer, E. (Ed.). (1983). *High school: A report on secondary education in America.* New York: Harper and Row.

Business–Higher Education Forum. (1983). *America's competitive challenge: The need for a national response.* Washington, DC: Business–Higher Education Forum.

Cawelti, G. (1987). Why instructional leaders are so scarce. *Educational Leadership, 45*(1), 3.

Clark, D., Lotto, L., & Astuto, T. (1984). Effective schools and school improvement. *Educational Administration Quarterly, 20*(3), 41–86.

Cohen, M. (1982, January/February). Effective schools: Accumulating research findings. *American Education,* 13–16.

Coleman, J. S., et al. (1966). *Equality of educational opportunity.* Washington, DC: U.S. Government Printing Office.

Denham, C., & Lieberman, A. (1980). *Time to learn.* Sacramento, CA: California Commission on Teacher Preparation and Licensing.

Domaine, B. (1990). Making education work. *Fortune, 121*(12), 12–22.

Donaldson, G. (1987). The Maine approach to improving principal leadership. *Educational Leadership, 47*(1), 43–45.

Dwyer, D., et al. (1982). *The principal's role in instructional management: Five participant observation studies in action.* San Francisco, CA: Far West Laboratory for Educational Research and Development.

Edmonds, R. (1979). Some schools work and more can. *Social Policy, 9*(5), 28–32.

Edmonds, R. (1982). Programs of school improvement: An overview. *Educational Leadership, 40,* 5–11.

Education Commission of the States Task Force on Economic Growth (1983). *Action for Excellence.* Denver, CO: Education Commission of the States.

Effective schooling practices: A research synthesis (n.d.). Portland, OR: Northwest Regional Educational Laboratory.

Levin, H. (1984). About time for educational reform. *Educational Evaluation and Policy Analysis, 6*(2), 151–163.

Lyons, T. S. & McDonough, J. T. (1990). *Critique of the effective schools literature.* Unpublished manuscript. Tempe, AZ: Arizona State University.

Mann, D. (1987). Business involvement and public school improvement. *Phi Delta Kappan, 69*(123–8), 228.

Murphy, C. (n.d.). *Effective principals: Knowledge, talent, spirit of inquiry.* Research brief. San Francisco, CA: Far West Laboratory for Educational Research and Development.

Nelson, H. (1986). *The principal as an instructional leader: A research synthesis.* Springfield, IL: Illinois State Board of Education, Illinois Renewal Institute.

Peters, T., & Waterman, R. (1982). *In search of excellence: Lessons from America's best-run companies.* New York: Harper and Row.

Program for effective teaching (PET) (n.d.). Little Rock, AR: Arkansas Department of Education.

Purkey, S., & Smith, M. (1982). Too soon to cheer? Synthesis of research on effective schools. *Educational Leadership, 40,* 64–69.

Rosenholtz, S. (1985). Effective schools: Interpreting the evidence. *American Journal of Education, 93*(3), 352–388.

Rowan, B., et al. (1983). Research on effective schools: A cautionary note. *Educational Researcher, 12*(4), 24–31.

Snyder, K., & Giella, M. (1987). Developing principals' problem-solving capacities. *Educational Leadership, 45*(1), 38–41.

Tikunoff, W., et al. (1981). *Part I of the study report. Volume II: Success indicators and consequences for limited English language proficiency students in the SBIF study.* San Francisco, CA: Far West Laboratory for Educational Research and Development.

Westbrook, J. (1982). *Considering the research: What makes an effective school?* Austin, TX: Southwest Educational Development Laboratory.

Part Seven

Projections for the Future

Education for the Twenty-First Century   **Chapter 18**

Chapter 18

Education for the Twenty-First Century

All education springs from some image of the future. If the image of the future held by a society is grossly inaccurate, its educational system will betray its youth.

Alvin Toffler
Learning for Tomorrow: The Role of the Future in Education *(1974)*

It was midday on August 17, 2020. Cheryl Woo sat down at her networking console (home/work/school station) and started her interactive video system. In moments, she was connected with the Tate Gallery in London and the Louvre in Paris. She checked the computer menu and accessed a printout of the works of Rodin. In seconds she retrieved a series of holograms. Now she could put the finishing touches on the multimedia project she was completing for summer session credit from Cambridge University. Next, she accessed the Worldwide Electronic Bulletin Board and sent a message to her classmate Donna, who was finishing her summer term at the Sorbonne.

Cheryl's younger brother Todd was downstairs working with his keyboard emulator. Physically handicapped since birth, Todd had very limited mobility but was able to control his computer by merely gazing at the terminal screen.

A red light flashed across the center wall accompanied by a subliminal sound. It was their mother, Dr. Audrey Woo, who was calling while en route home from Singapore where she consulted with the World Congress of Biomedical Scientists the day before. She was calling from Concorde II to tell Cheryl and Todd that she expected to arrive home by the dinner hour. She also reminded Cheryl to reprogram SRV3, their household robot, so that dinner would be ready when she arrived.

What type of curriculum do you expect to be in place by the year 2020? What type of individual would be most suited for teaching in the year 2020? Do you anticipate that you will still be teaching in the year 2020? Why or why not?

Although we do not yet live in the world of Cheryl, Todd, and Audrey Woo, much of the technology described in the scenario is already being developed. This chapter examines these technological advances along with societal trends that may characterize the next century and their impact on education. These trends include the expansion of minority and aging populations, economic transformation, changing work force, changing family configurations and lifestyles, globalization, and technological advances. The chapter also describes a curriculum for the future in the context of these trends. The information in the chapter will enable you to:

- Discuss what schools must do to meet the needs of a growing minority student body.

- Examine the phenomenon of the aging population and its effect on the school and the educational process.

- Describe how the future economy may influence the educational enterprise.

- Discuss the changing workplace, the changing nature of work, and the worker of the future.

- Identify what schools must emphasize to accommodate the changing workplace.

- Describe how the school will be called upon to accommodate the lifestyles of the families of tomorrow.

- Explain the impact of a global society and global interdependence on the curriculum.

- Speculate on some of the technological advances of the twenty-first century and how they might influence the schools and learning.

- Indicate how the study of the future might be integrated into the existing curriculum.

Few would argue that we live in a global society that has experienced unprecedented change. Those changes have included transitions from an agricultural world to an industrial world and, during the twentieth century, to an information-oriented world. What will the world of the twenty-first century look like? What will its educational system look like? Numerous hypotheses attempt to answer these questions. One way to glimpse the education of the next millennium is to study projected societal trends. The Historical Note on page 564 discusses an early "futurist's" attempt to answer similar questions.

Societal Trends for the Twenty-First Century

Expanding Minority Populations

It is estimated that the minority population in the United States will increase at a faster rate than the general population. Approximately one in every three children will be African-American, Hispanic, or Asian-American by the turn of the century. Boyer (1988) projects that by the year 2000, approximately one-third of all students will be minorities and a sizeable number of them will be from socially and economically disadvantaged families. Furthermore, it is projected that minority population growth will take place primarily in large urban areas (Wegmann, 1980) and in southern and western states (Furner, 1984).

Boyer (1988) found that in urban high schools at least four out of 10 students are absent on any given day. According to Boyer, almost 50% of the Hispanic students who are enrolled in public schools tend to drop out before graduation. Students who live in urban settings are most vulnerable to dropping out of school. For example, during the 1987 school year in Philadelphia, the dropout rate was 38%, in Boston, 43%, and in Chicago more than 50%. Of those who managed to receive a diploma, only one-third were reading at the twelfth-grade level. Figure 18.1 describes the population changes anticipated from 1980 to 2030 by ethnicity and race. A more detailed discussion of the current minority population and its impact on education was presented in Chapters 8 and 9.

Educational Implications

To meet the demands of a growing minority student body, educational personnel will need to be well versed in a variety of forms of multicultural, multiethnic, and bilingual education. The research on mentoring and modeling behavior tells us that teachers, administrators, support personnel and school governing bodies will need to be sensitive to the problems of students from different cultural and linguistic backgrounds, and also should be representative of those diverse backgrounds themselves.

The increased concentration of minorities in urban areas will place a heavier demand on the limited resources of older, inner-city school districts.

These demands will increase as baby boomers begin to retire and to compete for federal and state revenues for medical care and other services (Footlick, 1990). There will be a need to find innovative ways to redistrict school populations as well as to seek creative financing of public education (Connecticut ASCD, 1989).

In the future, the parents of minority children will exercise unprecedented political clout and will demand high-quality education (Connecticut ASCD, 1989). Legislators and school boards will be hard pressed to respond. The increasing number of children in American schools by the turn of the century probably will necessitate significant increases in federal aid to education. Unless the public school system can do a more effective job of keeping children in school, society may face a crisis of an undereducated and underprepared future workforce.

Have minority parents been active in education politics in your community? What have been their school concerns and issues?

The Aging of America

The aging, or "graying," of the United States population will be bolstered by yesterday's baby boomers who will be 64 years old by the year 2010. It is estimated that by the year 2030, the entire baby boom population, which includes 77 million people or one-third of the current population, will become senior citizens (Beck, 1990, p. 62). It is also anticipated that in the next millennium the population will enjoy increased life expectancy. For example, it is projected that by the year 2000 average life expectancy will be 80 years or more (see Figure 18.2). Approximately 13% of Americans will be past the age of 65 and approximately 3% of the population will reach 80 years of age or older (see Figure 18.3).

It is also projected that as the population ages, people will opt for later retirement. After 1994 when the federal government rescinds mandatory re-

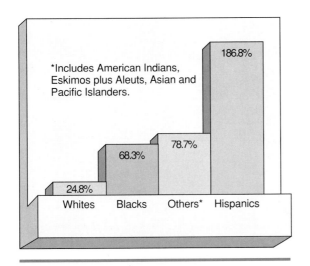

Figure 18.1: Projected Population Growth, 1980–2030 (percent, by race)

*Includes American Indians, Eskimos plus Aleuts, Asian and Pacific Islanders.

Whites	Blacks	Others*	Hispanics
24.8%	68.3%	78.7%	186.8%

Source: Footlick, J. K. (Winter/Spring, 1990). What happened to the family? (p. 16). *Newsweek.* Reprinted with permission.

564

Historical Note:
Nostradamus—Astrologer, Physician, and Futurist

Nostradamus (Michel de Nostredame) was born in 1503 at St. Remy in Provence and died in 1566. An astrologer, physician, and adviser to Henry II and Charles IX, as well as Catherine de Medici, Nostradamus was well known for his predictions of the future. In 1555 and in subsequent years he published 10 "Centuries" or books, each containing 100 rhymed quatrains of predictions of the future. For example, he predicted with accuracy the fatal death of Henri II, the decline of the Catholic Church, and the details of the French revolution and the Napoleonic period.

During his lifetime, futuristic prophecy was considered taboo and was condemned. As a result, he was forced to disguise his prophecies by using symbolism, hidden meanings, and terminology from several languages including French, Spanish, Portuguese, Italian, Latin, Greek, and Hebrew.

The fame of Nostradamus continued beyond his lifetime. Generations of followers have regarded his quatrains as serious prophetic messages. For example, several contemporary commentators have alleged that he foresaw World War II in great detail. As we anticipate the next millennium, Nostradamus enthusiasts will no doubt be particularly interested in his predictions and visions for tomorrow.

Source: Cavendish, R. (Ed.) (1983). *Man, myth and magic.* New York: Marshall Cavendish.

---

tirement at age 70, we may witness a growing number of senior citizens in the labor force.

The extraordinary growth of our elderly population is not without economic consequences. Pension and Medicare costs for this population exceeded $1 billion in 1988 (Shane, 1989). One might expect that a significant increase in expenditures will be necessary to meet the social security and medical needs of tomorrow's elderly population.

Figure 18.2: Life Expectancy at Birth for the Years 1920–2000

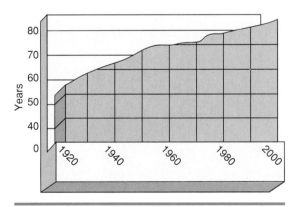

Source: Cetron, M., & Davies, O. (1989). *American renaissance: Our life at the turn of the 21st century* (p. 379 and projections). New York: St. Martin's Press. Copyright © 1989 by Marvin Cetron and Owen Davies. Reprinted with special permission from St. Martin's Press, Inc., New York.

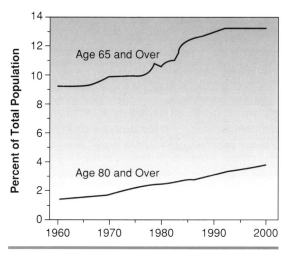

Figure 18.3: The Aging of America for the Years 1960–2000

Source: Cetron, M. & Davies, O. (1989). *American renaissance: Our life at the turn of the 21st century,* (p. 381 and projections). New York: St. Martin's Press. Copyright © 1989 by Marvin Cetron and Owen Davies. Reprinted with special permission from St. Martin's Press, Inc., New York.

By the year 2000 the average life expectancy will be 80 years.

Educational Implications

The aged population's need for more and more of society's resources probably will have a deleterious effect on the financing of education. Not only will there be competition for limited resources, but an aged population that does not have children enrolled in school may resist supporting public education (Connecticut ASCD, 1989).

On a more positive note, a significant number of these senior citizens may take advantage of occupational and postsecondary educational opportunities. Tomorrow's postsecondary institutions may witness an entirely new student body, the septuagenarians.

Economic Transformation

There are diverse opinions concerning the economic forecast for the future. For example, some *futurists* have projected economic prosperity, marked by affluence, low interest rates, and low inflation rates (Cetron, Rocha, & Luckins, 1988). Other futurists take a more pessimistic view and point out that the foreign-financed "invasion" of the United States—including $165.5 billion of property purchased by Japan, Britain and other countries—and the increasing debt of approximately $7 trillion owed by the government, corporations, and consumers (Shane, 1989) pose a threat to America's economic future.

Still others argue that by the year 2040, when the baby boomers stop paying toward Social Security benefits and begin reaping those benefits themselves, the Social Security system may face bankruptcy. The vulnerability of both the Social Security system and the Medicare Hospital Trust Fund could have an unfavorable impact on the nation's economy (Beck, 1990).

John Naisbitt and Patricia Auburdene's (1990) forecast for the future takes an optimistic view and projects that worldwide free trade will characterize the 1990s. According to Naisbitt and Auburdene, we are moving toward a unitary global economy, demonstrated by increasing economic agreements between countries. They point to Brazil and Argentina negotiating toward what might become a South American common market. They foresee that a global economic boom in the next decade will lead to a decade of accelerating competition, and that the United States along with other countries will benefit from the international economy of the future. Other trends for the 1990s projected by Naisbitt and Auburdene are listed in Figure 18.4.

An additional economic trend worthy of mention is the shift from an industrial/manufacturing–based economy to a service/information/technology–based economy (Benjamin, 1989). This major shift will have profound implications on the future workforce, as will be discussed later in this chapter.

Educational Implications

Futurists suggest that the society of tomorrow will require a citizenry that can think critically, reason, and inquire using scientific processes (Benjamin, 1989). Furthermore, with the accelerating changes anticipated by a global

What are the implications for the teaching profession of eliminating the mandatory retirement age at 70 years?

Figure 18.4: Toward the Millennium

1. There will be a global economic boom in the decade of the 1990s.

2. Leisure time activities and spending will shift to an emphasis on the arts.

3. There will be an emerging . . . "free market socialism."

4. Global lifestyles and cultural nationalism will characterize the world at the turn of the century.

5. There will be a global shift from the welfare state to privatization.

6. The [increasing importance] of the Pacific Rim will reflect the millennium.

7. Women will play key leadership roles during the 1990s.

8. Biology and biotechnology will characterize the new age.

9. As the world approaches the year 2000, we will witness a revival of spirituality but a decline in organized religion.

10. There will be a new respect for the individual with a demise of the collective.

Source: Naisbitt, J., & Auburdene, P. (1990). *Megatrends 2000: Ten new directions for the 1990s.* New York: William Morrow. Reprinted with permission of William Morrow and Company, Inc./Publishers, New York.

economy, students of tomorrow will need to be prepared to be world citizens who are intellectually flexible and can screen the information that will inundate them. Figure 18.5 provides a series of questions that focus on teaching students to evaluate the quality of information in an age that will be overloaded with information.

Students of the next millennium will need to be able to process information about complex systems, think holistically and abstractly, and above all, be creative. In short, higher cognitive skill development will be a necessary component of education. Since tomorrow's economic forecast emphasizes a shift to a service-oriented global society, we probably will experience more active involvement of students in service/learning experiences. Volunteerism in hospitals, museums, and community service across the globe will become an integral aspect of the teaching/learning process. New forms of yesterday's Peace Corps, VISTA, or Teacher Corps may surface.

If the projections about the nation's future economy are correct, the schools of tomorrow will need to prepare youth for the challenge of growing old in a society whose government programs may be inadequate to meet the demand for services.

If you had the opportunity to volunteer for a particular social service activity, which would it be?

Changing Workforce

Each of the future trends described in this chapter will have profound implications for the changing workforce. Similarly, the changing workforce will influence the trends of tomorrow in significant ways. The very nature of work will continue to evolve throughout the coming decades. Approximately 45% of the workforce is currently involved in information processing as a

Figure 18.5: Teaching Students to Evaluate the Quality of Information in the Information Age

1. What is junk information?

2. What is quality information in terms of relevance, of accuracy, of dealing with the significance of the information itself?

3. When is the most recent information not the best information?

4. What is a reliable source of information versus an unreliable one?

5. What is a media event, staged for the media, versus a spontaneous newsworthy event?

6. How can we tell when video interviews have been skewed to emphasize one point of view?

7. How do the technologies themselves, individually, influence and shape the information they carry?

8. What are the economic forces that shape information? The strategic and regulatory forces? The political ones?

Source: From *What Curriculum for the Information Age?* (p. 62) by M. A. White, 1987, Hillsdale, NJ: Lawrence Erlbaum Associates, Inc. Copyright 1987 by Lawrence Erlbaum Associates, Inc. Reprinted with permission.

Tomorrow's workforce will be dependent on significant numbers of women and minorities.

result of computer technology. Another 25% provides human services. And while much of the industrial workforce has shifted to *robotics* to increase productivity (particularly in the automotive and consumer appliance industries), 25% has not (Connecticut ASCD, 1989).

One of the dramatic implications of the use of robotics has been more effective manufacturing productivity with fewer workers engaged in production (Cain & Taber, 1987). Tomorrow's workforce will continue to shift from manufacturing or industrial employment to service or information processing. It is estimated that by the twenty-first century, only 5% of the total workforce will be employed in manufacturing, food production, or industrial goods production. The remaining 95% will be employed in service and information processing (Cain & Taber, 1987).

Production of food will be accomplished by a relatively small segment of the total workforce, an estimated 2%. Tomorrow's agriculturalist no longer will be an unskilled farm worker, but will need to be a highly skilled geneticist, economist, environmentalist, technologist, and globalist (Connecticut ASCD, 1989).

A number of futurists view information-processing employment as a subcategory of service employment and speculate that individuals who are employed in such jobs will be vulnerable to changing job requirements due to continually advancing technology. As a result, retraining of employees will become commonplace, and the worker who is most receptive to retraining will be the most valued by the employer of tomorrow (Cain & Taber, 1987).

In the future more women will enter and remain in the workforce, a trend that has increased steadily in recent decades (see Figure 18.6). Minorities (see Figure 18.7) and elderly workers will constitute the majority of tomorrow's new workforce. It is estimated that this trend will continue beyond the turn of the century. By the year 2027, Americans will be obligated to remain on the job until age 67 to receive maximum Social Security benefits (Beck, 1990). As

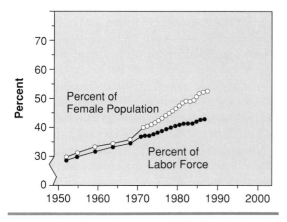

Figure 18.6: Women in the Workforce, 1950–2000

Source: Cetron, M., & Davies, O. (1989). *American renaissance: Our life at the turn of the 21st century* (p. 364). New York: St. Martin's Press. Copyright © 1989 by Marvin Cetron and Owen Davies. Reprinted with special permission from St. Martin's Press, Inc., New York.

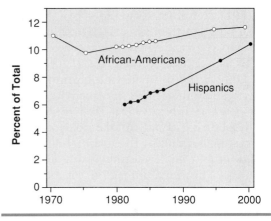

Figure 18.7: Minorities in the Labor Force, 1970–2000

Source: Cetron, M., & Davies, O. (1989). *American renaissance: Our life at the turn of the 21st century* (p. 345). New York: St. Martin's Press. Copyright © 1989 by Marvin Cetron and Owen Davies. Reprinted with special permission from St. Martin's Press, Inc., New York.

a result of this policy change and the possibility of raising the mandatory retirement age even beyond age 70, by the year 2050 the workforce may indeed include much older and more experienced employees.

Educational Implications

To prepare a workforce for tomorrow, the schools will need to do a better job of teaching basic skills such as verbal, mathematical, and scientific literacy in addition to logical reasoning (Drucker, 1989). Other higher-order cognitive skills will be fundamental to the school curriculum, such as creativity, flexibility, decision making with incomplete data, complex pattern recognition, information evaluation/synthesis, and holistic thinking (Dede, 1989). Since there will be more stringent demands placed on the worker of the future for social performance and responsibility, the schools will have to be concerned with moral education and ethics in addition to liberal education and technical education (Drucker, 1989).

Schools will need to change their curricula to reflect the technology in the workplace. As a result of technology, a greater emphasis will be placed on group task performances, collaborative learning, and solving real-world problems using concepts and skills from multiple subject areas rather than from a single-subject-centered discipline. New types of interpersonal skills also will be needed for the coming decades; therefore the school curriculum and instructional practice will need to place a greater emphasis on a variety of forms of communication, both verbal and nonverbal (Dede, 1989).

Which type of interpersonal skills do you anticipate will be needed in the coming decades?

The Changing Family

U.S. family life has undergone dramatic changes in recent years, changes that have not necessarily been positive. For example:

- The divorce rate has doubled since 1965.

- Half of all first marriages end in divorce.

- Six out of 10 second marriages will probably collapse.

- One-third of all children born in the past decade will probably live in a stepfamily before they are 18.

- One out of four children is being raised by a single parent. (Footlick, 1990, p. 16)

The very definition of family is being reconstituted and expanded to include a variety of types of households and nontraditional relationships. Those relationships include gay and lesbian couples, many of whom have children; unmarried heterosexual couples; stepfamilies; and so-called *skip-generation families* in which grandparents step in and raise their children's children (Seligmann, 1990).

There is every reason to believe that the kinds of American families will continue to evolve. It is projected that by the year 2000, married couples will represent approximately 50% of households, the lowest percentage in our history. The traditional family of two parents and children will constitute approximately one-third of American families, with stepfamilies and single parent families comprising the remaining two-thirds (Connecticut ASCD, 1989).

Already we are witnessing some profound shifts in childbearing patterns. As shown in Figure 18.8, the decline in the birth rate is projected to grow

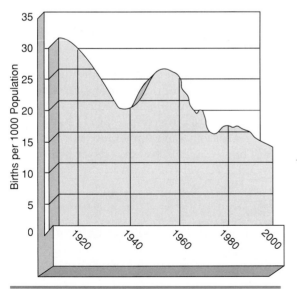

Figure 18.8: Birth Rate, 1920–2000

Source: Cetron, M., & Davies, O. (1989). *American renaissance: Our life at the turn of the 21st century* (p. 377). New York: St. Martin's Press. Copyright © 1989 by Marvin Cetron and Owen Davies. Reprinted with special permission from St. Martin's Press, Inc., New York.

Comprehensive and quality child care will be a high priority of future policy-makers.

steeper as we approach the year 2000. For example, in 1987 the number of childless couples outnumbered those who had children. At the same time, an increasing number of unmarried women are opting to become mothers, a trend that will continue in the next decades (Connecticut ASCD, 1989).

A number of these changes and transitions have contributed to the fragmentation of the American family. The net result has been fewer school-age children having a parent at home who is actively involved in the child's educational pursuit (Connecticut ASCD, 1989).

Educational Implications

As more families have less time to devote to the responsibilities of parenthood, schools may be requested to take on more of those surrogate-parenting tasks. It is expected that schools will be asked to expand their curriculum to include additional before-school and after-school programs and supervision for school-age children whose parents are working.

The need for safe, affordable, quality care for infants and children whose parents are working continues to plague families, in particular poor families.

Numerous legislators continue to work toward the development and implementation of a comprehensive child care policy at the national level.

The combination of the high turnover rate and low salaries of child-care workers will continue to be a major issue of the 1990s and beyond. Because of the problems associated with the lack of adequate child-care facilities, the schools of the future may be asked to include programs for very young children, such as three- and four-year-olds.

It is also projected that public support for education will continue to decline commensurate with the decline in the numbers of households with school-age children. For those families that do have school-age youngsters, the scheduling of classes, conferences with parents or guardians, and parent/teacher organizations will need to be redefined to accommodate the lifestyles of the families of tomorrow.

Since the general health and well-being of families is pivotal to the health and well-being of the nation, a number of congressional representatives have called for federal initiatives for families during the next decade (Schroeder, 1989). There will no doubt be more legislative agendas that focus on family needs in the future.

If you were to design a federal initiative to aid families during the next decade, what would the initiative entail?

Globalization

One of the most positive trends projected for the future is the possibility of global interdependence. Advances in telecommunication satellites and fiber optics already have provided almost instantaneous communication between nations. These advanced telecommunication technologies will make it possible for us to expand our knowledge of the world in significant ways. In short, we have the capability of creating a new twenty-first century world citizen.

As the economic system of the United States becomes increasingly linked to the economic systems of other nations, the English language probably will emerge as the global language. Naisbitt and Auburdene (1990) speculate that more than one billion individuals around the globe currently speak English; two-thirds of all scientific papers are published in English; and an increasing number of Chinese are mastering English, a trend that is expected to continue. As the international boundaries become more permeable and a global identity emerges, having mastery of English in addition to other languages will be an asset.

In the coming decade we will witness the expansion of multinational corporations and industries in unprecedented numbers. These new industries will reflect a more cooperative model of doing business, compared to the competitive model that has persisted for decades. We also will experience more collaborative projects and joint ventures between countries in manufacturing, marketing, banking, law, agriculture, research and development, science and technology, education, medicine, and the arts.

Educational Implications

As the world shrinks, schools will need to rethink their curriculum and plan for a global society. Part of that planning will require an expansion of the number of foreign languages taught. In addition to French and Spanish, we will find numerous school districts adding Russian, Chinese, and Japanese to their course offerings. The study of foreign language also will need to begin earlier, preferably at the elementary school level (Connecticut ASCD, 1989).

Schools of tomorrow will have to redesign and reconceptualize their view of the world. In place of the classical curriculum that features the history and culture of Western civilization, we will need a new interdisciplinary approach that focuses on world cultures, world history, world geography, and the humanities taught from a global perspective.

Preparing the world citizen for the information age will necessitate different instructional strategies, new learning methods, and the application of technology to the schools. Schools no longer will be defined by their four walls. Rather, geographic and cultural boundaries will be penetrated and the students of the future will have an opportunity to experience other cultures firsthand.

What could you contribute to a cross-cultural collaborative project? How important is it that students design such projects?

This type of *global education* model already is being piloted by a collaborative project between 12 schools in New York and 12 schools in the Soviet Union. The New York State/Soviet project incorporates a variety of forms of distance-learning strategies, including voice and image communication through the use of telephone devices that incorporate voice conferencing and slow scan video. This advanced technology has made it possible for groups of children from different countries to talk with one another and observe each other via a series of still monochrome photos that can be printed or displayed on a large-screen monitor (Morton & Copen, 1989). Similar collaborative designs are being tried in the area of teacher training. United States and Soviet teachers are learning how to develop curriculum projects using international communications in the classroom (Morton & Copen, 1989).

Technological Advances

Technologies, in particular electronic technologies, have had a dramatic impact on the economy, the workforce, the media, and the school. Several futurists speculate that the future economy will be dominated by new technologies including microelectronics, *biogenetics,* physics, robotics, and telecommunications (Benjamin, 1989).

One of the most advanced technologies of the future is *artificial intelligence.* Artificial intelligence research began approximately 30 years ago and has produced an artificially intelligent computer that has the capacity to learn how to learn (Cain & Taber, 1987). Artificial intelligence is not intended to compete with human intelligence, but to supplement and enhance our ability to think, create, and solve problems. It is estimated that by the year 2001, artificial intelligence will be used by business, industry, government, and education.

There are numerous other projections of how technology will transform our planet in the years to come:

● New developments in advanced computer technology will provide future robots with improved interactive multisensory capabilities (Higgins, 1986).

- By the year 2000 a new system of communication by satellite network will make it possible to transmit audio, video, or computer data and will serve as an interactive communication system with isolated areas (Shaw, 1986).

- The transportation of tomorrow will include 200 mph trains that will float on magnetic cushions (Cetron, Rocha, & Luckins, 1988).

- The Net console, an interconnected communications system that will serve as a home/work/school station, will become available. The Net console will incorporate a variety of computer interface devices such as microphones, video cameras, video disc recorders, biofeedback units, etc. (Cain & Taber, 1987).

- By the year 2000, $100 billion will be spent on genetic engineering and on medical advances including artificial blood, human growth hormones, memory-recall drugs, and disease immunities for newborns (Cetron, Rocha, & Luckins, 1988).

New and advanced technologies have the capacity to transform our home, school, and work environments.

Figure 18.9: Questions About Lifestyles and the Electronic Household

1. Will we become a stay-at-home society that does its shopping, banking, and corresponding electronically?

2. Will the family unit become more tightly knit as a result of living in "electronic cocoons"?

3. Will leisure become more home-based as video games, videocassette recorders, and cable TV find their way into family media centers?

4. Will "distance learning" in the home take over as more and more students enroll in electronic colleges and universities?

5. Will the home become the center for health and medical care by means of electronic house calls from physicians?

6. Will the electronic home be available only to the affluent, thus increasing the gap between the haves and have-nots?

7. Will government programs be needed to provide access to electronic services for the poor and handicapped?

Source: Shane, H. G. (1987). *Teaching and learning in a microelectronic age* (p. 15). Bloomington, IN: Phi Delta Kappa Educational Foundation. Reprinted with permission.

The microelectronic age also will herald significant changes in the home. A number of questions about the prospect of the electronic household and how it might affect lifestyles in the future are presented in Figure 18.9.

Educational Implications

Since World War II, the technological revolution has improved the quality of life immensely and it now has the potential to transform schooling. Advanced technology has opened the door to new opportunities for teaching and learning. However, technology alone will not be sufficient to transform or revitalize the school. Many futurists and educators recommend radical restructuring of the school commencing with a redesign of teacher and administrator preparation programs, school organization and management, and instructional delivery. Nonetheless, technology can serve as a catalyst for bringing about new models of education (Mojkowski, 1989).

What examples of trans-disciplinary education can you envision that include your discipline?

With the assistance of technology, in particular electronic technologies, learning and instruction in the future can be focused on broad-based ideas and problems, not fragmented or discrete subjects. Benjamin (1989) refers to such learning as *transdisciplinary education* or *holistic education* and suggests that tomorrow's students will need to draw solutions from their knowledge of a variety of disciplines or fields of study. Such an integrated view of learning will be compatible with the complex, interdependent, and global nature of the world.

To augment transdisciplinary education, all students will need to be computer literate. Knowledge of word processing and information retrieval will be pivotal to providing real-world contexts and real-world problems for students to solve. Video writing assignments in language arts, micro-based laboratories (MBLs) in science, microcomputer simulations and computer-based adventure games in social studies, database management software for organizing student research projects in a variety of subjects, synthesizers in music, computer graphics in art, CD-ROM (compact disk–read only memory) laser disk systems in science, voice-activated keyboards, and interactive television will be as commonplace in the classroom of the future as chalkboards and erasers were in the schoolhouse of the past (Gibbon, 1987).

Electronic technology of the Information Age will incorporate multimedia and multidisciplinary learning environments in numerous ways. However, schools of the future will need to do careful planning to maximize the use of technological innovation. Figure 18.10 enumerates five basic technological principles that schools should consider as they plan for the use of advanced technology in the classroom.

Cetron and Davies (1989) summarize the challenge facing both the teacher and the learner of the twenty-first century:

> Today's educational system cannot begin to prepare students for the world they will enter upon graduation from high school. By the time today's kindergartners graduate from high school, the amount of knowledge in the world will have doubled four times. The Class of 2000 will be exposed to more information in one year than their grandparents encountered in their entire lives. They will have to assimilate more inventions and more new information than have appeared in the last 150 years. And by 2010, there will be hardly a job in the county that does not require skill in using powerful computers and telecommunications systems. (p. 63)

Figure 18.10: Technological Principles for Schools

1. To select appropriate hardware and software, schools must decide on the desired uses and purposes of technology. Effective software can help retrieve and sort information, solve problems, dramatize events or issues, or assure mastery of skills. The first step is to establish where technology can accomplish tasks more efficiently or effectively than humans.
2. In planning for broader implementation of technology, careful provision must be made for the time and expense involved in training personnel in its use.
3. In the computer field, early attention is given in selecting programs to assure balance between instructional applications that provide "drill and practice" and those that make more open-ended, creative uses of the technology.
4. Care is taken to provide equity in access to technology as a learning tool in order to assure that neither teachers nor students are denied the opportunity to learn in this manner.
5. Students receive training in how to access, synthesize, and present information, and they participate regularly in assisting teachers in the presentation of such information to other students.

Source: Cawelti, G. (1989). Designing high schools for future. *Educational Leadership, 47*(1), 30–35. Reprinted with permission of the Association for Supervision and Curriculum Development.

Ask Yourself:
Are You a Futurist?

KEY: (High) 5, 4, 3, 2, 1, 0 (Low). The larger numbers should be used to indicate a high degree of agreement with the statement or tendency to act a certain way.

Circle response that most nearly reflects *how you feel about yourself:*

5 4 3 2 1 0/ 1. I am interested in emerging ideas and information about most things.
5 4 3 2 1 0/ 2. I am flexible and adaptable in most situations.
5 4 3 2 1 0/ 3. I think of myself as being in relative control of my life now and in the future.
5 4 3 2 1 0/ 4. I am generally confident of my powers to analyze, synthesize, interpret, and apply myself to new facts, conditions, and events.

Circle response that most nearly describes *your work behavior:*

5 4 3 2 1 0/ 5. I regularly and systematically examine broad goals and specific objectives to assure responsiveness to emerging conditions.
5 4 3 2 1 0/ 6. I periodically reassess professional goals and growth relative to changes in my field.
5 4 3 2 1 0/ 7. I keep an open mind to the possibility that I may choose to retread myself professionally or be nudged/forced to do so.
5 4 3 2 1 0/ 8. I regularly read a variety of published materials to update my work-related knowledge, skills, and attitudes. My reading includes materials directly related to my field and at least some in fields not commonly thought to be relevant (but which *may* directly or indirectly yield information or ideas which are mindstretching or adaptable/useful).
5 4 3 2 1 0/ 9. I periodically participate in seminars, workshops, conferences, and/or courses directly related to my field or indirectly useful, in the sense noted in #8.

Circle response that most nearly describes *your personal life:*

5 4 3 2 1 0/ 10. I commonly reflect on my personal values and seek to revitalize them.
5 4 3 2 1 0/ 11. I read a variety of books, journals, and magazines which collectively stimulate creative imagination and thinking about myself and others, for example, through science fiction, poems, novels, travel books and articles, materials on the arts, scholarly articles on alternative futures, etc.

Educators will find it increasingly difficult to remain current in their discipline or subject field because of the rapid increase of knowledge and information. Like their students of the next millennium, they will look to advanced technology for part of the solution to the knowledge explosion.

Futures Education

Futures education or futurism has grown in popularity during the past 25 years. The majority of formal courses in futurism, however, have been found primarily at the university level rather than the elementary or secondary lev-

5 4 3 2 1 0/   12. I engage in a variety of leisure-time and cultural activities that are pursued for personal enjoyment and growth, that are not directly work-related and that have no predetermined objective.

5 4 3 2 1 0/   13. I cultivate and maintain a variety of friendships—not just persons who are work-related, within the "expected" friendships based on socioeconomic class, neighborhood, college ties, etc.

5 4 3 2 1 0/   14. I feel comfortable about my lifestyle, my values, and my aspirations—and neither feel threatened by those who are different nor inclined to pressure others to become more like me.

Circle response that most nearly describes *your behavior as a citizen, parent, or member of groups:*

5 4 3 2 1 0/   15. I tend to encourage others to think about the possible future, which starts in the next minute—and the aspects of it that we should prepare ourselves for, adapt to, or block.

5 4 3 2 1 0/   16. I stimulate others to learn the processes by which they can develop and continually revitalize personally meaningful values and to use those processes with discretion.

5 4 3 2 1 0/   17. I stimulate others' futuristic thinking and behaving, for example, through various types of rewards, praise, and recognition.

5 4 3 2 1 0/   18. I try to provide a role model of an informed, rational person who is guided in part by futuristic knowledge and processes.

5 4 3 2 1 0/   19. I participate in futuristic group activities, in futures-oriented groups and in groups with occasional emphases on alternative futures, and try to create a societal receptivity toward futurism as a means of improving the quality of life and attaining positive social goals.

5 4 3 2 1 0/   20. I demonstrate the values of futuristic thinking in my roles as a citizen, parent, and/or group member.

Your "score": Add up the numbers you have circled. The closer you are to a score of 100, the more likely you are to be a "futurist."

Source: Copyright by Joel L. Burdin, November 6, 1979. Used with permission.

els. For those elementary and secondary educators who desire to introduce their students to the study of the future, there are a variety of program formats that can be used in the classroom. Pulliam (1987) describes five approaches to the study of the future that can be integrated easily into the existing educational curriculum.

    1. *Interdisciplinary approach.* The focus is on an interdisciplinary core curriculum and the relationship between a variety of subjects or disciplines, such as the relationship between biology and economics or science and social studies. The application of such an interdisciplinary approach in an elementary school might include a combined science and social studies unit that focuses on the anticipated impact of the greenhouse effect on the natural ecological

balance of the future and its relationship to economic development. Synergetic, integrated, holistic, core, and interdisciplinary studies are basic to a futures curriculum.

What other problems/issues might you recommend for problem analysis by secondary school students?

2. *Problem-analysis approach.* The purpose of the study of the future is to prepare students to analyze and solve problems and to probe for underlying cause-and-effect relationships. The application of such a problem-analysis approach in a secondary school might include an exploration of the moral and ethical considerations of genetic engineering. Such a problem-analysis approach would stress the power of the individual or group to alter the environment.

3. *Optimistic locus of control.* In spite of the skepticism of today's society, futures education typically takes an optimistic world view. Futurism stresses the positive and empowering capabilities of the human race. The application of an optimistic approach to studying the future in an elementary school might include a unit in language arts in which students write science fiction stories that exemplify current technological solutions to global problems.

4. *Open-ended, inquiry-based methodology.* The study of the future attempts to avoid the dissemination of mere facts and information. Instead, much of the curriculum includes hypothetical simulations or scenarios that pose probable alternative solutions. The application of an open-ended, inquiry-based methodology in a secondary school might include the development of exploratory predictions of the future through attitude surveys, brainstorming techniques, future games, or the delphi technique. The delphi technique offers a means of forecasting or polling based on group consensus. Such a methodology might be best suited for a course in journalism, political science, history, or sociology. Students are encouraged to project themselves into a variety of probable future scenarios and to extrapolate creative solutions to problems. The major goal is to teach creative thinking skills. For example, journalism students might be asked to publish a high school yearbook for the year 2050.

5. *Values tracking in the futures.* Most futures courses emphasize values and the choice among future alternatives. Futurism requires students to reexamine the values of society, the nation, and the world as well as their personal convictions. The application of a values component in an elementary school might include a unit in social studies that grapples with the question "What might the ideal education be in the future?" The challenge of a futures curriculum that examines the nature of choice and decision making offers the type of classroom interchange that leads to values identification and clarification—prerequisites for creative problem solving.

As educators, we need to help prepare our students to cope with the complexity of change. In spite of the uncertainty of the future, there is much we can do to aid our students in preparing for it. The study of the future offers an important vehicle for learning how to analyze, clarify, generalize, and make critical judgments; in short, how to cope with tomorrow's major problems. Moreover, the study of the future offers numerous creative opportunities for imagining and designing the best possible alternatives or visions for tomorrow.

"Ask Yourself" on pages 578–79 presents an informal personal assessment to help you determine the extent to which you yourself think, believe, or act as a futurist.

Summary

Projecting the future is never without its risks. A number of societal trends are so marked, however, that there is reason to believe that they will extend into the next century. Each of these trends will affect education in significant ways. Two of the trends that will affect education the most are the growing minority student body and the aging population. Both have the potential of placing a heavy financial burden on the economy, which in turn may have a deleterious effect on the financing of education. As discussed in Chapter 13, the great debate of this and future decades may concern the competition between the needs of youth and those of the aging population.

One of the most visible trends is the advances in technology. Of the projected technological advances, artificial intelligence is one of the most innovative and has the greatest potential to enhance our ability to solve problems creatively. Yet, while the educational implications of technology are limitless, they are not going to be the panacea for curing all the ills of education. A total redesign of the educational enterprise, including the curriculum, may be necessary for the technology to be most effective.

The complexity of tomorrow's world requires a certain type of knowledge and skill that enables one to adapt and cope with ongoing change. A futures curriculum can help develop the necessary skills to cope with the uncertainty of tomorrow's future.

Key Terms

Artificial intelligence	Global education
Biogenetics	Robotics
Futures education	Skip-generation families
Futurist	Transdisciplinary (holistic) education

Discussion Questions

1. Much of the conjecture about the future centers around global interdependence. What elementary, secondary, and postsecondary curriculum recommendations would you advance to best prepare the world citizen for tomorrow's global society?

2. It is hypothesized that the technology of the future, in particular electronic technologies, will have a profound impact on the school. Design a home/work/school station of the future that integrates the use of advanced technology in your subject matter discipline.

3. If you were designing a curriculum for the study of the future, which of Pulliam's five approaches would you choose and why?

4. Approximately twenty years ago the renowned psychologist Carl R. Rogers (1970) wrote an essay entitled "From Interpersonal Relationships: U.S.A. 2000" for a symposium sponsored by the Esalen Institute. In his essay he discussed such topics as relationships between men and women, parents and children, individuals in the workplace, and religion as interpersonal living. If you were invited to write an essay on "Interpersonal Relationships in the Next Millennium," what key points would your essay include?

5. In 1966, John R. Platt wrote the following for the American Association for the Advancement of Science: "A lifetime ago we made the transformation to education for living. It is time now to make the transformation to education for wholeness, for delight, and for diversity" (p. 1139). What do you think Platt meant by this statement? Does the quote still apply for the future (i.e., the year 2000)? If yes, how? If no, why not?

References

Beck, M. (Winter/Spring, 1990). The geezer boom. *Newsweek,* 62–63, 66, 68.

Benjamin, S. (1989). An ideascope for education: What futurists recommend. *Educational Leadership, 40*(1), 8–14.

Boyer, E. L. (1988). The future of American education: New realities, making connections. *Kappa Delta Pi Record, 25*(1), 6–12.

Cain, E. J., & Taber, F. M. (1987). *Educating disabled people for the 21st century.* Boston: Little, Brown.

Cetron, M. J., & Davies, O. (1989). *American renaissance: Our life at the turn of the 21st century.* New York: St. Martin's Press.

Cetron, M. J., Rocha, W., & Luckins, R. (1988). Into the 21st century: Long term trends affecting the United States. *The Futurist, 22*(4), 29–40.

Cetron, M. J., Soriano, B., & Gayle, M. (1985). *Schools of the future: How American business and education can cooperate to save our schools.* New York: McGraw-Hill.

Connecticut ASCD (1989). *Curriculum for the new millennium: Trends shaping our schools.* Fairfield, CT: CASCD.

Cox, H. G. (1969). *The feast of fools: A theological essay on festivity and fantasy.* Cambridge, MA: Harvard University Press.

Dede, C. (1989). The evolution of information technology: Implications for curriculum. *Educational Leadership, 47*(1), 23–26.

Drucker, P. F. (1989). How schools must change. *Psychology Today, 22*(5), 18–20.

Footlick, J. K. (Winter/Spring, 1990). What happened to the family? *Newsweek,* 14–18, 20.

Furner, B. (April, 1984). *Activity, essentials, and excellence: Language arts 2000.* Paper presented at the annual meeting of the National Council of Teachers of English, Columbus, OH (ERIC Document Reproduction Service No. 243 144).

Gibbon, S. Y., Jr. (1987). Learning and instruction in the Information Age. In M. A. White (Ed.), *What curriculum for the Information Age?* (pp. 1–23). Hillsdale, NJ: Lawrence Erlbaum Associates.

Higgins, M. (1986). The future of personal robots. *The Futurist, 20*(3), 43–46.

Mojkowski, C. (1989). *Transforming curriculum and instruction with technology.* Paper presented at the annual meeting of the American Educational Research Association, San Francisco, CA.

Morton, C., & Copen, P. (April, 1989). *Connecting countries: Distance in time, space, and culture—Linking students in a learning dialogue.* Paper presented at the Northeast Distance Learning Conference: Strategies for Implementation, Springfield, MA.

Naisbitt, J., & Auburdene, P. (1990). *Megatrends 2000: Ten New Directions for the 1990s.* New York: William Morrow.

Pallas, A. M., Natriello, G., & McDill, E. L. (1989). The changing nature of the disadvantaged population: Current dimensions and future trends. *Educational Researcher, 18*(5), 15–22.

Platt, J. R. (1966). Diversity. *Science, 154,* 1139.

Pulliam, J. D. (1987). *History of education in America.* Columbus, OH: Merrill.

Rogers, C. R. (1970). From interpersonal relationships: USA 2000. In M. Dunston and P. W. Garden (Eds.), *Worlds in the making: Probes for students of the future* (pp. 320–325). Englewood Cliffs, NJ: Prentice-Hall.

Schroeder, P. (1989). Toward a national family policy. *American Psychologist, 44,* 1410–1413.

Seligmann, J. (Winter/Spring 1990). Variations on a theme. *Newsweek,* 38–40, 44, 46.

Shane, H. G. (1989). Educated foresight for the 1990s. *Educational Leadership, 47*(1), 4–6.

Shaw, S. J. (1986). New satellites provide links to remote terminals. *Interpreter, 19*(11), 37–44.

Wegmann, R. (January, 1980). *Educational challenges of the 1980s.* Prepared for the Subcommittee on Elementary, Secondary, and Vocational Education in the 1980s: A Compendium of Policy Papers (ERIC Document Reproduction Service No. ED 194 476).

Appendix A

Selected Federal Legislation Supporting Education

1785   Northwest Ordinance—Reserved the sixteenth section of each township for the support of education.

1787   Northwest Ordinance—Endowed public institutions of higher education with public lands.

1802   First federal institution of higher education established—the U.S. Military Academy at West Point (the Naval Academy was established in 1845, the Coast Guard Academy in 1915, and the Air Force Academy in 1954).

1862   First Morrill Act—Provided land grants to the states for the support of agriculture and industrial colleges.

1867   Federal Department of Education established.

1890   Second Morrill Act—Provided money grants to each state to support land grant colleges; no grant would be provided to any state that denied admission to the land grant college on the basis of race unless it provided for separate institutions.

1917   Smith-Hughes Act—Provided grants to support teachers' salaries in vocational education at precollege level.

1918   Vocational Rehabilitation Act—Provided grants for rehabilitation training of World War I veterans.

1920   Smith-Bankhead Act—Authorized grants to states for vocational rehabilitation.

1933   Civilian Conservation Corps—Provided vocational and basic skills training to youth 18 to 25 enrolled in the corps.

1935   National Youth Administration—Provided part-time employment to high school and college students to help them remain in school.

1935   Bankhead-Jones Act—Provided grants to land-grant colleges.

1941   Lanham Act—Provided aid to school districts affected by the location of federal tax exempt property.

1943   Vocational Rehabilitation Act—Provided rehabilitation assistance to disabled veterans.

1944   Servicemen's Readjustment Act (G.I. Bill)—Provided financial assistance to veterans to continue their education.

1944   Surplus Property Act—Authorized transfer of surplus government property to educational institutions.

1946   Fullbright Act—Provided for international educational exchange.

1950   National Science Foundation (NSF) Act—Established the National Science Foundation to promote basic research and education in the sciences.

1950 Public Law 815—Provided funds for school construction to districts in which federal tax exempt property was located within the district.

1950 Public Law 874—Provided funds for operating expenses to school districts in which federal tax exempt property was located within the district.

1958 National Defense Education Act—Provided financial assistance to state and local education agencies to strengthen instruction in areas deemed critical to national defense (e.g., mathematics, science, and foreign languages); for the improvement of guidance counseling and testing service; educational media; and student loans and scholarships.

1962 Manpower Development and Training Act—Provided training for unemployed and underemployed persons to enable them to become wage earners.

1963 Higher Education Facilities Act—Provided funds to institutions of higher education to construct classrooms, laboratories, and libraries.

1964 Economic Opportunity Act—Established the Job Corps and Project Head Start as part of its antipoverty program.

1965 Elementary and Secondary Education Act—Provided assistance to local school districts for children in low-income families, for library and instructional materials, for supplemental educational centers, and for research and training.

1965 Higher Education Act—Provided funds to institutions of higher education for construction and improvement of facilities and for student loans and scholarships. Established National Teacher Corps.

1965 National Foundation on the Arts and the Humanities (NFAH) Act—Established the NFAH and authorized grants and loans to encourage production and scholarships in the arts and humanities.

1966 Adult Education Act—Authorized grants to states to establish and expand educational programs for adults, including the training of adult education teachers.

1967 Education Professions Development Act—Provided grants to improve the quality of teaching and meet the shortage of trained education personnel in specific areas.

1968 Bilingual Education Act—Provided funds to school districts to provide bilingual education to students with limited English proficiency.

1972 Education Amendments of 1972—Provided support for a number of postsecondary education programs; established the National Institute of Education, a Bureau of Occupational and Adult Education, and a bureau level Office of Indian Education; prohibited sex discrimination in admissions to institutions of higher education.

1975 Indian Self-Determination and Education Assistance Act—Mandated increased participation of Native Americans in the operation of their educational programs.

1975 Education of the Handicapped Act—Required that all handicapped children ages 5 to 18 be provided a free appropriate education designed to meet their unique needs.

1978 Career Education Incentive Act—Authorized the creation of a career education program for elementary and secondary schools.

1979 Department of Education Organization Act—Established a Department of Education.

1981 Education Consolidation and Improvement Act—Consolidated 42 federal programs into 7 block grants.

1984 Carl D. Perkins Vocational Education Act—Provided grants to states to make vocational education accessible to all persons, including the disadvantaged, the handicapped, single parents and homemakers.

1986 Handicapped Children's Protection Act—Allowed courts to award attorneys' fees to parents of disabled students who are successful in challenging district actions under the Education of the Handicapped Act.

1986 Drug Free Schools and Communities Act—Provided support for drug abuse education and prevention programs.

1988 Education and Training for a Competitive America Act—Authorized new and expanded programs in literacy, math-science, foreign languages, vocational education, international education, and technology training and transfer.

1990 Education of Children With Disabilities Act—Revised and extended programs established under the Education of the Handicapped Act, changed the name of the Act and all references from handicapped children to children with disabilities.

1990 Displaced Homemakers Self-Sufficiency Assistance Act—Provided assistance to states to provide employment training programs and referral support services to displaced homemakers.

1990 School Dropout Prevention and Basic Skills Improvement Act—Extended support to secondary education programs for basic skills improvement and dropout prevention and reentry.

1990 National Environmental Education Act—Provided support for environmental education programs and training of professionals in environmental fields.

Appendix B

Selected National Education Reports: 1982–1989

Adler, M. H. (1982). *The paideia proposal.* New York: Macmillan.

American Association of Colleges for Teacher Education. (1985). *A call for change in teacher education.* Washington, DC: AACTE.

American Association of Colleges for Teacher Education. Two reports from the National Commission for Excellence in Teacher Education. (1986). *The dynamics of change in teacher education,* vol. II. Washington, DC: ERIC Clearinghouse on Teacher Education.

American Federation of Teachers. (1986). *The revolution that is overdue: Looking toward the future of teaching and learning.* Washington, DC: ERIC Clearinghouse on Teacher Education.

Boyer, E. L. (1983). *High school: A report on secondary education in America.* New York: Harper & Row.

Boyer, E. L. (1987). *College: The undergraduate experience in America.* New York: Harper & Row.

Boyer, E. L. (1987). *The early years.* New York: Harper & Row.

Business–Higher Education Forum. (1985). *America's competitive challenge: The need for a national response.* Washington, DC: B–HEF.

Carnegie Forum on Education and the Economy. (1986). *A nation prepared: Teachers for the 21st century.* Washington, DC: Carnegie Forum on Education and the Economy.

Carnegie Foundation for the Advancement of Teaching. (1983). *Secondary education in America.* Washington, DC: Carnegie Foundation.

College Board Educational Equality Project. (1983). *Academic preparation for college: What students need to know and be able to do.* New York: The College Board.

Committee for Economic Development. (1985). *Investing in our children: Business and the public schools.* New York: CED.

Council of Chief State School Officers Study Commission. (1986). *Education and the economy.* Washington, DC: CCSSO.

Council of Chief State School Officers, Committee on Teacher Certification, Preparation, and Accreditation. (1984). *Staffing the nation's schools: A national emergency.* Washington, DC: CCSSO.

Education Commission of the States Task Force on Education for Economic Growth. (1983). *Action for excellence: A comprehensive plan to improve our nation's schools.* Denver, CO: ECS.

Education Commission of the States. (1986). *Transforming the state role in undergraduate education.* Denver, CO: ECS.

Education Commission of the States. (1986). *What next? More leverage for teachers?* Denver, CO: ECS.

Forum of Educational Leaders. (1983). *Educational reform: A response from education leaders.* Washington, DC: FEL.

Goodlad, J. I. (1984). *A place called school: Prospects for the future.* New York: McGraw Hill.

Griffiths, D. E., Stout, R. T., & Forsyth, P. B. (Eds.). (1988). *Leaders for America's schools: The report of the National Commission on Excellence in Educational Administration.* Tempe, AZ: University Council for Education Administration.

The Holmes Group. (1986). *Tomorrow's teachers: A report of The Holmes Group.* E. Lansing, MI: Holmes Group.

National Board for Professional Teaching Standards. (1989). *Towards high and rigorous standards for the teaching profession.* Washington, DC: NBPTS.

National Commission on Excellence in Teacher Education. (1985). *A call for change in teacher education.* Washington, DC: American Association of Colleges for Teacher Education.

National Commission on Excellence in Education. (1983). *A nation at risk: The imperative for education reform.* Washington, DC: U.S. Government Printing Office.

National Governors' Association Center for Policy Research and Analysis. (1986). *Time for results: The governors' 1991 report on education.* Washington, DC: NGA.

National Science Foundation. (1983). *Educating Americans for the 21st century: A report to the American people and the National Science Board.* Washington, DC: National Science Foundation.

Sizer, T. R. (1984). *Horace's compromise: The dilemma of the American high school.* Boston, MA: Houghton Mifflin Co.

Southern Regional Education Board. (1985). *Improving teacher education: An agenda for higher education and the schools.* Atlanta, GA: SREB.

Twentieth Century Fund Task Force on Federal Elementary and Secondary Education Policy. (1983). *Making the grade.* New York: Twentieth Century Fund.

U.S. Department of Education. (1986). *First lessons: A report on elementary education in America.* Washington, DC: U.S. Government Printing Office.

U.S. Department of Education. (1984). *What works: Research about teaching and learning.* Washington, DC: U.S. Government Printing Office.

Glossary

Academic freedom. The teacher's freedom to determine the most appropriate instructional materials and the most appropriate teaching strategies without censorship, interference, or fear of reprisal.

Academic learning time (ALT). The amount of engaged time (ET) that the student works with materials or activities and experiences a high success rate.

Academy. A type of private secondary school operating in the 1800s, designed to teach subjects useful in trade and commerce.

Accountability. A concept in which the school and teachers are held responsible for the accomplishment of expressed educational goals.

Acquired immune deficiency syndrome (AIDS). A serious health condition caused by a virus that destroys the immune system and leaves the body incapable of fighting disease.

Activity curriculum. A curriculum that is determined to a large extent by student interest and that emphasizes self-expression through games, singing, or other creative and spontaneous activities.

Adequacy. The extent to which funding for programs and learning opportunities is sufficient.

Administrative council. An assembly of school district administrators that meets regularly to plan, hear reports, and make administrative decisions about the operation of the school district.

Administrative law. The formal regulations and decisions of state or federal agencies.

Adult education. Education, for credit and noncredit, provided to individuals who are beyond the age of compulsory attendance, who have either completed or interrupted their formal education.

Aesthetics. The branch of philosophy concerned with values in beauty, especially in the fine arts.

Affirmative action. Affirmative steps to recruit and hire, or recruit and retain, individuals from groups who are underrepresented in the workplace or the classroom.

Alternative certification. State provisions or regulations for awarding a teaching license to a person who has not followed the traditional teacher education program; exceptions typically are related to completion of a concentrated professional education sequence, teaching internships or prior experience, or credits for work experience.

Alternative schools. Schools that offer specialized programs and learning experiences not normally found in the public schools, or that provide greater individual attention for students who are not making normal progress.

Amalgamation. A form of diversity that supports the "melting pot" notion and envisions American culture as emerging from the best elements of many cultures.

American Federation of Teachers (AFT). A national labor union for teachers; an affiliate of the AFL-CIO.

Apparent reality. The reality made up of day-to-day experiences and life events.

Artificial intelligence. Technology that allows the computer to perform functions that traditionally have been the realm of human intelligence, such as thinking and problem solving.

Assimilation. A response to population diversity that requires conformity to a single model, which is largely defined by traditional British political, social, cultural, and religious institutions.

At risk. A term used to describe students who are achieving below grade level expectations or are likely to experience educational problems in the future, as well as students who are likely to experience physical and mental health problems.

Attorney general. The chief legal officer of the state who serves as legal advisor to official agencies of the state.

Axiology. The branch of philosophy concerned with the nature of values.

Back-to-basics movement. A revival of essentialism begun in the 1970s and echoed in education reform reports of the 1980s which emphasizes the three R's, a core curriculum, and more rigorous academic program requirements.

Behavioral objectives. Action-oriented statements that indicate specific behaviors or knowledge that students are expected to learn or demonstrate upon completion of an instructional sequence.

Behaviorism. An educational theory predicated on the belief that human behavior can be explained in terms of responses to external stimuli. The basic principle underlying behaviorism in education is that behaviors can be modified in a socially acceptable manner through the arrangement of the conditions for learning.

Bibliotherapy. The use of books as a therapeutic intervention.

Bilingual education. Instruction to non-English-speaking students in their native language while teaching them English.

Biogenetics. The study of the development and generation of living organisms, especially concerned with factors related to inheritance and maturation.

Block grants. Allocations of funds that may be used for general educational purposes and programs to local school districts from either the federal government or state governments.

Bloom's Taxonomy of Educational Objectives. List and organizing scheme containing expected learnings for students.

Building principal. The person responsible for the administration and management of a school.

Career ladder. A career development plan that provides differential recognition and rewards for teachers at steps of the plan, which coincide with increased experience and expertise.

Cartesian method. A process proposed by Descartes which involves the derivation of axioms upon which theories can be based by the purposeful and progressive elimination of all interpretations of experience except those that are absolutely certain.

Categorical funding. The practice of state funding of specific educational programs or activities (e.g., bilingual education, education of handicapped pupils, pupil transportation, or in-service programs).

Categorical imperatives. Universal moral laws that guide our actions and behaviors.

Certification. The authorization of an individual by the state to teach in an area where the state has determined he or she has met established state standards.

Charity (pauper) schools. Schools in colonial New England designed for children who could not afford to attend other fee-charging schools.

Chief state school officer. The elected or appointed executive officer of the state department of education, responsible for elementary and secondary education, and sometimes for higher education; often referred to as the superintendent of public instruction or the commissioner of education.

Child abuse. The repeated mistreatment or neglect of a child which can result in physical, emotional, verbal, or sexual injury or harm.

Child benefit theory. The legal theory that supports providing state aid to private education when the aid benefits the private school child rather than the private school itself.

Child (student)-centered curriculum. Curriculum designed with the child's interest and needs at the center of the learning process; learning takes place through experience and problem solving.

Choice. Power or authority of (1) a local school board to select the instructional program and level of funding to be provided students in the school district, or (2) parents to select the school that their child can attend.

Classical conditioning. A type of behaviorism that demonstrates that a natural stimulus that produces a certain type of response can be replaced by a conditioned stimulus.

Clinical depression. A serious depression with persistent symptoms that typically last for at least two or more weeks.

Cluster suicides. A series of suicides that are closely related in time and place.

Cognitive styles. The alternative processes by which learners acquire knowledge.

Common schools. Publicly supported schools started during the mid-1800s attended in common by all children.

Compensatory education. Special educational programs designed to overcome the educational deficiencies associated with the socioeconomic, cultural, or minority group disadvantages of youth.

Competency testing. Testing designed to assess basic skills and knowledge.

Competitive grants. A method of allocation of state education (or federal education) funds whereby districts compete for funds through an application process.

Comprehensive high school. A public secondary school that offers curricula in vocational education, general education, and college preparation.

Constitution. A written contract for the establishment of a government; the highest level of law.

Continuing education program. Postsecondary education programs for adults, including career development programs, degree programs, and vocational offerings.

Continuity. The repetition of major curriculum elements to ensure that skills can be practiced and developed.

Cooperative learning. Instructional system that assumes that students will study and work together in a supportive relationship rather than competitively.

Core curriculum. A curriculum design that emphasizes the required minimum subjects and topics within subjects that all students are expected to learn.

Cosmology. The branch of philosophy concerned about the nature of the universe or cosmos.

Cost-of-living index. A measure of the change in the price of goods purchased by consumers.

Crisis intervention team. Volunteer teachers, counselors, administrators, social workers, school nurses, and school psychologists who network with each other and identify the student who appears to be overwhelmed by stress, or displays suicidal gestures or suicidal threats.

Critical thinking. The process of thinking and problem solving which involves the examination and validation of assumptions and evidence and the application of logic to the formulation of conclusions.

Cult. A group bound together by devotion to a person, belief system, or a set of practices.

Cultural literacy. Assumed body of knowledge about which persons should be able to demonstrate mastery if they are to function at an optimal level in society.

Cultural pluralism. A form of diversity that emphasizes the multiple cultures in the larger society.

Culture. The behavioral patterns, ideas, values, religions and moral beliefs, customs, laws, language, institutions, art and all other material things and artifacts characteristic of a given people at a given period of time.

Culture of the school. Social interactions of the students and adults in the school environment and the ways in which their behavior is influenced by the official rules and established mores of the school.

Curriculum. All the educational experiences of students which take place in the school.

Curriculum alignment. The correlation between what is assessed and what was planned and taught.

Dame school. The elementary school in the New England colonies, usually held in a kitchen or living room and taught by women with minimal education.

***De Facto* segregation.** Segregation existing as a matter of fact, regardless of the law.

***De Jure* segregation.** Segregation sanctioned by law.

Deductive logic. Logic that deduces concrete applications from a general principle or general rule.

Delinquency. A juvenile offense that includes the committing of adultlike crimes.

Demonstration instruction. Instructional technique in which students learn through doing and/or observing.

Deschooling curriculum. A curriculum based on the belief that the values promoted by formal educational institutions are unhealthy and harmful, that the public school system should be discontinued, and that the curriculum should be determined by what the learner likes, not what will be useful to someone else.

Desegregation. The abolition of racial, ethnic, or gender segregation.

Discrimination. Showing bias or prejudice in the treatment of individuals because of their race, ethnicity, gender, or handicapping condition.

Distance education. Education delivery system characterized by a separation in space and time for teaching and learning activities. Teaching takes place mostly through audio, video, computer, and print technologies, and learning is through independent study.

Drill and practice. Instructional technique in which the assumption is that learning is enhanced through repetitious activities, i.e., memorizing and reciting the multiplication tables.

Dropout. A pupil who leaves school for any reason except death, before graduation or completion of a program of studies and without transferring to another school or institution.

Due process. The process by which individuals are provided fair and equitable procedures in a matter affecting their welfare (procedural due process) and are protected from unfair deprivation of their property.

Economic distortions. Instances when the impact of a tax contributes to a change in consumer decisions concerning such actions as the site at which they secure services or purchases or their place of residence.

Educational foundations. Charitable or not-for-profit entities established to receive and/or distribute funds that can be used to enrich the educational opportunities for students.

Educational goals. Broad general statements of desired learning outcomes.

Educational objective. A clearly defined, observable, and measurable student behavior that indicates learner progress toward the achievement of a particular educational goal.

Educational overburden. A condition that exists in many urban districts because of the relatively larger number of pupils in these districts who require high-cost educational programs and the fact that the costs of goods and services to provide instruction are higher.

Efficiency. The ability to increase productivity without increasing costs, by such means as reductions in administrative costs, increased use of educational technology, and higher standards for pupils.

Emergency (temporary) certificate. A certificate issued to a person who does not meet the specified degree, course, or other requirements for regular certification; issued with the presumption that the recipient teacher will obtain the necessary credentials for regular certification.

Eminent domain. The right of the government to take private property for public use.

Engaged time. The time students spend working with materials or engaged in activities.

English as a second language (ESL). A form of bilingual education in which standard English is taught to limited-English-proficient students.

Epistemology. The branch of philosophy concerned with the investigation of the nature of knowledge.

Equal opportunity. A legal principle which when applied to education requires that school districts and other agencies develop policies and procedures to ensure that the rights of employees and students are protected and that they are given equal treatment in employment practices, access to programs, or other educational opportunities.

Equity. The equal treatment of persons/students in equal circumstances.

Essentialism. An educational theory that focuses on an essential set of learnings that prepare individuals for life, by concentration on the culture and traditions of the past.

Ethics. The branch of philosophy concerned with the study of the human conduct and what is right and wrong or good and bad.

Ethnic group. A subgroup of the population distinguished by having a common heritage (language, customs, history, etc.).

Ex post facto **law.** A law passed after the fact or after the event.

Existentialism. A philosophic belief that focuses on personal and subjective existence; the world of choice and responsibility is primary.

Experimentalism. A process of inquiry or philosophy that focuses on the things that work; the world of experience is central.

Expository instruction. A teacher-centered instructional method designed to convey information through formal lecture, informal lecture, and teacher-led discussion.

Expulsion. Exclusion of students from school for periods of time in excess of 10 days.

Field (clinical) experience. Applied learning experiences of education students provided prior to and in addition to the internship or student teaching experience.

Flat grants. A method for allocation of educational funds based on the allocation of a uniform amount per student, per teacher, per classroom, or other unit.

Formative evaluation. Form of evaluation designed to provide feedback while an activity is underway to improve the manner in which the activity is conducted.

Foundation plan. State school finance system that provides a base amount per pupil to local school districts from a combination of state and local tax sources with the amount of state funds per pupil received by a local school district being in inverse relation to the fiscal capacity per pupil of the local school district.

Free schools. Private schools, popular during the 1960s and 1970s, which promoted the value of out-of-state activities, informal study in the community, and students discovering for themselves what they want to learn.

Full state funding. School finance system whereby all funds for the support of the public schools come from the state and from state-level taxes.

Futures education (futurism). The study of the future.

Futurist. An individual concerned with the study of the future and the projection of trends for the future.

Gateway drugs. Substances such as alcohol, tobacco, and marijuana, which may serve as stepping-stones for a child's later use of hard drugs.

Global education. Curricular content related to the ways in which individuals, groups, and nations interact in mutually dependent relationships and the implications for societies and cultures.

Grammar school. A secondary school, originating in ancient Rome and continuing into the nineteenth century, which emphasized a classical education; forerunner of the high school; in current usage, an elementary school.

Great Books. The great works of the past including literature, philosophy, history, and science, which represent absolute truth according to perennialist theory.

Group instruction. Instructional system in which teachers divide the class into groups of students (often five to eight students) and structure instruction and learning activities for this smaller number of students.

Hermeneutics. The art or science of the interpretation of lived experience.

Hidden curriculum. The rules, regulations, rituals, and interactions that are part of the everyday life of the school.

Holistic education. An approach to education that emphasizes the need to draw from the knowledge of several disciplines.

Home schooling. The education of children outside the school setting and in the home; a form of private education.

Horizontal equity. In the financing of schools or the treatment of individuals, the principle that states that those who are alike should be treated the same; the equal treatment of equals.

Hornbook. Wooden board on which a sheet of parchment was placed and covered with a thin sheath of cow's horn; used in colonial New England primary schools.

Humanism. The dominant philosophy of the Renaissance which emphasized the importance of human beings and promoted literature and art of classical Rome and Greece.

Humanistic education. An educational program reflecting the philosophy of humanism.

Idealism. The oldest philosophic belief which views the world of the mind and ideas as fundamental.

In loco parentis. In the place of a parent.

Incentive pay. Paying teachers more for different kinds or amounts of work (e.g., master teacher plans or career ladder plans).

Incompetence. Lack of legal qualification, inability or capacity to discharge the required duty. In regard to teachers' incompetence, falls into four general categories: (1) inadequate teaching; (2) poor discipline; (3) physical or mental incapacity; (4) counterproductive personality traits.

Independent learning. A range of student-centered teaching methodologies that include programmed instruction, self-paced instruction, contract learning, and performance-based instruction.

Indian education. Term used to refer to educational program specifically designed for Native Americans.

Indirect compensation. Payments or fringe benefits that employees receive in addition to payments in the form of money; classified as either employee benefits or employee services, such as health and life insurance, long-term disability protection, or leaves with pay.

Individualized education program (IEP). Program designed by a team of educators, parents, and at times the student to meet the unique needs of the child for whom it is developed.

Individualized instruction. Instructional system in which teachers work with students on a one-on-one basis and structure instruction and learning activities for each student.

Inductive logic. Logic that begins with a combination of facts and from those facts a general principle or rule is formulated.

Infant school. A type of public preelementary school introduced in the U.S. in the nineteenth century to prepare children aged four to seven for elementary school.

Inquiry instruction. Problem-oriented instructional system in which students assume major responsibility for designing and structuring their learning activities and teachers serve as resource persons and facilitators.

Instructional time (IT). Classroom time spent on academic learning.

Insubordination. The persistent and willful violation of a reasonable rule or direct order from a recognized authority.

Integrated curriculum. A curriculum design that combines separate subjects from within the same discipline, and in some instances content from two or more branches of study.

Integration. The coordination of skills and knowledge across disciplines in the curriculum.

Intelligence quotient (IQ). A number intended to indicate an individual's level of mental development or intelligence.

Intermediate education service agency (IESA). State-authorized governmental entity that serves one or more local school districts; the functions of such entities vary by state. In individual states, the entities perform a variety of functions, i.e., providing special education and vocational education programs, in-service training, or financial accounting and reporting services between local school districts and the state.

Intervention programs. Programs or strategies directed at providing assistance to children and adolescents who are already at risk.

Junior college. An educational institution that offers courses for two years beyond high school. These courses may transfer to a four-year institution or may be complete career or vocational programs.

Junior high school. An intermediate school between elementary and high school that includes grades 7 and 8 or 7, 8, and 9.

Law. A body of rules of action or conduct prescribed by controlling authority and having binding legal force.

Learning disability. Having a disorder or delayed development in one or more of the processes of thinking, speaking, reading, writing, listening, or doing arithmetic operations.

Least restrictive environment. The educational setting that enables the handicapped child to have an educational experience most like that of a nonhandicapped child.

Lemon test. A tripartite test used by the courts to evaluate claims under the establishment clause. Asks three questions: Does the action or policy (1) have a primarily secular purpose, (2) have the primary effect of advancing or inhibiting religion, or (3) foster an excessive entanglement between the state and religion?

Life adjustment education. An educational program, popular in the mid-twentieth century, which focused on youth who did not attend college, rejected traditional academic studies, and stressed functional objectives, such as vocation and health.

Limited open forum. The condition said to exist when schools provide noncurriculum student groups the opportunity to meet on school premises during noninstructional time.

Linguistic minority. Nonnative English speakers and others who are native speakers of English, but have been exposed to another language in the home since birth.

Logical positivism (logical empiricism). The view that no proposition can be considered scientifically valid unless it can be verified on logical or empirical grounds.

Magnet school. A school offering specialized and unique programs designed to attract students from throughout the district, thereby promoting racial integration.

Mainstreaming. The placing of handicapped children, to the maximum extent possible, into the regular classroom where they have contact with nonhandicapped children.

Malpractice. Failure on the part of a professional to render a reasonable amount of care in the exercise of his/her duties with resultant injury or loss to another.

Master teacher. A teacher who is given special status, pay, and recognition, but remains in the classroom as a role model for other teachers, or is released from a portion of the regular classroom assignment to work with other teachers in a supportive, nonsupervisory role.

Mastery learning. Instructional system in which the desired learnings and performance levels are identified and teachers work with students until they attain the desired level of performance.

Mentoring. Formal and informal relationships between a beginning teacher and an experienced teacher(s) that are sources of information and support for the beginning teacher.

Merit pay. Differential pay awarded to individuals with the same job description on the basis of the quality of their performance.

Metaphysics. The branch of philosophy concerned with the nature of reality and existence.

Multicultural education. An educational strategy that provides for those students whose cultural and linguistic backgrounds may prevent them from succeeding in the traditional school setting that historically reflects the dominant Anglo-Saxon culture.

Municipal overburden. A burden caused by the need for a greater range of social services in urban areas that must be paid for by the same taxpayers who support the schools.

National Assessment of Educational Progress (NAEP). A series of tests that are given to a sample of school children throughout the nation to provide national information about the general level of performance of elementary and secondary school students.

Naturalism. A philosophic or educational philosophy that emphasizes the natural world, the freedom of the individual, and the development of that which is natural in humans.

National Education Association (NEA). A professional organization for teachers and other educators in the United States.

Negligence. A failure to do (or not do) what a reasonable and prudent person would do under the same or similar circumstances, the result of which is injury to another.

Neo-Thomism. A traditional philosophy that bridges the dualism of idealism and realism and emphasizes the existence of God which can be known by both faith and reason.

New basics. A curriculum composed of English, mathematics, science, social studies, computer sciences, and foreign languages for those aspiring to college.

Nongraded school. A school in which grade divisions are eliminated for a sequence of two or more years.

Normal School. Institutions established in the 1800s for the purpose of training teachers.

Null curriculum. Those things that are not included in the formal curriculum because of their controversial nature, because they represent different values, or because of the lack of resources or information.

Object lesson. An instructional activity that centers on concrete materials within the child's experience and involves discussion and oral presentation.

Ontology. The branch of metaphysics that is concerned about the nature of existence and what it means for anything "to be."

Open classroom. An architectural design for elementary schools popular during the 1960s which consisted of large open instructional spaces not divided into traditional walled classrooms.

Operant conditioning. A type of behaviorism in which any response to any stimulus can be conditioned by immediate reinforcement or reward.

Paideia. The general body of knowledge that all educated individuals should possess.

Parochial school. A private elementary or secondary school supported or affiliated with a church or religious organization.

Perennialism. An educational theory that focuses on the past, namely the universal truths and such absolutes as reason and faith. Perennialists believe the purpose of the school is to cultivate the rational intellect and search for the truth.

Phenomenology. The study of the consciousness and experiencing of phenomena in philosophy.

Philosophical analysis. The process of systematic questioning of assumptions, values, theories, procedures, and methods designed to help formulate and clarify beliefs about teaching and learning.

Philosophy of education. The theory of philosophic thought that defines our views about the learner, the teacher, and the school.

Plenary. Absolute, as the power of the state legislature to enact any legislation controlling the schools that is not contrary to the federal Constitution or the state constitution.

Policies. Guidelines or principles for action adopted by a local school board to provide direction for administrative rules and regulations used in administering a local school district.

Postvention programs. Strategies or programs designed to help the school return to normal in the aftermath of a crisis, which include grief counseling, support groups, interacting with the media, and follow-up care.

Power equalization. State school finance system in which the governing board of each local school district determines its spending level per pupil. For each unit of local tax rate, the state will provide sufficient funds to ensure a guaranteed amount; state funds will be in inverse relation to the fiscal capacity per pupil of the local school district.

Premack principle. The principle that states that because organisms freely choose to engage in certain behaviors rather than others, providing access to the preferred activities will serve as a reinforcement for engaging in nonpreferred activities.

Prevention programs. Strategies including programs, activities, and services designed to reduce the occurrence of at-risk behaviors in children and adolescents.

Profession. An occupation involving relatively long and specialized preparation on the level of higher education and governed by its own code of ethics.

Professional development. Activities designed to build the personal strengths and creative talents of individuals and thus create human resources necessary for organizational productivity.

Programmed instruction. A teaching method that enables individual students to answer questions about a unit of study at their own rate, checking their own answers and advancing only after answering correctly.

Progressivism. A theory of education that is concerned with "learning by doing" and that purports that children learn best when pursuing their own interests and satisfying their own needs.

Project method. An instructional methodology that attempts to make education as "lifelike" as possible through the use of educative activities that are consistent with the child's own goals.

Property right. The right to specific real or personal property, tangible and intangible; e.g., the right to continued employment or the use of one's name.

Proprietary school. School operated by an individual, group, or corporation for profit to serve the educational needs of a particular clientele.

Provisional certificate. A certificate issued to a person who has not met the requirements for a standard certificate.

Proximate cause. The primary act or mission that produces an injury and without which the injury would not have occurred. A standard used to determine a teacher's liability in the cause of an injury.

Rate bill. A tuition fee based on the number of children paid by the parents during the mid-1800s.

Real reality. A form of reality that includes the realm of ideas, eternal truths, and perfect order in the philosophy of idealism.

Realism. A philosophy in which the world of nature and physical matter is superior to the world of ideas. Matter exists whether the mind perceives it or not.

Reduction in force (RIF). A reduction in the total number of employees needed by a school district because of enrollment declines, curriculum changes, or other occurrences.

Reflective thinking. Thinking that is characterized by deliberate inquiry into all assumptions, claims of knowledge, evidence, and one's own thought processes.

Restructuring. A buzzword of the 1990s, connoting a number of prescriptions for education: parental choice, year-round schools, longer days and longer years, recast modes of governance, alternative funding patterns, and all-out commitments to technology.

Revenue elasticity. Capacity of a tax source (i.e., sales, income, or property tax), to yield more or less revenue as the economy expands or contracts.

Reverse discrimination. Discrimination or bias against members of one class in an attempt to correct past discrimination against members of another class.

Robotics. The technology involving the use of robots in business and industry, usually for performing repetitive tasks.

Scholasticism. The philosophy of Thomas Aquinas which serves as the foundation for Catholic education and holds that man is a rational being who possesses both a spiritual nature and a physical nature, that truth can be arrived at through the deductive process, and that when reason fails, man must rely on faith.

School board. As created by the state, the governing body for a local school district, with members generally selected by popular vote.

School effectiveness. The level at which students are performing in the basic skills.

Scientific method. The systematic reporting and analysis of what is observed and retesting of hypotheses formulated from the observations.

Secondary school. A program of study that follows elementary school, such as junior high school, middle school, or high school.

Secretary of education. The executive officer of the U.S. Department of Education; a member of the president's cabinet.

Secular humanism. Allegedly a faith that denies God, deifies man, and glorifies reason.

Sense realism. The belief that learning must come through the senses.

Separatism. A form of diversity that suggests that by maintaining a separatist position, minority groups can build strength, maintain their identity, and gain power.

Sequence. The arrangement of learning experiences in curriculum to ensure that successive experiences build upon preceding ones.

Seven liberal arts. The curriculum that includes the trivium (grammar, rhetoric, and logic) and the quadrivium (arithmetic, geometry, music, and astronomy).

Sex bias. The biased behavior that results from believing in sex role stereotypes.

Sex discrimination. Any action that denies opportunities, privileges, or rewards to a person or persons because of their gender, in violation of the law.

Sex equity. In education, this term refers to the concepts of equal treatment and equal opportunity for all students, regardless of their sex.

Sex role stereotyping. The attribution of specific behaviors, abilities, personality characteristics, and interests to one's gender.

Sexual abuse. Contact or interaction between a child and an adult when the child is being used for the sexual stimulation of the perpetrator or another person.

Simulation. In teaching and learning, making the educational environment and experiences resemble the situation in which the learning will be applied as near as possible.

Single salary schedule. A salary schedule for teachers that provides equivalent salaries for equivalent preparation and experience.

Site-based management. Delegation by a school board of certain decision-making responsibilities about educational program and school operations to individual schools. Usually provides that teachers, parents, and the principal serve as the decision-making group.

Skinheads. Neo-Nazi gang.

Skip-generation families. Families in which the grandparents are their grandchildren's primary caretakers.

Slack time. Time for teachers that is not scheduled for necessary activities, but during which they have some independence.

Social class. A social stratum in which the members share similar characteristics, such as income, occupation, status, education, etc.

Social mobility. The movement upward or downward among social classes.

Social reconstructionism. An educational theory that advocates change, improvement, and the reforming of the school and society.

Social reconstruction curriculum. A curriculum design that aims to engage students in a critical analysis of society and prepare them to effect change and create a more equitable society.

Social selection. A position that suggests schools serve the wealthy and powerful at the expense of the poor.

Socialization. The process by which persons are conditioned to the customs or patterns of a particular culture.

Society. A group of persons who share a common culture, government, institutions, land, or set of social relationships.

Socioeconomic status. The social and economic standing of an individual or group.

Socratic Method. A dialectical teaching method employed by Socrates using a questioning process based on the student's experiences and analyzing the consequences of responses, leading the student to a better understanding of the problem.

Sovereign immunity. The government's freedom from being sued for money damages without its consent.

Spiral curriculum. Curriculum in which a subject matter is presented over a number of grades with increasing complexity and abstraction.

Stare decisis. Let the decision stand; a legal rule that states that once a court has laid down a principle of law as applicable to a certain set of facts, it will apply it to all future cases where the facts are substantially the same and that other courts of equal or lesser rank will similarly apply the principle.

State board of education. A state agency charged with adopting regulations and monitoring local school districts to ensure implementation of the constitutional and statutory mandates related to the operation of the state system of schools.

State department of education. The operating arm for the administration of state education activities and functions.

Statutory law. That body of law consisting of the written enactments of a legislative body.

Strategic planning. A planning process that involves the establishment of a mission statement, the specification of goals and objectives, and the linking of funding priorities to the accomplishment of program priorities.

Subculture. A group of people distinguished by ethnic, racial, religious, geographic, social, economic, or lifestyle traits.

Subject-centered curriculum. Curriculum designed with the acquisition of certain knowledge as the primary goal. The learning process usually involves rote memorization and learning is measured using objective test scores.

Subject-area curriculum. A curriculum design that views the curriculum as a group of subjects or a body of that subject matter which has survived the test of time.

Suicide gesture. A behavior that suggests a willingness to commit suicide.

Suicide ideation. Thoughts about suicide.

Suicide threat. An expression of an intention to commit suicide.

Sunday schools. Educational programs of the later 1700s and early 1800s offering the rudiments of reading and writing on Sunday to children who worked during the week.

Superintendent of schools. The chief executive officer of the local school district whose educational program and related responsibilities include planning, staffing, coordinating, budgeting, administering, evaluating, and reporting. This person informs and works with the local school board.

Suspension. Exclusion of students from school for a period of time of 10 days or less.

Tabula rasa. Literally, blank slate: applied to the concept of the human mind which says that children come into the world with their minds a blank slate.

Tax benefits. Tax deductions and tax credits designed to benefit patrons and nonpublic schools.

Teachers' institute. A teacher training activity begun in the nineteenth century, lasting from a few days to several weeks, where teachers met to be instructed in new techniques, informed of modern materials, and inspired by noted educators.

Tenure. The status conferred on teachers who have served a specific period which guarantees them continuation of employment, subject to the requirements of good behavior and financial necessity.

Theory. A hypothesis or set of hypotheses that have been verified by observation or experiment, or a general synonym for systematic thinking or a set of coherent thoughts.

Theory of education. Systematic thinking or generalization about schooling.

Time on task. Amount of time that a student or teacher spends actively involved in the teaching or learning process.

Tort. A civil wrong that leads to injury to another and for which a court will provide a remedy in the form of an action for damages.

Transdisciplinary education. Method of instruction that involves a variety of disciplines that focus on broad-based ideas rather than on discrete subjects.

Tutorial program. Instructional system in which one person is assigned to assist, instruct, and/or examine a student; may be a professional employee of the school district, a fellow student, or an out-of-school volunteer adult.

Vernacular schools. Elementary schools originating in Germany in the sixteenth century that offered instruction in the mother tongue or vernacular, and a basic curriculum of reading, writing, mathematics, and religion.

Vertical equity. The assumption that groups that have different needs should be treated differently and also that those within each group should be treated in the same way.

Vocational education. Secondary and postsecondary programs of education designed to provide an alternative to college preparation and to prepare students for employment in all occupations except those requiring at least a baccalaureate degree.

Voucher. A grant or payment made to a parent or child to be used to pay the cost of the child's education in a private or public school.

Whole-child movement. An educational movement emphasizing totality of the child as the composite of the social, emotional, physical, and mental dimensions.

White flight. The exodus of middle and upper class white families from urban school districts to avoid desegregation.

Author Index

Addis, M., 319, 341

Adler, M. J., 78–79, 98, 203–204, 233, 483, 514–515, 531, 589

Aldeman, N. E., 19, 32

Anderson, D. R., 243–244, 269

Anderson, J. D., 131, 137

Anrig, G. R., 32

Apple, M. W., 246, 269, 496–497, 499, 501, 523, 531

Arends, R. I., 10–12, 33

Arias, M. B., 294, 306

Aristotle, 198

Arland, H., 252, 270, 280, 307

Ascher, C., 326, 341

Astuto, T. A., 26–27, 32, 556

Auburdene, P., 566–567, 573, 583

August, D., 293–294, 306

Austin, G. R., 547

Axtell, J. L., 79, 98

Bagley, W. C., 151–152, 169

Bane, M. J., 252, 270, 280, 307

Baratz-Snowden, J., 254, 256, 261–262, 269

Barnard, H., 101

Barnes, G. M., 314, 344

Barnes, H. E., 224, 233

Barone, T., 516, 531

Barrett, T. C., 341

Barrow, R., 66, 98

Bass de Martinez, B., 13, 32

Bates, J. A., 213, 233

Beck, A. G., 65, 98

Beck, M., 563, 566, 569, 582

Beebe, R. J., 24, 32

Beentjes, J. W. J., 244, 269

Bell, T. H., 32

Benjamin, S., 566, 574, 576, 582

Bentler, P. M., 313, 343

Berlender, D., 539, 543, 545, 547, 556

Berman, A. L., 322, 341

Bete, C. L., 333–334, 336–337, 341

Bialo, E. R., 327, 341

Bickers, P. M., 269

Binder, F. M., 111, 113, 115, 118, 137

Black, H. C. 347, 355, 376

Bloom, A., 204, 233

Bloom, B. S., 507–508, 531

Blum, R., 550, 556

Bock, R. D., 260, 269

Bondi, J., 495, 502

Bonjean, L. M., 328, 330–331, 341

Bonner, T. N., 145, 169

Book, C., 12, 32

Borkow, N. B., 12, 32

Bortner, M. A., 337, 339, 341

Bowen, J., 66, 68, 98

Bowers, C. A., 497, 501

Bowles, S., 246, 269

Boyer, E. L., 15, 32, 483, 493, 553, 556, 562, 582, 589

Braddock, J. H., II, 280

Brameld, T., 221, 233

Brandt, R., 511, 527, 531

Brecher, E. J., 328, 343

Bridgman, A., 441–442

Brody, J., 249, 269

Brookover, W., 506, 531

Brousseau, B., 12, 32

Brown, W. S., 13, 33

Bruner, J., 157, 487

Buckley, B., 526, 531

Burdin, J. L., 578–579

Burns, R., 507, 531

Buscemi, M., 318, 341

Bush, G., 2

Butler, J. D., 181–182, 197, 550, 556

Butts, R. F., 126, 129, 137

Cain, E. J., 569, 574–575, 582

Cambron-McCabe, N. H., 350, 367, 369, 376, 383, 385, 389, 391, 393, 413, 415, 472

Cameron, C. E., 274, 306

Campbell, R. F., 424, 426, 434, 442
Carelli, A. O., 297–300, 306
Carlson, K., 19, 34
Carriedo, R. A., 98
Carter, D., 257, 260–261, 269
Carter, T. P., 129, 137
Casanova, W., 292, 306
Castle, E. B., 64, 69, 98
Cave, W. M., 238, 269
Cavendish, R., 564
Cawelti, G., 493, 501, 549–550, 556, 577
Cetron, M. J., 564–566, 569–571, 575, 577, 582
Chesler, M. A., 238, 269
Chira, S., 527–529, 531
Church, R. L., 157, 160, 169
Cimbolic, P., 323, 342
Clark, D. L., 26–27, 30, 32, 367, 376, 556
Clinton, D., 106
Clume, W. H., III, 452, 472
Coffman, C. Q., 27, 32
Cohen, D., 252, 270, 280, 307
Cohen, M., 536, 556
Cohen, S. S., 86, 90–92, 94–95, 98
Cohen-Sandler, R., 322, 341
Coleman, J. S., 247–249, 252, 269, 536–537, 556
Collier, V., 292, 307
Collins, G. J., 348, 353, 376
Collins, P. A., 243–244, 269
Commager, H. S., 105
Conant, J. B., 169, 215, 233, 438, 442
Confucius, 236
Conners, E. T., 414
Coons, J. E., 452, 472
Copen, P., 574, 583
Cornbleth, C., 478, 501
Costa, M., 302, 306
Counts, G. C., 151, 221, 233, 495, 501
Cowan, J., 303, 306
Cox, H. G., 582
Crain, R. L., 280
Craver, S. M., 181–184, 187–189, 192, 194, 197, 218, 228
Cremen, L. A., 90, 93–94, 98, 103, 107, 109, 115, 118, 138, 146–148, 153, 161, 169, 491, 501
Cruickshank, D. R., 16, 32
Cruz, J., Jr., 16, 32
Cryer, N., 329, 342
Cuban, L., 516, 531

Cubberley, E. P., 86–87, 98, 454, 472
Cunningham, L. L., 424, 426, 434, 442

David, I., 339, 341
David, L., 339, 341
Davies, O., 564–565, 569–571, 577, 582
Dawe, H. A., 4, 32
Dawson, C., 288, 308, 429, 443, 452, 472
DeBlassie, R. R., 322, 342
Dede, C., 526, 531, 570, 582
Delattre, E. J., 216, 233
Delon, F. G., 388, 414
Denham, C., 556
Descartes, R., 182–183
Dewey, J., 192, 197, 208, 218, 233
Dezseran, C., 333, 341
Distad, L., 333, 341
Doll, R. C., 490
Domaine, B., 554, 556
Donaldson, G., 553, 556
Dong, F., 275, 277, 280, 308
Dorman, G., 314, 341
Douglas, W. O., 504
Drucker, P. F., 570, 582
Due, J. F., 472
Duke, D. L., 515, 531
Dunham, H. M., 323
Durbin, J., 287, 306
Dwyer, D., 540, 556

Eaton, W. E., 59
Edmonds, R., 536–537, 556–557
Egbert, R. L., 9, 33
Eisner, E., 495, 497, 501
Elam, S. M., 29, 33, 527, 531
Ellis, A. K., 491, 501, 519, 531
Elmore, R. F., 287, 306
Elson, D. E., 304, 306
Emmer, E. T., 211–212, 233
Estes, T., 525, 531
Ezell, J. S., 460, 472

Fennema, E., 265–267, 269, 298, 306
Ferguson, W. E., 322, 342
Finegan, T., 17
Finkelhor, D., 333, 341
Finn, C., 527, 529, 531
Fischer, L., 356, 385, 389, 394, 414
Flygare, T. J., 410, 414
Footlick, J. K., 563, 571, 582

Ford, P. L., 88–89, 98
Forsyth, P. B., 590
Fox, J. N., 45, 59
Foxe, J., 87
Franklin, B., 93
Frantz, N. R., Jr., 304, 306
Frase, M. J., 326, 342
Frazer, D., 133, 138
Frazier, S. H., 322–323, 342
Freeman, D., 12, 32
Freire, P., 222, 233
Friedman, M., 472
Frymier, J., 312–313, 321–322, 342–343
Furner, B., 562, 582

Gage, N. L., 4, 33
Gallegos, E. M., 287, 307
Gallup, A. M., 30, 367, 376, 527, 531
Galluzzo, G. R., 10–12, 33
Gansneder, B., 312–313, 342
Garber, H., 547
Garcia, E. E., 293–294, 306
Gareiss, R., 339, 342
Gayle, M., 582
Gee, E. G., 384, 414
Geiger, K., 527, 532
Geldof, D., 314, 341
Gerald, D. E., 265, 269
Gersten, J. C., 312–313, 342
Gibbon, S. Y., Jr., 577, 582
Gibney, F., 339, 342
Gideonse, H., 19, 34
Giella, M., 552, 557
Gilbert, W. S., 346
Gillette, M., 13, 33, 68, 80, 82, 93, 98
Gintis, H., 246, 252, 269–270, 280, 307
Gipp, G. E., 295
Giroux, H. A., 246, 269
Glatthorn, A., 496, 501
Glenn, A. D., 491, 501, 519, 531
Good, C. V., 4, 33, 39, 59
Good, H. G., 67, 98
Goodlad, J. I., 16, 33, 483, 492–493, 502, 590
Goodwin, D. A., 304, 308
Goodwin, T., 322, 344
Goren, P. D., 98
Graham, L., 334, 342
Graham, P. A., 13, 33, 120, 138
Grant, C. A., 13, 33
Gray, R., 142, 169

Greene, B. Z., 326, 342
Greene, J. E., 29, 33
Greene, M., 230, 233
Greuling, J. W., 322, 342
Grieder, C., 419, 425, 432, 442
Griffiths, D. E., 590
Grossnickle, D. R., 326–327, 342
Guskey, T., 513–514, 521, 532
Gutek, G. L., 86, 93, 95, 98, 105–106, 112–113, 117, 119–120, 122, 124–125, 133, 138, 149, 169
Gutman, C. J., 525, 531

Haberman, M., 14, 33
Hackett, G., 339, 342
Haddock, V., 339, 342
Hahn, A., 254, 269
Haig, R. M., 452, 472
Hamar, R., 288–289, 308
Hand, P. A., 132
Hanes, M. L., 19, 33
Hare, N., 133, 138
Harrington-Lueker, D., 275
Harris, L., 39, 53, 59, 242, 343
Harris-Hart, M., 334, 342
Harrison, E. K., 525, 531
Hart, V., 282
Haskins, R., 260, 269
Havighurst, R. J., 241, 247, 270, 297, 307, 416
Hawley, W. D., 22, 33
Hayes, L., 327, 342
Hayes, R. L., 329, 342
Heffernan, H., 148, 169
Hegel, G. W. F., 184
Henderson, R. I., 29, 33
Herman, P., 333, 335, 342
Hersch, P., 336, 342
Heyns, B., 252, 270, 280, 307
Higgins, M., 574, 582
Hipple, J., 323, 342
Hirsch, E. D., 525, 532
Holmes, O. W., Jr., 378
Holt, J., 227, 233
Howsam, R. B., 59
Hudgens, H. C., Jr., 357–358, 376
Hughes, R. D., 333–334, 343
Hunkins, F. P., 492, 502
Hussar, W. J., 265, 269
Hussey, M. A., 322, 344
Hutchins, R. M., 203, 233

Hyde, J. S., 263–264, 270
Hyland, C. R., 254–256, 258, 269

Ihle, E., 226–227, 233
Illich, I., 222, 233, 246, 269, 495–496, 502
Ingle, M. E., 322, 344
Irwin, P. M., 462–464, 472
Ishler, R. E., 10–11, 33

Jacks, M., 67, 98
Jarvis, P., 307
Jefferson, T., 41, 363
Jencks, C., 252, 270, 280, 307
Jenkinson, E. B., 371, 376
Jensen, S., 330, 343
Johns, T., 288, 308, 429, 443, 452, 472
Johnson, J. H., 322, 342
Johnson, L. B., 272
Johnson, S. M., 27, 33
Jones, J. G., 333, 342
Jordan, K. F., 12, 16, 32–33, 40, 59, 419, 424,
    428, 432, 437, 442–443, 470, 472

Kagay, M., 39, 53, 59
Kant, I., 184
Kaplan, G., 166, 170
Kaye, A., 302, 307
Kelly, C., 356, 385, 389, 394, 414
Kerr, C., 153
Kidwell, C. S., 126, 128, 138, 150, 170
King, R. A., 322, 341
King, S. E., 499, 502
Kirkland, E. C., 143, 170
Klopfer, L., 528, 532
Knapp, M. S., 254, 270
Kneip, W., 529, 532
Kneller, G. F., 182, 193, 195, 197, 200–201, 206,
    218, 224–226, 233
Knight, E. W., 153, 170
Kohl, H. R., 6–8, 33
Kourilsky, M., 506–508, 532
Kozol, J., 226–227, 233, 307

Lachance, L., 328, 342
LaMorte, M. W., 449, 451, 472
Landauer, W. L., 389, 414
Landers, S., 264, 270, 336, 342
Laurie, S. S., 75–76, 98
Lawton, M., 321, 342
Lawton, S., 288, 308, 429, 443, 452, 472
Leichenko, S., 39, 53, 59

Levin, H., 547–548, 557
Levine, D. U., 241, 247, 270, 297, 307
Levine, M., 108, 138
Lewis, A. C., 484, 502
Lieberman, A., 556
Light, A., 275, 277, 280, 308
Lightman, M., 319, 341
Lines, P. M., 18, 33
Linn, M. C., 263–264, 270
Lipman, M., 532
Littlefield, G. E., 88
Locke, John, 79
Long, L., 226–227, 233
Lotto, L., 556
Luckins, R., 566, 575, 582
Lykavitz, B., 254, 269
Lynch, R. H., 297, 307
Lyons, T. S., 534, 557

MacDonald, D. I., 314, 343
Mackey, J. A., 491, 501, 519, 531
Madsen, D. L., 103, 105, 109, 122–123, 138
Magee, J. B., 229–230, 233
Mahar, M., 440, 442
Manarino-Leggett, P., 27, 32
Mann, D., 553–555, 557
Mann, H., 36, 63
Maritain, J., 203, 233
Marler, C. D., 182, 197, 225, 233
Massialas, B., 518, 532
Mayer, F., 80, 82, 98
McCabe, N. H., 276–277, 307
McCarthy, M. M., 245, 271, 276–277, 307, 350,
    367, 369, 373, 376–377, 381, 383, 385, 389,
    393, 395, 403, 414–415
McCarthy, T. L., 297, 307
McCleary, L. E., 433, 442
McCutcheon, G., 499, 502
McCutcheon, S. M., 322, 342
McDaniel, T. R., 167, 170, 500, 502
McDill, E. L., 258, 270, 583
McDonald, D. M., 262, 270, 296–297, 307
McDonough, J. T., 534, 557
McEwen, T., 308
McGarrahan, E., 328, 343
McKeown, M. P., 470, 472
McKibbin, M. D., 20, 33
McLaughlin, M. W., 54, 59, 287, 306
McPartland, J. M., 280
Medina, A., 330, 344
Metha, A., 323

Meyer, A. E., 66–67, 73–74, 98
Meyer, R. H., 304, 308
Michelson, S., 252, 270, 280, 307
Michie, J. S., 288–289, 308
Mitgang, L., 260, 264, 266, 270
Moffett, W., 304, 307
Mojkowski, C., 576, 583
Monroe, P., 69, 98
Moore, E. G. L., 260, 269
Morris, V. C., 177–179, 184, 188–189, 194, 197, 201, 203, 225, 233–234
Morrison, H. C., 454, 472
Morrison, J. R., 330, 343
Mort, P. R., 472
Morton, C., 574, 583
Mrela, C., 321, 343
Muraskin, L. D., 304, 308
Murphy, C., 542, 557
Murray, F. B., 15, 33
Myerson-Katz, B., 333, 341

Naisbitt, J., 566–567, 573, 583
Natriello, G., 258, 270, 327, 343, 583
Neill, A. S., 226, 234
Nelson, H., 548–549, 557
Newcomb, M. D., 313, 343
Nickerson, R., 528, 532
Nicklos, L. B., 13, 33
Nystrand, R. O., 19, 34, 424, 426, 434, 442

Ochoa, A. M., 286, 307
O'Conner, M. C., 258, 270
Ogbu, J. U., 245, 270, 307
Olson, N., 550, 556
Omark, D. R., 286
Orfield, G., 258, 270
Orlosky, D. E., 433, 442
Orstein, A. C., 440, 443, 492, 502
Ovando, C., 292, 307
Ozmon, H. A., 181–184, 187–189, 192, 194, 218, 228, 234

Pacheco, R., 286
Pai, Y., 177–179, 184, 188–189, 201, 203, 234
Pallas, A. M., 258, 270, 583
Pankratz, H., 408, 415
Panzerger, J., 254, 269
Parelius, A. P., 253, 270
Parelius, R. J., 253, 270
Partelli, J. P., 228, 234
Pearl, D., 243, 270

Perkinson, H. J., 147, 151, 170
Peters, T., 557
Peterson, J. M., 142, 169
Peterson, N. L., 283–284, 307
Pettis, K. W., 333–334, 343
Pfeffer, C., 321, 343
Pfeifer, R. S., 54, 59
Phillips, D. C., 210, 234
Phipps-Yonas, S., 331, 343
Pierce, T. M., 419, 425, 432, 442
Pifer, A., 129–131, 138
Pitzi, M. J., 261, 270
Plato, 62, 67, 182, 197, 300
Platt, J. R., 583
Pollack, J., 254, 256, 261–262, 269
Portelli, J. P., 478, 495, 502
Posner, G. J., 487–488, 502
Power, E. J., 186–187, 197
Price, V., 244, 270
Protheroe, N., 459, 472
Pulliam, J. D., 102, 115, 122, 124, 133, 136, 138, 147–148, 151, 170, 491, 502, 579, 583
Purkey, S., 542, 557
Purpel, D., 246, 269

Quaranta, L., 506–508, 532
Quintilian, 69

Radeki, T., 243, 270
Ralph, J., 288–289, 307
Ramey, C. T., 260, 269
Ravitch, D., 154–155, 162, 170, 496, 502
Red Horse, J., 297, 307
Reed, H. B., 303, 307
Reed, S., 253–254, 270, 336, 343
Reeves, M. S., 261–262, 270, 295, 307
Resnick, L., 528, 532
Richardson, S. N., 374, 377
Rickover, Adm. H. G., 216, 234
Rippa, S. A., 98, 104–105, 110, 112, 124, 134, 138
Rist, R. C., 260, 270
Ritchie, D., 244, 270
Rittenmeyer, D. C., 328, 330–331, 341
Roberts, D. F., 244, 270
Robertson, N., 313, 343
Robinson, G. E., 459, 472
Rocha, W., 566, 575, 582
Rock, D., 254, 256, 261–262, 269
Rogers, C. R., 227, 234, 583
Rogers, J., 87

Rosauer, R., 330, 343
Rosenberg, M., 279–280, 307
Rosenholtz, S., 536–537, 543, 549, 553, 557
Ross, A., 476
Ross, J. M., 275, 277, 280, 308
Roth, R. A., 21, 33
Rowan, B., 540, 557
Rowls, M. D., 19, 33
Ruch, C., 19
Ruof, S. R., 343
Rush, B., 103

Sadker, D., 298, 308
Sadker, M., 298, 308
Saks, J. B., 253, 270
Salmon, R., 288, 308, 429, 443, 452, 472
Salzman, K. P., 318, 343
Salzman, S. A., 318, 343
Sandefur, J. T., 18, 34
Sandza, R., 339, 342
Santayana, G., 100
Sautter, R. C., 253–254, 270, 336, 343
Savage, D. G., 288, 308
Scarborough, B., 314, 341
Scheffler, I., 229, 234
Schimmel, D., 356, 385, 389, 394, 414
Schlesinger, A. M., 166, 170
Schmuck, P., 298, 308
Schroeder, P., 573, 583
Schulman-Miller, J., 319, 341
Schwartz, W., 326, 341
Schweinhart, L., 289, 308
Sedlak, M. W., 157, 160, 169
Selakovich, D., 241, 246, 270, 308
Seligmann, J., 571, 583
Sequra, R. D., 129, 137
Shamis, S., 312–313, 342
Shane, H. G., 498, 564, 566, 576, 583
Shapiro, A., 433, 442
Shaw, S. J., 575, 583
Sherman, J. D., 343
Sherman, R. R., 239, 244, 250–251, 271, 277, 280, 308
Shields, P. M., 254, 270
Shore, K., 282, 285, 308
Silberman, 226–227, 234
Singer, M. T., 319–321, 343
Sivin, J. P., 327, 341
Sizer, T. R., 590
Skilbeck, M., 493, 502

Skinner, B., 518–519, 532
Slavin, R., 511–512, 532
Smith, B. O., 4, 34
Smith, D. C., 19, 34
Smith, G. P., 34
Smith, M., 252, 270, 280, 307, 542, 557
Snider, W., 472
Snyder, K., 552, 557
Soltis, J. F., 175, 197, 210, 229, 234, 487, 502
Soriano, B., 582
Sowell, T., 160, 170
Spanfer, J. H., 389, 414
Spano, J., 343
Spencer, H., 119
Sperry, D. J., 384, 414
Spring, J., 105–106, 117, 134–135, 138, 151, 159–160, 170, 246, 270, 481–482, 485, 502
Stark, E., 343
Stedman, J. B., 428, 437, 443, 470, 472
Stein, C. B., Jr., 290–291, 308
Steindam, S., 298, 308
Stout, R. T., 590
Strahan, R. D., 370, 377
Strayer, G. D., 452, 472
Streibel, M., 523, 532
Strickland, D. C., 304, 306
Strother, D. B., 321, 343
Sugarman, S. D., 452, 472
Swanson-Owens, D., 54, 59
Swift, D. W., 126, 128, 133, 138, 150, 170
Sylvester, D. W., 72
Szasz, M. C., 127–128, 138, 150, 170

Taber, F. M., 569, 574–575, 582
Tabler, M. B., 498
Teller, J. D., 67, 98
Tetreault, M. K., 298, 308
Thomas, D. R., 246–247, 270
Thomas, S., 245, 271, 373, 377
Thorne, J. M., 288–289, 308
Tikunoff, W., 540, 557
Tippeconnic, J. W., III, 295, 308
Toffler, A., 560
Tollett, K. S., 161, 170
Tom, A., 514, 532
Topping, K., 108, 138
Tsang, S. L., 261, 271
Turiel, E., 243, 271
Turner, D. L., 370, 377
Tyler, R. W., 487–489, 502

Updegraff, H., 452, 473
Usdan, M. D., 424, 426, 434, 442

Vacca, R. S., 357–358, 376
Valente, W. D., 354, 377, 389–390, 415
Valentine, J., 157, 170
Van der Voort, T. H. A., 244, 269
Van Horn, B. F., Jr., 389, 414
Vican, L., 339, 344
Vocke, D., 529, 532

Walden, T., 260, 269
Walker, D. E., 487, 502
Walker, R., 451, 473
Wallace, H. W., 330, 344
Wallace, S., 297, 307
Ward, H., 310
Washburn, J. S., 308
Washington, G., 103
Waterman, R., 557
Waters, M. M., 13, 34
Webb, L. D., 245, 271, 373, 377, 433, 442
Webb, R. B., 239, 244, 250–251, 271, 277, 280,
    308
Weeks, J., 330, 344
Wegmann, R., 562, 583
Weikart, D., 289, 308
Welch, F., 275, 277, 280, 308
Wells, H. G., 3, 140
Welte, J. W., 314, 344

West, E., 131–132, 138
West, L. J., 319, 343
Westbrook, J., 546, 557
White, M. A., 568
Wilder, G., 254, 256, 261–262, 269
Wiles, J., 495, 502
Wilkins, A. S., 69, 98
Will, G. F., 172
Williams, B. I., 288–289, 308
Wilson, R., 257, 260–261, 269
Wingo, G. M., 174–175, 181–183, 185, 197,
    214–215, 224, 234
Winn, C., 67, 98
Wirt, J. G., 304, 308
Wittgenstein, L., 229, 234
Witthuhn, 261–262
Wittrock, M. C., 211, 234
Womack, S., 522, 532
Woodward, W. H., 74–75, 98
Worsham, T., 525, 532

Yaber, W. L., 168, 170, 331–332, 344
Yeaworth, C. R., 322, 344
Yee, S., 54, 59
Yinger, J. M., 279–280, 308
York, J., 322, 344

Zevin, J., 518, 532
Zigler, E., 157, 170
Zimpher, N. L., 17, 34

Subject Index

Absenteeism, 562
Academic freedom, 395–396, 591
Academic learning time, 547, 591
Academies, 67, 90–91, 96, 105, 108, 109–111,
    118–119, 121, 591
  Franklin, 93–94, 109
  Philadelphia, 93
  teachers in, 133
  women, 109
Accountability, 448–449, 469–470, 485, 543, 591
Achievement, 486
Acquired immune deficiency syndrome, 165,
    168, 313, 331–333, 336, 383, 410–412, 591
Activity curriculum, 83, 85, 591
Adequacy, 448, 470, 591
Adler, Mortimer, 78–79, 201, 203–205, 483,
    491, 497
Administrative council, 436–437, 591
Administrative law, 349, 357, 593
Adult education, 300–303, 305, 479, 586–587,
    591
Adult Education Act, 300, 586
Aesthetics, 176–177, 187–188, 194, 591
Affirmative action, 390, 400–401, 591
Agassiz, 216
Age Discrimination in Employment Act
    Amendment, 24
Age of Enlightenment, 78–82, 90. *See also specific
    philosophers*
Aging of America, 563–566, 569–570, 581
Aguilar v. Felton, 372, 376
Air Force Academy, 585
Alan Guttmacher Institute, 330, 341
Albee, Edward, 196
Albertus Magnus, St., 202
Alcohol abuse, 313–318, 322, 327, 336
Alcuin of York, 73, 75
Alexander, Lamar, 420
Alternative certification, 19–20, 31, 591
Alternative schools, 209, 227, 496, 499, 591
Amalgamation, 246–247, 591

Ambach v. Norwick, 382, 388, 413
American Association for Counseling and
    Development, 57
American Association for Supervision and
    Curriculum Development, 484, 493
American Association for the Advancement of
    Science, 484
American Association of Colleges of Teacher
    Education, 9, 11–12, 19, 32, 40, 589
American Association of Community and Junior
    Colleges, 302
American Association of School Administrators,
    57, 318, 433, 442, 484
American Baptist Mission Society, 131
American Broadcasting Company, 302
American Civil Liberties Union, 319
American College Test, 12–13, 261, 264, 266
American Colonization Society, 130
American Council of Life Insurance, 331, 341
American Federation of Teachers, 18, 21, 27, 37,
    42, 44, 54–56, 58, 156, 484, 589, 592
  history of, 55–56
American Institute of Instruction, 113
American Journal of Education, 115, 125
American Library Association, 57
American Lyceum, 113
American Missionary Association, 131
American Normal School Association, 56
Amish, 247, 374
Anable v. Ford, 404, 413
Analytic approach, 174–175
Analytic philosophy movement, 228–230
Anglican Church, 77, 94
Anglican Society for the Propagation of the
    Gospel, 102
Annapolis, 109
Antioch, 124
Apparent reality, 178–179, 592
Apperception, 80
Apple, Michael, 246
Apprenticeship system, 87, 95

Apprentice teachers, 51–52
Aptitude tests, 148
Aristotle, 67–68, 73, 97, 179, 184–185,
    187–188, 198, 216, 249
Arline standard, 410
Armstrong, General Samuel Chapman, 131
Army Specialized Training Program, 153
Articles of Confederation, 102
Artificial intelligence, 574, 581, 592
Asians, education of, 256, 260–261, 289, 294,
    562–563
Assimilation, 127–128, 246–247, 280, 290–291,
    295, 592
Association for Supervision and Curriculum
    Development, 57
Association of Colleges and Schools of
    Education, 10–11
Association of Junior Leagues, 318
Athens, 64–65, 71
Atlanta University, 131
At-risk youth, 297, 311–340, 464, 592
    acquired immune deficiency syndrome, 313,
        331–333, 336, 410–412, 591
    child abuse, 312–313, 333–336, 385, 593, 601
    cult participation, 313, 318–321, 594
    delinquency, 313, 322, 337–340, 594
    dropouts, 253–254, 256, 262, 289, 297,
        312–313, 326–329, 331, 340, 405, 447, 515,
        527, 555, 562, 587, 595
    drug abuse, 312–318, 322, 327, 331, 333, 336,
        339, 596
    runaways, 313, 323, 333–337
    suicide, 311–313, 321–325, 336, 593–594,
        603
    teenage pregnancy, 300, 312–313, 327–331,
        336
Attorney general, 160, 357–358, 375, 592
Augustine, St., 218, 223
Autonomy of teachers, 39–41
Axiology, 175–177, 179, 180, 592
    existentialism, 194–195
    experimentalism, 190–191
    idealism, 182–183
    neo-Thomism, 188–189
    realism, 186–187

Baby boom, 153
Back-to-basics movement, 216, 227, 491, 493,
    592
Bacon, Francis, 78, 84 187
Bagley, William, 151–152, 156, 216–217

Bankhead-Jones Act, 585
Baptists, 92, 131
Barnard, Henry, 80, 101, 113, 115, 125, 134
Basic skills, 538–540, 587
B. Dalton Bookseller's National Literacy
    Initiative, 302
Beckett, Samuel, 196
Beecher, Catherine, 109, 115, 125, 134
Beginning teachers, 51–53
Behavioral objectives, 212–213, 487, 507–508,
    592
Behaviorism, 200, 210–213, 231, 592
Beilan v. Board of Public Education, 351, 376
Bell, Terrel H., 14, 420
Bellmer v. Lund, 404, 413
Bennett, William, 420
Berea College, 130
Bestor, Arthur, 151, 154, 156, 216–217, 491,
    497
Bethel School District No. 403 v. Fraser,
    406–407, 413
Bibliotherapy, 334, 592
Bilingual education, 161, 209, 289, 291–294,
    349, 479, 562, 586, 592, 595
Bilingual Education Act, 161, 292, 356, 586
    amendments, 294
Bilingual maintenance, 293
Bill for the More General Diffusion of
    Knowledge, 104
Bill of Rights, 104
Bill of Rights for Handicapped Children,
    281–283, 286–287
Binet, Alfred, 148
Binet-Simon scale, 148
Biogenetics, 574, 592
Birdwell v. Hazelwood School District, 396, 413
Birthrates, 571–572
Black Codes, 129–130
Black Muslims, 247
Blacks, education of, 128–133, 136, 255–260,
    274, 276–277, 280, 290–292, 326, 562–563
    civil rights movement, 159–162, 274, 291
Blacks in teaching, 131, 274
Block grants, 464, 592
Bloom, Allan, 204–205
Bloom, Benjamin S., 507–508, 512, 592
Boarding schools, 127–128, 150
Board of Education, Island Trees Union Free
    School District No. 26, v. Pico, 396, 406, 413
Board of Education of Westside Community
    Schools v. Mergens, 364, 367, 375–376

Board of Education v. Rowley, 287
Board of Regents v. Roth, 392
Boards of education
　local, 383, 428, 433–435, 437, 481–482, 528,
　　602
　state, 114–115, 422–425, 428, 451, 481, 603
Boston English High School, 118
Boston Latin School, 88, 90
Boyer, Ernest L., 483, 493, 497
Brameld, Theodore, 221, 223, 495, 497
Brennan, William J., 363
British Open University, 302
Brookings Institution, 128
Broudy, 497
Brown University, 91, 96
Brown v. Board of Education of Topeka, 63,
　　159–160, 169, 274–276, 306, 361, 376
Bruner, Jerome, 157, 487
Brynes, James F., 363
Bryn Mawr College, 124
Buber, Martin, 194
Buckley Amendment, 409–410
Budgets, 458–459, 481
Bugenhagen, Johann, 76
Burch v. Baker, 413
Bureau of Education, 419
Bureau of Indian Affairs, 128, 150, 262, 295,
　　357
Bureau of Occupational and Adult Education,
　　586
Bureau of the Census, 142, 147, 153, 170, 254,
　　257, 259–261, 267, 271, 290, 308
Burnout, 53–54
Bush, George, 165–166, 279, 420, 553
Business-education partnership, 553–555
Business-Higher Education Forum, 553, 589
Busing, 275–276, 278
Butts v. Dallas Independent School District, 407,
　　413

California Basic Education Skills Test, 11, 18
Calvin, John, 76–77, 84, 87
Cambridge University, 122
Camus, Albert, 195
Cardinal Principles of Secondary Education,
　　120–121
Career Education Incentive Act, 586
Career ladder plans, 26, 41, 46, 51–52, 58, 592
Carey v. Piphus, 403, 413
Carl D. Perkins Vocational Education Act, 304,
　　587

Carnegie Forum, 13, 15–16, 32, 43, 589
Carnegie Foundation, 483, 589
Carpio v. Tucson High School District No. 1,
　　354, 376
Carter, Jimmy, 162
Cartesian method, 183–184, 592
Case law, 349, 355, 357
Categorical funding, 451, 453–454, 592
Categorical imperatives, 184, 593
Catholics. See Roman Catholic Church
Cavazos, Lauro, 420
Censorship, 369–371, 396–397, 407–408
Center for Disease Control, 332
Center for Population Options, 330
Center on the Study of Democratic Institutions,
　　203
Certification, 16–21, 38, 43–44, 55, 58, 135,
　　143, 167, 355, 357, 380–382, 390, 428, 593
　alternative programs, 19–20, 31, 591
　emergency, 21, 595
　interstate, 21
　national, 43
　principals, 437
　professional, 38, 44
　provisional, 8, 601
　recertification, 19, 44
　superintendents, 436
Chalk, Vincent, 383
Chalk v. U. S. District Court Cent. Dist. of
　　California, 383, 413
Changing Education, 55
Chapter 1, 159, 287–289, 462
Characteristics of teachers, 5–6
Charity schools, 87, 95–96, 108, 112–113,
　　115–116, 593
Charlemagne, 70, 72
Chautauqua Institution, 156
Cheyney State College, 130
Chicago Federation of Labor, 56
Chicago Teachers Federation, 56
Chief state school officer, 422–425, 593
Child abuse, 312–313, 333–336, 385, 593, 602
Child benefit theory, 371, 593
Child care, 572–573
Child-centered curriculum, 145, 491, 493–495,
　　497–499, 593
Child labor laws, 119
Children's Defense Fund, 253, 269
Childs, John, 221, 223
Child study movement, 147–148
Choice, 448, 470, 593

Church of England, 92, 94
Church-state relations, 363–375
Cigarette smoking, 313–314, 316
Citizenship of teachers, 380, 382
City of Richmond v. J. A. Croson Co., 400, 414
City superintendents, 117
Civilian Conservation Corps, 149–150, 585
Civil Rights Act, 24, 160–161, 293, 356, 403
Civil rights movement, 159–162, 274, 291
Civil War, 118–119, 122, 129
Clark University, 147, 156
Classical conditioning, 210, 593
Classroom management
    behaviorists, 211–213
    essentialists, 215, 217
    existentialists, 225, 228
    perennialists, 202–203, 205
    progressivists, 207, 209
    reconstructionists, 220, 223
Cleveland Board of Education v. Laudermill, 392
Clinical experiences, 9–11, 16, 596
Clinton, De Witt, 106
Cluster suicides, 325, 593
Coast Guard Academy, 585
Cochran v. Louisiana State Board of Education,
    364, 371, 376
Cognitive styles, 291–292, 593
Cold War, 153, 155
Coleman, James S., 247–249, 252
Coleman Report, 249, 252, 536–537
Coleridge, Samuel, 184
Collective bargaining, 394
College Board Educational Equity Project, 589
College of New Jersey, 92, 102. See also Princeton
    University
College of Philadelphia, 94, 102
College of Professional Teachers, 113
College of Rhode Island, 91, 102. See also Brown
    University
College of William and Mary, 95–96, 102, 104,
    460
Collegiate School, 91. See also Yale University
Collins v. Chandler Unified School District, 367,
    376
Colombian School, 134
Colonial America, 77, 83–97
Columbia University, 92, 96, 136, 146, 148, 151,
    156, 209, 453, 460
Comenius, Jan Amos, 78–80, 84, 93
Commager, Henry Steele, 105

Commissioner of Education, 101, 116, 423, 593
Commission on the Reorganization of Secondary
    Education, 120–121, 482
Committee for Economic Development, 447, 589
Committee for Public Education and Religious
    Liberty v. Nyquist, 373, 376
Committee for Public Education and Religious
    Liberty v. Regan, 371, 376
Committee of Ten, 120–122, 125
Common schools, 106–119, 123, 125, 132,
    353–354, 593
    teachers for, 134–135
Compensatory education, 287–289, 291–295,
    297, 305, 479, 593
Competency testing, 11, 13–14, 16–19, 32, 38,
    44, 58, 380–382, 593
    national, 18–19, 21
Competitive grants, 451, 453–454, 593
Compliance rates, 455–458
Components of learning, 548–549
Comprehensive high schools, 118, 121, 482, 593
Compulsory education, 86, 114, 119–120,
    373–374, 398
Computers, 523–524
    artificial intelligence, 574, 581, 592
Comte, Auguste, 192
Conant, James, 154, 156
Confucius, 236
Congregationalists, 131
Connecticut ASCD, 563, 566, 569, 571–572, 574,
    582
Connick v. Myers, 392–393, 413
Constitution, U.S., 63, 70, 102, 348–354, 375,
    381, 418–419, 593
    Bill of Rights, 104
    Eighth Amendment, 352–353, 403
    Fifth Amendment, 351–352
    First Amendment, 350–351, 363, 366, 370,
        375, 396, 402, 408
    Fourteenth Amendment, 353, 363, 381, 391,
        402, 409
    Fourth Amendment, 351, 404
    general welfare clause, 348–349, 419
    obligations of contracts clause, 350
Constitutions, state, 353–354, 375, 418, 450–451
Continuing education, 300–303, 552, 593
Continuity, 487, 489, 593
Contracts, 380, 383–384, 433
Controlled choice plans, 275
Cook County Normal School, 145, 156

Cooperative education service agency, 426–427
Cooperative learning, 509–512, 593
Copyright laws, 385–387, 412
Core curriculum, 492–493, 497, 594
Corporal punishment, 69–70, 75, 78, 97, 352–353, 389, 402–403
Correlation, 80
Cosmology, 176–177, 594
Cost-of-living index, 24, 594
Council for Exceptional Children, 56, 58
Council of Chief State School Officers, 312, 589
Council on Basic Education, 154, 156
Counts, George C., 151, 156, 221, 223, 495, 497
County superintendents, 116–117
Courts, 358–363. *See also* Supreme Court, U.S.
Court schools, 75
Cousin Report, 113
Crisis intervention team, 325, 594
Critical perspective, 487–488
Critical thinking instruction, 515–517, 519–520, 522, 594
Cubberley, E. P., 121
Cult Awareness Network, 318, 320, 341
Cults, 313, 318–321, 594
Cultural literacy, 525, 530, 594
Cultural pluralism, 246–247, 291–292, 594
Culture, 238, 241, 245, 594
  of the school, 537, 542, 594
Curriculum, 41, 477–500, 594
  academic freedom, 395–396
  activity, 83, 85
  alignment, 539, 594
  behaviorist, 211, 213
  bias, 368–371
  child-centered, 145, 491, 493–495, 499, 593
  colonial universities, 90
  core, 492–493, 497, 594
  cultural literacy, 525, 530
  cycle, 499–500
  deschooling, 495–497, 594
  development, 487–489
  essentialist, 211, 214–215, 217
  existentialist, 224–225, 228
  future, 573–574, 576
  global education, 529–530, 532, 573–574, 596
  hidden, 245–246, 496–499, 597
  individual differences, 69
  influencing forces, 478–486
  integrated, 491–492, 497, 598
  interdisciplinary approach, 579–580

Curriculum, *continued*
  national goals, 526–529
  Native Americans, 295, 297
  null, 497–498, 600
  patterns of organization, 488–498
  perennialist, 205, 210, 211
  progressivist, 206, 209
  reconstructionist, 219–220, 223
  social reconstruction, 495, 497, 603
  spiral, 157, 487
  subject-area, 145, 488–491, 497–498, 500, 603
Curriculum reform movement, 499

Dame schools, 87–88, 90, 96, 594
Dartmouth University, 91, 96, 102, 122, 126, 138, 460
Darwin, Charles, 192
Dayton Board of Education v. Brinkman, 276–277, 306
Decurion system, 107
Deductive logic, 176–178, 181, 594
Definitions of teaching, 3–4
Delinquency, 313, 322, 337–340, 594
Delphi technique, 580
Demand for teachers, 22–23
Demonstration instruction, 515–518, 594
Department of Agriculture, 149
Department of Commerce, 456–457. *See also* Bureau of the Census
Department of Defense, 421, 464
Department of Education, U.S., 5, 7, 22–23, 30, 34, 58–59, 144, 162–164, 170, 252–253, 256, 271, 288, 303–304, 308, 316–317, 326, 328, 344, 357, 419–421, 440, 443, 446, 464–469, 585–586, 590
  Office of Civil Rights, 162, 357
Department of Education, state, 418, 422–426, 451, 481, 603
Department of Education Organization Act, 586
Department of Health and Human Services, 314–315, 333, 344
Department of Justice, 162, 339
Department of Labor, 357
Department of the Interior, 262, 357
  Bureau of Indian Affairs, 128, 150, 262, 295, 357
Depression, 129, 148–153, 322–323, 593
Descartes, René, 182–183, 592
Deschooling curriculum, 495–497, 594
Descriptive approach, 174–176

Desegregation, 160–162, 274–281, 305, 594
    controlled choice plans, 275
    freedom of choice plans, 275
    integration, 488–489, 598
    magnet plans, 275, 277
    majority-to-minority transfers, 275
    neighborhood attendance zones, 275
    one-way transfers, 275
    pairing and clustering plans, 275–277
    rezoning, 275–277
Dewey, John, 78–79, 83, 145–146, 151,
    155–156, 179, 188, 190, 192, 208–209, 216,
    218, 223, 436, 497, 518
Diana v. California State Board of Education,
    286, 306
Didascaleum, 65, 71
Disabled children, education of, 281–288, 305
Discipline, 401–403
    corporal punishment, 69–70, 75, 78, 97,
    352–353, 389, 402–403
    expulsions, 401–402, 596
    suspensions, 401–403, 407, 604
Discovery instruction, 515–519
Discrimination, 400–401, 594, 601
Dismissal of teachers, 387–392
    due process, 384, 391
    for cause, 387–390
    nonrenewal of contract, 387, 390–391
    reduction in force, 387, 390
Displaced Homemakers Self-Sufficiency
    Assistance Act, 587
Disputations, 73
Distance education, 302, 595
District superintendents, 116–117
Divorce, 311–313, 322, 336, 571
Dodd v. Rambis, 407, 414
Doe v. Donton Elementary School District, 410,
    414
Doe v. Renfrow, 404, 414
Donahue v. Copiague Union Free Schools,
    398–399, 414
Drill and practice, 523, 595
Dropouts, 253–254, 256, 262, 289, 297,
    312–313, 326–329, 331, 340, 405, 447, 515,
    527, 555, 562, 587, 595
Drug abuse, 312–318, 322, 327, 331, 333, 336,
    339, 478, 587, 596
Drug Abuse Resistance Education, 318
Drug Free Schools and Communities Act, 315,
    587
Drug testing, 404–405

Du Bois, W. E. B., 131
Due process, 283, 285, 350–351, 353, 384, 391,
    401–403, 595
Dutch Reformed Church, 91

Ecclesiastical perennialists, 201–203
Eckmann v. Board of Education, 388, 414
Economic distortions, 455–456, 458, 595
Economic growth, 244–246, 267
Economic Opportunity Act, 158, 586
Edubba, 64
Educational foundations, 130–131, 460–461,
    595
Educational goals, 506–507, 595
Educational objectives, 506–508, 595
Educational overburden, 451, 595
Educational Research Service, 25, 32
Educational Testing Service, 11, 18, 264, 465
Education and Training for a Competitive
    America Act, 587
Education Commission of the States, 465, 482,
    553, 589
Education Consolidation and Improvement Act,
    164, 287, 421, 462, 587
Education for All Handicapped Children Act,
    161–162, 281–283, 286–287, 356, 463, 586.
    See also Individuals with Disabilities
    Education Act
Education Law of 1647, 86
Education of Children with Disabilities Act, 587
Education of teachers, 7–16, 19–20, 38, 40, 43,
    77, 114, 143, 576
    history of, 131, 133–136
    minorities, 12–14
    quality of, 10–12
    reforms in, 14–16
Education of the Handicapped Act, 281–283,
    286–287, 586–587
Education Policies Commission, 152, 169
Education Professions Development Act, 586
Edwards, v. Aguillard, 364, 369, 376
Effective principals, 548–553
Effective schools, 537
Effective teachers, 543–548
Efficiency, 448–449, 470, 595
Eighth Amendment, 352–353, 403
Eight Year Study, 151
Eisenhower, Dwight D., 160
Eisner, Elliot, 495, 497
Elementary and Secondary Education Act,
    158–159, 164, 272, 287, 292, 420, 425, 586

Elementary school teachers, 133–135
  demand for, 22–23
  education of, 9–10
  perceptions of, 30
  salaries of, 17, 25
Eliot, Charles, 120, 125
Emergency certificates, 21, 595
Emerson, Ralph Waldo, 184
Eminent domain, 354, 595
Employee benefits, 29
Employee services, 29
Endowed schools, 95–96
Engaged time, 547, 591, 595
Engel v. Vitale, 364–366, 376
English as a second language, 288, 293, 301, 595
English Classical School, 118
English Only movement, 294
Epistemology, 175–177, 180, 595
  existentialism, 193, 195
  experimentalism, 190–191
  idealism, 181, 183
  neo-Thomism, 188–189
  realism, 185–186
Epperson v. Arkansas, 364, 369, 376
Equal Access Act, 356, 367–368
Equal Employment Opportunity Act, 24
Equal Employment Opportunity Commission, 357
Equality of Educational Opportunity Report, 249, 252, 536–537
Equal opportunity, 400, 595
Equal Pay Act, 24, 356
Equity, 448–449, 455–458, 460–461, 470, 595, 597, 604
Erasmus, Desiderius, 74–76
ERIC, 27, 33, 523
Essentialism, 151–152, 200, 206–208, 211, 214–217, 231, 490, 497–498, 596
Essentialist Committee for the Advancement of American Education, 216
Ethics, 176–177, 179, 186, 188, 191, 194, 570, 596
  of teachers, 48–50
Ethnic groups. See Minorities, education of
Evaluation
  behaviorists, 212–213
  essentialists, 215–217
  existentialists, 225–226, 228
  perennialists, 203, 205
  progressivists, 207–209
  reconstructionists, 220–221, 223
  of teachers, 45–47

Everson v. Board of Education, 364, 371, 376
Existentialism, 173, 192–196, 200, 224–228, 231, 596
Experimentalism, 173, 188–192, 196, 206, 497, 596
Expository instruction, 515–517, 520, 596
Ex post facto law, 350, 596
Expulsions, 401–402, 596
Extracurricular activities, 28–29

Fair Labor Standards Act, 24
Families, 238–241, 267, 536
  changing, 570–573
  skip-generation, 571
Family Educational Rights and Privacy Act, 356, 409–410
Federal aid, 462–465
Federal grant universities, 153
Field, Stephen J., 363
Field experiences, 9–11, 16, 596
Fifth Amendment, 351–352
First Amendment, 350–351, 363, 366, 370, 375, 396, 402, 408
Fisher v. Fairbanks North Star Borough School District, 395, 414
Fisk University, 131
Flat grants, 451, 453–454, 596
Flinn Foundation, 330, 342
Ford, Gerald, 162
Formative evaluation, 208, 596
Fornaro v. Kerry, 398, 414
Forum of Educational Leaders, 589
Foundation plan, 451–453, 596
Fourteenth Amendment, 353, 363, 381, 391, 402, 409
Fourth Amendment, 351, 404
Franciscans, 83
Franklin, Benjamin, 93–94, 125–126, 460
Franklin Academy, 93–94, 109
Fraser, Matthew, 407
Freedmen's Bureau, 131–132
Freedom of choice plans, 275
Freedom of speech, 393–394, 402, 406–408, 412
Free schools, 95, 227, 496, 596
Free school societies, 105, 108
Freire, Paulo, 221–223, 497
Friedenberg, 497
Froebel, Friedrich, 82, 83, 85, 108, 145, 493
Fullbright Act, 585
Full state funding, 451, 453–454, 596

Funding of education, 349, 354, 428–429,
    432–433, 444–471
  budgeting, 458–460
  equalization programs, 451–454
  expense or investment, 447–448
  federal aid, 462–465
  Native Americans, 294–296
  nonpublic schools, 370–373
  nontax sources, 457, 460–462
  public policy goals in, 448–449
  sources of tax revenue, 454–458
Futrell, Mary Harwood, 19
Futures education, 578–580, 596
Futuristics, 492
Futurists, 564, 566–581, 596

Gang members, 337–339
Gano v. School District No. 411 of Twin Falls,
    409, 414
Garcia v. Miera, 403, 414
Garnett v. Renton School District No. 368, 376,
    403
Gateway drugs, 314, 596
Gaylord v. Tacoma School District No. 10, 389,
    414
General Education Board, 131
General education diploma, 301–302
G. I. Bill of Rights, 153, 355, 462, 585
Giroux, Henry, 246
Global education, 529–530, 532, 573–574, 596
Globalization, 566, 573–574
Goldberg, Arthur, 363
Goodlad, John, 483, 497
Goodman, 497
Gorgras, 66
Graded schools, 117–118
Grammar schools, 68, 71, 86, 90, 93, 95–96,
    102, 104, 109, 118, 121, 125–126, 596
  secondary, 88, 90
  teachers in, 133
Grammatistes, 65, 71
Great Books, 201–203, 205, 596
Great Society, 159, 287, 499
Greece, 64–68, 71, 97, 490. *See also specific
    philosophers*
Green v. County School Board of New Kent
    County, 275–276, 307
Gross v. Lopez, 403, 406, 414
Group instruction, 509–510, 596
Guarino da Verona, 75
Gymnasia, 65

Hadas, 216
Haig, Robert M., 452–453
Hall, G. Stanley, 122, 147–148, 156
Hall v. Tawney, 403, 414
Hampton Institute, 131
Hand, Pamelia A., 132
Handicapped, education of, 159, 161–162,
    281–288, 305, 397, 403, 420–421, 426, 432,
    463, 586–587, 598–599
Handicapped Children's Protection Act, 587
Harper v. Edgewood Board of Education, 409,
    414
Harris, William T., 490–491
Hartford Female Seminary, 109, 125
Harvard University, 87, 91, 95–96, 102, 120,
    122–123, 125–126, 154, 460
Hazelwood School District v. Kuhlmeier, 406,
    408, 414
Head Start, 158, 288–289, 586
Hegel, Georg Wilhelm Friedrich, 182, 184
Heidegger, Martin, 194–195
Herbart, Johann Friedrich, 80–82, 85
Herbartian methodology, 81
Hermeneutics, 194, 597
Heterogeneous groups, 524–525
Hidden curriculum, 245–246, 496–499, 597
Higher education, history of, 68–69, 71, 73–74,
    77, 90–92, 95–96, 102, 122, 130–131, 147,
    153
Higher Education Act, 159, 586
Higher Education Facilities Act, 586
Highet, 216
High schools, 110–111, 118–122
  comprehensive, 118, 121, 482, 593
  World War II, 153
Hispanic Policy Development Project, 256, 269,
    440, 442
Hispanics, education of, 128–129, 136, 159, 161,
    254–260, 276–277, 290–294, 326, 562–563
Hoffman v. Board of Education of the City of
    New York, 399, 414
Hogan, J. C., 402
Holistic education, 576, 579–580, 597
Holmes Group, 14–16, 33, 43, 590
Holt, John, 226–228, 495, 497
Homelessness, 313, 333–337
Home schooling, 374, 597
Homogeneous groups, 516, 524
Honig v. Doe, 403, 414
Hoover, Herbert, 363
Horizontal equity, 448, 597

Hornbooks, 87–88, 597
Horne, Herman H., 216–217
Horton v. Goose Creek Independent School District, 404, 414
Hortonville Joint School District No. 1 v. Hortonville Education Association, 392, 394
House Select Committee on Children, Youth, and Families, 335
Howard University, 131
Hufstadler, Shirley, 162, 420
Hughes, Charles Evans, 363
Humanism, 75, 597
Humanistic education, 209, 227, 493, 597
Hundreds, 104
Husserl, Edmund, 194
Hutchins, Robert M., 78, 203–205, 491, 497

Idealism, 67–68, 97, 173, 178–184, 187, 189, 196, 597, 601
Ignatius of Loyola, 77
Illich, Ivan, 221–223, 495–497
Illiteracy, 120, 302, 398, 527
Immersion, 293
Immorality, 388–389
Impact aid, 153
Incentive pay, 26, 597
    career ladder plans, 26, 41, 46, 51–52, 58, 592
    master teacher plans, 26, 41, 46, 51–52, 58, 599
    merit pay, 25–27, 32, 41, 46, 165, 167, 484–485, 599
Income taxes, 456–458
Incompetency, 388–389, 597
Independent instruction, 509, 512, 515–517, 520–522, 597
Indiana ex rel. Anderson v. Brand, 392
Indiana University, 123
Indian education. See Native Americans, education of
Indian Education Act, 161, 294, 297
Indian Education Amendments, 294
Indian New Deal, 150
Indian Self-Determination and Education Assistance Act, 161, 294, 586
Indirect compensation, 29, 597
Individualized education program, 282–283, 597
Individualized instruction, 509, 512, 515, 597
Individuals with Disabilities Education Act, 162, 281–283, 286–287
Inductive logic, 176–178, 187, 206, 597

Inequality of educational opportunity, 247–268
    ethnic groups, 254–262, 268
    gender differences, 256, 262–268
    social classes, 248–254, 268
Infant schools, 105, 108, 111, 125, 597
Ingraham v. Wright, 353, 376, 403, 406, 414
In loco parentis, 401, 597
Inquiry instruction, 66, 515–520, 598
Institutes, 135, 156
Instruction
    effectiveness, 536
    grouping students, 524–525, 530
    models of, 515–522
    technology, 522–524, 530
    types of, 509–514
Instructional time, 547, 598
Instrumentalism, 205–209. See also Progressivism
Insubordination, 389–390, 598
Integrated curriculum, 491–492, 497, 598
Integration, 488–489, 598
Intelligence quotient, 148, 156, 215, 217, 598
Intelligence tests, 148
Interborough Association of Women Teachers, 56
Interdisciplinary approach, 579–580
Interests, 80
Intermediate educational service agency, 418–419, 426–428, 432, 598
International Literacy Year, 303
International Reading Association, 484
Interstate Certification Agreement Contracts, 21
Intervention strategies, 598
    acquired immune deficiency syndrome, 332–333
    child abuse, 334–335
    cult participation, 319
    delinquency, 339
    dropouts, 328
    runaways, 337
    substance abuse, 318
    suicide, 325
    teenage pregnancy, 330–331
Ionesco, Eugene, 196

Jackson, Andrew, 113
Jackson, Robert, 363
Jaffree v. Wallace, 367, 376
Jager v. Douglas County School District, 367, 376
James, William, 192
Jay, John, 363
Jefferson, Thomas, 41, 103, 125, 363

Jesuits, 77, 83, 107

Job Corps, 158, 586

John Dewey Society for the Study of Education and Culture, 151

Johns Hopkins University, 147

Johnson, Lyndon B., 157–160, 162, 272, 287, 289

Johnson-O'Malley Act of 1934, 150

Joliet Junior College, 124

Jones v. Latexo Independent School District, 404, 414

Journals, educational, 113, 115

Junior colleges, 124–125, 147, 598

Junior high schools, 122, 598

Juvenile Awareness Project, 339

Kaiser Aluminum and Chemical Corporation v. Weber, 400, 414

Kalamazoo case, 119

Kant, Immanuel, 182, 184, 194

Karen B. v. Treen, 367, 376

Kay v. David Douglas School District, 367, 376

Kelson v. The City of Springfield, 325, 342

Kennedy, John F., 157–158, 160, 162

Kentucky Educational Television, 302

Kerr, Clark, 153

Keyes v. School District No. 1, 276–277, 307

Keyishian v. Board of Regents, 381, 392, 414

Kierkegaard, Soren, 192–195

Kilpatrick, William H., 146–147, 151, 156, 221, 223

Kindergartens, 82–83, 85, 108, 111

Kings College, 92, 460

Kingsville Independent School District v. Cooper, 395–396, 414

Kohl, Herbert, 495, 497

Kozol, Jonathan, 226–228

Lancaster, Joseph, 106, 108, 125

Land-grant colleges, 123, 131, 420, 585

Land Ordinance of 1785, 103

Lanham Act, 153, 585

Lanner v. Wimmer, 365, 376

Larry v. Wilson Riles, 286, 307

Lau v. Nichols, 161, 293, 307

Law, 347–358, 598
    administrative, 349, 357
    attorney general opinions, 357–358, 375
    case, 349, 355, 357
    constitutional, 348–354, 375
    statutory, 349, 354–356

Lay perennialist, 201, 203

Learning disabilities, 286, 598

Least restrictive environment, 283–284, 598

Lemon test, 365, 371, 598

Lemon v. Kurtzman, 364–365, 371, 376

Levitt v. Committee for Public Education and Religious Liberty, 371, 376

Liberal arts, 72–73, 84

Licenses to teach, 38, 42–44, 58

Life adjustment education, 154, 598

Limited open forum, 367–368, 598

Lincoln, Abraham, 123

Lincoln University, 130

Linguistic minority, 258, 598

Lions Club International, 318

Littlejohn v. Rose, 388, 414

Local schools, 437–439

Locke, John, 78–79, 84, 93, 103, 187, 249

Logic, 176–178, 181
    deductive, 176–178, 181, 594
    inductive, 176–178, 187, 206, 597

Logical empiricism, 229, 598

Logical positivism, 229, 598

Logography, 66

Lotteries, 457, 460

Lower class, 248–254

Lower-middle class, 248, 250–251

Loyalty oaths, 381

Loyola, 216

Ludus, 68, 71

Luther, Martin, 76–77, 84

Lutherans, 92

Lyon, Mary, 109, 125

Magnet plans, 275, 277, 599

Mainstreaming, 212, 282–283, 525, 599

Majority-to-minority transfers, 275

Malpractice, 398–399, 599

Management productivity model, 552–553

Mann, Horace, 78, 80, 105, 113–115, 125, 134

Manpower Development and Training Act, 157, 586

Marcel, Gabriel, 195

Maritain, Jacques, 203, 205

Marshall, John, 363

Martinez v. School Board, 410, 414

Marx, Karl, 218, 223, 249

Marxists, 246

Massachusetts Education Law of 1647, 87

Massachusetts Law of 1642, 86–87

Master teacher plans, 26, 41, 46, 51–52, 58, 599

Mastery learning, 509, 512–514, 599
McCollum v. Board of Education, 364–365, 376
McLean, John, 363
Measurement movement, 147
Media, 241–244, 267
Meek v. Pittenger, 372, 377
Mehary Medical College, 131
Melanchthon, Philip, 76
Men in teaching, 5
Mentoring, 52–53, 599
Meredith, James, 160
Meriam Report, 128, 150
Meritocratic position, 246
Merit pay, 25–27, 32, 41, 46, 165, 167, 484–485, 599
Merleau-Ponty, Maurice, 195–196
Metaphysics, 175–181, 599
    cosmology, 176–177
    existentialism, 192–195
    experimentalism, 189–191
    idealism, 178–179, 181, 183, 189
    neo-Thomism, 187, 189, 192
    ontology, 176–177, 600
    realism, 184–186, 189, 192
Methodists, 131
Methods of teaching, 199
    behaviorists, 211, 213
    essentialists, 215, 217
    existentialists, 225, 228
    perennialists, 202, 205
    progressivists, 206–207, 209
    reconstructionists, 220, 223
Mexican-American War, 128
Michigan State University, 12
Middle Ages, 70, 72–74
Middle colonies, 91–94, 96
Migrant students, 288
Military education, 64–65, 71, 109, 111, 153, 585
Milliken v. Bradley, 276–277, 307
Mills v. Board of Education of the District of Columbia, 281, 307
Milton, 216
Minorities, education of, 120, 123, 126–133, 136, 254–262, 274–281, 286–297, 305, 536, 562–563. See also specific minority groups
Minorities in teaching, 5, 12–14, 18, 31, 44, 131, 274
Mira v. Monroe County School Board, 400, 415
Mission schools, 126–127
Mitchell v. King, 381, 415

Monastic schools, 70
Monitorial schools, 105–108, 111, 113, 125
Montessori, Maria, 510
Montessori Method, 509–510
Moral Majority, 491
Moravians, 78, 92–93, 126
Morrill Acts, 123, 131, 420, 585
Mothers Against Drunk Driving, 318
Motivation, 548–549
Mount Healthy City School District v. Doyle, 392
Mount Holyoke College, 110
Mount Holyoke Female Seminary, 109, 125
Mozert v. Hawkins County Public Schools, 369, 377
Mueller v. Allen, 364, 373, 377
Multicultural education, 289–292, 492, 599
Municipal overburden, 452, 599
Murrow, Edward R., 157
Music schools, 65, 71

National Adult Education Initiative, 302
National Adult Literacy Congress, 302
National Advisory Council on Adult Education, 300, 307
National Assessment of Educational Progress, 252, 254–259, 261–264, 464–465, 599
National Association for the Advancement of Colored People, 131
National Association of Elementary School Principals, 57
National Association of School Superintendents, 56
National Association of Secondary School Principals, 57
National Board for Professional Teaching Standards, 44, 590
National Center for Educational Research, 421
National Center for Education Statistics, 465–469, 472
National Centers for Disease Control, 412
National Coalition for the Prevention of Drug and Alcohol Abuse, 318
National Commission on Excellence in Education, 14–15, 33, 216, 234, 246, 254, 270, 482, 493, 590
National Commission on Social Studies in the Schools, 484
National Committee for the Prevention of Child Abuse, 333
National Conference of Teachers of English, 56

National Council for the Social Studies, 56, 484, 529
National Council of Teachers of English, 484
National Council of Teachers of Mathematics, 56, 58, 484
National Defense Education Act, 155–157, 420, 462, 479, 586
National Education Association, 7, 18, 21, 27, 37, 42, 44, 54–56, 58, 101, 149, 162, 436, 441, 484, 527, 599
    Code of Ethics, 48–50
    Commission on the Reorganization of Secondary Education, 120–121, 482
    Committee of Ten, 120–122, 125
    Education Policies Commission, 152, 169
    history of, 54–56
    National Policies Commission, 149, 170
National Environmental Education Act, 587
National Foundation of the Arts and Humanities, 159, 586
National 4-H, 318
National goals, 526–529
National Governors' Association, 165, 528, 532, 590
National Herbartian Society, 81
National Institute for Education, 464, 586
National Institute of Education, 357
National Institute on Drug Abuse, 314
National Labor Relations Act, 40, 59
National Longitudinal Studies, 252–253
National Parent Teacher Association, 318
National Policies Commission, 149, 170
National Policy Board, 436–437, 442
National proficiency examinations, 18–19, 21
National Research Council, 331, 343, 484
National School Lunch Program, 149, 357, 420
National Science Foundation, 464, 585, 590
National Science Teachers Association, 56, 58, 484
National Society of the Scientific Study of Education, 82
National Teacher Examination, 18
National Teachers Association, 56
National Teachers Corps, 25, 586
National Youth Administration, 149, 585
Native Americans, education of, 126–128, 136, 150, 159, 161, 256, 261–262, 291, 294–297, 305, 349, 357, 586, 597
    boarding schools, 127–128, 150
    Meriam Report, 128

Native Americans, *continued*
    mission schools, 126–127
    public schools, 128
    reservation day school, 128, 150
Naturalism, 79, 85, 599
Naval Academy, 109, 585
Navy College Training Program, 153
Negligence, 397–398, 599
Neighborhood attendance zones, 275
Neill, A. S., 226, 228
Neo-Marxists, 246
Neo-Thomism, 173, 187–189, 192, 196, 201, 599
New basics, 216, 599
New Deal, 149–150
New England colonies, 86–91, 94–97
New England Primer, 87–89
New Jersey v. T. L. O., 404, 406, 415
New York College for the Training of Teachers, 136
New York State Normal School, 135
Nixon, Richard, 161–162
Nongraded schools, 209, 599
Nonpublic schools, 90, 92–96
    public support for, 370–373
    teachers of, 5–6
Nonrenewal of contract, 387, 390–391
Normal schools, 10, 114, 134–136, 145, 147, 156, 436, 599
Normative approach, 174–175
Northwest Ordinances, 103, 420, 585
Northwest Regional Educational Laboratory, 543
Nostradamus, 564
Nôtre-Dame, 73–74
Null curriculum, 497–498, 600

Oberlin College, 124, 130
Object lesson, 80, 600
Occupational Safety and Health Act, 354, 357
Odenheim v. Carlstadt-East Rutherford School District, 404, 415
Office for Educational Research and Improvement, 464
Office of Civil Rights, 162, 357
Office of Education, 154, 162, 419, 464
Office of Educational Research and Information, 421
Office of Indian Education, 297, 585
Oglethorpe University, 141
Ohio State University, 123

"Old Deluder Satan Law," 87
One-room schools, 107, 113, 117, 434, 439
One-way transfers, 275
Ontology, 176–177, 600
Open classroom, 209, 225–227, 499, 600
Open-ended, inquiry-based methodology, 580
Operant conditioning, 210, 212, 600
Organization of Petroleum Exporting Countries, 162
Owen, Robert, 108, 125
Oxford University, 73–74, 122

Page, David P., 135
Paideia, 78–79, 84, 600
Pairing and clustering plans, 275–277
Palace schools, 70, 72–73
Palestra, 65
Parent Teacher Association, 478
Parker, Francis W., 145, 156
Parochial schools, 91–96, 440
Participation fees, 460–461
Pauper schools, 87, 95–96, 108, 112–113, 115–116, 593
Pavlov, Ivan, 210, 212–213
Peabody Fund for the Advancement of Negro Education in the South, 130
Peace Corps, 158, 567
Pedagogical formalism, 146
Peer groups, 52–53, 241
Peer tutoring, 106, 107, 111, 511
Peirce, Charles Sanders, 192
Penn, William, 92
Pennsylvania Association of Retarded Citizens v. Commonwealth of Pennsylvania, 281, 307
Pennsylvania's Free School Act, 116
People v. Overton, 404, 415
Perceptions of teachers, 30–31, 38–40, 45
Perennialism, 200–208, 211, 214–216, 231, 497
Perkins, Carl D., 304, 587
Permanent records, 409–410
Perry v. Sandermann, 392
Personal systems of instruction, 520–522
Pestalozzi, Johann Heinrich, 78, 80, 85, 115, 145, 493
Pestalozzian methods, 80, 85, 113–114
Peter W. v. San Francisco Unified School District, 398, 415
Pharmaceutical Manufacturers Association, 316
Phenomenology, 194
Phi Delta Kappa Gallup Poll, 527

Philadelphia Academy, 93
Philosophical analysis, 230–232
Philosophies, 172–196. *See also specific philosophies*
    approaches of study, 174–175
    branches of, 175–178, 196
    definition, 174
    of education, 174–175, 178, 183, 186, 189, 191, 195, 199–232
Phipps v. Saddleback Valley Unified School District, 410, 415
Piaget, Jean, 148, 157, 179, 487
Pickering, Marvin, 393
Pickering v. Board of Education, 392–394, 415
Pierce v. Society of Sisters, 364, 374, 377
Plato, 62, 66–68, 97, 172, 178–179, 182–183, 187, 216, 218, 223, 249, 300
Plenary, 355
Plessy v. Ferguson, 133, 138, 361, 377
Plyler v. Doe, 373, 377, 406
Policies, 418, 600
Political activity, 394–395
Postvention strategies, 600
    cult participation, 321
    suicide, 325
Poverty, 249–250, 253–255, 257–258, 260, 420, 447, 536
    war on, 157–159, 253, 274, 287, 291
Power equalization, 452–454, 600
Pratt, General Richard, 127
Pregnancy Discrimination Act, 24
Premack, David, 213
Premack principle, 213, 600
Preparations for teaching, 7–16, 19–20, 38, 40, 43, 77, 114, 143
    history of, 131, 133–136
    minorities, 12–14
    quality of, 10–12
    reforms in, 14–16
Pre-Professional Skills Test, 11, 18
Presbyterians, 92
Prevention strategies, 600
    acquired immune deficiency syndrome, 332
    child abuse, 334
    cult participation, 319
    delinquency, 338–339
    dropouts, 327–328
    runaways, 337
    substance abuse, 315–318
    suicide, 324–325
    teenage pregnancy, 330

Primary schools, 108, 125
Princeton University, 92, 96, 123, 460
Principals, 435, 437–439, 536–538, 540–542, 545, 592
    effective, 548–553
    roles of, 550, 552
Private schools, 90, 92–96, 440–441, 496
    teachers of, 5–6
Problem-analysis approach, 580
Profession, teaching as, 37–54, 600
    development of, 43–54
Professional development, 48, 601
Professional organizations, 37, 39, 48, 54–58, 394, 484. *See also specific organizations*
Professional practices boards, 42
Professional teachers, 51–52
Profiles of teachers, 5–6
Profit-making activities, 460, 462
Program for Effective Teaching, 548
Programmed instruction, 211, 520, 601
Progressive education, 145–147, 151, 153–156, 493, 495
Progressive Education Association, 146–147, 151, 156
Progressive taxes, 455, 457–458
Progressivism, 200, 205–209, 214, 224, 231, 497–499, 601
Project Literacy U.S., 302
Project method, 146, 601
Property rights, 384, 391, 601
Property taxes, 450, 455–458
Proprietary schools, 441, 601
Protagoras, 66
Protestants, 76–77, 85–86, 112–113
Provisional certificates, 8, 601
Proximate cause, 397–398, 601
Prussian schools, 113–114
Public Broadcasting Service, 302
Public Law 94–142. *See* Education for All Handicapped Children Act
Public schools
    attitudes toward, 29
    teachers of, 5–6, 30
Public School Society, 108
Public Works Administration, 149–150
Pullout models, 288, 291
Purdue University, 123
Puritans, 77, 85–88, 92, 97, 129
Purposes of schooling, 244–247
    economic growth, 244–246, 267
    responding to diversity, 244, 246–247, 267

Purposes of schooling, *continued*
    socialization, 244–245, 267
    social mobility, 244, 246, 267
    social selection, 244, 246, 267

Quadrivium, 72
Quakers, 92–93, 106, 133
Queens College, 92
Quintilian, 69–70, 74–75, 78, 84, 97

Radcliffe College, 124
Raikes, Robert, 108, 125
Rate bills, 115–116, 601
Reading and writing schools, 87, 96
Reagan, Ronald, 162, 164–165, 302, 420, 553
Realism, 67–68, 78, 97, 173, 184–187, 189, 192, 196, 201
Real reality, 178–179, 601
Reasons for teaching, 6–7
Recertification, 19
Reconstructionism, 200, 218–223, 231, 497
Reduction in force, 387, 390, 601
Reflective thinking, 518, 601
Reformation, 76–78, 86–87
Regents of the University of California v. Alan Bakke, 400, 415
Regional education service agency, 426–427
Regressive taxes, 455, 457
Rehabilitation Act, 356, 383, 410
Reinforcement, 548–549
Renaissance, 74–76, 88
Renewal programs, 53–54, 58
Requirements for teachers, 380–387
Research About Teacher Education Project, 12
Reservation day schools, 128, 150
Residency requirements, 380, 382
Response reinforcement behaviorism, 210
Restructuring, 165, 167, 601
Retention, 548–549
Retirement, 358
Revenue elasticity, 455–458, 601
Reverse discrimination, 400, 601
Revisionists, 246
Revolutionary War, 102, 109, 122
Rezoning, 275–277
Rhetoricians, 66
Rickover, Admiral Hyman, 154, 216–217
Rights of students, 401–412
Rights of teachers, 380–401, 412
Roberts v. City of Boston, 130, 138
Robotics, 569, 574, 601

Rockefeller, John D., 131
Rogers, Carl, 226–228
Rogers, John, 87
Roman Catholic Church, 70, 73, 75–77, 83–85,
    111–112, 188, 201–202, 601
  parochial schools, 440
Rome, 68–71, 74, 97, 596
Roosevelt, Franklin D., 149–150
Ross v. Springfield School District No. 19, 415
Rousseau, Jean-Jacques, 78–80, 85, 145, 192,
    249, 493
Rowland v. Mad River Local School District, 389,
    415
Rugg, Harold, 146, 151, 156, 221, 223, 497
Runaways, 313, 323, 333–337
Rush, Dr. Benjamin, 94, 103, 113
Russell, Bertrand, 187
Rutgers University, 92, 96
Rutledge, John, 363

St. John's College, 115, 204
Salaries of teachers, 21–29, 38–39, 114, 356,
    394, 458–459, 585. See also Incentive pay
  extracurricular activities, 28–29
  history of, 134, 144, 162
  indirect compensation, 29, 597
  negotiating, 55
Sales taxes, 456–458
San Antonio v. Rodriguez, 450, 472
Sarason, 497
Sartre, Jean-Paul, 195
Schaill v. Tippecanoe County School Corp., 404,
    415
Scheffler, Israel, 229
Scholastic Aptitude Test, 12–13, 260–261, 264,
    266, 298
Scholasticism, 73, 75, 202, 601
School Board of Nassau County v. Arline, 383,
    392, 415
School boards, 383, 428, 433–435, 437,
    481–482, 528, 602
School District of Abington Township v.
    Schempp, 364, 366, 377
School districts, 116–117, 143, 355, 418,
    425–437, 447, 451
School Dropout Prevention and Basic Skills
    Improvement Act, 587
School effectiveness, 537–543, 602
School lunch program, 149, 357, 420
School of rhetoric, 67, 71
School reform movement, 535

Schumaker, Ann, 146
Schurz, Margaretha, 83
Scientific method, 185, 191, 203, 206–207,
    212–213, 602
Search and seizure, 351, 404–405
Secondary grammar schools, 88, 90
Secondary school teachers, 133, 135–136, 491
  demand for, 22–23
  education of, 9–10
  perceptions of, 29
  salaries of, 17, 25
Secretaries of education
  federal, 14, 420–421, 602
  state, 425
Secular humanism, 369–370, 478, 602
Segregation, 128, 130, 132–133, 136, 159, 258,
    274–280. See also Desegregation
  de facto, 128, 161, 276–277
  de jure, 128, 161, 275–277
Self-determination movement, 294–295, 297
Self-renewal, 53–54, 58
Senior teachers, 51–52
Sense realism, 78, 602
Separate but equal, 123, 130, 274, 276
Separatism, 246–247, 297, 602
Sequence, 487, 489, 602
Servicemen's Readjustment Act, 153, 355, 462,
    585
Seven liberal arts, 72–73, 84, 602
Seventh Day Adventists, 247
Sex bias, 298–299, 304, 602
Sex discrimination, 298–299, 602
  inequality of educational opportunity, 256,
    262–268
Sex equity, 297–299, 300, 305, 602
Sex role stereotyping, 298–299, 304, 602
Sexual abuse, 312–313, 333–336, 602
Sexually transmitted diseases, 332
  acquired immune deficiency syndrome, 165,
    168, 313, 331–333, 336, 383, 410–412, 591
Sheldon, Edward A., 80
Sheltered English, 293
Silberman, Charles, 226–228, 497
Simon, Theodore, 148
Simulation, 524, 602
Single salary schedules, 24–26, 602
Site-based management, 438–439, 441, 451,
    459–461, 537, 602
S. J. Lemoine v. St. Landry Parrish School, 350,
    377
Skeptics, 66

Skinheads, 338, 602
Skinner, B. F., 210, 212–213
Skip-generation families, 571, 602
Slack time, 539, 602
Slater Fund, 130
Smith-Bankhead Act, 585
Smith College, 124
Smith-Hughes Act, 124–125, 464, 585
Smith v. Board of School Commissioners, 370,
    377
Social classes, 248–254, 257, 260, 262, 268, 602
Socialization, 238–245, 267, 603
    families, 238–241, 267
    media, 241–244, 267
    peer groups, 241
    schools, 244–245
Social mobility, 244, 246, 267, 602
Social reconstruction curriculum, 495, 497, 603
Social reconstructionism, 151, 218–223, 497, 603
Social Security Administration, 332, 343
Social selection, 244, 246, 267, 603
Societies, 238, 603
Society for the Propagation of the Gospel in
    Foreign Parts, 92, 95, 126
Society of Friends, 92–93
Socioeconomic status, 248–254, 257, 260, 262,
    268
Socrates, 66–68, 182, 603
Socratic Method, 66–67, 71, 603
Sophists, 65–66
Southern colonies, 94–96
Southern Regional Education Board, 590
Sovereign immunity, 397, 603
Sparta, 64–65, 71
Spears v. Board of Education of Pike County,
    415
Special district, 426–427
Special education, 212, 281–288, 305, 312, 349,
    427–428, 433, 463, 525
Spencer, Herbert, 119
Spiral curriculum, 157, 487, 603
Sputnik, 155, 164, 479, 499
Standardized tests, 12–13, 484–486, 539
Stanford-Binet test, 148, 156, 399
Stanford University, 148
Stare decisis, 355, 603
State boards of education, 114–115
State educational agencies, 419, 422–427
State of Texas v. Project Principle, Inc., 381, 415
State superintendents of education, 116, 125

State University of Iowa, 124
Statutory law, 349, 354–356, 603
Stimulus substitution behaviorism, 210
Stone v. Graham, 366, 377
Story, Joseph, 363
Stowe, Harriet Beecher, 109
Stowe Report, 113
Strategic planning, 458–459, 603
Strategies of teaching, 514–522, 530
    critical thinking instruction, 515–517,
        519–520, 522
    demonstration instruction, 515–518
    expository instruction, 515–517, 520
    independent instruction, 515–517, 520–522
    inquiry instruction, 515–520
Strayer, George D., 452–453
Strayer-Haig model, 452–453
Strikes, 394
Student Rights Movement, 161
Student's Army Training Corps, 147
Student teaching, 9–10, 17, 19
Subcultures, 238, 241, 603
Subject-area curriculum, 145, 488–491,
    497–498, 500, 603
Submersion, 293
Substance abuse, 312–318, 322, 327, 331, 333,
    336, 339, 478, 586, 596
Sudbury Valley School, 226–227
Suicide, 311–313, 321–325, 336, 478, 593–594,
    603
    gestures, 321, 325, 603
    ideation, 321, 603
    threats, 321, 325, 603
Sumer, 64
Summerhill School, 226–227
Sunday schools, 105, 108, 111, 125, 603
Superintendents of education, 116–117
    city, 117
    county, 426
    district, 116–117
    local, 433–437, 604
    state, 116, 125, 423, 593
Supply of teachers, 21–23, 44–45, 58
Supreme Court, U.S., 63, 70, 122, 133,
        160–161, 274–277, 293, 348, 358–359, 361,
        363–375, 381–383, 389–394, 396–397,
        400, 403–408, 410, 450
Supreme Courts, state, 451
Surplus Property Act, 585
Suspensions, 401–403, 407, 604

Swann v. Charlotte-Mecklenburg Board of
    Education, 276, 308
Swilley v. Alexander, 394, 415

Tablet House, 64
Tabula rasa, 79, 84, 187, 604
Tax benefits, 372–373, 604
Taxes, 450–458
    income, 456–458
    progressive, 455, 457–458
    property, 450, 455–458
    regressive, 455–457
    sales, 456–458
    uniform, 452–453
Taxonomies of educational objectives, 507–508,
    592
Teacher Corps, 567
Teacher institutes, 135, 156, 604
Teachers College, 136, 146, 151, 156, 209
Teachers' institute movement, 115
Technical production perspective, 487–490
Technology, 522–524, 530, 561, 569–570,
    574–578, 581
    computers, 523–524
    impact of, 525–526, 530
Teenage pregnancy, 300, 312–313, 327–331,
    336
Teenage violence, 313, 337–340
Television, 241–244, 267
Temporary certificates, 21, 595
Tenure, 55, 380, 384, 390–391, 604
Terman, Lewis M., 148, 156
Tests, 215–217, 225, 513–515, 517–518, 520,
    528–529
    American College Test, 12–13, 261, 264, 266
    aptitude, 148
    intelligence, 148
    National Assessment of Educational Progress,
        252, 254–259, 261–264, 464–465, 599
    Scholastic Aptitude Test, 12–13, 260–261,
        264, 266, 298
    standardized, 12–13, 484–486, 539
    for teachers, 11, 13–14, 16–19, 32, 38, 44, 58,
        380–382
Texas A & M University, 123
Texas State Teachers' Association v. Garland
    Independent School District, 392, 394, 415
Textbooks, 486, 527
Theories of education, 199–232, 604
    behaviorism, 200, 210–213, 231, 592

Theories of education, *continued*
    essentialism, 200, 206–208, 214–217, 231,
        490, 497–498, 596
    existentialism, 200, 224–228, 231
    perennialism, 200–208, 214–216, 231, 497
    progressivism, 200, 205–209, 214, 224, 231,
        497–499, 601
    reconstructionism, 200, 218–223, 231, 497,
        603
Thomas Aquinas, St., 73, 84, 187–188,
    201–202, 601
Thomism, 73, 187
Thorndike, Edward L., 148, 156, 210, 212–213
Tillich, Paul, 196
Time on task, 546, 604
Tinker v. Des Moines, 393, 406–407, 415
Title I, 159, 287–288, 300
Title IV, 295
Title V, 425
Title VI, 159, 293
Title VII, 159, 292–293
Title IX, 161, 297–298, 357
Today's Education, 55
Tort liability, 397–399, 604
Town schools, 87–88, 90
Transdisciplinary education, 576, 604
Transfer, 548–549
Transitional bilingual education, 293
Trivium, 72
Troy Female Seminary, 109, 125, 134
Trustees of Dartmouth College v. Woodward,
    122, 138
Tuskegee Institute, 131
Tutorial programs, 523, 604
Tutors
    computers, 523
    peer, 106, 107, 511
Twentieth Century Fund Task Force, 482, 590
Tyler, Ralph, 487–489

Unemployment rates, 257, 260
Unions, 392, 394
United Nations Educational, Scientific and
    Cultural Organization, 203
United States v. Seeger, 369, 377
United States v. South Carolina, 381, 392, 415
Universitas, 73
Universities, 68–69, 71, 77, 95, 147. *See also*
    specific institutions
Updegraff, Harlan, 452–453

Upper class, 248, 250–251
Upper-middle class, 248, 250–251
U.S. Conference of Mayors, 332, 344

Values tracking, 580
Vassar College, 124
Vernacular schools, 76, 604
Vertical equity, 448, 604
Vienna Circle, 229
Violence, 313, 337–340
VISTA, 567
Vittorino da Feltre, 75
Vocational education, 120–121, 125, 127, 154,
    157, 159, 162, 254, 260, 298, 301–305, 349,
    374, 420–421, 426–428, 462, 464, 479, 585,
    587, 604
Vocational Education Act, 157, 159
Vocational Rehabilitation Act, 162, 585
Volunteers in Service to America, 158
Vouchers, 372–373, 604

Wallace v. Jaffree, 364, 367, 377
Walton, John, 90
Walton College, 131
Wardwell v. Board of Education of Cincinnati,
    382, 415
War on Poverty, 157–159, 253, 274, 287, 291
Washington, Booker T., 131
Washington, George, 103
Washington v. Davis, 276–277, 308, 392, 400,
    415
Watson, John B., 210, 212–213
Watts v. Seward School Board, 393–394, 415
Webster, Noah, 105, 113, 125
Wellesley College, 124
Welse v. United States, 369, 377
Western Institute for Women, 109

Western Literary Institute, 113
West Point, 109, 585
West Virginia State Board of Education v.
    Barnette, 364–365, 377
White, Byron R., 363
White flight, 280, 604
Whitehead, Alfred North, 187
Whole-child movement, 209, 604
Wilberforce University, 130
Willard, Emma, 109, 125, 134
William and Mary, 95–96, 102, 104, 460
William T. Grant Foundation, 289
Wisconsin v. Yoder, 374, 377
Witters v. Washington Department of Services
    for the Blind, 364, 373, 377
Wittgenstein, Ludwig, 229
Wolman v. Walter, 371, 377
Women, education of, 65, 67–68, 105, 109–110,
    118, 124, 256, 262–268, 292–300
Women in teaching, 5, 12, 108, 109, 115, 134
    Interborough Association of Women Teachers,
    56
Wood v. Strickland, 403, 406, 415
Wordsworth, William, 184
"Workhouse" schools, 95
Working class, 248, 250–251
Works Projects Administration, 149–150
World War I, 147–148
World War II, 152–153
Wygant v. Jackson Board of Education, 390, 392,
    400, 415

Yale University, 90–91, 96, 102, 123
Young, Ella Flagg, 436

Zorach v. Clauson, 364–365, 377